Marxism and the Crisis of Development in Prewar Japan

GERMAINE A. HOSTON

Marxism and the Crisis of Development in Prewar Japan

Princeton University Press Princeton, New Jersey

Published by Princeton University Press, 41 William Street,
Princeton, New Jersey 08540
In the United Kingdom: Princeton University Press, Guildford, Surrey

Library of Congress Cataloging in Publication Data will be found on the last printed page of this book

ISBN 0-691-07722-3 (cloth) 0-691-10206-6 (pbk.)

Publication of this book has been aided by a grant from
The Japan Foundation

This book has been composed in Linotron Times Roman

Clothbound editions of Princeton University Press books are printed on acid-free paper, and binding materials are chosen for strength and durability. Paperbacks, although satisfactory for personal collections, are not usually suitable for library rebinding

Printed in the United States of America by Princeton
University Press, Princeton, New Jersey

Dedicated to my mother

VERETTA L. HOSTON

CONTENTS

TABLES

PREFACE

As the victory of the Chinese Communist revolution in 1949 ushered in Marxian socialist revolutions elsewhere in Asia, Africa, and Latin America, it introduced a new theme into the study of comparative politics. The relationship between nationalism and Marxism has become the major *problématique* in the study of thinkers like Mao Zedong, Julius Nyerere, and Amilcar Cabral. Yet, despite the mutually supportive link between Marxism and nationalism in late-developing societies such as these, the sinification or africanization of Marxism involves much more than merely the pragmatic injection of the nationalistic impulse into Marxian theory. Rather, Marxists operating in twentieth-century Asia, Africa, and Latin America must confront fundamental and complex theoretical issues as they apply a schema developed on the basis of the nineteenth-century political and economic experience of Western Europe to their native contexts. A primary attraction of Marxist thought outside Europe lies in its claim to predict the inevitability of socialist revolution on the basis of the scientific analysis of the history of human society. Thus, for the theory to retain its persuasive power, its adherents must be able to demonstrate how its implicitly universalist observations about social change are manifested in the particular national histories of China, Tanzania, or Guinea-Bissau. In short, where peasantry, rather than proletariat, still form the oppressed mass in the society, and where capitalism is not uniformly or highly developed but must struggle against the inroads of European colonialism, Marxist theory must be reinterpreted. This must be done, however, without vitiating its predictive and persuasive powers by sacrificing its essential elements.

Nowhere has such an effort to apply Marxism to the new non-European context been more impressive than in prewar Japan. Yet, Japanese Marxism has never been analyzed systematically in these terms, because Japanese communism—meaning the history of the Japanese Communist Party (JCP) operating under Soviet guidance—and its failure to produce a successful socialist revolution in prewar Japan have diverted scholarly attention from the study of Japanese Marxist thought itself. The materials that form the basis of accounts of the Japanese Communist Party, Comintern and JCP documents, government reports, newspapers, and party journals, serve to obscure rather than to illuminate the diverse and innovative accomplishments of Japanese Marxism often made without direct association with the JCP. Moreover, scholars seeking the key to the alliance between Marxism and nationalism have chosen not to focus on a setting in which this alliance has been more suggestive of fascism than of the Leninist vision of revolution realized in China in 1949.

This study seeks to remedy this gap in the literature by examining the application of Marxism to Japan made by participants in the debate on Japanese capitalism (*Nihon shihon-shugi ronsō*) from its inception in 1927 to the present. The debate was launched by the abrupt departure of the Rōnō-ha (Labor-Farmer faction) from the JCP in opposition to the 1927 Comintern Theses calling for a two-stage (first bourgeois and then proletarian) revolution in Japan. Objecting to the Soviet premise that Japan was too backward and underdeveloped for an immediate socialist revolution, the dissidents presented their case for a single-stage revolution in their organ *Rōnō*. A vigorous controversy that grew increasingly scholarly and theoretical ensued as defenders of the JCP-Comintern line (the Kōza-ha) produced a series of studies culminating in the seven-volume *Nihon shihon-shugi hattatsu shi kōza* [Symposium on the history of the development of Japanese capitalism], published in 1932 and 1933. Scholars on both sides of the debate became Japan's first real social scientists as they defended their positions with an impressive wealth of new data on the history of Japanese political and economic development.

Because its central issue was the level of development of Japanese capitalism and its implications for the course of revolution in Japan, the debate on Japanese capitalism marked an important step in the adaptation of Marxism to an Asian context. In their historical schema of social change, Karl Marx and Friedrich Engels had originally envisaged that a socialist revolution would occur only when capitalism had developed sufficiently to create a dissatisfied and conscious proletarian majority and to sustain the production of plenty for all under socialism. When such a revolution failed to materialize out of the unrest in Europe in 1848, the founders briefly entertained the notion that socialism could emerge out of a less developed society such as Russia, which retained in the *mir* (peasant commune) a relic of primitive communal society. This optimism was tempered from the outset, however, by the belief that such a revolution in Russia could succeed only if it immediately sparked other revolutions in the advanced capitalist countries of Western Europe to support it. Eventually, Marx and Engels completely abandoned this notion, arguing that at best the *mir* represented a primitive institution that could not be a suitable basis for building a postcapitalist socialist society.

Of course, under V. I. Lenin and the Bolsheviks, Russia indeed became the first site of a successful Marxian socialist revolution. However, when the question of the suitability of the Marxian model for the relatively undeveloped Russian context became the subject of heated controversy between

Russia's *narodniks* and Marxists, Lenin himself skirted the adaptation issue. In his massive study, *The Development of Capitalism in Russia*, Lenin simply argued that the *narodniks* were wrong to insist that Russia had not developed capitalism sufficiently to support a proletarian socialist revolution. Nevertheless, Lenin shared Marx's view of Russia as "semi-Asiatic" and less developed than the Western European countries where Marx's socialism seemed to have its best prospects. Thus, Lenin too was concerned that the new Soviet society could not survive unless it was quickly supported by proletarian revolutions in the more highly developed capitalistic societies of the West. Lenin's hopes for such sustenance were short-lived: they perished in 1919 when the Spartacus uprising was crushed in Germany, and Lenin, like Marx and Engels before him, turned his sights eastward.

Beginning in 1919, then, the primary objective of Comintern policy became to foment revolution in the East. This shift in focus, however, did not substantially advance the adaptation of the Marxian schema of socialist revolution to the non-European context, because what Lenin envisaged in the East was not socialist revolution but movements of national liberation that could be propelled by Asia's massive peasantries rather than by its weak proletariats. Lenin wished to use nationalist anticolonial revolutions in China, India, and elsewhere in the East to break the crucial link by which Western European capitalisms were nourished by imperialistic expansion. National revolutions in Asia would disrupt the essential supply of raw materials and markets for European capital, inciting economic distress in Europe, and finally sparking the long-awaited proletarian revolutions in the West. This was an instrumentalist approach to revolution in Asia: it was merely a means to an end to be achieved elsewhere, a path to socialism not in the East but in the West. That Lenin's successors in the Comintern did not appreciably depart from this view is evident from the policies they pursued in Asia. In China, Soviet leaders supported Chiang Kai-shek's Guomindang in preference to the young Chinese Communist Party precisely because they believed that there was no viable prospect for socialist revolution where capitalism was so immature. Even in advising the Japanese Communist Party in the 1920s and 1930s, Nikolai Bukharin and other Comintern leaders firmly adhered to their expectation that only bourgeois-democratic revolution was possible immediately, despite the impressive growth of Japanese capitalism since the Meiji Restoration.

It was in opposition to this view that the Rōnō-ha provoked the debate on Japanese capitalism in 1927. The *Rōnō* faction maintained that the high level of finance capital, the rapid growth of trustification since World War I, and a powerful imperialist impulse all indicated Japan's status as an advanced capitalist power. The *Kōza*, or so-called feudal, school argued that the existence of semi-feudal remnants in Japan's political superstructure—

e.g., the emperor system, the Privy Council, and the dominant *kokutai* ideology—constituted proof that Japan's bourgeois-democratic revolution was not yet complete and would have to be finished before the JCP could embark on a socialist revolution. The Rōnō-ha was challenged to provide evidence of a significant transition to capitalism in the Japanese countryside as well as in the cities; while the Kōza-ha's feudal thesis led it to conduct extensive historical research as well on the process that had permitted Japanese capitalism to develop so rapidly while maintaining such powerful vestiges of backwardness.

Both factions were committed to the possibility of socialist revolution in Japan soon, if not immediately, and thus Marxists in both camps endeavored to do what their predecessors in the international movement had not: to furnish a meaningful adaptation of Marx's historical schema to a non-European context on the basis of a sustained and systematic analysis of the developmental experience of their own country. In the prewar era, this controversy led Japan's Marxists to address such issues as the Marxian periodization of Japanese history, the "Asiatic mode of production" concept, the origins of the development of industrial capitalism in Japan, and the nature and role of the emperor system in Japan's political economy. After the war, the changes wrought by the American Occupation served to lessen the significance of many of these issues. Yet the debate continues, if in diluted form, today. It defines the terms of the still widely influential academic Marxist discourse in Japan; and it affects the electoral policies of the Socialist and Communist parties.

The aim of this book, therefore, is twofold. Conceived as a case study in the adaptation of Marxism to an alien, non-European, twentieth-century context, the book assesses both the contributions of the Marxian framework to a fuller understanding of Japanese economic development in particular and of late-developing countries more generally, and the implications of the continuing controversy in Japan for the Marxist claim to historical and geographical universality. By analyzing the Marxist controversy within its political and economic context, the book offers a more complete picture of the nature of the crisis of development that Japan confronted in the Taishō and Shōwa eras. In trying to foment revolution, Japan's Marxists were seeking an alternative solution to the economic and political distress that their military leaders ultimately tried to resolve by going to war. Their confrontation with elements of this crisis in the debate on Japanese capitalism led them to raise issues that have received only scant or very recent attention from Western Marxists. More importantly, their ability or inability to interpret that crisis in Marxist terms ultimately represented a test of the integrity of Marxism as a universal theory of development.

Thus, the debate on Japanese capitalism is important as a subject of scholarly inquiry for three reasons. First, it marked the emergence of Japanese Marxism as an innovative and independent intellectual system that transcended the formulaic bounds of JCP and Comintern documents. Ironically, prior to the Kōza-ha–Rōnō-ha controversy, the most creative work of Japanese Marxism had been produced by Takahashi Kamekichi, an economic commentator who used Marxist categories to analyze Japanese capitalism. By means of an argument that closely resembled the as yet unarticulated Greater East Asia Co-Prosperity Sphere conception, the activist in the peasant movement and future member of the government's war planning board concluded that Japanese imperialist expansion in Asia was both necessary and legitimate and should be supported. Outraged and challenged by Takahashi's analysis, partisans of both the *Kōza* and *Rōnō* schools embarked on the search for an adaptation of Marxism to Japan that was true to the anti-imperialist impulses of Marxism-Leninism. With the aid of Marxist theory, Japanese economists and political activists analyzed the concrete dynamics of Japan's economic and political development from the mid-nineteenth century.

Second, participants in the debate produced a voluminous literature, offering interpretations of Japan's development that have been incorporated in piecemeal fashion even into American social scientific works on Japanese development. The original studies offer an integrated Marxian interpretation of the process that has culminated in Japan's current economic success. The debate, if presented in its original terms, can explain important aspects of Japan's capitalistic development, because the debate itself constituted a response to a particular stage of the development process. This explanatory power, coupled with the embedding of the debate in Japanese scholarship, has served to promote the continuing dominance of Marxism in Japan as the leading paradigm for the interpretation of modern Japanese history.

Finally, the Japan that was the object of this debate was a late-developing (relative to Western Europe) society that lay on the fringes of the Western state system when the Meiji oligarchy initiated its industrializing revolution from above in 1868. Because the debate arose in the context of crisis, as initially rapid growth slowed dramatically in the 1920s, many of the issues addressed by the Rōnō-ha and the Kōza-ha now serve to illuminate dilemmas of development in contemporary Third World countries. The implications of late development itself were evident to Japanese Marxists decades before they came to the attention of Western social scientists. Because of the prior development of Western Europe and the United States, the inputs into the economic development of late-developing societies differ not only in terms of indigenous factors but also in terms of powerful external forces. The deliberate pursuit of accelerated development involves the state in economic activity in a manner that differs fundamentally from its behavior in earlier developing capitalist societies. The resulting political centralization necessary to coordinate development in the economic and social spheres in turn may jeopardize the ideals of Western-style "bourgeois democracy" and social democracy. Is the goal of attaining democracy, then, antithetical to the goal of rapid economic growth in a late-developing society? Finally, the ability to observe the experience of countries that developed earlier offers thinkers in later developing countries the opportunity to assess critically the objective of "modernization" in the traditional capitalist sense itself. Perhaps such modernization necessarily entails social costs that are unacceptable. What, then, are the alternatives if one is to protect one's society from pressures exerted by earlier developing societies? In an era of tumultuous change in Asia, Africa, and Latin America, the debate on Japanese capitalism suggests both the contributions and the limitations of Marxist theory in comprehending and resolving such pressing issues as these. Furthermore, it helps to explain the appeal of Marxism as a revolutionary doctrine among political and intellectual leaders of less developed countries facing similar dilemmas today.

The ultimate objective of the participants in the Japanese debate was to promote a leftist revolution against what they perceived to be tremendous social and political costs resulting from Japan's rapid capitalistic development. By the 1920s Japan had attained the goals of the Meiji oligarchs to "enrich the country and strengthen the military" (*fukoku kyōhei*). Japan was preeminently successful as a capitalist world power in industry and finance and began to achieve recognition as such by the more firmly established powers of the United States and Great Britain when it was included in the naval conferences in London and Washington. Yet Marxism had become attractive in Japan because leading intellectuals like Kawakami Hajime were dissatisfied with some of the domestic consequences of the development of Japanese capitalism—poverty, overcrowded cities, the growth of an urban working class oppressed by long hours and poor pay. A disturbing schism between the new urban capitalist Japan and the traditional agrarian sector emerged. This gulf served to accentuate what became Kawakami's greatest concern: the sacrifice of certain traditional Japanese values, which remained intrinsically attractive, to antithetical values like human egoism, individualism, and the pursuit of profit that were associated with the rise of capitalism. For Japanese Marxists, the desirability of Western-style capitalism was called into question because the new order was perceived to have introduced new social tensions and cleavages into a hitherto harmonious society.

In a sense, then, the radical revolutionism of Marxism in Japan represented an effort to reinstate more traditional values like collectivism through further progress along the "Western" path through capitalism and on toward socialism, as described by Marx. Marxism offered a way to pursue these traditional values without calling for a return to the past. Ironically, the *Kōza*, or JCP, faction feared that "feudal remnants" like the emperor system required a two-step revolution to achieve socialism. Yet it can be argued that the persistence of older forms and values has in fact made Japanese capitalism more stable, more prosperous, more impervious to the Marxist revolution these theorists envisaged. The Japanese experience on which they reflected—one in which "tradition" merged with modern industrialism to create a capitalist economy that has earned international respect—is suggestive of analogous patterns of development emerging in the Third World today. The ambivalence of these Marxists concerning Japan's path has been echoed among socialists like Cabral and Nyerere in Africa, who, adapting Marxism to their native contexts, "felt an urgent need to reaffirm traditional values indigenous to their societies."[1] It is hoped that in making the content of Japanese Marxist thought about Japan's development more widely available, this volume will contribute to a fuller understanding of that experience in Japan and in other late-developing societies.

ACKNOWLEDGMENTS

So MANY American and Japanese scholars have helped me to complete this book that it seems impossible to thank them all. To Benjamin I. Schwartz I owe my greatest intellectual debt. His enthusiasm for the project and example of erudition of extraordinary depth and breadth were a powerful inspiration to me. Without his and Roy Hofheinz, Jr.'s, urging me to enlarge my study of Chinese politics to embrace Japan, I would not have discovered the contribution of Japan's prodigious Marxists to our understanding of political development in modern Japan. When my doctoral dissertation was completed, Professor Schwartz, along with John D. Montgomery, Joel S. Migdal, and Leo Ou-fan Lee encouraged me to seize the opportunity to develop a work on the much neglected subject of Japanese Marxism out of the thesis.

In Japan, I could not have accomplished my research without the support of my Japanese mentors. Ukai Nobushige provided me with valuable introductions to leading participants in the debate and patient explanations of the subtleties of Japanese political discourse. Ishida Takeshi and Baba Hiroji kindly arranged for me to be a Foreign Research Fellow in order to use the facilities of the University of Tokyo's Institute of Social Science and generously provided me with references to crucial books and articles to guide my research. I thank the other scholars at the Institute on both sides of the controversy—Shibagaki Kazuo, Okudaira Yasuhiro, Ōishi Ka'ichirō, Watanabe Osamu, and others—for their collegiality and Tsukagoshi Tsutako, Irite Fujio, and other Institute staff for their friendly support.

To participants in the debate on Japanese capitalism I owe a special debt of gratitude which, in all too many cases, it is too late to repay. I wish that I could convey my appreciation to the late Hirano Yoshitarō, Arahata Kanson, Minobe Ryōkichi, and Sakisaka Itsurō, all of whom offered me hours of discussion on the fine points of Marxist theory and practice in Japan. I am also grateful to Takahashi Masao, Moriya Fumio, Ōuchi Tsutomu, Ikumi Taku'ichi, and Watanabe Yōzō for sharing with me their experiences in the controversy and to Diet members Hori Masao, Doi Takako, and Yamamoto Masahiro for their observations on the impact of the debate on current Japanese politics.

Lengthy discussions with Maruyama Masao, Onabe Teruhiko, Fujita Shōzō, Fukushima Shingō, Hayashi Takehisa, Nakamura Takafusa, and Itō Makoto enriched my appreciation of the impact of Marxism in prewar and postwar Japan. Ishikawa Tadao, president of Keiō University, and Yamada Tatsuo and Ichiko Kenji, also of Keiō University, provided me with materials facilitating my comparison of Chinese and Japanese Marxism. I must thank Nakamura Tetsu, president of Hōsei University, and Nimura Kazuo, head of the Ōhara Institute for the Study of Social Problems, for access to handwritten documents. I am also appreciative of the warm hospitality of Horiguchi Rayko, who took me into her family's home, and Horiguchi Minoru, who made arrangements for my lodging in Kyoto.

While writing, I profited from the hearty support of my colleagues at Johns Hopkins and elsewhere. T. J. Pempel, Gail Lee Bernstein, George Armstrong Kelly, Richard E. Flathman, and J. Woodford Howard, Jr. read parts of the manuscript and offered suggestions. Katherine Verdery, Kristin Bumiller, Richard S. Katz, Steven David, and Matthew Crenson supported me with their friendship and, on occasion, logistical support. Emiko Moffitt, of the Hoover Institution, and Fumi Norcia, of the Library of Congress, made special efforts to facilitate my research here in the United States. For flawless typing, often under difficult conditions, I thank Catherine Grover. Lise-Ann Shea, Constance Rosemont, H. Kevin McNeelege, Deborah Kravitz, and Li-shing Wang provided crucial research assistance. Sanford Thatcher, of Princeton University Press, has been the kind of editor that every author hopes to have, with his indefatigable optimism and efforts on my behalf. I would also like to express my appreciation to David A. Titus and George Wilson for criticisms and suggestions that helped to make this a better book.

My doctoral research in Japan and at Asian collections in this country was made possible by generous funding by Harvard University, a Foreign Language and Area Studies Fellowship, and the American Association of University Women. From 1982 through 1984, as I travelled to Japan to update my materials, the International Federation of University Women, the National Endowment for the Humanities, and the Social Science Research Council provided essential financial resources.

Finally, but most importantly, I am thankful for the spiritual sustenance and forbearance of my mother and sister. To their constant support I owe my ability to bring this project to fruition.

Baltimore, Maryland
June 1985

Marxism and the Crisis of Development in Prewar Japan

ONE

The Setting: Political, Economic, and Intellectual Currents in Taishō Japan

The development of the world economic crisis is shaking the foundation of the entire capitalist order, and therefore also of Japan's capitalist system. The aggravation of the general crisis of capitalism, the catastrophic intensification of the depression that is proceeding on that basis, the menacing tension of international confrontation, and thus the incontestable intensification of class conflict and war—the sudden worsening of the situation of all these, which is already hard to conceal . . . has caused both the ruling class and its apologists now to proclaim the coming of a national crisis. "A national economic crisis!" they cry. "A national intellectual crisis! A national crisis unprecedented since the founding of the country!"

Imperialists upset by this pressing state of affairs probably cannot conceive of anything besides war and fascism. However, the resolution of the deadlock in economic development, the instability of political rule, and social unrest require a change . . . ; and without investigating the inevitable basic contradictions, it is probably impossible even to grasp a clue to the resolution of the problem. To examine the history of the establishment of Japanese capitalism, to investigate the special nature of its development, which was full of contradictions, is therefore the key to the discovery of the path of the fundamental resolution of the problems confronting Japanese capitalism. This *Symposium* seeks to provide that key. . . . Our hope is not to interpret history but to change it.

—Noro Eitarō, introducing the *Symposium on the History of the Development of Japanese Capitalism*

WHEN the debate on Japanese capitalism erupted in the late 1920s, it marked a vigorous response to actual political and economic developments in Japan's domestic and international contexts. The debate was not merely an arid intellectual controversy on the fine points of Marxist theory. Rather, it constituted an earnest effort by Japanese leftist political activists and scholars to seek in Marxism a solution to what they correctly perceived as a rising national crisis that would culminate in Japan's humiliating military defeat in 1945. The period of the debate on Japanese capitalism, from 1927 to 1937, was "the era when [Japan] turned from 'the conditions of Taishō democracy' to an age of war and fascism."[1] The origin and dynamic of the debate, then, must be understood in terms of its setting, against the backdrop of the tensions in Japan's economic and political affairs that resulted in large part from its rapid industrialization during the Meiji period (1868-1912).

During the Taishō era (1912-1926), on the eve of the Marxist debate, these difficulties were already very much in evidence and cried out for resolution. The issues that dominated the debate on Japanese capitalism involved the universal and special characteristics of Japan's industrialization, the continuing economic backwardness and distress in the countryside, and the persistence of apparently outmoded political institutions—the emperor system, the Privy Council, and the powerful informal influence of the *genrō* (elder statesmen) and military cliques—despite the introduction of Western constitutional forms associated with a multiparty parliamentary democracy. These issues comprised important aspects of questions concerning revolutionary strategy and tactics as formulated by the Communist International (Comintern), and they were discussed within the Japanese Communist Party (JCP) from the time of its establishment in 1922. By virtue of their theoretical significance within the framework of Marxist revolutionary thought alone, then, these issues gained a logical prominence at the center of the debate on Japanese capitalism. At the same time, these questions were also brought to the fore by actual political and economic developments during the Taishō period, although the resulting strains did not converge in a "road to fascism"[2] until the early Shōwa era (1926 to the present), when the debate was already underway.

When the Taishō period ended in 1926, the political, economic, and social crisis swelling beneath the veneer of "Taishō democracy" was undeniable. As the recession in the agrarian sector continued to deepen, rural rent strikes and tenant farmers' unions mushroomed, a temporary decline in labor strikes had reversed dramatically, and labor unions proliferated under the growing influence of the left. In the political arena, the facade of Taishō party government crumbled when instability at the highest levels left Japan with seven cabinets in the last five years of the period.[3] Throughout the Taishō years, Japanese scholars and activists increasingly rejected both traditional Japanese and classical Western approaches to society and polity as inadequate or inappropriate frameworks for the analysis and resolution of these problems. In their place, Marxism eventually emerged as an appealing intellectual system *cum* political program for those seeking to avert the kind of desperate recourse to militaristic expansionism that finally engulfed Japan in the 1930s and 1940s.

Yet Marxism was by no means the only alternative generated by Japan's resourceful intelligentsia. Theories ranging from the left to the far right emerged, as Japan's intellectual community offered solutions to the increasingly critical situation. Modifying Western liberal thought, for example, Tokyo Imperial University professor Yoshino Sakuzō advocated the implementation of *minpon-shugi* ("government for the people" rather than "government by the people"). Further to the left, Ōsugi Sakae led an anarchist movement until his murder by the military police in 1923. On the right, Kita Ikki drafted an *Outline for the Reorganization of Japan (Nihon kaizō hōan taikō)* (1919), Takabatake Motoyuki devised a doctrine of Marxist national or state socialism, and Akamatsu Katsumaro created "scientific Japanism."[4] The troubling political, economic, and social trends of the Taishō era that inspired these provocative schemes warrant closer examination because they also became the setting for the debate on Japanese capitalism.

Economic Crisis

Many of the economic difficulties that Japan experienced during the Taishō period were directly related to its status as a late developer. Much as Russian Tsar Alexander II did in response to the Crimean War of 1854-1856, the oligarchs ruling in the name of the Meiji emperor launched the Meiji reforms in the 1870s to strengthen Japan militarily enough to oppose external pressures from more advanced Western capitalist societies—"to expel the barbarians (*jōi*)."[5] The inability of the Tokugawa shogunate to resist the pressures of Commodore Matthew C. Perry and his successors had helped to precipitate armed rebellion among the feudal daimyo (lords) and the collapse of the shogunate. The new Meiji regime undertook massive industrialization under the slogan *fukoku kyōhei* ("enrich the country and strengthen the military"), its goal to match in a few short decades the achievements that England and France had required more than a century to produce.

Beginning with the 1868 Charter Oath's elimination of the class restraints characteristic of the centralized feudalism of the Tokugawa period, the Meiji regime emulated Western political and economic institutions and erased all legal arrangements that could be identified with feudal "backwardness." The *han* (feudal domains) were abolished, and administrative prefectures were established; a single Imperial military force with French-style training was formed; and a conscription law destroyed the former division of labor between samurai and commoner. The regime also established a single uniform currency, and a major reform in the system of agricultural land taxation helped to provide a stable financial basis for the state's industrialization efforts. Where taxes had been a percentage of agricultural yield paid in kind, a new law in 1873 fixed a monetary tax based on land value, so that the state's budget would no longer vary widely each year. The new tax was extremely effective, "provid[ing] 94% of the government's tax revenue at this time, and over half until almost the turn of the century."[6]

This new support for fiscal stability became an important factor in Japan's industrialization, for the Meiji state, like the Russian and German states, played a much larger and more direct role in industrialization than had the states of earlier industrializers like England and France. According to economists Kazushi Ohkawa and Henry Rosovsky, "Government investments generally exceeded those of the private sector until World War I: in 1884 they were 66 percent and in 1901 54 percent of the total."[7] The state, then, encouraged industrialization both indirectly, by providing essential preconditions of capitalism—a stable currency, a unified national banking system, efficient transportation and communication facilities, a mobile labor force—and directly, by participating in the economy itself. A major consequence of this state involvement was the creation of an expanded domestic market, which enabled Japan to achieve spectacular growth from the 1880s until the end of World War I, without relying too heavily on exports. In the words of William W. Lockwood,

> The growth of the market was also stimulated after 1880 by the heavy expenditures of the State for armaments, transport, communications, and supporting industries. These outlays were significant in economic terms chiefly because they were concentrated upon the metal, machinery, and shipbuilding industries, rather than because of their actual bulk. They helped materially to launch new enterprises in these fields and to get them over their first technological hurdles. In addition, government expenditures at home had a general expansionist effect on domestic industry and trade insofar as they were financed by credit creation or taxing agricultural incomes which would not otherwise have been spent in the market. An important share was actually devoted to purchasing arms and ships abroad. This also stimulated domestic production by encouraging the export of various commodities in payment.[8]

In this pattern of development lay the key to Japan's rapid transition from an agrarian economy to urban industrialized capitalism. Between 1895 and 1930, the ratio of Japan's urban population increased from 12 percent to 45 percent; and where only a tiny proletariat (workers in factories with five or more employees) of 400,000 existed in 1897, by the end of World War I there were over 1.7 million such workers.[9] In this process of intensive industrialization, however, lay many of the roots of the economic and social dislocation Japan suffered during the 1920s. A major effect of the rapidity of Japan's modernization was the emergence of a "dual economy," a schism between small-scale production in traditional sectors of the economy and large-scale, capital-intensive industries based on heavy concentrations of financial capital.[10] Because of the state's enormous role in the early development of capitalism in Japan, the concentration of capital occurred especially rapidly. Since the state was significant in both commerce and industry, there emerged the kind of fusion between bank capital and industrial capital that Rudolf Hilferding saw in Germany at the turn of the century in the form of "finance capital."[11] Like the cartels and industrial combines of Hilferding's Germany, the zaibatsu (financial cliques) were a dominant feature of Japan's capitalist economy by the Taishō period.[12] During the 1920s, the number of banks in Japan fell 50 percent,[13] and by the end of the Taishō period the "five large banks" (Mitsui, Mitsubishi, Sumitomo, Dai'ichi, and Yasuda), four of which were at the core of leading zaibatsu, controlled over 25 percent of the nation's bank capital (see table 1). At the same time, Japan made dramatic gains in industrial production in light industry (textiles) and even more in heavy industry (chemicals, machinery, and metals) on the basis of more advanced technology between 1868 and the 1920s.[14]

Despite these indicators of a high level of capitalist industrialization, the Japanese economy developed unevenly during these years, leaving a powerful traditional sector intact. This traditional sector included agriculture, cottage industry, and factories employing fewer than five workers. In contrast with other cases of late development, in its early years Japan's industrialization relied heavily on traditional technology,[15] rather than on advanced techniques imported wholesale from abroad. Nevertheless, the traditional sector prospered alongside the emergent heavy industrial sector, as the gradual introduction of mechanization, particularly in textiles, permitted the transformation of certain segments into the stage of light industrial production. Food production showed a 35 to 40 percent increase between 1894 and 1914, and textile production, even on the basis of relatively primitive technologies, also climbed.[16] Although the textile industry became increasingly mechanized, however, as late as 1930 over 50 percent of the total manufacturing labor force was employed in establishments of fewer than five workers.[17] Moreover, in 1920, more than half the labor force (51.7 percent) was still engaged in agricultural production.[18]

Within the traditional sector, however, agriculture fared less well. While gains in agricultural production occurred early in the Meiji period, the rural sector increasingly fell victim to the pressures caused by rising population and scarcity of land. The average size of agricultural holdings remained tiny, limiting the applicability of more advanced technologies.[19] Hence, agricultural production showed modest gains in the late Meiji and early Taishō periods.[20] Intense speculation drove rice prices upward rapidly toward the end of World War I, to which the rice riots of 1918 were a dramatic response.[21] After 1920, stagnation characterized the agrarian economy. Increases in agricultural production during the Meiji period had been based on improvements of traditional technology (e.g., improved seeds and the use of fertilizer), but opportunities for such improvements virtually disappeared by the

TABLE 1

Concentration of Bank Deposits in the Five Largest Banks
(In Millions of Yen)

Period Ending	Total deposits of all banks	Five largest banks							Regular banks excluding the five largest	Percentage of non-largest banks to total
		Mitsui	Mitsubishi	Sumitomo	Yasuda	Dai'ichi	Total	Percentage		
2d half 1923	7,705	418	307	344	565	344	1,978	25.7	5,727	74.3
1st half 1924	7,720	417	292	362	576	344	1,991	25.8	5,729	74.2
2d half 1924	7,914	409	303	377	573	346	2,008	25.4	5,906	74.6
1st half 1925	8,294	443	308	409	591	360	2,111	25.5	6,183	74.5
2d half 1925	8,702	440	312	416	572	366	2,106	24.2	6,596	75.8
1st half 1926	8,797	476	316	435	559	380	2,206	25.1	6,591	74.9
2d half 1926	9,031	456	329	435	623	391	2,234	24.7	6,797	75.3
1st half 1927	8,810	539	456	524	686	511	2,716	30.8	6,094	69.2
2d half 1927	8,906	560	471	553	713	521	2,818	31.6	6,088	68.4
1st half 1928	9,091	619	525	595	745	567	3,051	33.6	6,040	66.4
2d half 1928	9,215	606	562	643	722	597	3,130	34.0	6,085	66.0
1st half 1929	9,244	644	581	651	703	608	3,188	34.4	6,056	65.5

SOURCE: Takahashi Kamekichi, *Nihon shihon-shugi hattatsu shi* [History of the development of Japanese capitalism], rev. and enlgd. ed. (Tokyo: Nihon hyōron-sha, 1929), p. 255.

TABLE 2

Net Domestic Product in Agricultural and Nonagricultural Sectors at Market Prices: Constant Prices (1934-1936 Prices, in Millions of Yen)

Year	Agriculture (including forestry and fishing)	Total (NDP)	Private nonagriculture
(Meiji)			
1905	1,551	5,780	3,643
1906	1,902	6,628	4,228
1907	2,026	7,138	4,669
1908	2,082	7,043	4,483
1909	2,042	7,037	4,538
1910	1,917	7,166	4,771
1911	2,176	7,501	4,821
(Taishō)			
1912	2,172	7,656	4,990
1913	2,206	7,631	4,936
1914	2,232	7,927	5,217
1915	2,258	8,133	6,366
1916	2,521	10,058	7,085
1917	2,482	10,673	7,804
1918	2,479	11,071	8,238
1919	2,784	11,638	8,354
1920	2,545	10,838	7,865
1921	2,519	11,948	8,710
1922	2,491	12,173	9,055
1923	2,475	12,000	8,906
1924	2,539	13,157	8,451
1925	2,749	12,908	9,388
1926	2,565	13,093	9,676

SOURCE: Kazushi Ohkawa and Henry Rosovsky, *Japanese Economic Growth: Trend Acceleration in the Twentieth Century*, Studies of Economic Growth in Industrialized Countries (Stanford: Stanford University Press, 1973), p. 284.

beginning of the 1920s. Throughout the decade, the agrarian sector lagged far behind the performance of the economy as a whole (see table 2), recording only .44 percent growth annually between 1917 and 1931, where there had been 2.38 percent annual growth between 1897 and 1901.[22] After peaking in 1920, agricultural income declined steadily, suffering from rice imports from Taiwan and Korea. Moreover, agricultural prices were consistently lower than general price levels during the 1920s.[23] Thus, farmers suffered disproportionately greater distress during these years of recession and bank panics, and the rural population became increasingly receptive to programs for radical change offered by both the left and the right.

A major element in this distress was the extent of tenancy. In some estimates, tenancy reached almost 50 percent in this period, with rents remaining almost as high as feudal rents levied in the Tokugawa era.[24] In 1930, according to Lockwood, rents "absorbed two-thirds of the net income produced in Japanese agriculture."[25] In the countryside between 1920 and 1924, there were 7,115 incidents of tenants' strikes (in contrast with fewer than 500 in 1917), initiating a trend in which such disputes would rise to 11,136 between 1925 and 1929, and 19,139 between 1930 and 1934.[26] The impact of the survival of tenancy and the overall decline in agricultural production suggest that a major contributor to this unrest was the dual economy itself. By the 1920s, Japan's uneven development had produced a highly concentrated urban capitalist sector, one that contrasted sharply with conditions in the countryside that many Marxists came to see as vestiges of feudalism.

On the whole, however, the 1920s marked a difficult period for the entire Japanese economy, one that came to be viewed anxiously by contemporaries as a "deadlock" (*yukizumari*) in Japan's development.[27] Where Japan had made significant inroads into foreign markets by World War I, Japan's newly born capitalist economy was not excessively dependent on exports. During World War I, however, Japan capitalized on the opportunity offered by the preoccupation of the Allied Powers with military expenditures and took over many of the Allied markets. The resulting wartime boom in exports fueled an accompanying war prosperity in the entire domestic economy, in which the years 1914 to 1919 saw a 78 percent increase in total manufacturing production, and the profit rate rose from 40.8 percent in early 1914 to 55.2 percent in 1917-1919.[28] As foreign demand for Japanese goods soared, Japan experienced a consistent surplus on its current account. When the war ended, British and French recovery allowed the Allies to resume their markets, and Japan's war boom also came to an end. The slump in 1920 was followed by "readjustment," but the 1920s remained plagued by financial crisis. The Tokyo earthquake of 1923 aggravated the situation, and although a "reconstruction boom developed in the wake of the catastrophe, . . . this led into a banking crisis in 1927."[29] The few economic gains made during these years were uneven, affecting agriculture negatively, while the silk industry, for example, flourished in the worldwide prosperity of the late 1920s. Thus, where private nonagricultural investment had grown steadily through World War I, reaching 24 percent in 1915 and 1916, the years 1920 through 1925 experienced net declines in such investment; only a slight recovery occurred in 1927, before Japan joined the rest of the capitalist world in the Great Depression.[30] Where growth in gross national product averaged a healthy 4.56 percent between 1912 and 1917, the average growth rate between 1917 and 1931 was only 2.75 percent.[31]

This abrupt deterioration in Japan's economic performance was manifested in unrest in urban industrialized areas as well as the rural sector. The postwar economic decline followed on the heels of the Bolshevik revolution in 1917, and a reinvigorated left-wing movement enjoyed renewed successes among industrial workers. Strikes had occurred since 1897 in Japan.[32] However, unions and strikes were restricted under Article 17 of the Peace Police Law of 1900, and consequently, the labor movement had achieved only modest successes until World War I. Between 1914 and 1919 the number of factory workers doubled, and the heavy industrial sector, characterized by larger scale factories, expanded. The percentage of laborers employed in the sector rose from 13.6 to 24.2 percent over the decade ending in 1919; and laborers in factories of more than 100 workers increased from 43.6 to 55.6 percent. The prosperous wartime economy created favorable conditions for the labor movement, then, as workers both suffered from inflation and pressures to produce more rapidly and worked in situations that facilitated their appreciation of their common interests. The still illegal unions increased almost sevenfold, from 40 in 1911 to 273 in 1920.[33] In April 1921, the widely heralded strike at Ashio Copper Mines became a new rallying point for labor, when workers listed the right to unionization and collective bargaining among their demands.[34] When the JCP was founded the following year, the split of the anarcho-syndicalists behind Ōsugi Sakae from the "Bolsheviks" came to be mirrored in labor.[35] Splinterism plagued the national labor organizations—the General Federation and the Federation of Japanese Labor Unions—throughout the 1920s. However, both labor activism in the urban centers and tenants' unions in the countryside continued to make dramatic gains over the decade as symptoms of Taishō economic distress, fueling unrest in the political sphere as well.

"Taishō Democracy" and the Emergence of Marxism as a Political Movement

The economic distress of the Taishō years was accompanied by political developments that made many Japanese question the achievements of "Taishō democracy." Partly in reflection of these doubts, the political history of the Taishō period has been the subject of intense controversy. While there is some diversity in Western social science literature, with some scholars stressing the negative aspects of Taishō politics, far more common has been the premise that the Taishō period was the "Era of Party Rule."[36] This optimistic interpretation maintains that the successes of democracy—represented by newly activist political parties—outweighed its failures in this period. This view is based on a firm conviction that political parties are generally the best vehicle for "broadening the base of political participation and the scope of interest conciliation."[37] This stream in Western scholarship has emphasized the 1920s as an age when politics in prewar Japan most closely approximated the competitive democratic models of British and American politics. In this interpretation, steady progress toward parliamentary democracy was rudely interrupted when the parties lost initiative to right-wing military leaders and bureaucrats in the Shōwa period. There was, in this view, an essential discontinuity or "break" between Taishō politics and the militarism and fascism of the 1930s and 1940s that destroyed the fragile blossom of Taishō democracy.

Interestingly, this optimism dominating Western scholarship on the Taishō period coincides with the apparent disillusionment and pessimism felt among Japanese rightists during the period. While Japanese scholars, particularly on the left, overwhelmingly have treated the Taishō period with skepticism, insisting that Taishō democracy was but a myth,[38] contemporary observers on the right felt increasingly threatened by the democratizing tendencies in the era. If the mainstream of Japanese scholarship maintains that Taishō liberalism failed to introduce profound and enduring change into the conduct of Japanese politics, there was, nevertheless, growing fear on the right that the increased role of newly coherent and cohesive political parties distorted and betrayed the principles of the national polity (*kokutai*) stipulated in the Meiji Constitution. This disillusionment fueled the rise of right-wing forces and was most clearly articulated in the drive for a Shōwa Restoration among young military men in the 1930s. These critics of Taishō aimed to use the Shōwa period to restore the majestic traditions of Imperial Japan that had been sacrificed by rapid and indiscriminate Westernization in the political as well as economic spheres. Massive industrialization had destroyed venerable Japanese traditions of thought and behavior, introducing class conflict into a previously harmonious and ethnically united society. The cities teemed with workers alienated from their roots and seduced by Western ideas, leaving the agrarian countryside as sole repository of traditional values. *Nōhon-shugi* (agrarianism), which exalted traditional Japanese values and mores, swelled up in right-wing movements in the 1920s. In the 1930s, the traditional social structure and *weltanschaaung* of the countryside were exploited by the army's efforts to promote its nationalistic and militaristic ideology.[39]

The strength of this reaction against liberal developments of the Taishō era was evidenced in the proliferation of nationalist and national-socialist organizations after 1922, not coincidentally the year the JCP was founded. As prosecutor Baba Yoshitsugu wrote, "All these [groups] were active in the anti-socialist movement, taking as their first aim the prevention of communization." But they were more generally oriented toward conservatism, rather than united in a single restorationist or reformist ideology. Indeed, many of these groups consciously shared the aims of capitalists and their political parties and, in the name of patriotism, participated on their behalf in violent activity against the left.[40] Not all such groups were united in defense of the pure, unsullied politics of rustic Japan, but they shared a common desire to prevent the continued growth of Taishō democracy in any further movement toward the political left. Such groups gained legitimacy as the state suppressed more and more the advocates of radical and even merely reformist leftist politics in Japan, beginning with the "white terror" that followed the disastrous Tokyo earthquake of 1923. This task was facilitated when the Peace Preservation Law of 1925 made it illegal to participate in any organization with the intent of changing the *kokutai*. Notably, this legislation was initiated under Premier Katō Takaaki (Kōmei), whose government is most commonly described as the most progressive and democratizing of the Taishō cabinets.

Aside from disillusionment on the right, pessimism of another kind, born of skepticism about Taishō democracy, is far more prevalent in Japanese social science. While this negative view has drawn criticism in the West for its common association with Marxist perspectives on Japanese politics, it deserves close scrutiny, because it accurately reflects the apprehensions of Japanese political observers during the Taishō period itself. In this perspective, Taishō democracy initially held a strong element of promise, for the period was characterized by the rise of genuine mass political movements that sprang forth from below—the rice riots, the universal suffrage movement, the rise of labor unions and tenant farmers' associations, and the movement for a proletarian political party. Yet these democratic impulses from below remained separate from the behavior of the political parties, which were widely perceived as corrupt and closely tied to the huge financial interests of the zaibatsu and local elites.

This perspective, then, flatly rejects the rise of political parties as evidence of the massive democratization of Japanese politics in the Western liberal mode. In the words of historian Kato Shūichi, "What really distinguished Japanese society in the 1920s from the Western world was the very fact that the participation of the mass in politics still rested largely on votes in elections which were not much more than mere formalities."[41] While some may object that Japan was no less democratic than Great Britain in the mid-1840s, contemporary skeptics of Taishō politics saw that the peculiar institutional position of the emperor and his formal and informal advisors made the democratic tendencies that existed much weaker, and growing repression did not suggest that democratizing trends would blossom further in the future. The oligarchical politics of the Meiji period had indeed given way to "party rule" on the surface;[42] yet as the parties became more activist, they were increasingly integrated into the political establishment, and their maneuvers became barely distinguishable from the machinations of *genrō*, military men, and bureaucrats who had dominated politics in the Meiji era. The parties, in short, were not effective representatives of mass sentiment among a population that remained largely disengaged from politics. Consequently, those who did seek political action from below were finally compelled to generate reformist and then revolutionary alternatives to the Taishō political framework.

Contributing to the collapse of the myth of Taishō democracy were many factors congenial to Marxian analyses of the relationship between politics and economics. The elitism of the system was maintained, for example, by a suffrage that was initially severely limited on an economic basis. On the occasion of the first Diet elections of 1890, the 1890 Election Law had granted the right to vote only to males over twenty-five years of age (except priests, religious teachers, active servicemen, and the insane), who paid a hefty 15 yen in a national land or income tax. The law enfranchised only 1.5 percent of the population, one-third of whom were ex-samurai.[43] Under pressure from the universal suffrage movement from below beginning in 1919, the Diet considered a variety of measures to enlarge the electorate. In that year, the law still required a tax of 10 yen; the Hara (Kei) government's (Seiyūkai) conservative proposal to lower that requirement would still have enfranchised only 5.6 percent of the rural population and 3.2 percent of the urban population—less than 2.9 million of a total population of 56 million would have had the vote.[44] But the Diet elected dissolution over the liberalization of voting requirements. When the universal manhood suffrage act was finally passed in 1925, the twenty-five-year and male qualifications remained, but the removal of the tax requirement increased the voting population from 3 million to almost 14 million (of a total population of 59 million).[45] From the late Meiji to the late Taishō period, the expansion of the electorate failed to keep pace with overall population growth, reflecting the increased inequality of income distribution that accompanied Japan's rapid growth. The rising numbers of urban workers and farmers whose income was heavily consumed by high rents were effectively excluded from Taishō politics, as were, of course, women.

In addition to these restrictions on suffrage, party politics were also an elite matter. Where 98 percent of the population was excluded from the vote by requirements including a tax payment of 10 yen in 1919, even after universal manhood suffrage was passed in 1925, candidates had to post a bond of 2,000 yen, a fairly prohibitive fee.[46] Party membership, then, like the electorate as a whole, was disproportionately rural, reflecting the fact that rural landowners paid the heaviest so-called national tax, which was based on landownership; payment of this tax entitled one to vote. In the cities, larger-scale businessmen in the "modern" sector of the economy were those able to express themselves at the polls. Hence, the two major parties, the Seiyūkai and the Kenseikai, responded primarily to landowner interests in the countryside and zaibatsu interests in the cities.[47] In the Diet, parties maneuvered among themselves, with little connection to the population as a whole. The fledgling socialist parties were those closest to the "masses," for they controlled a number of labor unions. But unionization never involved a large enough segment of the population to establish a basis for a strong tie between urban workers and political party activity. This was particularly so because union activity was not officially permitted until the very end of the Taishō period, 1925.[48] These characteristics gave Taishō democracy a layered effect: at the grass-roots level, urban workers and rural tenants demonstrated their discontent with the distribution of political and economic power, often dramatically, as in the rice riots of 1918. Above them, unattached by the sort of link a less restricted suffrage might have provided, the parties tangled with one another and with the bureaucracy to make an impact on national policy. To be sure, party leaders were not unimpressed with public outbursts, and the younger parties, particularly the Kenseikai and Kokumintō, often took the initiative in proposing reformist legislation. But there was no basis for the organic tie between the parties and the population that is essential to the proper function of the party in facilitating democratic politics.[49]

In this fundamental respect, then, there was little to distinguish Taishō politics from Meiji politics. The institutional arrangements prescribed by the Meiji Constitution remained intact, severely limiting the possibilities for democratization during the Taishō period. The "power to rule" (*tōchiken*) or sovereignty officially resided with the emperor, under Article One of the Meiji Constitution. There was, therefore, no notion of popular sovereignty to legitimate the supremacy of political parties in the decision-making process. This interpretation of the locus of sovereignty instead operated to place a premium on those who could identify themselves most closely with the "Imperial Will." Those in the best position to accomplish this were not in the Diet but linked to the throne through institutional structure or custom: the *genrō*, the Privy Council, the Imperial Household Ministry, and, to a lesser extent, the House of Peers. The institution of popular representation, the lower House of Representatives, had little opportunity for leverage. Prime ministers were appointed by the *genrō*, not elected by party majorities. Even when the Taishō years produced a series of prime ministers who were party leaders, in most cases these men were also former bureaucrats, who, therefore, did not have a strong set of interests distinct from those of the bureaucracy. Indeed, party leadership in general reflected a steady growth in the proportion of former bureaucrats.[50] Maruyama Masao argued that this pattern had a negative effect on the development of parties and democracy in Japan. "Ex-politician-bureaucrats presently became ex-bureaucrat/politicians, until finally there was a deluge of bureaucrats-cum-officials, who were not really politicians at all. The autocratic sense of responsibility receded, and no democratic sense of responsibility arose to take its place.''[51] The parties themselves became increasingly bureaucratized, so that the claim that the Taishō period marked a replacement of oligarchical bureaucratic policy making by an era when ''the 'established parties' achieved a decisive measure of control over the cabinet''[52] does not in fact indicate the dramatic democratization it would seem to imply.

If the progressivism of the Katō Cabinet led ''many'' by 1927 ''to assume that party control over the cabinet was imbedded in Japanese parliamentary practice,''[53] other institutional arrangements carried over from the Meiji period made that a fallacious assumption indeed. Even the liberal measure of universal male suffrage did not render a Marxian critique irrelevant, for it was coupled with the repressive Peace Preservation Law, which sustained the efforts of the ''Thought Police'' through the 1930s.[54] Hence, when the debate on Japanese capitalism erupted in 1927, the extent to which the current state of politics in Japan constituted ''bourgeois democracy'' in any meaningful sense became a central issue of controversy. Even the Rōnō-ha, the Marxist dissident faction that seceded from the JCP in 1927 and maintained that a bourgeois-democratic revolution had already been achieved in the Meiji Restoration, conceded that there remained important ''bourgeois-democratic'' tasks to be accomplished in the imminent socialist revolution. By contrast, the Kōza-ha—the faction that remained loyal to the JCP and the Comintern's leadership—argued that the Meiji Restoration had initiated, but not completed, a bourgeois-democratic revolution, leaving feudal relations intact. Both the Rōnō-ha and Kōza-ha insisted that Taishō democracy suffered from major imperfections. In the Rōnō-ha view, power was largely held by the ''financial bourgeoisie,''[55] and thus any general Marxist criticism of bourgeois democracy as democracy for the few could be levelled against the Japanese state. While the Rōnō-ha stressed the fusion between the state and large finance capital,[56] the Kōza-ha repudiated the Taishō state as a feudal remnant, which the bourgeois revolution begun by the Meiji Restoration had failed to eliminate. This argument stressed the role of landlords—of which the emperor was the largest—in the political process.[57] This perspective was consistent with Kato Shūichi's description of the distortions of the democratic process by landowning interests in the Meiji/Taishō institutional framework.

> The Privy Council and the House of Peers held broad constitutional powers enabling them to reject any act of the House of Representatives [which did not have a broad popular base, in any case, given voting restrictions]. The cabinet, in the name of the Emperor, had the power

> to dissolve the Diet, intervene in elections, control information, and limit free speech and free assembly. Besides this, the cabinet could modify laws over the heads of the House of Representatives through the promulgation of Imperial ordinances. At the same time, the army, of which the supreme command was one of the Imperial prerogatives, had to a great extent independence from the cabinet, let alone from the House of Representatives. The leaders of the armed forces could appeal directly to the emperor without consulting the rest of the administration ("direct access to the throne").[58]

The view from below was disconcerting, indeed, for those who aspired to political democracy on the basis of some meaningful notion of representative government.

Finally, for advocates of Western-style liberalism in international relations as well as domestic affairs, foreign policy developments in the Taishō years were equally disturbing. The Japanese empire had been built on victories over China and Russia during the Meiji period, and the Taishō era saw further expansionist efforts. In addition to reaffirming Japan's special rights in Manchuria and Korea, the Lansing-Ishii Agreement with the United States in 1917 recognized Japan's interests and privileges in China. Two years earlier, Japan had presented China with Twenty-one Demands that were clearly designed to take advantage of China's weakened domestic and international positions and make China a virtual colony of Japan. The demands included recognition of Japan's succession to Germany's privileged position in Shandong, as well as economic concessions in Mongolia and Manchuria. These demands were met eventually through Japanese economic and military activity on the mainland throughout the 1920s, which was abetted by the Versailles settlement's ratification of Japan's position in Shandong. The Chinese vigorously resisted Japan's insistence on special privileges within China proper and on having Japanese advisors within the Chinese government. Japan continued to have substantial leverage in China, however, through loans to the government and its rapidly growing trade with China. These interests would, in 1928, fuel the army's effort (foiled by the government) to intervene against the unifying Northern Expedition of the Chinese Guomindang (Nationalist Party), and urge the assassination of warlord Zhang Zuolin to keep Manchuria out of the Nationalist orbit. Moreover, Japan's participation in the Allied intervention against the Bolshevik revolution in 1918 was especially vigorous. The army, enjoying some autonomy, committed troops for longer than any other Allied power, withdrawing only in 1922.

While there was clearly, as in this instance, some internal conflict between the government and parties on the one hand and the military on the other, it must be emphasized that there was a tacit consensus cutting across both groups on the desirability of acquiring and maintaining an exclusive Japanese sphere of military and economic influence on the Asian mainland.[59] The parties and their premiers could escape responsibility for neither imperialist expansion abroad nor repression at home. Katō, the premier most closely identified with liberal reform during these years, for example, was an active and involved foreign minister at the time of Japan's Twenty-one Demands on China. Throughout the Taishō years, this basic foreign policy consensus was reflected in the fact that the military budget consistently consumed at least 30 percent of the national budget, peaking at 49 percent at the height of the Siberian intervention in 1921. While Katō must be credited with decreasing the military share of the budget to 29 percent in 1925,[60] this was part of an overall financial retrenchment effort made in response to the worsening financial crisis. Katō apparently found it more difficult to placate party members on proposed cuts in funding for local projects than to reach an acceptable settlement with the military services. While the army was cut by four divisions, the saving achieved in so doing was to be applied to the introduction of more modern weapons; and naval costs were cut by retiring obsolete vessels.[61] These arrangements in no way challenged the ability of the military to dominate Japanese political life, as the 1930s would demonstrate.

Given the character of politics in the Taishō era, it is not surprising that a mass movement of discontented workers, farmers, and political activists should have risen from below. The founding of the Japanese Communist Party in 1922 received crucial external support from the Soviet Union; but the shortcomings of Taishō democracy nurtured the party and facilitated the spread of Marxism as an intellectual movement from within. Significantly, the party's Draft Program of 1922 called for what many felt should have been achieved already under the rubric of Taishō democracy: the abolition of major impediments like the emperor and the Privy Council; universal suffrage for all men and women over age eighteen; freedom of labor organization, assembly, and demonstration; the right to strike; and the abolition of the military police and the secret police (along with the more radical call to abolish the standing army and establish a people's militia). These were admittedly bourgeois-democratic slogans where basic democratic rights continued to be denied despite the constitutional structure of representative government.[62] In short, given the real conditions of the mythological Taishō democracy, the growth of a radical movement on the left was a natural development. In Kato Shūichi's words, "One of the striking paradoxes of Taishō liberalism was that the liberals were operating under such oppressive conditions that the fundamental ideas of political liberalism could not even be suggested in public, let alone put forward in a practicable program. In order to be consistent as a liberal, it was necessary to be a Marxist.''[63]

The Emergence of Marxism as a Political Movement

As these observations suggest, the failure of Taishō democracy contributed directly both to the right-wing mass movement and to the emergence of Japanese Marxism as a coherent political movement during the 1920s. The Taishō period was already ten years old, and the popular movement for universal suffrage had experienced at least three legislative defeats, when the Japanese Communist Party was founded in 1922. The young Japanese socialist movement had suffered a severe blow when its leader, the anarchist Kōtoku Shūsui, was convicted on charges of high treason and executed in 1911. The incident inaugurated the so-called winter period (*fuyu no jidai*) of the left-wing movement. After Kōtoku's execution, state repression effectively deterred socialists from political activism, and the movement virtually disappeared from the political stage for the remainder of the decade.

The revival of socialism in a Marxist-Leninist mold and its crystallization in the form of the JCP after World War I occurred with substantial moral and financial support from the Soviet Union. However, it was primarily a response to the internal political, economic, and social contradictions and crises of Taishō democracy. The upsurge of labor disputes during World War I and the rice riots immediately afterward demonstrated to Japanese socialists that rapid economic growth had introduced serious new tensions into Japanese society, producing a hotbed of mass discontent that could support the sweeping social changes that they advocated. The ripening of the economic preconditions of socialism in wartime growth, combined with the rise of a movement for economic and social justice from below, buoyed the hopes of leftists, aspirations that the realities of Taishō democracy dashed rudely. The repeated failure of the campaign for universal suffrage, the persistence of substantially oligarchical politics beneath the facade of Taishō democracy, and the inability to seek redress for economic grievances legally through labor organizations or parliamentary means all confirmed the socialists' belief that reformism within the existing structure of the Japanese state was not a viable option. The growth of Japanese Marxism as an active revolutionary political movement, in short, was nurtured in the womb of Taishō democracy.

Significantly, the resuscitation of Japanese socialism after the war entailed the differentiation of Marxian revolutionary socialism from other currents of socialism—anarcho-syndicalism, reformist social-democracy, and Christian socialism—for the first time in the history of the movement. The earliest years of the movement were characterized by an intermixture of a variety of strands of Western socialist thought. In 1898, Christian socialists led by Abe Isō, Katayama Sen, Kōtoku Shūsui, and Kawakami Kiyoshi founded the Shakai-shugi Kenkyūkai (Society for the Study of Socialism) in Tokyo to "study the principles of socialism and whether or not they were applicable to Japan."[64] For two years, the group studied the writings of Claude Henri Saint-Simon, Charles Fourier, and Pierre Joseph Proudhon, as well as Karl Marx. When Kōtoku's classic *Shakai-shugi shinzui* [The essence of socialism] was published in 1903, it referred to Marx as the "father of modern socialism" but drew liberally on these and other socialist thinkers. In 1902, Kōtoku did make a distinction between "two contradictory" categories of socialism: "that which expands the power of the state limitlessly" (e.g., state socialism) and that which implies the demise of the state (like anarchism). This differentiation, however, led Kōtoku to associate the thought of Marx and Engels with anarchism because of their emphasis on the withering away of the state after the proletarian revolution.[65] This identification of Marxian socialism with anarchism was challenged only after the birth of a new Soviet state after the Bolshevik revolution in Russia.

What early Japanese radicals sought in these conflicting schools of Western socialism was a solution to the ills that afflicted their society as a result of the massive growth of industrial capitalism since the Meiji Restoration. As cities became overcrowded with the influx of new, impoverished factory workers from the countryside, the economic forces set in motion by the Meiji Restoration generated "social problems" (*shakai mondai*) of the sort that Japan had not experienced before. Many felt that these economic ills were symptomatic of a much deeper malaise. New values that placed a premium on vigorous competition among individuals presented a more fundamental danger to the fiber of traditional Japanese society. The family-based agricultural unit was threatened, for example, by the advent of a technology that separated thousands of young women and girls from their homes to work in urban textile mills.[66] Traditional spiritual concerns were being superseded by material want to be satisfied by the new industries. The pioneers of Japan's socialist movement were adherents of traditional Confucian and Japanese *shishi* (samurai) values emphasizing social harmony and the dedication of individuals to the welfare of the whole; they were disturbed by the effects of the Meiji reforms that undermined those values. Meiji socialists shared a powerful concern with the moral issues raised by this erosion of values. Gail Bernstein has described this moralistic outlook in the Marxist pioneer Kawakami Hajime at the turn of the century: "Having suvived the threat to its existence as an independent nation, Japan was now being eaten from within: immorality—selfishness—was rampant. The cure had proven as bad as the illness. Whereas technology was the answer to Japan's material backwardness in the decades of the eighteen sixties and seventies, spiritual reform was necessary in Kawakami's time to temper the ill effects of Meiji economic reforms."[67]

The strength of this moral issue was the crucial link binding Japanese socialists to those who became known as "materialist" socialists (Marxists) who shared "universalist humanitarian concerns."[68] All embraced "socialism" as an ideology that opposed the "individualism" (*kojin-shugi*) that was at the root of capitalism's spiritual bankruptcy.[69] Meiji socialists uniformly rejected the "social Darwinist" perspective that had come to dominate intellectual discourse. The principle of "free competition" of the "British school of economics" placed a premium on "egoism" and individualism. Those were values alien to Japan's traditional social order based on the pursuit of the interests of the collectivity through the Confucian emphasis on harmony and on *jin* (benevolent love) as the guiding principle of human relations. In the view of Katayama, for example, "when seen as identical with the 'struggle for survival' . . . , 'free competition' [i.e., the capitalist organization of labor] was perceived to be 'in irreconcilable contradiction with morality and religion—[it was] animalism.' "[70]

The details of the salvation of Japanese society through socialism were supplied variously by Christian socialists, utopian socialists, anarchists, and those developing an affinity for Marxian socialism. This eclecticism was viable for a time as long as the particulars were not brought to the fore. Pacifism in international relations and the pursuit of social justice at home were the concerns that unified Meiji socialists until Japan's mobilization for war with Russia. The reality of international conflict introduced schisms that weakened the activist efforts of a movement that was already fragile under the shadow of the powerful Meiji state. The war with Russia in 1904 and 1905 marked a height of socialist agitation, when Kōtoku and Sakai Toshihiko founded the Heimin-sha (Commoner's Society) and published a newspaper to preach opposition to the war along with socialism.[71] Up to this time, eclecticism was evident in the few ill-fated efforts to organize socialist parties. In 1900, a group from the Shakai-shugi Kenkyūkai founded the more activist Shakai-shugi Kyōkai (Socialist Society). Of its six leaders five were Christians: Abe Isō, Katayama, Kawakami Kiyoshi, Kinoshita Naoe, and Nishikawa Kōjirō (Kōtoku was the exception). A year after this group was dissolved by the Home Ministry, Katayama, Kōtoku, and Abe tried to found the similarly short-lived Social-Democratic Party (Shakai Minshutō), in May 1901.[72] When the Russo-Japanese War raised the issue of the relationship between nationalism and socialism, sparking deep divisions in the most unified and successful incarnation of the movement to date, four groups emerged: a group of Christian socialists around Kinoshita, Abe, and Ishikawa Sanshirō, who thereupon launched the magazine *Shin kigen* [New era]; antiparliamentarian syndicalists around Kōtoku; a parliamentarist faction around Katayama and Tazoe Tetsuji; and a compromise faction led by Sakai.[73]

From this point until the dawn of the winter period, the Japanese socialist movement was engulfed constantly in tense conflict over political strategies. Converted to anarcho-syndicalism in 1906 and heavily influenced by the Russian anarchist Peter Kropotkin and the American syndicalist movement, Kōtoku advocated "direct action" (*chokusetsu kōdō ron*), such as strikes and terrorist activity, against the economic oppression of the enterprise and the Japanese imperial state as the shortest path to socialism.[74] Sakai, claiming to follow the Second International "orthodoxy" of German Social-Democrats Karl Kautsky and August Bebel, tried to offer a middle course between Kōtoku's antistatist extremism and Katayama's and Tazoe's advocacy of a parliamentary path to socialism. Since the Meiji state outlawed both labor unions and nongovernmental organized political activity, Sakai's was simply a theoretical position that muddled the distinction between Marxism and anarchism. Nevertheless, this compromise position barely prevailed in the conflict between direct action and parliamentarism at the Japan Socialist Party's (Nihon Shakaitō) Second Congress in 1907. Given the limitations imposed by the state, the victory of Sakai's view effectively nullified both strategies,[75] and the ideological conflict between the two lines continued to simmer after this party collapsed the same year and through the establishment of the JCP fifteen years later.

The conflict between reformist social-democracy (which, as advocated by Tazoe, received only two votes to Kōtoku's twenty-two and Sakai's twenty-eight at the Nihon Shakaitō congress) and the strategy of direct action makes an interesting contrast with the conflict between "economism" and Lenin's stress on political action in the early Russian socialist movement. Anarcho-syndicalists were "economists" in that they refused political action within the framework provided by the constitution, "since such a struggle signified to them the acceptance of the state principle," which they denied unequivocably. Anarchists felt that they should agitate among the masses in response to their economic needs for their economic rights. Lenin, by contrast, classified all such emphasis on economic demands along with the reformism of the German Social-Democratic Party as "revisionist." He contended that economism inevitably compromised the true long-term interests of the masses, who, regardless of minor improvements in working conditions, would continue to suffer the exploitation that was inherent in capitalist economic organization. Lenin proposed to crush the old tsarist state, but he also accepted the need for a temporary dictatorship of the proletariat as prescribed by Marx and Engels.[76]

Neither the alternative offered by Kōtoku's appeal to direct action nor Katayama's emphasis on using the Diet to achieve socialism through gradual reform transcended the conceptual framework of the "economism" that Lenin denounced so vehemently in Russia, although the Japanese socialists faced political conditions that were almost as repressive as those that had prevailed under the Russian tsar. Kōtoku rejected the state, but direct action did not mobilize political action against the state. Rather, inspired by the violent strike at the Ashio Copper Mines in January 1907, Kōtoku dreamed of laborers uniting in a general strike against their capitalist employers. Kōtoku correctly diagnosed the weaknesses of parliamentarism—its effect to dull the senses to the cruel realities inherent in the system—but his own strategy simply skirted the issue of political power as if it were unimportant to the outcome of the economic revolution he advocated. Thus, Kōtoku wrote in 1907,

> What the workers desire is not the conquest of political power, but the "conquest of bread," not laws, but food and clothing . . . I, at least, as a socialist, and as a member of the Socialist Party, believe that as far as the accomplishment of our goal, which is the fundamental revolution of the economic order and the abolition of the wage system, it is far more important to arouse the self-consciousness of ten workers, than to gather a thousand signatures on a petition for universal suffrage. It is far better to spend ten yen organizing workers than a thousand yen on an election campaign. One simple conversation with workers, I am convinced, is worth more than ten lofty speeches in parliament.[77]

That Kōtoku almost defeated both the Sakai and Katayama views was testimony to the fact that "the power of anarchism and syndicalism was tremendous and had an overwhelming influence in the movement in the late Meiji period." The effect of this trend, particularly after the 1905 Russian revolution, was "to draw younger participants away from the study of Marxist thought."[78] As a result, Marxist economic theory became the concern of academics like Kyōtō Imperial University professor Kawakami Hajime, who at this time was still outside the socialist movement.

Anarchism continued to dominate the weak and docile socialist movement in the remaining decade until World War I, the October Revolution, and the unprecedented rice riots of 1918 brought an end to the winter period following Kōtoku's trial and execution. This succession of events provoked renewed effort to study Marxism within the socialist movement itself. The rising interest in Marxism in the form that had finally cast off the tsarist autocracy prepared the Japanese socialist movement for the founding of its own party.

Yet the implications of the revolutions in Russia were not immediately clear to Japan's socialists. Most Japanese viewed Russia as extremely backward both economically and politically, and the Japanese socialist community initially responded to the February and October revolutions with shock. As the anarchist Arahata Kanson would later recall, it seemed incredible that "the absolute autocratic monarchy would crumble in Russia, the 'headquarters' of European reactionary forces." In response to the February revolution, Sakai secretly drafted a congratulatory message from the Japanese socialists to the new Russian provisional government, expressing their hope to see the " 'imperialist' war" in Europe ended quickly. The message was dispatched by way of organs of foreign socialist parties and published in English by Katayama in the American paper *Heimin* [Commoners], in the IWW's *International Socialist Review*, in *Shin intanashonaru* [New international], as well as in Russian newspapers.[79]

The ensuing confusion among Japanese socialists concerning the character of the revolution in Russia was deepened by their unfamiliarity with most of its leading figures. Before the October Revolution, certain Russian revolutionary leaders—George Plekhanov, Vera Zasulich, Lev Deych—were well-known in Japan, but not Lenin and the Bolsheviks. As Arahata wrote in February 1917, "We knew the difference between the Social Revolutionary Party and the Social-Democratic Party, but it was probably the first time anyone heard the terms Menshevik and Bolshevik. There was virtually no one who knew the names Kerensky, Lenin, and Trotsky."[80] Just before the October Revolution, Sakai characterized Lenin as an anarchist, and as late as April 1920 he maintained that "Bolshevism somewhat resembled syndicalism."[81] The anarchist Ōsugi Sakae, who would shortly repudiate Bolshevism for its statist aspects, declared in 1918 that "Bolshevik tactics are the tactics of anarchism."[82]

Japanese socialist interpretations of the Russian revolution tended to reflect pre-existing ideological tendencies. Sakai, in keeping with his view of Russia as more backward than Japan, conceded that it was a Marxist revolution but emphasized Russia's laggard political development. Labor leaders regarded the revolution as a victory for Russian workers.[83] Anarcho-syndicalists and moderate socialists alike heralded the revolution as a positive world-historical development, but the *ana-boru* (anarchist-Bolshevik) split was provoked within the movement when the revolution's outcome became more clearly defined. Specifically, the emergence of a strong Soviet state after October presented the predominantly anarchist movement with a reality that shook its preconceptions of socialist revolution. The Marxist Takabatake Motoyuki boldly exposed these realities in his column in *Shin shakai* [New society], precipitating a debate with Yamakawa Hitoshi by 1919 that presaged the permanent anarchist-Bolshevik rupture of 1922 and 1923.

Takabatake was relieved to see the events in Russia challenge the view that socialism should "ignore all authority"; this was the common conception of anarcho-syndicalists who saw "the state, authority, and further, government in general . . . as [a matter of] bourgeois morality or ethics."[84] As early as August 1917, Takabatake had pointed out that Lenin was not an anarchist, but a left-wing member of the Social-Democratic Party. Noting the Kerensky regime's indifference to imperialism, socialism, and popular desire to end the war, he predicted that the provisional government would soon collapse, while Lenin's faction would gain more power.[85] When the Bolsheviks acceded to power in October, Takabatake drew lessons from the Russian experience to apply to Japan. At this point, he exhibited the commitment to the state as a necessary institution for the maturation of socialism that would provide the basis for his own state socialist doctrine and that would provoke his break with the rest of the socialist movement in 1919. Both the anarchist Ōsugi and statist Takabatake agreed that the Soviet dictatorship of the proletariat demonstrated that Marxism was statist in practice. This view allowed Takabatake to continue to accept Marxism, while it compelled Ōsugi to reject it and reaffirm his earlier loyalty to Kōtoku's doctrine of direct action. The lessons Takabatake deduced from the Russian revolution enabled him to transcend the old direct action versus parliamentarianism controversy in the Japanese socialist movement. In this process he found himself engaged in a protracted debate with Yamakawa Hitoshi, the anarchist. The controversy gradually transformed Yamakawa's position.[86] Yamakawa's new perspective in turn eventually produced his *hōkō tenkan ron* (change of direction theory), on which the new JCP was built.[87]

At issue was Takabatake's professed intention to destroy the prevailing dichotomy between "political movement-parliamentarism" and "economic movement-direct action." Takabatake had supported Sakai's unsuccessful candidacy in the thirteenth general election in 1917 because, in light of Russia's February Revolution, he believed practical political activity was now possible and had rendered obsolete the abstract dichotomy that had dominated Japan's socialist movement since its inception. The Bolsheviks, he argued, succeeded as a revolutionary party precisely by transcending this debate. Writing in *Shin shakai* in February 1918, then, Takabatake asserted that neither parliamentarism nor syndicalism could be the whole of the socialist movement. Yamakawa responded that Takabatake had set up a "straw man": the slogan "parliamentary policy-political movement" in fact never implied that political action and economic action were taken in isolation from each other; rather, the two were always pursued in combination. Takabatake in turn argued that while this theoretical conflict was convulsing Japan's socialist movement, Lenin, Liebknecht, and Luxemburg opposed neither parliamentarism nor unionism but relied on both.[88] But Takabatake failed to convince his colleagues of his views on this issue and on national socialism and promptly removed himself from their circle at the Baibun-sha publishing house. He was impatient with Sakai's inability to perceive the end of the winter period and seize the initiative when the rice riots erupted, and he detested the individualistic antisocial and antistatist attitudes of Ōsugi and his anarchist followers.

Yamakawa, however, began to alter his position. Seeing the Hara Kei cabinet as a representative of bourgeois political power, he called for the establishment of a proletarian political party.[89] After he and Arahata organized a study group in 1918 "to criticize Marxism" and to spread anarcho-syndicalist ideas through its organ *Aofuku* [Blue uniform], Yamakawa gradually reconciled himself with the statist elements of Bolshevism. In December 1919, he defended the Soviet state against charges of being undemocratic and unfaithful to Marxism. Citing Marx and Lenin, Yamakawa reiterated Marx's critique of bourgeois democracy and argued that a strong state was required to defend this relatively backward lone socialist country against more economically advanced forces of reaction.[90] It was not until 1922, however, that Yamakawa decisively abandoned anarcho-syndicalism and adopted many of Takabatake's own arguments in his "change of direction" essay in the magazine *Zen'ei* [Vanguard].[91]

As Ōsugi remained committed to the late Kōtoku's direct action program while most other socialists accepted Bolshevism and fell into line behind Yamakawa, the *ana-boru* controversy peaked in 1922 and 1923. Between the Yamakawa-Takabatake debate and the founding of the JCP, anarchists and Bolsheviks cooperated as the outcome of the Russian revolution awaited firm resolution in the Siberian intervention. The Japanese Socialist League (Nihon Shakai-shugi Dōmei), which Sakai founded in December 1920, for example, encompassed not only anarcho-syndicalists and Bolsheviks, but national socialists (except Takabatake) as well. Sakai and Yamakawa joined the still nonactivist Kawakami Hajime to edit the journals *Shin shakai* (reorganized after Takabatake left Baibun-sha, and later retitled *Shin shakai hyōron* [New society review]), *Shakai-shugi kenkyū* [Studies in socialism], and *Shakai mondai kenkyū* [Studies on social problems]; all became important vehicles for introducing Marxist thought into Japan. Meanwhile, the Comintern began to show interest in Japan as Asia's sole imperialist power, and Japanese Marxists reciprocated by publishing articles on the Comintern.[92] During these years, the Japanese movement as a whole acquired a more decidedly Marxist hue in contrast with the eclecticism of its early years. Ironically, it was the anarchist Ōsugi who made the first Japanese contact with the Comintern. When offered 10,000 yen by Gregory Voitinsky at the October 1920 conference of Far Eastern socialists in Shanghai, Ōsugi accepted the funds at a time when Sakai and Yamakawa (both later Rōnō-ha leaders) were hesitant to establish relations with the Comintern.[93]

Nevertheless, a final split between the Bolshevists, now prepared to submit to Comintern authority, and the anarchists was not long in coming. The Japanese Socialist League was officially banned in 1922, but not before internal tensions between the two groups had already weakened the organization from within.[94] Latent ideological antagonisms surfaced at the League's Second Congress in May 1921 and intensified until the dispute resulted in the establishment of the Rōdō Kumiai Sōrengō (General Association of Labor Unions) in September 1922.[95] As Yamakawa's *Zen'ei* (launched in January 1922) waged an ideological war against Ōsugi's anarchist organ, *Rōdō undō* [Labor movement], members of the Japanese Socialist League aligned with one faction or the other. Leninists like Tokuda Kyūichi and Takase Kiyoshi formed splinter groups such as the Suiyōkai (Wednesday Society) around Yamakawa, while Arahata moved from anarchism toward Bolshevism after being influenced by events in the Italian movement. The Bolshevists, aided by a revolutionary philosophy that stressed organization, gained more and more momentum. In April 1922, Ichikawa Shōichi founded the journal *Musan kaikyū* [Proletariat], which merged with Sakai's and Yamakawa's *Shakai-shugi kenkyū* (or *Zen'ei*) a year later. That year, on the third annual commemoration of May Day, the slogan demanded "Recognition of workers' and peasants' Russia!" The Japanese Bolsheviks scored a conclusive victory over anarchism when the JCP was founded in 1922 by the Bolshevists in Japan and overseas Japanese socialists led by Katayama Sen.[96] If only for five years, former anarcho-syndicalists like Arahata and Yamakawa tempered their anarchist and nationalist instincts resisting Comintern authority to lead the new Communist Party in the face of heavy-handed government repression.

For the rest of the prewar period, the JCP endeavored to implement the revolutionary strategy prescribed in the Comintern's theses on Japan. Within a year after the party was established, however, the state launched a series of massive "roundups" of communists and suspected fellow-travellers. As the party struggled to maintain its increasingly precarious existence in Taishō Japan, Marxism wielded less influence as an activist movement effectively mobilizing large numbers of urban workers on the Russian model and gained increasing significance as an intellectual trend in the critical Taishō and Shōwa years.

Intellectual Currents: Traditional Japanese and Imported Theories of Society and Polity

By the time the debate on Japanese capitalism began late in 1927, significant changes had altered the intellectual milieu of Taishō Japan. By the end of the Meiji period, Marxism began to rival the influence of classical Western—primarily British—schools of economics in Japan's leading Tokyo

Imperial and Kyoto Imperial universities, the training grounds for Japan's bureaucrats and nongovernmental political leaders. By the late 1920s and early 1930s, Marxism contended with orthodoxy in the economics and *kokushi* (history) departments and law schools of Japan's elite universities. Yet the Marxist-Leninist approach to political change was by no means the sole alternative to Taishō democracy generated by its critics. Traditionalist schemes for the restoration of the grandeur of the Meiji period, varieties of national-socialism, and Western-style liberalism enriched the intellectual context in which the debate on Japanese capitalism occurred. These were the foils against which Marxists in the Rōnō-ha and Kōza-ha directed their political programs and innovative interpretations of Japanese society and its polity.

As a result of the Meiji oligarchy's purposive efforts to articulate an official state ideology and to disseminate it through a universal education system,[97] a fairly coherent body of "traditional" Japanese political thought dominated Japanese intellectual circles in the Meiji period and continued to wield a powerful influence in the Taishō period. Not only did this body of thought shape the consensus of Taishō political leaders on the nature of the Japanese polity; but because the ideology permeated the educational system up to the university level,[98] it also influenced the political preconceptions of Japanese Marxists, most of whom were educated through the highest levels of the selective educational system. This traditional thought, then, is significant not only as the governing ideology and steadfast opponent of Marxism, but as a belief system that could be expected to affect the patterns of the adaptation of Marxist and other Western ideas to Japan.

The emperor (*tennō* or *mikado*) occupied the central position in official Meiji political thought. It compressed the concepts of nation and state into one and demonstrated the extent to which traditionally the state—the political organization—absorbed the nation—the political community or society in general—in indigenous Japanese thought. The *tennō* was at the apex of both, as the patriarchal head of the uniquely Japanese *kokutai* (which can be translated only inadequately as "national polity" or "national body"), incorporating race, ethnicity, lineage, and spirituality into a single concept; and as the political ruler of a constitutional monarchic form of state (*seitai*). Within the context of the militaristic international system to which the Meiji Restoration itself was a response, the *tennō* was at once "(1) a constitutional monarch, the monarch of an authoritarian state as established by the Meiji Constitution granted by the emperor [not demanded by the people]; (2) the generalissimo (*daigenshi*), the monarch as the summit of authority of supreme command over the armed forces, independent from the control of the cabinet; and (3) a monarch of divine right, a monarch representing religious or spiritual authority in place of that of the West's Christianity."[99]

This conception of the emperor system represented an amalgam of religious elements drawn from traditional Japanese Shintō thought, moral elements adopted from Tokugawa Confucianism, and German theories of state sovereignty imported through the influence of German constitutional scholars like Rudolf von Gneist, Lorenz von Stein, Hermann Roesler, Georg Jellinek, and Johann Kaspar Bluntschli.[100] During the Tokugawa period, real political power had lain with the shogun, the military ruler, rather than with the emperor. The emperor remained throughout, however, a symbolic figure whose authority was maintained through the Shintō mythology of his divine origins and of his position as the head of the extended Japanese national (ethnic) family.[101] The framers of the Meiji Constitution invoked German political thought in order to reconcile this traditional conception with contemporary constitutional monarchical forms. Roesler was most influential in making this formulation. Roesler conceived of the emperor playing a supra-political role that would permit him to transcend the divisions and petty infighting of party politics. Thus, even though Roesler did not accept the traditional mythology of the emperor, his attribution of the sovereignty to the emperor in Article One of the Meiji Constitution was reinforced by the structure of traditional Japanese beliefs about him.[102]

The effect of this combination of traditional and imported elements was to give the Meiji polity and its ideology a decidedly antiliberal cast, and to create a system of politics that was resistant to liberal appeals to popular rights and sovereignty. This effect was evident even within the popular rights movement of the late nineteenth century. Left-wing civil rights theorists like Ueki Emori (1857-1892) protested the "irrationality" of the monarchical system and repudiated the imperial institution until about 1880. After 1882, however, as the new ideology became more systematized, even these theorists gradually abandoned such arguments, and the legitimate existence of the emperor became the premise for their advocacy of "constitutional democracy."[103]

Nevertheless, the conception of imperial sovereignty permitted some flexibility. By the end of the Meiji period two schools of thought had evolved from this set of basic assumptions about the *kokutai* and the Meiji Constitution. The "absolutist" interpretation systematized by legal scholars Hozumi Yatsuka and Uesugi Shinkichi emphasized the unique divine nature of Japan's emperor. By contrast, drawing on the organic state theories of Bluntschli and his successors, Minobe Tatsukichi's "emperor-organ theory" (*tennō kikan setsu*) maintained that the Japanese emperor should be treated on the same basis as all national monarchs. According to Minobe, the state was a sovereign organic body, and the emperor, as a legal but not divine person, was but the highest of its many organs. The Diet thus shared the power to rule with the emperor.[104] In opposition to the *lèse-majesté* implied by Minobe's conception, Uesugi developed a more nationalistic and authoritarian theory of a patrimonial state that countered that sovereignty (*taiken*) lay not in the state but in the emperor himself.[105]

Significantly, this controversy evolved solely as a purely legal or constitutional debate on the interpretation of Article One of the Meiji Constitution. Political theory as such was not subject to debate, particularly insofar as it concerned the emperor in this period of the consolidation of the Meiji oligarchy's state- and nation-building efforts.[106] Indeed, the basic similarities between the two major schools illustrate an underlying consensus on the nature of the emperor. Both Minobe and Uesugi had been influenced by German state theory, and neither questioned the origins of the emperor system. Nor did they, like the classical political theorists Thomas Hobbes, John Locke, and Jean-Jacques Rousseau, examine the basis of the state in order to legitimate the origins of government itself. Minobe, like Uesugi, accepted the validity of the emperor system itself; but in Uesugi's view, the emperor's absolute authority was natural and positive in itself.[107] For a time, from about 1903 through the Taishō period, Minobe's interpretation attained considerable influence in academic circles, and its legitimacy was unofficially recognized by the government.[108] However, the basic constellation of assumptions supporting the authoritarian interpretation remained intact, and in the 1930s the government explicitly supported it in order to promote nationalistic sentiment for the war effort. That both the emperor-organ theory and Minobe himself were formally censured by the Diet in 1935[109] testifies to the continued vitality of the family-state *kokutai* conception in Japanese political thought through the 1920s and 1930s.[110] Indeed, as educational textbooks indicate, by 1910 something of a reaction against the legalistic nation-state of the Western conception had already occurred. Texts of 1903 emphasized the theme of *chūkun-aikoku* (loyalty to the monarch and patriotism toward the state), which was replaced in 1910 with the theme of the unity of filial piety in Japanese sentiment toward the emperor.[111] Clearly the continued dominance of this family conception of the state (*kazoku kokka*) effectively delimited the range of development of political life even within the framework of the notion of Taishō democracy. Hence, even the liberalism of Japan's spokesman for the most Western liberal conception of the polity, Yoshino Sakuzō, fell far short of claiming popular sovereignty. His advocacy of *minpon-shugi* or "government for the people" was consistent with a set of political ideas that attributed constitutionalism and civil rights to the grace of the emperor rather than to natural "rights."[112]

Kokutai, then, with its mixture of Confucian and distinctively Japanese elements, was the mainstream traditional view of the Japanese polity, the backdrop against which Western ideas were introduced into Japan. This family conception of the state was an organic theory in which the Japanese nation was conceived as a natural extension of the family. The Confucian bonds of loyalty and piety that existed within a properly Confucian family were to characterize the polity as well.[113] While the communal aspects of this conception would appear to make intellectuals in Meiji and Taishō Japan more receptive to socialism, in fact, its particularism[114] and religious undertones had the opposite effect. When socialism was first introduced into Japan, Inoue Tetsujirō, a philosophy professor at Tokyo Imperial University, "and other 'national morality' spokesmen" argued that the universality of socialism violated the Japanese *kokutai*. This objection troubled Japanese socialists for some time thereafter.[115] Moreover, spokesmen for the *kokutai* idea, like the authors of the official textbook *Kokutai no hongi* [The true meaning of *kokutai*] (1937), were emphatic on the contradictions between this indigenous mode of thought and Western ideologies based on egoistic individualism:

> The individualistic aspect of human beings abstracts only one aspect of an individuality and overlooks the national and historical qualities. Hence, it loses sight of the totality and concreteness of human beings and deviates from the reality of human existence, the theories departing from actualities and running off into many mistaken channels. Herein lie the basic errors underlying the various concepts of individualism, liberalism, and their developments. The nations of the West have now awakened up to these errors, and various ideologies and movements have sprung up in order to overcome them. Nevertheless, these ideologies and movements will eventually end in regarding the collections of people as bodies or classes, or at the most in conceiving a conceptual state; so that such things will do no more than provide erroneous ideas to take the place of existing erroneous ideas, and will furnish no true way out or solution.[116]

Marxism, with its emphasis on class and the conceptual state, was clearly such a response to Western-style individualism. Was this "solution" required where there was no indigenous rampant individualism to produce the terrible consequences it had wrought in the West?

The fundamental conflict between the traditional *kokutai* conception on the one hand and both liberal and post-liberal Western political thought on the other predictably created significant difficulties for the application of Marxism in Japan. *Tenkōsha*, or those who renounced communism in the critical Shōwa years of mounting war crisis, frequently returned to the *kokutai* conception;[117] some, including Sano Manabu, tried to reconcile these ideas with Marxism in the form of a Marxian national socialism.[118] For both the public, exposed to JCP slogans for the demise of the emperor system, and

Marxists attempting to analyze the state in Marxist terms, the continued influence of this *kokutai* conception obstructed the full acceptance of Marxism in Japan and its application to analyze the state in abstract terms. As *tenkōsha* Kobayashi Morito claimed, "In a case such as Japan, in particular, where *minzoku* [nation or ethnic people] and *kokka* [the state] were one," the JCP and its Comintern-inspired slogans were truly alien.[119] To abolish the emperor as the JCP demanded implied the destruction of the Japanese nation itself, making socialism impracticable.

Despite the incompatibility of traditional *kokutai* thought with Western liberal political thought, classical Western economic theory—and even social theory like that of Max Weber—found a hearty reception among university scholars seeking an understanding of the forces behind the state's capitalist industrializing efforts. The economic theory of capitalism posed none of the difficulties of liberal political thought for the Meiji regime. Indeed, as Gail Bernstein has noted, *kokutai* thought "affirmed capitalism as the basis of Japanese economic organization."[120] Thus, by the end of the Meiji period, British classical economics, the work of Adam Smith, James Mill, Thomas Malthus, and David Ricardo, quickly became a main current of academic work in the imperial universities, where Japan's intellectual, political, and business elites were trained. Yet, given the role of the Meiji state in promoting Japan's industrialization, laissez-faire economics was never accepted without qualification in Japan. Thus, the study of British economics was paralleled by the pursuit of the work of German social policy theorists. At the turn of the century, the two schools were represented by the *Tōkyō keizai zasshi* [Tokyo economics journal], edited by Finance Ministry official Taguchi Ukichi for the laissez-faire school, and by the *Kokka gakkai zasshi* [National studies association journal], edited by law professors at Tokyo Imperial University for the social policy school.

The German social policy approach was the state-centric theoretical basis for Otto von Bismarck's economic and social policies; since these were designed to cripple the appeal of the German social-democratic movement, they were an attractive model for scholars sympathetic to the Meiji state. In addition, the German social policy theorists like Roger Wagner were more consistent than classical British economics with the statist and national concerns of the Meiji state.[121] Their profession of social concern resounded with the *kokutai* conception's portrayal of the emperor as a moral and benevolent ruler with profound concern for the welfare of his subjects. As a member of the social policy economic school in the first decade of this century at Kyoto Imperial University, the later Marxist Kawakami Hajime advocated social policy in a manner suggestive of this relationship between traditional Japanese political ethics and the German school.

> The major difference between the West and Japan lies in the difference between individualism and nationalism. In the West even socialism is based ultimately on the individual. This is also true of social policy in the West, which has as its goal the fulfillment of the individual. In our country, we can say that social policy has still not been realized. For example, even though we have moved toward establishing factory laws, the goal of these laws is not the reverence of the workers' personality or the increase of the class profit of the working class. As much as possible we consider [the workers] to be the tools of national industry. The improvement of these tools is necessary for the healthy advancement of the nation's industry.[122]

In response to the political, economic, and social crisis rising in the Taishō years, an emphasis on this kind of conception of the state emerged repeatedly in non-Marxist alternatives generated by Japanese intellectuals seeking radical political and economic change. Kita Ikki's *Outline for the Reconstruction of Japan* (1918-1919) criticized the official *kokutai-ron* conception as a mythological perversion of a true *kokutai*, which was essentially social democratic.[123] But his vision of a Japanese state or national socialism later became a banner for the right-wing ultranationalist movement among young military officers in the 1930s. Similarly, Takabatake Motoyuki, the first to produce a complete Japanese translation of the three volumes of *Capital*, created a system of Marxist national socialism. Asserting that "Marxism was originally statism,"[124] Takabatake cited Thomas Hobbes and other Western state theorists to support the notion that the state preceded class society and would not wither away after a proletarian revolution. To guard against external threats and to organize economic activity at home—against the possibility of proletarian imperialism on the part of Soviet Russia, for example—a socialist Japan would require a powerful state.[125] Later, in 1924, another Marxist, Akamatsu Katsumaro, advocated a doctrine of "scientific Japanism" and subsequently espoused his own version of national socialism, which also emphasized the role of the state in Japan's economic development.[126] Finally, presaging the mass *tenkō* of the 1930s, in 1927 a group of imprisoned Marxists led by Mizuno Shigeo renounced Marxist internationalism in favor of a theory of national socialism based on the Imperial Household.[127]

While the dynamics of this pattern in twentieth-century Japanese political thought are deservedly the subject of a separate study, this brief survey does suggest the range of thought against which the Marxist interpreters of Japanese capitalism pitted themselves. After the Russian revolution the importation of Marxist thought into Japan accelerated, and Marxism won an increasing number of adherents in the country's leading academic institutions.

The mounting economic and social crisis of the Taishō period both stimulated such academic concern about economic issues and heightened political activism among those who were attracted to Marx's ideal of revolutionary socialism. As the post-World War I distress in agriculture and industry deepened, it provided fertile ground, particularly in the countryside, for the growth of right-wing influences supporting a return to agrarian traditionalism or resort to military expansion. The economic crisis thus weakened a potentially democratic constitution that was already fragile and threatened the dreams of liberals and socialists, who could exercise little effective power under the restrictions imposed by the state.

The political and economic doctrine of Marxism armed disgruntled intellectuals with a powerful weapon against the crisis of Taishō. While its economic interpretation of capitalism and its theory of the state helped Japanese dissidents to analyze the causes of the current malaise, its theory of revolution offered a ready blueprint for resolving it. In their effort to define a solution to the crisis of Taishō democracy without reverting to the traditional *kokutai* conception or conceding to the chauvinistic impulses of national socialism, the partisans of this new school of political, economic, and social thought in Japan confronted a vital challenge. The decade of the 1920s established the theoretical and organizational foundations for their impassioned endeavor.

TWO

Internal Factors Shaping the Debate: The Evolution of Marxism in Japan to 1927

THE DEBATE on Japanese capitalism marked a watershed in the development of Marxist thought in Japan. The controversy demonstrated that the basic tenets of Marxism and Marxism-Leninism had been absorbed in Japan sufficiently to permit their innovative application to analyze the peculiarities of Japanese political and economic development. Significantly, the controversy initially emerged out of the practical efforts of the Japanese Communist Party from the time of its founding in 1922 to resolve pressing questions of revolutionary strategy and tactics. The course of the debate itself from its inception in 1927 to its abrupt silencing by the police in 1937 mirrored this overall pattern in the maturation of Japanese Marxism, signalling a rapid progression from relatively mechanistic "applied Marxism" to higher, more abstract and sophisticated levels of analysis. The complex, more historical and theoretical Marxist scholarship that finally emerged in the course of the debate by the mid-1930s would in turn provide the basis for the outstanding contribution to Marxist political economy made by Japanese Marxists after World War II.

The contours of the debate and the character of the scholarship that it produced were shaped by factors both internal and external to the evolution of the Japanese Marxist movement. Following the brief overview of the debate below is an analysis of the trends within Japanese Marxism itself and in the larger international context that stimulated the controversy on Japanese capitalism.

Overview of the Debate

Japanese scholars have generally distinguished two periods in the debate on Japanese capitalism.[1] The first period, from 1927 to 1931, began with the exit of the dissident faction (Rōnō-ha) of former Japanese Communist Party leader Yamakawa Hitoshi from the party. Yamakawa's group opposed the existence of the Japanese Communist Party as a vanguard revolutionary party under Comintern leadership; and the group's departure from the party in November 1927 was triggered by the party's adoption of the Comintern's July 1927 Theses on Japan. According to the '27 Theses, the persistence of "feudal remnants" in the agrarian sector of the economy and in the political superstructure—the emperor system *(tennō-sei)*, the Privy Council, the extra-legal influence of the *genrō*, the *Naidaijin* (Lord Keeper of the Privy Seal), and Imperial Household minister—indicated that the bourgeois revolution begun by the Meiji Restoration had not yet been completed. Therefore, a strategy of two-stage revolution was necessary: a bourgeois-democratic revolution led by the proletariat would complete the tasks abandoned by Japan's weak bourgeoisie and then be followed immediately by a socialist revolution.[2] Yamakawa's group rejected the Comintern's depiction of Japan as too backward for an immediate socialist revolution and in December 1927 launched the journal *Rōnō* [Labor-farmer], after which the faction was named, to conduct vocal criticism of the Japanese Communist Party and to present its case for a single proletarian socialist revolution.

The early period from 1927 to 1931, then, was defined by the advocacy of a one-stage revolution by Rōnō-ha leaders Yamakawa and Inomata Tsunao (1889-1942) and its rebuttal by JCP loyalists writing in such left-wing journals as *Marukusu-shugi* [Marxism] and *Taiyō* [The sun].[3] Labor leaders in the JCP like Noro Eitarō, Watanabe Masanosuke (1899-1928), Ichikawa Shōichi (1892-1945), and Takahashi Sadaki (1905-1935) attacked the Rōnō-ha in defense of the Comintern's formula of two-stage revolution. At this stage the controversy focused on practical questions of political party organization and revolutionary strategy and tactics, the issues that had driven the Rōnō-ha from the JCP at the outset. What originated as an intraparty dispute, however, quickly spilled over beyond the party and its dissenters to embrace an increasing number of nonparty academic Marxists.[4] To such scholars, it was self-evident that the question of a one-stage or a two-stage revolution ultimately rested on an interpretation of the current level of Japanese political and economic development, which could only be understood in terms of the past.

This intellectual concern combined with changes in the domestic political situation by 1932 to draw the debate into its second phase. Official repression of the revolutionary movement had grown steadily during the 1920s, particularly with the passage of the Peace Preservation Law in 1925. Under this law, the Japanese police conducted massive arrests of JCP members and suspected sympathizers in the March 1928, April 1929, and February 1930 roundups. Such government repression forced the *Marukusu-shugi* to cease publication in April 1929, and finally made open debate on practical issues virtually impossible.[5] Indeed, it was the increasing pressure by Japan's Special Higher (Thought) Police that drove the debate underground early in the 1930s before quashing it completely by 1940.[6]

The second period of the debate consequently reflected these pressures. In 1932, the Comintern issued new theses on Japan reasserting the need for a two-stage revolution to destroy the deeply rooted "feudal remnants" in Japanese society before proceeding with a socialist revolution. Coincidentally, efforts by JCP loyalists to conduct their own Marxist analyses of Japan appeared in the form of the seven-volume scholarly *Nihon shihon-shugi hattatsu shi kōza* [Symposium on the history of the development of Japanese capitalism], the publication that gave the Kōza-ha its name.[7] The appearance of the *Kōza* marked the emergence of the rigorous and increasingly abstract and theoretical contributions that characterized the second stage of the debate on Japanese capitalism. As the Rōnō-ha–Kōza-ha debate intensified, writers of both factions assembled a wealth of empirical data; and the period yielded a rich variety of Marxist scholarship, much of which remains the underpinning of Japanese work on the history of Japan's economic development even today.

During this period, battle lines hardened, and the arguments offered by the two sides became more coherent. Although there was no official membership in the factions, their supporters were readily identifiable by the views they espoused. Prominent names included:

(1) For the Kōza-ha, Aikawa Haruki, Hani Gorō, Hat(t)ori Shisō, Hirano Yoshitarō, Ikumi Taku'ichi, Inoue Harumaru, Kobayashi Ryōsei, Noro Eitarō, Sakamoto Sanzen, Shinobu Seizaburō, Tatsuda Nobuo, Tanaka Yasuo, and Yamada Moritarō.

(2) For the Rōnō-ha, Aono Suekichi, Arahata Kanson, Fujii Yonezō, Inomata Tsunao (until circa 1930), Itō Yoshimichi, Kitaura Sentarō, Kushida Tamizō, Okada Sōji, Ōuchi Hyōe, Sakai Toshihiko, Sakisaka Itsurō, Suzuki Mosaburō, Tsuchiya Takao, and Yamakawa Hitoshi.

(3) Holding a middle ground: Moriya Fumio (closer to Kōza-ha), Kimura Masanosuke (Kawai Etsuzō), Toda Shintarō, and Tsushima Tadayuki (closer to Rōnō-ha).[8]

The works considered most representative of the respective factions were two books of essays by Hirano and Yamada assembled from the *Kōza* and refutations of these penned by Rōnō-ha theorists. Yamada Moritarō's *Nihon shihon-shugi bunseki* [An analysis of Japanese capitalism] (1934), which resembled V. I. Lenin's *Development of Capitalism in Russia* (1899), became the "Bible" of the Kōza-ha.[9] Its complex structural economic approach was complemented by the emphasis on political aspects of Japanese development in Hirano Yoshitarō's *Nihon shihon-shugi-shakai no kikō* [The structure of Japanese capitalist society] (1934). Rōnō-ha responses to these analyses were presented in Kushida Tamizō's *Nōgyō mondai* [The agrarian problem] (1935) and Sakisaka Itsurō's *Nihon shihon-shugi no sho mondai* [Problems of Japanese capitalism] (1937). Moreover, the subdebate focusing specifically on the origins of capitalism in Japan (the so-called manufacture debate) was conducted between Hattori Shisō for the Kōza-ha (*Ishin shi no hōhōron* [Methodology of the history of the Restoration] [1933]) and Tsuchiya Takao for the Rōnō-ha (*Nihon shihon-shugi shi ronshū* [Collected essays on the history of Japanese capitalism] [1937]). Besides these major works, essays supporting the Rōnō-ha and Kōza-ha appeared in journals closely identified with one faction or the other. Vehicles for Kōza-ha ideas included *Rekishi kagaku* [Historical science], published from May 1932 to December 1936; *Keizai hyōron* [Economic review] (September 1934 to October 1937); and *Yuibutsu ron kenkyū* [Studies in the theory of materialism], launched in November 1932. In addition to *Zen'ei* [Vanguard], which succeeded *Rōnō* in 1932, support for the opposition was carried in *Senku* [Pioneer], launched in June 1935, and *Ōhara shakai mondai kenkyūjo zasshi* [Magazine of the Ōhara Institute for the Study of Social Problems], revived in July 1934. Both *Chūō kōron* [Central review] and *Kaizō* [Reconstruction] have been identified with the Rōnō-ha, but in fact published essays from all perspectives. Centrists tended to publish in *Shakai hyōron* [Social review] (March 1935 to April 1936) and *Sarariiman* [Salary man].[10]

The second period of the debate on Japanese capitalism, then, saw the original antagonisms between the two factions harden and deepen to a more theoretical level. On the one hand, between 1932 and 1937, the debate increasingly focused on the theoretical points raised by the '32 Theses: their depiction of the Japanese state since the Meiji period as an absolutist state resembling English, French, German, and Russian absolutisms based on feudal or semi-feudal landowners; the extent to which the main causes of the Restoration itself were purely external or were partly the internal dynamics of Japanese capitalist development (addressed in the "manufacture debate"); and the related issue of landownership relations in the countryside, that is, whether agrarian land rents were still feudalistic or capitalistic in nature. At the same time, the basic differences in approach to party organization that had appeared in the Rōnō-ha split from the JCP in 1927 remained in evidence. The Rōnō-ha, experiencing recurrent internal disputes throughout the period,[11] continued to identify itself as a "non-Communist party Marxist" group[12]—a faction that was Marxist but not Leninist—and sought to build not a vanguard party but a single proletarian political party that would seek an immediate transition to socialism. This measure, in fact, helped to shelter the Rōnō-ha from police pressures while most JCP members found themselves in prison in the early 1930s.

Indeed, when the Rōnō-ha broke with the "union of the international revolutionary vanguard" dominated by Soviet Russia,[13] it deliberately sought to distinguish itself, in the eyes of the authorities, from the orthodox members of the JCP following the Comintern line. This step was directly linked to the March 15 (1928) government repression of the left-wing movement, in which 1,568 persons were arrested, and the April 16 incident (1929), in which the Council of Japanese Labor Unions (Nihon Rōdō Kumiai Hyōgikai), the Labor-Farmer Party (Rōdō Nōmintō), and the Proletarian Youth League (Musan Seinen Dōmei) were all banned.[14] Yamakawa rejected the label "social-democracy" that Watanabe would apply to the *Rōnō* group in the latter's essay "Nihon kyōsantō kenkyo to shakai minshu-shugisha no demagōgu" [The arrests of the Japanese Communist Party and the demagoguery of the social-democrats].[15] Insisting that the Rōnō-ha was but a different school of Marxism, Yamakawa, Inomata, and Arahata carefully distinguished themselves from the more "extremist" and dangerous communist elements who should rightly be repressed. Uchida Jōkichi and Nakano Jirō have quoted and explicated the joint Yamakawa-Inomata-Arahata statement, which appeared in the May 1928 issue of *Rōnō*:

> "The bourgeoisie, just as the extreme leftist *bunretsu-shugisha* [splinterists/Fukumotoists] have said, has deliberately confused the *vanguard party and the three left-wing groups* that are open mass groups as phenomena of the same nature and has ordered [their] dispersion. This is the first step of the expression of the ruling class's intention to repress all proletarian groups thoroughly." [Emphasis is Uchida's.] According to the point in the preface, this is tantamount to saying that it is natural that the vanguard party [the JCP] be repressed, and we, separately, do not oppose that. But since there is a difference between vanguard "extreme left" elements and us, do not carry out any further repression than this [against us].[16]

Such statements immediately drew the wrath of Watanabe and other JCP loyalists, including Comintern representative Katayama Sen, who published essays attacking Yamakawa's group from late 1928 to January 1929 in foreign and domestic magazines. In the summer of 1928 at its Sixth Congress, the Comintern, having had the JCP expel the Rōnō-ha, rejected in principle the existence of a laborers' and peasants' political party outside the Communist Party.[17] While the Rōnō-ha as a group came into conflict with the Comintern, however, it was not unanimous in its attitudes toward the Comintern and toward the international communist movement in general. Yamakawa led those who questioned "the very existence of the Comintern" and objected in principle to "the control and leadership over the [Japanese] movement by any international organ." By contrast, Inomata contended that the Rōnō-ha should endeavor "to make the Comintern regard the Rōnō-ha as the orthodox form of Japanese Marxism, by proving the correctness of the Rōnō-ha's theory and practice."[18]

The group's efforts to avoid arrest by dissociating itself from the Japanese Communist Party and its theory, however, proved to be fruitless under the pressures brought by the widening of the war in China. The Popular Front

Incident of 1936 and the Professors' Group arrests at Tokyo Imperial University in 1938 saw the authorities specifically target the Rōnō-ha, rounding up even those academics merely suspected of being fellow travellers, and the Rōnō-ha was effectively crushed by 1940.[19] One could argue that the futility of the Rōnō-ha's efforts to protect itself by abandoning illegal underground activity betrayed the error of its optimism on the progress of bourgeois democracy in Japan. The group ultimately was not permitted to continue to operate politically, or even refer to Marxist theory, without the threat of arrest. The persistent pressures of the thought police accorded more fully with the Kōza-ha's view that Japan's political superstructure was so backward that political democracy was but a facade crying out for completion of the bourgeois revolution begun by the Meiji Restoration.

If there was a central theme linking the two phases of the debate on Japanese capitalism, it was the effort to adapt Marxist theory to Japanese conditions. At a time when the Japanese military was riding a crest of ultranationalist sentiment, this overarching dimension of the debate among its Marxist opponents was not without its own nationalistic implications. Whether on the question of correct party organization or on the theoretical issue of the historical development of Japanese capitalism, the fundamental choice lay between accepting or rejecting a Soviet Marxist interpretation of Japan's backwardness and its prospects for revolution, in adopting or repudiating Leninist modes of organization and the authority of the Comintern. From the outset, the Rōnō-ha questioned not only the Comintern's analyses, but its authority as well: the Comintern view invited doubt in large part because it was Russian and Soviet in origin. It may not be insignificant in this respect that Rōnō-ha leaders Yamakawa and Arahata had been so closely identified with the anarchist movement before the Japanese Communist Party was formed.[20]

On the level of theory, the Rōnō-ha simply rejected Leninism, as represented in the history of the Russian revolution, as a universally valid model of socialist revolution. Yamakawa, for example, wrote explicitly in his autobiography on the limitations of the Russian model of two-step revolution:

> That Bolshevism is a development of Marxism does not mean that it is the only [possible] development from Marx's basic theory . . . but means that it made Marx's basic theory develop within the practice of the revolutionary movement, in response to the special conditions of the Russian revolution. In that sense, the revolutionary movements of individual countries must develop their own respective revolutionary theories. . . . It does not mean to imitate German social-democracy or Russian communism (Bolshevism); it is necessary to return to Marx and begin from there.[21]

In short, the group around Yamakawa did not accept the Comintern's analogy between Russia's February and October revolutions on the one hand and an overthrow of the Japanese emperor system followed by a proletarian revolution on the other.[22] In the words of one scholar with Rōnō-ha leanings, Yamakawa's secession from the Japanese Communist Party "also signified a split between a Marxism that was becoming indigenized in Japan and a Marxism native-born to Russia."[23] Hence, the Rōnō-ha as a whole has repeatedly cast aspersions on the Kōza-ha by characterizing it as a mere passive follower of the Comintern line. Rōnō-ha historian Tsushima Tadayuki, for example, has argued that "Kōza-ha theory is the academic foundation of the '32 Theses. The existence of serfdom in agrarian relations, the absolutist rule in the state—it academically provided a basis for these [points] and thus tried to make the accuracy of the two-stage strategy theory [a] necessary [conclusion]."[24]

It is correct that there was substantial agreement between the *Kōza* and the '32 Theses. However, such complete identification of the Kōza-ha with the '32 Theses is misleading given the chronology of the publication of the *Kōza* itself and of the earlier works by Noro that were its inspiration. Noro had published several essays in the thirteen-volume *Marukusu-shugi kōza* [Symposium on Marxism], edited by Ōyama Ikuo and Kawakami Hajime. Under the collective title "Nihon shihon-shugi hattatsu no rekishi-teki jōken" [The historical conditions of the development of Japanese capitalism], Noro's work appeared in three parts published in March and June 1928 and March 1929 (volumes 5, 7, and 13). In mid-1931, shortly after the publication of the 1931 Draft Political Theses, Noro proposed to publisher Iwata Yoshimichi (1898-1932) that he plan a *kōza* (symposium) to offer "the key to fundamental solutions of various immediate problems" through a complete analysis of the "conditions of the development of Japanese capitalism, its basic peculiarities, and its fundamental contradictions."[25] For this effort, Noro gathered theorists and scholars from within and outside the party, particularly those already involved in the Association for Research in Proletarian Science (Puro-ka) and the Industrial Labor Research Bureau (Sangyō Rōdō Chōsajo).[26]

By the time the 1932 Theses were published, then, most contributions to the *Kōza* had already been completed. That there was so much agreement between the *Kōza* and the new theses is not fortuitous, of course. The Kōza-ha had been heavily influenced by the '27 Theses, which the '32 Theses supported. Nevertheless, at Noro's urging, the group refused to allow the publication of the 1931 Draft Political Theses—which severely jolted party members by lending more support to the Rōnō-ha position[27]—to alter their writings already in progress.[28] It would be as incorrect, then, to devalue the *Kōza* on the grounds of its support of the Soviet analysis as to characterize the Rōnō-ha position as equally blind opposition to Soviet views. Both factions offered what they believed to be valid applications of Marxist theory and method to Japan's specific features. The driving force of the debate as a whole was the intellectual need to fit Japan into the context of Marx's theory of economic and political development in order to legitimate a socialist revolution, whether it was to occur in two stages or one.

The achievements of the debate on Japanese capitalism rested on foundations laid during what may be termed loosely the "prehistory" of the debate. On the one hand, indigenous efforts to assimilate Marxist theory and then to Japanize it in application to existing conditions had made significant progress on the eve of the debate. In the early 1920s, the translation and interpretation of major Marxist works accelerated, and Japanese Marxists made the first tentative steps in applying Marxist categories of analysis to Japan. At the same time, within the Japanese Communist Party, leaders Yamakawa Hitoshi and Fukumoto Kazuo (1894-1983) formulated, in succession, opposing doctrines of party organization in order to realize their Marxist revolutionary aspirations in Japan. In combination, these two trends fueled a controversy on revolutionary strategy and tactics that engulfed most of Japan's Marxist movement through the 1920s. A second stimulus to the debate, which will be covered in the succeeding chapter, came from without in the form of the Comintern's theses on Japan from 1922 to 1932.[29] The theses established the terms of the debate by defining the issues and a preliminary range of possible interpretations of contemporary conditions in Japan. Yet the internal prehistory of the debate furnished its Japanese contributors with the experience, consciousness, and intellectual tools to overcome the limitations of Comintern analyses drafted by Soviet leaders unfamiliar with the Japanese context.

The Theoretical Assimilation of Marxism in Japan

When Marxism was first imported into Japan, it appealed to progressive intellectuals in large part because it, like social Darwinism, was perceived as a doctrine at the forefront of Western thought.[30] From the late Meiji period through the 1920s, Marxism and then Marxism-Leninism were disseminated, alongside other Western theories and ideas, with increasing rapidity through translation and exegesis by Japanese writers. It is important to note, however, that Marxism arrived in Japan in far less coherent fashion than it had come to be understood by Western European and Russian Marxists. Consequently, the Marxism that the participants in the debate on Japanese capitalism had at their disposal was the doctrine elaborated—even revised, some would argue—by Friedrich Engels and Russian theorists after him.[31] It was the historical materialism that Engels systematized as "scientific socialism''[32] that was imported into Japan, not the complete Marxist conception of state and society that rested on many of Marx's and Engels's earlier writings.

The most important early vehicles for the assimilation of Marxist thought in the 1890s were the Shakaigaku Kenkyūkai (Association for the Study of Sociology) and the Shakai-shugi Kenkyūkai (Association for the Study of Socialism). The latter, founded by Christian socialists associated with Tokyo Imperial University, drew widely on the ideas of Saint-Simon, Fourier, and Ferdinand Lassalle, as well as Marx and Engels.[33] In addition to translations of *Social Problems* by Henry George and of a work by the American Christian socialist Richard Ely (rendered in Japanese *Shakai-shugi to shakai kairyō* [Socialism and social reform]),[34] several partial translations of Marxist works were published and studied in the period up to 1903. Works that were not available in translation were often read in other languages. Yamakawa Hitoshi, for example, endeavored to read the 1902 English edition of *Das Kapital* (published in the United States) during his imprisonment.[35]

During the Russo-Japanese War, in 1904-1905, the Heimin-sha (Commoner's Society), organized by Sakai Toshihiko and Kōtoku Shūsui in November 1903, played the leading role in the translation and publication of Marxist writings. Advocating social change within the scope of the law, the Heimin-sha's socialism was eclectic, drawing from the writings of Lassalle, August Bebel, Leo Tolstoy, Peter Kropotkin, and Marx and Engels.[36] In the service of Marxism, however, the group performed two important functions. First, the Heimin-sha helped to establish contact between Japanese socialists and the Russian Social-Democratic Labor Party and other European parties affiliated with the Socialist International. The March 13, 1904 issue of the *Heimin shinbun* [Commoner's paper] carried an open letter to the Russian party, calling for its unity with Japanese socialists during the war, against the common enemies of ''patriotism and militarism''; and its number 37 published the reply of *Iskra*. In addition, the paper carried an account of the Russian 1905 revolution and published articles on other socialist parties.[37] Its members, meanwhile, became leading figures in translating the Marxist classics. Sakai, later the first to introduce writings by Lenin into Japan, was also the first to publish a translation of the *Communist Manifesto* in November 1904 in the first anniversary issue of the *Heimin shinbun*.[38] The *Manifesto* and Engels's *Socialism: Utopian and Scientific* were the basis for the two most sophisticated presentations of Marxism available in Japanese on the eve of the Russo-Japanese War. Katayama Sen's *Waga shakai-shugi* and Kōtoku Shūsui's *Shakai-shugi shinzui*, however, did no more than explain Marxist theory on the basis of *Socialism: Utopian and Scientific* and the social reformism of the Second International.[39] Katayama and Kōtoku stressed the theory of surplus value, class struggle, and the materialist interpretation of history as crucial concepts. Their concern, typical of Meiji socialists, for the ills that accompanied Japan's rapid industrialization was reflected in their analysis of two major contradictions of capitalist society: that between "social production and capitalist ownership"; and that between "organized factory production and the anarchic general market."[40] Most importantly, Marxism was appreciated in these works as a scientific theory, the culmination of the long historical development of Western socialist thought.

Hence, by the time the first Japanese translation of *Das Kapital* (by Takabatake Motoyuki) was published in 1920, the "scientific socialism" systematized by Engels constituted the core of Marxism as imported into Japan. Before the October Revolution, Russian interpretations exercised little influence; nor was Lenin preeminent among the first Russian socialists to be translated into Japanese. Rather, George Plekhanov's *Fundamental Problems of Marxism* was the first Russian socialist work to be translated before 1921, when Lenin's *Immediate Tasks of the Soviet Government* (translated by Yamakawa and his wife Yamakawa Kikue) was published as a separate volume.[41] During the 1920s Lenin's influence remained secondary in Japan, and Bukharin became by far the most widely read and respected Russian Marxist.[42] Two of his major works, *The ABC of Communism* (with Yevgeny Preobrazhensky, 1919) and *Historical Materialism: A System of Sociology* (1921), were promptly translated into Japanese by mid-decade and read as basic textbooks of Marxism.[43] These works offered a fairly mechanistic presentation of Marxism, underscoring existing notions of Marxism as "scientific socialism" in Japan. The earlier, more humanistic writings of the young Marx—*The Economic and Philosophic Manuscripts* (1844), *The German Ideology* (1845-1846), *Critique of Hegel's Philosophy of Right* (1843)—were not available even to Western Marxists until the late 1920s and 1930s and thus had no role in the assimilation of Marxism before the debate on Japanese capitalism. Other available translated works, Kautsky's *Ethics and the Materialist Conception of History*, Marx's *Wage Labor and Capital*, Engels's *Origin of the Family, Private Property and the State*, and Bukharin's *Economics of the Transition Period* (1920), *Imperialism and World Economy* (1917), and *Imperialism and the Accumulation of Capital* (1924-1925), reinforced the emphasis on scientific economic analysis stressed in *Das Kapital* and *Socialism: Utopian and Scientific*.[44] Marx's link with his philosophical ancestor, G.W.F. Hegel, was not entirely unappreciated in Japan.[45] However, the consequence of the unbalanced introduction to Marxism was that, for Japanese Marxists, as for Lenin and German Social-Democrats, "without the components concealed in these books [by the young Marx], many sides of the Marxian idea of politics were exceedingly difficult to grasp."[46] The writings of the young Marx contained the analysis of the German state and broader interpretations of the notions of alienation and pre-capitalist society that were lost in later works' stress on the dynamics of capitalism.

In the context of the debate on Japanese capitalism, this effect was of major significance. It would contribute to the polarization of Japanese Marxist theorists into two irreconcilable factions, particularly on the question of the Japanese state. Indeed, it may be argued that the flexibility and creativity of both groups were severely hampered by these constraints on the extent and nature of Marxist theory as it had been introduced into Japan by the late 1920s.

Nevertheless, the progress made by Japanese Marxists in comprehending and assimilating Marxist theory by the time of the debate must not be underestimated. The mid-1920s were a time of fierce debate on the proper interpretation of such crucial concepts as "surplus value." At the same time, the first efforts outside the organizational framework of the Japanese Communist Party were made to apply Marxian categories of analysis to Japan. A major stimulus to the development of studies in Marxian economics, in fact, lay in Japan's actual situation. Japan's severe economic distress following World War I, which most seriously affected the agrarian sector, was aggravated through the 1920s by growing overpopulation and seemed to reflect the general crisis of postwar world capitalism proclaimed by the Comintern. As a consequence, Japanese Marxists became more deeply absorbed in the study of Marx's economic theory in order to support the burgeoning labor and agrarian movements. Under the influence of the work of Bukharin, Rosa Luxemburg, and Lenin on imperialism, in the early 1920s the study of Marx's economics turned toward the application of the concepts of monopoly capitalism and world capitalist collapse to Japan's political and economic structures.[47] This work in turn set the stage for the original contributions made by Japanese theorists in the debate on Japanese capitalism. The assimilation of Marxism in Japan in the prewar period culminated in the effort to produce "original" interpretations by Sakai (*Yuibutsu shikan no tachiba kara* [From the perspective of historical materialism] [1919] and *Kyōfu, tōsō, kanki* [Fear, struggle, joy] [1920]) and Yamakawa (*Shakaishugisha no shakai kan* [A socialist's world-view] [1919]). These, however, did not yet involve "the study of the Japanese state and Japanese capitalism as a whole"[48] requisite to the formation of a truly Japanese brand of Marxism.

The burgeoning interest in Marxism outside the JCP coincided with the establishment and development of economics as an independent discipline in Japan. In April 1919 the economics department became independent of the law faculty at Tokyo Imperial University, a precedent that was followed shortly at Kyoto Imperial University.[49] It is ironic that this development should have accompanied the beginning of the serious study of Marxism, for Marxist philosophy fused the political and the economic in the concept of political economy, and the political was not autonomous but an outgrowth of the economic realm. In any case, in the early 1920s there was a virtual explosion in the study of Marx's economics in Japanese economic circles. Technical writings on aspects of Marxian economic theory supplanted the broad, unfocused surveys of European social movements and vaguely philosophical and humanistic reflections on socialism that had dominated left-wing writings up to that time. Politics, however, remained the domain of the Japanese Communist Party leadership, and only later, in the debate on Japanese capitalism, did Japanese Marxists approach the subject in a holistic manner integrating the philosophical and political with the economic aspects of Marxism.

Progress in the assimilation of Marxian economic theory occurred through intense debate on the proper understanding of its key concepts. A central figure in these controversies was Kawakami Hajime (1879-1946), the pioneering Marxist economist at Kyoto Imperial University, whose career reflected many of the tensions inherent in the effort to adapt the Marxian analytical framework to the Japanese context.[50] Like other Meiji Marxists, Kawakami had been attracted to Marxism in an effort to comprehend and rectify the social ills that accompanied capitalist industrialization in Japan. Thus, without access to Marx's early humanistic writings, Kawakami struggled constantly to reconcile the ethical humanitarian concerns expressed in his own early work, *Binbō monogatari* [Tale of poverty] (1916), with the scientific concerns of Marx's political economy. His "idealist" critique of human "selfishness" drew the fire of younger Marxists, like his student Kushida Tamizō (1885-1934);[51] and, at their urging, he turned to economic theory. Founded in 1919, Kawakami's journal *Shakai mondai kenkyū* [Studies on social problems] was a major force in the study and dissemination of Marxian thought until its demise in October 1930. This journal became a leading forum in which Kawakami engaged others in debate on the basic tenets of Marxist economics. Having aroused considerable controversy over the concept of "capital" as early as 1916, during the 1920s Kawakami confronted Sakai Toshihiko on moralism (*dōtoku-ron*), economist Fukuda Tokuzō on Marx's notion of wage labor and the origins of capital, and sociologist Takata Yasuma on surplus value. He challenged Fukumoto on historical materialism and Yamakawa, Takabatake, Kushida, and others on Marx's labor theory of value.[52]

Thus the progress made by Japanese Marxists in absorbing Marxist economics was reflected in Kawakami's own works. In the early 1920s, Kawakami penned relatively simple presentations of Marxism as historical materialism: *Shihon ni arawareru yuibutsu shikan no danpen* [Fragments of historical materialism seen in *Capital*] (1920), *Kinsei keizai shisō shiron* [Historical treatise on modern economic thought] (1920), which was subsequently expanded into his *Shihon-shugi keizaigaku no shi-teki hatten* [The historical development of capitalist economic studies] (1923), *Shakai soshiki to shakai kakumei* [Social organization and social revolution] (1922), and *Yuibutsu shikan ryakkai* [A brief explanation of historical materialism] (1922). He also completed translations of Marx's *Wage Labor and Capital* (1921) and *Wages, Profits and Value* (1921).[53]

The mid-1920s, however, marked a turning point for Kawakami. In response to his many critics, Kawakami pursued a more integrative approach, pursuing Marxian economics with its philosophical basis firmly in grasp. By the late 1920s, Kawakami's works mirrored significant progress, especially in the economic sphere. In addition to his *Marukusu-shugi no tetsugaku-teki kiso* [The philosophical basis of Marxism] (1929), Kawakami published several economic works: *Marukusu-shugi keizaigaku* [Marxian economics] (1928), *Keizaigaku taikō* [General principles of economics] (1928), *Marukusu-shugi keizaigaku no kiso riron* [Basic theory of Marxian economics] (1929), and others.[54]

During the same period, Marxists also began to take that first crucial step toward the systematic application of Marxist theory to Japan's social and economic history and to contemporary Japanese capitalism that would be attained fully only in the *Rōnō-Kōza* debate. Sano Manabu (1892-1953), as lecturer in economic history at Waseda University and then a Central Committee member of the newly established Japanese Communist Party, began to move in this direction as early as 1922. In that year he published *Nihon shakai shi joron* [A preface to Japanese social history], and in the following year *Nihon keizai-shi gairon* [Outline of Japanese economic history].[55] These early pieces were "not written from a thoroughly materialistic or Marxian point of view," a shortcoming which Sano himself readily acknowledged.[56] Similarly, Honjō Eijirō (1888-1973), a Kyoto Imperial University professor of economics who had studied in Europe and the United States, wrote a series of books analyzing Japanese social and economic development in terms of Marxist categories, albeit "from the liberal but not Marxian point of view."[57] At mid-decade, Honjō published three major works: *Nihon shakai shi* [History of Japanese society] (1924); *Kinsei nōson mondai shiron* [Treatise on the modern agrarian problem] (1925); and *Nihon zaisei shi* [The financial history of Japan] (1926).[58] Like Sano's work, that of Honjō represented a fairly rudimentary effort to locate phenomena in Japanese social, political, and economic history to which Marxian concepts could be applied.

None of the works by either Sano or Honjō could by any means be regarded as wholly within the Marxist tradition. Nor, therefore, did they make any significant contribution to the ensuing debate on Japanese capitalism. At best, Sano and Honjō made an important step beyond the issues of economic theory pursued by Kawakami, Kushida, and others. They posed—

but did not answer—the question that would become central to the debate: To what extent did the Marxist notions that became popular in the 1920s reflect any aspect of Japanese socio-economic reality? Presaging Sano's endeavor after his 1933 *tenkō* to formulate a uniquely "oriental" brand of Marxism by rejecting the applicability of the notion of class conflict to Japan's nonindividualistic society,[59] Honjō treated the concept of class struggle with skepticism. His *History of Japanese Society* essayed "an analysis of the pre-Meiji period to see whether this history is exemplified in a class struggle or whether interclass struggle is greater than intraclass struggle."[60] Sano, on the other hand, continued to contribute articles on various aspects of the politics of Marxism in such left-wing non-party journals as *Marukusu-shugi, Shakai kagaku*, and *Musansha shinbun* [Proletarian news] through 1930. But like his earlier work, these essays were not particularly creative in applying Marxist political thought to Japanese realities.[61]

Ironically, the most provocative and innovative work that emerged in the mid-1920s applying Marxian analysis to the study of Japanese political and economic development was the product of Takahashi Kamekichi, whose theory of "petty bourgeois imperialism" (*puchi teikoku-shugi*) could only be regarded as an apology for Japanese imperialism. Takahashi's systematic application of Marxism to Japan helped to foment the debate on Japanese capitalism by drawing the fire of both Rōnō-ha dissidents and Japanese Communist Party loyalists. (See chapter 4.) In the early years, however, efforts to Japanize Marxism occurred primarily within the Japanese Communist Party under the tutelage of the Soviet-led Comintern.

Early Efforts toward the Japanization of Marxism: From Yamakawaism to Fukumotoism

The Bolshevik revolution of October 1917 brought an abrupt end to the winter period of the socialist movement. Spurred by Soviet efforts to encourage revolution in the East from without and by rice riots and strikes at home, the Japanese Communist Party was founded in mid-1922. During the decade between the October Revolution and the beginning of the debate on Japanese capitalism, Marxist revolutionaries in Japan eagerly imported the classics of Marxist-Leninist theory and took the first tentative steps to Japanize it in application to their own context. The revolutionary strategies of Yamakawa Hitoshi and Fukumoto Kazuo constituted the first such efforts to Japanize Marxism, that is, to forge a unity between Marxist theory and the practice of the Japanese revolution.

It is significant that the assimilation of Marxist economic and political theory was still in its early stages when the first efforts to Japanize Marxism occurred. The still low level of knowledge of Marxist theory in Japan in the early to mid-1920s imposed major constraints on its application. Aside from the idiosyncratic national socialism of Takabatake Motoyuki,[62] Japanese Marxist theoretical work worthy of the label "original" during these years yielded only the dogmas of Yamakawaism and Fukumotoism. Produced by leaders of the struggling JCP eager to implement Soviet guidelines on the organization of a revolutionary party in Japan, these doctrines represented opposite extremes in this effort. The two leaders sought to formulate theoretical foundations for a Leninist party that was at once a radical left-wing party and a more broadly based coalition that could respond properly to the clarion call "To the masses!" issued by the Third Comintern Congress of mid-1921.[63] These contradictory requirements for a mass communist party constructed to spearhead a bourgeois-democratic revolution that would explode rapidly into proletarian revolution were reiterated throughout subsequent Comintern theses on Japan.[64] Until the debate on Japanese capitalism erupted when the Comintern repudiated both Yamakawaism and Fukumotoism in 1927, Japanese Marxists remained mired in these dogmatic organizational theories. Marxists followed the general intellectual tendency of the period, in the view of leading Japanese scholars, "to import theory [directly] from Western society and not from the empirical facts" of Japanese existence.[65] It was not until Marxist theory had been absorbed more fully among both party and nonparty Marxists that Japanese theorists could conduct the analysis of concrete Japanese conditions that was preliminary to any true Japanization of Marxism.

The Japanese Communist Party furnished the organizational support for the two most prominent efforts to Japanize Marxism in the early 1920s, Yamakawaism and Fukumotoism. If, as the JCP's first leader, Yamakawa emphasized the need to remedy the alienation of vanguard intellectuals from the Japanese masses when the JCP was born, Fukumoto Kazuo stressed those elements of Lenin's vanguard party conception that subordinated the potential revolutionary energy of mass spontaneity to the requirement for an ideologically tempered elite.[66] Both doctrines responded to half of the requirements set forth by the Comintern, and neither reflected a coherent Marxian analysis of peculiarly Japanese conditions analogous to that offered by Lenin of Russian conditions.

Since Yamakawaism became the foundation for many elements of the Rōnō-ha's approach to the Japanese revolution, it would be useful to look more closely at Yamakawa's early ideas. There later emerged three primary tenets of Rōnō-ha thought: the desire to "dissolve the Communist party and replace it with a social-democratic political party (a united front party)"; the assertion that "feudal remnants in the village are not rooted in the land system, so a struggle over land is not of major importance" to the revolution;

and the belief that "the emperor system since the Meiji period has been essentially a bourgeois monarchy, and absolutist structures are merely . . . remnants that are no longer of any significance. Thus a bourgeois-democratic struggle to overthrow the emperor system is not necessary."[67] The origins of all three elements were already apparent in Yamakawa's first approach to Marxism by way of anarcho-syndicalism circa 1907-1908, in the Yamakawaist strategy that was formulated in 1922, in the Yamakawa-led movement to dissolve the party in 1924, and in the theory of organization that Yamakawa developed to oppose Fukumoto's growing influence in 1925. The Rōnō-ha's split from the Japanese Communist Party thus began as early as 1925; it became "decisive," however, only after the issue of the '27 Theses.[68] The publication of the journal *Rōnō* in response to the theses heralded the reemergence of Yamakawaism in the form of Rōnō-ha theory.[69]

Yamakawa first developed his strategy for the Japanese proletarian movement when the JCP was formed. Published in *Zen'ei* in August 1922, his essay "Musan-kaikyū undō no hōkō tenkan" [A change of direction in the proletarian movement] called for the "massification" (*taishū-ka*) of the new party and a shift to political struggle and rebellion rather than the passivity on the part of socialist and labor leaders that had been characteristic of the winter period. Responding in large part to the Comintern's 1921 slogans "To the masses!" and "Advance toward political struggle,"[70] Yamakawa went on to advocate a united front political party in 1924-1925. In his essay "Tan'itsu musan-kaikyūtō ron" [On a single proletarian political party], Yamakawa argued that the Communist Party had opened the path for the proletariat to organize and act in an open, legal, and independent political movement. Rejecting Lenin's vanguard party conception as unsuitable to new conditions in Japan, Yamakawa assigned the role of political struggle to this single legal proletarian political party. Yamakawa's "united front" would combine into this party "all organized and unorganized laborers, peasants, and lower levels of the middle class and all anticapitalist movements and organizations."[71] Since this vision attributed no special role to the Communist Party as a vanguard, if not elite, party, Yamakawaism was criticized by many as "Japanese-style legalism and dissolutionism."[72] Moreover, as a theory, it came under attack for its neglect of the emperor system in analyzing the Japanese state, and consequently for its inability to justify its rejection of the vanguard party idea.[73]

Yamakawa's ideas on revolutionary organization were soon implemented as official JCP policy. Only a year after the party was founded, a combination of events pushed many JCP members to consider dissolving it. On the one hand, government repression increased: after an initial "roundup" of party members in June 1923, the police used the crisis of the Tokyo earthquake as a pretext to launch a "white terror" in September and conducted mass arrests of JCP members. At the same time, the government made efforts to co-opt the left with the appealing promise of universal manhood suffrage—which would become law in 1925. Thus, by the time Arahata returned to Japan in November 1923 from reporting on the founding of the new party to the Comintern in Moscow, he was dismayed to find widespread talk of dissolution.[74] Yamakawa and JCP cofounder (and later Rōnō-ha member) Sakai Toshihiko were leading advocates of dissolution, arguing that an illegal vanguard party was no longer either necessary or desirable in Japan. Such a party, Yamakawa claimed, would inevitably become alienated from the masses and attract further government repression. Revolutionary Marxists should operate instead through mass organizations, including labor unions, peasant associations, and a legal proletarian political party that would prepare the way for a mass communist party. Yamakawa's influence as party leader was decisive on this matter, and the JCP was dissolved in March 1924, less than two years after it was born.

After leading the move to dissolve the first JCP, Yamakawa used his organizational formula once again to oppose the emergence of a competing organizational theory offered by Fukumoto Kazuo. This step established an essential link between Yamakawa's advocacy of dissolution in 1923 and his leadership of the Rōnō-ha secession that sparked the debate on Japanese capitalism four years later. Yet, between 1924 and 1926, Yamakawa's formula was not entirely opposed to Comintern policy, which called for a united front. Indeed, while Yamakawa's original interpretation of Japanese capitalism and the Japanese state of 1922-1924 differed radically from the 1922 Draft JCP Program, by 1926 there was a temporary change in the Comintern interpretation that brought it closer to Yamakawa's view. Prefiguring the 1931 Draft Political Theses, the "Moscow Theses," passed at the Sixth Comintern Executive Committee Plenum of February-March 1926, emphasized that "the bloc political power of capitalists and landlords hitherto under the hegemony of the landlords now was completely under the hegemony of the bourgeoisie." Possibly this revision was a response to Japanese political developments of the previous two years—the passage of the universal suffrage bill and progressive labor legislation under the Katō Cabinet. The Moscow Theses went on to deny the need for a bourgeois revolution,[75] a step equally unnecessary for Yamakawa, whose idea of a legal united front party presumed a liberal bourgeois-democratic setting. The Moscow Theses introduced a predictable confusion into Japanese Marxist circles that was relieved only by the 1927 Theses' return to the premises of the 1922 Draft Program.[76]

Yet the Moscow Theses, like the 1931 Draft Political Theses, marked but a momentary aberration in a pattern that found Yamakawaism ranged against the Comintern and JCP line throughout the 1920s and 1930s. This antagonism was immediately apparent in the succession of Yamakawaism by Fukumotoism. The influence of Fukumoto as a leading theorist in the left-wing movement rose in 1925 and 1926 as the Comintern's angry response to the dissolution of the first JCP produced a vigorous effort to reorganize it.[77] Yamakawa's critique notwithstanding, the Comintern never abandoned the concept of the JCP as a vanguard party, and Fukumoto supported this conception in his organizational theory. By the time the JCP was officially reborn in December 1926, Fukumotoism had become the dominant tide in the movement.

Yamakawa's united front proletarian political party strategy had sought to implement the slogan "To the masses!" quite literally, for it aimed to break down all potential barriers between revolutionary leaders and masses by concentrating on mass rather than vanguard organization. Yamakawa's strategy was formulated with an eye toward the practical possibilities opened up by the passage of universal manhood suffrage. By contrast, Fukumoto's doctrine placed theoretical concerns at the forefront, for the school teacher had studied Marxism in Europe and become well-versed in the abstract principles of dialectical materialism and the writings of Rosa Luxemburg, Karl Liebknecht, and others in the German socialist movement, with which Fukumoto had become involved as a law student in Germany. As an editor of the journal *Marukusu-shugi* and as the founder of his own journal *Marukusu-shizumu no hata no moto ni* [Under the banner of Marxism], which appeared from June to December 1926, Fukumoto published critical theoretical essays regularly.[78] His writings were dense and abstruse, but they were very appealing to Japanese left-wing intellectuals who took pride in their understanding of Marxism.[79] Fukumoto's organizational doctrine rested on intellectual exclusivism, since the JCP would include only those with a sufficient revolutionary "consciousness" and deep understanding of Marxist theory. The Fukumotoist era of the JCP, which lasted until Fukumoto was condemned by the '27 Theses for his preoccupation with "artificially and arbitrarily formulated abstractions" and "principles of logic,"[80] began when his virulent attacks on Yamakawaism in late 1925 and early 1926 gained widespread support. His rejection of Yamakawa's method as unsophisticated and his politics as the politics of compromise rather than revolution formed the point of departure for the articulation of his own theory.[81]

Fukumoto's views on the correct constitution of the party were both consistent with the Comintern's depiction of Japan's backwardness and reflective of Fukumoto's personal penchant for what his critics saw as sterile intellectualism.[82] Accepting the Soviet view that Japan's political superstructure was still dominated by absolutist forces, Fukumoto found Yamakawa's premise of the feasibility of operating openly in a democratic arena foolish and inclined toward the "unionism" or "economism" that Lenin had attacked in pre-1905 Russia. Opposing Yamakawa's "liquidationism" (or "dissolutionism"), Fukumoto reasserted the need for a vanguard party in Japan and took the Leninist conception a step further. To avoid falling into the "opportunist-unionist" weaknesses of Yamakawaism in working with the masses, Marxists must first separate themselves from all other progressive elements, immerse themselves totally in Marxist thought, and crystallize (*kesshō*) themselves as pure Marxists before uniting with others. This "division before unity" principle (*bunri ketsugō ron*) was essential, in Fukumoto's view, to the creation of an effective vanguard party in Japan. "Theoretical struggle" against those who were weak in consciousness had to occur within the party as well as between Marxists and other groups.[83] Marxists must first purify themselves inwardly before they could extend their influence to the masses, Fukumoto asserted. This was a view that emphasized a depth of consciousness among the few, a devotion to theory preliminary to praxis.

When the JCP opened its Third (Reconstruction) Congress in December 1926, it reconstituted itself on the basis of Fukumotoism. Not surprisingly, under Fukumoto factional conflict thrived within the party and within the labor movement it was seeking to dominate. Thus, even before Fukumoto was attacked by the Comintern, he came under fire in Japan as well. Not only was he counterattacked by Yamakawa and his supporters, but he was more widely denounced for promoting "sectarian splinterism" in the movement; Kuroda Hisao borrowed Lenin's words to label Fukumotoism as a "left-wing infantile disorder."[84] Fukumoto's personality, his pedantic manner, and his increasing influence on the party's policies alienated many within the JCP and in the broader left-wing movement. Many felt, as Kawakami Hajime did, that "so-called Fukumotoism was not Marxism even though it resembled it." Fukumoto had merely gained ascendancy through intimidation, by pretentiously quoting Lenin's *What Is To Be Done?* at length and by claiming to present a truly Leninist doctrine of dialectical materialism.[85] During Fukumoto's absence early in 1927, opposition to him crystallized to the point that a group including Sano Manabu, Sakai Toshihiko, Arahata Kanson, and Yamakawa began to plan an anti-Fukumoto magazine. This extreme disaffection came to be shared by the Comintern when it heard a report by Nabeyama Sadachika in Moscow that was critical of Fukumotoism and of its potentially harmful effects on the movement.[86]

Despite such criticisms of both Fukumoto and his predecessor, however, Fukumotoism marked the high point of the adaptation of Marxism to Japan before 1927. Contributions to the true Japanization of Marxism that would avoid the rightist and leftist extremes of Yamakawaism and Fukumotoism would not appear until Japanese Marxists were able to conduct their own analyses of Japanese conditions. Until then, however, the Soviet leadership of the Comintern furnished the most coherent Marxist analysis of Japanese society.

THREE

The Stimulus from Without: Comintern Theses on Japan, 1922–1932

As Marxist political and economic theory was increasingly assimilated in Japan during the early years of the Japanese Communist Party, the determination of political orthodoxy for Japan's Marxism came from outside Japan. Issued from the Soviet-dominated Comintern, these designations of the "correct" line served as parameters for early Japanese Marxist endeavors to analyze the political and economic forces propelling them toward proletarian socialist revolution. Both Yamakawaism and Fukumotoism, the first systematic efforts to adapt Marxism to Japan, were formulated in response to Comintern directives from Moscow. The contributions made by Japanese Marxists in the debate on Japanese capitalism, too, were in large part stimulated, if not constrained, by the Comintern's instructions to the JCP.

Between 1922 and 1932, four major documents on the revolution in Japan emanated from Moscow. The 1922 Draft Program of the JCP, the 1927 (July) Theses on the Japan Problem, the 1931 Draft Political Theses, and the 1932 Theses on the Situation in Japan and the Tasks of the Communist Party all offered Marxist interpretations of Japan's political development and recommendations on revolutionary strategy and tactics. The resolutions marked Soviet responses to both developments within Japan and perceived changes in the international arena; and at times, they reflected vicissitudes of Soviet internal politics of which Japanese Marxist leaders were entirely unaware. Yet, before the debate on Japanese capitalism, the Comintern's theses offered the most coherent applications of Marxist theory to Japan, and their claim to authority, whether accepted or not, made them documents to which all others endeavoring to adapt Marxism to Japan were compelled to respond. Thus, the Comintern's theses—particularly the '27 Theses, which precipitated the Rōnō-ha's split from the JCP—not only were the catalyzing external stimulus to the debate on Japanese capitalism. They also established the basic terms on which the controversy was conducted, challenging Japanese theorists to produce a more satisfying Marxist interpretation of their own society.

CHAPTER THREE

THE INTERNATIONAL CONTEXT: UNITED FRONT TACTICS AND THE REVOLUTION IN JAPAN

The Soviet leaders who penned the Comintern's resolutions on Japan did so with some consultation with Japanese representatives like Katayama Sen, but they had virtually no firsthand knowledge of Japan. The theses relied heavily on implicit analogies between conditions in Japan and Russia in 1905 and 1917. But, more significantly, the theses were always formulated within the context of the Comintern's pursuit of revolution worldwide, particularly in China. For the internationalists in the Comintern, the success of individual national revolutions was always contingent on the conditions of the entire world capitalist system. The dominant view of the changing nature of this system determined Comintern strategy for revolution worldwide and in turn was reflected in the Comintern's resolutions on Japan.

The Communist International was born in 1919 out of the Bolshevik faith in the inevitability of an international revolution. It also emerged out of the fear that the new Soviet state, besieged from within by armed White Russian resistance and from without by hostile intervention by the capitalist powers, could not long survive without the support of a similar revolution elsewhere. Ideally, this proletarian revolution would come in an advanced Western European country, which would have a powerful economic base with which to support Soviet development. Otherwise, in Lenin's view, the relatively less advanced Russian regime would soon collapse. The brutal crushing of the Spartacus uprising in Germany in January 1919, however, dashed these hopes, and the Bolsheviks had to make their revolution elsewhere. They looked, then, to colonial peoples in Asia and Africa, and Soviet leaders hoped to see the *smychka* (alliance) between workers and peasants that had made the Bolshevik revolution reproduced successfully on an international scale. On the basis of their theories of imperialism, Lenin and later Bukharin (in 1923-1926) saw the colonized peoples of the East as the weakest link of world capitalism. Nationalistic revolutions in these largely peasant countries would sever this vital link between the Western metropolises and their colonies, precipitating revolutionary crisis in the West. The proletariat in the advanced capitalist countries would join the peasant masses of the East in a *smychka* to catalyze the international revolution the Bolsheviks so anxiously awaited.[1]

Yet Soviet expectations of the success of this scenario varied over the 1920s, and these changed perspectives were reflected in repeated adjustments in the Comintern's "united front" strategy. Lenin's and Bukharin's interpretations of imperialism both suggested that imperialist wars, like World War I, and revolutions arising therefrom were inevitable. In the early years of the Comintern, this optimistic view was reinforced by the belief that world capitalism was in crisis, on the brink of revolution. By the late 1920s, however, the failure of the capitalist states to collapse under tremendous postwar economic distress led Bukharin to a new perception of the "third period" of world capitalism. He concluded that "capitalism's 'third period' witnessed not internal breakdowns but further stabilization on a higher technological and organizational level."[2]

In an age of imperialism, the state and the economy, as Bukharin had argued a decade earlier, were becoming increasingly fused into organized state capitalist trusts, making the capitalist state more impervious to the threat of revolution from its own proletariat. While the war and militarization of the economy had seen statization—the establishment of state control—from above, after the war, the " 'process of the fusing of the largest centralized enterprises, concerns, trusts and the like with organs of state power' was proceeding primarily 'from below.' The state was becoming 'directly dependent on large and powerful concerns or combinations of concerns,' a development Bukharin called '*trustification* of state power itself.' . . . '[A]ll this reflects a peculiar form of *state capitalism,* where the state power controls and develops capitalism.' "[3] The mutual dependence between capitalism and the state, in short, was intensifying. This statization of capitalism was occurring on the basis of a higher level of technology than ever before attained, uniting the state and capitalist management into a single organization capable of rationalizing and regulating not only the economy but the whole of society as well. In 1927, this view made Bukharin very pessimistic about the prospects for world revolution, but his interpretation was roundly denounced by Josef Stalin, with whom he shared the Soviet leadership. When Stalin had outmaneuvered Bukharin by 1929, Bukharin's view of "capitalist stabilization" was discarded along with all other theoretical contributions associated with Bukharin.[4]

These changes in the Soviet view of the international situation were matched by shifts in the overall united front strategy it prescribed for global revolution. Discouraged by developments in Europe, in December 1921, the Comintern's "Directives on the United Front" sent national communist parties "To the masses" with united front tactics, "a method of organizing the masses on a programme of transitional demands." In 1924, as Yamakawa led the movement to dissolve the first JCP, the Fifth Comintern Congress reinterpreted the united front strategy more narrowly, to call for a united front "from below" under tutelage of the communist parties in individual countries. Pursuit of the united front "only from above," that is, through the cooperation of communist party leaders with social-democratic and other progressive or reformist leaderships, was now strictly prohibited.[5] Changes in Comintern policy that occurred after this time developed primarily in the sphere of application rather than in the theoretical realm; and toward the end of the decade, these changes were increasingly linked to the political turmoil in the Soviet Union.

Indeed, when Stalin and Bukharin attacked Trotsky's Left Opposition, the Japanese Communist Party was drawn into the Soviet power struggle. According to former party leader Kazama Jōkichi, the Stalinist faction in the Comintern accused the ultraleftist Fukumotoists of being associated with Soviet Trotskyism. Meanwhile, Gregory Zinoviev, now allied with Trotsky, had been removed from his post at the head of the Comintern in 1926 after being expelled from the Soviet Communist Party's Politburo and Central Committee and just before being expelled from the party itself in 1927. Gregory Voitinsky, long associated with Japan policy, had left the Far Eastern Bureau. And, finally, Bukharin replaced Zinoviev as formal head of the Comintern, a position which limited the time he could spend on Japan policy but which also assured that his influence would be felt. Between March and June of 1927 Bukharin chaired the Comintern subcommittee formed to address the Japan problem and particularly Fukumotoism.[6]

By the time the committee formulated the '27 Theses, however, its judgment of the situation in Japan was heavily colored by a traumatic new development in the international situation, Chiang Kai-shek's betrayal of the Chinese Communists in the Shanghai coup of April 1927. The application of the Comintern's united front tactics had varied according to national conditions. In China, a less developed country "where there was no labour movement of any size or significance to which overtures for a united front could be made," the Stalin-Bukharin formula was to subordinate the Communist Party to the leadership of Chiang's Guomindang (KMT) as the leading anti-imperialist force. This policy was criticized by Trotsky as foolhardy, particularly after Chiang's Canton coup against the left in 1926. Stalin's policy, Trotsky claimed, was based on the false premise "that the KMT was not primarily a class party, but a party of all anti-imperialist groups and classes." The Stalin-Bukharin policy thus required that overzealous revolutionary activity on the part of workers and peasants in China be restrained lest the broad anti-imperialist front in China be ruptured.[7] The strategy of the Chinese revolution quickly became a major political issue within the Soviet Union, a tool in the internal power struggle that dwarfed the consideration of all other national revolutionary movements in the Comintern. The failure of Comintern policy in China (and in England as well) provoked an overall review of united front tactics resulting in a switch in emphasis from temporary unity among all potentially revolutionary classes and parties to the "third period's" slogan of vigorous "class against class" struggle.

The theoretical justification for this change did not emerge until February 1928, at the Comintern Executive Committee's Ninth Plenum. In mid-

1928, Bukharin elaborated on these resolutions, arguing that "as social-democracy was becoming more bourgeois and imperialist, more and more an integral part of the bourgeois state, 'the fight against bourgeois labour parties must be intensified.' "[8] It is clear from the '27 Theses that in mid-1927, Comintern thinking on the united front was still in flux. The theses continued to stress the formation of a united front by the Communist Party with "such left-wing legal mass organizations as the Rōnōtō (Labor-Farmer Party) and the Tōitsu Dōmei (Unification League)" and between such organizations as the Rōnōtō and "mass social-democratic and centrist organizations."[9] At the same time, the '27 Theses' argument that in such a united front "the communist party absolutely must not lose its independence," that such a "united front struggle will be carried out on a class basis and make no ideological concessions,"[10] suggests that the lessons of the Chinese revolution were not lost on the Comintern's Japan committee. In comparison with the 1922 Draft Program, class struggle was to be radicalized through a bourgeois revolution moving without interruption into a proletarian revolution.

The relationship between events in China and elsewhere and the development of Comintern strategy for Japan did not end with the '27 Theses and Bukharin's departure from the Comintern leadership. Indeed, some have argued that the dramatic change in policy that occurred with the 1931 Draft Political Theses and the about-face of the '32 Theses shortly thereafter can only be understood in light of events in China[11] and in the Soviet Union. Aside from increased official repression, changes in Japan's domestic situation were not significant enough to warrant the shift in the 1931 Draft Political Theses that saw Japan as less feudal than bourgeois and seemed to call for one-step revolution. This change in Japan policy coincided with the short tenure of Li Lisan and the implementation and failure of the Li Lisan line of urban insurrection in China in 1930 and 1931.[12] In this view, a strategy of one-step proletarian revolution was applied to Japan in tandem with the policy of urban uprisings in China and was withdrawn in the 1932 Theses with the rapid demise of the so-called Li Lisan line. The return to the premise that Japan was semi-feudal, especially in the agrarian sector, was supported by the particularly bad economic situation in Japanese agriculture in 1931 and 1932.[13]

More importantly, however, we must note the potential impact of Bukharin's political fall on this turn of events. Much as Stalin had repudiated and then adopted the Left Opposition's theory of "socialism in one country" domestically, the 1931 Draft Theses might have reflected a turn against Bukharin's interpretation, followed by its reaffirmation (minus Bukharin's name) in 1932. Certainly the Rōnō-ha–Kōza-ha debate was affected by Bukharin's fate. The Kōza-ha followed the Comintern's official denunciation of "Bukharinism," even while writing the *Symposium* to support the Bukharinist premise of a semi-feudal Japan. The Rōnō-ha remained relatively free to apply Bukharin's theories of "state monopoly" or "organized capitalism" (even while acknowledging the need to deny Bukharin's influence) to support its own premise of a highly developed imperialistic Japan.[14]

The difficulty was, of course, that neither Japanese faction would deny either the existence of semi-feudal remnants or the high level of capitalistic development in the urban sector. The problem was how much weight should be given to each factor in determining whether the revolution in Japan should proceed in two stages or one. This is why Bukharin's views could be cited to support the positions of both factions. This also explains why, for Japanese Marxists dissatisfied with the depth of knowledge that Soviet leaders had about Japan, the Comintern theses raised more questions than they resolved about the character of Japan's recent development.

THE 1922 DRAFT PROGRAM OF THE JAPANESE COMMUNIST PARTY

Bukharin's influence on Marxism in Japan was most clearly stamped on those theses most often attributed to him, the 1922 Draft Program of the newborn JCP and the 1927 Theses. The difficulties in applying Marxism to Japan—apparent in the irony of the subsequent conflict between the Bukharinist tendencies of both Rōnō-ha and Kōza-ha—were already in evidence in 1922; and Bukharin himself must be credited with setting forth the "issue of the complex nature of class relations in capitalist Japan"[15] at the outset.

Japan's industrial development had occurred in such a way that neither the strategies devised for the colonial peoples of the East, on which Soviet attention was concentrated,[16] nor those of the defunct movements in Europe were applicable. The 1922 Draft Program of the JCP marked the first effort to resolve this complex problem. The program was formulated at the Fourth Comintern Congress in November 1922 in Leningrad by a Comintern Commission on Japan headed by Bukharin,[17] in which Katayama Sen also played a major role.[18] From this early document, it was already clear that the continued existence of the emperor system (*tennō-sei*) posed major theoretical difficulties. Extensive debate on the provision that the party seek to abolish the emperor system ensued when party leaders deliberated on the draft in March 1923 at the Shakujii Conference. It was only after prolonged debate that the party agreed to accept the Comintern's mandate on the emperor system. Some, including Sano Manabu, remained unpersuaded, conceding the issue only reluctantly. A major concern in this early debate was pragmatic: it lay not in the positive or negative evaluation of the emperor system itself, but rather in whether it would be politically prudent for the new party to risk alienating large numbers of potential Japanese followers by adopting so radical a slogan. While the Draft Program recognized the economic gains Japan had made during World War I, many felt, "it ignored the general national[istic] sentiment that had emerged as a result."[19] In addition, the continued existence of the traditional emperor system posed a major theoretical problem in defining the nature of Japanese class relations and the state, and hence the character of the emerging revolution and the role of the Japanese Communist Party.

More so than in the subsequent '27 Theses, the Draft Program emphasized the emperor system in characterizing Japanese society as backward.[20] Likening the progress of capitalist development in Japan in 1922 to that of prerevolutionary Russia, the program equated the position of the Japanese emperor with that of the tsar,[21] an analogy that would clearly prove to be untenable for Japanese believers in the uniqueness of the Japanese *kokutai* and of the emperor at its apex. At the same time, Japan was acknowledged to be a "special" case, where feudal remnants ruled alongside the bourgeoisie, making the specification of the party's strategy a particularly difficult task. As the program stated,

> The Japanese Communist Party, while based on the common demands of the communist parties of all countries, must consider the peculiarities of the development of Japanese capitalism. Since the world war did not affect Japan to the same extent that it affected other countries, Japanese capitalism attained extraordinary development during the war; however, today Japanese capitalism still retains some traces of the feudal relations of the previous era. Most of the land is in the hands of large semi-feudal landlords; the greatest among those is the emperor (*mikado*) as the head of the Japanese government. On the other hand, most of the land which these large landlords own is rented to tenant farmers; tenant farmers have their own agricultural implements and cultivate [the land] with them. Thus, as a result of fierce competition for land, rents have risen increasingly, and now have reached the level of so-called starvation land-rents (*kiga-jidai*). The remnants of feudalism still occupy a dominant position in the state structure today: the state organs are still held in the hands of a bloc comprised of a certain part of the commercial and industrial bourgeoisie and large landlords. The special semi-feudalistic nature of state power is expressed clearly by the major and guiding role that the *genrō* (note: read "nobility") have in the constitution. Under such conditions, the forces opposed to the existing state power not only arise from the working class, the peasants, and the petty bourgeoisie, but also arise from a broad segment of the so-called liberal bourgeoisie—they too are opposed to the existing government.[22]

The worsening economic and political crisis marked by intensified "class struggle" that developed in the wake of Japan's wartime economic boom presented the Japanese Communist Party with a potentially revolutionary situation. Because of the limitations on bourgeois development evident in the continued economic and political power of Japan's large landowners, it was clear that the immediate requisite was the completion of the bourgeois revolution begun by the Meiji Restoration. "The bourgeois revolution in Japan will be achieved only when a sufficiently powerful proletariat and revolutionary peasantry have appeared. Therefore, the completion of the bourgeois revolution can become the immediate prelude to a proletarian revolution aimed at the domination of the bourgeoisie and the realization of proletarian dictatorship."[23]

Interestingly, the Bukharin formula emphasizing the backwardness of Japan enabled the application to Japan of virtually the same strategy defining a major revolutionary role for the bourgeoisie as the Comintern had devised for the "semi-colonial" countries of India and China, Japan's clearly superior economic development and role as an imperialist power notwithstanding. This occurred despite Lenin's plea at the Third Comintern Congress for the need "to study in depth the concrete developments in the revolution in advanced capitalist countries,"[24] and it suggests that the Soviets tended to categorize Japan uncritically along with less developed Asian societies.[25] In this light, the Rōnō-ha's insistence that the Soviets knew nothing of Japan, and suspicion that the Comintern's Japan policies were in fact responses to events in China, are understandable.

The revolutionary role that the Draft Program assigned to the JCP was based on premises that bore a close resemblance to Leon Trotsky's theories of "combined and uneven development" and "permanent" (or "uninterrupted") revolution. Trotsky had argued that Russia's rapid economic development under state tutelage, first under Peter the Great and then after the Crimean War, had caused unusual features to emerge. The bourgeoisie, whose entrepreneurial role was assumed by the state, never fully developed, and certain features of feudal society remained intact. The result was a peculiar combination of both the capitalist and feudal modes of production in which aspects of each existed side by side. This innovation in Trotsky's analysis of Russia seems to have been applied by Comintern representative Gregory Voitinsky in his notes on "Class Struggle in Japan." According to Voitinsky, despite Japan's high level of industrial development, a significant feature of Japanese politics lay in the conflict between the landed aristocracy and a bourgeoisie that was still rather weak. On the one hand, the impulse toward imperialism suggested that the Japanese bourgeoisie was very highly developed. In Voitinsky's words, "A tendency was arising among Japan's progressive bourgeoisie to try to conquer economically the markets of China and Siberia without relying on war, and of course this was but one factor leading Japan's bourgeoisie to imperialistic tendencies." Nevertheless, the inability of this relatively young bourgeoisie to break completely the fetters of the feudal model of production was reflected in the fact that "feudal lords, moving almost always in alliance with powerful military cliques, are still a powerful social and political force. For that reason, the struggle between the feudal lords and the bourgeoisie will doubtless come to have a revolutionary character."[26]

As Trotsky's theory of uneven and combined development had suggested with reference to Russia, Japan's rapid industrialization under the tutelage of the Meiji state meant that "a pre-industrial urban bourgeoisie, which Trotsky considered so essential to the subsequent growth of an independent bourgeoisie, had never come into being, [but] a post-industrial business or 'capitalist class' [in Japan, e.g., the large zaibatsu] did suddenly spring up."[27] The result of this pattern was the failure of the bourgeoisie to transform the rural economy, and thus ultimately what contemporary scholars of Japan have called the "dual structure" of the Japanese economy.[28] Furthermore, "just as in the economy there was no mediation between the lower, agricultural foundations and the higher, industrial ones, so in the social structure there was no mediation between, on the one hand, the lower classes and, on the other, the upper classes engaged in industrial production. And for this reason the capitalist class was itself fundamentally weak for it lacked a wider social basis on which it could rely in a confrontation with the state. Moreover, it lacked the tradition of fighting for its interests: 'Big capital obtained its economic rule without a struggle.' "[29]

It is undeniable that both Russia and Japan shared a pattern of backwardness and accelerated economic development from above yielding a combination of aspects of different modes of production in both cases. Neither Voitinsky nor the Draft Program made reference to Trotsky's work. But Comintern leaders did indeed draw such an analogy between tsarist Russia and Japan, and the logical links that were missing in the argument of the Draft Program could be found in Voitinsky's notes. The notion of combined and uneven development explained why the Japanese bourgeoisie was too weak and cowardly to carry its own revolution to completion. Similarly, the notion that the impending revolution would be a bourgeois revolution that would rapidly become a proletarian one was essentially Trotsky's maligned notion of "permanent" revolution, "an idea that connects the liquidation of absolutism and feudalism with a socialist revolution."[30] The Communist Party would be the concrete expression of this linkage.

Voitinsky described the inability of Japan's bourgeoisie to complete the bourgeois revolution on its own. "History shows us that until the end of the war the bourgeoisie was always manipulated by feudal forces and military cliques, and could not represent a united front with the rising proletariat; therefore, nor could it gather its strength for class struggle.''[31] The postwar economic and political unrest offered the Japanese Communist Party the opportunity to seize the banner of bourgeois revolution and carry it through to completion. Trotsky had observed that the young proletariat held disproportionate strength. ''[The] political power [of the bourgeoisie]—which was primarily based on a large army—did not embody the economic power which should have been derived from industry. Instead, it was the proletariat which, in a sense, by default, inherited this economic power. Industry without capitalism, in short, meant not only a working class without a bourgeoisie, but a working class with the capacity to rule over industry.''[32] As the proletariat's vanguard, according to the Draft Program, the JCP would ''have to call for the overthrow of the imperial government and the abolition of the monarchy as temporary slogans, and further would have to lead the struggle for universal suffrage.'' These bourgeois-democratic slogans would be abandoned immediately and the party would work toward proletarian dictatorship, however, once the preliminary goal of overthrowing the existing government had been achieved.[33]

These prescriptions went unfulfilled, for police pressures drove Japanese leaders to dissolve the party before deliberation could be completed and the draft formally adopted as the party's official program.[34] Ironically, however, in leading the movement to dissolve the party, Yamakawa Hitoshi drew support from Voitinsky's analysis. Yamakawa too argued that neither the bourgeoisie nor the petty bourgeoisie could complete the building of democracy in Japan. ''The revolutionary spirit of a rising class had disappeared in the Japanese bourgeoisie from the outset,'' and in the 1920s, ''the bourgeoisie was continually being intimidated by the emergence of the proletariat that is awakening as a class, from beneath it.'' The proletariat then was ''the most powerful'' force contributing to Japan's democratization, particularly if it made use of the newly granted suffrage rights through a proletarian political party.[35] This formula posed the true dilemma for the left movement: while such a party would have to incorporate both workers and peasants, ''the more inclusive the proletarian party is, the greater the danger that its political movement might stray from the main current of the revolutionary movement and fall into mere reformist parliamentarianism.''[36] Nevertheless, in the aftermath of government repression, Yamakawa's solution was to seek to build a broad basis for the movement by work in mass organizations such as labor and peasant unions, while similarly repressive conditions in Russia had led Lenin to his conception of the illegal vanguard party.

Yamakawa's arguments failed to persuade men like Ichikawa Shōichi, who charged that the party's dissolution betrayed the leadership's

" 'shameless petty bourgeois' character" and was in fact widely resisted.[37] Ichikawa joined Watanabe Masanosuke, Shiga Yoshio, Noro Eitarō, and others to publish essays in the journal *Marukusu-shugi* (1924-1929) in support of the Comintern's effort to form a new vanguard party under the Draft Program.[38] In the June-July issue Ichikawa argued, for example, that the Communist Party must be preserved as the party of the proletariat during the bourgeois-democratic revolution, even while the proletariat would support "a united front party forming into a political league all oppressed strata," with the proletariat itself as the leading force. Here Ichikawa differed not only with Yamakawa but also with the Fukumotoist views of men like Murayama Yōshirō, who supported an exclusive, ideologically pure vanguard party.[39] When the new Comintern theses ratified Ichikawa's position late in 1927, the Rōnō-ha seceded and formulated its theory that collapsed the bourgeois-democratic and proletarian revolutions into a single, uninterrupted revolution.[40]

THE 1927 THESES ON THE JAPAN PROBLEM

The occasion for the issuance of the July 1927 Theses was the successful reorganization of the JCP under Comintern tutelage in 1926. Condemning both Yamakawaism and Fukumotoism for their opposing "deviations" in leading the Japanese party to date, the Comintern presented a fresh plan of action to the new party. The '27 Theses, then, reiterated many points of the defunct 1922 Draft Program's analysis of Japanese political and economic development and updated the program in accordance with new domestic and international developments. The premise of Japan's backwardness, particularly in the countryside, was retained as the foundation for the Comintern's policy of two-stage revolution in Japan. The proletariat, for which the JCP acted as "the revolutionary vanguard . . . fighting for the fundamental historical interests of the working class as a whole," would lead the peasantry and "urban petty bourgeois" in the struggle to complete the bourgeois-democratic revolution begun with the Meiji Restoration. According to the theses, "the Japanese proletariat must link its struggle for a socialist revolution with a struggle of all toilers of Japan, under the hegemony of the proletariat, for a bourgeois-democratic revolution."[41]

Despite the Comintern's explicit call for this conception of a two-stage revolution, however, the internal ambiguities and contradictions of the 1927 Theses became a major precipitant of the debate on Japanese capitalism. Like the 1922 Draft Program, the new theses were authored by Bukharin, as head of the Comintern's special committee on Japan. The new directive was consistent with the old in its emphasis on Japan's backwardness, particularly as manifested in the "feudal remnants" in the Japanese state. Yet it was precisely in the theses' treatment of the state and its economic basis that the new document faltered. The Comintern's analysis of Japan's current domestic and international situation led it to place far more emphasis in the new theses on the high level of Japanese development; and this assertion came into conflict with the premise of the dominance of feudal remnants that was essential to support the policy of a two-stage revolution.

The peculiarities in Japan's development resulting from its relatively late start, as described in Voitinsky's application of Trotsky's notion of combined and uneven development, suffice to account for the Comintern's self-contradictions. Those attempting to apply Marxism to Japan were faced with a backward political superstructure that was incongruent with its highly advanced economic base. The economic base, moreover, was split between a highly urbanized capital-intensive industrial sector and a traditional rural sector. In theoretical terms, the problem was that a mechanistic application of Marxism as simple stage theory was inadequate. In the words of the theses, "there is a two-fold process of lending to the old feudal forms a bourgeois content and of transforming the bourgeoisie into a counter-revolutionary force."[42] The theses attempted to resolve the problem by postulating the existence of absolutism in which both feudal remnants and bourgeoisie coexisted in the institutions of the Japanese state. To support their policy of two-stage revolution, Comintern leaders had to attribute great strength to feudal forces—otherwise, there would be no need to complete the bourgeois revolution before moving on to proletarian socialist revolution. Nevertheless, the Comintern also found it necessary to stress in the new theses the high development of the capitalist urban sector of the economy and the controlling position of the bourgeoisie in order to account for Japan's increasingly expansionist behavior.

From the theses' opening assertion that "Japanese intervention in China [against the revolution] is an accomplished fact," it is evident that the reason for the contradiction in the Comintern's position in 1927 lay in preeminently practical concerns.[43] The Soviet leaders now saw in Japanese imperialism an urgent threat to the world revolution and to the Soviet state, and the correct interpretation of Japanese imperialism was thrust to the forefront of their concerns. Confronted with the rise of "Japanese imperialism . . . on a rising curve of development," the Comintern had to explain the militaristic behavior of Japan in terms of the interests of a bourgeois state.[44] Here Bukharin drew on his own theoretical work on the advanced capitalist state. "The present Japanese government is in the hands of a bloc of the capitalists and the landlords," the theses argued, but as the architect of Japan's imperialist policies, the bourgeoisie was clearly dominant. While the two major political parties, the Seiyūkai and the Kenseikai, differed in some respects—the Seiyūkai being closer to the nobility and the military and the latter acting as a "quasi-liberal" bourgeoisie—both simply represented conflicting bourgeois interests. As Japanese capitalism continued its upward course of development, Bukharin saw closer and closer ties between state and economy, higher and higher levels of trustification emerging.

> The Japanese state is in itself a powerful element of Japanese capitalism. No European country has come as close to adopting state capitalism as Japan, where according to some estimates 30 per cent of all capital invested in industry and finance, not including the railroads, which are almost entirely in the hands of the government, belongs to the state. The Mikado [emperor] is not only a big landowner, but also a very rich stockholder in many stock companies and combines; he also has his own bank, with assets of 100 million yen.[45]

In short, the theses depicted the Japanese state as a capitalist state but not as a truly bourgeois-democratic state. Unlike China's bourgeoisie, "the Japanese bourgeoisie already holds power and is making extensive use of the government machinery with all its feudal attributes and relics for the organization and protection of capitalist exploitation." The self-contradictions of this position, particularly when juxtaposed with the theses' continued emphasis on the "extreme backwardness" of the rural economy and the state structure, are fully evident in the following paragraph:

> The struggle for the democratization of the Japanese state, the abolition of the monarchy, and the removal of the present ruling cliques from the government in a country with such a high level of capital concentration will therefore inevitably change from a struggle against feudal survivals into a struggle against capitalism itself. The bourgeois-democratic revolution of Japan will rapidly grow into a socialist revolution precisely because the contemporary Japanese state, with all its feudal attributes and relics, is the most concentrated expression of Japanese capitalism, embodying a whole series of its most vital nerves; to strike at the state is to strike at the capitalist system as a whole.[46]

Not surprisingly, Yamakawa asserted that the '27 Theses supported the Rōnō-ha view, claiming that they presented the Comintern's doctrine of a single-stage revolution.[47] Hence, one could argue that the contradictions in the theses were directly responsible for igniting the controversy between Marxists arguing in favor of a two-stage revolution and those advocating a one-stage revolution. The new theses supported the 1926 Moscow Theses, which had confused the new party by asserting that capital had gained hegemony in the landlord-capitalist bloc ruling the Japanese state.[48] As Rōnō-ha sympathizer Tsushima Tadayuki has argued, theoretically "the establishment of bourgeois hegemony in state power and the holistic existence of absolutism cannot be reconciled.''[49] In other words, the Comintern had established a strategy of revolution that was inconsistent with its own analysis of the current political situation. Even Kōza-ha sympathizers Koyama Hirotake and Kishimoto Eitarō have conceded, therefore, that the document presented an ''untenable formula of the revolution as 'a bourgeois revolution versus bourgeois power,' and reproduced in more obvious form the contradictions and confusion of the previous 1926 Moscow Theses.''[50]

Nevertheless, the Comintern was determined to establish the theses as a policy of two-stage revolution. The full text of the '27 Theses was not available in Japan until early 1928, and its availability then simply intensified the debate.[51] But, to enforce this interpretation of the directive, the Comintern immediately designated a new JCP Central Committee including permanent members Watanabe Masanosuke, Sano Manabu, Nabeyama Sadachika, Ichikawa Shōichi, and Arahata Kanson, as well as Sugiura Kei'ichi, Kokuryō Goichirō, Nakao Katsuo, and Yamamoto Kenzō.[52] From 1927 to 1931, the '27 Theses were the official program of the JCP, as the debate on Japanese capitalism gathered momentum.

A Change in Course: The 1931 Draft Political Theses

Between the '27 Theses and the publication of the *Kōza* in 1932-1933, the Comintern issued two more major documents on Japan: the 1931 Draft Political Theses and the 1932 Theses. The debate on Japanese capitalism had already begun, but these contradictory programs exacerbated the Japanese debate by lending support to the theoretical positions of both sides.

It was in the 1931 Draft Political Theses that the Rōnō-ha could find the most explicit Comintern support for its strategy of one-stage revolution. Perhaps in a Stalinist effort to purge ''Bukharinist'' influences from Comintern policy,[53] maybe in response to repression by the Hamaguchi Cabinet,[54] and possibly in response to the worldwide economic depression that descended in 1929,[55] the 1931 Theses ratified the Comintern's abandonment of the united front in favor of intensified class struggle and called for an immediate one-step ''proletarian revolution broadly embracing bourgeois-democratic responsibilities.''[56] Formulated in late 1930, the Comintern's new theses completely rejected the analysis of the '27 Theses, arguing that the Japanese state was dominated by monopoly capital. Such a highly developed capitalistic country required a proletarian socialist revolution rather than a bourgeois-democratic revolution. This strategy was to be implemented by an ''emergency communist party'' (*hijōji kyōsantō*) under Kazama Jōkichi beginning in the spring of 1931.[57] The short era of Kazama's leadership marked the only time in the prewar period in which a one-step strategy of revolution was official Comintern orthodoxy.[58]

Although the policy shift of the 1931 Theses seemed abrupt, in fact there was a certain continuity with changes in Comintern policy dating back to 1927-1928. It will be recalled that the demise of the revolutionary party in China in April 1927 prompted a reconsideration of the whole united front idea, and that the ambiguities of the '27 Theses reflected this process. As Tsushima has observed, "The resolutions of the Sixth Comintern Congress of 1928 and the Sixth Plenum of 1929 had [already] demanded changes and a revision of the July [1927] Theses. This point was deliberated early within our [the Japanese] party and within the international leadership."[59] In mid-1928 Bukharin's position was still relatively secure in the Comintern, so Stalin's need to repudiate his influence could provide only a partial explanation for the policy change at that time. At the same time, the policy change was linked to Stalin's increasingly vigorous attack on Bukharin's theory of the stabilization of capitalism in the Comintern's Oriental Bureau shortly after Bukharin's fall and the Executive Committee's Tenth Plenum.[60] The process by which the theses were drafted and transmitted to Japan illustrates the impact of this development in Soviet politics.

According to Kazama, the theses originated in August 1930 at the Fifth Congress of the Profintern. In an unusual move, a special subcommittee on Japan was formed under Profintern head A. Lasovsky. Japanese Profintern delegates served on the committee along with Chinese, Korean, and other representatives of the Profintern's Oriental Bureau: Soviet leaders Piatnitsky, Karl Radek, Georgy Safarov, and Yevgeny S. Iolk. Several months earlier, in April, Stalin had already launched his attack on Bukharin's theory of capitalist stabilization. The onset of the Great Depression suggested that such stabilization was merely temporary, and that a proletarian revolution in a country such as Japan could succeed if the stage of bourgeois-democratic revolution were bypassed. The Profintern published theses critical of the "opportunistic" trends in the Japanese labor movement, but it left the suggestion that the Japanese revolution be proletarian and not bourgeois to the Comintern. It was Georgy Safarov who finally produced the Draft Political Theses. Kazama carried them by memory back to Japan, where he put them into writing as a revision of the '27 Theses. It remained a "draft," for it was never formally approved by the many high-level JCP officials who were in prison at the time.[61]

It would be incorrect to argue, as some have, that the 1931 Draft Political Theses marked but another progression in a series of increasingly optimistic Comintern appraisals of the revolutionary situation in Japan.[62] On the contrary, the document was an aberration that would be called "adventurist" in Marxist terms, a deviation from a deep-seated belief in the backwardness of Japan's political superstructure and a departure from the pessimism that permeated the 1922 Draft Program, the '27 Theses, and particularly the '32

Theses, all of which called for the completion of a bourgeois-democratic revolution as a prerequisite for socialist revolution. The short-lived Draft Political Theses continued to acknowledge the problems posed by Japan's emperor system and the feudal landlords supporting it, but argued that these could be solved within the context of a proletarian revolution.[63]

This argument rested on a sustained analysis of the development of capitalism and the state in Japan that challenged the tenets of the '27 Theses. Most importantly, the Draft Theses argued that the Meiji Restoration had indeed constituted a bourgeois revolution, if incomplete:

> The Meiji Revolution of 1868 was caused by the increase of rising capitalistic forces internally and by the attack of . . . "cheap commodities"—"the coming of the black ships." But the question of whether to become a colony of foreign capitalism or whether to carry out a great revolution in order to become a capitalist country could not be resolved as a "revolution from below" such as we saw in France, because at that time the Japanese bourgeoisie was still extremely weak. However, nor was it carried out as a "revolution from above" as in Germany. Domestic and foreign relations made this revolution very incomplete; but without a doubt, it was a bourgeois-democratic revolution that opened the path to capitalist development. Feudal lords were abolished, but the establishment of private landownership made most of them landlords; and as a result, those who had held substantial land before the revolution emerged as new landlords. Thus, on agricultural lands, most peasants were exploited as [if they were] landless serfs, almost in the same way as before the revolution. . . . [Nevertheless,] no matter how incomplete this revolution was, that it was the first bourgeois revolution in the Orient, that it had among its neighbors tsarist Russia and feudalistic China and Korea, and that the attention of the advanced capitalist powers was turned not toward the Orient but toward Western Europe—all these [factors] provided good conditions that made the early development of Japanese capitalism rapid.[64]

As a result of these historical circumstances, Japan's weak bourgeoisie had been unable to resolve the agrarian problem thoroughly and had been unable to perfect bourgeois democracy. Thus, Japan had "entered the stage of imperialism without passing through an age of [European-style] liberalism."[65] It was the political situation in 1931, however, that dwarfed the significance of feudal remnants and indicated that "in Japan the preconditions of socialist revolution are maturing rapidly."[66]

The theses argued that "Japan is now a highly developed imperialist country." Its "state power is in the hands of the bourgeoisie and landlords, in which finance capital has hegemony." The power of landlords remained significant but was subordinate to that of the bourgeoisie. Japanese imperialism could therefore easily be explained by Lenin's formula of "imperialism as the highest stage of capitalism." Japanese industry had become highly concentrated, with 34.9 percent of all the industrial labor force employed in enterprises of over five hundred employees, and 58 percent in enterprises employing one hundred or more persons. "Power over banks, industry, and mining was held by the . . . five financial cliques of Mitsui, Mitsubishi, Yasuda, Sumitomo, and Dai'ichi"—a concentration of financial power even greater than that in Germany. Led by the power of finance capital, "the emperor system . . . has become a powerful instrument of fascist oppression and exploitation of the ruling classes against the . . . laborers and toiling exploited peasant masses. Thus the fundamental class contradiction in this period is the opposition between the bourgeoisie and the proletariat," the Draft Theses concluded.[67] The continuing agrarian problem would be solved by the proletarian dictatorship established after the revolution.[68] The framers of the 1931 Theses were optimistic about this proletarian revolution, because they felt that "the deepening of the economic crisis in Japan, the intensification of class contradictions, the extraordinary increase of the mass of unemployed, and the pressures of new imperialist wars" all signalled the imminent demise of Japanese capitalism and the ripening of the political situation for immediate socialist revolution.[69]

The presentation of a one-stage revolutionary strategy in the 1931 Draft Political Theses placed the JCP leadership in the awkward position of seeming to adopt wholesale the Rōnō-ha's analysis of the Japanese revolution. The party central that had been established early in 1931 under Kazama and Iwata Yoshimichi immediately endeavored to differentiate the Comintern's new formula from that of the dissident faction. A fundamental difference between the two, it was argued unconvincingly, lay "in the recognition and evaluation of the bourgeois-democratic responsibilities to be embraced within the basic responsibilities of the socialist revolution." Specifically, the Rōnō-ha did not believe that agriculture remained semi-feudal, and "consequently the emperor system had already become but an ornament of the bourgeoisie without any real [economic] basis." Therefore, there was no need, in the Rōnō-ha view, for the socialist revolution to undertake any bourgeois-democratic revolutionary tasks. On this basis the JCP was able to continue to reject the Rōnō-ha interpretation while accepting the Comintern's one-step strategy as official party policy.[70]

Japanese Militarism and the 1932 Theses

This official Comintern version of the one-stage revolutionary strategy was short-lived. By August 1931, the Draft Political Theses had been denounced as "Trotskyist," its author, Safarov, had been removed from the Comintern, and the Comintern was at work on a new draft on JCP strategy. Completed by October 1931, the new "Theses on the Situation in Japan and the Tasks of the Communist Party" "were issued not in the name of the Comintern's Executive Committee but in the name of the Comintern's *West European Bureau*" in May 1932. Often called the "Kuusinen Theses"[71] after their author O. Kuusinen, a close associate of the deposed Bukharin,[72] the '32 Theses invoked the Bukharinist analysis of the Japanese state to return to the two-stage revolutionary strategy of the 1922 Draft Program and the '27 Theses.

The most interesting aspect of this document is its even greater emphasis on international affairs, particularly Japanese imperialism, which had advanced into Manchuria. In addition to internal developments in the Soviet Union and the vicissitudes of the Chinese revolution, the Manchurian War loomed large in the formulation of the '32 Theses. Highly emotional language describing Japanese society as "barbaric," "backward," and "feudalistic" revealed heightened Soviet fears of Japanese militarism on the Asian continent. The '32 Theses forged a new interpretation of the linkage between rising Japanese imperialism and the feudal elements in the emperor system and ruling military cliques, and called for a bourgeois-democratic revolution to overthrow these semi-feudal elements.[73]

Comintern delegates from Japan, Katayama and Nosaka Sanzō, helped to formulate the new theses. Nosaka was particularly vocal on the importance of the new theses as a reversal of the erroneous 1931 Theses. Opposing the 1931 "draft's theory of 'proletarian revolution with broad bourgeois democratic duties,' " Nosaka argued that the 1932 Theses correctly diagnosed the need for the "overthrow of the monarchy and the confiscation of land for the peasants."[74] The JCP accepted the theses as official policy and published a Japanese translation in July,[75] but not without some discomfiture on the part of the party central. The leadership was acutely embarrassed at its sudden shift in policy, conceding that the shift had to be explained, "since the new theses may appear to have been produced 'abruptly.' " The Central Committee was careful to note that the Comintern shared responsibility for the change. It is apparent that the JCP leaders did not feel that they had underestimated the agrarian problem or the "militaristic police emperor system," which had pressed so heavily on the newly organized JCP in the incidents of April 16 and July 15. They accepted the change, they asserted, "in the spirit of democratic centralism" to express "unity" with the views of the Comintern leadership.[76] The leadership also claimed that the 1931 Draft Theses had criticized the '27 Theses but were never intended "*to erase the historical and practical achievements* [of] the 'July Theses.' "

Two major aspects of the 1932 Theses became central to the debate on

Japanese capitalism. These were the tasks of the agrarian revolution in Japan, and the nature of the emperor system as the "principal bulwark of political reaction and of all the relics of feudalism in the country."[77] These emphases reflected domestic and international developments in 1931 and 1932. The Japanese economy was affected by the world depression in that interim; and as the crisis deepened, the labor and agrarian movements grew with strikes and tenant walkouts. Internationally, in the words of Koyama Hirotake, "aggressive military elements who sensed the crisis in the emperor system plotted a domestic coup and military activities in Manchuria."[78] The 1932 Theses produced a theory of the state incorporating an analysis of the agrarian economic base with an interpretation of the superstructural emperor system into a unified whole.

On the agrarian question, the '32 Theses returned to the 1922 and 1927 emphasis on "the feudal remnants" in Japan's social structure. While Japan enjoyed a form of highly developed predatory "monopoly capitalism," "Japanese capitalism expanded under militaristic and police relations and on the basis of feudal remnants domestically." Furthermore, "finance capital systematically and thoroughly utilizes cottage industry, petty handicraft industry, and manufacture, remnants of feudalism, and thereby supports the merciless exploitation of the working class." Not to be neglected, therefore, was the significance of "the Asiatically backward semi-feudal rule in the villages that obstructs the development of Japan's agrarian forces of production and accelerates the deterioration of agriculture and the impoverishment of the main masses of peasants."[79]

This rural structure was the basis of Japan's existing "absolutist domination," "which is no less a phenomenon than fascism in other capitalist countries in that it is oppressive as a form of dictatorship of the bourgeoisie and landlords over toilers." "Japan's emperor system, on the one hand, rests on a parasitic feudal class mainly as a landlord, and on the other hand, also stands on a rapacious bourgeoisie that is becoming wealthy rapidly." While the power of the landlords indicated that "one of the basic responsibilities of the Japanese revolution is *agrarian revolution*," a task which must not be underestimated,[80] most importantly, the revolution must destroy this absolutist state power that was oppressive within and militaristically expansive without. The theses then proceeded to outline three major tasks of the Japanese "bourgeois-democratic revolution with a tendency to change perforce into a socialist revolution": "(1) the overthrow of the emperor system; (2) the abolition of large landownership; and (3) the realization of the seven-hour labor system, and—under the relations of the revolutionary situation—the fusion of all banks into a single state bank, and the execution of a regime based on workers', peasants', and soldiers' soviets vis-à-vis these banks, large capitalist management, and especially the production of all concerns and trusts."[81]

A pessimistic document indeed, the '32 Theses posited a strategy based on a recognition of those most troublesome and unique aspects of Japanese society that had plagued Bukharin and the JCP from the outset. Here the Comintern combined an analysis of these peculiarities with an outlook that placed Japan at a stage of development on a par with that of tsarist Russia, prescribing the "workers', peasants', and soldiers' " soviets that were familiar from the Russian revolution. These theses were the last systematic analysis of Japan presented by the Comintern. As the most complete and provocative interpretation of the Japanese state, they had a significant impact on the continued debate on Japanese capitalism that had begun with the '27 Theses. The two major problems discussed in the document subsequently became major issues in the Rōnō-ha–Kōza-ha controversy, and the debate escalated sharply along these lines until it was forcibly terminated in 1937.

Conclusions

Before and during the early years of the debate on Japanese capitalism, the Comintern's theses offered a major stimulus to the Marxist controversy in Japan. Where native leaders of the Japanese Communist Party, Yamakawa and Fukumoto, had made major efforts to Japanize Marxism, these had severe limitations. Both focused on organizational theory and responded to short-term developments in Japanese domestic politics. Neither pursued a sustained historical analysis of the development of the Japanese economy and state in Marxist terms. Only the Comintern, its leaders poorly acquainted with Japan but far more comfortable with Marxist theory than the leaders of the Japanese movement, endeavored to undertake such an analysis. Significantly, its analysis was always formulated in the context of longer range developments in the international situation. The virtual identity between the international body and the Soviet state meant that this attention to international circumstances often resulted in distorted interpretations of Japan that vacillated sharply with changes in perceived Soviet national interests and Japanese state policies.

This interest in Japanese international behavior, however, was not the monopoly of Soviet Marxist theoreticians. Japanese socialism had a long history of opposition to Japanese militarism. The first socialist organizations, like the Heimin-sha, had risen in pacifist opposition to the Russo-Japanese War. In the early 1920s, the leaders of the new JCP opposed the prolonged Japanese presence in Siberia after the allied intervention against the Bolshevik revolution in 1919. As the appreciation of Marxist theory in Japan deepened during the 1920s, Japanese Marxists gained access to the theories of imperialism offered by Luxemburg, Bukharin, and Lenin. Not surprisingly, by the late 1920s, Japanese Marxists too felt prepared to apply their newly acquired theoretical knowledge to advance their own analyses of Japanese imperialism. Significant new developments in Japanese Marxism occurred, as Japanese imperialism came to be treated as a consequence of the limitations imposed on Japan's economic development by its status as a late developer in an increasingly inhospitable international environment. Writing on this theme in 1927, Japanese Marxist Takahashi Kamekichi offered the most competent and innovative Marxian analysis of the historical development of Japanese capitalism; and, like the Comintern, he linked his far more comprehensive interpretation to a prescription for Japan's proletarian movement. His conclusions, however, drew the wrath of both JCP loyalists and party dissidents, sparking in effect the beginning of the academic debate on Japanese capitalism. His indigenous contribution effectively challenged fellow Marxists to surpass the Comintern's analysis by engaging in a more intensive study of Japan's economic and political development than any Marxist had undertaken to date. Takahashi Kamekichi's controversial theory of "petty imperialism" was at least as important a stimulus to the debate on Japanese capitalism as the Comintern theses offered from without. Long neglected by both Japanese and Western scholars, Takahashi's work is of such significance that it deserves detailed discussion.

FOUR

The Challenge: Takahashi Kamekichi and the Theory of Petty Imperialism

Takahashi Kamekichi and the Challenge to the Left

He feels obliged to metamorphose my historical sketch of the genesis of capitalism in Western Europe into an historico-philosophical theory of the *marche générale* imposed by fate upon every people, whatever the historical circumstances in which it finds itself, in order that it may ultimately arrive at the form of economy which will ensure, together with the greatest expansion of the productive powers of social labour, the most complete development of man. But I beg his pardon. (He is both honouring and shaming me too much.)

—Karl Marx

It is not unusual for scholars today to disparage Japanese Marxism in the 1920s and 1930s by charging that both the Rōnō-ha and the Kōza-ha offered equally dogmatic and formulistic responses to "Comintern orthodoxy."[1] In this view, the *Nihon shihon-shugi hattatsu shi kōza* was published in 1932-1933 to offer blind support to the 1932 Theses;[2] and the Rōnō-ha simply opposed the Comintern's analysis in a similarly unimaginative fashion. It is indeed correct that the occasion for the Rōnō-ha's angry departure from the Japanese Communist Party late in 1927 was the publication in July of the Comintern's '27 Theses and their adoption by the JCP. In this sense, a major precipitant of the debate on Japanese capitalism was external; it grew out of the controversy on strategy and tactics aroused by the Soviet analysis of conditions in Japan.

It would be incorrect, however, to regard the debate solely as a response to such a factor external to Japanese Marxism itself. A far more powerful stimulus was offered by Takahashi Kamekichi (1891-1977) in his theory of "petty imperialism." This thesis was a thinly veiled apologia for Japanese expansionism in Asia, that, ironically, was based on the most competent and innovative Marxian analysis of Japan's capitalistic development produced by a native Marxist. Takahashi's thesis, presented in April 1927,[3] was that the distinctive characteristics of Japanese economic development rendered V. I. Lenin's critical conception of *Imperialism, the Highest Stage of Capitalism* inapplicable to Japan. The argument was offensive to the leadership of the left not merely because of its call for Japanese military might to "liberate" Asia from the grip of the more advanced European powers. More fundamentally, Takahashi's thesis called into question the universality of Karl Marx's original theory of capitalistic development, thereby threatening Marxism's claim to scientific truth and thus its legitimacy as revolutionary ideology in Japan.

Half a century earlier, Marx's disclaimer to the populist N. K. Mikhailovsky had offered support to the notion of alternative paths of development. Nevertheless, Marx and Engels had eventually abandoned their vague notions concerning "oriental society" precisely because they recognized that any implication of alternative paths of development would violate a claim to truth that was based on the universal validity of the laws of historical materialism.[4] Lenin shared this conviction when he justified his own revolutionary activities by arguing in *The Development of Capitalism in Russia* (1899) that the growth of capitalism in Russia had followed the same course as that of Western Europe, even if Russia's economic progress had been delayed by certain "Asiatic" features. Similarly, for Japanese Marxists in the 1920s, if a Marxian socialist revolution was to occur in Japan, it was because Japan's secure position in the Marxist-Leninist historical framework made it inevitable. Takahashi's theory implied that Japan had pursued a different path; and it challenged its Marxist revolutionaries to demonstrate, as Lenin had done, that whatever the peculiarities of Japanese development described in the JCP's Draft Program and the Comintern Theses, Japan still fit neatly into Marx's original paradigm. Immediately after the presentation of his theory of petty imperialism, then, Takahashi was attacked vigorously by Marxist theoreticians of the left-wing movement. The petty imperialism debate, raging through December 1927, when the first issue of *Rōnō* appeared, involved future spokesmen for the Rōnō-ha and Kōza-ha and is widely regarded as the prelude to the debate on Japanese capitalism.[5]

Takahashi Kamekichi was an economic reporter for the Tōyō Keizai Shinpō-sha (Oriental Economic News Agency) until 1926, when he became an independent economic historian. In 1932, Takahashi formed his own economics institute and subsequently acted as consultant to the Japanese colonial administrations in Manchuguo and Taiwan and as advisor to the Japanese government in a variety of posts, most notably serving in the cabinet's War Planning Office.[6] He had been educated at the private Waseda University and, because of financial difficulties, did not pursue graduate studies in economics or law, as did so many of his Marxist contemporaries. He was self-educated in Marxian economic theory, much in the manner of Georges Sorel. An avid observer of domestic and international economic events during his rapid rise on the staff of the *Tōyō keizai shinbun*, he cultivated a preference for empirical analysis and a healthy distrust of pure theory. At the newspaper, Takahashi was assigned responsibility for a new column on foreign economic affairs that reflected the increased linkage between Japan and European economies following the economic boom Japan enjoyed during World War I. Takahashi felt acutely the need for studies of Japanese and Western economics that did not rely on the prevailing liberal economic theories of James Mill and Adam Smith, theories that seemed to have been rendered obsolete by wartime developments. Takahashi found Marxist works like Rudolf Hilferding's *Finance Capital*, Nikolai Bukharin's *Economics of the Transition Period*, and Lenin's *Imperialism* more valuable tools of analysis. Yet he was also convinced that events since the World War necessitated if not revision, then at least a serious reconsideration of certain points in Marxist economics on the basis of concrete research.[7] Drawing on his own statistical studies for his news column, in the 1920s Takahashi became a prolific writer, producing several dozen works in political economy by the end of World War II.

Unlike many of his contemporaries in the early 1920s, Takahashi did not join the Japanese Communist Party, and thus he never felt compelled to accept the Comintern's analyses of Japanese development. He was active in the social movement for a time, however. On a visit to Europe and the United States in 1919 and 1920, he had met Japanese socialists Taguchi Unzō and Katayama Sen, although he claimed ignorance of their Communist ties at the time. After returning to Japan, he drew closer to Yamakawa Hitoshi and Sakai Toshihiko, leaders of the newly born JCP. Takahashi became a founding member of the left-wing Seiji Kenkyūkai (Political Studies Association), where his rightist leanings became increasingly apparent. He withdrew from the group when a split between its JCP members and "right-wing" social-democrats resulted in its dominance by the Communist left. In 1926, Takahashi became deeply involved in the Nihon Nōmintō (Japanese Farmers' Party), a group that exhibited both leftist and rightist leanings.[8] After 1928, when he ran unsuccessfully for office as a Nōmintō candidate, Takahashi severed all connections with the social movement.[9] With the outbreak of full-scale war with China in 1937, Takahashi became linked with more explicitly right-wing nationalist groups, such as the Shōwa Kenkyūkai (Shōwa Research Association), a research group that supported the goal of establishing Japanese military and economic dominance in Asia.[10]

Takahashi's background and activities, then, made him a very unusual Marxist in prewar Japan. Although he enjoyed a strong reputation in government and business circles, his education at a private university rather than at the prestigious Tokyo Imperial University, which produced most leading Marxist scholars, gained him less esteem among fellow Marxists. Nevertheless, by 1927, he had become highly regarded by Marxist and non-Marxist scholars of economic development because of his pioneering work in Japanese political economy.[11] His *Nihon shihon-shugi keizai no kenkyū* [Studies on the Japanese capitalist economy] (1924), which presented his thesis of the "deadlock" of the Japanese economy (*yukizumari-ron*), became widely influential in the proletarian movement. At this time virtually all Marxists agreed that the development of capitalism in Japan had been very slow, even "stagnant," after the Meiji period, particularly in agriculture. At a time when the Soviets were talking of a "general crisis of world capitalism," Takahashi was not the first to argue that Japan was experiencing a deadlock in its economic development, but he offered carefully compiled statistics to present an argument that struck a harmonious chord with the prevailing sentiment among his contemporaries.[12] Moreover, Takahashi's was the most provocative and innovative work that emerged in the 1920s, combining as it did Marxian analysis with the study of Japanese political and economic development.[13] When he published his controversial pieces on petty imperialism in April 1927, he had been writing regularly in such left-wing journals as *Marukusu-shugi* [Marxism], *Shakai-kagaku* [Social science], and *Taiyō* [The sun]. The petty imperialism theory, however, immediately drew the fire of leaders of the left-wing movement.[14] Takahashi suddenly found that he could no longer publish in *Marukusu-shugi* or *Shakai-kagaku*; and the left-wing publisher of Takahashi's earlier books, Hakuyō-sha, responded to a left-wing boycott by refusing to publish him.[15] The attack both by Marxists loyal to the JCP (the Kōza-ha) and by later Rōnō-ha leaders was violent but, objectively speaking, ineffective. The controversy merely exposed the many tasks that remained to be accomplished in the study of Japanese development, tasks that the debate on Japanese capitalism would fulfill to a significant extent over the next decade.

Japanese Marxists, then, found that they could not simply ignore Takahashi's work, even though they objected to his conclusions. For Takahashi's essays posed what became the pivotal problem for Japanese Marxist theoreticians in the 1920s and 1930s: How could Japanese political and economic development be analyzed so that it fit neatly into the model provided by Marx and Lenin? If the "universal laws of history" did not apply to Japan, there was no historical necessity for the kind of Marxist-Leninist revolution these leaders wished to make. To neglect the task had dangerous practical implications, as exemplified in Takahashi's work: even a leftist, it seemed, could easily manipulate the Marxian framework to legitimate an ultrarightist policy of military expansionism.

The Theory of Petty Imperialism

What was most troubling for his contemporaries in the left-wing movement was that Takahashi's argument was logically compelling, however unpalatable his conclusions were for Marxist opponents of political and economic oppression at home and abroad. Takahashi's theory endeavored to explain the unmistakable growth of increasingly expansionist Japanese militarism concurrent with the consolidation of the Meiji state and "Taishō democracy." The trend was evident in the defeat of China in 1894-1895; the 1905 victory over Russia; the presentation of the Twenty-one Demands to China in 1915; the occupation of former German territories in China through the terms of the Versailles Treaty; the Japanese participation in and extension of the Siberian expedition against the new Soviet Russian regime; and the preparation during the 1920s for a military move into Manchuria.

Takahashi offered the petty imperialism thesis in two essays in 1927,[16] although his argument can only be comprehended fully in terms of his earlier studies of Japanese development.[17] His essay on "The Imperialistic Position of Japanese Capitalism" opened with the question, "Is it possible to apply in its given form, the so-called 'imperialism as the final stage of capitalism' [theory of Lenin] to Japanese imperialism?" The extent to which Lenin's theory was applicable, Takahashi argued, would affect "in no small measure, such matters as the program, policies, and strategy of our proletarian movement," since a proletarian revolutionary strategy must differ in countries subjected to imperialism from that strategy in advanced imperialist countries. Takahashi sought to challenge the theoretical leadership of the left-wing movement in Japan, which, he felt, was proceeding blindly on the assumption that Japan was an "imperialist" power, in the Leninist sense. This implied the presumption that Japanese expansionism indicated that capitalism in Japan had already peaked and was on the verge of collapse.[18]

Lenin had identified five characteristics of modern imperialism:

> 1) the concentration of production and capital has developed to such a high stage that it has created monopolies which play a decisive role in economic life; 2) the merging of bank capital with industrial capital, and the creation, on the basis of this "finance capital," of a financial oligarchy; 3) the export of capital as distinguished from the export of commodities acquires exceptional importance; 4) the formation of international monopolist capitalist combines which share the world among themselves; and 5) the territorial division of the whole world among the biggest capitalist powers is completed.[19]

By applying these characteristics of imperialism, Takahashi concluded that Japan was not an imperialist power. Because of the peculiarities of the late development of Japanese capitalism, Lenin's theory could not explain Japanese expansionism; Japanese capitalism "had not yet attained the stage of imperialism" in Lenin's usage. "If you look at Japanese capitalism internationally," he argued,

> it may indeed be imperialist*ic*. However, at the most, it is an imperialist*ic* country as the petite bourgeoisie is to the grande bourgeoisie. If we take the term *petit bourgeois* and establish the category of petty imperialism, Japan is but a petty imperialist country. Thus, just as the interests of the petite bourgeoisie coincide with those of the proletariat and are not one with the interests of the grande bourgeoisie, the interests of petty imperialist countries coincide more with those of countries subject to imperialism than with those of large imperialist countries.

Indeed, Takahashi went on to assert that there was considerable evidence that Japan too "is in the position of a country subject to imperialism." "Consequently, [Japan's] international class role, rather than coinciding with that of imperialist countries like Britain and the United States, coincides far more with that of China, India, and other countries subject to imperialism." Japan's wars with Russia and China and its annexation of Korea were merely "nationalistic wars" waged in order to establish Japan as an independent state. Its proletarian revolutionary movement, therefore, should not despise nationalism, as the Comintern's program urged the JCP to do. Rather it must incorporate nationalistic elements into its movement in the manner prescribed by Lenin for the colonial areas, and, from its relatively advantaged position vis-à-vis China and India, take the lead in liberating the oppressed peoples of Asia. If the left failed to appreciate this objective need for nationalism in its revolutionary program, Takahashi warned, the Japanese masses would soon turn to the right, and the left itself would be to blame for the rise of fascism in Japan.[20]

The methodological weaknesses of Takahashi's article on "The Imperialistic Position of Japanese Capitalism" rendered his effort to justify Japanese expansionism more transparent. His application of Lenin's five features of the international phenomenon of imperialism to the single nation-state was itself, as Inomata Tsunao charged, of doubtful validity. In denying their applicability to Japan, Takahashi exhibited considerable recklessness and inconsistency, although such instances in fact served to demonstrate the difficulties of applying Marxist-Leninist categories rigidly to a late-developing country such as Japan. Takahashi was confronting the problem of Japan's dual economy,[21] for example, when he denied a high degree of concentration and monopolization in industrial production except in certain peripheral industries like flax spinning, plate glass, and dyes. In agricultural production, in which over half of Japan's labor force was engaged, Takahashi argued, small-scale agricultural and commodity production prevailed, with a substantial proportion of factories still employing fewer than five workers. Takahashi denied the absolute domination of finance capital (referring, in the Hilferding-Lenin usage, to a merger of bank with industrial capital); this was a surprising contention given the role of the zaibatsu in the Japanese economy. In addition, he was imprecise in his employment of the term "petty imperialism." At times he included the United States in that category, and at others he placed the United States and Germany alongside Britain as large imperialist powers.[22] Finally, the article placed considerable emphasis on the inherent inequity of the international system in a most unmaterialistic fashion. In an argument heavy with racialist overtones, Takahashi deplored Japan's large population coupled with inadequate resources. Japan was subject to the negative effects of imperialism, because the imperialist powers of Europe and America had appropriated resources and markets far out of proportion to the needs of their peoples. North America, for example, possessed only 6.6 percent of the world's population and 28.7 percent of its natural resources and foodstuffs. Yet in fear of the "yellow peril," the United States was prohibiting the "colored races" from its territories, while the Japanese strained under a population density ten times greater than that of America and Europe.[23]

Yukizumari-ron: Problems in the Development of Japanese Capitalism

These points made Takahashi's petty imperialism thesis extremely vulnerable to attack from enraged left-wing theorists. In its more refined version, however, his thesis was a remarkable application of Marxian analysis to Japanese economic development that drew, by Marxist-Leninist standards, counter-intuitive conclusions, given the phenomenon of Japanese expansionism and Lenin's theory of imperialism. At the same time, Takahashi's views managed to incorporate what would be the Rōnō-ha's emphasis on Japan's rapid industrial development with the future Kōza-ha's stress on Japan's underdevelopment relative to other industrialized countries. Finally, while it referred specifically to Japanese conditions, the argument was also suggestive of patterns of development in other "backward" countries. These were patterns that could not be explained without some adjustment in Marxist-Leninist theory.

The petty imperialism theory was premised on the notion of a current *yukizumari* (impasse or deadlock) in the development of Japanese capitalism. The *yukizumari* thesis had already become widely influential in Marxist and non-Marxist scholarly circles because it reflected the genuine economic problems Japan experienced in the 1920s. A burst of economic growth during World War I, when Japanese exports took over the markets of the warring European powers, was followed by a severe recession during the 1920s, which was particularly acute in the agricultural sector. Until the "readjustment" process was completed in the early 1930s, the decade of the 1920s was a series of financial panics, deflation, and agrarian crises.[24]

These conditions led Takahashi to assert that Japanese capitalism, which had still not developed to its highest possible level, had become "deadlocked." Unlike advanced countries which had reached the monopoly stage, however, Japan was suffering from a *yukizumari* that could be broken through deliberate state policies that would permit capitalism in Japan to resume its normal course to peak and inevitably decline. Takahashi wrote, "The soil which has nurtured the development of our capitalism from its infancy to maturity has . . . become exhausted of its main nutritive elements; . . . many contradictions inherent in the development of capitalism have intensified, and thus it has become impossible for our economy to continue the capitalistic development such as [it has sustained] up to now."[25]

According to Takahashi, the ingredients of Japan's spectacular growth from the Meiji Restoration (1868) to the end of the Meiji period (1912) had been the following: (1) the growth of productive forces achieved through copying, adaptation, and refinement of "modern science and technology" from Europe and the United States; (2) the effect of the first factor [having been] to render the rich natural resources that had lain undisturbed under feudalism useful; and (3) a rich supply of cheap labor beneficial for competition with foreign industries. As evidenced by statistics showing trends in land cultivation and mining from the early Meiji period to 1927, however, Japanese capitalist development had peaked and then in the late Taishō and early Shōwa (from 1925) had begun to stagnate. The economic boom of World War I was short-lived and quickly reversed in all respects. Copper production declined 44 percent from 1919 to 1927; silver production fell 39 percent from 1917 to 1927; coal production declined 11 percent from 1919 to 1922 and rose again but fell short of its 1919 level in 1927; oil production collapsed from its peak of 1919 by 44 percent in 1927; and sulphur production in 1927 was less than half its 1917 level. Meanwhile, the total area of cultivated land peaked in 1922 at 6,090,000 *chō* (1 *chō* = 2.45 acres) and declined gradually to 6,081,000 *chō* in 1927. Takahashi's figures also indicated a sharp decline in average agricultural productivity after a brief peak at the end of World War I (see table 3). These trends indicated that "despite the extraordinary support of the government during this period," Japanese capitalism had reached an impasse in its growth. The conditions that had fostered Japanese economic development during the Meiji period had disappeared (see table 4).

In addition, new domestic and international conditions created further impediments to the development of Japanese capitalism. Most significant among these were: (1) "the increase in labor wages" partly as a result of the growth of union activities since the Russian revolution; (2) "the poisoning [or undermining] of capitalist supports" like import duties and other protectionist government policies; (3) "the aggravation of the burden of imperi-

TABLE 3

Yields of Major Agricultural Products per One-Tenth Hectare

Average	Rice (Koku)	Barley (Koku)	Rye (Koku)	Wheat (Koku)	Soy beans (Koku)	Sweet potatoes (Kan)
1879-1883	1.20	0.91	0.79	0.60	0.52	188
1884-1888	1.34	1.06	0 75	0.71	—	—
1889-1893	1.40	1.07	0.84	0.71	—	—
1894-1898	1.42	1.28	1.01	0.86	0.69	259
1899-1903	1.48	1.28	0.93	0.78	0.76	262
1904-1908	1.63	1.41	1.02	0.90	0.77	283
1909-1913	1.69	1.58	1.14	1.02	0.72	320
1914-1918	1.83	1.52	1.16	1.08	0.81	337
1919	1.96	1.84	1.18	1.16	0.81	372
1920	2.02	1.37	1.22	1 07	0.90	371
1921	1.76	1.71	1.06	1.08	0.85	347
1922	1.93	1.74	1.16	1 14	0.82	344
1923	1.76	1.59	1.04	1.06	—	—

SOURCE: Takahashi Kamekichi, *Nihon keizai no yukizumari to musan-kaikyū no taisaku* [The deadlock of the Japanese economy and the countermeasures of the proletariat] (Tokyo: Hakuyō-sha, 1926), p. 64, table 1.

NOTE: 1 *koku* = 4.96 bushels; 1 *kan* = 8⅓ pounds.

alist policies'' for Japanese at home through rising taxes; (4) ''the intensification of industrial development and competition therefrom in backward countries, especially China''; and (5) ''setbacks in imperialist development,'' particularly because of the rise of a nationalistic revolutionary movement in China.[26] (See table 5.)

Two key factors causing not only Japan's *yukizumari* but also the peculiar nature of Japanese expansionism resulting from this stagnation were Japan's lack of raw materials and the previous partition of the world by the more advanced capitalist states, which deprived Japan of access to essential raw materials and markets abroad. If Japan's capitalist development was so limited, however, how could its imperialistic maneuvers be explained? In response to this question, Takahashi denied the universality of Lenin's definition of imperialism ''as the highest stage of capitalism,'' citing the phenomenon of imperialism on the part of less developed countries (LDCs).[27] Because of Japan's status as a late developer, there was a qualitative difference in the 1920s between Japanese nationalistic expansionism and the imperialism of the advanced capitalist states, the United States, Great Britain, and Germany. Given its dearth of raw materials, Japan had been unable to flourish as a producer of heavy capital goods, as opposed to light industrial and consumer goods like textiles. That fully 73 percent of Japanese exports from 1921 to 1925 were textiles reflected the fact that there

TABLE 4

Increases and Decreases in Arable Land and Mineral Production

Year	Farm land area: Rice fields (1,000 *chō*)	Farm land area: Dry fields (1,000 *chō*)	Farm land area: Total (1,000 *chō*)	Silver (*kan*)	Copper (1,000 *kin*)	Coal (1,000 metric tons)	Oil (1,000 *koku*)	Sulphur (1,000 *kin*)
1874	—	—	—	728	3,516	208	3	968
1878	2,614[a]	1,799[a]	4,313[a]	2,638	7,094	680	19	3,586
1888	—	—	—	11,297	22,291	2,023	40	31,660
1898	—	—	—	16,118	35,040	6,696	281	17,202
1908	2,874	2,631	5,504	31,972	67,755	14,825	1,642	55,699
1913	2,945	2,848	5,794	39,007	110,835	21,316	1,694	99,081
1917	2,997	2,956	5,953	58,992	180,064	26,361	2,509	118,089[b]
1919	3,022	3,050	6,072	42,822	130,739	31,271	1,964	50,631[b]
1922	3,050	3,040	6,090	32,841	90,210	27,701	1,799	34,642[b]
1926	3,119	2,962	6,080	36,496	104,271	29,262	1,450	45,675[b]
1927	3,131	2,949	6,081	35,942	100,908	31,199	1,406	58,464[b]

SOURCE: Takahashi Kamekichi, *Nihon shihon-shugi hattatsu shi* [History of the development of Japanese capitalism], rev. and enlgd. ed. (Tokyo: Nihon Hyōron-sha, 1929), p. 335, table 1.
NOTE: 1 *chō* = 2.45 acres; 1 *kan* = 8⅓ pounds; 1 *kin* = 1⅓ pounds; 1 *koku* = 4 96 bushels.
[a] These figures are based on the distinction at the time of the land reform circa 1877. Other areas of arable land are based on agricultural statistical tables. Mineral production quantities are taken from statistical yearbooks.
[b] From 1917 on, sulphur figure is in metric tons.

TABLE 5

Increases in Military Expenditures Relative to Japan's Total Central Annual Expenditures (In Millions of Yen)

Category	Actual Figures: 1881	1894	1904	1914	1925	Percentages: 1881	1894	1904	1914	1925
Administrative expenditures	31 3	37.7	210.4	328.3	892.2	44	48	76	51	58
Military expenditures	11.3	20.6	32.7	170.9	426.7	17	25	12	26	27
National debt expenditures	27.7	19.7	33.8	149 1	230.7	39	27	12	23	15
Totals	70.3	78.0	276.9	648.3	1549.6	100	100	100	100	100

SOURCE: Takahashi Kamekichi, *Nihon shihon-shugi hattatsu shi* [History of the development of Japanese capitalism], rev. and enlgd. ed. (Tokyo: Nihon Hyōron-sha, 1929), p. 347, table 2. Takahashi based his table on Tōyō Keizai Shinpō-sha, comp., *Meiji Taishō zaisei shōran* [Detailed survey of Meiji and Taishō finance], preface

was no room in the international market for the expansion of Japanese heavy industry that was essential to a mature capitalist economy.[28]

As a late developer, Japan had also been deprived of the benefits of free trade. Tariff barriers had already been erected and economic spheres of influence established in Asia and Africa by the time Japan entered the world market. Even as Japan approached the height of its capitalistic development, the advanced economies of Western Europe and America abruptly changed the "rules of the game." After World War I, advanced capitalist "status quo powers," seeking to protect the colonial and semi-colonial spheres of influence that they had acquired through international violence, suddenly took up the cry for peace, working through the League of Nations and arms reduction talks. These maneuvers were purposeful efforts on their part to protect their territories from rising LDCs; their effect was to place additional obstacles in the path of Japan's development.[29] As a consequence, "no matter how much their economic power declines, and how they may fall into indolence, the now advanced countries of Europe and America will remain perpetually in a superior position and [their peoples] can continue to enjoy a high living standard unsuited to their [true] capabilities."[30]

These conditions, in Takahashi's view, made it virtually impossible for Japan to experience a pattern of economic development typical of the more advanced powers in the "imperialist age." Japan would not enjoy the export of capital and heavy industrial products such as advanced imperialist countries like Great Britain, the United States, and Germany experienced in a second-stage prosperity built around their capital industries. On the contrary, Japan was becoming increasingly dependent on external sources of the materials essential to such capital industries, such as coal (see table 6). As a result, Japanese imperialism would continue to differ from that of Europe and the United States. From the outset of its capitalistic development, Japan's limited natural resource base had required that its imperialism rely on military expansion rather than economic expansion first. By contrast, Western European and American imperialistic development had been driven by a combination of financial forces and industrial power.[31] Japan's capital exports surged in 1924 and 1925, but Japan remained a net capital-importing country throughout.[32] For a short time after World War I, financial capital grew in Japan, and capital exports to China were encouraged. Nevertheless, these transactions consisted primarily of "political investment" loans to the weak Chinese government, while little capital export was undertaken, Takahashi asserted, that could stimulate the growth of Japan's heavy industrial sector. Finally, Japanese imperialism could not be powered by "finance capital" in the Leninist sense. Finance capital had grown prematurely in late-developing Japan, with the support of the Meiji

TABLE 6

Supply and Demand of Native Coal
(In Thousands of Metric Tons)

	Domestic Production	Imports	Exports
1913	21,315	576.7	3,870
1916	22,901	556.1	3,016
1917	36,361	713.0	2,813
1918	28,029	767.7	2,197
1919	31,271	705.2	2,016
1920	29,245	809.9	2,146
1921	26,220	789.6	2,406
1922	27,701	1,187.2	1,704
1923	28,948	1,712.8	1,586

SOURCE: Takahashi Kamekichi, *Nihon keizai no yukizumari to musan-kaikyū no taisaku* [The deadlock of the Japanese economy and the countermeasures of the proletariat] (Tokyo: Hakuyō-sha, 1926), p. 37, table 1.

state, in advance and in support of industrial capital. This process constituted a reversal of the development sequence of Europe and America. Consequently, the finance capital to be found in the zaibatsu was not identical with the finance capital Lenin and Hilferding had described as characteristic of the "age of finance capital."[33] These internal and international financial conditions placed severe constraints on Japanese economic expansion. Even where Japan had been able to execute imperialistic ventures, their benefits to Japanese capitalistic development and the extent of Japan's imperialistic exploitation were necessarily more limited than those gained through comparable activities by the United States, Great Britain, and Germany.

Takahashi's conclusions thereupon closely resembled the rationale for the official Greater East Asian Co-Prosperity Sphere policy of the 1930s.[34] Takahashi maintained that "while Japan has colonies in Korea, Taiwan, and Manchuria, these incursions do not necessarily signify what today's left calls 'imperialism.' " As a late developer, Japan had been relatively disadvantaged; its expansionism, therefore, was not of the same reprehensible character as the imperialism of the West, because its impetus came from elsewhere. Imperialistic expansion was absolutely essential for the survival of the still immature Japanese economy, a wronged party along with other LDCs in an international economic system that was inherently unfair. "Japan's wars with China and Russia and its annexation of Korea were all wars [waged] for the sake of Japan's independence and self-support," Takahashi declared.[35]

The notion of petty imperialism underscored this point by permitting the identification of Japan with other LDCs rather than with the imperialist powers of the West. Japan's "international position" not only made it "difficult to avoid its inevitably bearing the hues of a nationalistic movement in the [world] anti-imperialist movement";[36] indeed, in Takahashi's conception, it also urged upon Japan a positive political role. Joining hands with other oppressed LDCs in Asia, Japan could lead the struggle against the "international irrationality and immorality" that kept them under the "exploitation" of the "white races" of Europe and America. The low wages and living standards of Asia vilified by the advanced capitalist countries were not the deliberate policies of Eastern peoples to perpetuate "social dumping" in the West. Rather, they represented the "sacrifice of the Orient" for the benefit of Europe and America, the result of Western and not Eastern economic activities.[37]

This international context offered to Japan and its proletariat a unique historical mission. Japan would pioneer a "new international order" to rectify these wrongs. The seeds of the new order were already present: the low wages of the Orient and its importation of advanced technologies would help make its industries more competitive with those of Europe and America. But purely economic behavior would not suffice to mitigate the wrongs compounded by Western nation-states acting in support of their national capitalisms. An active military movement of national liberation would be necessary. Japan was the only Asian country in a position to lead that struggle, for Japan alone had built a massive military state on the basis of methods imported from the West.[38] Japanese expansion onto the Asian mainland would serve two purposes, then. It would enable Japan to break the *yukizumari* of its own capitalistic development by expanding its territorial natural resource base onto the mainland, thereby also eliminating the twin threats to Japan posed by Chinese economic growth and nationalistic revolution.[39] At the same time, Japan would fulfill the much larger world-historical role that Marx had envisaged for European capitalism: it would liberate Asia from economic stagnation and bring it back into the mainstream of human progress. Thus far, China had not yet been able to liberate itself from the yoke of European imperialism; Japan would help its fellow Asian peoples achieve victory in its war of national liberation from the "exploitation" of the "white races" and enable China and other late-developing Asian nations to achieve rapid industrialization under Japanese tutelage. In short, in Takahashi's view, to support Japanese imperialism was to support Asian anti-imperialist movements of national liberation. Marxists struggling for proletarian socialism would either embrace this nationalistic mission within their revolutionary program or risk losing the initiative to the right.[40]

The Attack from the Left: The Beginning of the Debate on Japanese Capitalism

On the level of practical politics, Takahashi's thesis offered a compelling account of the economic factors that would motivate Japan's militaristic expansion in the 1930s. It was curious that Takahashi, who so quickly allied himself with the official military cause of the right, presented his petty imperialism thesis in terms of the Marxian advocacy of proletarian socialist revolution in Japan. It is especially difficult to understand against what contingency Takahashi was warning with such remarkable foresight when he blamed the left's abdication of nationalistic leadership for the possible rise of fascism in Japan. Apparently, for Takahashi, "fascism" would comprise the military expansionism abroad and authoritarian domination at home that arose in the 1930s. His own revolutionary strategy called for military expansionism to be linked with proletarian-led revolution at home. In his view, petty imperialism would enhance the potential for a successful socialist revolution in Japan by spurring the growth of Japan's proletariat. If the left refused to recognize this and support his petty imperialist strategy, the initiative in the nationalist-imperialist movement would be lost to the capitalist and landlord forces that formed the basis for fascism in Japan. Takahashi's argument, then, posed no necessary theoretical contradictions with the Comintern's policies elsewhere in Asia. Nevertheless, it did deny the universality of the Soviet interpretation of class relations in countries that had already demonstrated significant capitalistic development at home and expansion abroad; and it challenged certain specific Soviet views about Japanese capitalism and imperialism. Marxists who were committed to Comintern leadership in the mid-1920s and who had not conducted their own empirical studies of Japanese development could offer only angry but remarkably weak responses to Takahashi's argument.

Indeed, one could argue that Takahashi's views effectively revealed the internal contradictions of a Soviet interpretation of Japanese political development that was based on a rigid application of Marx's unilinear model of economic and political development. The petty imperialism argument was fully consistent with Lenin's prescriptions for the proper role of nationalism in revolution among colonial peoples. At the same time, it also exposed the fragility of Lenin's interpretation of imperialism and national liberation movements. Lenin had posited a simple bifurcation between "imperialistic" powers and "colonial peoples" when he wrote of "imperialist wars." On the outbreak of World War I, Lenin had urged fellow socialists not to support their national bourgeoisies in war, for the dualistic contradiction between bourgeoisie and proletariat at home was simply being duplicated on the international level. George Lukács has summarized Lenin's argument as follows:

> The choice is not *whether* the proletariat will or will not struggle, but *in whose interests* it should struggle: its own or that of the bourgeoisie. The question history places before the proletariat is *not to choose between war and peace*, but between imperialist war and war against this war: civil war. . . . Only when the working class recognizes world war as the logical result of imperialist development, when it clearly sees that *civil war is the only possible resistance* to its own destruction in the service of imperialism, can the material and organizational preparation of the resistance begin.[41]

In the advanced industrialized countries of Western Europe in 1914, this meant that there could be no "progressive" role for nationalism among their proletariats. Nationalism could be such a progressive force only among colonial peoples, Lenin argued after the war, and this view was the theoretical basis for Comintern policy for all Asian countries except Japan after 1921.

By arguing that Japan was relatively less developed as a capitalist power and remained in a disadvantaged position in an inherently "unfair" international system, Takahashi did not merely adopt for Japan the Leninist position on colonial wars over that on proletarian strategy in capitalist states. Rather, he rejected the Comintern's interpretation of the simple "bourgeoisie-proletarian" dichotomy as applied to both the domestic and international spheres for a new, intermediate group of late-developing countries. For Takahashi, given Japan's current international position, the interests of its proletariat and those of its bourgeoisie were indistinguishable, at least until the *yukizumari* of Japanese capitalistic development had been resolved. Bourgeoisie and proletariat would be partners in Japan's economic expansionism. If Japan's proletariat acted in accordance with Lenin's prescription for advanced capitalist countries, Japan's "civil war" would prohibit its ever attaining the stage of advanced capitalism required for socialist revolution.

Takahashi thus made a case for the presence of powerful nationalistic and statist elements in Japan's proletarian movement by arguing that Japan's "backwardness" determined a course of development distinct from that of the more advanced countries of Western Europe. Where Lenin had revised Marx on the subject of the development of advanced capitalist states in the era of imperialism, Takahashi would do the same for Lenin on the subject of the national development of LDCs in the new post-World War I period. That Marxian analysis transcended Leninism from the perspective of a have-not power, and its conclusions reflected a consensus between a "left-wing'' interpretation and a rightist analysis of the objective requirements of Japan's economic and political development. Nor was this convergence peculiar to Japan, given the terms of Takahashi's argument. It could occur in other states, like Italy, which shared many of Japan's disadvantages as a late-developing country. Lenin's analysis was invalid for Japan because it recognized only one historical path of development where history had provided at least two. ''The path of historical development in backward countries,'' Takahashi concluded, ''occurs under conditions that differ substantially from those in advanced countries.'' These conditions dictated that whatever the scattered outward signs of advanced capitalism in Japan, Japanese economic development was severely constrained by what had occurred previously in more industrialized countries. That development would be ''distorted'' from the Marxian model, and therefore one could not simply apply to Japan the same revolutionary strategy that was appropriate for Britain, France, or the United States.

The Comintern's Japan policy, however, was based on Lenin's formula concerning advanced capitalist countries, and it was both convoluted and politically transparent. On the one hand, because of the Russian heritage of intermittent hostilities with Japan, the Soviet leaders deeply feared Japanese aggression and used their analysis of Japanese capitalism to repudiate, as Lenin had, nationalism as a reactionary force. Thus, throughout the 1920s and especially after the Manchurian Incident in 1931, the Comintern theses called for the JCP to resist Japanese expansionism and intervention against the Chinese revolution. At the same time, in somewhat ''Orientalist'' fashion, the Soviets were predisposed to view Japan's development as inferior to that of Europe and Russia. The theses drafted under Bukharin's leadership stressed the backwardness of Japan's agrarian sector and its reflection in the political sphere, calling on the JCP to overthrow the ''semi-feudal'' emperor system. A two-stage revolutionary process was prescribed for the ''backward'' Japan, as it was for China; but in Japan there was to be no positive role for nationalistic sentiment.[42]

Takahashi Kamekichi's critics were remarkably ineffective because they remained entirely within the constraints of this Comintern doctrine.[43] In early 1927, the Comintern analysis was widely accepted by leading Japanese Marxists, for it accorded with the aversion to Japanese militarism that had nurtured a fledgling socialist movement born of opposition to the Russo-Japanese War. Inomata Tsunao, Noro Eitarō, and Sano Manabu successfully exposed methodological flaws and inconsistencies in Takahashi's argument; but their casual acceptance of Comintern doctrine severely debilitated their critiques. In their furious but feeble efforts to refute a thesis carefully supported by a wealth of statistics and an understanding of Japanese economic conditions that they themselves lacked, Inomata and Noro discovered the impotence of Japan's indigenous Marxism that they would seek to dispel in the debate on Japanese capitalism. Indeed, without Takahashi's challenge, Japanese Marxists may have taken considerably longer to proceed from the mere importation of Marxism to its enrichment through innovative interpretation of the lessons of Japanese development.

The responses to Takahashi involved several major points that were poorly organized and often themselves internally inconsistent. All critics of the theory were offended by Takahashi's proposal for a new nationalistic strategy for Japan's proletarian movement, and they immediately tried to attack it by refuting the contention that Japan was not yet a truly "imperialist" country.[44] Noro was particularly disturbed by the notion that Japan did not fit the pattern described by Lenin. Therefore, he argued that in fact Japan had met all but the last of the five criteria established by Lenin. (In other words, the territorial division of the world among the advanced capitalist powers was not yet complete, in Noro's view.) In addition, Noro pointed out that imperialism referred to an international phenomenon without reference to which Japanese behavior could not be explained.[45] Only Inomata, however, was perceptive enough to extend this point to criticize Takahashi's methodology. If imperialism was a world-historical phenomenon, one could not apply Lenin's criteria, as both Takahashi and Noro did, to the single national entity of Japan. In the imperialist age, it would be difficult to find individual countries that met all five criteria; but the dynamic of world capitalism as a whole would drive individual capitalist states to act "imperialistically."[46] Having made this point, however, Inomata failed to link an analysis of the capitalist "world system" with the process of internal development of individual states, as Takahashi had tried to do.

Indeed, it was in making their own alternative analyses of Japanese development that Noro and Inomata floundered helplessly. At what point had Japan reached the stage of finance capitalism? How could one explain the many signs of Japanese "backwardness" stressed by the Comintern, given the conviction that Japanese expansionism was the economic imperialism described by Lenin? On these crucial issues both Noro and Inomata were incoherent, although their interpretations diverged considerably. In Inomata's view, capitalism was "already becoming the dominant mode of production" at the time of the Sino-Japanese War; the Russo-Japanese War was Japan's imperialist war, and the annexation of Korea and its other rewards were the fruits of capitalistic imperialism. Yet, at the same time, Inomata admitted that Japan had not yet become a "finance capitalistic country" by 1904-1905. Japan's finance capital was, just as Takahashi had pointed out, "semi-bureaucratic" in nature. Given this relative backwardness, Japan's early, even "premature" embarkation on the path of imperialism had to be considered more a function of international than of internal economic conditions.[47]

By contrast, Noro argued that Japanese capitalism had developed through two stages of industrial revolution. The first, from about 1885 or 1886 to the Sino-Japanese War, was based on light industry, while the second, based on heavy industry, did not occur until the Russo-Japanese War. At the same time, finance capital began to mature rapidly because of the stage of development of world capitalism, Noro asserted. Thus, the Russo-Japanese War marked the beginning of Japan's development as an imperialist country, but that war itself was not yet an imperialist war. Rather, like the Boer War and the Spanish-American War, it was what Lenin had referred to as a transitional war, marking a new world-historical epoch.[48] While Noro disputed some of Takahashi's statistics, he did not offer evidence of the two "industrial revolutions" he cited; nor did he explain the internal conditions for the "transitional" Russo-Japanese War and the growth of Japanese finance capital that allegedly occurred at the time.

What Noro did offer, as historian Kojima Hinehisa has observed, was a bizarre image of Japanese imperialism based on both "capitalism that has developed to the imperialist stage and old absolutism."[49] Inomata seemed to ignore the peculiarities of Japanese development without offering persuasive data to support his own case for Japanese imperialism. Yet Noro's image of Japanese imperialism, which would continue to permeate Kōza-ha writings during the debate on Japanese capitalism, in fact left Noro with the implication he had originally found most disturbing in the petty imperialism thesis: that Japanese economic development was not typical at all of the patterns Marx and Lenin had observed in Western Europe. At this point, neither Inomata nor Noro was prepared to introduce into his Marxian analysis the flexibility that Takahashi had shown. Consequently, neither could explain the distortions in Japan's internal development that had been caused in part by its relatively late start in the age of imperialism. Indeed, until Uno Kōzō's analyses in the 1930s, no Japanese Marxist was fully prepared to develop this theme into the more complex "stage theory" of world economic development,[50] a more refined version of Leon Trotsky's notion of "combined and uneven development"[51] that Japan's circumstances seemed to require. To Noro and Inomata any such temptation to "revise" Marx and Lenin promised to lead to the convergence between left and right that Takahashi represented and that would, in fact, engulf Japan in the wave of mass conversions (*tenkō*) of Marxists to the national cause during the 1930s.[52]

Takahashi's challenge to orthodox Marxist-Leninists in 1927, then, was clear. The tension between the historical peculiarities of Japanese development on the one hand and the universality of Marx's model had to be resolved in favor of a socialist and anti-imperialist course. The possibility of multiple paths of development was to be laid to rest. Only a detailed concrete analysis of Japanese development by Marxists dedicated to these goals could produce a genuine indigenous Japanese Marxism without the rightist leanings of Takahashi Kamekichi. The debate on Japanese capitalism, erupting on the heels of the petty imperialism controversy, would become the left's enthusiastic response to the challenge.

FIVE

The Development of Capitalism in Japan

ONCE confronted by the culmination of Takahashi Kamekichi's analyses of Japanese development in the heretical theory of petty imperialism, those dedicated to defending the anti-imperialist orthodoxy of Marxism-Leninism accepted Takahashi's challenge to produce superior scholarship on Japan's political and economic history. This response assumed the form of the debate on Japanese capitalism as the discrepancies between Inomata Tsunao's and Noro Eitarō's critiques of Takahashi escalated into a direct confrontation between two theoretical schools. The factional split cut deeply into the academic community, establishing conflicting paradigms that would influence the study of Japanese development and comparative history for decades. At the same time, the rupture also reflected tensions that had been swelling within the Japanese Communist Party itself for several years. The divergent Marxist interpretations of Japanese development that emerged in the course of the debate on Japanese capitalism, then, are explicable only within the context of the controversy's linkage to the intraparty dispute on revolutionary strategy and tactics that was described in preceding pages.

The political discord within the socialist movement helped to shape the character of the debate from the outset. The faction of former JCP leader Yamakawa Hitoshi had long contested the influence of Fukumoto Kazuo. Yet the Comintern's denunciation of the latter in the 1927 Theses could not satisfy Yamakawa's desire to return as the party's theoretical leader, because the Comintern's repudiation of Fukumoto's "sectarianism" was coupled with a renewed condemnation of Yamakawa's "liquidationist" advocacy of a single "broad workers' and peasants' party."[1] Moreover, the JCP's acceptance of the theses made it clear that the Comintern would continue to be the final arbiter of the "correct" revolutionary line for a Leninist-style vanguard party. Thus, shortly after Noro and Inomata began to attack Takahashi's petty imperialism thesis, Yamakawa and his followers—including Inomata and the former anarchist Arahata Kanson—officially launched the debate on Japanese capitalism by leaving the party in November 1927. All JCP efforts to conciliate the so-called *Rōnō* dissident faction were met with indifference. When the Comintern invited Arahata to rejoin the party and to sit on its Central Committee, Arahata refused unless the Yamakawa faction was to be permitted to assume exclusive leadership of the party. Arahata also rejected an invitation to confer with Comintern representative Jacob Janson in Shanghai, and Yamakawa refused to attend a meeting with party leader Watanabe Masanosuke arranged by the Central Committee. The JCP finally replied in kind to the group's intransigence in February 1928, when the Central Committee formally expelled the dissidents from the party "under orders from the Far Eastern Bureau of the Comintern."[2]

As early as July 1927, Inomata had begun to publish analyses of Japanese capitalism, adopting a critical posture vis-à-vis both Takahashi's theory and the 1927 Theses that would support the Rōnō-ha's position. In addition to essays on "The Pattern of Stability and the Pattern of Decline of Japanese Capitalism" and "The Problem of the Present Stage of Japanese Capitalism,"[3] Inomata penned a piece on "The Political Position of the Bourgeoisie in Japan" that became one of the "classic articles" stating the Rōnō-ha interpretation of Japanese capitalism.[4] Now, as a founding member of *Rōnō*, Inomata offered a theoretical foundation for Yamakawa's united front political strategy by way of an instrumentalist approach to the Japanese state.[5] Viewing the existing regime as the instrument of a highly developed bourgeoisie, Inomata tied a description of Japanese politics in the 1920s directly to the issue of proletarian revolutionary strategy.[6] Along with Tokyo Imperial University economic historian Tsuchiya Takao (whose work focused more on the origins of Japanese capitalism, particularly in the agrarian sector), Inomata quickly emerged as a preeminent theoretician of the Rōnō-ha. Curiously, Inomata's work became its most theoretical only after he had split with Yamakawa in 1929.[7] Yet, except for an analysis of "Asiatic features" of Japanese agriculture published in 1937,[8] virtually all this later work continued in the vein of his early studies of finance capital and imperialism.[9] Inomata consistently drew on Nikolai Bukharin's ideas on the advanced capitalist state to support the Rōnō-ha's thesis that Japan was so highly developed a capitalist society that only a one-stage proletarian socialist revolution was necessary. Once Inomata no longer espoused Yamakawa's united front strategy, books like *Botsuraku shihon-shugi no daisan ki* [The third period of declining capitalism] (1930), *Nihon no dokusen shihon-shugi* [Japanese monopoly capitalism] (1931), and *Kyōkō moto no Nihon shihon-shugi* [Japanese capitalism in crisis] (1931) offered more "objective" scholarly studies of Japan's political economy, such as he had begun as a member of the Sangyō Rōdō Chōsajo research group. In keeping with his earlier theoretical approach, Inomata's new writings continued to be critical of the views adopted by Noro, the Comintern, and the JCP loyalists who formed the Kōza-ha.[10]

The fact that Inomata's writings first emerged in close association with Yamakawa's strategic doctrine meant that they tended to be confined to the analysis of Japanese capitalism as it existed at the time Inomata wrote. On the whole, until the early 1930s, when Tsuchiya Takao endeavored to refute Hattori Shisō's thesis that the late Edo period corresponded to what Karl Marx called the maufacture era by offering historical research of his own, the Rōnō-ha tended to emphasize current economic and political developments at the expense of a longer historical perspective. This pattern was, of course, consistent with the Rōnō-ha aim to demonstrate the existence of those new elements of a highly developed capitalism that demanded immediate proletarian revolution. In the Rōnō-ha view, the feudal elements of the Tokugawa period had been effectively swept aside by the bourgeois-democratic revolution of the Meiji Restoration and no longer warranted close scrutiny.

By contrast, the Kōza-ha, supporting the far more complex Comintern interpretation, necessarily adopted an historical perspective at the outset. The Kōza-ha needed an approach that could unravel the combination of feudal remnants (*hōken isei*) and new capitalistic features that made Japan at one and the same time "backward" and "semi-feudal" as well as capable of the imperialism of advanced capitalist states in the Leninist sense. Indeed, Noro's response to Takahashi revealed this mandate for a reexamination of the Japanese past through Marxist lenses.

Noro's refutation of Takahashi's theory of petty imperialism attempted to show that "in Japan monopoly capitalism and modern imperialism were maturing completely." For Noro, Lenin's theory of imperialism as the highest stage of capitalism could explain Japanese imperialism, even if Japan's capitalist economy did possess certain unique characteristics.[11] Here Noro diverged from Takahashi, but he also differed with Inomata, who rejected the Comintern's view that "extreme backwardness" in the agrarian sector and the continued political strength of "large landowners and the military and royal cliques" required a two-step revolutionary process.[12] Where Takahashi had attributed uniqueness to Japanese imperialism, Noro identified Japan's divergence from the Western European model of development by upholding this general Comintern outline of uneven development in town and countryside.[13] Inomata had expressed the Rōnō-ha's view that what Japan shared with other capitalist societies dwarfed the significance of any peculiarities: even in the countryside, peasants were now exploited by profit-seeking landlords through capitalistic taxes, farm rents determined by the market forces of supply and demand, and wage labor. But Noro argued that Japan's uniqueness lay precisely in the fact that Japanese agriculture was still very small in scale and had not yet been replaced by large-scale capitalistic agriculture. In short, Japan's agrarian sector had never fully emerged from the petty mode of production of feudalism. As Yamada Moritarō would argue in his *Analysis of Japanese Capitalism*,[14] capitalism had not supplanted feudalism in the Meiji period; rather, capitalism had risen on the basis of old feudal modes of exploitation. Hence, feudalism and capitalism coexisted in a mutually supportive relationship, distorting the universal characteristics of Japan's capitalism that were stressed by the Rōnō-ha.[15] Noro detected in the dual Japanese economy an imbalance between higher and lower modes of production, an imbalance that threatened to increase with the continued development of the industrial sector at the expense of the rural sphere. This disequilibrium could only be resolved by a thoroughgoing bourgeois-democratic revolution that carried the capitalist mode of production into the countryside.

At the beginning of his critiques of Fukumotoism and of Takahashi's petty imperialism thesis, Noro did not perform the solid Marxian analysis of Japanese development since the late Tokugawa period that was necessary to support these claims. By 1930, however, both Noro's *Nihon shihon-shugi hattatsu shi* [History of the development of Japanese capitalism] and Hattori's *Meiji ishin shi* [History of the Meiji Restoration] had made the first efforts in this direction.[16] Noro's book became the basis of the seven-volume symposium (*Nihon shihon-shugi hattatsu shi kōza*) that offered systematic historical research in support of an indigenous Marxian interpretation of Japanese development, which, appreciative of Japan's peculiarities, was closer to the Comintern position than to the Rōnō-ha view. To defend their own views against the *Kōza* faction's interpretation, Rōnō-ha scholars were then likewise constrained to adopt a more historical approach in the 1930s.

As the debate grew more historical, both sides offered solutions to central problems in the political and economic development of Japan since the late Tokugawa era (*bakumatsu*). To what extent did the pattern of this development conform to or diverge from the English model that had formed the basis of Marx's original theory of revolution? What were its universal characteristics and its unique aspects? To what may these differences be attributed, and what would be their implications for the promise of Japanese revolution in the early Shōwa era? Did the Meiji Restoration fulfill the tasks of a bourgeois-democratic revolution? To the extent that it failed to do so, how could one account for that deficiency, and how were its consequences manifested in the ensuing decades? Finally, and perhaps most fundamentally, precisely what was the balance between internal and external stimuli of the rapid economic and political development that occurred in Japan in the late nineteenth century? Did the Western intrusion in the 1850s have the decisive impact that Western scholars attribute to it today? Or had Japan already experienced in the *bakumatsu* indigenous capitalistic development? And indeed, if the latter was the case, what then precipitated the political reforms that accompanied the Restoration and the economic acceleration that characterized the 1880s and 1890s?

This last set of issues concerning internal and external sources of change was raised explicitly by Kōza-ha historian Hattori Shisō in 1933. The "manufacture controversy" aroused by Hattori's assertion that significant indigenous development of capitalism had occurred in Japan before the opening of the ports and the country's entry into the world capitalist system involved disagreement not only between the two major factions but within Hattori's own Kōza-ha as well. It was in response to this concern and the others raised above that the participants in the debate outlined several versions of the development of capitalism in Japan. Ideally, such an historical analysis would do for the Japanese Marxist movement what Lenin's *Development of Capitalism in Russia* had done for the Bolsheviks: it would demonstrate that whatever its national peculiarities due to "Oriental" or Asiatic characteristics, Japan's course of development coincided sufficiently with that of Western Europe to render Marx's revolutionary scheme applicable to Japan. The danger of maintaining that external stimuli were more important lay in the implication that Japan's "natural" indigenous course was not progressive change from feudalism through capitalism to socialism but rather the same Asiatic stagnancy that Marx saw in China and India.

Yet in outlining the development of capitalism in Japan, participants in the debate were not merely engaged in a mechanistic application of Marxian categories of analysis to reinterpret Japan's past and present. The relationship between history and theory is intimate in Marxism; and in pursuing their concerns historically, Japanese Marxists also emerged as theorists of political and economic change. Over the last several decades, Western Marxists like Maurice Dobb and Paul Sweezy have been engaged in a controversy on the character of the development of capitalism in Western Europe. In confronting the issue of whether an external force, world trade (Sweezy), or some factor inherent in the feudal system (Dobb) was the principal factor that precipitated England's evolution of industrial capitalism, these scholars have addressed important gaps remaining in Marx's original theory.[17] The participants in the debate on Japanese capitalism undertook this endeavor twenty years before Western Marxists did, and in their study of a non-Western case, spoke to the question of the relationship between the universal and the particular that is fundamental to any conception of political development, whether Marxist or non-Marxist. The following pages explore Rōnō-ha and Kōza-ha efforts to describe the development of capitalism in Japan, with particular attention to the so-called manufacture debate.

The Manufacture Debate: Internal and External Stimuli of Economic Development

The two basic analytical schemes—Rōnō-ha and Kōza-ha—that Japanese Marxists developed to interpret the history of Japanese political development were implicit in the intra party controversy surrounding the Comintern's theses on Japan. The Kōza-ha accepted the Comintern's belief that revolutionary change begun by the Meiji Restoration had still not produced a capitalistic economic base sufficiently uniform to generate a bourgeois-democratic monarchy in the political superstructure.[18] For these JCP loyalists, the Comintern's analysis offered a cogent explanation for the economic and political difficulties afflicting Japan in the late Taishō and early Shōwa periods. The emperor-system state, which was becoming increasingly repressive in "roundups" directed against the socialist movement, was clearly not effectively democratic; its glaring weaknesses far exceeded those of the admittedly imperfect bourgeois states in England and America. The state was not using the means of a bourgeois state to deceive its voting public into supporting it with the ballot; rather it was using the brutal physical force characteristic of a semi-feudal "absolutist regime."

Finally, the Comintern's analysis of Japan's uneven development was a persuasive explanation of the laggard economic performance of the agrarian sphere throughout the decade (see chapter 1). The Comintern had found in Japan "both the objective prerequisites for a bourgeois-democratic revolution (the feudal remnants in the state structure, an acute agrarian problem) and the objective prerequisites for the rapid transformation of the bourgeois revolution into a socialist revolution (the high level of concentration of capital, the growing number of trusts, the close relationship between the state and the trusts, the approximation of the economy to state capitalism, and the unity of the bourgeoisie with the landed nobility)."[19] In their early studies, Noro and Hattori began to supply the details of the historical process that had resulted in this complex economic and political structure.

On the other side, Rōnō-ha theorists Inomata and Tsuchiya endeavored to offer proof of the maturation of capitalism in city and countryside, in base and superstructure. The Meiji Restoration had constituted a bourgeois-democratic revolution, even if certain of that revolution's tasks remained to be accomplished. The land-tax reforms, abolition of *han* and establishment of prefectures, and the removal of feudal restrictions in the early years of the Meiji, they maintained, propelled Japan toward the rapid growth of industrial capitalism that was occurring by the turn of the century. The high concentration of capital and the growth of finance capital in the urban areas, Japan's embarkation on an imperialist course in Asia, constitutional rule, party cabinets, and the passage of universal suffrage in 1925 were all taken as indications that Japan was not "backward" at all, as the Comintern maintained. Rather, it had followed the classic course of transition from feudalism through bourgeois revolution that had been pioneered by England.[20]

It would appear that the difference between the two sides was not great—

that the disagreement concerned merely the extent and significance of changes during the Meiji period that all historians could agree had occurred. The issue was not, however, merely a quantitative one but a qualitative one. While Tsuchiya could concede that agrarian rents had remained as high as they were in the Tokugawa period, he argued that they had changed from feudal rents in kind to capitalistic money ground rents; their high rates were determined not by the extra-economic coercion characteristic of feudal society, but by the impersonal laws of supply and demand of land on the free market. Hirano and other Kōza-ha Marxists countered that while agrarian rents had changed in form they had not changed in essence; they remained semi-feudal in nature, as personalistic feudal mores persevered in the countryside.[21]

Nevertheless, the two paradigms were genuinely similar in their underlying assumptions about the sources of Japan's capitalist development. Hattori Shisō recognized that both Rōnō-ha and Kōza-ha assumed the primacy of external causation, the world market, in Japanese development, and when he attacked this assumption, he provoked the "manufacture debate." Drawing on Marx's and Lenin's treatments of the development of industrial capitalism in Western Europe and Russia, Hattori reexamined Japanese economic history to discover whether significant capitalist development had in fact occurred before the Western intrusion. His work led him to identify the late Tokugawa era before the arrival of America's black ships as Japan's "manufacture period." By the 1840s and 1850s, he argued, capitalist production in Japan had already advanced well beyond the stage of small handicraft industry and was preparing for the transition to large-scale mechanized industrial capitalism. In Hattori's view, such an interpretation made the prevailing assumption that Japan had been able to develop capitalism only as a result of external pressures untenable. When this argument was countered by Rōnō-ha and Kōza-ha Marxists alike, it aroused heated controversy on a major question in the analysis of the development of capitalism in Japan and elsewhere.

Japanese Capitalism as the Product of Western Intrusion

The controversy, which raged in 1933 and 1934, began when Hattori exposed and reexamined this assumption by means of a self-criticism of his own 1929 publication, *History of the Meiji Restoration*.[22] Hattori had penned this study in late 1927 and early 1928 to address the issue of the extent to which the Meiji Restoration had been the bourgeois-democratic revolution that the Rōnō-ha claimed it to be. At this point, the Rōnō-ha had simply stated in its strategic program its conviction that the Meiji Restoration constituted such a revolution but had not yet produced historical research to sustain this claim.[23] Not surprisingly, Hattori concluded from his own study that if the Meiji Restoration had initiated such a transformation, it was incomplete at best because of the peculiar set of circumstances under which it occurred in Japan. Specifically, Hattori referred to the interaction between internal contradictions afflicting Tokugawa society before the opening of the ports in the 1850s to foreign contact and trade, and the effects of the international economic system to which Japan was exposed. Japanese feudalism had been suffering from contradictions inherent in the feudal mode of production even before the arrival of Commodore Perry in 1854; but because of the abrupt end to the shogun's exclusionist policies coerced by the powers, Japanese feudalism began to decline. In Hattori's words:

> Because of the world capitalism that was firmly linked to Japan from the fifth year of the Ansei period (1858) a powerful disintegration . . . of feudalistic production methods and production relations began to proceed from their very bases within the country. However, because of the balance of foreign forces, this process of economic disintegration ended without inviting the misfortune . . . of united foreign military intervention—as in China.[24]

The preexisting contradictions in Japan's feudal society were resolved under the new conditions provided by interaction with the West. This process did not, however, entail a classic bourgeois-democratic revolution, Hattori argued. Such feudal contradictions existed in the antagonism "between the natural agrarian economy and the commercial and usury capital of the cities"; but they "were absolutely not of the kind that we generally discover taking the classical form of revolutionary resistance of merchants against warriors and warrior domination in a bourgeois revolution," as some seemed to assume. On the contrary, in Japan such contradictions merely "incited limitless disintegrative strife between peasants [on the one hand] and shogun, daimyo, and lower status retainer groups [on the other]." The new conditions occasioned by the opening of the ports required political changes that would open the domestic market, and the agents of this change emerged out of the discord among old feudal ruling groups—the warriors (*bushi*) who became radicalized and were able to form the most powerful political force equipped to carry out the Restoration. These samurai in turn immediately mobilized the vacillating commercial and usury capitalists (bourgeoisie). The new absolutist monarchical Meiji regime that emerged from this process was "a phoenix born from [the ashes of] the disintegration of the old system." Gathering its political energies, this regime thereupon resolved to "abolish the entire old system that had been its own womb, carry out the economic reformation that had been brewing since the opening of the ports, and take the first step in building the empire of 'capitalistic Japan.' "[25]

Because of the foreign pressures that galvanized it, then, the Meiji Restoration was a revolution from above pioneered not by a rising bourgeoisie, but by a class of warriors drawn from the old feudal structure of Tokugawa Japan. Hence the Restoration could not complete either the economic or political tasks that were accomplished by the "classic" bourgeois-democratic revolutions of Western Europe. Under the tutelage of the absolutist monarchy[26] "a series of bourgeois reforms" was carried out. Among them, the national reorganization of feudal domains (*han*) on the basis of prefectures helped to shift the locus of real political and economic power from old individual domains to the centralized government now under the nominal authority of the emperor. Old feudal classes were stripped of certain of their former privileges, and the new state promulgated a constitution and established a national Diet.

In Hattori's view, however, these reforms did not constitute a genuine bourgeois revolution, nor could they, given the circumstances under which they were effected. In Hattori's view of the French revolution of 1789—"a model (*tenkei-teki*) bourgeois revolution"—"what was overthrown along with feudalism was the absolute monarchy, and those who assumed responsibility for the liberation of all the oppressed people were the battling bourgeoisie." By contrast, in Japan, "the power of the absolute monarchy government itself was the agent of bourgeois reform." Yet, despite these reforms, the "power of *hanbatsu*, military cliques, and cliques of nobility" was maintained, and the Meiji regime did not abolish the economic basis of feudalism in the countryside, because agrarian feudalism was the economic foundation upon which the new state itself stood:

> The Restoration government, in 1871, began its unique bourgeois revolution "from above," but the agrarian revolution that forms the truly revolutionary content of a bourgeois-democratic revolution "from below" was not something that the Restoration government was able to do well. Despite the increasingly . . . semi-bourgeois nature of the Restoration government, it was itself a feudal power, and, except for bonds borrowed from bourgeois at high interest rates, it had only the peasants' land tax as its primary material basis. From the late 1870s indirect taxes and profits from state capital gradually increased, but even so, before the late 1880s generally the land tax comprised over 80 percent of current revenues. Therefore, if the Restoration government had not had the land tax, doubtless there would have been no industrial protection and promotion, state capitalism, militaristic enterprise, and consequently no future "first-echelon nation" imperialist Japan. In-

> deed, the Meiji government's acquisition of the land tax was the primitive accumulation that was indispensable for the birth of imperialist Japan.[27]

The land tax reforms changed the basis on which the tax was calculated from annual crop yield to land value and replaced miscellaneous feudal taxes and levies with a single unified land tax that provided the state with a stable source of revenue. Along with the elimination of prior bans on the purchase and sale of land, these reforms marked the Meiji state's response both to the increasing encroachment of a commodity economy resulting from international trade and to the decline of the natural agrarian economy. These reforms did provide a basis for a "modern" land ownership system (in which land itself was now an alienable commodity). Nevertheless, they did not "carry out a decisive agrarian revolution"; rather, they "reproduced feudal relations of exploitation between landowner and peasant based on large feudal landownership among new landlords, on the basis of modern landownership and tenant farmers." The amount of rent, as a proportion of peasant income, experienced no change at the time of the land tax reforms; but while the burden of state taxes on the peasant declined as a result of the reforms, the amount of peasant income that went to the landlord increased. Consequently, there was a tendency for independent farmers to lose their land, while landlords were able to merge lands under the provisions of the new land laws. Thus there was a net shift of independent farmers from independence to tenant-farmer status, and a group of "new landlords" emerged. A series of poor harvests compounded the hardships suffered by peasants under the new laws, with the result that the number of day-laborers and farmers who labored seasonally in the cities during the nongrowing season increased steadily. The result was that a large pool of potential urban proletarians was created in the countryside, but peasants were not moved from the countryside en masse. Rather, as independent farmers fell into "feudalistic" tenant-farmer status, a younger generation gradually moved into the urban areas to be exploited as workers.[28]

The Indigenous Development of Capitalism in Japan

This interpretation was consistent with the Comintern's view, as expressed in the '27 Theses. But, writing in mid-1933 on "Methodological Problems in the History of the Restoration," Hattori judged his own early analysis of the Meiji Restoration to have been founded on an erroneous tendency (which he much later called "Bukharinist"[29]) to seek the origins of the Meiji reforms—hence industrial capitalist development—in external causes and to underestimate the indigenous development of capitalism in Japan. In his 1927 analysis of the Restoration, Hattori saw the driving force of the rapid economic and political developments of the Meiji period in the contradiction between a capitalistic Western Europe and America and a feudalistic ("Asiatically" backward) Orient. In this view, the *bakumatsu* economy was described as dominated by handicrafts and peasant domestic industry, elements of the feudal mode of production. This is where the difficulties arose. Such a characterization of the Japanese economy was applicable to the pre-Kamakura era (which began in the late twelfth century) through the entire period of Tokugawa feudalism. This view failed to identify any process of change and specifically neglected the tensions affecting the economy on the eve of Commodore Perry's arrival. More importantly, if the growth of industrial capitalism was solely the result of coercion by foreign capital, then how could one explain China's and Japan's radically contrasting responses?[30]

In criticizing his own work, Hattori was also attacking Rōnō-ha scholars, whose analyses rested on the same erroneous premises. For example, the previous year Tsuchiya had written in an analysis of the late Tokugawa period that " 'The opening of Japan, following the opening of China, was significant [in that] it formed the final link in the process of the formation of a grand capitalist world market, which [had] originated in the sudden rise of British and American capitalism in the eighteenth century.' " In addition, like Hattori, Tsuchiya perceived virtually no indigenous development of industrial capitalism in the late Edo period; feudalism was the dominant mode of production, and only commercial and usury capital were being accumulated.[31] Similarly, the lesser known Ishihama Tomoyuki virtually ignored internal factors in the growth of Japanese capitalism; and Kōza-ha scholar Hani Gorō did not deny the significance of such factors, but he did stress Japan's Asiatic features and the impact of Japan's inclusion into the world capitalist market.[32] Thus, Hattori in 1927, Hani, Tsuchiya, Ishihama, and others had all acknowledged the existence of manufacture—cooperative production based on a division of labor, involving few capitalists and large numbers of workers, and done by hand and not by machine[33]—in the late Tokugawa; but they had "underestimated its internal revolutionary significance." Instead, they stressed the presence of commercial and usury capital, the impoverishment of the daimyo and lower-level samurai, and the aggravation of these internal tensions by the opening of the ports to the world capitalist market. Consequently, they reached the conclusion of a revolution by lower-class samurai who did not possess "capital" in the strict sense.

For the Kōza-ha, Hattori had thus determined that the Restoration was not a social revolution but merely a reorganization of feudal rule, with the Sat-Chō clique replacing the shogunate. Now Hattori decided that this argument was logically coherent, but was not supported by the facts of Tokugawa economic development. On the other side, the Rōnō-ha view was simply wrong in its entirety. Inomata argued that the Restoration, with its adoption of the *fukoku kyōhei* slogan and promotion of industrial capitalism, was a heroic revolutionary gesture undertaken to enable Japan to resist external encroachment. The historic mission of the Meiji regime, in this view, was to make Japan a link in the world capitalist system. But the lack of attention given by Inomata, Tsuchiya, and other Rōnō-ha theorists to internal factors made it impossible for them to explain Japan's ability to resist foreign encroachment, in contrast with China's humiliating reduction to semi-colonial status. In both cases, the argument was overdetermined by an analytical method that stressed the grand "systemic" conflict between Western capitalism and Oriental feudalism.[34]

Hattori was not the first to offer such a criticism of existing work on the Meiji Restoration,[35] but he was the first to present an alternative hypothesis accompanied by concrete historical evidence to support it. At this point, Hattori had already penned an article for the *Kōza* entitled "Revolution and Counter-revolution in the Meiji Restoration."[36] There he had stressed the presence of indigenous capitalistic development in the late Tokugawa period, calling it the "stage of relatively high-level development of early capitalism." In this essay, Hattori made three simple points. First, there was a significant presence of machine industry after the opening of the ports and before the Restoration.[37] Such machinery used for industry (as distinguished from irrigation machinery with much longer historical roots) was generally owned and managed not by individual citizens but by the shogun and domain lords. Nevertheless, its purpose was to produce not only for military needs (as in the Yokosuka shipbuilding industry) but also for civilian purposes (as in the Satsuma *han*'s sugar factory and spinning mills). Nor were these machine enterprises solely propelled by foreign impetus. The presence of such machine industry late in the Tokugawa era lent support to Hattori's second point: that manufacture in the narrow Marxian sense (i.e., without machines) had already developed well before the Restoration. Finally, Hattori noted that despite the existence of castle towns and commercial cities, the first capitalist production occurred outside cities in rural areas. Industries in which manufacture was widespread in the *bakumatsu*—metal refining, textiles, ceramics, and brewing of spirits—were dispersed in rural belts, and a smaller population center like Kiryū was more modern than Edo itself, given its position as a locus of manufacture and capitalistic domestic industry.[38]

Hattori's argument in the *Kōza* piece did not elaborate further on a theoretical level. After offering some examples to support these claims of pre-Meiji nascent capitalism, Hattori went on in this piece to analyze how these economic factors contributed to the political events of the Restoration itself.

In the controversial essay on "Methodological Problems," however, Hattori presented the more precise notion of "*gen mani jidai*" (the era of manufacture in the strict [Marxian] sense). Here he argued that the late Tokugawa period was "the era of manufacture in the strict sense," when "manufacture was the predominant form taken by capitalist production," according to Marx.[39] This era in turn internally prepared the conditions for the industrial revolution of the Meiji period. Marx had dated the manufacture period in Western Europe from the mid-sixteenth century to the last third of the eighteenth century; writing in early 1934, Hattori dated Japan's manufacture era from the Tenpō period (1830-1844)—before the arrival of Western ships at Yokohama—to the second decade of the Meiji era, a period of fifty to seventy-five years.[40] Controversy arose immediately in response to Hattori's thesis, the central issue being whether or not manufacture not only existed but was predominant in the late Tokugawa. The first to attack Hattori was Rōnō-ha economist Tsuchiya, who published a series of essays presenting historical evidence of his own. Ironically, the manufacture debate also served to reveal the diversity of interpretation within the Kōza-ha. Tsuchiya was able to draw on Kōza-ha critics of Hattori, like Hirano Yoshitarō, to fuel his own attack. While the controversy spurred much-needed scholarship on the *bakumatsu* economy, its major accomplishment may have been to illuminate the extent to which a mammoth task remained to be completed in unearthing and interpreting historical data before any firm conclusions on indigenous capitalistic development could be reached. After analyzing the complex difficulties posed by both method and paucity of data,[41] Hattori himself drew the debate to a close only one year after it had begun. Feeling he had exhausted the range of debate possible on the basis of existing data, Hattori turned his efforts to deep research into the primary documents on the *bakumatsu*, producing detailed studies of local industries during the period.[42]

The basis of Hattori's work was not only Marx's own writings in *Capital*, but also Lenin's application of Marxian economic theory to Russian development. Lenin had distinguished three stages in the evolution of capitalism in Russia: (1) "small commodity production (small, mainly peasant industries)," (2) "capitalist manufacture" (the focus of Hattori's analysis); and (3) "the factory (large-scale) machine industry."[43] Progress through these stages entailed departure from cottage industry "where agriculture and industry were unseparated" toward large mechanized industry where the two are completely divorced from one another. The first step in this separation occurred in handicraft or commodity production that was managed "capitalistically" on the basis of hired labor. According to Lenin, this first stage was connected to the latter two in a causal fashion: "The connection and continuity between the forms of industry mentioned is of the most direct and intimate kind. The facts show quite clearly that the main trend of small commodity production is towards the development of capitalism, in particular, towards the rise of manufacture; and manufacture is growing with enormous rapidity before our very eyes into large-scale machine industry.''[44] Hattori argued that to date Japanese Marxist economic historians had not considered Lenin's observations with respect to the late Tokugawa era. Even when they recognized in the *bakumatsu* the existence of domestic industry and the *toiya-sei* (putting-out system, *Verlag* system)—phenomena which are correlated with the early stages of capitalist production in Marxian economics[45]—their theoretical significance for the indigenous development of capitalism in Japan was ignored. Hani Gorō, for example, did acknowledge in his early contribution to the *Kōza* that such sprouts of capitalism were manifest, and indeed that even machine production had already been imported by the shogun and by daimyo in the southwestern areas of Saga and Kagoshima. Yet Hani maintained that the peasant cottage industry and trade guild handicrafts characteristic of feudalism dominated economic life in the period. "Thus, the revolution in production methods in Japan had to be coerced from outside by the influx of cheap commodities of modern industry—foreign commodities—and by the demand of European and American markets. In other words,'' Hani concluded, "capital at the end of the shogunate generally had still not reached the point of being endowed with the slightest revolutionary character.''[46] Similarly, Hattori himself had written in 1927 that the shogun's isolationist policies had prevented what manufacture that had emerged from ever becoming more than "a partial existence"; consequently, handicrafts and "the unity of agriculture and handicrafts'' continued to predominate.[47]

Clearly neither Hattori, in his early studies, nor Hani and Rōnō-ha theorists who emphasized the primacy of external factors fully appreciated Marx's own observations about the inherent character of manufacture; thus they underestimated both its revolutionary potential for Japan's indigenous development, apart from the impact of foreign trade, and limitations intrinsic to manufacture itself. Marx had written that even during "the manufacture period proper, i.e., the period during which manufacture is the predominant form taken by capitalist production, many obstacles are opposed to the full development of the peculiar tendencies of manufacture.'' Since the technical basis of manufacture remains handicrafts, for example, "capital is constantly compelled to wrestle with the insubordination of the workmen,'' hence, "during the period between the 16th century and the epoch of Modern Industry, capital failed to become the master of the whole disposable working time of the manufacturing labourers.'' Thus, manufacture itself was not revolutionary: if it dominated capitalist production, it never dominated the whole of social production. Yet, Marx's dialectic offered, with manufacture, the seeds of its sublation into machine industry in its potential to produce "the instruments of labour themselves, including especially the complicated mechanical apparatus then already employed"—machines. Machines in turn supplanted handicrafts as the technical basis of production. This occurred when, "At a given stage in its development, the narrow technical basis on which manufacture rested, came into conflict with requirements of production that were created by manufacture itself."[48]

In 1933, Hattori sought to apply these observations by Marx on the nature of nascent capitalistic development to *bakumatsu* Japan,[49] on the basis of the model supplied by Lenin's analysis of the *Development of Capitalism in Russia*. Positing the late Tokugawa era as the manufacture period proper, Hattori asserted that "Japanese capitalism had already entered the manufacture stage."[50] This formulation did not deny the presence of the petty feudal mode of production, "but rather saw feudal and capitalist elements in a transitional unity, on the basis of which stood manufacture." Therein lay the critical difference with China and Korea, which were not experiencing the manufacture stage at the time of the Western intrusion.[51] The impact of the West on Japan was simply to accelerate changes that were already occuring, leading to a spontaneous industrial revolution that Hattori dated in the late 1870s and 1880s. "Pressed by American and European large-scale industrial production that flowed in with the opening of the ports, and then stimulated by large-scale industry that was transplanted to Japan as well as by the large-scale industry [that was sponsored by] the Meiji government, the *kokusan* [*han*- and shogunate-managed] manufacture [that had existed] since the Tokugawa changed form" and experienced an "industrial revolution." This era of industrial revolution was the stage of "primitive accumulation" spearheaded by the power of the Meiji state. Both in England and in Marx's theory of capitalist development, Hattori reminded his readers, primitive accumulation was linked with the "total negation of the manufacture stage of capital."[52]

In making the argument that has been summarized briefly here, Hattori raised and endeavored to resolve a variety of complex issues through an often painfully detailed examination of manufacture in late Tokugawa Japan. His self-assigned task of demonstrating the predominance of manufacture over small commodity production was ambitious and, as Hattori himself acknowledged, too enormous for one scholar to achieve. Yet, he focused attention on such key questions as the variety of forms of production that fell under the rubric "capitalist." How was one to assess the significance of *toiya-sei* production and domestic labor, the existence of which during the late Tokugawa most economic historians readily concede? Finally, there were the larger but most significant issues that Western scholars approached with respect to Western Europe only much later. How was one to understand realistically the relationship between feudalism and capitalism during the era of the "transition"? Do not feudalistic and capitalistic forms coexist for some time? And what is the impact of external forces like international trade on the transition to capitalism: are they preconditions or merely features that tend to accompany the indigenous growth of capitalism? How do such factors help to distinguish the Japanese experience from the Western European one—or from the fate of the remainder of a seemingly stagnant, passive Asia?

Forms of Capitalistic Production in Late Tokugawa Japan

In identifying the birth of capitalism in England, Maurice Dobb has dated its "opening phase" "in the latter half of the sixteenth and the early seventeenth century when capital began to penetrate production on a considerable scale, either in the form of a fairly matured relationship between capitalist and hired wage-earners or in the less developed form of the subordination of domestic handicraftsmen, working in their own homes, to a capitalist in the so-called 'putting-out' system [*toiya-sei*]."[53] Hattori was familiar with Lenin's similar observation concerning the close relationship between manufacture and capitalist domestic industry (as distinguished from peasant domestic or handicrafts industry in precapitalist modes of production). In *The Development of Capitalism in Russia*, Lenin had written, "In Western Europe also, as we know, the manufactory period of capitalism was distinguished by the extensive development of domestic industry—in the weaving industries for instance."[54] Thus, in seeking the indigenous roots of capitalism in Tokugawa Japan, Hattori properly sought development beyond the most primitive form of capitalist enterprise (commodity production) not only in manufactories in the sense of individual craftsmen employed in the same workshop by a single capitalist, but also in the presence of the *toiya-sei* or putting-out system.[55] And he found such patterns to be particularly widespread in the cotton and silk goods industries.

In the cotton industry, Hattori disputed the prevailing notion that the petty mode of production and independent handicrafts continued to be "dominant" in the late Tokugawa era. Cotton production, he maintained, had already begun its departure from peasant cottage industry in the spinning stage—the first level of processing—and the cotton market had already grown to a national scale, supporting the commoditization of cotton production. Moreover, he argued, with each higher stage of cotton processing, the production process was still more removed from peasant cottage industry: as one moved from spinning cotton, to cotton willowing, to the transfer of cotton to bamboo spools, to the production of cotton thread, and finally to the fabrication of cotton cloth, as one approached the final stages of processing, the smaller was the proportion of work left to independent handicraftsmen, and the greater the ratio of those craftsmen laboring for buying-up capitalists who had lost their economic independence. As Takahashi properly noted in his analysis of the Tokugawa cotton industry, such domestic laborers included both skilled handicraftsmen and peasant hired laborers who worked to supplement meager agricultural earnings.[56]

Hattori's evidence from the silk goods industry was more detailed. The industry, dating back over a century, was based originally on imported raw silk thread. Ironically, the importation of raw silk thread peaked after the shogun's declaration of his *sakoku* (isolationist) policy, during the Kanbun years (1661-1672). When the outflow of gold became intolerable, the shogun imposed a quota on raw silk imports in 1685, and imports that had reached 200,000 catties (1 catty = 1.5 pounds) during the Kanbun years were limited to 70,000 catties per year. Gradually the indigenous production of Japanese raw silk was encouraged, and by the Bunka and Bunsei eras (1805-1829) domestic silk "not only completely drove imported raw silk thread out of the domestic silk goods industry but developed to the point where it was a major item among those that [Kaga merchant-shipper] Zeniya Gohei smuggled abroad." These developments, which spurred the evolution of an internal division of labor in the silk goods industry, provided what Marx claimed to be an essential prerequisite of manufacture[57] in that industry in Japan.[58]

This development of the silk goods industry occurred on the basis of a geographical division of labor. Since the warmer areas of the Osaka-Kyoto area, Chūgoku (where Hiroshima is located), Shikoku, and Kantō had been engaged in cotton cloth making, silk thread production came to be concentrated in the cooler Hokuriku districts. The production of Japanese silk thread grew to support the silk goods industry that had already risen on the basis of the formerly imported raw silk thread. As the native silk industry grew, at first raw silk was produced on the basis of peasant domestic industry, and there were many who thereby made a living on performing the entire production process, from planting mulberry trees and raising silkworms, to the final stage of making thread. Gradually an all-native silk goods industry emerged on the basis of independent handicrafts which supplanted peasant cottage industry, and the industry thereupon evolved through capitalistic handicrafts, capitalistic domestic labor, and finally manufacture in the Tokugawa era.[59] Thus, in the first decade of the nineteenth century in the Bunka period, the silk goods industry in Ashikaga "was already in the manufacture and domestic labor stage." Indeed, Hattori asserted, by the opening of the ports, the period of manufacture in silk thread production was already drawing to a close, and early mechanized production had begun. Historical data in support of this conclusion he drew primarily from Takahashi Kamekichi's *Studies on the Tokugawa Feudal Economy*. Takahashi had concluded from the same data that, on the whole, the silk industry in the late Tokugawa was still dominated by peasant cottage industry. By contrast, drawing on Lenin, Hattori saw the coexistence of the petty mode of production with manufacture and machine industry as "both capitalistic and feudalistic elements in a single progressive unity."[60]

Hattori was careful to point out that the existence of manufacture and capitalist domestic labor, as forms of production controlled by merchants, was "the initial form of the transformation of commercial capital into industrial capital." This form had arisen by mid-Tokugawa in castle towns, where later the urban poor joined with urban manufacture workers to form a nascent urban proletariat. Those samurai who worked on the side in such areas thus were to be viewed as proletarians at the same time that they were *bushi*. Yet of equal if not greater significance was the development of capitalist enterprise in rural areas. For example, in the indigo industry, the first subordination of direct producers to commercial capitalists occurred not through the direct hiring of peasants as domestic laborers, but rather when merchant capitalists "bought-up" indigo balls produced by the peasant households, which in turn were sold by the merchants on the market. Similar situations obtained as well in the production of textiles, mat facings, and wicker trunks. When the buyers-up paid producers in raw materials, then the producers became "de facto wage laborers," and the buyers-up their employers. This happened frequently both in cases where the *han* did the buying-up and in private buying-up; and although private enterprises were on occasion forcibly taken over by the *han*, on the whole private buyers-up maintained a superior and independent position.[61] Finally, Hattori cited the buying-up and putting-out activities of Zeniya Gohei as the most outstanding example of how, even before the opening of the ports, the conditions of industrial revolution were prepared as "accumulated large mercantile and usury capital began to change, partially but in large quantities, to industrial capital, because of the realization of the manufacture stage."[62]

In his last essay on the "Historical Conditions of the Manufacture Period," Hattori pushed his *gen mani jidai* thesis to its limit, clarifying fine points and elaborating on the question of the role of international trade in Japan's capitalistic development. First he noted that the manufacture period extended from the 1830s through the late 1880s and early 1890s—both before and after Japan's opening to the West. Thus, the Meiji Restoration was to be viewed as an internal process inherent to the manufacture period. Secondly, he noted that the "decisive historical condition" of the manufacture period was the transformation of labor power into a commodity by the development of the division of labor within Japanese society—i.e., "the process of primitive accumulation itself." According to Hattori, this process could occur in two ways: (1) nascent manufacture, in which the old feudal craft guild organization was openly repudiated; or (2) capitalist domestic labor, in which the external forms of craft guild organization were maintained, while de facto wage labor was created. In either case, the process of primitive accumulation was dependent on the growth of trade markets, and here the issue became whether it was the domestic market or external trade that accelerated the accumulation process.

Finally, Hattori addressed the question of which areas of production should serve as indicators of the existence of the manufacture period. Here, Hattori asserted that consumer goods sectors—which could be taken to show the extent of the ''dissolution of former peasant strata''—especially textiles and the raw materials that supply them, should be such indicators. The production of labor implements, he claimed in opposition to views expressed by Tsuchiya and Hirano Yoshitarō, marked not the formation of the manufacture era, but its conclusion. As for the fact that in England the manufacture period coincided with the phenomenon of wandering vagabonds, which did not occur in Japan until after the Restoration, Hattori argued that the English phenomenon was a result of enclosure in Flanders, and that in any case, the existence of manufacture was the premise for the willingness of these vagabonds to leave feudal estates.[63] But more theoretically significant than any of these issues was the question of the impact of trade in the international capitalist system on Japan's development.

A Reassessment of the Role of International Trade in Japan's Capitalistic Development

Following his analysis of what he believed to be the period of manufacture proper in the Tokugawa era, Hattori tackled the question of whether exposure to the international capitalist system had not been—as his argument presumed—a necessary precondition for the establishment of the manufacture period. By the time he penned this last essay, Hattori's position on this question was already clear. Several months earlier, he had written that ''the development of the social division of labor in the closed-country [isolationist] Tokugawa period . . . dissolved cottage industry in the strict sense and handicrafts, and from there went on transforming small enterprises that lost [their] independence, [as well as] capitalist domestic labor, and manufacture.''[64] Marx did write in volume 1 of *Capital* that ''the Colonial system and the opening out of the markets of the world, both of which are included in the general conditions of existence of the manufacturing period, furnish rich material for developing the division of labour in society.''[65] But it was in volume 3 of *Capital*, Hattori emphasized, that Marx described the conditions that were necessary for manufacture, and trade that was specifically external was not among them. The key prerequisite was an internal division of labor propelled by commerce, which promoted production for exchange value rather than for use-value.

Thus, it was the development of the internal market that was critical for the manufacture period; the expansion of the world market, which Marx felt was premised on the manufacture period, Hattori claimed, simply "accelerated greatly the internal division of labor in the society." In *The German Ideology*, Marx and Engels had noted that in both England and France, "manufacture first limited itself to the domestic market." Similarly, Hattori argued, in Japan too, during the era of the *sakoku* policy, "manufacture came into being along with the development of the domestic market from the mid-Tokugawa on." Indeed, this occurred, he argued, because the *sakoku* policy had stimulated the development of both domestic markets and Japan's internal division of labor.[66] Thus, Hattori considered it crucial to his argument to prove "the existence of a large nationwide market" in the late Tokugawa era;[67] and the arrival of Western ships on Japan's shores had far less impact than that attributed to it by Tsuchiya and others. Since a large internal market already existed and the manufacture period had evolved on that basis well before the opening of the ports, the era of isolation was already being destroyed from within. By the time the ports were opened, Tokugawa feudalism had already disintegrated to a large extent because of the contradiction between capitalist and feudal modes of production that characterized manufacture everywhere. In Europe, the end of the manufacture era culminated in England's Glorious Revolution and the French Revolution. In Japan, the consequence was the Meiji Restoration, which produced an absolutist regime resting on an equilibrium of bourgeois power and the lingering influence of the feudal nobility.[68] In short, the collapse of Tokugawa feudalism and the Meiji Restoration, which sponsored Japan's industrial revolution, evolved spontaneously out of mechanisms of the transition from feudalism to capitalism that Japan shared with Western Europe. To Hattori, there was no question that the course of capitalist development in Japan fit neatly the paradigm outlined in Marx's *Capital*: like England and France, Japan required no external impetus to assure its participation in the world-historical development of capitalism.

The Critique from the Rōnō-ha

Given the Rōnō-ha's view that Japanese capitalism was far more mature and uniformly developed by the 1920s than the Kōza-ha would acknowledge, it is ironic that Hattori's manufacture thesis positing indigenous capitalist development by the mid-nineteenth century should have met such powerful resistance from the Rōnō-ha.[69] Since Inomata Tsunao had severed his ties with the Yamakawa faction several years earlier, Tsuchiya Takao responded to the Hattori thesis from a Rōnō-ha perspective. Tsuchiya offered his first critique of Hattori in September 1933 in an essay on "Manufacture in the Tokugawa Period," charging that Hattori had not adequately substantiated his argument with historical data.[70] The debate between Tsuchiya and Hattori continued for about two years, interspersed with contributions by Kōza-ha scholars Yamada Shōjirō, Kobayashi Ryōsei, Hirano Yoshitarō, and Nagata Hiroshi.[71]

Despite his repudiation of Hattori's thesis as a claim that could not be proved on the basis of existing evidence, the overall tone of Tsuchiya's commentary was fairly conciliatory. In response to Hattori's *Kōza* essay on the Meiji Restoration and methodological critique of prior research on the history of Japanese capitalist development, Tsuchiya readily agreed with Hattori's repudiation of his own earlier work on the Meiji Restoration. Tsuchiya concurred that the prevailing understanding of Japanese-Western relations in terms of the schema "feudal Japan-capitalist Europe and America" was erroneous and should be abandoned. However, Tsuchiya could not accept Hattori's designation of the late Tokugawa era before the opening of Japan to the West as the period of manufacture proper.[72]

Tsuchiya saw Hattori's claim to be based on the basic differentiation among forms of capitalism prior to large machine industry on which there was already a substantial consensus among (Marxist) economic historians. As Tsuchiya understood them, these were: (1) handicrafts production, in which "wage laborers were employed instead of or alongside apprentices"; (2) "*toiya-sei* domestic labor or capitalist domestic labor"; and (3) manufacture. When manufacture is dominant over the other two forms, it is the manufacture period proper. Therefore, one can only determine the existence of such a period after conducting research on all three forms to ascertain the primacy of one form over the others. Yet Hattori drew his conclusions on the basis only of several examples of manufacture. For example, he argued that the manufacture period was drawing to an end in the spinning industry on the sole basis of the fact that there was machine spinning in Kōzuke (in Gunma prefecture) in 1859. Moreover, Hattori's examples of manufacture had been limited to Numa Kamoichiro's waterwheel-powered spinning machine, the Hiroshima *han*'s iron sand refinery, and silk goods production under entrepreneur Zeniya Gohei. Since Hattori conducted no corporative study of all three forms of premachine capitalist production, there was no factual basis for his conclusion that manufacture predominated.[73]

Tsuchiya then turned to the results of his own historical research, which he argued demonstrated that the putting-out system and capitalist domestic labor were far more common than manufacture in the late Tokugawa silk and cotton thread industries. This Tsuchiya maintained even though he also found evidence of frequent use of manufacture at the end of the shogunate and of some small machine industry on the eve of the opening of the ports. The examples of manufacture Tsuchiya then cited in his own article added to the list offered by Hattori. In the mid- to late eighteenth century, the head of Higo *han*, Hosokawa Shigekata, promoted silk production, establishing what were apparently manufactories for spinning and weaving in the castle town. Tsuchiya argued that the example of the Kōzuke waterwheel-powered spinning industry adduced by Hattori was insignificant, since the factory operated for only a few years. But Tsuchiya offered his own examples of other spinning and weaving manufactories and machine industry. These included the promotion of machine reeling in the spinning industry in Shinshū in the early 1860s; the promotion of spinning manufacture involving some use of machines and twelve female workers in the 1860s in Daishōuji under entrepreneur Tsuchimura Kanogentarō; and the increased productivity resulting from the development of a machine reeling and spinning industry in the Toyama area just before the Restoration. Yet, in the last case, and indeed in most of these cases cited by Tsuchiya, he was careful to note that the machines were used after the opening of the ports and, particularly in the Toyama instance, were copied under influence from other areas.[74]

Tsuchiya found additional examples of manufacture in the textile industry in Kiryū, Ashikaga, and Mino in the weaving of silk, cotton, and flax. As early as the 1840s, Tsuchiya reported, a dyeing shop with 120 looms and over 300 indigo vats formed a very large-scale manufactory in the production of blue-striped cotton cloth in Musashi and northern Adachi district. Still earlier there were records of velvet manufacture involving ten looms in Etchū after 1817, as well as the promotion of silk goods manufacture in a factory with several dozen workers in Fukui *han* in the 1820s. This was one of three instances Tsuchiya found in which official *han* funds were used to promote such industries. Nevertheless, despite these and additional examples cited by Ishihama Tomoyuki and Hattori himself, Tsuchiya argued that given the extensive existence of domestic industry as well, he could not conclude that manufacture was the dominant form of capitalist production in the textile industry.[75]

Tsuchiya's conclusions were the same as he examined production spheres that Hattori's study had not covered. In the brewing of spirits (sake) and soy sauce, as well as in magnetic sand refining, Tsuchiya cited numerous "handicraft factories" or manufactories. Since people normally made unrefined sake for their own use, the production of refined sake tended to be fairly low, and there were a large number of small-scale breweries that did not, in Tsuchiya's view, fit the criteria of manufacture. As early as the late seventeenth century, however, there were households in Ikeda brewing 1,000 *koku* of liquor (technically, the liquor produced using 1,000 *koku* of rice), a task that required more than ten persons. There were also large breweries, in the Noda area, for example, producing on the basis of a complex division of labor, in which all laborers in a particular capacity received specific wages. A similar situation obtained in soy sauce brewing, with evidence of production on a manufacture basis in Noda in the 1830s. But since in both soy sauce and sake brewing there were also large numbers of small establishments—presumably not organized on a manufacture basis—Tsuchiya hesitated again to pronounce manufacture dominant in that sphere.[76]

Finally, Tsuchiya raised a theoretical issue when he discussed the presence of manufacture in magnetic sand refining and wax making. There was no question that manufacture existed in magnetic sand refining in the Chūgoku area and the hill country of the Yamage region. In the Hiroshima *han*, this industry involved a complex that linked a factory for extracting magnetic sand (*kannaba*), a furnace shop, a charcoal factory, and a forging shop, each of which involved from seven to twenty wage laborers. These were more often private enterprises, but some were *han* owned and managed. Similarly, where wax had been imported in the early Tokugawa period, from the mid-eighteenth century to the Meiji Restoration wax manufactories were sponsored by the old Tsuwano *han*. Although at first the enterprise was run by local merchants, subsequently feudal lords purchased the raw materials and controlled both the production and sale of wax. In Tsuchiya's mind this raised the question of the true character of these particular enterprises. In any case, Tsuchiya's overall conclusion was that while his and Hattori's research had shown that there was far more manufacture in the Tokugawa period than had been originally suspected, the available materials were too sparse to permit any firm conclusions; more detailed research by teams of scholars was urgently required.[77]

Hattori responded to Tsuchiya's first critique immediately, concentrating on a countercritique of Tsuchiya's analytical method. At the outset Hattori correctly noted that Tsuchiya had misstated the forms of capitalist production that were the heart of the controversy. By separating capitalist domestic industry from manufacture, Tsuchiya committed a major error that undermined his critique. Citing Lenin, Hattori pointed out that although capitalist domestic industry could coexist alongside machine industry, it was most characteristic of the manufacture era; indeed it was hard to conceive of the manufacture period without it. Thus Tsuchiya simply misunderstood when he said that Hattori had claimed that manufacture predominated over handicrafts and domestic labor, because capitalist domestic labor was in fact "the most powerful sign of the predominant existence of manufacture." Nor was it helpful that Tsuchiya concluded that the prevalence of manufacture in textiles did not necessarily signify that manufacture was predominant, because domestic enterprise under the putting-out system was so widespread. As for

Tsuchiya's doubts on whether the *han*-promoted silk goods industry in Fukui *han* was manufacture or domestic labor, Hattori countered that Tsuchiya was unable to resolve the (incorrectly posed) question because he had neglected to examine the organization of labor in the enterprise. On the basis of the same document, Hattori found evidence of the existence of "a large market, large enterprise, and large capital"—all of which were to be found only after the beginning of the manufacture period. The Miyake Jōshirō factory employing several dozen workers was the core of a group of several small urban manufactories; and its head supervised urban weavers who could not deal independently with the market. The market included other *han*, and its capital was a sum made up of private Miyake funds and *han* resources. Moreover, the paragraph that Tsuchiya himself quoted described capitalist domestic labor under the control of commercial capital. Finally, Hattori stressed that the "semi-official" character of the Fukui example was irrelevant, since the crucial criterion was the "mode of exploitation": if labor did not take the form of wage labor (or payment according to output) but rather produced "without remuneration because of extra-economic coercion by feudal lords, then it was clear that it would not be capitalistic." In any case, Hattori reminded Tsuchiya that Lenin had noted that in the transitional manufacture period, capitalist relations tended to be embellished by such feudal "casings" as paternalism on the part of managers and survival of old customs.[78] Such feudal elements would be evident even when the entrepreneur was not a feudal lord.[79]

After reiterating his views in studies of the Tokugawa economy and domestic industry in the Edo period,[80] Tsuchiya borrowed from Hattori's Kōza-ha critic, Hirano Yoshitarō, to launch a counterattack of his own.[81] In his essay, "Central Points at Issue in the Study of Restoration History," Tsuchiya made several new points. First, he argued that Hattori had not adequately examined shops that produced the instruments of labor themselves, and he reiterated an earlier, rather ineffective charge that Hattori had failed to distinguish between the mechanization of production and that certain point to which manufacture developed when, according to Marx, "the narrow technical basis on which manufacture rested, came into conflict with requirements of production that were created by manufacture itself."[82] Secondly, citing Hirano, Tsuchiya argued that Hattori had emphasized the positive "hothouse" role of *han* enterprises, while neglecting their negative effects on Japanese development. On the role of external trade, Tsuchiya also agreed with Hirano's point that Marx had said only that manufacture was limited to the domestic market in England and France initially, during the beginning of manufacture itself, not during the manufacture period proper. (England was exporting woolen goods in the fourteenth century, while the manufacture era proper began in the mid-sixteenth century.) Finally, Tsuchiya argued that according to *The German Ideology* the disintegration of feudal retainer groups and the spread of vagabonds in the thirteenth to sixteenth centuries, providing a large pool of free laborers, were a precondition for the establishment of manufacture.[83]

These points were immediately followed by the presentation of still more historical data on the existence of manufacture in the *bakumatsu*. Offering diagrams from a variety of sources, Tsuchiya cited manufacture in the cast iron industry in Kawaguchi and Takaoka, where there were twelve "factories" established in the 1820s. There were *han*-managed wax enterprises in Uwajima, where crude wax was made under the putting-out system, and refined wax was produced by manufacture. In the 1820s, in such areas as Ki'i and Tosa, whale processing was also done in large-scale manufacture involving up to two hundred workers each organized in composites of workshops. Small-scale manufacture could also be found in salt-making and sardine compost-making industries, each enterprise employing about ten persons. Such plants lined the sand dune belt of the coast, and the products were sold wholesale to buyers-up in Edo and elsewhere and widely distributed from there to villages in the Kantō region. Finally, there was substantial manufacture activity in the coin-minting industry under the direct control of the shogunate. Located in Edo, the gold coinage mint was divided into six separate workshops and was organized on the basis of large-scale manufacture (as was the production of gold leaf/gold foil).[84]

Having presented these additional examples of manufacture in the late Edo period, however, Tsuchiya once again declined to endorse Hattori's conclusions. He protested that there was still no evidence in the most important category—manufactories producing the instruments of production themselves—a category that Hattori maintained would not signify the existence of the manufacture period proper but its conclusion. Tsuchiya claimed that he had not found much large-scale manufacture in textiles, nor had he had the opportunity to seek examples of manufacture in mining, ship-building, porcelain, and other categories. While there was much relatively simple, small-scale manufacture, he argued, many such enterprises had not yet "subordinated domestic labor to it," and if there was a manufacture period, as Hattori claimed, it was "of such a low [level of development] as to be incomparable with that era in Western Europe." On this basis, Tsuchiya allowed himself to draw two tentative conclusions: first, that Japan's manufacture was of a peculiar nature that should be made the real object of study; one must not "simply force it into one model." Yet at the same time, Tsuchiya drew another conclusion that suggested both that his own conception of Marx's schema remained muddled and that he himself believed there was indeed only one proper course of development. Marx had seen production of labor implements toward the end of the manufacture period, and Tsuchiya felt that such production was to be taken as an indicator of progress on the eve of the industrial revolution. Since there was no evidence of the manufacture of the tools of production, he asserted, "Japan's industry in the late Edo before the opening of the ports had not progressed to the point of requiring spontaneously [indigenously] an industrial revolution."[85]

The Kōza-ha and the Question of the Manufacture Period

Hattori Shisō's thesis that the late Tokugawa period represented the period of manufacture proper in Marx's conception was by no means exempt from criticism from his fellow theorists in the Kōza-ha. Indeed, not only did Kōza-ha scholars criticize Hattori's thesis in far greater numbers than did the Rōnō-ha—although they generally used such indirect means as omitting mention of Hattori by name and attacking Tsuchiya in the same breath. In addition, they manifested a range of independent views on problems in the history of the Meiji Restoration that reflected intensive individual research efforts of the *Kōza* scholars[86] and belied the notion that the faction was merely a group uniformly dedicated to bolster the Comintern's interpretation of Japanese economic and political development. The Comintern version, articulated in the 1927 Theses, the contradictory '31 Theses, and the 1932 Theses, was incomplete at best.[87] This left Kōza-ha scholars much room to maneuver and to engage in controversy among themselves, as they did in the manufacture debate.

In retrospect the Kōza-ha's wariness of the manufacture thesis is not surprising in view of the fact that Hattori had first offered the theory in implicit criticism of the work of fellow Kōza-ha members Yamada Moritarō, Hirano Yoshitarō, and Hani Gorō. Hani, along with others Hattori attacked in his first essay on manufacture, had placed primary emphasis on the role of Japan's inclusion into the world capitalist market. This tendency was consistent with Hani's and Hirano's emphasis on the importance of "Asiatic" characteristics in determining Japan's economic and political backwardness. For Marx had argued that only outside, necessarily brutal, intervention by the advanced capitalist West could break the pattern of "the unchangeableness of Asiatic societies."[88] On the whole, Kōza-ha critiques of Hattori's manufacture thesis, therefore, were premised on the conviction that Hattori's view positing the fundamental similarity between Japan's economic development in the late Tokugawa era and English development from the sixteenth to the eighteenth centuries was far too sanguine. Because of certain unique characteristics, Hirano and Yamada believed, Japan's early capitalist development was seriously distorted,[89] resulting in what Yamada called the "militaristic semi-serf character" of Japanese capitalism to the current day (1930s). Hattori's thesis could not adequately explain this peculiar pattern.[90]

As for Hattori, he later claimed that by the time he introduced the notion of nascent capitalism in his third piece for the *Kōza* ("Revolution and Counter-Revolution in the Meiji Restoration"), he objected to certain points of the Yamada-Hirano-Hani work of earlier volumes that had already come to be called Kōza-ha theory. He alleged that the three could not "completely overcome Rōnō-ha Kaitō-ha [dissolutionist faction] theory" on the basis of their view of the Meiji Restoration, and he has since stated that Noro wanted to restructure that view but never had the opportunity to publish his altered interpretation. In consultation with Noro, Hattori agreed to write the essays setting forth the manufacture thesis as an internal critique of Yamada, Hirano, and Hani, and Noro would make any desired revisions.

Hattori criticized Yamada and Hirano for arguing that Japanese feudalism represented a uniquely Japanese pattern. They had reversed "Trotskyist" errors by devoting inordinate attention to the agrarian problem and the feudal remnants, but dealt only crudely with the origins of capital and wage labor in Japan. Thus, while the Rōnō-ha saw the seeds of wage labor even in tenancy, Yamada and Hirano insisted on perceiving even wage labor as serfdom. "Even the unmistakably modern buds of capital and wage labor they stamp as feudalistic and Asiatic phenomena," Hattori contended, and Hani had borrowed this same perspective to write the political history of the *bakumatsu* and Restoration.[91]

There were, of course, those in the Kōza-ha who looked favorably on Hattori's thesis. Aikawa Haruki and Kobayashi Ryōsei, for example, joined Hattori in countering Tsuchiya's criticisms. Kobayashi made an effort to reconcile Hattori's thesis with the Kōza-ha's emphasis on Japan's backwardness, arguing that the definition of the *bakumatsu* as the manufacture period "was premised on the soil of feudalistic exploitation that was 'Asiatically backward.' " Since the further development of Japan's manufacture had been obstructed by the " 'Asiatically backward' feudal mire" of old landownership relations, Kobayashi continued, it required supplemental elements such as domestic labor.[92] Other charges levied by Kobayashi and Aikawa against Tsuchiya were less substantive: Kobayashi pointed out that Tsuchiya's *Nihon zaisei shi* [History of Japanese finance] was structured on the basis of Honjō Eitarō's book of the same title. And Aikawa argued that Tsuchiya's study of "Economics of the Transition Period" had borrowed quite heavily from Hani Gorō's *Kōza* essay on "The Socioeconomic Situation in the *Bakumatsu*."[93]

Nevertheless, these weak gestures of support for Hattori did not come from the most influential members of the Kōza-ha. Preceding even Tsuchiya in attacking Hattori was *Kōza* contributor Yamada Shōjirō. In his

Kōza essay on "The Development of Capitalism in Agriculture," Yamada, an economist trained at Tokyo Imperial University, argued that development from *toiya-sei* capital to manufacture had occurred only tentatively in such selected fields as dyeing, sake brewing, and mining and metallurgy.[94] Hattori's theory had overemphasized certain isolated facts, Yamada concluded, making it incumbent on others to conduct further research.

But Yamada Shōjirō's critique rested neither on new research nor on theoretical insights into the issues raised by Hattori's thesis. Hirano Yoshitarō's critique was powerful especially because of the attention Hirano devoted to theoretical issues. Directed explicitly against Tsuchiya but implicitly against Hattori as well, Hirano's brief discussion made several points. First addressing Tsuchiya's essay on "Manufacture in the Tokugawa Period," Hirano argued that the issue of whether manufacture was dominant or not was "neither a question of number or quantity nor only a question of the form of cooperation based on a division of labor"; Tsuchiya, in so treating it, had fallen into "crude empiricism." In addition, the examples of manufacture that Tsuchiya had offered (like some of those of Hattori, although Hirano did not so state)—wax, ceramics, and brewing—were insignificant, because what should be taken as indicators of manufacture were "workshops that produced labor implements themselves." Likewise, Hirano pointed out, when considering mining, metal extraction work should be cited as evidence of the development of early capitalism, not workshops used for extracting elements used for coinage like silver and gold.[95] Hattori later responded that the kind of indicators Hirano proposed were appropriate for gauging the transition from manufacture to large industry, since Marx had written that a revolution in the method of production begins with labor power in manufacture and with the tools of labor in large industry. It was the organization of labor, the unity of workers cooperating on the basis of a division of labor, Hattori countered, that was of revolutionary significance in manufacture. Moreover, he maintained that manufacture in consumption goods like clothing was pivotal in determining the maturity of the manufacture era, for such production indicated the dominance of a commodity economy.[96]

These were relatively minor considerations for Hirano, however. Far more important were the questions he raised concerning semi-official enterprises and the impediments to capitalistic development existing in the late Tokugawa period. Key to Hirano's handling of these two issues was his concern with the political dimensions of Japan's transition to capitalism. The theme of Hirano's article on "Civil Rights" was that "the objective character of the civil rights movement and its limitations were attributable to the special character and contradictions of the maturation of industrial development in Japan." In other words, the Meiji civil rights movement was abortive because of deformities "within the womb" of Japanese capitalism. Both of Hirano's last two objections to Hattori's manufacture thesis revolved around such alleged perversions in Japanese development. Hirano contended that in order to uncover such peculiarities it was essential to distinguish between manufacture enterprises that were privately owned and managed and *han*-sponsored manufacture. Hattori had treated the *hans*' establishment of workshops as equivalent to the mercantilist policies of Western European monarchs which supported industry in the age of manufacture.[97] Hirano could not agree. The crucial issue was how the means of production were accumulated in the hands of capitalists. Unless one examined the distinction between private and official or quasi-official capital, one could not analyze the "powerful imbalance in changing relations of production—a large peculiarity in this country." It was crucial not to overlook the "historical preconditions" contributing to the "immaturity of the bourgeois revolutionary political consciousness of the burghers" and the "de facto wage laborers" (now) being able "to liberate themselves bourgeois-democratically from feudal compounds."[98]

Implicit here was the suggestion that semi-official enterprises had stunted the growth of Japan's proper bourgeoisie, and this was related to Hirano's final point. The entire economy of the *bakumatsu*, he argued, had to be examined systemically, with attention not only to those aspects of its structure that (like *han* enterprises) promoted capitalist production in a "hot-house" manner but also those elements obstructing further development. These included an "Asiatically backward" feudal system exploiting "petty cultivating peasants," and "the domination of commercial capital and usury capital" that lived "parasitically" off that feudal exploitation. This structure crippled the subsequent development of the Japanese capitalist economy and the civil rights movement and helped to account for the widespread existence of *han*-run and semi-official enterprises.[99] In addition, Japan's isolation from the world market, imposed to protect the feudal rule of the shogun, denied Japan an important condition for the transformation of commercial to industrial capital.[100]

Finally, Hirano indicated three basic models in the process of the evolution of industrial capital: "(1) from manufacture to factory industry; (2) from putting-out system industry to manufacture; and (3) from putting-out system industry to factory industry (omitting the change from handicrafts)." Espousing a systemic analysis of Japan's early capitalist development, Hirano stressed the need to examine both the linkages among handicrafts, *toiya-sei* industry, and manufacture ("three basic patterns") and the conflict between the necessity for the three kinds of change indicated above on the one hand and elements impeding those processes on the other. Interestingly, Hirano's account of the premachine industry forms of capitalist enterprise bore a closer resemblance to Tsuchiya's than to that of Hattori;[101] like Tsuchiya and unlike Hattori, Hirano saw an important distinction between domestic industry under the putting-out system and manufacture. Although Hirano did not elaborate on this perspective, one might suggest that in Hirano's mind the greater use of domestic labor under the putting-out system rather than the concentration of workers in manufactories enabled the system more easily to maintain the Asiatic feudal characteristics that Hirano emphasized so heavily. In addition, there is no question that, in view of Marx's understanding of the revolutionary character of capitalistic production and the origins of proletarian consciousness, the growth of manufactories was a more significant development than the putting-out system, which spared the capitalist certain expenses and left the worker in his former (feudal) work environment.

Aikawa Haruki tried to minimize the conflict within the Kōza-ha, contending that the differences between Hirano and Hattori were merely "a 'matter of emphasis.' "[102] But Hirano never did accept the designation of the late Edo period as the manufacture period proper. Indeed he argued that the transition from the putting-out system to manufacture was "*decisively* hindered."[103] On the other side, Hattori was suspicious of Hirano's motivations in raising such issues as the distinction between private and *han* enterprises. He later charged that Hirano was trying to promote the notion of a uniquely Asian pattern of development, to argue that while capitalism had sprouted "normally" in Europe, Japan had manifested a unique pattern. Such an emphasis on Japan's uniqueness came dangerously close to the heretical exceptionalism of Takahashi Kamekichi's petty imperialism thesis. Thus, Hattori could not accept such a view, for it implied that "laws that Marx and Engels drew from the history of Europe did not obtain in Asia, and thus it was acceptable if there was no manufacture stage in Japan."[104]

Conclusions

Despite the theoretical and methodological differences between them, Hattori, Hirano, and Tsuchiya all agreed that a final resolution to the controversy must await further historical research. Although the manufacture controversy reached no definable conclusion in the prewar period, it did serve a number of useful functions. By questioning the exclusive emphasis placed on the role of external causation in Japanese development, the manufacture thesis stimulated Japanese historiography, particularly on indigenous economic development in the late Tokugawa and early Meiji periods. In addition, the controversy helped to force the participants of the larger debate on Japanese capitalism to speak to the issues in more concrete terms and to lengthen their historical perspective by tracing the roots of Japanese capitalism back further into the Edo period than they had done hitherto. Nevertheless, the manner in which the controversy itself was waged was not conducive to a resolution of the issues. Kōza-ha critics focused on methodological and theoretical concerns, while Tsuchiya concentrated on the lack of historical evidence available to support Hattori's thesis. There was debate on what kinds of phenomena should be treated, and there was a glaring gap in the historical scholarship that could be brought to bear on the issues. Hattori accurately perceived these difficulties and called an end to the debate pending the publication of additional research on the period.

Nevertheless, the manufacture controversy revived during and after the war,[105] exploring major issues in the study of political and economic development in Japan and elsewhere. By positing the manufacture thesis, Hattori raised two crucial questions. First, he raised the very general issue that has absorbed the attention of Western Marxists like Maurice Dobb and Paul Sweezy. What is the relative weight that one should attribute to internal and external factors in analyzing the transition from feudalism to capitalism, not only in Japan but in Western Europe as well? Secondly, regardless of how one answered this question for Western societies, how was one to assess the similarities and differences between the capitalist development of England or France and that of Japan? For all his objections to the Yamada-Hirano schema emphasizing Japan's special properties, Hattori's manufacture thesis helped to clarify just how different Japan's developmental course was from that of Western Europe. Yes, his detailed historical studies offered much evidence of manufacture in the late Tokugawa period. But his work and that of his critics also demonstrated that the existence of manufacture in general must not obscure the peculiarities of its manifestation in Japan: its extraordinarily heavy reliance on domestic labor through the putting-out system, the significant role of feudal lords in promoting capitalistic production, and the absence of thorough change in feudal landownership relations in the early stages of capitalist development. As Kōza-ha Marxist Takahashi Kōhachirō would later note in the Dobb-Sweezy controversy, these features distinguished the failure of feudalism to collapse in Japan as it had in France and England before the completion of the great bourgeois revolutions. These differences signalled that in Japan "the erection of capitalism under the control and patronage of the feudal absolute state was in the cards from the very first"; and consequently, the achievement of liberal democracy was a far more protracted and agonizing task in Japan.[106]

Hattori chose not to stress the role of the West in producing the peculiar aspects of Japanese development, as had Takahashi Kamekichi in his petty imperialism thesis. Yet, like the interpretation of Takahashi Kōhachirō, the manufacture controversy suggested that such peculiarities as those stressed by Hirano and other Kōza-ha theorists could be accommodated within

Marx's original model. To argue that Japan's development differed in important ways from that of Western Europe was not to posit, as Hattori alleged, a Japanese pattern that was so unique that it violated the universal(ist) premises of Marxism. One needed only to determine the precise combination or balance of general "laws" and historical peculiarities. The controversy on the Asiatic mode of production, which compared Japanese development with that of other Asian societies, marked still another attempt to delineate this balance.

SIX

The Asiatic Mode of Production and the Periodization of Japanese History

IN HIS manufacture thesis, Hattori Shisō asserted that capitalism had sprouted indigenously in Japan well before the arrival of America's "black ships" in Yokohama harbor in 1854. This argument implicitly rejected the suggestion that Japan might have required external pressure from the more "advanced" Western powers in order to achieve industrial capitalism. Hattori's claim that the late Tokugawa era corresponded to the era of "manufacture proper" that Karl Marx had described for Western Europe affirmed that an internal dynamic of development inhered in Japan as well as in the West; and on this ground Japan was to be distinguished from other so-called oriental societies.

Other participants in the debate on Japanese capitalism did not so easily dispose of the question of the relationship between Japan's development and that of the rest of the East. Japanese Marxists of the 1920s and 1930s were well acquainted with Marx's writings on the "orient," and they appreciated the difficulties that Marx's views posed for the application of Marxist economic theory to an Asian context. Marx had treated Asian societies in the "Orientalist" manner, to borrow Edward Said's terminology,[1] that had been characteristic of Western political thinkers since Plato and Aristotle. This perspective had reached its fullest expression in the eighteenth century in the works of Charles Montesquieu, who depicted the East as the seat of a pervasive despotism that was social as well as political in character.[2] Marx himself contributed to this tradition by explicitly excluding Asian societies from the schema of socio-economic development that he had discovered in France and England and presented systematically in *Capital*. Writing in the New York *Daily Tribune* on British imperialism in India, Marx maintained a Hegelian perspective on the Orient as a civilization now bypassed by history, asserting harshly that the only hope for change in an Asia lacking any internal dynamic of development had to come from Western imperialism.

> English interference having placed the spinner in Lancashire and the weaver in Bengal, or sweeping away both Hindoo spinner and weaver, dissolved these small semi-barbarian, semi-civilised communities, by

> blowing up their economic basis, and thus produced the greatest, and, to speak the truth, the only *social* revolution ever heard of in Asia.
>
> Now, sickening as it must be to human feeling to witness those myriads of industrious patriarchal and inoffensive social organisations disorganised and dissolved into their units, thrown into a sea of woes, and their individual members losing at the same time their ancient form of civilisation, and their hereditary means of subsistence, we must not forget that these idyllic village communities, inoffensive though they may appear, had always been the solid foundation of Oriental despotism, that they restrained the human mind within the smallest possible compass, making it the unresisting tool of superstition, enslaving it beneath traditional rules, depriving it of all grandeur and historical energies. . . . We must not forget that this undignified, stagnatory, and vegetative life, that this passive sort of existence evoked on the other part, in contradistinction, wild, aimless, unbounded forces of destruction and rendered murder itself a religious rite in Hindostan. . . .
>
> England, it is true, in causing a social revolution in Hindostan, was actuated only by the vilest interests, and was stupid in her manner of enforcing them. But that is not the question. The question is, can mankind fulfill its destiny without a fundamental revolution in the social state of Asia? If not, whatever may have been the crimes of England she was the unconscious tool of history in bringing about that revolution.[3]

In his discussion of oriental societies such as India and China, then, Marx rejected the notion that anything of lasting humanistic value could be found in them, and he justified the exercise of dominion and repression by the European imperialist powers over them.

Marx's normative assessment of oriental society would appear to conflict with his claim to have analyzed "scientifically" the Asiatic mode of production. In the preface to *A Contribution to the Critique of Political Economy* (1859), where he described the materialist conception of history, Marx wrote, "In broad outlines Asiatic, ancient, feudal, and modern bourgeois modes of production can be designated as progressive epochs in the economic formation of society."[4] Marx defined oriental society as the product of a special mode of production in which small-scale agriculture was carried out on the basis of production relations involving communal property ownership and cooperation. Oriental society, then, had its own peculiar economic base in the Asiatic mode of production and was characterized by small, scattered agrarian communities, the absence of private property, and a despotic superstructure. At the very outset, it is clear why the concept of the Asiatic mode of production should have become problematic for Marx's followers. What should have been a precise distinction between the Asiatic mode of production and oriental society was muddled, largely because Marx devised the conception of the Asiatic mode of production "to account for a type of society outside the mainline of Western development."[5] As a result, the apparent contradiction between a view of allegedly static oriental societies that was geography-specific and the implication that the "Asiatic mode of production" was intended to be a general, universal category of dynamic socio-economic change without a necessary geographic reference has aroused continual controversy among Marxists on the subject of Asian societies. Notably, this conflict reached a peak circa 1930, as Marxists within the Comintern endeavored to devise a suitable strategy for revolution in the East. The controversy was revived after World War II, when the Chinese Communist Party emerged victorious in 1949, and as national liberation movements proliferated in the territories of crumbling European empires elsewhere in Asia and Africa.[6]

When Joseph Stalin rejected the Asiatic mode of production concept at the Leningrad Conference of 1931, he neither resolved the issues that divided Soviet scholars of oriental societies nor prevented the resurrection of the Asiatic mode of production theory itself in East or West. However, Maurice Godelier's acceptance of the "Asiatic mode of production" as a valid and useful socio-economic concept is by far the minority viewpoint that has emerged from this long debate.[7] Much more representative has been the assessment of E. J. Hobsbawm, who asserts that in "the field of the study of oriental societies," "Marx combines profound insight with mistaken assumptions, e.g., about the internal stability of some such societies."[8] Perry Anderson's recent historical analysis of state forms likewise concurs with the judgment that on the Asiatic mode of production concept, "Marx was both empirically and theoretically wrong in establishing this concept and so are those Marxists who try to give it a new lease on life."[9]

Nevertheless, the twin conceptions of oriental society and the Asiatic mode of production were not so easily dismissed by Asian activists and scholars who found in Marx's general paradigm the key to the resolution of pressing dilemmas of development arising in their own societies. If the "universal laws of history" were not effective in East as well as in West, then there was no objective necessity for a Marxist-led revolution (whether in two stages or one) to succeed in the "orient." Nevertheless, the business of altering ever so slightly the theory of the orthodox version of Marxism-Leninism to conform to Japanese realities was a frightening alternative that did not resolve this dilemma. By the late 1920s, Japanese participants in the debate on Japanese capitalism had already witnessed Takabatake Motoyuki's transformation of Marxism into a theory of national/state socialism (*kokka shakai-shugi*) by means of a modification of Marx's "erroneous" theory of the state.[10] And they had been revolted by Takahashi Kamekichi's revision of the Leninist understanding of imperialism to produce a justification for Japanese military expansion onto the Asian mainland that could scarcely be differentiated from official and rightist pronouncements on Japanese foreign policy.[11] Marxists in Japan in the 1930s, then, had to steer a precarious course between the Scylla of an empty formalistic and mechanical application of Marxism to interwar Japan and the Charybdis of an interpretation that was so flexible that it rendered the underlying theory meaningless and deflated any real (historically valid) opportunity for successful revolution in Japan.

The difficulties posed by the concept of the Asiatic mode of production did not concern Asian Marxists alone, however, because they inhered in the conception of oriental society itself, and they carried dangerous implications for the validity of the Marxist theoretical framework as a whole. Leszek Kolakowski best identified these theoretical issues as he contemplated the reasons that the Asiatic mode of production was excluded from Stalin's Marxist orthodoxy.[12]

> Firstly, if a large part of humanity had lived for centuries with an economy of a type all its own, there could be no question of a uniform pattern of development for all mankind. The progression from slave-owning through feudalism to capitalism would apply only to one part of the world and not to the rest, so that there could be no universally valid Marxist theory of history. Secondly, according to Marx the peculiarities of the Asiatic system were due to geographic factors; but how could the primacy of technology over natural conditions be maintained, if the latter could bring about a different form of social development in a large part of the globe? Thirdly, the Asiatic system was said by Marx to have involved the countries concerned in stagnation from which they were only rescued by the incursion of peoples whose economic development had been on different lines; apparently, then, "progress" is not a necessary feature of human history but may or may not happen, according to circumstances. Thus, the "Asiatic mode of production" appeared contrary to three of the fundamental principles that orthodox Marxists generally attributed to historical materialism: the primary role of productive forces, the inevitability of progress, and the uniformity of human evolution in society. It might seem that the doctrine applied only to Western Europe and that capitalism itself was an accident.[13]

The Asiatic mode of production concept was also plagued by issues pertaining to the relationship between the state and economic development (arising out of the contention that the "oriental despot" prevented the development of private property and capitalism) as well as the normative dilemmas that arose out of the implications of the oriental society construct for the legitimacy of imperialism.

These issues assumed greater proportions for Marxists operating in an Asian context. The model for many Japanese endeavoring to analyze Japanese economic development in Marxist terms was V. I. Lenin's *Development of Capitalism in Russia* (1899). There, while arguing against the populist view that capitalism was not emerging to a significant extent in Russia, Lenin nonetheless conceded that Russia's semi-Asiatic characteristics (see below) had hindered its development of industrial capitalism. Yet Lenin was careful to distinguish Russia from fully Asiatic societies like India, Persia, and China. Unlike these societies, in which the stagnancy portrayed by Marx and Engels appeared to stifle completely the development of private property, feudalism, and capitalism, Russia had in fact experienced not only feudalism but also a growing, if hybrid, capitalism.[14]

The fact that Marx had made passing reference to nineteenth-century Japan as the prototype of feudal society did not mitigate the difficulties that the concept of oriental society posed for Japanese Marxists.[15] Rather, the similarities between Japan's experience of late development under external pressure from more "advanced" Western societies and that of Russia suggested that many of Lenin's observations concerning the impact of Russia's "Asiatic" characteristics were equally if not more applicable to Japan. Military pressures from abroad in the mid-nineteenth century had compelled the elites in both countries to borrow Western technologies and stimulate an economic revolution from above from one mode of production to another. Lenin's depiction of a hybrid capitalism produced by Asiatic features could also help to explain the continued oppressiveness of the Japanese state and other aspects of Japanese society, like the emperor system, that seemed more characteristic of a feudal system heavily stamped with Asiatic features than of capitalism. This application could be used to justify either of the positions adopted by the rival *Kōza* and *Rōnō* factions in Japan: that Japanese feudalism continued to thrive and required a bourgeois-democratic revolution, or that despite feudal vestiges, Japanese society had in fact experienced sufficient capitalist development to recommend immediate proletarian revolution, respectively.

Yet the issue was naturally more salient for the Kōza-ha, given its support of the Comintern view that Japan's capitalism remained underdeveloped because of remnants of its feudal and prefeudal past. Hence, virtually all controversy on the Asiatic mode of production occurred within the Kōza-ha group.[16] The Rōnō-ha chose not to appeal to the concept, for its view that Japanese capitalism was ripe for socialist revolution rendered the oriental society conception with its implications of stagnancy and backwardness virtually a nonissue for them.[17] Where Japanese Marxists were favorably inclined toward this concept, however, there remained logical difficulties in their efforts to apply it to Japan. If they accepted Marx's scheme of oriental society as valid, how could they explain how Japan happened to avoid a stagnancy that afflicted the rest of Asia without legitimating the destructive role of imperialism? It was far simpler to apply the theory of oriental society to China, and many Japanese Marxists did precisely that. Indeed, in the 1930s, as Japan's Marxists were subjected to increasing pressures to remold their ideas to support the war effort, some combined Marx's claim that oriental countries required an external stimulus to end Asiatic stagnancy with an advocacy of Asia-for-Asians in order to justify Japanese imperialism in China.[18] But this is merely a side issue. To understand why many participants in the debate on Japanese capitalism found the concept of oriental society useful to analyze Japan itself, it is necessary to review briefly the elements of Marx's original conception.

Oriental Society and the Asiatic Mode of Production in Karl Marx

For Japanese Marxists, the key issue arising out of Marx's writings on oriental society and the Asiatic mode of production was the question of whether alternative paths of development were possible in different geographical areas of the world. This possibility was raised as the conception of oriental society began to take shape in Marx's correspondence with Engels in 1853 and in Marx's articles in the New York *Daily Tribune* on "Revolution in China and Europe" (June 14, 1853) and "The British Rule in India" (June 25, 1853). The conception was elaborated further in the three volumes of *Capital* and in Engels's *Anti-Dühring* (1878). Because Marx's comments on the subject are scattered and somewhat fragmentary, some scholars have distinguished between two and even three separate conceptions of oriental society.[19] Donald Lowe, for example, argues that three separate versions appear in the writings of the young Marx, *Capital*, and *Anti-Dühring*, and that each version stresses a different element. The 1853 version "emphasized the phenomena of self-enclosed village communities and of governmental control of water works," reflecting the influence of the "political economy" of Adam Smith, Richard Jones, J. S. Mill, and François Bernier; the *Capital* version discussed the Asiatic as a variant of the ancient mode of production (vol. 1, chap. 1, sec. 4), emphasizing the self-contained village community and the state's appropriation of surplus value, with less emphasis on the absence of private property and waterworks; and the *Anti-Dühring* version stressed the self-enclosed village community to the neglect of waterworks.[20]

Although Japanese Marxists had gained access to Marxism primarily on the basis of Marx's later writings and Engels's works, in the writings of the debate on Japanese capitalism are all the components of the Asiatic mode of production theory provided in both the early and the late writings of Marx and Engels. Taken together, these accounts of the Asiatic mode of production provide a complete picture of the essential causal links contributing to what Marx saw as "the current (stagnant) state of oriental society." Climatic conditions → need for irrigation/large-scale waterworks → growth of despotism on the basis of dispersed, self-contained agrarian village communities → the absence of the development of private landownership and therefore an inability to evolve feudalistic and capitalistic modes of production.[21]

In this chain of causation, the key element diminishing prospects for further development was the "absence of [private] property in land," which Marx and Engels argued was permanent because of the presence of the oriental despot.[22] Originally, the community (or village commune) in such primitive societies owned the land, and the birth of the oriental state represented the classic instance Engels described in *Anti-Dühring*, in which a state arose out of a need to perform certain common social functions for the benefit of the community or society as a whole. Because of arid climatic conditions, Engels argued, "only in the form of Oriental despotism did such societal dominance based on public function [rather than class interest] spread far and last long."[23] In this case, the state preceded class rule rather than arising out of it; and the "exploitation of man by man exists without private property in land."[24] Under the new state, landownership resided in "an individual representing the community":[25] "*the king is the sole and only proprietor of all the land.*"[26]

This despotic state, which monopolized landownership and ruled absolutely in the absence of class conflict, was the most distinctive feature of oriental society, distinguishing the Asiatic mode of production from the ancient, feudal, and capitalist modes of production. The mutually supportive relationship between this form of political superstructure and its economic base was crucial, since in Marx's view it effectively prevented a smooth transition to a higher mode of production. The despot as exploiter was the "principal owner of the surplus-product" in the form of rent in kind. This surplus was normally appropriated in the form of surplus labor or compulsion (what Lenin would later call *corvée* labor), since the sole landowner was the despot, who in turn applied this labor to the execution of the large public works for which purpose the state was originally created.[27] The people over whom the monarch arrogated to himself despotic power were direct producers subordinated to the state. There existed private (by individuals) and public (by the village community) possession and use of land for production, but there was no private ownership of land. Nor could such private landownership arise in oriental society as it did in France, for example, because of the peculiar character of the Asiatic state, which owned its people as well as the land in the phenomenon Marx described as "general slavery." The state "stands over [the people] as their landlord and simultaneously as sovereign, [and therefore] . . . rent and taxes coincide, or rather there exists no tax which differs from this [labor] form of ground-rent. . . . Sovereignty here exists in the ownership of land concentrated on a national scale."[28]

It was this system of concentrated landownership and labor tax = rent that formed the basis for the "stationary social conditions" that Marx and Engels found in Asia.[29] In Marx's view, "the Orient had not evolved anything corresponding to private property in land: unquestionably one of the preconditions of genuine feudalism."[30] Thus, in Asia, the oriental despot effectively prevented the rise of a property-owning class that might have become the driving force of economic change; the despotic state preemptively quashed any indigenous bourgeois impulse to develop the forces of production to a higher level. Indeed, where there were no economic classes, there could be no class struggle—which was essential to the dynamic of socioeconomic change in Marx's schema.[31]

This "scientific" analysis of the nature of the political superstructure characteristic of the Asiatic mode of production furnished the vital link to Marx's normative view of oriental society.[32] While his analytical method focusing on objective, material forces of production distinguished Marx's view from Hegel's mystical account of oriental "stagnancy," Marx's and Hegel's conclusions were identical in their pessimism concerning the future prospects for change in the constitution of Asiatic society. Such a society lacked an internal dynamic of change, since a major source of such change—class conflict arising out of private property relations—had been stifled by the presence of the oriental despot. Even usury, normally a powerful agent of change, Marx declared, encountered stubborn resistance in oriental society and could not dissolve its structural components.[33] The only possible source of change in the constitution of Asia, Marx concluded, was necessarily external to the system itself and appeared to him in the form of the restless bourgeoisie of the West, where the dynamic furnished by private property had spurred England and France to evolve from antiquity through feudalism to industrial capitalism.

> The bourgeoisie, by the rapid improvement of all instruments of production, by the immensely facilitated means of communication, draws all, even the most barbarian nations into civilization. . . . It compels all nations, on pain of extinction, to adopt the bourgeois mode of production; it compels them to introduce what it calls civilisation

> into their midst, *i.e.*, to become bourgeois themselves. In one word, it creates a world after its own image. . . . Just as it has made the country dependent on the towns, so it has made barbarian and semi-barbarian countries dependent on the civilised ones, nations [of] peasants on nations of bourgeois, the East on the West.[34]

Yet, even his general optimism about the international empire of Western capitalism did not allow Marx to be sanguine about the future of Asia. Almost fifteen years after his initial commentary on British imperialism in India, Marx observed in *Capital* that "the obstacles presented by the internal solidity and organisation of pre-capitalistic, national modes of production to the corrosive influence of commerce are strikingly illustrated in the intercourse of the English with India and China." In India, he noted, "this work proceeds [only] very gradually. And still more slowly in China, where it is not re-enforced by direct political power [like that the British wielded over India]."[35]

This pessimism concerning the future of oriental societies supports an interpretation of Marx's overall schema of development from Greek and Roman antiquity through feudal and then capitalist modes of production as a description of a unilinear process of Western historical development that excludes Asia. As George Lichtheim argues, "When Marx describes 'Asiatic, ancient, feudal, and modern bourgeois modes of production' as 'progressive epochs in the economic formation of society,' he takes the unilinear view of history common to his age; that is to say, he assumes that slavery, feudalism, and capitalism are definite phases in the development of Western society, unknown to the Orient whose historical stagnation is viewed as the consequence of the dominant 'Asiatic mode of production.' " As we have seen, however, "Marx does not share the prevailing optimism in respect of 'progress.' There are hints that every advance has to be paid for by the relinquishment of achievements possible only under more primitive conditions."[36] Nor is it clear, in view of the resistance of Asiatic societies even to the onslaught of world capitalism, that such "progress" will always be made.

Marx's and Engels's ideas on oriental society found in *Capital* and *Anti-Dühring* were further elaborated by the Russian Marxist George Plekhanov, who was widely read among Japanese Marxists in the 1920s. In response to the growth of the revolutionary movement in Russia and the need to adapt his own formerly pan-Slavic and populist inclinations to Marxist theory, Plekhanov emphasized the idea of communal property and geography in providing for alternative paths of development. These two separate issues had originally become intertwined in Marx's own writings, when he analyzed the possibilities for revolution in Russia in the 1870s, as prospects for socialist revolution collapsed in Western Europe. When Marx denied to the *narodnik* N. K. Mikhailovsky that his schema prescribed identical Western European and Russian paths through capitalism to socialism, he was endeavoring to inject a note of optimism about the prospects for revolution in a society Marx himself had once considered the "bastion of reaction" in Europe. Support for the conception of distinct paths of development for East and West was only obliquely offered in *Capital*, where Marx intimated that societies diverge at the stage of primitive society into the oriental form, in which we see a despotic ruler as a supreme landlord ruling over small village communities described above, on the one hand, and a Western form, typified by Greek (or classical) antiquity. This divergence was outlined more explicitly in the *Grundrisse*, where Marx's discussion of varying types of property and communities included a description of the Slavonic community—a modified form of oriental communal property.[37] The persistence of the Slavonic community in Russia into the late nineteenth century posed the special "historical circumstance" of Russian development. By responding to the questions raised by Russian intelligentsia concerning this problem, Marx established the logical link between communal property and a separate pattern of development for the East that would become a focus of Japanese Marxist debate on the *kyōdōtai* (rural community).

Marx's presentation of social history in the *Grundrisse* and other works began with communal society and stressed "the 'artificial' nature of private property, and especially of capitalism, in that they involve the historical destruction of quite different prior social systems."[38] Marx underscored the point in his *Critique of Hegel's Philosophy of Right*, arguing that the bourgeois state based on private property produces the Rousseauean schism between public and private man (*citoyen* versus *homme*) that could only be overcome by a return to socialized man. The existence of communal property at the beginning of human history helped to make a postcapitalist communist society conceivable. In the 1870s, now anxious to encourage the revolutionaries in Russia, Marx and Engels conceded that the persistence of the peasant commune (*obschina*) into the nineteenth century offered Russia a communist future in the nearer term, despite the apparent backwardness of Russia in comparison with Western Europe. Surrounded by advanced capitalist systems, the Russian "commune has the theoretical possibility of taking over the technological fruits of capitalism without taking over its production relations, or repeating [in isolation] a path of development as long and arduous as the West underwent."[39] Marx and Engels later qualified this argument: only "if the Russian Revolution becomes a signal for a proletarian revolution in the West, so that both complement each other, [will] the present Russian common ownership of land . . . serve as the starting-point for a communist development."[40] Russian communist development through revolution, in other words, was once again dependent on external support from revolutions in the more advanced West.

As the appeal of Marxism moved eastward to Russia, the Russian peasant commune became an issue in Plekhanov's work on the Russian revolution, and the conception of oriental society played a central role in his discussion. As a *narodnik* in his early years, Plekhanov had stressed differences between Russia and the West; and this emphasis continued to be evident in his writings as a Marxist. Plekhanov now saw Russia as "an oriental society breaking down under the impact of Western influences." The tsar was a despotic ruler constructed "on the basis of a primitive agricultural economy."[41] In 1895, Plekhanov argued, " 'Old Moscovite Russia was distinguished by its completely Asiatic character. Its social life, its administration, the psychology of its people—everything in it was alien to Europe and very closely related to China, Persia, and ancient Egypt.' " The development of its despotic rule was reinforced on the one hand by "the need to support an expanding administrative apparatus and the pomp of an imperial court" in the new political center at Moscow, and on the other by the even more important need to support "a massive military establishment" against external pressures. The state thus assumed ownership of all property in order to meet these needs.[42] In Plekhanov's view, the reforms of Peter and of Nicholas I in the nineteenth century were superficial, maintaining the state in its despotic relation to Russian society. "To these subjects [of the state] the state allotted land and thus the right to live, but only on condition of service to the state, military administrative for some, labor-fiscal for most." Just like any despotic oriental society, Russia had a "vegetative, non-developmental character." The result was stasis, a lack of any internal dynamic promoting change to new modes of production.[43]

As a populist, Plekhanov had hoped that the commune would enable the Russian revolution to bypass European capitalism. Now as a Marxist, even when he believed that Europeanization was proceeding in Russia and would culminate in a proletarian revolution, Plekhanov still fully appreciated the implications of Russia's oriental characteristics.[44] Russian leaders since the time of Peter the Great, he observed, had been compelled to borrow Western ideas and technology to defend Russia against the growing economic and military power of the West.[45] It was in response to this external threat that rapid industrialization ensued under Peter the Great and, after the Crimean War in the mid-nineteenth century, in a massive drive from above that was very shortly excelled by Japan's Meiji regime.

Thus Plekhanov provided the most important aspect of the Marxist oriental society conception by going on to argue (in *Fundamental Problems of Marxism*) that geographical differences had played a major role in creating separate paths of Western and Eastern development after the demise of clan or communal society.[46] Some Marxists have downplayed the geographical significance of the Asiatic mode of production, arguing that "the idea of 'Asiatic society' is a socio-historical rather than a geographical concept," because of Marx's frank acknowledgment that Tokugawa Japan was a feudal society and because he extended the conception to apply to Peruvian and Mexican society.[47] According to Plekhanov, however, geographical circumstances were preconditions determining historical development and could determine specific relations of production; thus, by implication, the development of the forces of production was decisively influenced by geographic conditions.[48] Moreover, to explain the economic stagnation resulting from oriental despotism, Plekhanov observed that "there arises between the superstructure and the base an *interaction* which provides the key to an understanding of all those phenomena which *at first glance* seem to contradict the fundamental thesis of historical materialism." One way in which oriental despotism inhibits the emergence of private property, for example, is in its "decisive influence on the entire mentality of social man."[49] As Lenin argued in *The Development of Capitalism in Russia*, the despotic state inhibits the emergence of "conditions required for capitalist production" such as "[a] class of people . . . who were accustomed to work for hire." "Agriculture in general, and the peasantry in particular, are weighted down most heavily by the traditions of a distant past, the traditions of patriarchal life, as a consequence of which the transformative effects of capitalism (the development of the productive forces, the changing of all social relations, etc.) manifest themselves here most slowly and gradually."[50]

Thus, both Plekhanov and Lenin suggested that Russia's Asiatic past and continuing semi-Asiatic nature was the source of its tardiness in developing capitalism. Moreover, they discovered that when capitalism finally did appear in Russia, it emerged in a hybrid form. Russia's experience was not merely a transition from feudalism to capitalism that was typical of Western progress. Rather, it was a special product of Russia's Asiatic past that "capitalist elements began to appear in Russia not after the liquidation of serfdom [as] in the West but while feudal-serf relations were still developing vigorously."[51] Lenin, like Plekhanov, was ambiguous about the future of Asiatic societies; the Asiatic mode did not necessarily preclude further development along the typically Western path, for Asiatic Russia had evolved a form of feudalism. Yet Asiatic despotism, with its natural economy, did not allow Russia "to participate in the overseas expansion that spurred the commercial revolution in the West."[52]

Plekhanov's work on Russian development and its Asiatic past alluded to Trotsky's notion of "uneven and combined development." Similarly, it was the effect of combined development on the shape of Russian capitalism that Lenin analyzed when, paradoxically, he sought to emphasize Russia's peculiarities, especially its Asiatic features, to make Marx's revolution seem viable and applicable to Russia. Despite all evidence to the contrary, Lenin asserted, capitalism had developed, albeit in a peculiar form because of Russia's semi-Asiatic past. The transition to capitalism had been delayed because "the conditions required for capitalist production did not yet exist" and because "the old corvée system of economy had been undermined, but not yet completely destroyed." Moreover, "the possibility of exercising 'other than economic pressure' [(a characteristic of feudalism)] remained in the shape of the peasants' temporarily-bound status, collective responsibility, corporal punishment, forced labor on public works, etc." Consequently, Lenin argued,

> The only possible system of economy was, accordingly, a transitional one, a system combining the features of both the corvée and the capitalist systems. And indeed, the post-Reform system of farming practised by the landlords bears precisely these features. With all the endless variety of forms characteristic of a transitional epoch, the economic organization of contemporary landlord farming amounts to two main systems, in the most varied combinations—the labour-service [corvée] system and the *capitalist* system. . . . It is quite natural that the combination of such dissimilar and even opposite systems of economy leads in practice to a whole number of most profound and complicated conflicts and contradictions, and that the pressure of these contradictions results in a number of the farmers going bankrupt, etc. All these are phenomena characteristic of every transitional period.[53]

It is unclear from Lenin's language whether he regarded Russia's semi-Asiatic experience as historically unique. But it is clear that his observations on uneven and combined development in Russia carried powerful implications for Japanese Marxists trying to understand the applicability of the oriental society construct to Japan's development. Lenin's interpretation was attractive, for it reconciled apparently conflicting aspects of Marx's paradigm. Despite its own Asiatic features, Russia, like Japan, had attained both feudalism and capitalism. With the aid of the notion of uneven development, one could invoke the concept of oriental society to explain the persistence of "backward" elements in the Japanese economy and polity, without condemning Japan to the fate of passive, undeveloping China. Perhaps it was because of Lenin's success in applying the oriental society conception to Russia and then emerging to lead the Bolsheviks to revolutionary victory that the Asiatic mode of production and oriental society conception emerged repeatedly in Kōza-ha contributions to the debate on Japanese capitalism. To the extent that Japan did develop feudalism, it could be argued that characteristics of oriental society had made that feudalism less progressive than its counterpart in the West and continued to restrain Japan's transition to capitalism.

During the 1930s, as the paths of China and Japan diverged more sharply than ever before under the shadow of rising Japanese expansionism, writings on Asiatic society proliferated in Japanese Marxist circles. The intensity of writing and publication on this subject reflected the fact that many saw the Asiatic mode of production conception as "a 'key' in the study of the special characteristics of the individual historical eras of development in Japan" from antiquity to Meiji.[54] The remainder of this chapter will describe how the Asiatic mode of production paradigm was interpreted variously to produce Marxian periodizations of Japanese history and how participants in the debate on Japanese capitalism appealed to Japan's "Asiatic" characteristics to explain the peculiarities of Japan's transition from feudalism to capitalism.

Competing Paradigms of the Asiatic Mode of Production

There were two separate tasks to be accomplished by Japanese Marxists seeking in the Asiatic mode of production theory a key to the history of Japanese economic development. These were first to establish a coherent paradigm from the competing versions of the theory of the Asiatic mode of production then circulating among Western Marxists; and then to apply the paradigm to establish the succession of political and economic eras—from primitive clan society to the Meiji Restoration—in Japan's own history.

In undertaking the preliminary task of understanding Marx's conception of the Asiatic mode of production, Japanese Marxists drew heavily on the many contributions that Soviet Marxists made on the issue during the controversy on the debacle of the Chinese revolution in 1927-1928. The views of participants in the debate on Japanese capitalism were as divergent as those of their Soviet counterparts, but the debate in Russia did not restrict the range of interpretation in Japan. On the contrary, the Japanese Marxists discussed here were fully aware that the Asiatic mode of production theory had been repudiated by the Leningrad Conference in February 1931;[55] yet many maintained that the theory was still a useful tool for analyzing the socio-economic development of Japan and its neighbors in the East. Those Japanese Marxists who did reject the Asiatic mode of production theory in general did so independently and for their own reasons, and they nonetheless often retained some elements of the original Marxist conception to reinterpret Japan's economic history.

Soviet Thought on the Asiatic Mode of Production

The major Soviet scholars who influenced Japanese thinking on the issue fell into two major groups. One circle formed in the mid- to late 1920s around the work of Soviet economists Eugene S. Varga and Ludwig S. Mad'iar. Both Hungarian emigrés to the Soviet Union, Varga and the more junior Mad'iar applied Marx's views on Asia to analyze contemporary China, and they strongly endorsed the validity of the Asiatic mode of production concept from their different vantage points. Active in Comintern activities, Varga headed the Soviet Institute for the Study of the World Economy and World Politics from 1927 to 1947, and he quickly established a reputation as the foremost Soviet authority on the world economic crisis. Beginning in 1925, however, Varga published extensively on the Chinese economy and revolution.[56] In these essays, Varga further elevated Soviet interest in Marx's ideas on the Asiatic mode of production, which had been assembled in an earlier article entitled "Marx on India and China," published by David B. Riazanov, head of the Marx-Engels Institute, in 1925.[57] Writing in the same year, Varga had asserted that Chinese society was dominated by a scholar-bureaucrat ruling class that controlled waterworks owned by the government and erected for productive and defensive purposes. The Chinese economic elite, in other words, was not a group that held private property but rather a class that controlled public property. Subsequently, Varga went on to identify China explicitly as an Asiatic society that differed in crucial respects from feudal society.[58]

Mad'iar endorsed the application of the Asiatic mode of production concept to analyze China, but he developed a perspective that differed from Varga's view on the basis of his own firsthand experience in China. Mad'iar followed Comintern advisor Mikhail M. Borodin to China in 1926-1927. As a China specialist, Mad'iar produced a series of works on the Chinese rural economy, in which he boldly defined contemporary China as a society still dominated by the Asiatic mode of production.[59] Mad'iar, like Varga, argued that the Asiatic mode of production was a separate mode of production that differed from feudalism in that there were no feudal property and no feudal lords. Mad'iar, however, emphasized that floods and the need for water control and artificial irrigation were the crucial factors leading to the formation of this special mode of production. In his view, the need for public works was the key to the establishment of a despotic state, which owned the land and the water, out of ancient communal societies based on rural communities (what Japanese Marxists called the *kyōdōtai*). Mad'iar saw oriental society as a class society, and he opposed those who would see the rise of oriental despotism on the basis of provision of public works as a kind of supra-class state. Nevertheless, he argued, in a manner that was consistent with Varga's view, that in this class society, the main antagonism lay between peasants and the state.[60]

By 1930, there had evolved an overt conflict between Mad'iar and Varga, on the one hand, and the group of scholars who would prevail at the Leningrad meeting a year later. Led by Mikhail Godes and Yevgeny S. Iolk, and joined subsequently by the historian of ancient society, Sergei I. Kovalev, this group maintained that the Asiatic mode of production was not a separate mode of production at all, but rather was merely a variant of some other mode of production. Neither Iolk, a Soviet academic who had served as a translator in China from 1925 to 1927, nor Godes had published extensively on the issue prior to 1930.[61] Yet the attack on the Asiatic mode of production scholarship of Varga and Mad'iar was launched by these two men. This undoubtedly occurred with the support of Joseph Stalin, who had now eliminated Nikolai Bukharin and Gregory Zinoviev, both of whom had led the Comintern in Far Eastern policy in the mid- and late 1920s.

The political motivation behind the attack on advocates of the oriental society paradigm was undisguised in Godes's report at the Leningrad "Discussion on the Asiatic Mode of Production." Of course, the language of the report itself offers nothing to support Karl Wittfogel's allegation that the Asiatic mode of production theory was rejected because it implied the possibility of an Asiatic "restoration" of bureaucratic class rule in Stalin's Russia. Both Godes and Iolk did, however, couch their attack on Mad'iar, Varga, Riazanov, and, by implication, the fallen Bukharin—none of whom was invited to participate in the discussion[62]—in terms of the repeated failures of the Chinese revolution under Comintern leadership since the bloody Shanghai coup of April 1927. In the words of Iolk:

> If we deem it possible to discuss the question of the "Asiatic mode of production," then it is primarily because we are concerned with the political conclusion to be drawn from the theory of the Asiatic mode of production.
>
> We are not here because, as Comrade Kokin said, we "need at last to study the history of the Orient and include it in world history." This is not the reason we are discussing the Asiatic mode of production, but in order to turn the practical history now being created by the heroic struggle of the exploited masses of China, Indo-China, and India, to the interests of the labouring masses by means of the correct method. . . .
>
> And so, if we approach things from this perspective, . . . then it is perfectly clear that the interpretation of individual statements by Marx and Engels on the Orient, presented to us in the guise of a superficially perfected theory about a particular Asiatic mode of production, is absolutely unacceptable from a political point of view.[63]

As this passage illustrates, the controversy on the Asiatic mode of production was an integral part of the debate on China policy, which in turn formed a key element of the factional conflict between Stalin, on the one hand, and his now powerless rivals in the Soviet Communist Party, Leon Trotsky and Nikolai Bukharin. It is not coincidental that the rejection of the Asiatic mode of production theory occurred at precisely the same time as the Comintern's temporary *volte-face* on Japan policy in the 1931 Draft Political Theses (see chapter 3). Both measures served to repudiate the theoretical influence of eminent scholars associated with Bukharin. As Stalin consolidated his stranglehold on the Soviet party apparatus, these purges of the theoretical influences of Bukharin, Trotsky, and others drove the final nail into the coffin of their effective political power in Russia and abroad. The fact that the politics of intraparty struggle took precedence over scholarship and intellectual rigor in the Leningrad discussion of the Asiatic mode of production, then, helps to explain why this concept—like Bukharin's notion of "state capitalist trust"—nevertheless continued to provoke interest and controversy among Japanese Marxists in the 1930s and 1940s. Kōza-ha scholars seeking to comprehend Japanese history in a Marxian framework simply could not be satisfied with the anti-intellectual and cavalier treatment given the concept of oriental society at the Leningrad Conference.

What were the crucial points that emerged from this discussion? Even if Godes and Iolk failed to give the Asiatic mode of production serious academic treatment, their critique did serve to pinpoint some of the conceptual weaknesses both in the Comintern's view of China in the 1920s—a product of Stalin as well as of Bukharin—and in the views of Varga, Mad'iar, and Wittfogel. In 1926 and 1927, Stalin had begun to stress the role of feudal remnants in Chinese society, and in 1928 the Chinese Communist Party itself, at its Sixth National Congress in Moscow, yielded to Stalin's influence by emphasizing feudal relations in the Chinese countryside and rejecting the Mad'iar-Wittfogel view of China as an Asiatic society.[64] Yet one of the difficulties of the Mad'iar view lay precisely in his assertion that the "remnants" of the Asiatic mode of production coexisted alongside the "remnants" of feudalism: in other words, at some point private property and feudalism had in fact emerged in China and elsewhere in the Orient.[65] While it was conceivable that remnants of both feudalism and the Asiatic mode of production could coexist, in the Soviet discussion feudalism and the Asiatic mode of production represented contradictory alternative models of the current state of Chinese society. The Asiatic mode of production, as originally presented in Marx's writings, seemed to preclude the rise of private property; and the de facto existence of private property, in the form of the hereditary right to land and serfs, was an essential element of feudalism. Thus, Mad'iar could sustain his interpretation only by making some alteration in Marx's original views on the static nature of oriental society.

Mad'iar made this adjustment by speculating on the possible effects of an encounter between an oriental society and the dynamic West. He assumed that European imperialism had encountered the Asiatic mode of production when it invaded India and China and had presumably triggered the move from the Asiatic to feudal and capitalist relations of production. As Godes perceptively noted, this proposition posed a variety of theoretical problems: Did the Asiatic mode of production fall, and if so, precisely how? In addition, Godes found other inconsistencies in Mad'iar's interpretation of the history of the East.

> If the Asiatic mode of production ended in China in the Chou dynasty, then Mad'iar is incorrect in bringing it down to the nineteenth century. If Mad'iar is right when he considers that the European incursion found the Asiatic mode of production, then how does he explain the economic and social structure of contemporary China? . . . If Mad'iar is right, and if the survivals of feudal relations predominate in China, then by what miracle, in an era of European intrusion, did the Asiatic mode of production evolve into the feudal mode of production? And if to the present day the survivals of the Asiatic mode of production dominate [as Varga asserted], then how do you connect this with the pronouncements of the Communist International on the question of the character of the Chinese revolution?

Godes charged that none of these issues could be resolved satisfactorily on the basis of the Varga-Mad'iar Asiatic mode of production theory. More importantly, this theory, which Iolk alleged to "reflect well-defined foreign influences" (Germany's Wittfogel, perhaps), challenged the Stalinist view and thus was "the wet nurse for the theoretical position of Trotskyism."[66]

Godes proposed a solution to the problem that was essentially semantic: "The Asiatic mode of production is nothing other than feudalism. The Orient, in a very unique fashion, went through the same stages of social development as Europe." Careful study, Godes argued, would lead one to discover in East, as in West, the essential characteristics of feudalism, which he defined as follows: "land-ownership is the basis for the accumulation of the surplus product; the direct producer conducts his own independent economic operation; in the relations between the owner of the means of production and the direct producer, extra-economic compulsion prevails; the hierarchy of land-ownership corresponds to the hierarchy of political power." Godes did not deny that the elements that Mad'iar and M. Kokin and G. Papaian identified as accoutrements of the Asiatic mode of production existed in the East. However, he did reject the notion that these characteristics could "either individually, or taken together, . . . fulfill the main requirement for the construction of a separate mode of production."[67] Thus, in practice the Chinese gentry were to be considered not "Asiatic-bureaucratic" but feudalistic in character. Moreover, the notion that a state bureaucracy, based on public management rather than its private ownership of land and other means of production, could comprise a ruling class was denounced as un-Marxist. With a single stroke, Stalin's critics of the Asiatic mode of production theory thus relegated the peculiarities of Asian societies like China and Japan to insignificance and allowed Comintern Marxists conveniently to ignore Marx's embarrassing remarks on the positive role of Western imperialism in the East.

Godes's formulation that the Asiatic mode of production did not really constitute a separate mode of production at all but was merely a variant of the feudal mode of production dominated Marxist discourse on Asia until Stalin's death, but it was not the sole Soviet resolution of the issues raised above by Godes at the Leningrad meeting. Another critique of the Mad'iar-Varga understanding of oriental society was offered during the 1930s by the historian Sergei I. Kovalev of the University of Leningrad. Kovalev, best known for his 1935 work *Istorija drevnevo mira* [History of the ancient world], was the leading Soviet theorist on antiquity. Kovalev agreed with Godes that the Asiatic mode of production was not an independent economic formation, but he argued that the so-called Asiatic mode of production was actually the slaveowner formation as it appeared in the East. Along with the work of Wittfogel, Varga, and Mad'iar and the critiques of Iolk and Godes, Kovalev's thesis exercised a significant influence on Japanese Marxists assessing the Asiatic mode of production conception for themselves in the 1930s.

Japanese Paradigms of the Asiatic Mode of Production

Beginning in 1931, shortly after the Leningrad discussion and as the *Symposium on the History of the Development of Japanese Capitalism* was being prepared, Japanese Marxists began to address the issue of the Asiatic mode of production. A controversy within the Kōza-ha on the application of the conception to Japanese economic history rapidly gained momentum until the late 1930s, when the debate on Japanese capitalism as a whole succumbed to police repression. During these years, a small group of Marxists debated the applicability of the notion of the Asiatic mode of production, to what period in Japanese history it most closely corresponded, and to what extent its lingering impact might still be felt in the economics and politics of contemporary Japan.

Out of this controversy emerged several definitions of the Asiatic mode of production and two major patterns of interpretation of its role in Marx's historical schema. The judgment of the Leningrad discussion notwithstanding, many—including Aikawa Haruki, Moritani Katsumi, and Hirano Yoshitarō—accepted the Asiatic mode of production as a separate mode of production. A second group, including Akizawa Shūji and Hayakawa Jirō, agreed with Godes and Iolk that the Asiatic mode of production was not a separate mode of production but a variant of some other social formation. Hattori Shisō went on to agree with Godes that what Varga and Mad'iar had interpreted as the Asiatic mode of production was actually a variant of feudalism, while Hayakawa drew heavily on Kovalev's work to argue that this was simply the oriental version of slave society. Virtually all the Marxist scholars engaged in this controversy used the concepts of oriental society and the Asiatic mode of production to some degree to analyze Japanese economic history. For Kōza-ha Marxists seeking the reasons for Japan's continued backwardness in the agrarian economy and in the political sphere, the paradigm proved to be very useful.

This position of the Asiatic mode of production controversy in the larger debate on Japanese capitalism was evident in Aikawa Haruki's essay on "The Reactionary Nature of the Theory of the 'Asiatic Mode of Production,' " published in April 1933. There, by assessing the implications of the Soviet controversy on oriental society for the Rōnō-ha–Kōza-ha debate,[68] Aikawa set a bold, independent tone for the Japanese debate. He attacked Soviet Marxist Riazanov for "abstract dogmatism" and for "sabotaging . . . concrete research on historical development" and criticized at length both Soviet advocates of the Asiatic mode of production theory and their critics. The flawed views of both Mad'iar and Iolk, he asserted, were intimately linked to the arguments of Inomata and Rōnō-ha economist Kushida Tamizō, who had argued that Japanese capitalism no longer had a special nature.[69]

Aikawa was not content with Mad'iar's conception of the Asiatic mode of production, which argued that Eastern and Western societies diverged after the primitive communal stage as a result of a geography-based necessity for waterworks in the East. According to Mad'iar, Marx's and Engels's early writings indicated four characteristic features of oriental society: "1) An absence of private land-ownership; 2) A necessity for artificial irrigation and, connected with this, a necessity for the organization of public works on a grand scale; 3) The rural commune; 4) Despotism as a form of government." This Eastern pattern converged with the Western path once again in feudalism and capitalism because of the impact of military pressures from more advanced Western societies. Yet Eastern feudalism, including Japanese feudalism, still bore the imprint of the Asiatic mode of production and its stubborn remnants.

Mad'iar acknowledged that in many respects Japan appeared to be an exception to the general pattern of stagnant oriental societies being victimized by Western imperialist exploitation. Nevertheless, he contended that Japan too bore the legacy of the Asiatic mode of production, particularly in the "method of exploitation" that predominated in the countryside. In Mad'iar's words:

> It hardly bears repeating that at the present time, in all countries of the Orient, including Japan, the product is extracted from the peasantry primarily in the form of rent in kind, or secondarily, in the form of money rent, as a transformed variety of rent in kind. Of course, merchant usury, tax, and imperialistic exploitation of the peasant masses play a tremendous role. But at the same time, it would be incorrect and would not correspond to the state of things to search the social order of these countries, and the agrarian order in particular only for remains and survivals of the feudal order of exploitation and to mobilize the workers and the peasants against them.

The continued "extraction of a rent/tax" in the countryside along with survivals of village communal landownership demonstrated, in Mad'iar's view, that "along with the remains of feudalism, the remains and survivals of the Asiatic mode of production could be found in the Orient" as late as the 1920s.[70]

In evaluating the extent to which Japan's late-developing capitalism continued to be backward because of the imprint of "Asiatic characteristics," Aikawa and others had first to establish the correct interpretation of the Asiatic mode of production theory for themselves. If it did constitute a separate mode of production that was geographically contingent, then one would expect its long-term impact on the distinctive aspects of capitalist development in Japan to be far greater than if Marx's notion of oriental society were taken to represent merely the specific manifestations of universal developmental stages—antiquity (Kovalev), feudalism (Godes), or as an era of transition from one stage to another (Aikawa).

Aikawa adopted a literal interpretation of Marx's enumeration of the Asiatic, ancient, feudal, and capitalist modes of production as "progressive" epochs in man's social history in the 1859 "Preface to a Critique of Political Economy." He saw the Asiatic mode of production as the first form of antagonistic or class society, preceding Greek and Roman antiquity, the classic slaveowner formation; and Marx's references to "oriental" or "Asiatic" society were to be interpreted to refer to the social forms of the ancient East, as discovered in Marx's research on Egypt, Turkey, Persia, India, and Tartar. Marx had drawn on François Bernier's description of the ancient Moghul empire to explain the patriarchal social structure of ancient Asia. Moreover, Aikawa maintained, Marx had found in these Asian peoples the historical bases of Greek and Roman antiquity and of ancient Germany, and this was the reason he had named it the Asiatic mode of production. The category was universal, not geographically specific, in this view.

Thus Aikawa was critical of those like Mad'iar and Riazanov, who stressed the role of waterworks and argued that arid conditions merely constrained the community (*kyōdōtai*) or state to support sedentary agriculture and communal landownership by engaging in irrigation. [71] Here, although Aikawa did not emulate Godes in discarding the Asiatic mode of production as a "hypothesis," he did share Godes's view of a unilinear pattern of historical development.[72] Subsequently, however, in an essay on "The Tendency toward the Formation of an Asiatic Concept," he rejected those aspects of Godes's views that would neglect the study of the "individual national peculiarities" of societies like Japan.[73]

Over the course of the controversy, Aikawa became increasingly critical of Godes's views. Although Godes had rejected the Asiatic mode of production as a separate social formation, he had maintained the same undifferentiated conception of the East that characterized the perspectives of Mad'iar, Varga, and other advocates of the Asiatic mode of production theory. Thus, Aikawa argued that Godes's reference to the "unique feudalism of the Orient in general" obliterated the dramatic differences between a country like Japan, which had a pure feudalism remarked by Marx himself, and India, where small-scale agriculture and handicrafts continued to exist on the basis of communal landownership. "We must eliminate this concept of the Orient in general," Aikawa asserted.[74] Therefore, Aikawa opposed both the view that there was no essential difference in the developmental experiences of East versus West and the view, common among other Kōza-ha Marxists, that the Asiatic mode of production conception was valid as a geographically specific category and could be applied productively to understand the peculiar aspects of Japan's feudal and capitalist development.

Aikawa's position was supported by Moritani Katsumi, who also saw the Asiatic mode of production as a pre-ancient epoch common to all societies. Moritani had written extensively on the subject before, but he reconsidered the issue after reading the Japanese translation of Kovalev's *Theory of the Ancient World*. Moritani took issue with Kovalev's understanding of the Asiatic mode of production as slavery in the East; and he repudiated Kovalev's treatment of the concept as a social formation peculiar to oriental antiquity. Having admitted ignorance on the Far East, Kovalev had identified in ancient Egypt "a classic example of the Asiatic mode of production," and while he recognized that this formation did not necessarily exist everywhere in the East, he had concluded that it was the dominant mode of production there. Moritani argued, however, that if Marx saw the Asiatic mode of production as demarcating a major social epoch, then it could not have been merely an oriental variant of slavery, as Kovalev alleged, or of feudalism, as Godes claimed.[75]

According to Moritani, the ancient and feudal modes of production were experienced in the East after the Asiatic mode, but those formations did not mature fully. The pre-"ancient" Asiatic mode was the era of the "primitive agrarian *kyōdōtai*" and common ownership of the land, he argued. This *kyōdōtai* system marked the disintegrating stage of primitive communal society, and thus it was to be distinguished from the preceding *kyōdōtai* based on blood kinship ties. In its original form, the *kyōdōtai* involved cooperative labor as well as communal landownership; but the agrarian *kyōdōtai* that characterized the Asiatic mode of production was "the first social unit of free men unbound by blood ties." Only land was held in common and periodically redistributed among community members, and eventually each member cultivated and owned the product of the land he had been given. These arrangements had been termed "Asiatic" not because they were to be found only in Asia, but because Marx had discovered their prototype in Asia.[76]

In his treatment of the issue, Moritani accepted the validity of an Asiatic mode of production conception, but he rejected as its characteristics many features that Soviet Marxists like Varga and Mad'iar had identified with it. For example, he argued that the Asiatic mode of production could not have involved state or monarchic ownership of the land, nor could it have referred to variations of slavery or serfdom. Rather, although it may have predated the written history of many peoples, it was the starting point of the development of many cultures in the East, which then progressed to the ancient and feudal modes of production. Although the remnants of the primitive agrarian *kyōdōtai* tended to be considerable, progress did occur in the East, according to Moritani, because the economic basis of the Asiatic mode of production was a dual presence of primitive communal ownership and private ownership, which emerged as the original blood-kinship *kyōdōtai* was dissolving.[77]

Although Moritani's interpretation resembled Aikawa's view of the Asiatic mode of production in some respects, Moritani was critical of what he saw as inconsistencies and ambiguities in Aikawa's view. For instance, Moritani pointed out, Aikawa had seen the Asiatic mode of production as a class social formation preceding Greek and Roman antiquity. Yet, Aikawa saw the slave-slaveowner relationship as the first class antagonism; thus his Asiatic mode of production was necessarily a kind of slaveowner formation, a "patriarchal form of slavery" to be distinguished from the slavery of Greek and Roman antiquity. But, Moritani pointed out, Marx had never identified patriarchal slavery as a distinguishing characteristic of the Asiatic mode of production, nor did he see the Asiatic as the first antagonistic social formation. Finally, Aikawa had seen both "primitive *kyōdōtai* relations" and patriarchal slavery in the Asiatic mode of production; but there was a contradiction between the notion of the primitive *kyōdōtai* and patriarchal slavery, which involved class divisions. Nor could Aikawa support his claim that a patriarchal slave system had preceded Greek and Roman antiquity.[78]

Moritani was equally critical of the views of the Soviet historian Kovalev, which seemed to suffer from some of the same inconsistencies that afflicted Aikawa's interpretation. In an early essay, Kovalev had designated the Asiatic as an Eastern class social formation preceding Greek and Roman antiquity, and he seemed to see Eastern peoples as having lived their entire lives in stagnation under this social structure. The characteristics of this social formation included common ownership of the means of production on the basis of the primitive agrarian *kyōdōtai*; an upper class of *bushi* (warriors) and landowners, which lived on rents; and antagonism between the *kyōdōtai* and these privileged groups, who in effect controlled the *kyōdōtai*. Kovalev then distinguished the Asiatic mode of production not from the ancient but from the feudal mode of production, stressing that individual exploitation was secondary to collective exploitation and that collective ownership under the Asiatic mode was to be contrasted with private ownership in feudalism. Although Kovalev slightly modified his views subsequently, Moritani saw fundamental errors in his basic interpretation. Kovalev no longer sought a pre-antiquity epoch, and he abandoned his view of an Asiatic mode involving the collective exploitation of the *kyōdōtai* by landowners. Now he saw that in East as well as West slavery was the first class formation; and the Asiatic mode of production took on a dual meaning: a variant of slavery in Asian antiquity and a modified feudalism in the middle ages in the Orient. Moritani firmly rejected this view, arguing that the Asiatic mode of production was not essentially a class social formation but was based on the primitive agrarian *kyōdōtai*.[79]

Despite Moritani's criticisms, Kovalev's and Godes's views of the Asiatic mode of production as merely oriental versions of the ancient and feudal modes of production gained dedicated adherents among Japan's Marxists. Both Hani Gorō and Hayakawa Jirō found the Asiatic mode of production concept useful, but, like Kovalev and Godes, they did not accept it as an independent mode of production. Hani had developed a special interest in the Asiatic mode of production well before Aikawa did, while tracing the growth of capitalism in the East;[80] and he identified the special characteristics attributed to Asiatic societies by Marxists and other scholars from Hegel to Wittfogel as follows:

> the collective or state concentration of the ownership of slaves and land; a tributary system [appearing] as an undifferentiated unity of ground rent and taxes; . . . many instances in which communal or state enterprises of artificial water irrigation facilities or agrarian *kyōdōtai*

system were employed by the rulers; stability of the unity between petty cultivation and handicraft industry in the household; the isolation of rural *kyōdōtai*; the absence of communication/transport (*kōtsū*); adherence to a status class system; the persistence of patriarchy; an incomplete differentiation of production labor; the extreme bondage of . . . freedom of character . . .; the difficulty of the industrial development of urban handicrafts; restraint on the freedom or independence of cities; the enormity of the bureaucratic stratum; the pressure of despotism and the stubborn petrification and stagnancy of these special characteristics; the atrophy of overall growth; the cruelty of famine; general poverty; and the difficulty of the emergence of the premises of movement to a higher stage of development from the narrowness of this general mode of life, mode of culture, stagnancy, and cycles.[81]

While Hani acknowledged that these characteristics were common to Eastern societies, he maintained that the combination of these elements could not suffice to constitute a separate precapitalist mode of production. Rather, echoing Kovalev and Godes, he asserted that the so-called Asiatic mode of production was best "regarded as a primitive form or metamorphosis of the two [precapitalist] modes of production," the ancient and feudal. It was the result of the incomplete emergence of the first class society, based on slavery; and "the adhesion, stagnancy, or preservation of the relations" of primitive clan society (*gentes*) made the ensuing precapitalist forms, slavery and feudalism, "more contradictory, stagnant, cruel, and oppressive."[82]

Other Kōza-ha scholars, including Hattori Shisō, Hayakawa, and Akizawa Shūji, agreed with this position. According to Akizawa, if a mode of production was defined as "the mode of the unity between labor power and the means of production" and, in class societies, "the form in which surplus labor is extracted from the direct producers and laborers," then an Asiatic structure conceived "*as an independent mode of production is not possible*."[83] Similarly, Hayakawa maintained that the term "Asiatic mode of production" was used by Soviet scholars merely "for convenience," and that it was "not to be placed in a position alongside the primitive communist, slave, feudal, and capitalist modes of production." The problem was that the set of characteristics that Soviet scholars had identified in the East "invariably collapse[d] when [they came] in contact with historical realities." Hayakawa recognized that "in some Eastern countries despotic rule and irrigation were linked to 'state landownership,' [and] that in some cases the underdevelopment of cities could be explained by 'state landownership.' " What he could not support was any notion of an Asiatic mode of production that posited that these relationships always existed.[84]

Given these objections to Varga's and Mad'iar's formulations of the Asiatic mode of production, how were Japanese Marxists to understand Marx's use of the term? Could it still be used to analyze the peculiarities of Japanese development? Akizawa joined Iolk and Godes in asserting that the so-called Asiatic mode of production referred to nothing more than the several special characteristics of Asian societies. The most significant of these peculiarities was the "stubborn preservation of the agricultural *kyōdōtai*," which occurred "under the unique historical conditions of the despotic countries of Asia." Yet Akizawa saw that this view meant that one would still have to analyze the concrete historical and social conditions within individual Asian societies in order to diagnose the mode of production that predominated in each.[85] Others, like Hattori Shisō, agreed that abstract debate on the Asiatic mode of production and its mechanistic application to Japan had to give way to a detailed study of late Tokugawa history by scholars armed with a valid understanding of the concept. For Hattori, the Asiatic mode of production was one form of feudal relations, the special character of which lay in "the state ownership of land and therefore the identity of rents and taxes." Understood in this sense, Hattori contended, "it was indisputable that the Asiatic mode of production existed in Japan in the late Edo and Meiji Restoration periods," as indicated by the reform measures of the Restoration itself.[86]

Similarly, Hayakawa joined those associated with the Institute for the Study of the China Problem (Shina Mondai Kenkyūjo) and accepted the term Asiatic mode of production to refer strictly to "state landownership." His understanding of this term, however, led Hayakawa to conclusions that contradicted Hattori's view. Hayakawa interpreted "state" landownership to mean landownership not by the state, but on a national scale, as opposed to the parcelization of land among feudal lords, as in Tokugawa Japan and medieval Europe. Thus, the identity of rents and taxes described by Marx meant that there were no longer any forms of tax that differed from the form of ground rent. All those subject to this system were directly subordinate to the state both politically and economically. In Marx's words, "In such a case, the state is the highest landlord, and 'sovereignty' is nothing other than landownership concentrated on a national scale."[87] Hayakawa concluded that in this narrower sense, "there is no doubt than an 'Asiatic mode of production' society once existed," and he went on to develop one of the most coherent periodizations of Japanese history.[88]

Hayakawa's position stirred considerable dissent among fellow Kōza-ha Marxists. Yet his interpretation is not unrepresentative of the stance on the question that Japanese Marxists adopted on the whole. Hayakawa had begun by repudiating the Rōnō-ha's assumption that the history of Japan's development was essentially no different from the universal pattern of world history in general. Nevertheless, Hayakawa and others could not easily accept the emphasis on the uniqueness of the East that was as central to the views of oriental society advocates Mad'iar and Varga as to those of their critics Godes and Iolk. Such a perspective, whether graced with the label "Asiatic mode of production" or not, amounted to "geographical materialism," in Hayakawa's view, and vitiated the efficacy of Marx's theory of history to guide Japan's revolution.[89] Nevertheless, one could not simply discard Marx's and Engels's writings on Asia because they were inconvenient. As a result, Hayakawa and others found themselves not only retaining some (broad or narrow) conception of the Asiatic mode of production, but also incorporating the notion as an integral element of their understanding of Japan's socio-economic development.

The Periodization of Japanese History

The controversy on the Asiatic mode of production led directly into a debate on the correct periodization of Japanese history. This occurred at the same time and for the same fundamental reason that Marxists in revolutionary China engaged in a parallel controversy on Chinese social history. In both countries, Marxist scholars and revolutionary activists firmly believed that the integrity of Marx's social theory required a correct identification of the mode of production that dominated contemporary Japan or China.[90] In addition, for Kōza-ha Marxists who believed that Japan had not yet reached the apex of its capitalist development but was saddled with the fetters of remnants from earlier eras, it was absolutely essential to trace the path of the prior development of Japan's economic and political arrangements from antiquity to the 1920s and 1930s.

The Asiatic mode of production conception figured centrally in the effort to periodize Japanese history, for here Marx's casual observation that mid-nineteenth-century Japan was a prototypical feudal society clashed with his presumption of the overall stagnancy of societies of the East straining under despotic rule. For this reason, the consideration of the Asiatic mode of production theory led participants in the debate on Japanese capitalism to propose a variety of interpretations of Japan's putative progression from primitive communal society to a modern capitalism crippled by remnants of earlier modes of political and economic organization. This discussion will examine the alternative periodizations of Japanese history offered by Marxist theorists of the Asiatic mode of production, and their appraisals of the impact of "Asiatic" elements on Japan's transition from feudalism to capitalism.

The fundamental issue in this controversy was ultimately the relationship between universality and particularity in the history of Japanese socio-economic development—the same basic issue dividing the Rōnō-ha from the Kōza-ha in the debate on Japanese capitalism as a whole. Did Japan experience the classical slavery of ancient Greece and Rome? If not, did its distinguishing characteristics fit the conception of the Asiatic mode of production? If Japan was an "oriental society" in the slave era, whence came the dynamic that moved it to feudalism, and what were the lasting influences of early "Asiatic characteristics" on that feudal formation and subsequently on the evolution of Japanese capitalism?

Generally, most Kōza-ha scholars responded to these issues by incorporating some notion of the Asiatic mode of production into their periodizations of Japanese history. Much of the discussion revolved around the transition from primitive communal society to feudalism, for it was here that the conflict between Marx's view of a stagnant oriental society and the reality of Japan's development of feudalism and capitalism was most apparent. The problem was that if one found in Japan's past the Asiatic mode of production, then, according to Marx's analysis, there could have been no emergence of private property. Yet Japan had developed feudalism, which required the existence of private property. Somehow, then, private property had to have developed sufficiently to sustain the emergence of feudalism in Japan. This problem was especially urgent for participants in this controversy, because they sought the source of the transition to feudalism within Japanese society, and not in the external force of Western imperialism, to which Mad'iar had attributed the rise of feudalism in the East. As applied to Japan, the concept of the Asiatic mode of production required some internal dynamic, and to this extent, the interpretations of Kōza-ha scholars had to move beyond what had been accomplished by Western scholars from Marx to Mad'iar.

The solution for those who insisted on using elements of the Asiatic mode of production idea to explain Japan's peculiarities was to equivocate on the issue of private property. Thus, Akizawa, who did not designate any specific era as dominated by the Asiatic mode of production in Japan, stressed the growth of private property as the key to the transition to slavery and ultimately feudalism; while Hayakawa discerned the disintegration of the primitive *kyōdōtai* as a dialectical process. With the emergence of private property, there arose class cleavages that tended to pull the primitive community apart, yet its "Asiatic" characteristics held the community together enough to allow for the transition to a tributary system of state landownership. Yet private property was not completely suppressed. It remained a significant enough force to move Japan to feudalism and eventually to capitalism. Such an assessment of the role of private property became important to the periodization of Japanese history, whether the Asiatic mode of production was accepted as a completely separate social formation (Aikawa and

Hirano) or merely as a variant of slavery or of feudalism (Akizawa, Hayakawa, and Hori). In any case, the "Asiatic" peculiarities of Japanese society dating back to the era of primitive communal society were said to have imbued the subsequent stages of Japanese development with elements of political and economic "backwardness."

It was Hayakawa Jirō who sparked a "debate on Japanese social history" when he conceived an elaborate periodization of Japanese history beginning in late 1933. Having repudiated the view of the Asiatic mode of production as a separate mode of production, Hayakawa argued that the only valid understanding of the notion was to refer narrowly to the "tribute system" based on state landownership. He went on to examine Japan's economic and social structure, arguing that the Taika reforms of the seventh century marked the collapse of the primitive communal clan system and the beginning of the Asiatic mode of production, defined in this narrow sense.

Hayakawa's point of departure was Marx's and Engels's characterization of the Asiatic mode of production and classical slavery as successive epochs. Engels had argued in *Anti-Dühring* that where the *kyōdōtai* persisted, it became the basis of the Asiatic mode of production and its "crudest form of state"; where it collapsed, old mores were shed and peoples continued to progress to a new class-based society, slavery. Historically, Hayakawa observed, Engels's hypotheses were confirmed by the facts: such an Asiatic mode of production could neither precede primitive communal society nor follow capitalism. The slaveowner formation had fallen with the destruction of the opposing classes and was followed by the birth of feudalism, which in turn had led only to capitalism. Consequently, Hayakawa reasoned, the Asiatic mode of production could only have existed at the end of primitive communal society. It probably took the form of the tributary system, from what Marx himself had written in volume 2 of *Capital*: "under slavery, serfdom, and *(as far as the primitive kyōdōtai is concerned) tribute system relations*, those owning products and consequently those who sold [them] were slave owners, feudal lords, and states receiving tribute [respectively]."[91]

In Hayakawa's view, the tributary state system explained many of the alleged peculiarities of Eastern history. This was the basis, in his view, of state landownership in the East, and artificial irrigation in turn was a secondary consequence of this "form of state landownership." Subsequently, the *kyōdōtai*, which had stubbornly persisted longer in the East than in Greece and Rome, did gradually disappear, but the powerful state it had engendered continued to have an impact on the subsequent course of Eastern development. This powerful role was manifested in the "state feudalism" of Chinese antiquity, and in the persistence of state landownership alongside private landownership in Japan's Nara and Heian periods (the Ōchō or Dynastic era, 710-1184).[92]

Hayakawa went on to argue that the emergence of the tribute system—his "Asiatic mode of production"—could be traced from Engels's description of the collapse of primitive communal society in *Anti-Dühring*. According to Engels, this collapse had occurred in two ways. In the first process, the development of the forces of production imbued excess labor with value; thus, war prisoners who had previously been deemed useless and killed were transformed into slaves, and the classical form of slavery identified with Greek and Roman antiquity emerged. In *Origin of the Family*, however, Engels offered a second path for the collapse of primitive society. New cleavages within the primitive *kyōdōtai* between rich and poor and between slave and freeman accompanied the beginnings of commodity exchange and private property. Such internal divisions eventually destroyed the old *kyōdōtai* and communal land cultivation, in Engels's account, and land was turned over—first temporarily and then permanently—to the use of individual families and became an alienable commodity that could be bought and sold.[93] But in Hayakawa's interpretation, the emergence of new cleavages in the *kyōdōtai* in this second historical pattern initiated only a tentative disintegration of the *kyōdōtai* and marked the point of departure for the rise of the Asiatic mode of production, interpreted narrowly to refer to the tribute state system.

In making this argument, which he had systematized by December 1933 in his *Nihon Ōchō jidai shi* [History of the Dynastic age in Japan], Hayakawa was careful to stress those aspects of Japanese history that were shared in common with other societies, in order to avoid vitiating Marx's historical schema as a universally valid paradigm.[94] Thus, initially, Hayakawa wrote, "there can be no slaveowner formation based on anything other than 'classical slavery.' In this sense, [since Japan did not experience classical, or "mature" slavery], one cannot conceive of the 'existence' of a slaveowner formation in Eastern history." He then hurriedly noted that there were at least three cases in which such a lack of a mature slaveowner formation was possible. First, conceivably, primitive societies might, with the support of advanced proletarian-socialist countries, attain socialism and bypass intermediate modes of production. A second case was historically evident in the German conquest of Rome, as the result of which the development of German society was "grafted" onto the development of the preceding Roman society. In this case, technically, the German peoples would not have experienced a slaveowner formation directly. Finally, the history of the East represented a third case. In China and Japan slavery was not truly absent, as in the first two cases. There was an economic system of slavery, but it remained undeveloped, containing the seeds of a completed and dominant social formation, but never reaching the point of maturing into ancient Greek and Roman slavery.[95] Conversely, he argued, some form of class society had preceded classical slavery in Greece and Rome, but this tributary system had never attained the status of an independent social formation; it was merely a pattern that emerged at the close of the primitive clan system.[96]

In Hayakawa's view, the tributary system, or the Asiatic mode of production, had emerged out of the collapse of primitive communal society, through warfare among individual *kyōdōtai*. Dominant members of a single *kyōdōtai*, who collected rents and taxes from poorer members, endeavored to expand their power base by conquering neighboring communities; and when successful, they collected tribute from the vanquished communities.[97] The conquering *kyōdōtai*, now the tributary state, then assumed a leading role in economic projects, when large-scale projects, such as irrigation, were necessary. When dominant communities fell into decline, the relations that had predominated there were reproduced on the periphery. As a result, the transition to a new "slaveowner formation" was more difficult than it was where the growth of production forces had caused a more immediate collapse of *kyōdōtai* relations. As Hayakawa contended, " 'tributary relations' persisted for an extremely long period because of the stagnancy of the *kyōdōtai* itself and the possibility of the 'retrogression' of history."[98]

In this interpretation, the main cause of the so-called Asiatic mode of production was not geographical environment, or the need for irrigation, as Mad'iar or Kovalev would have it. Rather, the underdevelopment of commercial relations contributed to the stubbornness of *kyōdōtai* relations, which in turn produced the seeming lack of a slaveowner formation in the East. The apparent relationship between geography and this underdevelopment after the collapse of primitive communal society was merely coincidental.[99] Eastern societies, like Western ones, were on the path to the development of a slaveowner formation, but the underdevelopment of commerce hindered this movement in the East.[100]

But how could the "lack" or skipping over of classical slavery in the East be reconciled with Marx's historical schema? Hayakawa argued that the "lack" of a slaveowner formation in the East was comparable to the absence of a true epoch of bourgeois-democratic revolution in Russia. In Russia, this gap was compensated by the presence of "bourgeois elements in both the preceding and succeeding eras"; and in Japan, the remains of immature slavery in the Nara period compensated for its lack of a mature slaveowner formation.[101] This conceptualization in no way denied the basic progression postulated by Marx: primitive society → slaveowner formation → feudalism → capitalism. While the characteristics of primitive society, *kyō-*

dōtai relations, remained dominant in the East long after they had disappeared in the West, the forces of production continued to develop therein, and eventually produced a rapid birth of feudal society when *kyōdōtai* relations finally collapsed. This perspective denied the assumption of the stagnation of production forces that was integral to the picture of oriental society contained in Marx's writings. At the same time, it repudiated the need for a formal abstraction of a special slaveowner formation period, or the claim that the pre-Taika reform (645-649) period or Nara era was equivalent to Greek and Roman antiquity. Instead, Hayakawa argued, it was sufficient to note that characteristics of the slaveowner formation were still in evidence in the feudalisms of Han China and Nara Japan.[102]

Thus, Hayakawa's schematic periodization of Japanese history appeared as follows:

	Taika reforms (645-649)		Nara (710-794) and Heian (794-1184) (Ōchō or Dynastic era)	
primitive communal society based on the tribal *(shizoku) kyōdōtai*	→	(slaveowner formation) tribute system (Asiatic mode of production)	→	feudalism, characterized by remnants of state landownership and slavery

The Taika reforms marked the transition from primitive communal society to the era of the tribute system, in which "state landownership" was dominant. The split between rich and poor within the *kyōdōtai* that triggered this development began to appear in the central Kinai area of Japan, where the Imperial Household was established, as early as the sixth and seventh centuries.[103] In this periodization, the Dynastic age already saw the emergence of feudalism in Japan, but it was characterized by the remnants of the tributary system, specifically the coexistence of state land ownership alongside the private land ownership that had emerged by the time the primitive blood kinship *kyōdōtai* began to collapse. What became problematic in the application of Hayakawa's interpretation of the Asiatic mode of production to Japan was the status of the *benotami*, the servants of the Imperial Household and nobility who existed in clan society and after the Taika reforms. Were not these *benotami*—compared to the helots of ancient Sparta—slaves in the classical sense? Or were they more analogous to serfs? What was the position of this subjugated group in the history of Japanese socio-economic development?

The point of departure for Hayakawa's treatment of this issue was the suggestion by others that the *benotami*—and the helots of Sparta—were slaves. This argument would have suggested that an era of classical slavery preceded the Taika reforms, and it was essential for Hayakawa to dispose of this claim. Hayakawa distinguished among three forms of slavery—domestic or household slavery, classical slavery, and a system of state-owned slaves—in order to analyze the differences between Japan's *be* system, Sparta's helots, and the classical slavery of Athens and Rome. A system of household slaves, he pointed out, could not be the basis of a social formation, since such slaves could not be the "basis of production." Rather, domestic slavery was merely a precursor to the classical system of the Roman and Athenian variety, but depending on the characteristics of the society, a mature classic slave system might or might not evolve. State slavery may supplement domestic slavery in a still relatively primitive society. Or, it may supplement a predominant system of classical slavery, as in Sparta (in contrast with Athens, which was based entirely on classical slavery as described by Marx and Engels). It was because of its need for state slavery—its underdevelopment, in other words—that Sparta could not be cited as a model of Greek and Roman antiquity.[104]

Hayakawa applied these distinctions to Japan, by arguing that neither the helots nor the Japanese *be* represented slaves in the classical sense. He saw the helots as proto-slaves, a subjected group of agrarian laborers who developed toward slaves.[105] The helots thus appeared to precede classical (mature) slavery; as a form of subjected labor, these agrarian laborers developed prior to domestic slavery. Similarly, in Japan, he claimed, the *be* appeared where domestic slavery had reached the limits of its development, but where the conditions for "classical slavery" were partially absent. The *be* were formed after domestic slavery had come into being, and when a society that was not completely free of clan *kyōdōtai* relations conquered another society at an even lower level of development and enslaved its people. Unlike the helots, the *be* were not the group property of conquerors but the property of individuals;[106] and unlike the slaves of classical antiquity, the classic Japanese histories the *Kojiki* and *Nihon shoki* showed that the *be* were exchanged as ransom or given away rather than bought or sold. In addition, the *be* resembled serfs in that even before the Nara era, the so-called *tabe*, who worked as forced labor in the cultivation of colonized land and in granaries as agricultural workers on lands controlled by the imperial court, lived in specific villages and had to produce their own subsistence as well. Hayakawa thus argued that classical slavery was replaced in Japan by a sort of tribal slavery (*shuzoku-dorei*), a "state slavery," which arose out of the conquest of one community by another. Citing Kovalev, he pointed out that in such an underdeveloped agricultural economy, state slavery "was the cheapest form of exploiting slaves."[107] Yet, because the *be* were only one category of subjected persons that existed in ancient Japan, and because they were individually owned, Hayakawa was not prepared to identify Japan's *be* system fully with "state slavery."[108] In any case, when the state undertook the Taika reforms and distributed and redistributed land to individual peasants (called *handen* peasants), the *be* system gradually disappeared, as wage labor emerged and industrial production spread among *handen* peasants. As private property overtook state landownership and feudalism flourished in the Nara and Heian eras, Hayakawa noted, the remnants of the *be* became feudal retainers or lived as the poorly treated *burakumin* in separate villages.[109]

Hayakawa's periodization, then, bore some resemblance to the views of the Soviet scholars he had criticized. Even his limited definition of the Asiatic mode of production led him to postulate a separate path of development for the East. In a peculiar twist, however, Hayakawa was arguing that while conditions were not ripe for classical slavery to develop in the Taika era, an extremely rapid development of the forces of production—facilitated by intercourse with China—had enabled Japan to "leap over" or "skip over" the era of mature slavery, and move to a system of centralized feudalism after the Taika reforms. The Asiatic mode of production constituted a sort of transition from clan to feudal society.

This assumption of the "skipping over of slavery" in Japan gained many adherents among Japanese Marxists, including Rōnō-ha theorist Tsuchiya Takao. In his *Outline of Japanese Economic History* (1934), Tsuchiya denied that slavery was ever significant enough in Japan to form the core of its own mode of production:

> These conditions formed the basis for the establishment of a *feudal* centralized state, in a sense, in the Taika reforms. Clearly slavery existed in the great ancient society, but generally *serf relations, as in the "be"*, were predominant. Thus, what was established as a result of the Taika reforms, the *decisive purge of class organization, was not* an *ancient state* based on slavery. Rather it is erroneous to define the society previous to that as a slave society. It is true that at the time slavery existed, but its significance in production was not major.[110]

Thus, in Tsuchiya's view, the correct periodization was as follows:

pre-Taika era				
the *shizoku* (clan) system & patriarchal family, the *benotami*, serf-type relations	⟶	Taika reforms	⟶	centralized feudalism based on state landownership *komin* or serfdom

Similarly, Hori Toshio also argued that Japan had not experienced an era of classical slavery, but, unlike Hayakawa, Hori posited the Asiatic mode of production as a variant of feudalism.

primitive communal society based on rural *kyōdōtai*, characterized by patriarchy	Taika reforms ↔	feudalistic state (Asiatic mode of production based on state landownership)

In Hori's view, serfs and slaves coexisted in pre-Taika society, but slavery did not predominate. Slaves, which had been expropriated by rural *kyōdōtai*, were distinguished from the *benotami*, whom Hori saw as exploited *kyōdōtai* members. In this view, the Taika reforms marked the end of patriarchal *kyōdōtai* relations, including proto-slavery and communal landownership.[111]

Nevertheless, despite this influence of Hayakawa's ambitious periodization of Japanese history, it was somewhat muddled in its application of the Asiatic mode of production concept. Not surprisingly, it immediately drew fire from other Kōza-ha scholars. Aikawa Haruki, who adopted a literal interpretation of the "Asiatic mode of production" to refer to a separate pre-antiquity mode of production, was among the first to challenge Hayakawa's views on the issue of slavery in Japan. As Aikawa interpreted the latter's argument, an extraordinarily rapid development of production forces enabled Japan to "leap over" the classic slavery stage. Thus the Taika reforms marked the collapse of the primitive clan society, but until the maturation of feudalism in the Ōchō era, state landownership continued to predominate over the slowly evolving private ownership of land; and this intermediary period was the "Asiatic mode of production" that Hawakawa defined as the tributary system.

To Aikawa, this scheme seemed to be inconsistent with Marx's thesis of the progressive succession of one mode of production by another. There was no question that Japan in the Asuka or Suiko era (592-710) was heavily influenced by Tang China, importing handicrafts techniques, medical arts, Chinese characters, religion, and metalworking, all of which "accelerated the development of the forces of production and spiritual civilization" in Japan. But, in Aikawa's view, Hayakawa had erroneously attributed primacy to a secondary factor, like "the importation of production forces" and culture, ignoring the internal development of forces and relations of production in Japan. The crucial question that Hayakawa had left unanswered was, what did the historical evidence reveal about patterns of landownership and production relations in the period that Hayakawa had identified as the Asiatic mode of production?[112]

Aikawa charged that in labelling post-Taika society as feudalistic, Hayakawa was applying mechanistically to Japan the results of research on the formation of a centralized feudal society in China. He had prematurely seen the various forms of subjugated groups as serfs, rather than slaves. Aikawa saw a different pattern of development before and after the Taika reforms. He argued that slavery began to develop under the old clan system; in Japan, where modes of transportation flourished rapidly, slavery spread quickly, abetted by wars of conquest. In order to protect themselves from external enemies, conquering tribes gathered in cities, where they developed a league of clans, based on common property. (Private ownership remained in a subordinate position on the eve of the Taika reforms.) With the growth of production forces and slavery, tribal heads became more powerful, and a centralization of authority occurred. The Taika reforms legalized this arrangement, codifying state landownership in Japan.[113]

In short, Aikawa challenged Hayakawa's thesis of the "skipping over" of slavery in Japan by locating a slavery formation in his own periodization. Yet Aikawa, like Hayakawa, gave the Asiatic mode of production a position as a transitional stage in his schema. This similarity underscores the fact that Hayakawa and others who had denied that the Asiatic constituted a separate mode of production in fact reintroduced the Asiatic mode of production concept through the back door, thereby resurrecting the very same possibility of alternative paths of development for East and West that had prompted Soviet critics to repudiate the concept at the outset.

Nevertheless, Aikawa was more faithful than was Hayakawa to Marx's enumeration of the primitive, Asiatic, ancient, feudal, and capitalist stages as progressive modes of production. Maintaining that there was an "inseparable relationship" between slaves engaged in productive labor and household slaves, Aikawa insisted that a slave society existed in Japan after the Taika reforms. In his view, patriarchal slavery arose out of the gradual disintegration of the primitive clan *kyōdōtai*, as forces of production developed, the division of labor proceeded, and private property came into existence. The Asiatic mode of production was the process of this transition from primitive communal society to class society. Here Aikawa claimed that Kovalev had neglected the significance of patriarchal slavery as the precursor of classical slavery in ancient Greece and Rome.[114] This observation implied that the Asiatic mode of production, as a transitional era, was common to East and West. But Aikawa did not say this explicitly, and the peculiarities versus the universalities of Japan's experience remained unspecified.

What Aikawa did do was adduce historical evidence on forms of landownership and class differentiation in Japan circa the Taika reforms. In the classic *Chronicle of Japan*, Aikawa found intermediary forms of large landownership between communal *kyōdōtai* ownership and private landownership by individuals. He also discovered that in addition to the nobility, common citizens, and servants of the imperial court, there was a large group of *yakko*, or pure slaves, the unfree poor and outcasts who had neither family names nor the status of a social unit as a household. These had emerged out of conquest, much in the same manner that Hayakawa had described. As the clan lineage *kyōdōtai* was transformed into a geographically based *kyōdōtai*, and ultimately into the unitary patriarchal family, class distinctions such as these were sharpened.[115]

Despite their differences on the question of slavery in Japan, both Aikawa and Hayakawa agreed that pre-Taika Japan was the era of primitive clan society,[116] and both cited the role of the Asiatic mode of production in its transition to feudalism. Among the participants in the controversy, only Akizawa Shūji consistently repudiated any application of the Asiatic mode of production concept to Japan. Yet even Akizawa felt the need to cite a "special Japanese form of the slaveowner formation" to explain the peculiarities of Japan's subsequent development. This discussion, in turn, led Akizawa perilously close again to the concept of oriental society through a consideration of Japanese "state feudalism."[117]

Like Aikawa, Akizawa firmly rejected any notion that Japan had "skipped" the slaveowner formation. While he acknowledged that in Japan slavery "did not take the form of the so-called 'classical slavery' " of Rome and Greece, he protested Hayakawa's view that there was only one genuine slaveowner formation. Instead, Akizawa agreed with Aikawa in arguing that the *be* circa the Taika reforms more closely resembled slaves than feudal serfs. The *be* were "tribute-paying clansmen privately owned by hereditary nobility"; they were directly subject to the nobility, not serfs bound to the domains of feudal lords. For Akizawa, then, there was no question that slavery once existed in Japan, for it was the first class social formation that was a universal development in all societies. The only issue was the special form this would take under varying historical conditions. Drawing on Engels's discussion in *Origin of the Family*, Akizawa argued that the key to the special character of slavery in Japan lay in the "*special form of the disintegration of kyōdōtai relations in the formation of class society*" in Japan.[118]

Akizawa adopted as valid Hayakawa's distinction between an economic structure and a mature social formation, and the view that Greek and Roman slavery represented the most developed pattern of slavery. Akizawa argued that Hayakawa had erred, however, in assuming that the absence of the Greek-Roman pattern signified the absence of a slaveowner formation in the East.[119] According to Akizawa, it was entirely possible that slavery could appear only as an economic system and not as a social formation because either (1) it was merely the sprouts of the new slaveowner formation or (2) it was already only a remnant of the slaveowner formation in the next social formation. Thus, that feudal production relations had already emerged, e.g., in serfdom, did not preclude the continued existence of a slaveowner constitution.[120]

This was an important point, for Akizawa had already identified the ancient Japanese state as a form of "state feudalism."[121] He had not yet, however, analyzed the relationship between this form of feudalism and state landownership and how the rise of labor productivity caused the emergence of slavery and state feudalism as a necessary consequence.[122] Adducing archeological evidence, Akizawa found that in the early Iron Age (from the first century A.D. to the Asuka era, 593-710), there were large-scale tombs in which luxury items had been buried. These indicated the accumulation of individual wealth by nobility as well as a large pool of slave labor, which the construction of such large tombs necessitated. The existence of slavery was corroborated by passages from the *Gokansho tōi retsuden* [Biographical series on the Eastern barbarians of the book of the later Han dynasty], revealing that slaves were exported to China at the time (circa 108 A.D.), and that in Japan "the majority of noblemen owned slaves." Other records of Japanese society in the second and third centuries, like the *Gishi wajinden* [Chronicle of ancient Japanese history in the *History of Wei*], indicated that at the beginning of the Iron Age, the growth of classes and slavery accelerated. Slaves were initially provided by captives taken in conquest and were owned first by tribes and clans; then, with the growth of private property, they were owned privately by families to serve households and in productive labor.[123] Ultimately, a centralized tributary state emerged in the Kinai area out of warfare among clan-based *kyōdōtai*. The story of the rise of this state was supported by the mythological accounts of the classic *Kojiki* and *Nihon shoki*, and other records illustrated the state's collection of tribute and the enormous wealth and numerous slaves owned by the Imperial Household.[124]

What Akizawa found in documentary and archeological records fit nicely Engels's description of the collapse of the clan-based *kyōdōtai*, and the rise of private property, social classes, and slavery. This was the Yamato state, described in the *Gishi wajinden* as the most powerful state established from the second to early third centuries. Tribute was paid to the center, and the *benotami* system, which Akizawa identified as a Japanese variant of slavery involving both the *be* quasi-slaves and pure slaves, flourished. The evolution of private large-scale landownership by nobles and the growth of slavery mutually sustained and promoted one another and in turn hastened the demise of the kinship-based *kyōdōtai*. In general, slavery evolved from tribal-community owned slavery, to "patriarchal slavery," household slavery, and finally the classical slavery of Greece and Rome. The *Nihon shoki* revealed that even before the Taika reforms, slaves owned by nobility, temples, and shrines engaged in both agricultural production and handicraft production. Finally, the ancient *Man'yōshū* anthology of poems (volumes 2 and 7) offered evidence that slaves were the primary source of labor power in agriculture, and their use on private cultivated fields was a general phenomenon. Indeed, slavery had become "an essential component of the social system," once large landownership by the nobility had developed. Although Akizawa maintained that in pre-Taika Japan production by "semi-slave" *be* had "*decisively* greater significance than even production by slaves," nevertheless the system of slaves (*dohi*) had "essential significance" in understanding the role of the universal category of slavery in Japanese history. Citing household registers and the other sources cited above, Akizawa concluded that in Japan on the eve of the Taika reforms, slavery took not the classical Greek-Roman pattern, but the form of patriarchal or household slavery. In short, pre-Taika Japan had a household or patriarchal slavery "in transition to a large-scale system of slave labor."[125]

Even after the Taika reforms, while the slave system was crucial to production, the form of the *benotami* was predominant. Thus, Akizawa contended that the slave economy "was not a slave system in which a superstructure rose on the basis of huge numbers of slaves and their forced labor, as in the Athenian form of classical slavery at its height." Slaves were expensive, because of the inadequacy of their supply both before and after the Taika reforms; and as private property spread and demanded more labor power, the *be* system flourished as a supplement to slavery. Conversely, slavery itself hastened the demise of the *kyōdōtai* by necessitating that more of its members be transformed into *be*. In conclusion, Akizawa argued that "the *benotami* system was a Japanese variant of slavery."[126]

The impact of the Taika reforms was to weaken and ultimately destroy the state tribute system and establish a centralized despotism. While land was declared to be state-owned and redistributed to peasants, nobles, and government workers, private landownership survived in the form of large lands owned by some nobles, temples, and shrines. Nor were all *be* liberated. Meanwhile, slavery continued to develop along with private property; but slave ownership by nobles, temples, and shrines gradually evolved toward serf relations, as the large lands owned by nobles were transformed into feudal manors during and after the Ōchō period.[127]

The special historical factor that contributed to this peculiar variety of Japanese slavery identified by Akizawa was "uneven development" among the various regions of ancient Japan. The more slowly developing Ainu were a major source of slaves circa the Taika reforms, but captured Ainu could not immediately be used as slaves because of their low technical level. More important was the disparity in rates of development between clans in the central Kinai area, which formed the core of the ancient state, and the development of clans in outlying areas. This helped to explain both the concentration of slavery in the center and the coexistence of large landholdings approaching feudal manors on the one hand and the rural *kyōdōtai* on the other. Finally, this disparity accounted for the intense demand for slaves in some areas and the dearth of people with a sufficiently high level of development to function as slaves, hence the proliferation of the *be* semi-slave form. Finally, the continued underdevelopment of outlying localities impeded the development of slavery as a whole in Japan to the "classic" form it attained in Greece and Rome, and *kyōdōtai* relations were able to persist far longer than in the West. These further hindered the growth of commodity production and exchange as well as of commercial capital.[128]

While these special forces impeded the maturation of slavery in Japan, the growth of large landownership toward a manorial system enabled Japan to move into a feudal system after the Taika reforms in the Ōchō era. Indeed, the factors that determined the peculiar form of slavery in Japan necessitated the reforms and set the stage for this subsequent path of development. The uneven development of ancient Japan, the inadequate supply of slaves, made it necessary to use land distribution measures, based on the existing system of land division internal to the *kyōdōtai*, to break down the local communities that remained and to complete the establishment on the national scale of private property. As a result, commerce prospered somewhat, and private landownership flourished into a system of (feudal) rents. While immaturity in production prevented the Taika regime from abolishing the *be* completely, the growth of private landownership eventually enabled the remaining organizations of *be* to be dissolved and for "feudal" relations to mature.[129] The following, then, is the periodization schema that emerged from Akizawa's analysis:

	Taika reforms (645-649)	Ōchō era (Nara & Heian, 710-1184)
primitive clan *kyōdōtai* society ⟶	Slaveowner formation ⟶ slavery = dominant mode of production *be* = Japanese variant of slaves	state feudalism

What Akizawa left unresolved was whether Japan's "Asiatic" characteristics had made any contribution to the specific state feudalist form—especially in the superstructure—that emerged after the slavery era. This became a key issue that could not be avoided for Japanese Marxists who confronted the nature of Tokugawa feudalism and who sought therein the answer to Japan's continued underdevelopment in the countryside and in the political superstructure as late as the 1920s.

"Asiatic" Elements and the Transition from Feudalism to Capitalism

The participants in the debate on Japanese capitalism were somewhat less successful in specifying a materialistic interpretation of the "Asiatic" characteristics of Japanese feudalism than they were in analyzing ancient slavery. This was especially unfortunate, because the analysis of feudalism formed the crucial link tying a periodization of Japan's Asiatic past to the elements of Tokugawa feudalism that the Kōza-ha claimed persisted through the Meiji era and continued to impede and pervert Japan's capitalistic development as late as the 1920s. Since so much of this discussion is intimately linked to the broader debate on the agrarian question (explored in chapter 8), the material that follows will focus on the broad issues of geographical determination and of "state feudalism."

It was in fact in the context of the discussion of Tokugawa feudalism and the incompleteness of the Meiji Restoration as a bourgeois revolution that the entire issue of oriental society and the Asiatic mode of production first emerged in Kōza-ha writings. Those involved in the preparation of the *Kōza* drew support from the Comintern's explicit reference, less than a year after the Leningrad Conference, to the negative impact of Asiatic characteristics on the Japanese countryside: "The second of the main component parts of the ruling system of Japan is landlordism—this backward, Asiatic, semi-feudal system in the Japanese villages that hinders the development of productive forces, increases the degradation of agriculture, and pauperizes the peasant masses."[130] Marxists writing for the *Kōza* tended to interpret this passage to suggest that it was the Asiatic characteristics of Japanese agriculture that gave it its particularly oppressive character. Hayakawa, Aikawa, Hattori, Hani, and especially Hirano Yoshitarō took the lead in identifying the sources and qualities of these Asiatic characteristics and their implications for the nature of Japanese feudalism and its transition to capitalism.

The manner in which each of these scholars approached the analysis of feudalism was closely linked to his interpretation of the Asiatic mode of production. Hayakawa Jirō, for example, had followed the lead of Godes and Iolk and rejected the distinction of the Asiatic mode of production as a separate constellation of production forces and relations from the ancient, feudal, and bourgeois modes of production. Nevertheless, he did retain the term to refer narrowly to a system of tribute relations among *kyōdōtai*; and he allowed its application to Japan to refer strictly to such a set of arrangements based on state landownership. Hayakawa's conception of state landownership involving landownership on a national scale, rather than the mere coincidence of rents and taxes, was such that it would challenge the views of both Godes—who saw the Asiatic mode of production as simply a variant of feudalism unique to the East—and the mainstream views of Safarov, Mif, and the Institute for the Study of the China Problem, advocates of the notion that "Asiatic feudalism" was state feudalism, its main characteristic the identity of rents and taxes.[131] According to Hayakawa, even if the Asiatic mode of production were correctly understood to be a variant of feudalism, it did not exist in the Tokugawa era.

In Hayakawa's interpretation, the crucial characteristic of state landownership was its extension of authority over the land on a nationwide (*kokumin-teki*) scale. However, this definition did not apply where sovereignty over the land was divided among feudal lords, as in Tokugawa Japan (or medieval Europe). The shogunate did impose taxes on the daimyo and their peasants periodically; "but in the Edo period," Hayakawa argued, "taxes and ground rent were different forms." Hayakawa drew support for his usage of the notion of state landownership from the writings of Marx and Engels on Java and Tokugawa Japan.[132] In the Tokugawa era, in addition to "so-called local landlords," there were feudal lords who shared in state power. But this phenomenon alone was not sufficient to support a reference to state landownership in this period, for on this basis one would have to call twelfth-century France also an instance of state landownership, which Marx and Engels never did. Finally, there was, of course, the fact that Marx had, in *Capital*, declared Tokugawa Japan to be a version of feudalism that was more pure than even that of medieval Europe.[133]

A more appropriate example of state landownership, according to Hayakawa, was to be found in the feudalism of the Ōchō era. During this period, there were both private and state landownership, slaves as well as serfs, with serfs outnumbering slaves almost ten to one. The collection of ground rent was ordered and dominated by the center; a portion was given to the state, the rest allocated to nobility designated by the state. In this system, the nobility did not collect ground rent directly from the peasantry, as was the practice in the Edo period, but obtained it through the state. This Hayakawa designated a case of "state landownership." Here was a system that prevailed throughout Japan, in which ground rent was collected by state officials despatched by the center to the local areas.[134]

These generalizations were substantiated by government documents from the period. Along with classics like the *Nihon shoki*, they also portrayed the maturation of feudalism in Japan as the state landownership first established by the Taika reforms slowly gave way to the proliferation of private domains. During the Ōchō period, Japan had already begun to see the beginnings of a manorial system that spawned private armies for powerful families like the Genji and Heishi clans. Nevertheless, state landownership continued to coexist alongside private manors into the Kamakura period (1185-1382). In many cases, the boundaries between the administrative powers of provincial and district officials and property rights of manor lords were so vague that there were in effect double or triple ownership rights over the same piece of land.[135]

This state of affairs was further complicated by the Kamakura *bakufu*'s designation of manorial overlords or guards. These appointees were given authority—parallel to that of the daimyo themselves—over specific areas, and they levied taxes on manors within their purview. Over the years, these overlords competed with provincial governors and manorial lords for domination over the manors, and the system gradually progressed toward large feudal landownership. The civil strife on the Shōkyū War (1221) and the short-lived Kenmu Restoration led to the establishment of the Ashikaga shogunate, which centralized the state and advanced the process of the unification of landownership, which finally came to an end in the Warring States period (1467-1558). The form of feudal landownership established in this era, when the power of the center fell to its nadir, closely resembled the feudalism of the medieval period in Europe. After Toyotomi Hideyoshi unified the country, the Tokugawa regime simply legalized a system of feudalism that had already come into being in the Warring States period.[136]

Hayakawa's interpretation of the relationship between the political power of the state and the economic structure of feudalism from the Ōchō era to the Tokugawa period offers a plausible general schema within which to comprehend the changes that occurred historically in the character of Japanese feudalism. It is less successful, however, in its endeavor to trace the long-term impact of the Asiatic mode of production on Japanese development in the nineteenth and twentieth centuries. If the Asiatic mode of production was a tributary system based on state landownership, did it end with the Taika reforms, or only with the Warring States period? Hayakawa's analysis of the economic basis of the authority of the Tokugawa shogunate inadequately presented the qualitative difference between the power of this *bakufu* and that of the weak Ashikaga shogunate. Finally, Hayakawa's discussion offered little to illuminate those factors that continued to make the Japanese countryside "Asiatically backward," as the Kōza-ha and Comintern charged it to be as late as the 1920s.

Fellow Kōza-ha Marxist Hirano Yoshitarō was far more effective in this respect than was Hayakawa. Hirano's analysis of the impact of Asiatic characteristics on the transition from feudalism to capitalism was similarly based on a general interpretation of the applicability of Marx's "progressive epochs."[137] Hirano was concerned with the problem of the Asiatic mode of production because he believed that the deeply ingrained cultural patterns of submissiveness and passivity, etched by the ancient experience of "Asian despotism," were crucial factors explaining the failure of the revolution launched by the Meiji Restoration to produce a liberal-democratic bourgeois society—either the ideal or the reality—in Japan.[138]

Although Japan advanced rapidly to a European-style feudal system, Hirano argued that the impact of its experience with "Asiatic despotism" remained in evidence well after the Meiji period both in economic organization, particularly in the countryside, and in the cultural and political spheres. During the controversy on oriental society in the 1930s, Hirano traced this impact first in the Asiatic features of Japanese feudalism and then in the inadequacies of the Meiji Restoration. In Tokugawa feudalism, Hirano, like Hattori Shisō, saw special Asiatic elements remaining from the ancient Asiatic mode of production as the cause of the aggravation of an already severe degree of exploitation that was inherent in feudalism itself.[139] Yet, the arguments of the two Kōza-ha Marxists varied somewhat. Hattori did not develop the complicated historical schema that Hirano advocated, which saw the Asiatic mode of production as a system of total slavery that could occur in East or West. Rather Hattori had followed Godes closely and defined the Asiatic mode of production simply as the "most stubborn" and cruel form of feudalism, the defining characteristic of which was the pronounced lingering impact of earlier, more oppressive modes of production. Thus, in Hattori's view, a hallmark of the Asiatic form of feudalism as it existed in Japan was the existence of "starvation rents" (*kiga jidai*). In Japan, feudalism exhibited the "Asiatic special characteristic of taking the entire feudal ground rent in the form of taxes," "neither killing [the peasant] nor allowing [him] to live." Although private landowning grew throughout the Tokugawa period and the role of the state in oppressing the peasantry economically declined, Hattori argued that the state did use its power to revive aspects of the Asiatic mode of production, even in the late Tokugawa period. Hattori cited the Tokugawa regime's prohibition on the buying and selling of land, limitations on the merger of existing properties, the *shichikō-sanmin* tax law requiring that 70 percent of a year's crop be paid as ground rent, tribute, or tax to the feudal lord and only 30 percent kept as peasant income, and the imposition of even higher tax rates. That these measures ultimately failed to prevent the collapse of this Asiatic feudalism was the result of peasant revolts and the growth of contradictions inherent to feudalism, and not any lack of effort by the Tokugawa to make the system more durably oppressive.[140]

Hirano did not concur with Hattori's adoption of Godes's definition of the Asiatic mode of production as simply a more oppressive form of feudalism, but he did agree that Asiatic elements from the past were the key to the peculiarly backward, cruel, and stubborn form of feudalism in Japan. Certain of the special characteristics of Tokugawa feudalism, like "starvation rents" and the *han*'s powerful role in commodity production and exchange exercised through "state production offices," helped to hinder the progression from feudalism to capitalism.[141] Hirano did acknowledge the considerable extent to which the feudal system was gradually undermined during the Tokugawa period, concurring with Hattori's judgment on the growth of manufacture in dyeing, ceramics, sake brewing, and ore extraction and refining, the growth of commercial capital, and the spread of the putting-out (*Verlag*, or *toiya*) system. Nevertheless, this process of the collapse of feudalism and growth of capitalism was "deformed" because of the peculiarities of the feudal system in Japan, Hirano argued. For example, feudal lords boosted their deteriorating position by dominating commodity circulation through state production offices in their individual *han*, increased their oppression of serfs, and themselves became engaged in managing economic enterprises.[142] This activity was analogous to the economic role the state had played under the Asiatic mode of production.

As a result of these patterns, the growth of the bourgeoisie was stunted, and feudal production relations were reinforced rather than eroded. Consequently, it was not a rising bourgeoisie that propelled forward a bourgeois-democratic revolution. Rather, peasant uprisings, in response to more severe exploitation under increased tributes and miscellaneous *han*-imposed duties and forced labor, were the motive forces of the Meiji reforms. Significantly, these uprisings erupted most frequently in the areas most penetrated by a commodity economy and particularly in *han* where state production offices had emerged (e.g., Tosa, Suo, and Awa in Tokushima prefecture), or where there had been forced cultivation (e.g., Saga and Kagoshima). Moreover, because of the weakness of the "indigenous industrial bourgeoisie," the feudal system did not simply collapse but was unified in the Restoration and "immediately reorganized feudalistically vis-à-vis the peasantry." Since the bourgeoisie was not powerful enough to gain ascendancy at once, the successor to Tokugawa feudalism became the transitional "absolutist" state described by Marx, and the civil rights movement did not succeed until it became allied with the burgeoning labor movement in the late Meiji.[143]

Indeed, Hirano went on to argue that during what he saw as the reconstruction of feudal possession in the Meiji Restoration, "the ancient Asiatic system was recalled and ancient laws [were] copied" until as late as 1871. This reflected the "immaturity and low degree of development of bourgeois production forces in Japan" and was a key difference between the absolutism of Meiji Japan and the more progressive absolutism of Western Europe.[144] The reason for this stunted development lay in the original Asiatic characteristics of Tokugawa feudalism. As Hirano wrote:

> Japan's petty serf system, with special characteristics in an Asiatic mode of exploitation conditioned by a low-level agricultural mode of production, shrank the living resources of the petty serfs, the direct producers, to the lowest limit necessary to the body in the sense of only a vegetable existence [by starvation rents]. [In the latter Tokugawa era, this resulted from] the progression of exploitation based on the poverty of feudal lords in the period of the dissolution of feudalism that accompanied bourgeois development. Consequently, [the system] did not generally expand nation-wide its scale of production, the development of technology, agricultural implements (like threshers . . .), and commercial fertilizers; and in many instances this made agriculture solely dependent on such natural conditions as the fertility of the land and the weather.

In Hirano's view, this was a "mode of production that stabilizes and renders life stationary": both capital and labor lacked the dynamism essential to the birth of a capitalist economy. Thus, despite the signs of indigenous capitalist development cited by Hattori and others, petty handicraft production remained tightly linked to agriculture, as handicraftsmen were compelled to supplement their incomes by laboring in agriculture, and *han* enterprises survived on increased tribute paid by farmers.[145]

Even after the Meiji land tax reforms, the tribute relationship persisted between peasant and landlord, according to Hirano. At best, the post-Restoration land system was semi-feudal, as the Kōza-ha maintained that the content of agrarian rents remained customary and feudalistic in character, rather than capitalistically determined by free market forces (see chapter 8). Hirano and others argued that rents remained as high after the reforms as they had been in the Tokugawa era, discouraging the cultivation of rice as a commodity and leaving the peasant as little of his crop for personal income as had been the case before the land tax reforms. Hirano used the data presented in table 7 to support this argument. The Meiji state, resting on relations in the countryside that continued to be "Asiatically backward" and "semi-feudal," used the rural land system and the land tax to "coerce the process of the primitive accumulation of capital," a task the weak bourgeoisie could not perform.[146]

Hirano's notion of Asiatic feudalism as an explanation for Japan's continued backwardness in the agrarian and political spheres was widely shared among Kōza-ha scholars, even if they could not agree on a single conception of the Asiatic mode of production. Only Aikawa rejected any notion of Asiatic differences in Japanese feudalism, although in his essay on the

TABLE 7

Relative Proportions of Product Distributed to Landlords and the State

	State	Landlord	Tenant	Total
Percentages under tribute tax in kind in Tokugawa era	37%	28%	35%	100%
Percentages in accordance with land tax reforms	34%	34%	32%	100%
Percentages under tax reduction of 1877	30%	38%	32%	100%

SOURCE: Hirano Yoshitarō, *Nihon shihon-shugi shakai no kikō* [The structure of Japanese capitalist society] (Tokyo: Iwanami Shoten, 1934), p. 25.

"Agrarian Panic" for the *Kōza*, he had referred repeatedly to Japan's "Asiatically stagnant semi-feudal structure in the countryside" and its "Asiatically backward feudalistic petty agriculture." Aikawa criticized his own early position, fearing that aspects of social structure that were peculiar to Japan would be "dissolved" in a notion of Asiatic traits that indiscriminately lumped together peculiarities of China, India, and Japan. Thus he embarked on a concrete historical study of late Tokugawa feudalism, relying on Yamada Moritarō's classic *Analysis of Japanese Capitalism*.[147]

Aikawa began this analysis by rejecting the thesis that the Meiji cash land tax was identical to feudal ground rent, because, he argued, that formula led to "the 'Asiatic' mystification that the state was the collector of ground rent and a monopolistic land holder." Instead, Aikawa redefined the Meiji state as a "semi-feudal capitalist state": semi-feudal in that it "reaffirmed the basis of the land tax in cash ground rent (seizure of surplus product)," yet capitalist "insofar as it mobilized the cash 'land tax' system as the lever of the primitive accumulation of capital." In other words, the Meiji state relied on a feudalistic land system to pursue capitalist ends. The resulting system was only semi-feudal, because certain adjustments were made in the land system to pursue these new ends. The Meiji regime partially dissolved the large land holding "form" through its reforms, and the cash land tax "differed structurally from the tribute or ground rent in kind of the old feudal system"; yet agrarian rents (*kosakuryō*) still retained "the essence of feudal tribute, and part of it was still paid through the landlords as the land tax." This meant that the Asiatic characteristic of the whole of feudal ground rent being collected in the form of taxes had already been destroyed. By the Meiji era, then, the single subordination of the peasant to the state through taxes that were equivalent to ground rent had been replaced by a system of "two-layered" subordination in which the peasant paid ground rent to the landlord and tax to the state.[148]

Aikawa did not state explicitly where he believed that the "Asiatic" system had already been replaced by this dual system in the Tokugawa era. His repeated references to Tokugawa feudalism as "pure feudalism," however, suggest that he did not find the notion of "Asiatic feudalism" applicable to Tokugawa Japan. The elements alleged to characterize Asiatic feudalism were the following: 1) "State landownership" "characterized by 'the unity of feudalistic land possession and feudalistic landownership' " and the formal unity of rents and taxes; 2) The "village unit system," the *goningumi*, the "self-governing" units established by the shogun for the common people, modeled on the ancient *goho* system organizing groups of five households; 3) "The unity of petty agriculture and domestic industry"; and 4) The nature of urban organization and forms of industry, and of commercial and usury capital; the notion that "officials, merchants, and landlords" were all the same group of people. Aikawa argued that these characteristics applied to Tokugawa Japan less well than the definitions of classical feudalism supplied by Marx and by Soviet authorities Godes and I. I. Smirnov. In Aikawa's view, if one applied the notion of Asiatic feudalism postulating the unity of ground rents and taxes to the Tokugawa era, one would be arguing that the *han* lord was the highest landlord. That would be untenable. By contrast, the political hierarchy in which the shogun exercised domination over *han* lords neatly fit the classic conception of the hierarchical structure of feudalistic landownership.[149]

In this analysis, however, Aikawa never went on to identify the peculiar national characteristics of Tokugawa feudalism that he feared would be "dissolved" in a notion of Asiatic feudalism. Thus, Aikawa never satisfactorily evolved an alternative to the oriental society conception to resolve the question of the peculiarity versus universality of feudalism in Japan.

Conclusions

The Asiatic mode of production concept, whether originally intended to carry a geographical connotation or not, was the only answer Karl Marx offered to explain why the development of the East—especially China and India—failed to fit precisely the schema he evolved out of his own historical materialism. He himself knew very little of the non-Western world, having conducted no extended scholarly research on it; and it came to his attention almost as an afterthought, through the medium of Western European imperialism. Rather than performing his own study of social formations in the East to match his work on the West (which admittedly would have been a good deal to ask), Marx relied heavily on perceptions of the East offered by Hegel, Montesquieu, and others. Thus, the notion of the Asiatic mode of production may have originated as the product of Marx's systematic consideration of precapitalist economic formations in the *Grundrisse*. But the articulation of this mode of production remained incomplete; and the category of "oriental society," replete with assumptions drawn from "idealist" Western writings, became a convenient catch-all to apply to non-Western societies that fell too far short of the ideal patterns described by the "ancient," "feudal," and "capitalist" modes of production.

Marx's depiction of nineteenth-century Japan as pure feudalism would seem to defuse the Asiatic mode of production issue for Japanese Marxists. However, the extended discussion above demonstrates that it did not. Rather, the Asiatic mode of production theory became as problematic for Japanese Marxists as it was for their Chinese contemporaries. The reason for the persistent concern is that the problems of applying Marx's historical schema to a non-European setting that had originally compelled Marx to formulate a separate "Asiatic" mode of production remained unresolved. Therefore, the efforts of Stalinists to quash the discussion of the Asiatic mode of production at the Leningrad Conference of 1931 were destined to fail among native Asian Marxists. For them, it was still necessary to demonstrate a fit between Marx's schema and the socio-economic development of their countries, or their position that socialist revolution was historically inevitable was untenable. Godes, Iolk, and other critics of the Asiatic mode of production concept offered no convincing alternative means of doing this.

Godes had asserted that the theory was "politically harmful and methodologically incorrect" and "must be discarded," but it was clear that his conclusions were politically motivated by the power struggle in the Soviet Union and were not the product of a deep familiarity with the histories of China, India, and Japan. Thus, his claim that "the Asiatic mode of production is nothing other than feudalism," that "the Orient, in a very unique fashion, went through the same stages of social development as Europe,"[150] had a hollow ring to it. Anyone with the kind of knowledge about Chinese and Japanese history shared by indigenous historians and economists recognized immediately that such a fit between these experiences and those of England and France was difficult, if not impossible, to prove. Moreover, Godes's reference to the single "very unique fashion" in which the Orient repeated the European pattern simply begged the central question, while it upheld the old "Orientalist" premise of a vast, undifferentiated East. It is not at all surprising that, despite the conclusions of the Leningrad Conference, Japanese Marxists determined to examine the Asiatic mode of production question for themselves.

Since it was the Kōza-ha that saw in current Japanese development more significant departures from the Western pattern, it was the Kōza-ha that undertook this project. They studied the issue in the context of the massive historical scholarship and theoretical contemplation that was the hallmark of their contribution to the overall debate. But were they, on the basis of their historical research and acquaintance with Western theory, any more successful than Marx, Godes, and Iolk in evolving a satisfactory resolution to the issues underlying the theory of the Asiatic mode of production? Were they able to transcend the mystical concept of "oriental society" in identifying the peculiarities of Japanese development and reconciling those with Marx's general schema?

The writings examined here suggest that Japanese Marxists may have made significant progress in this direction, but they did so by referring to the Asiatic mode of production or to the possibility of parallel paths of development. All except Aikawa actively used the concept of the Asiatic mode of production to explain certain peculiarities of Japanese development. Aikawa himself maintained the Asiatic in the strict schema of unilinear progression prescribed by Marx; but his post-*Kōza* abandonment of the idea of "Asiatic feudalism" neglected the task of explaining Japan's deviations from that schema. Akizawa, Hayakawa, and Hattori all followed Godes in rejecting the notion that the Asiatic mode of production was a separate social formation, but their analysis of ancient Japanese slavery led them to reintroduce it, and it continued to carry some geographical specificity. Hirano probably offered the most satisfying interpretation, but this he never fully elaborated as an effort to periodize Japanese history, and we are left only with his more satisfying interpretations of Japan's recent political development as a consequence of its earlier experience.

Hirano's work is also compatible with that of Hani Gorō on the long-term consequences of Japan's Asiatic characteristics. Both Hirano and Hani developed interpretations of the peculiarities of Japanese capitalism by incorporating certain elements commonly identified with the Asiatic mode of production theory; but they did so without becoming enslaved by that somewhat muddled conception. Hani, like Hirano, drew on the writings of Wittfogel, Mad'iar, Varga, Max Weber, Guo Moruo, D. R. Gadgil, Pavel Mif, and S. M. Dubrovsky. They clearly had access to the contemporary debates on the Asiatic mode of production in the Soviet Union and China; yet, since their primary concern was to analyze Japanese capitalism, which had properties different from the political economies of Russia and China, they wisely drew their own conclusions.

Hani firmly rejected interpretations of the Asiatic mode of production based on water control (although he identified this theory not with Wittfogel but with Simcox, Weber, and Mad'iar), "conflict with nomadic peoples," and "surplus population." Instead, Hani adopted the view that the Asiatic mode was merely a variant of slave or serf society, in which coercion and oppression were especially cruel. Deeply imprinted with the characteristics of the ancient *kyōdōtai*, this "Asiatic mode of production" may indeed have taken the form of "unlimited ownership of the persons of the producers."[151] Thus, he wrote, "In such a sense and only in this sense can we speak of an Asiatic mode of production and a society based on it. *The Asiatic mode of production* is nothing more than *essentially* the *slave* or *serf mode of production*; however, it is more cruel and plagued by levels of contradictions because of the maintenance of backward, late-clan society relations."[152] Asiatic society, then, did not exist prior to class divisions; its state was based on class antagonisms, not only on the performance of common functions. And for Hani, as for Hirano, such an oriental society was not inconsistent with the development of feudalism and capitalism. China developed a feudal system with Asiatic characteristics, Hani argued, and this "feudal despotic structure" was forced to dissolve by the intrusion of foreign capitalism.[153]

According to Hani, in Japan the characteristics of Asiatic society were manifested in its ancient *be* system of community slave ownership. Since community ownership of land was also characteristic of this period, the development of private property, a requisite for feudalism and capitalism, was made more difficult. When private landownership appeared with commodity production, it retained some characteristics of the old tribal society, so that land came to be concentrated on a "state scale." Similarly, the *kōmin* (citizens) were not serfs of private landowners, but rather serfs of the state. These Asiatic characteristics of ancient Japan persisted in the feudal era; and the state at each point hindered the development of free economic activity among the populace. This explained the peculiar form of Japanese feudalism, and the difficulty of transforming commercial capital gained from *han* granaries and production offices into industrial capital. The Asiatic remnants of Japanese feudalism also accounted for the failure of Tokugawa feudalism to produce an absolutist government immediately. The forces of world capitalism forced the demise of Tokugawa feudalism and the rapid ascent of Japanese capitalism to the imperialist stage, even while Japan's Asiatic legacy made the completion of an indigenous bourgeois-democratic revolution impossible. Having lived under Asiatic despotism, the Japanese had lost all aspirations to individual freedom. "Feudal production relations . . . under the Asiatic form . . . were now maintained in order to repress the people under imperialism." Only the newly awakened proletariat could complete this bourgeois-democratic revolution so long after Japanese capitalism had advanced to the imperialist stage.[154]

These observations by Hirano and Hani on the Asiatic mode of production and its manifestation in Japan formed a tiny part of the voluminous writings of the Kōza-ha. Nevertheless, they had great significance for the Kōza-ha's position in the debate on Japanese capitalism. On the one hand, they made significant progress in reaffirming the position of Japan and other non-European countries in Marx's theory of social development and revolution. In Hani's words, "the so-called colonization of India, the semi-colonization of China, and Japan's opening of ports and Meiji Restoration are none other than the oriental historic expression of world-historical laws."[155] At the same time, the notion of oriental society helped to attest to the peculiarities of Japanese capitalism that required that it still undergo a bourgeois-democratic revolution. The notion thus helped to fill some crucial gaps in the Kōza-ha theory, particularly concerning the state. The emperor system and its ideology could be recognized as a mere myth "common to Asia's monsoon belt."[156] This emperor system was not harmless, however, for it maintained a material basis in economic arrangements, particularly in the agrarian sector, that continued to be tinged with Asiatic characteristics. If these Asiatic-tinged remnants of feudalism and absolutism were not destroyed through bourgeois-democratic revolution, the proletarian revolution advocated by the JCP simply could not materialize.

These remarks best summarize the outcome of the debate within the Kōza-ha on the Asiatic mode of production. The Rōnō-ha, of course, always maintained that the Japanese experience did not diverge significantly from that of the West, and never acknowledged the need to examine the Asiatic mode of production more closely. To this extent, whatever the shortcomings of the Kōza-ha analyses, it is to their credit that they recognized the need for this difficult theoretical task and undertook the massive scholarly endeavor required to accomplish it.

SEVEN

The Emperor System and the Marxist Theory of the State

THE MASSIVE role of the state in Japan's economic development since the Meiji period gave the analysis of the state a central place in the debate on Japanese capitalism. For participants in the controversy, the existing Japanese state represented a decidedly mixed legacy. The Meiji oligarchs' "revolution from above" had constituted a sort of "enlightened despotism" that saved Japan from the fate of China.[1] Yet, in the words of historian E. H. Norman, "the speed and manner of the transition from feudal to new Japan" in the Meiji period involved tremendous costs: "a disproportionally heavy tax burden on the agricultural classes, . . . the stunting of enterprises less vital than those connected with defense, and . . . a general impatience at any sign of unrest or democratic protest which might precipitate a domestic crisis and so hinder or retard the task of reconstruction."[2] It was against these social costs and this repressive state, the roots of which lay deep in the Meiji period, that Japanese Marxists in the 1920s and 1930s championed revolution.

THE THEORY OF THE STATE AND THE DEBATE ON JAPANESE CAPITALISM

In the debate on Japanese capitalism, the issue of the state demanded special attention because it posed major problems for the adaptation of Marxist theory to Japan. Two major issues were: (1) how to interpret the leading role of the Meiji state in Japan's economic development in Marxist terms; and (2) how to interpret the class character of the imperial state as it had evolved by the Shōwa period. The first issue was raised by the success of the purposeful intervention of the Meiji state in the economy. In Karl Marx's original paradigm, the state was part of a superstructure that was determined by the economic basis of a given society.

> It is always the direct relationship of the owners of the conditions of production to the direct producers—a relation naturally corresponding to a definite stage in the development of the methods of labour and thereby its social productivity—which reveals the innermost secret, the hidden basis of the entire social structure, and with it the political

> form of the relation of sovereignty and dependence, in short, the corresponding specific form of the state.[3]

Marx saw "the centralized State power, with its ubiquitous organs of standing army, police, bureaucracy, clergy and juridicature—[as] organs wrought after the plan of [i.e., stemming from] a systematic and hierarchic division of labor."[4] While Marx and Engels acknowledged that the political might have some effect on the economic sphere, the latter remained dominant in the classical Marxian conception.

In recent years, however, the study of economic revolutions conducted from above—as in Meiji Japan and Bismarckian Germany—has led many contemporary Marxist scholars to revise this classical conception by introducing the notion of the "relative autonomy" of the state.[5] In this view, the basic classical Marxist notion of the state remains intact: the state is "a set of administrative, policing, and military organizations headed, and more or less well-coordinated by, an executive authority. Any state first and fundamentally extracts resources and deploys these to create and support coercive and administrative organizations." Yet, the traditional Marxian conception is modified in that the state is "at least potentially autonomous from direct dominant class control."[6] The state has its own life, its own rationality, a raison d'être that may conflict with the interests of the dominant socio-economic class. This perspective releases one from the confines of a strict Marxian class analysis where it may be least appropriate—when a "modernizing" society is in transition from traditional social and economic patterns to new ones, particularly if this occurs under external pressure. Such an approach also permits one to view the state as an independent actor initiating, rather than simply reflecting, economic change. The notion of the "relative autonomy of the state" may even approach a reversal of the classical Marxist causal relationship between base and superstructure when it is used to support an analysis of modernizing revolutions from above. Applying this reinterpretation of Marxism to Meiji Japan, for example, Ellen Kay Trimberger has completely rejected the characterization of Tokugawa Japan as feudalistic and has emphasized the role of "autonomous" state bureaucrats instead of lower samurai and merchants in executing the Meiji regime's "revolution from above."[7]

In the 1920s and 1930s, such a revision of Marxist theory to accord with Japan's historical realities was not a palatable option for the participants in the debate on Japanese capitalism. Their task was to support the premise of an inevitable revolution, whether pursued in one stage or two, by demonstrating that Japan's economic and political history fit the orthodox Marxian categories of social transformation from feudal to capitalist and then socialist modes of production. This was a disturbing problem indeed, since Japan's developmental experience since the Meiji period differed so markedly from the pattern that Marx and Engels had observed in France and England. Fifty years before the notion of the "relative autonomy of the state" gained currency among Western Marxists, Japanese Marxists confronted the phenomenon in their own national history and endeavored to explain it with as little deviation as possible from Marx's original schema. This self-appointed task challenged them to wrestle with complex issues not only with respect to the theory of the state, but also with regard to the tensions between the universality and particularity of Marxism itself.

The difficulty arose largely because the pattern of Western European capitalist development itself assured that the process in later developing ("follower") nations would diverge from the original British and French models. The development of capitalism in Western Europe, in short, could not be duplicated because this pattern forever obliterated the international conditions that had nurtured English and French development. Thus, even if the internal conditions of follower societies could be identical, which in any case was unlikely, the international environment that permitted Britain and France unhampered capitalistic development had all but disappeared. By the latter third of the nineteenth century, capitalist development in Britain and France had culminated in the formation of a global capitalist system, as the Western powers carved out spheres of influence through colonization and trade in Asia, Africa, and the Americas.[8]

This transformation of the international milieu had at least three effects on regions outside Western Europe. First, because the superior military technology of industrial capitalism clearly established its ability to dominate "traditional" economies in Asia and Africa, scholars and statesmen of the non-Western world increasingly identified capitalist industrialization with "modernization" and accepted it as the objective and normative future of their own societies. Besieged by the military prowess of Britain, France, and the United States, leaders of the Meiji Restoration, like China's self-strengtheners, finally, if reluctantly, embraced the path of the West as their own destiny, rejecting many indigenous social and economic institutions as "backward" and useless.[9] Secondly, just as "late developers" adopted the dream of industrial capitalism, the new international system effectively denied them certain mechanisms that had promoted industrial capitalism in Western Europe. As Takahashi Kamekichi observed in the 1920s (see chapter 4), the free trade and colonial expansion that had helped to sustain the growth of European capitalisms were no longer feasible in a world that had already been divided into exclusive economic zones. In addition, as Marxist Uno Kōzō would argue in the 1930s, certain markets, and therefore development strategies, were preempted by the prior paths of development pursued by England, the United States, and Germany. Just as Germany depended on heavy industry and chemicals because it could not compete with the textile industry that had been the core of England's early capitalist development, so Japan could not readily develop an export trade in heavy industrial goods because it could not compete in this field with the United States, England, and Germany.[10]

Finally, as a result of the political, economic, and military pressures imposed by advanced Western European states, capitalist industrialization came to be pursued by follower nations in a deliberate goal-oriented fashion, rather than through the willy-nilly process that had characterized English and French development. As such societies have "typically searched for substitutes to the factors which were conditions of development in the advanced countries,"[11] the state has assumed a comparatively larger role in the economic development of follower nations than it did in the model of capitalism described by Marx and Engels. Seeking "to overcome the sources of their own instability which arise from the special tensions created by backwardness,"[12] governments in late industrializers of Asia, as in Germany and Russia, have played a major role "in furthering economic modernization, especially in mobilizing and spending investment funds."[13]

Japanese Marxists knew of the German experience; the founders of the Meiji regime had relied heavily upon its example to create the constitution and institutions of the new state. Nevertheless, Japanese Marxists were understandably loath to associate the destiny of their own country too closely with that of Germany, for by the late 1920s and early 1930s, the collapse of the Weimar Republic into fascism was clearly imminent. Moreover, if Japan's Marxists did not wish to identify Japan fully with the stagnant despotic Asia of Marx's conception, how then could they reconcile the dominant economic activity of their own state with the orthodox Marxist view of the state as the mere tool of the ruling class?

This issue was related to a second problem: the dual character of the Japanese economy and of the state in late Taishō and Shōwa Japan. On the one hand, there appeared to be a dichotomy in the state structure—elements of both bourgeois democracy and feudal autocracy—that corresponded to the dual structure of the economy as a whole: the coexistence of a highly concentrated, capital-intensive heavy industrial and financial sector alongside a small-scale, labor-intensive agricultural and light industrial sector.[14] At the same time, as the Comintern's '27 Theses noted, there seemed to be a disparity between the nature of the economic base—which bore many of the features of highly developed and trustified finance capitalism—and the political superstructure, which, despite the formal constitutional structure of parliamentary democracy, was characterized by remnants of an earlier era: the emperor, the Privy Council, the *genrō*, and powerful military advisors. Marx's writings on the state were sufficiently ambiguous to leave open a wide range of interpretation of this phenomenon. Although Marx postulated a direct relationship between the nature of the economic base of a society and its political superstructure, he also substantially weakened this formula by asserting that this link "does not prevent the same economic basis—the same from the standpoint of its main conditions—due to innumerable different empirical circumstances, natural environment, racial relations, external historical experiences, etc., from showing infinite variations and gradations in appearance."[15] Marx's ambiguity on the state enabled Japanese Marxists to defend a position stressing either the universality of the Japanese state (the Rōnō-ha) or its peculiarities (the Kōza-ha).

The question of the monarchy quickly emerged as pivotal in this controversy. The continued presence of what the Kōza-ha labelled the "emperor system" (*tennō-sei*) signalled to JCP loyalists that the state power born of the Meiji Restoration and becoming increasingly authoritarian under military pressure in the early Shōwa period was not bourgeois democracy.[16] The emperor and its supporting institutions were remnants of the past that thwarted the realization of parliamentary democracy in Japan and had to be removed before the tasks of bourgeois-democratic revolution begun by the Restoration could be deemed complete. Thus, *Kōza* theorists fully supported the demand to abolish the emperor system that had been written into the JCP's original program, at Comintern insistence but only after protracted debate, in 1922.

By contrast, for theorists of the *Rōnō* position, the presence of the emperor did not negate the democratic nature of the Meiji state, which was amply evidenced by the existence of the Diet, political parties, cabinet rule, and government by constitution (as opposed to government by fiat). The minor inadequacies of democracy in Japan did not prevent the revolution from proceeding immediately to the proletarian stage. The imperial institution, in effect, did not occupy a central position in the current regime for Rōnō-ha Marxists; like the British throne, it was a "bourgeois monarchy." The Rōnō-ha drew a distinction between the imperial institution, as a bourgeois monarchy relatively independent of the class conflict within the society, and the "emperor system" that the Kōza-ha identified more strongly with feudal forces and with uniquely Japanese elements. To the extent that feudal forces continued to impair Japanese democracy, their influence would gradually decline until the *tennō-sei* itself disappeared. If this did not occur until the state itself "withered away" after the proletarian revolution, this would pose no theoretical problem for *Rōnō* Marxists.[17] For the Kōza-ha, then, the emperor was the determining element of the Japanese state structure, the key to identifying its underlying class basis; for the Rōnō-ha, it was a mere appendage of the state apparatus.

But was the emperor system truly "meaningless" in the Rōnō-ha critique? Or did the Rōnō-ha's opposition to the Comintern's call to abolish the emperor system signify a strong sentimental attachment to the imperial institution that Russians in the Comintern could not possibly comprehend? Could such an attachment explain the reluctance of many Japanese Marxists to treat the *tennō-sei* in the objective terms required by Marx's theory of the state and to attack it as revolutionary theory demanded? The failure of certain participants in the debate on Japanese capitalism, particularly on the Rōnō-ha side, to analyze the emperor system in a dispassionate manner reveals certain constraints on the acceptance of Marxism as a theoretical system and suggests the limits of its adaptability to Japan.

This interpretation is supported by the phenomenon of *tenkō*, which finally engulfed, with few exceptions, Marxists of all factions by the 1940s.[18] In attempting to reintegrate *tenkōsha* (apostates from communism) into Japanese society, the government attempted to distinguish among those who abandoned the communist movement for political, religious, and social reasons.[19] Nevertheless, all Marxists of this generation had been inculcated in the traditional Japanese family-state *kokutai* conception,[20] an idea that combined religious, political, and social elements into a single notion of the "national polity." To call oneself a Marxist, to apply the Marxist theory of the state to Japan's allegedly unique imperial institution, and to accept the Comintern directive to endeavor to abolish the emperor system was to provoke in a Japanese revolutionary a kind of identity crisis. To do this was to define oneself outside of the Japanese political, civil, and spiritual community, for all three aspects were entwined in the mystical notion of the *kokutai*.[21]

Despite this cultural dilemma confronting Japanese Marxists, participants in the debate on Japanese capitalism tackled the theory of the state with vigor. Marxism had become appealing in Japan precisely because it was perceived to be the most advanced scientific and universal political theory available, yet the *kokutai* family-state ideology presumed the uniqueness of the Japanese polity.[22] The emperor was the pivotal element in official *kokutai* thought, articulated in the Meiji period and disseminated thereafter through a universal education system. In indigenous Japanese thought, the emperor (*tennō* or *mikado*) conjoined the concepts of nation and state: the political body of the state was one with the ethnic and social community of the nation. The emperor headed both as the spiritual and ethnic patriarch of the uniquely Japanese "national polity" (*kokutai*) and as the political ruler of the constitutional monarchic state. Since the Meiji Restoration, the emperor had been an authoritarian monarch to whom Article One of the Meiji Constitution gave full sovereignty. He was the supreme commander of the armed forces, whose military authority was independent of the cabinet. And he was the paramount spiritual authority, analogous to the medieval Western king who ruled by "divine right."[23]

This conception of the Japanese polity had powerful mystical elements drawn from Shintō mythology concerning the emperor and the origins of the Japanese people (*minzoku*). Its heavily particularistic content modified the impact of the general theories of state sovereignty offered by German scholars like Hermann Roesler, who influenced the drafting of the Meiji Constitution.[24] The conventions of Meiji and Taishō Japan, supported by the state's effective police network, had prohibited direct discussion of the emperor system itself and discouraged speculation on the legitimate origins of government in abstract and universalist terms.[25] Even the heated controversy between Uesugi Shinkichi's authoritarian interpretation of the Meiji Constitution (*tennō shuken ron*, the view that sovereignty resided in the emperor) and Minobe Tatsukichi's emperor-organ theory (the notion that the emperor and Diet were both mere organs of the state, and the state was the locus of sovereignty) was conducted entirely in legalistic terms, as a debate between broad and narrow constructions of Article One of the Meiji Constitution delineating the power of the throne. For both Uesugi and Minobe, the emperor system was a given. Its legitimacy was not open to judgment by abstract general theories on the origins of government.[26]

In the early Meiji period, the German *Staatsrecht* thought of J. K. Bluntschli and Georg Jellinek had been foremost among Western theories contributing to the development of Japanese political thought. Along with the less influential British constitutional theory, which supported Japan's party cabinet system in the 1890s, this strand of German thought was combined with the Kokugaku school's *sonnō* (revere the emperor) thought of the Tokugawa period to form the emperor-centered official orthodoxy of the Hozumi Yatsuka school at Tokyo Imperial University.[27] Apace with the consolidation of Meiji imperial power, these imported European theories were absorbed into Shintō and *kokutai* thought, their abstract generality gradually but steadily superseded by the special elements of native Japanese thought on the emperor system. Thenceforth these legal ideas on the state no longer fulfilled the role of a universalist theory untainted by the mystification and particularism of the emperor system ideology.

In Marxism, then, Japanese intellectuals of the third generation since the Restoration for the first time found a tool with which to analyze politics in general. The abstract categories of Marxist thought could be applied systematically to study the relationship between state and society, concepts hitherto collapsed, or undifferentiated, in traditional Japanese thought. The heretical implications of this general theory were no deterrent to its application by Japanese Marxists: until the early 1930s, intellectuals working as university scholars were treated less harshly by the police and were left relatively free to dabble in the application of Marxist thought on the state to Japan.[28] To such scholars, the debate on Japanese capitalism offered an opportunity to reexamine with a critical eye all they had previously accepted about their society and polity, but Marxist theory itself would not emerge unscathed. To the extent that Japan's experience diverged from Marx's generalizations about states in Europe as well as in Asia, participants in the controversy discovered lacunae in what many have argued is the least developed aspect of Marxist thought—the theory of the state.[29] Consequently, many of the insights produced in the controversy on the Japanese state anticipated developments in Western Marxism over the past decade and implicitly raised issues that have been neither addressed nor resolved in the West. The debate is examined here, then, for what it reveals concerning Japan's political development as well as for what it suggests about the strengths and weaknesses of a Marxist approach to the state itself.

The Rōnō-ha and the Advanced Capitalist State

Yamakawaism and the Rōnō-ha's Analysis of the Japanese State

The strategic formula of Yamakawa Hitoshi (Yamakawaism), which dominated the first JCP from its birth until its dissolution in 1924, provided the framework for the Rōnō-ha's approach to the Japanese state. After the Rōnō-ha seceded from the party late in 1927, Yamakawa continued to write short pieces about practical revolutionary work and did not contribute directly to the kind of sustained theoretical analysis that Inomata Tsunao performed on behalf of the Rōnō-ha. Nevertheless, Yamakawa's judgment that the political and economic situation was ripe for an immediate socialist revolution steered the Rōnō-ha toward a treatment of the contemporary state that differed dramatically from the Kōza-ha's analysis. Indeed, this view has persisted, with some modifications, to the present day, in the form of the political program of the left wing of the Japanese Socialist Party articulated by the late Sakisaka Itsurō.

The Kōza-ha's concern with the "semi-feudal" character of the emperor-system state led it to seek the historical roots of the state and its imperfections in Meiji "absolutism" (*zettai-shugi*). The Rōnō-ha, however, declared that the emperor system since the Meiji Restoration was a "bourgeois monarchy, and [that] absolutist structures are merely . . . remnants that are no longer of any significance."[30] Thus, the Kōza-ha probed the historical development of "structural" links between the "feudal remnants" in the state and economic backwardness in the countryside; but the Rōnō-ha asserted the primacy of capitalism in contemporary Japan and viewed the state as a composite of bourgeois factions producing policies designed to serve the interests of Japanese capitalism.

The premises of Yamakawaism guided the Rōnō-ha to a straightforward approach to the relationship between politics and economics that Western Marxists have recently come to label "instrumentalist." Based on the notion that the state is the mere "*instrument* of the ruling class" because it is controlled by a self-conscious ruling class,[31] this approach examines "the nature of the class which rules, the mechanisms which tie this class to the state, and the concrete relationships between state policies and class interests."[32] Because such a perspective on the part of the Rōnō-ha reaffirmed the supremacy of capitalist economic relations in Japan, it strengthened Yamakawa's case for the elimination of a communist party geared to conditions of underdevelopment and its replacement by a united front proletarian political party that would pursue a single-stage socialist revolution immediately. Finally, in breaking with the JCP, the Rōnō-ha asserted that the peculiarities of Japan's situation in the late 1920s precluded the kind of analogies the Comintern drew with Russia before the February revolution of 1917.[33] Nevertheless, at the same time, their strict ("instrumentalist") adherence to the dictum in the *Communist Manifesto* that "the executive of the modern state is but a committee for managing the common affairs of the whole bourgeoisie"[34] induced them to submerge the peculiar attributes of the Japanese state in universal characteristics alleged to typify all capitalist states. Many weaknesses of the Rōnō-ha's analysis then were also the weaknesses of an instrumentalist approach.

Still other difficulties in the Rōnō-ha's approach to the state stemmed from problems in the faction's guiding strategic doctrine, Yamakawaism. Against the Comintern's view that Japan's uneven development and backwardness in the agrarian sphere required a vanguard party to lead a two-stage revolution, Yamakawa and Inomata counterposed a model of a highly advanced capitalist state dominated by the "imperialist bourgeoisie."[35] In his essay launching the organ *Rōnō*, "Toward a Political United Front!" (December 1927), Yamakawa established the basis for Inomata's theoretical analysis of the state by reviewing briefly the historical course by which Japan had attained the "stage of monopoly finance capital." Yamakawa thereupon described the consequences of this development for contemporary politics and related these elements to his prescription for a united front political party.

Yamakawa asserted that the Meiji Restoration had "proclaimed the transition from feudal society to capitalist society" in Japan, even though it had been carried out not by its "weak and immature" bourgeoisie but by "mainly lower-stratum *bushi* (samurai)." The latter, having lost their own feudal economic basis, "could stand on the economic base of the rising bourgeoisie and represent that class's interests . . . as [the *bushi*'s] only means of survival.'' Since political power did not fall into the hands of the bourgeoisie immediately, a transitional absolutist *hanbatsu* government[36] emerged, and the completion of the tasks of bourgeois revolution required an additional fifty years. The *hanbatsu* regime was a bureaucratic and military government that lacked any economic basis of its own and represented the interests of the still rising bourgeoisie. These ''absolutist remnant forces'' were gradually assimilated into the forces of the bourgeoisie during capitalist development through four processes: (1) the maturation and strengthening of the bourgeoisie relative to feudal forces; (2) the increased importance of state capital and a lessening of its dependence on private capital; (3) the decline of the significance of agriculture and the transformation of landlords into capitalists; and (4) the deepening of the imperialist character of Japanese capitalism, reflecting the expansion of monopolistic finance capital and the increase in the ''reaction'' of the bourgeoisie. As a result of these changes, ''the nobility, bureaucracy, *gunbatsu* [military cliques], etc. no longer constituted any fundamental opposition to the bourgeoisie.'' They were simply integrated, as they were, into the structure of bourgeois political power. Moreover, ''the landlord class [had] become completely subordinated to the bourgeoisie.'' The final consolidation of bourgeois rule was manifested in the birth of a party cabinet system. As Yamakawa wrote in 1928 and 1929, then, the proletariat confronted an ''imperialistic, reactionary, bourgeois political power which [had] assimilated and strengthened the absolutist remnant forces.''

An alliance between the ''imperialistic bourgeoisie'' and rural landlords was evident in economic concessions made by the former to the latter. Thus, by 1928, the Comintern view, which saw an antagonism between landlord forces in the Seiyūkai and the urban commercial and industrial bourgeoisie, represented by the Kenseikai, was completely mistaken, Yamakawa argued. Rather, the combination of the two forces, abetted by the extension of universal suffrage, had resulted in ''the bourgeoisie and the proletariat not only being for the first time . . . mutually antagonistic classes, but also being the only two classes directly opposing each other.'' This situation paralleled the Russian case not on the eve of but after the February revolution and the fall of the tsarist autocracy.[37]

This analysis of capitalist development in Japan supported Yamakawa's organizational doctrine of a united front proletarian political party. By the late 1920s, Yamakawa argued, ''forces which formerly had had a reactionary character . . . are rapidly forming, around the forces of monopolistic finance capital, into a powerful reactionary, imperialistic force.'' The strategy of this bourgeois political force was ''to cause the complete isolation of the proletariat and its allies, the peasants.'' Therefore, Fukumotoism, or "splinterism within the proletarian movement, . . . [essentially] cooperates with this basic policy of the bourgeoisie." To the self-defeating strategy of Fukumotoism, Yamakawa counterposed his organization, which would conduct revolutionary struggle by operating as an open political party. It would constitute a united front because it would "fuse a powerful anti-bourgeois political force against the reactionary imperialist bourgeoisie, mobilizing all classes and social strata to function as an . . . opposing force." Finally, it would be a proletarian party, because "it is the proletariat which is made to bear the leading responsibility in the anti-bourgeois political force; . . . its allies are poor peasants—primarily semi-proletarian tenant farmers"—while the petty bourgeoisie was merely a potential, but unreliable, ally. The proletarian political party was thus a "special form of the united front," in the shape of a political party whose aim "was not necessarily socialism but a struggle to obtain democracy." This struggle for democracy was not equivalent to the JCP's demand for "bourgeois democracy" against "absolutist autocracy," but rather constituted the struggle of "the workers, peasants, and all other laboring peoples and oppressed people demanding democracy against the rule of the imperialist bourgeoisie." The goals of this party, therefore, were limited, and, accordingly, "the influence of [revolutionary proletarian] vanguard elements" must be restricted: "The vanguard can grow and mature only in relationship to the masses."[38]

If this presentation of Yamakawa's notion of a "political united front" appears muddled, it reflects the confusion in the conception itself. It is not clear if Yamakawa's ultimate goal remained socialism, and, if so, how his united front proletarian political party would advance that goal. Moreover, Yamakawa never adequately responded to the question of why the Japanese left-wing movement required a proletarian political party as a "special form of the united front." He vaguely mentioned the "specialness" of the Japanese state, but instead of describing the state's special features in detail, Yamakawa simply defended himself by attacking the "sectarian splinterists" in the JCP. Indeed, he went so far as to argue that the Fifth Comintern Congress of June 1924 had actually provided support for him by criticizing the "sectarians" opposed to the merger of the existing Japanese proletarian parties.[39] In 1928, there was a need for such a merger of the four proletarian political parties, a need, Yamakawa argued, imposed by a mass demand for a "united front" "boiling up . . . from below."[40] But could this demand be met? If so, how? Was the single proletarian political party a viable and defensible strategy under Japan's "special" conditions? Did not the oppressive measures of the Thought Police preclude such a strategy? To Inomata Tsunao fell the task of answering these questions by means of a detailed analysis of the contemporary Japanese state.

CHAPTER SEVEN

Inomata Tsunao and the Nature of the Advanced Capitalist State

Inomata Tsunao's "Gendai Nihon burujoajii no seiji-teki chi'i" [The political position of the contemporary Japanese bourgeoisie], published in the November 1927 issue of *Taiyō*, presented the theoretical position of the Rōnō-ha on the character of the Japanese state. Inomata's point of departure was the '27 Theses' stipulation that "The contemporary Japanese state, despite all its feudal appendages and remnants, is the most concentrated expression of Japanese capitalism and the embodiment of its entire major life nervous system."[41] Inomata agreed with the JCP and the Comintern Theses that the Meiji state had been a "paternalistic, autocratic," and absolutist government that had promoted the growth of capitalism in Japan. He also conceded that the remnants of the feudal forces involved in Meiji absolutism (*zettai-shugi*) continued to exercise influence in the 1930s, through institutions such as the Privy Council, the House of Peers, and the *i'aku jōsō* (the military's direct access to the throne), as well as in feudalistic ideology.[42] Like others in the Rōnō-ha, however, Inomata did not ascribe to the imperial institution itself a dominant feudal character; and he perceived in the Japanese state from Meiji to Shōwa much more fundamental change than did the Kōza-ha. The embourgeoisement of landlords in Japan, as in England, he argued, had eroded the material basis of the feudal forces that had dominated the Meiji state. As this bourgeoisified landed class allied with the burgeoning forces of monopoly finance capital, particularly after World War I, rule by feudal autocratic forces gave way to a mature bourgeois state in Japan. In making this argument, Inomata not only offered a reinterpretation of modern Japanese political history; he also developed an instrumentalist analysis of the state that showed how the Taishō and Shōwa state acted on behalf of the now powerful bourgeoisie.

FEUDAL ABSOLUTIST FORCES AND THE EMERGENCE OF A CAPITALIST STATE IN JAPAN. In *Gendai Nihon kenkyū* [Studies on contemporary Japan], a series of articles published in 1927 and 1928, Inomata offered an historical perspective on the role of "so-called feudal absolutist forces" in the Meiji state and in the emergence of Japanese capitalism. This historical interpretation was key to Inomata's support for the Rōnō-ha's position, for it was here that Inomata explained the replacement of the dominance of feudal forces in the Meiji era by the supremacy of the bourgeoisie in the 1920s and 1930s. Inomata admitted that "feudal remnant forces" had not been effectively resisted and eliminated in Japan, presumably until the Taishō and Shōwa eras, when the influence of the civil and military bureaucracy declined vis-à-vis that of bourgeois political parties. The problem was that Inomata could not deny the peculiarity of the conditions that had resulted in the tenacity of these feudal remnant forces. From the outset, then, there was a conflict in Inomata's analysis between the need to explain the persistence of feudal absolutist institutions in the state and then to demonstrate and explain their sudden loss of significance—particularly in the face of the rising influence of the military in the late 1920s and 1930s—in an advanced capitalist state.

This dilemma was sharpened by Inomata's limited perceptions of the role of the military. While he drew heavily on Nikolai Bukharin's observations on the nature of advanced capitalist states,[43] he neither developed Bukharin's theories any further nor exploited Bukharin's ideas on the military to support the Rōnō-ha's view of the state. The military might have been viewed as either a feudalistic or a capitalistic force, depending on which class interests it served. Thus, Bukharin had observed that the age of imperialism had caused the military to assert increasing powers in capitalist states. One of Inomata's fellow Rōnō-ha members, Okada Sōji (1902-1975), agreed with Bukharin that "what is 'militarist' today is not just [peculiar] to Japanese capitalism, but is a characteristic common to all capitalist countries."[44] Yet, Inomata, anxious to disprove the Comintern's thesis that "feudal autocratic" militaristic forces remained dominant in Japan, never challenged the Comintern's assumption that the military in Japan was a feudal force in the 1920s and 1930s. As a result, Inomata confined himself to what he saw as indicators of the steadily rising influence of the bourgeoisie from Meiji to Shōwa, and the military did not figure prominently in his description of the contemporary state. Here, Inomata's eagerness to defend the Rōnō-ha position on the state by submerging the particular into the general served to weaken his analysis. As a result of a historical discussion that led him to underestimate the peculiarities of the Japanese state in the 1920s and 1930s—particularly those in the emperor system and the military—Inomata's work could not fully justify Yamakawa's political strategy.

Yet Inomata was not unaware of the role of the military in helping to propel Japan's capitalist development "by huge wartime establishments and successful wars."[45] Japan had been spurred on to imperialist expansion "based on military [rather than financial] supremacy" early in its development, Inomata argued, because of the scarcity of its own resources, "the weaknesses of neighboring oriental countries and the pressures of the imperialist countries on them." Japanese capitalism then grew apace with the acquisition of territories and economic rights abroad in the Sino-Japanese, Russo-Japanese, and the First World wars. As a result of this military activity, Japan gained a solid position in world silk and other commodity production and was exploiting colonies and semi-colonies "capitalistically," even while it remained a net importer of foreign capital. Yet, this constant warfare also generated "rapid growth in armaments, along with militarization and financial difficulties,'' which enabled the military to maintain an important role long after the traditional *bushi*'s economic basis had disappeared.[46]

The military establishment that supported this expansionist activity, as well as the nobility, a large landlord class, and the bureaucracy, were feudal remnants whose material basis had been the feudal landownership system of the Tokugawa period, Inomata argued. This distinctive system, which did not produce the large estates and powerful landlords that characterized prerevolutionary Russia and Germany, was one of many ''internal natural and social conditions and international circumstances''[47] that made the development of capitalism in Japan unique. It was this uniqueness that in turn allowed feudal remnant institutions in the state to exercise significant political and ideological power as late as the 1920s, long after they had lost their material basis with the decline of feudal landownership in the Meiji period.[48]

The absolutist Meiji regime, acting on behalf of the bourgeoisie, moved quickly to promote a capitalist economy. First, it swept away what was left of the feudal agrarian land system by restructuring the land tax system, and thus it prevented the establishment of Russian-style, semi-feudal, large-scale landownership. On the positive side, ''under high protective tariffs, trustification and cartelization evolved early in some industries, [and the regime] prepared [the conditions for] the monopoly stage by developing state capital and large capital closely linked to it.'' Thus, the young state promoted the completion of a state-owned national rail network, the development of the textile industry, heavy industries, electrical enterprise, and the general industrialization process in Japan.[49]

Because of the unique circumstances of the Meiji bourgeois-democratic revolution, there never occurred the ''fierce struggle'' between the bourgeoisie and the landlord class such as evolved in late nineteenth- and early twentieth-century Russia and Germany. Nevertheless, from the outset, the Diet saw the gradual decline of landlord class forces and their replacement by capitalist forces; landlord parties, deprived of their old economic base, were gradually transformed into capitalist forces. This occurred so smoothly in Japan because there were no large landlords comparable to those in Russia and Germany. According to Inomata, in late nineteenth-century Russia there were over 700 men who held lands of over 10,000 hectares each, and 62 percent of all land was owned by nobility. Similarly, in Germany in 1907, 30 percent of all arable lands were fields of over 100 hectares, and 52 percent were fields of more than 50 hectares each. By contrast, in Japan in 1924, 5,000 landowners of fields of 50 hectares or more held only 7 percent of all arable land. The Japanese landlord class lacked the power to struggle with the rising bourgeoisie, and the bourgeoisie remained ''cowardly, indecisive, and compromising.'' As a consequence, capitalism could mature only under the tutelage of the government of semi-feudal bureaucrats and military cliques, and the survival of these feudal remnants became extremely prolonged. Only gradually, with the growth of ''the entire financial oligarchy,'' was state capital ''transformed into a component of the state capitalist trust'' as the basic structure of political and economic rule by finance capital.[50]

The weakness of the Japanese bourgeoisie was manifested in its intimate link to the autocracy rather than with forces of liberal change. Through 1877, the Meiji government, acting on behalf of the bourgeoisie, suppressed resistance to its efforts to open the way to capitalist development. Thus, it was the landlord class, mobilizing large numbers of peasants, that led the beleaguered civil rights (*jiyū minken*) movement. This position of the bourgeoisie in relation to the landed class began to change only with the rapid economic development occasioned by the Sino-Japanese and Russo-Japanese wars. While the landlords became ''bourgeoisified,'' both early political parties, which they had dominated, also became ''bourgeoisified,'' and engaged in a struggle for constitutionalism against the *hanbatsu* and then the ''bureaucratic-military cliques'' (*kanryō gunbatsu*). When these groups would not surrender their power, the bourgeoisified landlord class joined the bourgeoisie in ''choosing a path of moderate sober-minded compromise . . . with autocratic rule and absolutist remnant forces.'' The passage of universal male suffrage in 1925—which signalled the ''decisive victory of the bourgeoisie'' over the traditional landlords and ruling bureaucratic military clique—was achieved ''from above,'' and was possible only because of the political awakening of the upper-stratum petty bourgeoisie and the proletariat. Yet both these groups were natural opponents of monopoly capital. As the bourgeois-democratic movement of ''Taishō democracy'' exploited ''the political resistance of the petty bourgeois stratum,'' it also led ''the labor movement, the peasant movement, the movement for social equality, and the outbreak of the rice riot incidents, and . . . the socialist movement.'' The labor movement flourished further, as Japan's expanding capitalism transformed peasants and petty bourgeois into proletarians and semi-proletarian agrarian workers.[51]

By the time of the Russo-Japanese War, the Japanese bourgeoisie, then, had changed from compromising passivity to an actively intimidated political force, threatened by the peasant and workers' movements that had sprung up under the leadership of late Meiji socialists. In addition, Japan's bourgeoisie now confronted not ''the Europe of feudalistic reaction forces trying to hinder liberalism and bourgeois-democracy, [but rather] . . . the imperialist world of finance capital. Thus, Japan's bourgeoisie, which had never praised liberty from its heart, had become reactionary early on, as an imperialist bourgeoisie."[52] This occurred as the bourgeoisie was on its way to establishing dominance over feudal absolutist elements, which occurred as Japan made the final leap to the most advanced stage of capitalism with the war boom of 1914 to 1919. As Japan changed from a debtor country to a creditor country during these years, " 'bureaucratic politics' gave way to the age of political party government." Yet having gained power "without receiving the baptism of 'liberty,' " the bourgeoisie now acted in collusion with feudal remnants to suppress the "political upsurge of the proletariat."[53]

The continued role of "feudal remnants" was sustained in part by the link between the capitalist economy and a state power that was absolutist in the early Meiji period. According to Inomata, then, even in the 1920s, "when the true power of political rule appertain[ed] to the bourgeoisie, there [was] no complete democracy, and there [were] feudalistic absolutist remnants" in ideology and in political institutions. The "ideology of absolutist domination and submission," which was born along with the "imperialist bourgeoisie," was disseminated through the country's universal education system, while the exercise of force by the old pillars of centralized autocratic power, the army and the police, was brutal and naked.[54]

THE STATE STRUCTURE OF JAPANESE MONOPOLY CAPITALISM. The instrumentalism of Inomata's analysis entered here: he needed to dispose of "the *surprising strength*" of absolutist remnants in the Japanese state in order to defend his thesis that the Japanese state was but a tool of the bourgeoisie. The key to his argument was the assertion that the bourgeoisie had come to "dominate Japanese politics because they control production," in an economy that had been transformed from a "semi-agrarian country to an industrial nation." As the concentration of capital increased, particularly after the war years, so did the concentration of political power in the hands of the bourgeoisie. According to Inomata, by 1923, 84 percent of all stock company capital came from a mere 8 percent of the existing joint-stock companies; and 2 percent of large companies controlled 61 percent of all capital. The state, then, was but "the 'central committee' of the Japanese industrial club, the public organ that determines and promulgates the high-level policies of Japanese monopoly capitalists."[55] The dominance of the bourgeoisie over feudal remnant forces was manifested, in Inomata's view, in the activities of different components of state power. Thus, Inomata's analysis focused on the machinations of political parties as representatives of the bourgeoisie on the one hand, and the "civil and military bureaucracy" as representative of feudal remnant forces on the other. Finally, he stressed that such feudal forces remained influential in the Japanese state only insofar as they had been incorporated into the bourgeoisie.

In short, just as Meiji landlords had been bourgeoisified, so too while "the casing of the Japanese state is still embellished with many feudal remnants, its content is becoming bourgeois," Inomata argued. This was true both of the political parties and of the bureaucracy, in his view. While the Comintern had identified the Seiyūkai with rural landlords and the opposing Kenseikai (predecessor of the Minseitō) with more urbanized bourgeois elements, by the 1920s both the Seiyūkai and the Minseitō acted on behalf of monopoly capitalists. The two parties had become virtually indistinguishable in the "professional backgrounds of their affiliated M.P.'s (Diet members), local distributions of influence, and even in the policies they support[ed]."[56] Even in the Privy Council and the House of Peers, officials who were large landowners had become a minority, "and even that minority frequently depend more on capital income. The majority have become, if not capitalists, their direct or indirect agents." As the embourgeoisement of landlords proceeded, the political linkage between landowners and bourgeois tightened, because their economic interests were less in conflict and more in harmony.[57] Together absolutist remnant forces and the monopolist bourgeoisie acted to extend the sphere of capitalist exploitation and to mitigate the intense contradictions that accompanied the rapid growth of Japanese capitalism.

The interaction between the state institutions associated with the bourgeoisie and those identified with feudal absolutist institutions was clarified by Inomata's analysis of specific political incidents. Writing just before the financial panic (*kin'yū kyōkō*) of April 19, 1927, for example, Inomata cited the Kenseikai Cabinet's proposal that an urgent imperial decree rescue collapsing banks. The Privy Council unanimously rejected the proposal, whereupon the cabinet resigned. This behavior on the part of the absolutist remnant institution (the Privy Council) could be regarded as an attempt to undermine bourgeois rule. This effort failed when a new cabinet was formed under Tanaka Gi'ichi of the Seiyūkai, which was a "bourgeois political party." The Tanaka Cabinet resolved the crisis through loans from the Bank of Japan and a three-week moratorium on bank payments. This conclusion of the incident firmly established the supremacy of the so-called five large banks (*godai ginkō*)—the Mitsui, Mitsubishi, Sumitomo, Yasuda, and Dai'ichi banks—the core of the dominant finance capitalist zaibatsu, in Inomata's interpretation. Clearly, in the age of Japanese finance capitalism, the "absolutist remnant forces" lacked sufficient material basis to undermine the basic unity of the state in support of large capital. Yet the bourgeoisie remained unwilling or unable to eliminate feudal absolutist forces completely. This task, essential to the fruition of bourgeois democracy in Japan, fell to the revolutionary proletariat.[58]

To Inomata, observing the trends of economic growth and crisis in the

1920s, it was clear that "a transformation of production relations" was occurring in Japan: capitalism was moving toward its final form, a "state capitalist trust" (*kokka shihon-shugi-teki torasuto*).[59] The politics of the contemporary state could only be understood in terms of Bukharin's theoretical understanding of this development. Bukharin had observed, a full decade before Inomata wrote, that as laissez-faire capitalism developed into monopoly capitalism through the increasing concentration of wealth and the transformation of industrial capital into finance capital, the national economy became an increasingly regulated system of "organized capitalism." As monopolies and finance capital flourished, all the advanced capitalist countries became national trusts, Bukharin claimed; and since "trustification had come to involve a merging of industrial and financial interests with state power itself, he termed it a 'state capitalist trust.' "[60]

Trustification brought with it a changed role for the state, and it was this aspect of Bukharin's work that Inomata found most applicable to the analysis of the Japanese state in the 1920s. According to Bukharin, "organized state capitalism" arose out of the efforts of increasingly powerful finance capitalists to manage the inevitable contradictions of capitalism that resulted in a declining rate of profit. As the "executive committee of the bourgeoisie," the state played a role in this process, until it had been transformed from a mere instrument into an active participant in the economy: it became " 'a very large shareholder in the state capitalist trust' and 'its highest and all-embracing organizational culmination.' "[61] Ultimately, the contradictions that national bourgeoisies resolved internally were reproduced on the level of the world capitalist economy. These took the form of imperialist wars, as state capitalist trusts all endeavored to extend their spheres of political, military, and economic influence by competing for colonies and colonial empires, Bukharin wrote.[62]

Inomata placed his analysis of the Japanese state within the context of these international economic developments. World War I and the postwar economic panic had marked the collapse of world capitalism into chaos, as production and international trade declined and international exchange rates collapsed. While the world economy experienced some temporary stabilization, contradictions inherent in capitalism continued to plague it, and they would continue to do so as the concentration of capital and trustification proceeded in each country.[63] In the postwar years, Inomata observed, "The contradiction between the forces of production and the market intensified, so much so that (1) monopoly capitalism, via monopoly prices, increased the scissor price gap [the scissors crisis] of agriculture,[64] (2) monopoly capitalism produced chronic unemployment, forcing [economic] rationalization, and (3) monopoly capitalism raised tariff barriers while vigorously dumping goods abroad." As these symptoms of economic disruption grew,

TABLE 8

Production Increases in Major Japanese Commodities

Year	Pig iron (thousands of metric tons)	Steel materials (thousands of metric tons)	Coal (millions of tons)	Raw silk thread (millions of *kan*)	Cotton thread (millions of *kan*)	Paper-making (millions of *sun*)	Cement (millions of barrels)
1914 (Prewar)	317	282	22	3.7	88	208	3.6
1919 (Wartime High)	595	552	31	6.3	93	942	6.6
1920	529	537	29	5.8	79	—	7.8
1921	480	561	26	6.2	84	—	9.0
1922	559	662	28	6.4	98	—	10.8
1923	599	619	29	6.7	91	873	13.0
1924	585	906	30	6.1	98	941	12.8
1925	685	1,102	31	—	109	1,079	14.5

SOURCE: Inomata Tsunao, *Gendai Nihon kenkyū—Marukishizumu no tachiba yori* [Studies on contemporary Japan: From a Marxist standpoint] (Tokyo: Kaizō-sha, 1928, 1929, 1934), pp. 24-25.
NOTE: 1 *kan* = 8⅓ pounds; 1 *sun* = 1/10 foot, 1.2 inches.

the social crisis deepened, and class conflict intensified. Internationally, such domestic tensions also served to intensify competition among the advanced capitalist countries.[65]

As Inomata wrote in the 1920s, Japan too was affected by the contradictions described in Bukharin's treatment of the advanced capitalist state. The war boom had enabled Japanese capitalism to enter the monopoly stage, Inomata wrote. Postwar production of pig iron, steel, coal, raw silk and cotton thread, paper, and cement all equalled or surpassed their wartime highs by 1925. Many doubled, tripled, or increased fivefold their prewar levels. Other commodities, including crude oil, copper, sugar, and textiles, also showed significant production increases (see table 8). Most importantly, finance capital grew rapidly. State capital rose to the most important position in this development, with the capital of several huge concerns closely tied to it. State monopoly now predominated in transport, shipbuilding, armaments, and steel making, and in mining and heavy industry it was merged with the capital of giant concerns. Most major industries became cartelized, with bank or finance capital dominating the cartels.

Yet, during the 1920s, Japan's economic growth slowed along with that of the world economy, and the domestic economy was continually subjected to financial panics and depressions. As in the world economy, the contradiction between the contracted postwar market and expanding production became a major problem in Japan. The Panic of 1920 was one manifestation of the magnitude of the resulting problem of surplus capital, which was especially severe in the military-related heavy industries. In addition, Japan was increasingly dependent on other countries for supplies of raw materials, such as lumber, pig iron, and coal, and foodstuffs. China, a promising supplier of such raw materials and a suitable investment site for Japanese capital, was experiencing its own capitalistic development as well as a nationalist surge and thus was becoming increasingly hostile to Japanese interests. As markets for Japanese capital export shrank, moreover, new pressures arose for the use of military power to coerce capital exports to unwilling recipients like China. These contradictions in the Japanese economy were linked to still other factors: the fact that Japan had entered the stage of monopoly capitalism remarkably soon after its capitalist development had begun; the persistence of a system of excessively small-scale petty agriculture alongside large-scale industrial capitalism; and extremely large numbers of cottage industries and small capitalist enterprises (both characteristics of Japan's dual economy).[66]

These pressures required restriction of gold export, domestic cooperation among industrialists to lower production costs, and relief measures adopted by the government, lest these negative factors force retrenchment in Japan's economic growth. However, such measures fueled resistance by the proletariat and other groups who bore the costs of lowered wages and imperialist thrusts abroad. The state, the bourgeois parties, acting as the instrument of capital, thus took countermeasures against the political forces of the workers and peasants, on the one hand, while they pursued a "cooperative line" promoting the further concentration and monopolization of capital, on the other. In the face of the new challenges, capitalists tried to "rationalize" domestic industry with the support of the state through the merger of weak enterprises, the disposal of surplus capital, the conclusion of price agreements, and the formation of cartels and syndicates.[67]

Efforts by the state to resolve these tensions further exacerbated the concentration of capital and development of monopoly capitalism. The 1920 panic, for instance, had helped to elevate the five largest banks to even greater dominance in the financial sphere. Panics, such as that of 1927, continued to occur because of the weak basis of Japanese finance capital, which had been abruptly transformed from mere bank capital during the abnormal wartime economic boom. Finance capital, in turn, endeavored to handle this weakness by accelerating the merge of private with state capital and assimilating it with state power. "The entire effort of the finance capitalist bourgeoisie now," wrote Inomata, "is concentrated on the organizational construction of a strong state capitalist trust."[68] Thus, Japan was undergoing the "final form" of the transformation that Bukharin had described in 1916: it was becoming a state capitalist trust.[69]

Of course, the state had always played a massive role in Japan's capitalist development, but there was a qualitative difference between the economic role of the state in the Meiji period and its role after World War I. The new phenomenon was based on monopoly capitalism, which did not exist at the time of the Meiji Restoration, Inomata argued. As of late 1928, "the capital of state enterprises in production areas ha[d] reached a huge figure totalling 4.28 billion yen" in the fields of mining, industry, and transportation. Since the private capital of private enterprises in these areas totalled 8.4 or 8.5 billion yen, "state capital comprise[d] 34 percent of all capital" in these spheres.[70] Moreover, monopoly was "the common characteristic of enterprises" in printing, armaments, and minting, which employed over 500,000 workers, and 20 percent of all workers in mining, industry, and transportation (a ratio exceeding that of all other capitalist countries). At the same time, state capital merged with private capital in other monopolies, including the Manchurian Railway, Sakhalin Mining, Japan Radio, and Japan Airlines. The state had established direct control over finance capital, managing the Bank of Japan, the Bank of Taiwan, the Bank of Korea, and several others which together held about 4 billion yen in currency. Finally, the state was a huge purchaser of commodities, spending about 1.5 to 1.6 billion yen annually. The state's control expanded, furthermore, at the expense of private monopoly capital, which declined relative to state capital.[71]

As a result of this increasingly intimate linkage between the state and finance capital, "it has become impossible to hide the state as an organ of class rule," Inomata claimed.[72] Bonds floated by the state (loans) helped to form state capitalist enterprises. During the panic of 1927, the state's "special finance" relief measures enabled the huge banks to strengthen their monopoly on currency and on the bond market. Of 400 million [yen in] local bonds and 2.4 billion yen in state bonds held by banks, 60 percent were concentrated in the hands of twelve large banks, and 40 percent in the five largest banks.[73] The Japanese state, never a laissez-faire institution at any point in its development, used regulatory activity more and more openly to rescue capital from the "basic contradictions of capitalism." Duties imposed on major commodities were clearly aimed at the protection of monopolies in such areas as coal, paper making, rayon, cotton thread, and sugar. The effect of state actions to increase monopolization was especially evident in finance. From 1923 to 1929 over nine hundred banks perished, up to eight hundred of these because of mergers. "The revised bank laws that contributed to bank mergers will destroy about 240 (with about 300 million yen in capital) this year and next," Inomata predicted.[74]

These trends were congenial to Inomata's application of an instrumentalist approach to the Japanese state. Not only specific political parties, but individual names and their economic interests could be associated with state policies. Inomata wrote of the 1927 panic:

> The previous Minseitō cabinet collapsed, defeated in struggle with the Privy Council because it tried to rescue the Suzuki concern against the wishes of finance capital; the succeeding Seiyūkai cabinet fell because it was unable to assemble a reduced budget for the deflation policies that finance capital desired. The Hamaguchi Minseitō cabinet was able to outrival the Privy Council this time because it was still useful for finance capital—witness these [instances]. And, who has provided funds for the support and election of the bourgeois political parties?! Of which concerns are Shidehara, Sengoku, Sakurauchi, the two Yamamotos, Kuhara, Mutō, and Takahashi representatives?!—It's okay if we do not recount such details, because they are too widely known.[75]

Despite the state's relatively effective management of economic tensions in Japan by regulations and cartelization, as Bukharin argued, these internal adjustments were ultimately inadequate, and the contradictions of the domestic economy were simply transferred to the international level. Thus, Inomata observed, in the postwar era, "monopoly capitalism reveal[ed] its own decay and parasitism and chaos . . . shamelessly." Thus, the state turned outward, competing internationally with other state capitalist trusts for scarce markets and resources.[76] Inomata's application of Bukharin's theory of state capitalism to analyze the internal behavior of the Japanese state, therefore, led him directly to an explanation of Japanese imperialism.[77]

THE CAPITALIST STATE AND JAPANESE IMPERIALISM. Inomata's conception of imperialism was influenced by Rudolf Hilferding and closely resembled Bukharin's equilibrium theory of accumulation and theory of imperialism. Inomata, like Bukharin, preferred to think in terms of a single world capitalist system. Competition among countries at the core of the world capitalist system seeking to resolve the internal contradictions of their individual capitalist economies formed the international setting of Inomata's commentary on imperialism.[78] This context was central both to his defense of the Rōnō-ha view that the proletarian revolution in Japan must oppose the imperialist bourgeoisie rather than "feudal remnants," and to his critique of Takahashi Kamekichi's effort "to turn the Japanese proletarian struggle [against something] other than imperialism."[79]

Inomata rejected Takahashi's distinction between Japanese expansionism and the economic imperialism of which Lenin wrote. Instead, he argued that World War I, by stimulating rapid economic development in Japan, had merely "enabled Japan to shift from militaristic imperialism to capitalist imperialism."[80] However, Inomata also claimed that Japan had previously reached a sufficiently high level of capitalist development for its wars against China (1894-1895) and Russia (1904-1905) to be classified as imperialist ventures.[81] Furthermore, Inomata rejected Takahashi's application of Lenin's description of imperialism as a world system to individual capitalist states. The very notion of imperialism, Inomata argued, "implies mutual competition among advanced capitalist countries, and means the subjugation and exploitation of semi-civilized peoples and uncivilized peoples by such competitive countries."[82] Competition such as this could only occur within an international framework.

Thus, the world system itself had to be imperialist, as it was by 1894-1895, and "Japan [had] established itself decisively as an imperialist country ('in the modern sense') via the Sino-Japanese War." A modern imperialist power also had to be capitalist, engage in aggressive policies abroad, possess power to struggle for a monopolist position in the world system, and require warfare to maintain its expansionist and monopolist position.[83] Such a power must also "operate its own capital externally, as finance capital," as Japan did when it built the Seoul-Inchon and Seoul-Pusan railways in Korea. Finally, Inomata argued, within the world economy, there were national differences in the rates of the development of monopoly and finance capital; but such a lag in one area should not preclude a nation's being categorized as an imperialist power. In pre-World War I Japan, state monopoly was supreme, while finance capital was less developed. As Lenin argued, Japanese imperialism needed to supplement its monopoly of finance capital with a monopoly on regional military power.[84]

Thus, by the early twentieth century, Japan was an imperialist country, and after the growth of finance capital in World War I, it pursued the "typical policies of imperialism." These policies became the lifeblood of the Japanese state, the product of an internal need for the bourgeoisie "to overcome the deep contradictions between production forces and markets, between industrial production and raw materials." Colonies like Taiwan and Sakhalin provided sites for capital investment and sources of raw materials and foodstuffs, while Korea became a market solely for Japanese capital. Meanwhile, Japan grasped a colonial stronghold in the South Seas archipelago, while developing a monopoly position in Southern Manchuria and Inner Mongolia, and in steel production in China. Investments of over 2.5 billion yen made Japan the leading economic power in China, influencing not only the Chinese government (via loans) but also Chinese development of railroads, coal mines, steel making, textiles, commerce, and finance. Japan's position in East Asia, Inomata observed, was further strengthened when World War I resulted in the demise of Russian imperialism and the retreat of German and French imperialism. As the United States, which also thrived on war, advanced upon China, the possibility of direct conflict between the United States and Japan increased steadily.[85]

Given American, British, and Japanese competition for dominance in Asia, Inomata devoted considerable attention to the relationship between Japanese imperialism and the Chinese revolution. The nationalist revolution in China threatened the very existence of Japanese capitalism, which would perish if it could not expand. China was the site of 90 percent of Japanese foreign investment, which was concentrated in the pivotal Chinese commercial centers of Shanghai, Qingdao, Hankou, and Tianjin. In turn, Japanese capital had an enormous impact on the Chinese economy. Japanese capital controlled about 25 percent of the 25 million tons of annual Chinese coal production, over 90 percent of the 1 million tons of iron ore produced annually in China, and 60 percent of the Chinese spinning industry, the only sphere in China to have achieved "modern industrial development." Japanese ships matched British strength and comprised 30 to 40 percent of all ships involved in the China trade, and an equal proportion of major telephone and telegraph lines, like the Shanghai-Nagasaki, Fuzhou-Taiwan, and Dairen-Sasebo lines. Japanese banks issued widely circulated currencies and financed major capital enterprises in China. Finally, Japan was the most significant of the thirteen creditor countries making loans to China, holding 20 percent of all railroad loans, 90 percent of all telegraph loans, and 50 percent of all loans to local organizations.[86]

This flow of Japanese capital truncated the natural development of the Chinese capitalist economy and exploited China's laborers and its state. Chinese resistance to Japanese capitalism soon provided an added stimulus for Japanese military intervention against the Chinese revolution, Inomata argued. A victory for the nationalist, anti-imperialist forces in a land so vital to Japan for markets and raw materials was a real danger for a Japanese economy that required imperialist expansion to accommodate the increased production forces in postwar Japan. In 1919, the boycott of Japanese goods resulted in an 80 percent decline (173,000 tons) in freight carried by ships in the ports of Hankou and Shanghai; and in 1923 Japanese exports to China fell 20 percent (32 million yen) in the first six months and 15 percent (50 million yen) for the entire year.[87]

A continuous trade deficit (see table 9) also demonstrated the importance of the China market and Chinese sites for overseas enterprises to balance imports. When Japan's trade deficit reached 440 million yen in 1925, 80 percent of inflowing capital (420 million yen) came from Chinese sources. The China market also absorbed 25 to 30 percent of the approximately 2 billion yen in goods exported by Japan in that year. Japan was heavily dependent on Chinese foodstuffs (legumes and grains), salt, coal, and pig iron (which supplied half that needed for Japanese steel production). Clearly,

TABLE 9

Development of Japanese Import and Export Trade
(In Millions of Yen)

Year	Exports	Imports	Total volume	Exports-imports (balance of trade)
1914				
(Prewar)	591	595	1,186	-4
1919				
(Wartime High)	2,098	2,173	4,272	-74
1920	1,948	2,336	4,284	-387
1921	1,252	1.614	2,866	-361
1922	1,637	1,890	3,527	-253
1923	1,447	1,982	3,427	-534
1924	1,807	2,453	4,260	-646
1925	2,305	2,572	4,878	-267
1926	2,044	2,377	4,422	-322

SOURCE: Inomata Tsunao, *Gendai Nihon kenkyū—Marukishizumu no tachiba yori* [Studies on contemporary Japan: From a Marxist standpoint] (Tokyo: Kaizō-sha, 1928, 1929, 1934), p. 26.

China was the most important component of the Japanese imperialist economy in its monopoly stage. The Chinese revolution threatened to aggravate the gap between Japanese production forces and markets, slow the rate of Japanese economic growth, and thus hasten the demise of Japanese capitalism. These threats urged the Japanese bourgeoisie to intervene desperately in China (although it was the military that was in fact the main political force here) and possibly occasion yet another world war, which would abet the decline of the entire world capitalist system.[88]

Inomata considered this range of possibilities when he supported Yamakawa's strategy for the Japanese proletariat. His analysis of the capitalist state and of its position in the world economy led to discouraging conclusions on the outlook for revolution in a capitalistic country as highly developed as Japan. Nevertheless, a more positive outlook arose from Inomata's search for allies for the Japanese proletariat in the "colonial masses and those of semi-colonial countries, . . . as well as existing proletarian states," all of which opposed imperialism. In his view, a war with China, like the war that toppled first the Russian tsar and then the provisional government, could be beneficial to the Japanese proletariat. The proletariat must scrutinize carefully the China policy of the Japanese state, "because the anti-imperialist revolutionary struggle in China and the reactionary policies of imperialist Japan against it foster instability in close interaction with Japan's financial disturbances." Finally, the proletariat could act to divide the bourgeoisie against itself, exacerbating conflicts between the so-called Mitsui Seiyū and the Mitsubishi Kensei political parties.[89]

Here there were important differences between Yamakawa and Inomata on the matter of revolutionary strategy, differences that may have led Inomata to part with the Rōnō-ha in the 1930s. Inomata proposed a revolutionary strategy that he felt coincided with the strategy of world revolution since October 1917.[90] Partly because Inomata was more conciliatory toward the Comintern and accepted the need to coordinate Japan's proletarian movement with other revolutionary movements, his strategic theory was in fact a compromise between one-stage and two-stage revolutionary strategies. There were clearly a "step 1" and a "step 2" in Inomata's revolution, and he was not averse to using the analogy of Russia between February and October 1917 to make his argument. Indeed, like the October Revolution. Inomata's revolution embraced the completion of bourgeois democracy in Japan and a role for poor peasants that would be different in each stage.[91] The divergence between Inomata and Yamakawa was clear; for the direct support that Inomata gave to Yamakawa's united front political party was sparse indeed, as the former concentrated on a theoretical analysis of the Japanese state.

However, Inomata did share Yamakawa's optimism about a socialist revolutionary process that would come earlier than that envisaged by the JCP, and it is in this optimism that the weaknesses of Inomata's interpretation of the state are evident. Despite the impressive power that Inomata's analysis of Japan as an advanced capitalist state brought to bear on the understanding of certain fiscal policies and Japanese imperialism, he was not fully consistent in his assessment of the continuing impact of the so-called feudal remnants in the Japanese state. Inomata conceded that absolutist remnants like the Privy Council continued to rule in the 1920s without any material base. Even large landlords, who held only a small proportion of arable land, did "not themselves manage large agricultural enterprises," Inomata asserted; their only link with capital lay in income received from interest and dividends.[92] Yet, in support of the Rōnō-ha view that such feudal forces had become bourgeoisified and were now part of an advanced capitalist state, rather than a transitional state, Inomata insisted that in the state apparatus they acted on behalf of capital. This was not fully consistent with his own analysis of the behavior of the Privy Council and other feudal remnants, which, he asserted, acted in opposition to the interests of capital. Inomata's confidence in the possibility of an immediate socialist revolution on the basis of Yamakawa's united front political party idea, then, was partly attributable to an underestimation of the continued economic and political power of such forces as the emperor system, its ideology, the *genrō*, and the military in a period when party rule was not undisputed and domestic repression was on the rise. It fell to the Kōza-ha, then, to analyze the emperor system and its supporting institutions in connection with the continuing duality in the economic base of Taishō and Shōwa society.

THE KŌZA-HA: A STRUCTURAL ANALYSIS OF THE JAPANESE STATE

The Kōza-ha's works on the Japanese state, like those of Inomata Tsunao, were responses to the challenge raised by Takahashi Kamekichi's theory of petty imperialism. On behalf of the Rōnō-ha, Inomata's response to Takahashi's effort to justify Japanese imperialism was to demonstrate that Japan had already reached the stage of monopoly finance capitalism and therefore fulfilled Lenin's definition of imperialism. The task of the Kōza-ha, however, was more difficult. Loyal to the Comintern's view that Japan's basic status as a capitalist society was complicated by feudal backwardness in the agrarian economy and in the political superstructure, the Kōza-ha had first to locate the historical roots of Japan's continued backwardness and then to explain the complex mechanisms that enabled the more advanced and less developed aspects of the society to operate as an integral whole.

To identify the reasons for Japan's hybrid economy and state structure, Kōza-ha analysts of the state were forced to delve into Japan's economic history in great depth, while Inomata could be content with summarizing the highlights of Japan's steady progress in capitalist development and concentrate more on the interpretation of current policies. The Kōza-ha confronted the interaction between the old feudal forces they claimed continued to wield significant political power and the representatives of the new capitalist structure. To analyze this relationship, the Rōnō-ha's instrumentalist approach, which slighted elements that were inconsistent with the assumption of advanced capitalism, was inadequate. Instead, the Kōza-ha adopted a "structural" (*kōzō-teki*) perspective on the state and society, an approach that coincides both nominally and substantively with what Western Marxists fifty years later call a "structuralist" approach to the state.

Structuralists object to the instrumentalist assumption that a self-conscious ruling class purposely pursues policies advantageous to itself through the state apparatus. Structuralists cite Marx's argument that men's consciousness is conditional and limited by the material conditions in which they live.[93] This assertion "leads one to expect the degree of rationality of politically implemented strategies certainly to be restricted and marked by 'false consciousness,' so that we cannot take a coherent and consistent class consciousness of the ruling-class as a starting-point for a reconstruction of the class-character of the state activity—even if we assume the Influence Theory argumentation to be correct empirically."[94] Structuralists claim, therefore, that "the functions of the state are broadly determined by the structures of the society rather than [as in the instrumentalist approach] by the people who occupy the positions of state power."[95] It is not class consciousness or purposive rationality that is important, but the larger constraints of the society that delimit the activity of the state and its functionaries. These constraints derive from "the systematic functional interrelationships among" "the concrete social institutions that make up a society."[96] Hence, while Inomata's analysis followed the behavior of actors responding to domestic and international events to protect the interests of Japan's "state capitalist trust," the Kōza-ha, led by Noro Eitarō, examined the structural links between the dual economic base and its political superstructure.[97]

Interestingly, Noro and Inomata had begun their study of the state together, several years before the debate on Japanese capitalism erupted. On March 1, 1924, the General Labor Federation (Rōdō Sōdōmei) spawned the Industrial Labor Research Bureau (Sangyō Rōdō Chōsajo) to support the strategy of the labor movement. After ideological tensions ruptured the Sōdōmei in May 1925 and the left-wing Council of Japanese Labor Unions (Nihon Rōdō Kumiai Hyōgikai) was formed, the Industrial Labor Research Bureau carried on independently, launching its own organ, *Sangyō rōdō jihō* [Industrial labor times] in September. A subgroup of this organization, the Association for the Study of Capital (Shihon Chōsa Kai), produced the Research Bureau's most lasting contribution to the development of Japanese Marxism. Takahashi Kamekichi and Inomata headed the group, and Noro, along with JCP official Nosaka Sanzō and future Kōza-ha member Shiga Yoshio, produced most of its work. Embracing a variety of interpretations, the association made the first sustained academic effort to organize the Marxist study of Japanese political economy. They published their results in a thirteen-volume *Shakai mondai kōza* [Symposium on social problems]. Issued between March 1926 and June 1927, on the eve of the proclamation of the '27 Theses, the series offered detailed analyses and diagrammatic presentations of Japan's political and economic structure.[98]

In a sense, then, the Industrial Labor Research Bureau became a breeding ground for the full range of the leading Marxist approaches to the state that developed in the prewar period. It was during his years with the bureau that Takahashi began to develop his unorthodox theory of petty imperialism. Similarly, Shiga criticizing Akamatsu Katsumaro's "scientific Japanism," offered an interpretation of the Japanese state that advanced beyond the 1922 Draft JCP Program and anticipated the views of the '27 Theses. As early as 1925, for example, Shiga stressed that "feudal remnants '*occupy the dominant position* in the state structure.' " "The state organ is held in the hands of a bloc formed of a certain part of the commercial and industrial bourgeoisie and large landlords," Shiga claimed. He went on to adopt an aspect of Marx's Asiatic society model when he declared that "the government of the emperor . . . is a 'landlord government' oppressing the peasantry.''[99] The involvement of some of the most eminent participants in the debate on Japanese capitalism in such a dynamic, scholarly association prepared them to carry the intraparty dispute on strategy and tactics to a higher theoretical plane when domestic and international events forced them to do so.

Given this common experience, how did Inomata and Noro adopt such divergent theoretical approaches to the state? The answer lies partly in the differing evaluations of current conditions and predilections about revolutionary strategy that colored their interpretations of the data. While Inomata was sanguine about the possibilities offered by democratic institutions and party rule in Japan, the repression the JCP had suffered during ''Taishō democracy'' indicated to the Kōza-ha that these institutions were deeply flawed: the continued presence of the emperor system and the rising powers of the military and special police betrayed these faults. Hence, the Kōza-ha felt that there was little to be gained from treating the Japanese state as a typical bourgeois monarchy like that of England, with the universal characteristics of bourgeois democracies. Instead, they concentrated on the peculiarities of Japan's capitalist development, a subject for which the structural approach was more appropriate, since it did not rest on the assumption of bourgeois rationality. The risks of this course were many: by emphasizing the particular, the Kōza-ha would move further away from the Marxist model of European capitalist development that was the premise for their revolution. Similarly, in response to Takahashi's theory, the Kōza-ha claimed that the impetus for Japanese imperialism came from an alliance of surviving feudal ruling classes and the military coupled with those of the rising capitalist structure. This notion placed them in a difficult position vis-à-vis Lenin's general theory of imperialism. Nevertheless, however much the Kōza-ha was influenced by Comintern views, theirs was a more flexible approach that enabled them to confront the harsh realities in Japan that the Rōnō-ha ignored: the survival of the emperor system, the persistence of a military power with roots deep in Japan's ''feudal past,'' and the failure of the state to draw the countryside into the industrial capitalist age. Ironically, this analysis by loyalists to the radical JCP supported a far more pessimistic view than that of the Rōnō-ha of the possibilities for socialist revolution in a country that remained stubbornly semi-feudal in character and that seemed to draw sustenance from that backwardness.

The Kōza-ha and the Emperor System: Arguing from Superstructure to Base

The '27 Theses provided the point of departure for the development of the Kōza-ha's analysis of the state, but from the very outset of the debate on

Japanese capitalism, the Kōza-ha's interpretation of the emperor system expressed a pessimism about the prospects for socialist revolution in Japan that exceeded that of the Comintern. As early as 1928, Hattori Shisō independently undertook a theroetical study of the notion of "absolutism" in Marx and Engels, and he concluded that the Japanese state from Meiji to Shōwa was absolutist.[100] Absolutism, strictly speaking, was a state form of the last stage of feudalism; it arose where the bourgeois revolution had not yet been completed; and its "historical role lay in nurturing and promoting the development to a still higher stage of a bourgeoisie which still had not developed to [the point of] being an independent force accumulating political power."[101] Despite the remarkable growth in Japan's capitalist economy and the institutional symbols of Taishō democracy, then, Hattori argued that the emperor system in the 1920s remained in transition between feudal and bourgeois rule. This position on the state was elaborated by Hattori, Hirano Yoshitarō, and others while the *Kōza* was being prepared and quickly became the key to the Kōza-ha's analysis of the contemporary Japanese state.

The Kōza-ha's analysis of absolutism in prewar Japan was in place, then, by the time the Comintern's '32 Theses were published. Coincidentally, the new theses not only overturned the '31 Draft Political Theses, which had defined the Japanese state as a capitalist-landlord bloc in which capitalists held hegemony, but also went beyond this to present a much more sober view of the state than had the '27 Theses. Absolving itself from blame for the JCP's difficulties, the Comintern claimed that the absence of a correct interpretation of the absolutist emperor system had "hampered the objective analysis of Japanese capitalism," had led to an incorrect depiction of Japan's state power, and therefore had caused considerable confusion in the JCP's revolutionary strategy. While the state did link landlords with upper strata bourgeois, the theses claimed, it was not merely an instrument of those classes.[102] Rather, "Japan's emperor system has maintained its independent and relatively significant responsibilities and its absolutist nature, barely concealed by pseudo-constitutional forms." Apparently unaware of the work on absolutism already undertaken by Hattori and Hirano, the Comintern alleged that both the JCP and the Rōnō-ha had underestimated the significance of this absolutist system "by considering the Diet and the political party cabinet apart from the emperor system, as if they were bourgeois state forms independent of the emperor system." Japanese Marxists must look beyond the surface and seek the true economic basis of this absolutist state, which enjoyed relative autonomy under the rule of bureaucrats and the military. This material basis, "the second major component of the ruling system in Japan, is landownership—Asiatically backward semi-feudal domination in the countryside that hinders the development of the productive forces of Japanese agriculture and hastens the decline of agriculture and the impoverishment of the main masses of peasants.'' Such feudalistic ''domination of peasants in industrially advanced Japan'' resembled ''that of the most backward colonial countries.'' To be sure, finance capital was significant, as the third feature of the state power, but it relied on feudal remnants and the emperor system to exercise its rule and could not be analyzed apart from the other two components.[103]

To support this assessment of the emperor system as absolutist and to justify the Comintern/JCP strategy of two-stage revolution, Kōza-ha Marxists devised an argument that could raise serious methodological issues. Citing Marx's observations in *Capital* on the relationship between the state and the economic base, they argued from the nature of the superstructure, in a somewhat circular fashion, to substantiate their view that feudal production relations persisted in the economic base and required the prescribed bourgeois-democratic revolution. This contention was not threatened by the Kōza-ha's acknowledgment that the emperor was also the head of an imperialistic state. The Kōza-ha and the '32 Theses both described the Japanese emperor system as absolutist and feudalistic in nature, like ''the militaristic imperialist tsarist state'' and the German state under the kaiser.[104] The emperor system, as an absolutist state, rested on a balance of feudal forces and bourgeois forces. Yet in essence, the Japanese state was still feudalistic because its material base remained ''the exploitation of serfs, or rather, semi-serf peasants and independent small producers.''[105]

To accept the emperor system as absolutist—''on this there was no difference of opinion'' between Kōza-ha and Rōnō-ha.[106] The issue was how long after the Meiji Restoration the emperor system remained in the transitional stage of ''absolutism.'' The Rōnō-ha maintained that absolutism had given way to bourgeois rule by the 1920s and 1930s. According to Inomata, for example, this shift had occurred as early as the Meiji Restoration: the Meiji reforms had deprived absolutism of its material basis as feudal landlords underwent embourgeoisement.[107] Yamakawa's view was closer to that of the '27 Theses. He conceded that Japan remained absolutist after the Meiji reforms, but he argued that the tremendous expansion of Japan's capitalist economy during World War I had enabled the bourgeoisie to emerge victorious from a power struggle with feudal elements in the state. Thereafter, Yamakawa claimed, state power continued to be shared by capitalists and landlords, but the hegemony of the bourgeoisie was firmly established.[108] Once the Rōnō-ha had posited this early transition from an absolutism based on a balance of forces between two classes to a state premised on the hegemony of the bourgeoisie, their instrumentalist approach to the bourgeois state was justified.

The Kōza-ha, however, did not accept the Rōnō-ha's view that transitional absolutist rule had given way to bourgeois hegemony but instead argued that the emperor system remained absolutist from the Meiji era through the 1920s and 1930s. The problem for the Kōza-ha, then, was to prove that the feudal economic base of this absolutism had remained intact despite the evidence that the emperor system had become a capitalist, imperialistic state. Moreover, since the notion of absolutism posited significant autonomy for a state that was not the mere tool of a single class, an instrumentalist approach could not apply. Rather, the Kōza-ha in effect had no choice but to rely on a much more complex argument delineating how the feudalistic and capitalistic elements of the economic structure in prewar Japan were reflected in the emperor-system state.

Here, Hirano, Hattori, and others relied heavily on Yamada Moritarō's *Analysis of Japanese Capitalism*. Specifically, they argued that feudalism had never been entirely eliminated; instead, feudal remnant forces were simply incorporated into the new absolutist Meiji state, which in turn encouraged the development of capitalism. Although the Meiji regime was a transitional absolutist state, it never completed the transformation of Japan to a capitalist power by eradicating feudalism completely. Rather, feudal elements in the Meiji regime acted to preserve their material basis in the countryside. Thus, feudalism disintegrated only partially, in compromise with new elements needed to promote industrial capitalism. As a result, not only did the Meiji Restoration leave feudal remnants intact, but the power of these elements continued to grow as the state itself benefited from the development of capitalism and imperialism.

In this view, proof of absolutism lay in agrarian relations, in the relations of exploitation in the countryside that continued to be feudalistic in character.[109] The uniqueness of Japanese economic development since the Meiji Restoration lay in the fact that "capitalism was evolved to the stage of imperialism from a structure that could develop only on the basis of semi-feudal private landownership."[110] How was this peculiar pattern of development possible? Many, like Noro and Hirano, pointed to the continued influence of ancient "Asiatic" elements in both the economic base and its superstructure. According to Noro, one such Asiatic feature persisted in the post-Restoration state's continued role as the nation's highest landlord; as in the ancient Asiatic mode of production, the absolutist state levied feudal-type rents in the form of taxes on the direct producers (peasants). In Noro's words, "the land tax reform . . . did not immediately signify the abolition of feudal rents, but thereby, in reality, rents in kind (dues in kind) [paid] to feudal landowners were now merely changed into cash rents (cash land taxes) [rendered] to the state as the single highest monopolistic landowner."[111] Noro conceded Inomata's point that landownership in Japan was not predominantly large-scale landownership. But he argued that this fact alone could not prove that there was no material base for semi-feudal absolutist forces. Inomata was wrong to assume that only feudal agrarian systems such as those of nineteenth-century Russia and Germany could support absolutism. As Hirano argued, the test lay not in the size of landholdings, but in the relationship of those who held it vis-à-vis the direct producers. In Japan, this relationship was not a capitalistic one in which farmers hired wage labor in pursuit of profit; rather, tenant farmers themselves continued to be direct producers who used their own household's labor to produce a subsistence. Since the Meiji state retained the same levies as feudal rents, the feudal relationship remained; it was simply the state that took the surplus in the form of cash taxes instead of the feudal lord. As a transitional absolutist state, the emperor-centered structure used this surplus to accomplish primitive capital accumulation. The resulting juxtaposition of persistent semi-feudal relations of production in agriculture with the growth of capitalism in the nation as a whole became "one of the most fundamental contradictions of Japanese capitalism." This contradiction "could be resolved only by the sublation of the capitalist system itself," that is, by the elimination of the emperor system, by agrarian revolution, and by the completion of a socialist revolution.[112]

One criticism that has been levelled at the Kōza-ha's analysis of the emperor system is that it was a static view. Although the concept of absolutism as a transitional regime is intrinsically dynamic, opponents of the Kōza-ha's application of the concept to prewar Japan claim that the Kōza-ha refused to acknowledge changes in the economic base and its superstructure that had occurred from the beginning of the Meiji period to the early Shōwa era. This may have been a risk inherent in the Kōza-ha's method of first stipulating the nature of the emperor system and then proceeding to analyze the character of its economic base. Once the Kōza-ha determined that their criticism of the emperor system could only be sustained by arguing that its economic base remained essentially feudalistic as late as the 1920s, the faction's theorists needed to deny the significance of the signs of capitalistic growth that the Rōnō-ha found so encouraging.[113] In addition, one could also suggest that the faction's conviction that the emperor system could never be compared to the British monarchy might have reflected the widely shared belief at the time in the *kokutai* ideology, which saw Japan's emperor system as unique by virtue of its religious and ethnic content. These criticisms notwithstanding, the Kōza-ha's contribution to an understanding of the dynamics of the relationship between the development of capitalism and the emperor system since the Tokugawa era is undeniable. Their structural approach yielded far deeper historical research than that produced by the Rōnō-ha. Theoretically, the Kōza-ha's application of Marx's ideas on absolutism and oriental society to the Japanese state was more subtle, more flexible, and ultimately more productive than the Rōnō-ha's perspective.

Absolutism and the Japanese State

According to the Kōza-ha, the Meiji regime fulfilled the functions of an absolutist state. It began the bourgeois-democratic revolution in Japan by undermining feudal political centers—through the abolishment of the *han* and the establishment of prefectures (*ken*)—in 1869 and by transferring sovereignty from the multiple feudal units (*kuni*) of the Tokugawa period to a single central head, the emperor, on a national level. The regime had cleared the path for the development of capitalism: by lifting, in 1872, the ban on the purchase and sale of land imposed in 1643; by legalizing private landownership; and by permitting redistribution and merger of lands by the removal, in 1875, of laws restricting individual ownership of land. Nevertheless, the Meiji reforms left intact an underlying system of agrarian relations that made the new Meiji state neither bourgeois nor entirely feudalistic.[114]

Noro summarized the Kōza-ha view on this point as follows:

> *Pure feudal landholding relations* were abolished for a time, along with the restrictions that accompanied it, by the reforms of the Meiji Restoration. Even so, this fact does not imply that it, as he [Inomata] says, "abolished the *land system* of feudal agriculture as the basis of feudal absolutism." It merely accomplished the removal of pure feudal landholding relations, i.e., abolished the relations of pure feudal landholding by the *bakufu* and three hundred daimyo, and in its place put unified landownership under the sovereignty of the absolute monarch. . . . In our country the state ["as before"] is the highest landlord, and sovereignty is landownership aggregated on a national scale. Our country's land taxes, both in their traditional conception and in reality, could not be essentially different from the form of ground rent.[115]

If the Meiji state "did not deliberately try to advance the development of large landownership," "it clearly opened the path for the concentration" of landownership through its land policies. As a consequence, in the late 1920s half of all arable land in Japan was tenant land, and "we still do not see notable development of capitalism in agriculture," even though the new state pursued protectionist policies to nurture the native bourgeoisie.[116] If this state was neither bourgeois nor purely feudal any longer, it could be described as "absolutist," a regime that pressed onward with reforms that would make Japan an industrial capitalistic society.

According to Hirano Yoshitarō, Tokugawa feudalism, like feudal societies in general, had sown the seeds of the development of capitalism in Japan and therefore the eventual causes of its own demise in the Meiji Restoration. Capitalist enterprises developed in embryo form under government production offices established by individual feudal domains. These businesses enabled merchants, usurers, and feudal daimyo themselves to accumulate capital in the form of currency. The shogun's *sankin kōtai* (alternate attendance) system spawned a network of internal water transport, and, as Hattori argued, manufacture developed under the *toiya* system, drawing cottage industry under the domination of commercial capital. The commercial capital produced by commodity circulation in the Edo period could easily have been converted to industrial capital, if the "feudal fetters" were removed, if the domestic market were fully integrated to transcend the boundaries of feudal domains, and if other conditions of the capitalist mode of production, such as the import of technology and participation in the world market, had been present.[117]

Indeed, the shogunate had encouraged the emergence of some of these conditions. For example, recognizing the importance of commercial capital and commercial cities, "the *bakufu* . . . brought all such cities as Edo, Osaka, Sakai, Kyoto, and Nagasaki under its direct rule, placed the Ikuno, Sado, and Ashio mines [under its] direct jurisdiction, and made the power to coin money [its] exclusive jurisdiction." The Tokugawa regime was also engaged in "primitive accumulation," in promoting industries, and in reorganizing the armies. But the bourgeoisie in the *bakufu*'s own domain was weak, so the shogun licensed (or chartered) monopolies to the bourgeoisie in commercial cities. Unfortunately, in Hirano's view, commercial cities such as Edo and Osaka, unlike commercial centers in Western Europe in the seventeenth century, were "parasitic," as they were merely entrepôts for products of a serf-based agrarian economy. Neither in the shogun's lands nor elsewhere did an industrial bourgeoisie become differentiated from the commercial bourgeoisie to propel the development of manufacture industry that would form a new mode of production in Japan. (Here Hirano differed with fellow Kōza-ha scholar Hattori Shisō.) Thus, it became impossible for Japan to develop a state form comparable to that in Western Europe, which had used these bourgeois as supporters against feudal lords to establish a fully centralized regime. Other *han* too encouraged "serf-commodity" production and circulation through government monopolies on rice and mining in the domains. Yet, despite these and the shogun's efforts to promote capitalism, the "perversion" of the development of the Japanese bourgeoisie by an Asiatically entrenched feudal system prevented the emergence of an industrial bourgeoisie to balance the feudal aristocracy. As a result, the Tokugawa regime could not immediately be transformed into a Western European-style absolutist state. The feudal domains developed relatively equally, balancing each other's power, so that a fully centralized transitional state did not emerge until the Meiji Restoration.[118]

Finally, the peculiarities of the Asiatic serf-agrarian system in the countryside prevented this rapidly growing commercial capital from developing into the industrial capital needed for the fruition of the capitalist mode of production. As commodity production and circulation increased, the rise of miscellaneous exactions (*kokinonari*), taxes on those engaged in shipping, fishing, and hunting (*unjō*), and forced labor that financed this development occasioned peasant uprisings in the last years of the shogunate. In these circumstances, worsened by the shogun's forcible isolation of Japan from the world market, the development of industry separate from agriculture was difficult. Merchants' and usurers' capital remained in the villages, where they led a parasitic existence on the serf system by financing loans to feudal lords. Thus, commercial and usury capital could not perform the revolutionary tasks of a bourgeois revolution, described by Marx and Engels, to bring about capitalism on a national scale. Such a feudal system as had developed by the late Edo period combined the tentative growth of commercial capital with the steady increase of feudal exploitation. Since it did not advance to produce an industrial bourgeoisie, the system began to stagnate, to disintegrate from within. It finally collapsed abruptly, "as when a mummy hits the air" when it made contact with the dynamic system of world capitalism, Hirano argued.[119]

The Tokugawa state, then, collapsed from a combination of internal and external factors. Internally, the economic developments described above, the emergence of nascent capitalism on the basis of, and in adhesion to, a semi-serf agrarian economy, produced antagonism between the Imperial Court and the shogunate, peasants and feudal lords, individual domains and the shogunate, lord and retainer. An important actor in these antagonisms was the warrior class, which came to be separated from the land. Beginning with the rule of Toyotomi Hideyoshi (1536-1598), warriors were gradually transformed into mere "parasitic holders of fief/stipend rights." Toyotomi had conducted land surveys and established separate areas of habitation for peasants and *bushi* (samurai), in a move that initiated the strict policy of fixed social status of Tokugawa feudalism. By the end of the Edo period, warriors lived off rice stipends from *bakufu* and *han* granaries. These samurai, in contrast to landed *Junkers* in Germany, were easily swept aside by the Meiji regime's introduction of compulsory commutation of stipends (*kinroku kōsai*), beginning in 1876.[120]

Another antagonism hastening the fall of the shogunate was its conflict with the feudal domains, a conflict that was not resolved until the Restoration government overthrew the shogun, abolished the domains, and established administrative prefectures. Finally, there were large samurai who stood in antagonism with the peasants. At the time of the Meiji Restoration, "there were 399,000 households of extremely large samurai bodies, who were able to live only as parasites, on the cruel extortion of serfs on the basis of an Asiatic petty serf system." Lower samurai, who numbered over half of this group, were extremely impoverished and played a tremendously destructive role in the Restoration. Many became participants in the reforms of the Meiji state. These political and economic conflicts were finally resolved in the demise of the Tokugawa system, abetted by the challenge of the West. Nevertheless, the system that replaced it, the Meiji state, was merely a transitional regime, its reforms leaving much of the old feudal system intact, as "semi-feudal" forces. Therefore, Hirano argued that "Not only was the traditional lord-vassal relationship retained, but as long as the general system of petty semi-serfs remained, it was possible for [the old feudal daimyo] to be made a political power supporting those forces resting on that semi-serf system." One example of this phenomenon was the continuity of political power wielded by the Satsuma, Tosa, Chōshū, and Hizen clans. The new government, the *hanbatsu*, "merely represented these four *han* and maintained a balance of power among them."[121]

As an absolutist state destined to execute the full transition to the capitalist mode of production, the Meiji regime faced major obstacles. The capitalism it inherited was from the Tokugawa period, "chipped and distorted" by its origins in a semi-serf system that had been attacked from without by more advanced capitalist countries. The Meiji regime had to carry out the tasks of primitive capitalist accumulation that the indigenous bourgeoisie had been too weak and immature to accomplish. Because of the coincidence of external military pressures and internal backwardness, this process was necessarily especially violent, as the Meiji state sought to accomplish in fifty years what the British had required two centuries to achieve. In so doing, it was necessary that the state retain the semi-serf system that had nurtured Japanese capitalism at the outset. The bourgeoisie that emerged from the Meiji period was thus a "serf-landlord bourgeoisie." "Since the nascent bourgeoisie itself was based on a serf system and reproduced it, it furthermore embossed the entire system with the form of semi-serf capitalism, and the entire basis of such an economic structure caused the political rule to be characterized in the same way."[122]

The structure of the emperor system regime as it emerged during the Meiji era reflected this same search for continuity while promoting change toward contemporary models of industrial capitalist societies found in the West. The *kokutai* ideology that sustained the system was a faithful replication of this process: the ancient philosophical traditions of Shintō and Confucianism were combined with nineteenth-century German thought on the state and society. A national Diet was created, but in accordance with the Meiji oligarchy's claim to "restore" power to the imperial throne, the Meiji Constitution accorded full sovereignty to the emperor. The continuing active and independent roles for the Privy Council, the *gunbatsu*, and the genrō assured that the new state would not be overwhelmed by "bourgeois" influences, even as the economic strength of the bourgeoisie increased with the growth of industrial capitalism. The emperor, then, balanced the bourgeois and feudal elements in the state structure, enabling the state to retain some autonomy from the interests of both classes. Yet, the burden of the Kōza-ha's challenge to the Rōnō-ha position lay in stressing the conservative nature of an absolutist regime that had achieved momentous change in the urban economy. Thus, the Kōza-ha characterized the Meiji state as "a composite unified system of feudal possession" under the dictatorship of the old feudal clans. The bureaucracy, staffed by former samurai, opposed any possibility of bourgeois democracy, such as the civil rights movement, by reviving feudal remnants. Moreover, aspects of the ancient Asiatic despotic system were recalled, and old laws copied into new legal codes, even while the political system of King Friedrich II of Prussia (1740-1786) was adopted as the model for the new state. The revival of such old forms was evident in the regime's use of "extra-economic coercion toward the peasantry and urban workers" and its strict regulation of and reliance on forced labor in accumulating capital. At the same time, the government established intimate relationships with commercial capitalists—such as the Mitsui and Shimada families, which had originated in the *han* industries and would combine to form zaibatsu in the succeeding decades—on which it relied heavily for loans.[123]

Most importantly, the threat from abroad forced the Meiji state to accomplish primitive accumulation rapidly and in a manner that would strengthen the nation militarily. This helped to account for the continued power and autonomy of the military in the modern state.

> The Meiji government was not only a powerful lever in the transitional process of primitive accumulation of capital, but it could even possibly have been the parent of the birth of capitalist production itself. Because of this relationship, the protection and nurturing of capitalist production, the importation of technology, and the transplantation of industry had to be conjoined with the official patriarchic organization of the Meiji government. Thus, it was not an accident that this patriarchic tutorial protectionist bureaucratic organization (*bevormundende Bureaukratie*) structured the entire state system, as an indispensable framework for the establishment and development of capitalism. The appearance of that state structure was the process of the formation of the Meiji regime.[124]

If internal constraints made one facet of this regime its base in a semi-serf land system, the international threat gave it its militaristic character, which was encouraged through the state's promotion of heavy industry and "a huge military structure = key industry system," financed by the backward land system. As described by Yamada, the Meiji state was a "militaristic semi-feudal" absolutist state, which endeavored immediately to build a strong regular army to repel foreign capitalists and an oppressive police network to control advocates of democratic liberation at home. It created the Tokyo munitions factory, the Osaka munitions factory, and naval shipbuilding enterprises, many of which relied on formerly *han* structures. As a consequence of this tutelage of the Meiji state, Japanese capitalism developed its heavy industry first, and then its light, consumer industries, although *han*-sponsored enterprises had given capitalism a head start in the latter category. By the turn of the century, Japan had achieved self-sufficiency in the communications and transport network required for a powerful military structure, whereas in 1872 it had been almost completely dependent on British aid to lay the Tokyo-Yokohama railroad line.[125]

Neither this pattern of development nor the absolutism that sustained it was unique to Japan. Economically, Japan from the early Meiji period to the 1920s might be compared with Germany from the early nineteenth century until the founding of the empire in 1879 through the turn of the century (see Hirano's comparison of the two cases in table 10).[126] In Germany, as in Japan, the external threat (the French revolution, in the former case) was a powerful determinant of the manner in which the state promoted capitalist development; and both sides diverged from the classic French pattern of bourgeois revolution from below. Marx and Engels had described the rise of such absolutism after incomplete bourgeois revolutions in 1848-1849 in Germany and Austria and in Russia in 1905. Drawing on these writings, Hirano endeavored to place Japan in what he saw as a geographical pattern in the execution of such revolutions. Bourgeois-democratic revolutions first occurred in 1648 England and in 1789 France; these were thoroughgoing events, which saw the birth of the liberal democratic ideology that Marx and Engels identified with the bourgeoisie. Such ideas, however, were unknown in oriental despotic and feudal regimes, like China and India. Capitalism and bourgeois ideology had been brought to the East only from without, forcibly, by the eastward expansion of world capitalism. "In Japan too," Hirano argued, "this 'freedom' held by the laws of commodity production of world capitalism, if forcibly, has shaken the old forms of production in Japan on the basis of the adoption of the new capitalist mode of production, and is bringing about so-called 'liberty.' " While the notion of "bourgeois liberty" was deeply flawed, as Marx argued, its achievement was still an essential stage in the path toward socialism. But because of the weaknesses

TABLE 10

Comparison of Scale and Pace of Industrial Production in Germany and Japan

	Agrarian population	Industrial workers in factories	Handicraft industry workers per 1,000 pop.	Spindles (thousands)	Coal production (millions of tons)	Pig iron production (thousands of tons)
Germany						
1786	—	165,000	—	—	—	—
1812[a]	—	—	—	256	—	—
1816[b]	78%	—	38.8	—	—	—
1843	—	—	—	—	3.0	—
1846	—	551,000	52.1	474[a]	—	—
1849[b]	64%	—	—	—	—	—
1850	—	—	—	—	—	223
1860	—	—	—	—	—	529
1861	—	—	59.1	170[b]	—	—
1865	50%	—	—	—	—	—
1870	—	—	—	—	26.3	1,391
1882	—	2,990,000[c] 4,300,000	—	—	—	—
1895	35%	5,950,000 4,700,000	—	—	—	—
1900	—	—	—	8,000	109.2	8,400
1907	28%	8,950,000 5,300,000	—	—	—	—
1908	—	—	—	9,882	—	—
1913	—	—	—	—	279.0	19,304
Japan						
1873	78%	—	20.6[d]	—	—	—
1886	—	149,000[e]	—	—	—	—
1888	—	—	—	114	—	—
1889	—	—	—	—	1.9	13
1920	51%	—	43.3[f]	—	—	—
1924	—	1,586,000[g]	—	—	—	—
1929	—	—	—	6,109	32.9	—
1930	—	—	—	—	—	1,187

SOURCE: Hirano Yoshitarō, "Meiji ishin ni okeru seiji-teki shihai keitai" [The form of political domination in the Meiji Restoration], in *Nihon shihon-shugi hattatsu shi kōza* [Symposium on the history of the development of Japanese capitalism] (Tokyo: Iwanami Shoten, 1932-1933), 5:59n.

[a] Data for Saxony only. [b] Data for Prussia only.

[c] Beginning in 1882, German statistics differentiate between factories employing 6 or more workers (top figure) and those employing 5 or fewer workers (bottom figure).

[d] Averaged from data collected 1873-1877.

[e] Averaged from data collected 1886-1889.

[f] Data from *Nihon tokei nenkan* [Japanese statistical yearbook], vol. 49 (1930).

[g] Factories employing 5 or more workers only.

of Japan's bourgeoisie, and because of similar consequences of backwardness in the constitutions of Germany and Austria, neither the political institutions nor the ideological superstructures in these countries evolved the mature notion of bourgeois democracy.

Similarly, in Japan, Hirano noted, to the extent that democratic institutions existed, they were handed down from above by the emperor, and throughout the era of the absolutist state, these institutions were always vitiated by the influence of the ideology of absolutism.[127] The Meiji regime's family-state idea of the national polity, which had been systematized to support the state's economic revolution from above, dictated that the "Imperial Will," rather than the popular will, was the basis of political legitimacy. It was this ideological superstructure—itself based on the balance of material forces in the Meiji Restoration—that in turn sustained the potential autonomy of the emperor-system state. These circumstances, which explained why a bourgeois-democratic revolution had yet to be completed in prewar Japan, could only be appreciated in terms of a structuralist approach to the state. Yamada expressed this structural aspect in Kōza-ha work succinctly when he argued that the distinctive feature of Japan's "militaristic semi-serf" capitalism was the "relationship of mutual regulation between semi-serf petty cultivation and capitalism."[128] In the Tokugawa era, capitalism had flourished on the basis of a semi-feudal agrarian system in such a way that it could not survive without that base. As capitalism grew from Meiji to Shōwa, feudal elements did not disappear but were strengthened, and the concentration of power in the Meiji state merely reinforced these tendencies. Thus, feudal remnants were reflected in the political superstructure, even while the regime's close ties to usury capital and commitment to build a large military regime promoted the growth of monopoly capital and imperialism. The emperor system reflected the absolutist character of such a regime.

Yet Kōza-ha writings presented a variety of interpretations of this absolutism. Hattori Shisō followed Karl Kautsky's interpretation very closely, emphasizing the balance, or equilibrium, among class forces.[129] By contrast, Hirano rejected this criterion, arguing that there could be no equilibrium between bourgeoisie and landed aristocracy where the bourgeoisie did not struggle. He stressed instead semi-serfdom in large landownership and the concentration of power into a kind of state feudalism under the Meiji oligarchy. This was not pure feudalism, but feudalism in its final stages, hence absolutism. Finally, Noro acknowledged no large-scale landownership but argued that the Meiji state had promoted capitalism by facilitating concentration of landholding.

In almost all these cases, into the emperor system was injected some analysis of its Asiatic origins and its consequences. Indeed, the very depiction of the Meiji state as absolutist seemed very closely bound to the notion of oriental despotism, as Hirano, Noro, and Hattori all took a cue from the Comintern theses and made some mention of the state acting as the highest landlord. While the analytical distinction between absolutism and oriental despotism was clear to Kōza-ha Marxists, in their view, only the peculiarities carried over from its Asiatic past could have made Japanese feudalism exhibit all the peculiarities they discerned. This link between the continued backwardness of the emperor system and its "oriental past" was strongly suggested by repeated references to petty agriculture as the basis of Meiji absolutism: Marx, of course, had identified small isolated peasant agricultural communities as the seat of oriental despotism. This picture of the development of the Japanese state from Tokugawa to Shōwa contrasted dramatically with Inomata's portrait of an increasingly liberal bourgeois monarchy resting on a highly developed capitalist base. For the Rōnō-ha, Japan was merely another example of a bourgeois-democratic state. For the Kōza-ha, its peculiarities—which could explain the survival of the emperor system, the growth of the military, and the intensification of repression at home—were so overwhelming that they warranted special attention.

The Debate on Japanese Capitalism and Problems in the Marxist Theory of the State

At first glance, the weaknesses of both factions in the controversy on the Japanese state seem all too evident. Each side emphasized one aspect of the whole to the neglect of the other. On the one hand, the Rōnō-ha accepted with few reservations the myth of Taishō democracy and treated the contemporary state as if it coincided precisely with the model of the state in advanced capitalist society described by Bukharin. On the other hand, in contrast to the Rōnō-ha's acceptance of the formal structure of the state—its constitution and institutions of parliamentary democracy—the Kōza-ha was deeply troubled by the imperfections of bourgeois democracy in Japan. Neglecting the operation of the political parties, the Kōza-ha stressed the emperor system and its supporting institutions as the key to the discrepancy between the increasingly repressive and militaristic political reality in Japan and the ideal of the bourgeois-democratic state that Marx had described.

Hence, while both major factions applied some notion of absolutism to the post-Restoration Meiji state, the *problématique* of the Kōza-ha became the emperor system, while that of the Rōnō-ha was the phenomenon of monopoly capitalism (a subject that few Kōza-ha writers, with the exception of Shinobu Seizaburō, a student of Hattori, elected to study).[130] The Rōnō-ha's preference for an instrumentalist approach yielded a descriptive account of the role of bourgeois economic interests in state politics in the Taishō and

Shōwa periods. The Kōza-ha's emphasis on the emperor system encouraged the development of a historical and structuralist approach not only to the state but to the whole of Japanese political economy since the mid-nineteenth century. Thus, the Rōnō-ha's contribution to an historical analysis of state-building was sparse, while the Kōza-ha left the dynamics of contemporary Japanese politics to inference. Yet, ironically, it was the Kōza-ha's concentration on the historical evolution of the absolutist state that was more conducive to an understanding of the rise of the military in contemporary Japan. The Rōnō-ha's assumption that the emperor system had lost significance in the Taishō and Shōwa eras offered them no basis for understanding the autonomy of the civil and military bureaucracy. Their premise that absolutism had given way to bourgeois democracy led the Rōnō-ha to neglect the continuing influence of *kokutai* thought and the efficacy of the appeal to the "Imperial Will," which the military exploited unhesitatingly in its rise to dominance in the 1930s. Nevertheless, Inomata's work perceptively noted the role of China in Japan's economic well-being and was nicely predictive of the prospects for war in the Pacific between the world's two newest capitalist powers, the United States and Japan.

Besides these insights into Japan's national and international development in the 1930s and 1940s, the controversy on the Japanese state also offers a view of some theoretical difficulties in the Marxist theory of the state as a whole. This is particularly so on the side of the Kōza-ha, which, equipped with the perspectives of Marx's early writings and drawing freely on non-Marxist works, accepted the risks posed by emphasizing the peculiar over the universal aspects of the Japanese state. Japanese Marxists confronted a pattern of political development that did not easily fit the orthodox Marxist model of political change: the coexistence of an apparently feudalistic and Asiatic emperor system heavily imbued with religious content alongside highly developed finance capitalism and the formal political structure of bourgeois democracy. By investigating the mix of peculiarly Japanese elements with aspects shared with other capitalist states and with "backward" societies, Japanese Marxists ventured beyond the limits of Soviet orthodoxy and discovered the possibility of new, mutant forms of the state. In this sense, many participants in the controversy—particularly Yamada, Hani, and Hirano—did not merely describe the state in the theoretical terms of others, but fully deserve to be recognized as theorists. Certain of their theoretical insights antedated and surpassed the work of prominent Western scholars like Barrington Moore and Immanuel Wallerstein.

The significance of the contribution of these Kōza-ha Marxists is suggested by the point at which their work on Japan diverged from that of Trotsky on Russia. In his study of Russia, Trotsky had acknowledged the powerful role the state had played in promoting economic development in response to external threat, but he had concluded that the resulting strains in the society made revolution inevitable. As Yamada, Hani, and Hirano demonstrated, however, this conclusion did not apply to Japan. The Meiji state had been able to accomplish what Qing China and tsarist Russia could not: it combined old and new political ideas to establish a solid basis of political legitimacy, a quintessential "Socratic Lie," in emperor-centered *kokutai* thought, to support its modernizing reforms, thereby preempting the potential for revolution from below. Kōza-ha Marxists like Hirano analyzed effectively this example of a backward country responding to international pressures without risking a revolution from below. The Kōza-ha readily acknowledged the significant role of the Meiji state in encouraging a pattern of economic development that could sustain a defensive posture of militarism vis-à-vis more developed capitalist states. Unlike many Western Marxists, then, the Kōza-ha was not crippled by the fear that their recognition of such a relationship between base and superstructure would challenge the integrity of Marxism as a whole. Rather, they in effect recognized the Meiji Restoration as a revolution from above—however imperfect—made in response to pressures imposed upon a late-developing Japan by the prior development of an expansive system of capitalism in Europe. The Kōza-ha also perceived that this course affected negatively the possibility for the maturation of true bourgeois and then socialist democracy from within. Finally, Hirano observed similarities with Russia, with Italy, and with Germany that not only raised frightening prospects for the fate of democracy in Japan but also implied that this was a course that might be shared by other late developers as well.[131] It remained for others in the Kōza-ha to explain these aspects of Japanese political development in terms of the persistence of feudal relations in the countryside in the prewar and then the postwar eras.

EIGHT

The Agrarian Problem: The Dual Economy and the Revolution in the Countryside

In spite of the stormy development of capitalism in the cities, the countryside is still remarkably backward, externally, technologically, and socio-economically. The lack of land and extreme poverty prevail among the peasants. While 5.5 million peasant families, i.e., 80 percent of the entire peasantry, cultivate an average of only 1.1 *chō* (2.7 acres), only .1 percent of the peasantry own 80 percent of all arable land. Furthermore, a system of usurious ground rent has spread throughout Japan. About half of the harvest gathered from 40 percent of all cultivable land is paid as rent by tenants to landlords. These few figures demonstrate fully the severe intensification of the agrarian problem in Japan, at the same time that they indicate that the peasant revolution in Japan has already ripened and that the problem of the bourgeois-democratic revolution has become a very real one.
—The '27 Theses

THE CONTROVERSY on the agrarian problem (*nōgyō mondai*) was at once both a central and a peripheral component of the debate on Japanese capitalism. On the one hand, the assessment of the current level of development of the agricultural sector of the Japanese economy rested on a theoretical understanding of the transition from feudalism to capitalism in general. The consideration of the agrarian problem with respect to the abstract concepts of *Capital* quickly gave rise to narrowly focused disputes on Marxist economic theory, and these esoteric discussions failed to engage as large a circle of Japanese Marxists as the theory of the state or the Asiatic mode of production. Nevertheless, the agrarian problem as a whole was a crucial part of the larger debate on Japanese capitalism. The issue drove a wedge between the Rōnō-ha and those who remained loyal to the Comintern's interpretation of the economic situation in Japan; and the conflict touched on the main theme of the debate on Japanese capitalism as a whole, the relationship between the universal and the particular aspects of Japanese development.

For participants in the debate, the agrarian problem was the touchstone of the analysis of the current stage of Japanese capitalism. Insofar as the growth of capitalism had failed to transform the Japanese countryside as rapidly as the concentration of capital had proceeded in the cities since the Meiji Restoration, the seeming disparity between the English pattern of socio-economic development and that of Japan from Meiji to early Shōwa signified to Marxists of both major factions that Japan remained "backward" in the agrarian sphere, regardless of the tremendously rapid advances that had been made in the urban industrial sector. Clearly, the dual economy existed in interwar Japan. Consequently, while it was relatively easy to analyze Japan's industrialized urban sector in terms of Marx's paradigm of the capitalist mode of production, the persistence of a lagging agrarian sector significantly complicated the effort to interpret the economic situation in order to evolve an effective revolutionary strategy in prewar Japan.

The Comintern theses of July 1927 argued that the gap between the West European and Japanese experiences in the agrarian sphere was of qualitative significance. In Japan in the mid- to late 1920s, over 50 percent of the population was still engaged in agriculture[1] (although agriculture produced only about 25 percent of national income, a decline from almost 40 percent from the Meiji period),[2] and the agrarian sector reeled from recurrent depressions (see chapter 1). In such a setting, the Comintern theses portrayed the imbalance between the development of the industrial sector and that of the agrarian sphere as a key element determining the need for a two-stage revolution in Japan. It was the persistence of entrenched "semi-feudal" landownership and landlordism in the countryside that demonstrated the inadequacy of the Meiji Restoration as a bourgeois-democratic revolution. These elements, which comprised the material basis for Japan's "absolutist" emperor system, were to be dismantled when the bourgeois-democratic revolution in the countryside was completed. Only then would the high level of development of capitalism in the urban areas allow the proletarian-socialist revolution to proceed.

By contrast, the *Rōnō* group believed that the admittedly backward elements of Japanese agriculture did not carry the significance imputed to them by the Comintern. In support of their strategy of immediate socialist revolution, then, Rōnō-ha leaders Inomata Tsunao and Kushida Tamizō produced theoretical and historical studies to support the premise of an agrarian sphere that had experienced substantial capitalistic development. Their work was consistent with the overall Rōnō-ha tendency to understate the peculiarities of Japanese development while stressing its coincidence with the Western European model. In their view, "the feudalistic elements remaining in capitalist Japan were merely remnants of older systems without economic and material backing, and were quantitatively fading and disappearing with the development of capitalism."[3]

This stress on the universal elements of the Japanese experience in the countryside led Rōnō-ha theorists to abstract discussions that became significant for later developments in Japanese Marxian economics, but remained peripheral to the more pressing concrete issues tackled in the debate on Japanese capitalism. The controversy on the theory of ground rent (*jidai ronsō*), for example, was similar to a discussion that engulfed Marxist theoreticians in the Soviet Union and Western Europe as well.[4] This issue was intimately related to the agrarian problem, for the interpretation of the character of the Japanese countryside turned on the question of whether agrarian rents in the 1920s were essentially capitalistic or feudalistic in nature. Kushida and others challenged the claim of Hirano Yoshitarō and other Kōza-ha theorists that no fundamental change in agrarian land rents had occurred since the late Tokugawa era.[5] The ensuing debate on the theory of ground rent took on a life of its own, spiraling to increasingly abstract levels of analysis, and moving away from the immediate issues concerning the current state of agriculture in Japan. Indeed, neither Yamakawa nor Inomata devoted more than sparse attention to this issue in discussing the agrarian problem.[6] Accordingly, the abstract debate on ground rent and the related controversy on the Marxist theory of value are treated here only insofar as they pertained directly to the question of the nature of Japanese political and economic development to the 1930s.

The debate on the agrarian problem did not gain momentum until almost 1930, when the pattern of declining agricultural prices had become firmly established.[7] Yet, the roots of the controversy on agriculture date back to the birth of the JCP in 1922. The party's Draft Program frankly acknowledged the difficulties of analyzing Japanese capitalism because of the backwardness of the agrarian sphere:

> While the Japanese Communist Party is based on the common demands of the communist parties of all countries, it must consider the special character of the development of Japanese capitalism. . . . Japanese capitalism now still has the vestiges of the feudal characteristics of a previous era. The greater part of the land is in the hands of semi-feudal large landlords, and the largest of them is the emperor. . . . On the other hand, most of the arable land owned by these large landlords is rented to tenant farmers, and tenant farmers cultivate with their own agricultural implements. Thus, as a result of fierce competition over the land, ground rents have risen to the point now of reaching so-called "starvation ground-rents" (*kiga jidai*).[8]

As this passage indicates, the continued backwardness of the agrarian sector was at the forefront of the difficulties the Comintern leaders saw in the effort to develop a suitable strategy for the newly founded JCP. The economic base of the semi-feudal authoritarian emperor-system state, a system that still carried the hues of an "oriental society" in which the emperor was the highest landlord, lay in an agrarian sphere that stood curiously in contradiction with highly developed and increasingly concentrated capitalism in the urban sphere.

Yet the Comintern's emphasis on the agrarian problem varied in subsequent theses. The 1927 Theses, drafted when Comintern leaders were desperate for revolutionary success in the East after the crushing defeat in China, stressed the characteristics of highly developed capitalism in Japan. Drawing on Bukharin's insights on the advanced capitalist state and the movement toward state capitalism, the new theses emphasized changes in the urban sector and their reflection in the power of the imperial regime rather than the backwardness of the rural economy.[9] Nevertheless, big semi-feudal landlords continued to figure prominently in the theses' analysis of "the feudal elements, lords, and military cliques who play a large role in the government."[10] After the brief acknowledgment of the political "hegemony" of "finance capital" in the 1931 Draft Political Theses,[11] the agrarian problem reemerged prominently in the emphasis the '32 Theses gave to feudal features of the Japanese state. The landlord system received equal billing with monopoly capital, and the theses called for the "overthrow of the emperor system," "the elimination of large landownership," as well as the fulfillment of labor's demands against capital, in that order.[12] The overall pattern of the Comintern's view of Japanese agriculture was evident. Japanese agriculture was viewed as "Asiatically backward" and thus in need of thorough revolution in the countryside. Where the '27 Theses had recognized a system of "usurious rents" in Japan, this statement, used by the Rōnō-ha to support its premise of capitalist agriculture,[13] posed no necessary contradiction with the view of Japan as Asiatic; for Marx had noted that stagnant Asiatic systems seemed immune even to the pervasive progressive effects of usury capital (see chapter 6).

These abrupt shifts in the Comintern's emphasis on the agrarian problem were largely attributable to factors extraneous to the situation in Japan: events in China and the power struggle in the Soviet Union. Nevertheless, throughout the 1920s and 1930s, the Comintern's erratic attention to the agrarian problem was superseded by a consistent rise in interest in the issue among Japan's indigenous Marxists, particularly within the dissident *Rōnō* faction. Alarming economic trends, and social unrest in response to these, were responsible for this growing attention to the agrarian problem.[14]

During these years, as the Japanese economy as a whole experienced a contraction after the boom of World War I, the gap between the agrarian and industrial sectors became increasingly evident. Agriculture had shared in the relative prosperity occasioned by the war, when prices soared and rural productivity and income also rose significantly; but after the war, the rural sector abruptly fell into a decline from which it would not recover until after World War II. At the same time, farmers were also hurt by the postwar industrial recession, as the number of factory jobs shrank, driving many back to the countryside to pursue the more difficult and less rewarding livelihood of a rural day laborer or tenant farmer. As Marxist scholar Nishiyama Take'ichi observed in mid-1927, "the surplus of Japan's rural population can not be absorbed by the cities and is stagnating in the countryside."[15] Net migration from villages to cities, then, declined substantially from 1.21 percent of total agricultural laborers in 1921 to .85 percent in 1930. In the meantime, landownership became concentrated in fewer hands, and agricultural prices fell below overall price levels.[16]

Symptomatic of the sharp deterioration in the fortunes of the Japanese peasantry was the equally dramatic rise in incidents of tenant unrest in the countryside. The more than tenfold increase in reported rural disputes, from 256 in 1918 to 2,700 in 1926, according to one account, aroused a "sense of crisis" even in government circles, since the countryside had been "long regarded as the nation's ultimate guarantee of social stability." Contemporary observers sought the causes of this unrest in rural poverty, the proliferation of radical ideologies including Marxism coupled with the stirring example of the Russian revolution, and the effects of universal education and conscription. A recent Western study, however, has argued persuasively that none of these factors alone can explain the startling incidence of tenant disputes during these years. Rather, the pattern of wartime economic growth which raised expectations among farmers, particularly in the rapidly industrializing southwestern part of Japan, was coupled with the withdrawal of landlords, now moving their capital as well as their homes in many cases to the cities. These two factors together have been identified as the principal contributors to the rising crisis in the villages during the 1920s.[17]

Those Marxists associated with the Kōza-ha and the Rōnō-ha did not have access to the data and techniques that produced this particular understanding of the agrarian problem. But their firsthand observation of the overall pattern of economic distress coupled with social unrest alerted them to the need to study the agrarian problem in depth. Although some work on this issue was begun before the schism in the JCP, the Rōnō-ha's rejection of the '27 Theses destroyed the assumption that the Comintern's analysis was an adequate basis of revolutionary strategy and presented an opportunity to pursue the issue and its implications for the Japanese revolutionary movement at length.

Between 1927 and 1937, Marxists of both factions tackled the agrarian question. In the West, both sides have been taken to task for a one-sided approach to the issue, the Rōnō-ha for emphasizing the universalities of Japanese agrarian development, and the Kōza-ha for stressing its peculiarities.[18] This discussion of the controversy will argue that whatever their infirmities, both Rōnō-ha and Kōza-ha were fundamentally correct in their perception of the problems posed by the dual economy in Japan. The Kōza-ha view may have had more merit for recognizing that the problem of uneven and combined development was far more severe than the Rōnō-ha was prepared to acknowledge. In any case, these scholars properly sought in the imbalance between town and countryside a major reason for the economic crisis that would culminate in expansionist war.

The Rōnō-ha and the Development of Capitalism in the Countryside

The Challenge to the Comintern's View of the Undevelopment of Japanese Agriculture

Yamakawa Hitoshi and his supporters had left the JCP because they could not accept the Comintern's conclusion in the '27 Theses that backwardness in the agrarian sphere effectively relegated Japan to the status of a less-developed country and condemned it to a strategy of two-stage revolution. Yet the Rōnō-ha faced the same incontrovertible facts that sustained the Comintern-JCP view: the Meiji reforms notwithstanding, many characteristics of the agrarian economy that had emerged late in the Edo period persisted decades later. The late Tokugawa landlord system and the small-scale family agricultural enterprise were retained long after the Restoration. Tenancy still involved almost half of all peasants and half of all agricultural lands at one time. Rents in kind remained, reaching 50 percent of harvest, and landlord-tenant relations continued to be imbued with "feudal" customs from the Edo period.[19] At the same time, while there was no evidence of large-scale commercialization of agriculture, many landlords invested their rental incomes in industry and finance and engaged in usury, thereby establishing links with the industrial sector that had not existed before.[20]

This context offered evidence for both the persistence of feudalism and the inroads of capitalism in the agrarian sphere; but to support their one-stage revolutionary strategy, Rōnō-ha Marxists needed to demonstrate that "capitalism" was predominant in the agrarian as well as in the urban sector. Simply to show the existence of state capitalism was insufficient; the Comintern had done so and still advocated a preliminary bourgeois-democratic revolution directed against feudal remnants that maintained a powerful economic base in large feudal landholding.

Although Yamakawa, as the faction's political strategist, did not undertake the sustained economic analysis that Inomata, Kushida, and Sakisaka Itsurō would produce to accomplish this task, the broad outlines of the Rōnō-ha's argument could be found in the essay with which Yamakawa launched the group's organ *Rōnō*. There Yamakawa argued that the landlords that the Comintern had designated as "semi-feudal" had become a relatively less powerful force in the economy as Japanese capitalism developed rapidly. In addition, Yamakawa claimed, the landlords had become "bourgeoisified": they had taken on some of the characteristics of capitalists, by investing in commerce, industry, and finance. Given this line of argument, it is not surprising that Yamakawa did not view agrarian development as sufficiently problematic to occupy a larger position in his strategic theory as a whole.[21]

As economists, however, Inomata, Kushida, and Sakisaka saw the technical and theoretical difficulties of proving this argument. Recognizing that it formed a crucial link in their refutation of the Comintern's strategy for Japan, they pursued the agrarian problem more seriously. These Rōnō-ha theorists rejected the Comintern's analysis for its lack of dynamism: it saw, they claimed, essentially no positive development in Japanese agriculture from the late Tokugawa era to the 1920s. They also repudiated the argument of Yamada Moritarō and other Kōza-ha theorists that semi-feudal landownership in the agrarian sector had provided the primary resource for primitive capital accumulation that had in turn given birth to a militarist semi-serf pattern of capitalism in Japan.[22] According to Rōnō-ha scholars, it was absurd to claim that capitalism could have evolved on an essentially feudalistic base, since capitalism was generally built on the demise of feudalistic landownership. In their view, the Meiji land tax reforms established a system of "modern" (i.e., capitalist) landownership; free market competition for land explained the persistence of high ground rents, high land prices, and the generally low standard of living of the peasantry.[23] Furthermore, as Sakisaka asserted, the "nondevelopment" characteristic of Yamada's interpretation of Japanese capitalism had to be replaced by a dynamic analysis reflecting the universal laws of capitalist development described by Marx. Such an approach would show that although "the capitalisms of individual countries have their respective special natures, nevertheless, such special structures are dissolved into universality or generality with the development of capitalism." Whatever might have been the peculiar characteristics of Japan in its feudal era, "in both Russia and Germany the feudalism that remained deeply embedded gradually disappeared with the development of capitalism"; "there is no reason to expect Japan to be an exception to this [pattern]," Sakisaka argued.[24] It was this concern with the universal characteristics of the transition from feudalism to capitalism that led Rōnō-ha Marxists to stress the changed character of agrarian landlords in Japan and thereby to become deeply embroiled in the controversy on ground rent.

The Embourgeoisement of Landlords and the Controversy on Ground Rent

It was Inomata who took the first steps for the Rōnō-ha in undertaking a sustained economic analysis to support the group's political position. Early on, Inomata protested that Kōza-ha theorists, writing in the journal *Marukusu-*

shugi [Marxism] in 1928 in criticism of early *Rōnō* essays, had distorted the true position of the dissidents in claiming that they were neglecting the agrarian problem. In response, Inomata asserted that the Rōnō-ha had never claimed that agrarian landlords had lost the material basis necessary for them to function as an independent political force. Rather, in his own essay, "The Political Position of the Contemporary Japanese Bourgeoisie," Inomata recalled, he had merely stated that this group's continued importance in national politics was recognized in its role as part of a bourgeois-landlord bloc. But the Rōnō-ha argued that a struggle against "feudal absolutism" should not be the main thrust of Japan's revolution because in Japan "landlords and other feudal remnant forces were no longer powerful political opponents of the bourgeoisie, for they had lost the material basis necessary to act as a potent antagonistic force."[25]

In April 1928, Inomata outlined what he believed to be the special characteristics of the agrarian problem in Japan, but he raised more questions than he answered.[26] Inomata began with the observation that in the late 1920s, the peasant movement was proceeding as part of a larger labor movement, rather than as an independent force in Japanese politics. The issue at hand was whether this should continue to be the case, given the "objective" situation in the countryside. Analyzing that situation, Inomata stressed that the "peculiar" character of Japanese agriculture was directly attributable to Japan's position as a late-developing country:

> Capitalism in backward Japan, which has a variety of peculiarities, both made agricultural production capitalistic and raised [the level of] its forces of production. [But] before carrying out its proper historical task of transforming the majority of the rural population into proletarians, [it] has already become a link in the chain of world capitalism in the era of [its] collapse. Japanese capitalism, born late, could grow only by seizing the surplus value that peasants produced, under (reactionary) government policies.

Finally, Inomata noted, capitalism, in pursuit of profits as its foremost objective, had failed to dominate the agrarian sector and thus left agricultural cultivation to proceed on the most primitive technical level. Hence, the continued "extreme poverty" of the peasantry and "the special content of the agrarian problem" in Japan.[27] Nevertheless, Inomata argued that the trend was toward the increasing dominance of capitalism in the countryside.

In this view, capitalism had failed to transform the agrarian sphere rapidly in Japan because of the downturn in the world capitalist economy; but Inomata did not explain precisely why this was so. However, he did offer one reason for the high level of agrarian rents in Japan. A "surplus rural population" had been inherited from the feudal era, and "the speed of the development of capitalism after the Meiji Restoration was not rapid enough to absorb that surplus population.[28] This development left in the countryside a large peasant population competing for land that was in increasingly short supply. Finally, in this early analysis, Inomata contested the Comintern's claim that large feudal landowning in the countryside was the basis of the emperor system. "The land [reforms] of the Meiji Restoration," Inomata argued, "made impossible the establishment and continued existence of a semi-feudal large landowning system such as [those] of prewar Russia and Germany." He equivocated on the implications of this difference, however. On the one hand, he claimed that the reforms made it "impossible for special forms of exploitation like the serf-landlord system to continue."[29] At the same time, however, the absence of a large landholding system like that of England did not facilitate the development of capitalist agricultural enterprise in Japan.[30]

At this point, Inomata did refer briefly to two points that would become critical to the Rōnō-ha's interpretation of the agrarian problem: the thesis of the "bourgeoisification of landlords" and the notion of "usury ground rent." Inomata elaborated on Yamakawa's assertion that the landlords to which the Comintern referred as feudal had in fact taken on many characteristics of the bourgeoisie.

> With the development of capitalism, many of our landlords, who were merely passively collecting ground rent, gradually became cash capitalists. Instead of reinvesting in land and agriculture, they turned the surplus value paid by tenants into time deposits in banks and invested in government bonds, stocks, and corporate bonds. Also, quite a few large landlords are specifically the directors of enterprise companies and bank presidents, and some of them are large-scale usurers. Thus, having lost the special character of agricultural landlords, they gradually were assimilated into bourgeois ideology and stand under the banner of finance capitalism.[31]

Thus, even if landlords had not become entrepreneurs in large-scale commercial agriculture, still, since the Meiji Restoration, Japanese landlords played an increasing role in the finance of urban capitalist industrialization through investment. This was the point where the interests of capitalists and landlords—who shared state power, in the Rōnō-ha view—converged. By using the rents paid by peasants to promote urban development, these landlords became exploiters of the proletariat as well as the peasantry, as "ground rent had become the blood and bones of capitalism." Moreover, since the landlords had thus shed some of their feudal character, Inomata reasoned, the distinction between landlord and capitalist was blurred, and the capitalist-landlord ruling bloc in Japan was even less imbued with "feudal characteristics'' than it would have been otherwise. Inomata offered no statistics on the number of landlords who had been so ''bourgeoisified''; but clearly he and other Rōnō-ha theorists believed that this was a significant proportion of the group.[32]

The link between these agrarian landlords and industrial capitalism in the cities lay in what Inomata called ''usury ground rent.'' It was in the discussion of this notion that we see crucial difficulties involved in analyzing a Japanese agricultural economy that was in an ambiguous process of transition. Here Inomata and Kōza-ha theorist Noro Eitarō looked at the same phenomenon—the collection of rents that closely resembled the high ground rents levied in the era of Tokugawa feudalism—and drew diametrically opposite conclusions. The discussion on this point in turn led Rōnō-ha and Kōza-ha into a twofold controversy on the nature of agrarian ground rents. The first issue lay in the proper interpretation of the nature of ground rents in the Japanese countryside in the 1920s. Were they still essentially feudalistic, reflecting the persistence of a feudalistic mode of exploitation and manifested in rents in kind, as the Kōza-ha maintained? Or did the form of ground rents mask an essential change in the nature of exploitation that had accompanied the penetration of capitalism in the countryside, as the Rōnō-ha argued? To the extent that these rents were perceived to be capitalistic, Marxists were then challenged to apply correctly Marx's observations on the nature of ground rent in order to understand the transformation that they were convinced had occurred in Japan, as elsewhere.

Inomata argued that whatever the formal similarities between Tokugawa ground rents and agrarian rents collected in the 1920s, the new rents were qualitatively different from their feudal predecessors. By virtue of collecting such rents, now regulated by market forces rather than by ''extra-economic coercion'' that Marxists commonly associated with feudalism, using them as a lever to impose usurious interest rates on peasants who could not pay, and investing collected rents in capitalist finance and industry in the cities, the landlords of Shōwa Japan were ''new'' landlords. They had a dual character: they were at once feudalistic and capitalistic. While Inomata was unclear about in which respects these landlords remained feudalistic, he maintained the Rōnō-ha argument that the dominant trend was toward the capitalistic transformation of the countryside.

Inomata readily acknowledged that the forms of contemporary ''usury ground rents,'' specifically the continued prevalence of their payment in kind at high rates of often 50 percent of harvest, were ''holdovers'' from the feudal tribute (*nengu*) collected by feudal lords. However, their content had changed in two ways. First, the new ground rents, which Kushida termed ''precapitalistic ground rents,'' comprised wages and average profits as well as ground rent in its original sense.[33] As Kushida would argue, these payments were conceptualized as currency by the peasants. It was Kushida's view that "in situations where the capitalist mode of production prevailed, even if a system of payment in kind was widely implemented, one could not immediately say that this was feudal ground rent and that landlord-tenant relations were feudal collection relations. Why? Because payment in kind itself was being conceptually converted into currency in the minds of landlords and tenants."[34]

The second crucial difference between the old and the new ground rents lay in their origins. The new rents were firmly rooted in a structure of small-scale individual landownership that was capitalistic, and their excessively high levels were the result of the inequality of land distribution in a capitalist society. The feudal tribute system of the Tokugawa era grew out of a system of landholding based on status relations that was fundamentally in conflict with a system of freely marketed land. As Marx had argued in his discussion of capitalist ground rent in *Capital*, "Landed property [in capitalist society] . . . receives its purely economic form by discarding all its former political and social embellishments and associations, in brief all those traditional accessories, which are denounced . . . as useless and absurd superfluities by the industrial capitalists themselves."[35]

Inomata, Kushida, and other Rōnō-ha theorists asserted that agrarian ground rents had already been stripped of these traditional elements. The feudal system of land tenure, in which the payment of tribute depended in part on customary status relations, was destroyed by the modernizing Meiji land tax reforms, they argued. These reforms "legalized private ownership that had already been coming into existence within the womb of feudal society; precisely because this was so, they . . . opened a new stage in the development of too-small scale agricultural production."[36] The Meiji Restoration was revolutionary because it had established what Marx considered to be the prerequisites for the development of capitalist agriculture by sweeping away feudal arrangements, including serfdom, in the countryside. Under the new capitalist system, in the context of a surplus agrarian population, high ground rents and land prices were the direct result of "the too-small scale agricultural system that accompanied legalized private landownership."[37] As agricultural labor became more productive and each peasant was driven by a desperate need to obtain land for his household to farm, fierce competition for scarce land drove rents and prices higher.[38]

As Marx's original discussion of ground rent as the transformation of a portion of surplus value in a capitalist society indicates, this understanding of the reasons for high ground rents even in an agrarian sector presumed to be capitalist was inadequate.[39] Clearly this Rōnō-ha position on the transformation of feudal to capitalist ground rents required a fuller understanding of the origins of the latter and the dynamics contributing to its high levels in

Shōwa Japan. Consequently, Rōnō-ha theorists were disproportionately represented in the separate but related controversy on the theory of ground rent itself. The controversy on ground rent initially emerged out of a larger debate on Marx's theory of value, in which non-Marxist economists responded to the increasing influence of Marxist economic theory in academic circles in the early 1920s by seeking to prove that its basic concepts were flawed. Because the discussion of ground rent had practical as well as theoretical implications, it in turn evolved into a dispute between supporters of the Comintern's diagnosis of the agrarian problem and their opponents. Rōnō-ha partisan Kushida explained this relationship between the ground rent controversy and the agrarian problem:

> There are currently two controversies in progress in the Japanese press. One is the inquiry into the Marxist schema of differential ground rent, and the other is the discussion of the current stage of Japanese agriculture. The former is the question of how to understand the final pattern of bourgeois-democratic revolution: while it differs from country to country, generally, it is an objective of countries in which the growth of capitalism is slow. . . . The latter is the question of to what extent contemporary Japanese agriculture has approached this goal, and through what process it is approaching it.[40]

The non-Marxist economist Hijikata Seibi launched the ground rent controversy in April 1928 with an essay provocatively entitled "The Collapse of Marx's Theory of Value as Viewed from the Theory of Ground Rent." Hijikata, and later fellow economist Takada Yasuma, asserted that there were fundamental inconsistencies between Marx's theory of ground rent and his theory of value, as well as in Marx's depiction of differential ground rent as "false social value."[41] The theoretical problem was twofold. First, in discussing market prices in general, Marx had argued that, because of the mechanism of competition the market value of a given commodity was established on the basis of the socially average labor embodied in it, even though individual items might have separate (labor) values as a result of differing production conditions within that sphere of production. Yet, when discussing differential ground rent, Marx no longer spoke in terms of the determination of the market price-value of agricultural products on the basis of average value; rather, he spoke in terms of the individual values of commodities produced under the poorest conditions (i.e., on the poorest land).[42] For, according to Marx, ground rent in capitalist agriculture "is always a differential rent." "It invariably arises from the difference between the individual production price of a particular capital having command over the monopolised natural force [land], on the one hand, and the general production price of the total capital invested in the sphere of production concerned, on the other."[43] This seemed to violate Marx's general theory of value. Moreover, if the market value of agricultural products was determined by the individual values of items produced in the poorest conditions, then it appeared that ground rent was no longer surplus value. In industry in general, where average value-price determined market prices, surplus profits generated under optimal production conditions and the minus surplus profit produced under the worst conditions simply cancelled each other out; and the sum of individual values corresponded to total market value. If, in the case of agricultural produce, however, the commodities produced on the worst land determined market value, there would be no such cancellation of surplus profit, and the total of the market value would be greater than the sum of individual commodity values. It was thus that a "false social value" emerged, as a part of this surplus profit was transformed into ground rent: ground rent was a reward to the landowner, in effect, for his " 'natural ability to monopolize' the land."[44] This process of the creation of ground rent explained the "continuous inflation of rents"; landlords could pocket a product of social development created without their help. The process itself, as Marx also noted, served to impede the development of capitalist agriculture, because "the tenant farmer avoids all improvements and outlays for which he cannot expect complete returns during the term of his lease."[45] Nevertheless, Marx's critics in Japan argued, this concept of differential ground rent representing false social value was not surplus value, and this was problematic for the consistency of Marx's theory as a whole.[46]

It was in responding to these critiques of Marxian economics that conflict arose among Marxist economists themselves, reinforcing the Rōnō-ha–Kōza-ha split and often dividing Rōnō-ha Marxists among themselves. Inomata was one of the first to respond to the criticisms of Takada and Hijikata, but he did so by misinterpreting Marx's theory of ground rent. He saw average value as the determinant of the market value of agricultural products as for manufactures, and he argued that the only reason that the value of commodities produced on the worst land would determine market value was that such land comprised most agricultural lands. In opposition to this view, Kushida argued that much of differential rent derived from surplus labor within agrarian society. Finally, Sakisaka identified the shortcoming of Kushida's view by noting that ground rent was to be interpreted not in physical terms but in terms of value/price. Ultimately, Sakisaka defended the consistency of Marx's theory of ground rent with the theory of value by showing the operation of the law of market value within the context of the limited nature of land of quality. Thus, Sakisaka was also able to show that differential rent was a form of the "redistribution of a part of surplus value of society as a whole through commodity circulation."[47]

Kōza-ha Marxists would find Sakisaka's defense of Marx's economics unsatisfactory on both pure theoretical and political grounds. On the one hand, it suggested that what Marx had seen as false social value in differential ground rent was not false at all, because it seemed to confuse absolute and differential ground rent. According to Moriya Fumio, Kushida and Sakisaka failed to understand that "absolute ground rent arises out of the limited nature of landownership and the low level of organic formation of capital in agriculture," and they rather chracteristically ignored the special aspects of the agrarian economy in favor of treating it only in terms of the universal aspects of the theory of value. These theoretical shortcomings in turn were linked to the political conflict between the two factions. Yamada Moritarō, for example, argued that Marx's description of differential ground rent as "*ein falscher sozialer Wert*" was reinterpreted by Rōnō-ha Marxists to mean "improper" rather than "false" social value. Once differential ground rent was attributed substance, as this reinterpretation (and Sakisaka's assertion that it constituted a redistribution of a portion of surplus value) implied, it was possible to conceive of its persisting under socialism. Yet the fact that Marx had connected the "false social value" of ground rent to the existence of capitalism denied the validity of this reinterpretation; and if the transformation to socialism would not eliminate this "false social value," then a major argument in favor of socialism would be undermined.[48]

Ultimately, of course, the primary point of contention between the two factions on the matter of ground rent lay in the Rōnō-ha's claim that rents in the 1920s were capitalist ground rents. Where Kōza-ha theorists argued that extra-economic coercion persisted even after the Meiji Restoration and determined high feudal ground rents, the Rōnō-ha maintained that this was not so. Kushida claimed that "no case [was] known in which a landowner . . . prohibited a change of occupation by a tenant for fear of the loss of rent."[49] Feudal personalistic relations between landlord and tenant had been replaced by impersonal capitalist contracts; land prices and rents were now the product of supply and demand curves, not noneconomic means of coercion exercised by the feudal landlord. Japanese peasants were no longer serfs but free individuals acting in an open, competitive market. In this interpretation, "feudal remnant forces" in the countryside had been so weakened that they did not significantly obstruct the development of capitalism in the countryside. Rather, according to Inomata, it was capitalism that hindered itself by failing to develop rapidly enough in the cities to absorb surplus labor. Only at that point did feudal "remnants become shackles on the development of agricultural production forces and consequently become an absolute restraint on the even higher development of capitalism itself," Inomata asserted. Curiously, Inomata thus appeared to argue that the uneven development in Japan's dual economy was itself a product of uneven development, without ever explaining what factors inherent in the agrarian sphere may have resisted its early and rapid industrialization at the outset.[50] These factors Inomata eventually found in Japan's "Asiatic" characteristics, but only after he had left the Rōnō-ha and developed an interpretation of the agrarian problem that more closely approximated the Kōza-ha view.

Nevertheless, the location of the ultimate source of the agrarian problem in capitalism itself was convenient for Inomata's effort to support the Rōnō-ha's revolutionary strategy. For if the problem was attributed to a pattern of unequal land distribution rooted in a capitalistic private property system, then only a socialist revolution that abolished that system could solve the problem. Moreover, if the landlords had been widely "bourgeoisified," one could hardly expect the "democratic" resolution of the land problem to be achieved by the "new" bourgeoisified landlords, who held a stake in the existing distribution of land and in high rents. Like Marx and Lenin, Inomata believed that "the peasants are not a social stratum that can form an independent political force."[51] Therefore, they could accomplish their primary objectives—rent reduction and land reform—only in cooperation with the proletariat.

Finally, Inomata asserted that these objectives of the peasantry were in fact bourgeois-democratic goals in a late-developing country where capitalism had still not fully transformed the countryside and where institutions like the Privy Council signalled that the state was far from democratic. However, these bourgeois-democratic tasks were only of secondary importance and could not be the primary objective of the Japanese revolution, as the Comintern and JCP argued. Land reform alone could not solve the agrarian problem, because the peasantry could not live "humanly" on the basis of small-scale cultivation on an average of slightly more than one *chō* of land per household. Rather, the forces of production in the agrarian sphere needed to be increased, Inomata argued, and this could only be accomplished in a socialist society where presumably land would be tilled in common larger tracts, and where farmers produced for society rather than for capital.[52]

Thus, like the Comintern and the JCP, Rōnō-ha theorists recognized that much of the bourgeois-democratic revolution had yet to be completed, and that the agrarian sphere was to be central in that process. Nevertheless, according to Inomata and others, the speed with which the Russian revolution had moved from one stage to the other suggested the foolishness of a formalistic effort to separate one stage of revolution from the next, as the two-stage theorists were wont to do. Therefore, "the bourgeois-democratic struggle of the Japanese proletariat does not precede the proletarian socialist struggle. It is not that when the first is finished the latter begins." Rather, "at the outset, the two are inextricably linked." Inomata declared that only by overthrowing the bourgeoisie could the united proletariat and peasantry remove "feudal remnants" and solve the land problem in the countryside.[53]

Ironically, Inomata made this argument by stressing the peculiarities of Japan's capitalist development. "Under historical conditions in Japan, the beginning of the proletarian revolution is manifested in the form of bourgeois revolution. The two are contracted into one stage instead of being dragged out into two stages."[54] The key phrase here for Inomata was "historical conditions in Japan," for these both necessitated the continued struggle for bourgeois democracy and weakened the revolutionary power of the proletariat. Bourgeois democracy had not been fully realized in Japan not just because of the persistence of former ruling groups, but primarily because "the Japanese bourgeoisie [had] gained power through compromise, without a decisive mass struggle."[55] When it finally became an imperialist bourgeoisie, it was threatened from both above (internationally) and below (by the proletariat) and could not fight the feudal remnant forces effectively. The "embourgeoisement of landlords and the reactionary imperialism of the bourgeoisie combined to make the completion of bourgeois democracy" "the responsibility of the proletariat." In this sense, while the JCP was wrong to compare the current situation in Japan with Russia before February 1917, an analogy of Japan in the 1920s with Russia between February and October 1917 was fully tenable: "in Russia, the responsibility for the completion of democracy [also] had to be linked with the overthrow of imperialism as the main task of the proletariat in an imperialist country with both the remnants of feudal forces . . . and a political structure that reflected them."[56]

This analysis of the agrarian problem by Inomata, Kushida, and later Sakisaka confirmed the validity of Yamakawa's call for a united front strategy for the revolution. The bourgeoisification of landlords made the peasantry the natural ally of a proletariat that was as politically immature as the bourgeoisie that had emerged through compromise rather than struggle in late-developing Japan.[57] The proletariat, therefore, had to follow Yamakawa's call to draw all antibourgeois forces, such as the Labor-Farmer Party (Rōdō Nōmintō) and the Japanese Labor-Farmer Party (Nihon Rōnōtō), together into a united front. Poor peasants—mostly tenants, peasants with no land, and peasants with land insufficient to apply the entire family's labor—would form the core of this alliance. Most of the poor peasants were also rural semi-proletarians, that is, the heads of the household, or perhaps sons, who also hired themselves out to work. The rural semi-proletariat plus those who comprised the agrarian proletariat formed a massive pool of discontented rural hand laborers who shared the urban proletariat's revolutionary aspirations. Middle peasants would be their temporary allies until a radicalized revolutionary process established a regime of proletarian-poor peasant political power.[58]

In many respects this strategy closely resembled the "permanent revolution" advocated by Leon Trotsky and implemented by Lenin in Russia. However, Inomata also wanted to make a more fundamental distinction between Rōnō-ha strategy and the JCP's two-stage strategy than was implied by the notion that two stages were simply telescoped into one. The Rōnō-ha's analysis of the agrarian problem provided the sole basis on which Inomata could argue that any conception of the bourgeois-democratic and socialist aspects of the revolution in terms of stages was fundamentally incorrect.

The Kōza-ha: The Persistence of Feudalism and the Need for Agrarian Revolution

The task of the Kōza-ha in refuting the Rōnō-ha analysis of the agrarian problem was less difficult, and supporters of the Comintern-JCP strategy lost no time in undertaking that task. Even in their own interpretations emphasizing change in the countryside since the Meiji Restoration, Rōnō-ha theorists had had to accept the premise of uneven development resulting in a dual economy that was strikingly evident in the late 1920s. From the outset, moreover, Inomata had been compelled to admit that "the development of capitalistic production methods in agriculture has not progressed."[59] Likewise, Kushida acknowledged, "the method of the determination of rent at the time of the land tax reform . . . in 1875 clearly followed from that prevailing in the Tokugawa period," and he saw that "more than half a century later in the ninth year of Taisho (1920) rent at this ratio is still the one prevalently adopted. . . . Hence, formally the remnants of the feudal system continue to exist even today."[60]

Thus, Rōnō-ha theorists found that they could not be entirely consistent in their interpretation of the Meiji Restoration. While Inomata, Kushida, and Sakisaka asserted that Tokugawa landlords had been transformed into "new" landlords who were heavily bourgeois in character, nevertheless, they found themselves discussing the continued significance of "semi-feudal" elements and the need for the Japanese revolution to accomplish "bourgeois-democratic" tasks left undone by the Meiji Restoration, especially in the countryside. Noro Eitarō, Hirano Yoshitarō, Yamada Moritarō, and other Kōza-ha theorists immediately leapt upon these weaknesses and produced scholarly analyses to support the Comintern line advocating a two-stage revolution.

While the Kōza-ha supported the Comintern's view of the agrarian problem as a central factor dictating a strategy of two-stage revolution in Japan, nevertheless, there was not full agreement between the Comintern and the Kōza-ha on the analysis of the problem. Lacking an intimate knowledge of the Japanese countryside, the Comintern simply presumed that the problem lay in a pattern of large-scale feudal landholding like that of prerevolutionary Russia.[61] Yet almost without exception, the Kōza-ha writers agreed with Rōnō-ha analysts that the system of land use and cultivation in Japan was based on plots "too small" to cultivate efficiently by introducing agricultural machinery. For Hirano and Aikawa Haruki, as for Inomata after his break with the Rōnō-ha, this was a peculiarity of Japanese agriculture that was attributable to the legacy of the Asiatic mode of production.[62]

Indeed, JCP loyalists initially had some difficulty in formulating a consistent position on the agrarian problem. In his 1927 work, *The History of the Development of Japanese Capitalism*, Noro had assumed that capitalism had developed apace in the countryside as in the cities and that landlords had been transformed into agricultural capitalists. Similarly, Nishiyama Take'ichi, writing in the *Symposium on Marxism*, registered agreement with the Rōnō-ha's perspective on the embourgeoisement of landlords, by noting that agrarian landlords were increasingly "close to the bourgeoisie in their investment of income in finance and in industry."[63] The conflict with the Rōnō-ha over the '27 Theses thus challenged supporters of the Comintern line to determine and prove "whether Japan's farmers were still serfs subordinated to large landlords, free peasants who came into being because of the bourgeois revolution of the [Meiji] Restoration, or laborers under agrarian capitalists. The tenants, who form the majority of today's small farmers [and to whom the JCP sought to appeal in the countryside]," Watanabe Masanosuke observed, "we cannot call laborers."[64]

In response to this challenge the Kōza-ha groped hesitantly toward a coherent interpretation of the agrarian problem that was consistent with their revolutionary strategy. Noro initiated this effort in 1929 by refuting Inomata's argument that the Meiji Restoration had swept away the basis of feudal landownership in the countryside. This argument was not unambiguous. Noro acknowledged the "capitalistic" character of rural landlords in the 1920s: The rents they collected were the sum of (1) "the average profit of capital that tenant farmers had put out for agricultural production" plus (2) "capitalistic ground rent, as the entire part of surplus value beyond that."[65] Thus, Noro did not object to the notion that the Meiji Restoration had begun the process of bourgeois-democratic revolution in Japan, but he did deny the significance Inomata attributed to it:

> Pure feudal land possession relations, along with restrictions appended to [those relations], were eliminated. Nevertheless, this does not immediately mean that [the Restoration] "abolished the *land system* of

> feudal agriculture as the basis of feudal absolutism." It simply eliminated pure feudal landownership relations, i.e., feudal landownership relations from the shogunate to 300 daimyo and merely replaced them with unified landownership under the sovereignty of an absolute despotic monarch.

Indeed, Noro went on to echo the Comintern's view of the relationship between landownership and political power in Japan as typical of an oriental society, as described by Marx. "In our country," Noro wrote, "the state is the highest landlord and sovereignty is landownership concentrated on a national scale. Our country's land tax, both in its traditionalist conception and in reality, could not be anything essentially different from the form of ground rent."[66] The transition to capitalism in the countryside was thus incomplete. "Agriculture continued to be done on the basis of a noncapitalist small-scale mode of production, and landlords, in place of feudal lords, now came to extract all surplus value from tenants," Noro asserted. Landlords had a dual character in this view, but it was only in the process of circulation, that is, in the landlords' investment of their income in capitalist industry and finance, that landlords were involved in capitalist economic relations.[67]

Here Noro made a point that became a key element of the Kōza-ha's interpretation of the role of agriculture in Japan's capitalist development. The effect of the Meiji Restoration, in this view, was not to abolish the conditions of feudal landownership, but rather to reorganize it in such a manner as to make it more efficient for state purposes. The reforms removed all obstacles to the purchase, sale, and annexation of lands, "for the purpose of expanded reproduction of the conditions of feudal exploitation on a national scale—and consequently for the most free execution of the primitive accumulation of capital" under the tutelage of the Meiji state.[68] Later, in Yamada's contributions to the *Kōza* (collected in his *Analysis of Japanese Capitalism*), this notion was systematized into the paradigm of "the militaristic semi-serf system nature of Japanese capitalism." According to Yamada,

> The Restoration reforms first caused the main part of petty cultivating serfs to change into semi-serf petty cultivating farmers who paid high rents (*kosakuryō*) of 51 to 56 percent or 58 percent to usury capitalist parasitic landlords, heirs to semi-feudal conditions of servitude that were [merely] a compromising dissolution form of large feudal land possession rights; secondly, [the reforms] directly and forcibly transformed the other major portion of petty cultivating serfs into semi-serf wage laborers. the counterpart to the change of the resources and

means of production of social life to capital, one end in the process of primitive accumulation.[69]

In other words, according to Yamada, the outcome of the Meiji reforms was not land parcelization or distribution to the peasants, as it was in the aftermath of the French revolution. Instead, the Meiji state, acting in lieu of Japan's poorly developed bourgeoisie, simply made revisions in agricultural organization to facilitate the primitive accumulation of capital in order to strengthen a late-developing country that was being pressured militarily by more advanced Western capitalist states.

There were two critical points in this analysis. One was the argument that the imbalance between town and countryside provided the basis for an "absolutist" Meiji state, a regime that was half capitalist and half feudal, if one followed Marx's analysis of absolutism in the "Eighteenth Brumaire."[70] Even if the historical mission of this regime was to lead the transition from feudalism to capitalism, its economic basis remained fundamentally feudalistic, because the path toward large-scale commercial agriculture had not been broken by the Meiji reforms. Rather, the traditionalist inequality of rural land distribution remained intact, leaving peasants to remain "petty cultivators" of plots of land that were too small to allow them to live comfortably after paying high feudalistic ("starvation") ground rents to landlords and taxes to the state. At the time of the land tax reforms, the area of arable land averaged .88 hectares per household; in late Meiji (1905), .94 hectares; and .94 hectares as late as 1929. While the specific pattern of cultivation varied from region to region (from Kinki to Tōhoku to Hokkaidō), throughout Japan small-scale agricultural cultivation was maintained from Meiji through Shōwa without any significant change.[71]

Kōza-ha writers did not deny that some changes signalling the "sprouts" of capitalism had occurred in the countryside. In his early article on "landownership relations," for example, Noro noted that "at the time [of the Meiji reforms] a large sector of today's landlords had formed a bourgeois stratum (rich peasants, merchants, usurers, etc.)." But Noro also argued that it was as a consequence of the Meiji land reforms, which strengthened the traditional land system in order to use it to raise capital for modernization efforts, that the landlords had gained the powers of domination in the countryside that they held by the late 1920s.[72] The peculiarity of the role of agriculture in Japanese development, according to the Kōza-ha view, lay precisely in the fact that the progress of the industrial revolution did not occur on the basis of a collapse of feudal agrarian organization; rather, once the land system was modified by the Meiji state, "semi-feudal" land relations and the growth of Japan's heavily militaristic brand of capitalism proceeded hand in hand, each supporting the other.

This is where the second major point of Yamada's *Analysis* emerges: the close link between the militaristic and seemingly prematurely imperialist character of Japanese capitalism and "semi-feudal" agrarian relations in the countryside. Noro had alluded to this relationship, as he engaged Inomata in controversy over Takahashi Kamekichi's heretical theory of petty imperialism. "Without a clear understanding of the special nature of agriculture in our country," Noro asserted, "one cannot expose the internal necessity of its imperialistic policies."[73] Specifically, in arguing that the Meiji Restoration did not constitute a complete bourgeois-democratic revolution, the Kōza-ha maintained that the high agrarian rents, still largely collected in kind, remained essentially feudalistic.[74] The Kōza-ha asked Rōnō-ha theorists why those rents had not declined if feudal landownership had been abolished by the Meiji reforms. The Kōza-ha found the Rōnō-ha's insistence that capitalist land relations were prevalent—and that rents in kind were "conceptually transformed into cash" by tenants and landlords—to be unconvincing. Instead, they argued that the reason ground rents continued to be high was that feudal or communal institutions remained in the countryside. In this respect, Ogura Takekazu, for example, had "found many examples of communal coercion to force peasants to pay rent."[75]

More importantly, the Kōza-ha here made a careful distinction between feudalistic and capitalistic ground rents. In Hirano's words, capitalistic ground rent is what "the large-scale capitalist entrepreneur pays with the objective of pursuing a profit," while feudalistic ground rent uses "extra-economic coercion to drain the entire surplus labor from the direct producers, who make their own livelihood for a life of starvation" with land they are provided and their own agricultural implements.[76] Rents in Japan in the 1920s were successors to the feudal ground rents of the Tokugawa period; they were not, as the Rōnō-ha saw them, determined by the laws of supply and demand of a capitalistic land market. Furthermore, the new land tax was simply a successor to feudal tribute collected under customary relations between peasants and feudal lords in the Tokugawa era.[77] Thus, when challenged by the Rōnō-ha to provide evidence of noneconomic coercion (*keizaigai-teki kyōsei*), Yamada, Hirano, and others cited the power of the Meiji state. Yamada argued that the militaristic nature of the Meiji regime was a product of internal as well as external factors. Not only did the Meiji regime have to cultivate the heavy industrial sector and military industry in order to defend itself against more advanced Western capitalist powers. This need was also reinforced by the necessity to "suppress the resistance of the laboring strata of semi-feudal petty cultivating peasants and semi-serf wage laborers" and to maintain intact the semi-feudal land organization that was to be the basis of its "primitive accumulation of capital" for rapid industrialization.[78]

Clearly, this was not the "normal path" of capitalist development, in which the emergence of large-scale commercialized agriculture paralleled the rise of large urban industry in Marx's historical schema. The preservation of semi-feudal ground rents in twentieth-century Japan was symptomatic of the fact that Japan did not follow the standard pattern of development in the countryside. According to Hirano, the classical progression of the forms of ground rent was as follows: "Labor ground rent → ground rent in kind → cash ground rent (the preceding are feudal ground rents) → ground rent in the transitional intermediate form toward free [private] landownership and capitalism → capitalist ground rent." This "normal progression," typical of Western Europe, depended on conditions that permitted a balance between the growth of capitalism in industry and the "rise in the productive forces of agriculture." Where this kind of balance existed, feudal landownership gave way to capitalistic landholding on the pattern of the English yeoman. Hirano wrote, "it was the peasantry of England, France, and western Germany that took the fully classical pattern in which feudal petty proprietors (*keieisha*) were changed into landowners, and these small enterprises blossomed and . . . [flourished] unrestrained and achieved the development of independence of a bourgeois-democratic character. So too it was only in these countries that this classical pattern [emerged]."[79]

While the Kōza-ha stressed the unique characteristics of the underdevelopment of Japan's agrarian sphere, Hirano and others who took a broad comparative perspective on trends of capitalist development saw that Japan was not alone in facing the difficulties of "uneven" or "unbalanced" development. According to Hirano, in contrast to England, France, and western Germany, the entire area east of Elbe, from Prussia to Japan, experienced this pattern of [late] development:

> In countries where land reform is incomplete, and there was no complete establishment of small landownership by partition, tenants who cannot become land owners remain limited to the status of semi-feudal tenants. Furthermore, since their product alone is insufficient to meet their living expenses, they form a category of "poor peasants" (and at the same time a semi-proletariat) dependent also on wage labor.
>
> From eastern Prussia, bounded by the Elbe to Poland, from Bulgaria and the Danube countries [Austria, Czechoslovakia, Hungary] to Russia, in the east, as far as Japan, the transformation of feudal petty cultivators to landowners—whose fully free and independent character was liberated—has not occurred.

Rather, in Russia and eastern Europe capitalist landlord enterprises were established "atop semi-feudalistic huge [land]ownership."[80] As we have seen, however, such large-scale landownership did not emerge in Japan. In explaining why productive forces in Japanese agriculture failed to develop as rapidly as they might have, and why small-scale "petty" agriculture rather than large-scale landownership and cultivation prevailed in Japan unlike Russia and eastern Europe, Kōza-ha theorists found themselves turning to the Asiatic mode of production concept.

As indicated in the earlier discussion, the conception of the Asiatic mode of production, with its various components describing the formal unity of rents and taxes, the phenomenon of general slavery, and the view of the "despot" as the highest landlord, came to form an important link in the Kōza-ha's analysis of the agrarian problem. This was the factor that explained the "stagnancy" in agricultural production forces resulting in Japan's inability to experience a classic bourgeois-democratic revolution.[81] The legacy of the AMP was also said to account for the continued prevalence of "too-small" peasant cultivation in Japan in the 1920s. In short, the AMP offered to many in the Kōza-ha the key to understanding the resistance of the agricultural sphere to the impulse of capitalistic development.

Yet, it was Inomata Tsunao, after his break with the Rōnō-ha circa 1930, who offered the most comprehensive interpretation of the negative impact of the AMP on economic development in the agrarian sphere. In 1934, Inomata embarked on a rural survey of two urban prefectures, sixteen additional prefectures, and forty-three villages in all regions of Japan. The results he published first in an essay on "the impoverished village" during the recent years of economic distress,[82] which he hoped would offer guidance to the peasant union movement. Three years later, Inomata offered a more comprehensive report of his findings in the volume *Introduction to the Agrarian Problem*, and it was here that he interpreted the issue in terms of the historical legacy of the AMP. While his treatment here closely approximated the Kōza-ha perspective, Inomata's flexible analysis approached a one-and-a-half-stage theory of revolution that avoided the pitfalls of Rōnō-ha and Kōza-ha efforts to fit Japanese agrarian development neatly into either the capitalist or feudal mode of production—clearly an impossible task given the wealth of self-contradictory evidence.

In the *Introduction to the Agrarian Problem*, Inomata focused on special "Asiatic" features of Japanese agriculture. Distinguishing its development from that of Western agricultural systems, Inomata drew heavily on Marx's and Engels's observations concerning the importance of water and irrigation in "Asiatic systems." In addition, Inomata also cited Marx's recognition that a mature feudalism had evolved in Japan in order to distinguish the Japanese experience from that of other "Asiatic" societies like China and India. Thus, much of what Inomata wrote here echoed the writings of Kōza-ha theorists like Aikawa Jirō and Hani Gorō. However, Inomata focused specifically on the forms of Japanese agriculture, especially the three-thousand-year tradition of "Asiatic" wet-field cultivation, that he felt made the transition to capitalism much more difficult. Like Hirano, Inomata saw the AMP as one of two modes of production based on slave labor. The legacy of the Asiatic mode, which was geography-specific because of climatic features, according to Inomata, included the suprisingly "high ratio of the farming population to arable land area, the terrible backwardness of agricultural techniques, and the [pervasiveness] of petty (small-scale) management." The current agrarian problem, in which the relationship between the agrarian sector and the capitalistic economy as a whole was in a state of "crisis," was precisely "the problem of the special Asiatic nature of [its] historical development."[83]

According to Inomata, in the Asiatic society that immediately followed primitive communal society, the bonds of the old agrarian *kyōdōtai* did not dissolve immediately, but remained strong enough to provide the basis for a despotic state that could fulfill the need for water control in such a society. The AMP reached the peak of its development in the Nara period and began to collapse shortly thereafter. Unlike China and India, Japan had less of a need for large-scale irrigation, and in Japan there were also relatively large uncultivated areas of land, without which the "tight binding" of the Asiatic slave to the land could have been supported much longer. Thus in Japan, unlike India and China, "internal contradictions" within the Asiatic system caused it finally to give way to feudalism beginning in the mid-Heian era. However, Japanese feudalism did not reach its complete form until the Tokugawa era, Inomata asserted. As a result, its history in the Asiatic mode was relatively long by comparison with its feudal era, and that earlier mode left a deep imprint on the character of Japanese agriculture centuries after its demise. Thus in analyzing the role of the agrarian sphere in the development of capitalism in interwar Japan, Inomata argued, only by considering the long-term impact of "Asiatic factors" could one fully appreciate the phenomenon of Japan's dual economy.[84]

By 1937, after his personal foray into the countryside, Inomata was far more willing than he had been as a Rōnō-ha spokesman to attribute major significance to "feudal" attributes of the countryside. As Trotsky had in *1905*, Inomata was now prepared to acknowledge the coexistence of "feudal" remnants with emergent "capitalist" features of the countryside, particularly in relatively backward countries like Russia and Japan. Kōza-ha writers had maintained such a view from the outset, but unlike them and their opponents in the Rōnō-ha, Inomata now resisted the impulse to apply the label "feudal" or "capitalist" to a sphere that was clearly in transition. Moreover, Inomata also reminded his fellow Marxists that "even in England, the motherland of capitalism, it took quite a long time to destroy and transform the feudal mode of production." One could only expect the remnants of feudalism to be "more numerous" in Japan where "capitalism required only sixty or seventy years to achieve four hundred years of development."[85]

Despite these changes in his thinking about the agrarian problem, Inomata did not adopt Trotsky's view that the problem was not simply a matter of feudal remnants persisting alongside capitalist forms. Inomata did not suggest that the uneven pattern of Japanese capitalist development had resulted in a pattern that was so qualitatively distinctive that the original categories of Marx's analysis, designed to describe pioneering Western societies unaffected by pressures from earlier developing states, needed to be revised or transcended.

Conclusions: Uneven Development, the Dual Economy, and the Rise of Japanese Militarism

In debating the agrarian problem, neither the Rōnō-ha nor the Kōza-ha transcended Marx's original analytical categories. In this respect, perhaps more so than in any other component of the larger debate on Japanese capitalism, Marxists of both major factions remained entrapped by existing categories of analysis that had emerged out of the founder's description of English development. Both sides clearly recognized that the agrarian problem in Japan itself was the product of "uneven" development resulting in a dual economy, but this phenomenon could not be accommodated by the simple notions of "feudalism" and "capitalism." The term "semi-feudal" was an inadequate substitute for a concept that could convey the impact of a qualitative change that left Japanese agriculture neither feudal nor capitalistic.

Yet it would be unfair to take Japanese Marxists alone to task for this shortcoming in their work. One could argue that Marx himself handled the issue no more effectively when he confronted German "backwardness" in 1843. In the Germany of Marx's time, there were conflicting indicators of modernity and backwardness, and the ambiguity of Germany's situation was evidenced by the self-contradictions of Marx's analysis. His primary critique of Hegel, of course, was that the Hegelian ideal state was nothing other than the existing German state; and this was the "bourgeois" state. In the introduction to this critique (written after the main text), however, Marx characterized Germany as a late-developing nation that had not yet experienced a bourgeois-democratic revolution. Large landowners, and not bourgeois, held the reins of political and economic power. Nevertheless, it was here that Marx first proposed the idea of a "universal class": the class that would liberate a Germany that had not yet experienced bourgeois democracy would be the urban proletariat, a class that was "only beginning to form itself in Germany, as a result of the industrial movement."[86] In short, in response to a political and economic situation that shared many of the ambiguities of Taishō and Shōwa Japan, Marx proposed the same solution that he offered to liberate highly developed capitalist countries like England and France. What Japanese Marxists confronted in the 1920s was not completely without analogue in Marx's own experience, yet he himself had generated no new categories tailored to the peculiarities of cases like the German one.

It is thus a great credit to Japanese participants in the debate on Japanese capitalism that they so readily identified the dual economy with a lagging agrarian sector as a critical problem in Japanese political and economic development. Their focus on the agrarian sphere has been ratified by recent work such as that of Barrington Moore, illustrating how the resolution of agrarian conflict is a key determinant of the path to modernity adopted by a given society.[87] In addition, Japan's Marxists, particularly those in the Kōza-ha who refused to dissolve the special features of Japanese agrarian development into general categories that were so broad as to be meaningless, were correct to focus on the agrarian problem as they sought to avert militarism through a socialist revolution.[88] The agrarian problem was closely linked to the rise of militarism in the 1930s in two respects. First, the very notion of the "agrarian problem" referred to the unbalanced or uneven development between town and countryside. The lagging development of the agrarian sphere clearly hindered the further progress of capitalism in Japan in general, as peasants were not being transformed rapidly enough into commodity producers and consumers to fuel the economy. Rising economic and social distress in the countryside, manifested in recurrent and deepening recession and tenant protest, contributed to the crisis perceived by leaders seeking a military solution to Japan's domestic political and economic problems. As Takahashi Kamekichi and others recognized, Japan's disadvantaged international position as a late developer contributed to the economic *yukizumari* that was most severe in the agrarian sphere. As the crises arising out of uneven development within Japan and between Japan and the Western powers intensified and increasingly alarmed civilian and military leaders in the 1930s, the possibility of resolving the crisis through external expansion grew increasingly attractive. The agrarian problem, then, was a significant element among the domestic forces propelling Japan toward expansionist war.

The attention devoted by Japan's Marxists to the agrarian problem during the debate on Japanese capitalism also underscores the role of tensions in the countryside—which resulted from efforts to achieve economic "modernization"—in supporting military expansionism in the Taishō and Shōwa eras. As noted in recent Western treatments of the relationship between rural communities and rising militarism in the 1930s and 1940s, there were many elements in agrarian populism (*nōhon-shugi*) that conflicted with the state-centered ideology of the militarist advocates of the Greater East Asia Co-Prosperity Sphere. Like agrarian populists in the United States, for example, Japanese agrarianists were fiercely opposed to large industry and a powerful centralized state. In Marxian terms, *nōhon-shugi* was a form of consciousness that resisted changes in both the forces and relations of production. Its advocates held a retrospective ideal, one that harkened back to self-sufficient agrarian communities that were permitted to live free of the intervention of the state fused with large capitalist industry that was essential to the expansionist dream of militarist leaders.[89] Nevertheless, *nōhon-shugi* emerged as a product of change in the countryside that was proceeding too quickly for most, yet left behind the coexistence of old and new that both Rōnō-ha and Kōza-ha Marxists identified. The Kōza-ha was correct to emphasize the extent to which peasants continued to be bound in submissive relationships with landlords through custom and tradition. As Ann Waswo has noted, much of the rural distress in the 1920s and 1930s arose out of protest by peasants who resented the manner in which their landlords were increasingly seduced away from their traditional village responsibilities by capitalist investment opportunities in the cities.[90] Rōnō-ha scholars accurately perceived these changes in the character of rural landlords, and while Kōza-ha Marxists were not anxious to point to a peasant preference for traditional relations of subordination, they properly stressed the close link between agrarian backwardness and the persistence of a passive ideological submission to emperor and nation.

These Marxist observations on the agrarian problem point to a second factor in the rise of militarism in the 1930s. Despite the antagonism between many elements of the *nōhon-shugi* reaction to rural change and distress and the statist nationalism of many Japanese leaders, militarism drew significant support from the victims of uneven development in town and village. The expansionist impulse of military leaders resonated with the call of agrarianists like Katō Kanji for colonialist emigration to the Asian mainland as a solution to the land problem.[91] Moreover, military organizations in the countryside helped to reinforce the "submissiveness to authoritarian leadership," "village-oriented holism" that stressed the good of the family, village, and nation over the individual, and the competitive nationalism that R. P. Dore has identified as characteristic of prewar rural communities that remained loyal to traditional spiritual values in the face of material change.[92] Agrarianism, then, rightly viewed as a symptom of the agrarian problem, "contributed to Japanese nationalism" by defining the essence of Japan as an agricultural premodern nation untainted by Western ideas and economic organization. Thomas R. H. Havens has described this link between the agrarian problem and prewar militarist nationalism as follows:

> Agrarian nationalism was sufficiently compatible with the prevailing statist outlook to provide at least tacit support for Japan's military rulers. Both the government and Nōhonshugisha [agrarianists] developed elaborate myths about the ethnic and religious uniqueness of the nation. Agrarianism was also institutionally conservative, advocating rural stability and overall social solidarity of a sort that would please a regime opposed to domestic change in a time of crisis. In addition, although it was more pro-Japan than actively anti-Western, to some extent Nōhonshugi thought probably predisposed its adherents to accepting war with America and the European powers by systematically attacking capitalism, party politics, colonialism, and the decadent values which had invaded Japan from abroad.[93]

The malaise in the countryside, in short, fed the crisis that Marxist activists feared would lead to militarist expansionism. In the view of both major factions, without a fundamental change in socio-economic relations in the countryside, a more democratic and equitable Japan could not emerge. After the war, Japan's Marxists discovered that they were not alone in this view, when American Occupation officials undertook a massive land reform. Nevertheless, an "agrarian problem," like other issues explored in the debate on Japanese capitalism, persists and continues to be debated today among Marxist scholars and politicians.

NINE

Postwar Developments: The Continuing Controversy

THE DEBATE between the Rōnō-ha and the Kōza-ha on the nature of Japanese capitalism and its implications for revolution in prewar Japan was forcibly ended when the left succumbed to the pressures of the police in the 1930s. As the nation mobilized for war, the imperial regime intensified efforts to crush those who would oppose military expansion abroad by fomenting social revolution at home. Already by 1930, the Special Higher (Thought) Police had "rounded up" thousands of known and suspected Marxists, beginning with the Japanese Communist Party itself. In 1931 and 1932, 200 leading party members were tried jointly in Tokyo District Court. Of these, 187 were convicted of violating the Peace Preservation Law and were sentenced to terms ranging from two years' to life imprisonment. Shortly afterward, in June 1933, the communist movement was stunned when Sano Manabu and Nabeyama Sadachika, leaders of the party's in-prison Central Committee, publicly renounced their communist ties and *tenkō*ed (converted) to the "national cause."[1] In the ensuing years, *tenkō* burgeoned into a movement of mass defections that was coopted by the police; and the combination of *tenkō* and escalating arrests finally "brought about the complete destruction of the Communist movement by the end of 1935."[2]

The Kōza-ha, most of whose members had some links to the JCP and its illegal advocacy of violent revolution, was the first to fall silent. The Rōnō-ha had rendered itself relatively secure from police pressures by abandoning the JCP in 1927, repudiating the notion of a secret vanguard party, and espousing a socialist "revolution" through a legal mass-based united front political party that would take advantage of the existing accoutrements of bourgeois democracy. However, with the eruption of full-scale war with China in 1937, the Rōnō-ha too fell victim to the police. Many of its leading members, including Yamakawa Hitoshi, Sakisaka Itsurō, and Ōuchi Hyōe, numbered among those arrested in the Popular Front Incident and the Professors' Group Incident in 1937 and 1938. Certainly by 1940 then, imprisoned or, in any event, unable to publish Marxist scholarship on Japan, the participants in the debate turned their attention elsewhere, and the controversy lapsed, its issues unresolved.[3]

If the outbreak of war forced the participants in the debate on Japanese capitalism into silence, it did not destroy the controversy itself. Many of its most prominent issues, such as the character of the imperial institution and the origins of Japanese imperialism, had been raised at the outset in an effort to stem the crisis of development that Japan's leadership tried to resolve by going to war. Precisely because of the crushing defeat in war and the fact that the controversy had been suspended without resolution, it was revived, along with the left-wing movement itself, immediately after the war. By 1947, as a new constitution was drafted under the American Occupation forces, Marxists of both prewar factions were publishing prolifically once again on the many aspects of the debate on Japanese capitalism. Indeed, the debate persists today, if in somewhat altered form, in academic circles as well as in the politics of the Japanese Socialist and Communist parties.

Many old issues of the prewar debate were pursued once again as they assumed new significance in the aftermath of the war. Nevertheless, the controversy itself was necessarily transformed in character after the war, to reflect the rapidly changing context of Japan under American Occupation. Determined that the Japanese invasion of Asia should never be repeated, the Supreme Commander for the Allied Powers (SCAP) General Douglas MacArthur launched sweeping democratizing and demilitarizing reforms in Japan's political and economic life. Under SCAP, Japan's military services were demobilized, paramilitary organizations were dissolved, armaments industries were dismantled, the top wartime leadership was purged, and the oppressive police apparatus was weakened and decentralized. When the emperor declared he was no longer to be considered divine and Shintō was disestablished as the official state religion, the core of the ideological apparatus of the prewar state targetted by its Kōza-ha critics was destroyed. Gradually, the *kokutai* myth that had supported the imperial regime before the war was enervated, forcing Marxist critics of the state in postwar Japan to recast their critiques.[4]

Since both the Rōnō-ha and the Kōza-ha had couched their analyses of the prewar state in terms of a diagnosis of the nature of its economic base, the postwar challenge to their positions was heightened by the economic reforms engineered by SCAP. Ironically, American Occupation officials apparently shared the Marxists' conviction of the intimate linkage between economics and politics: SCAP undertook extensive economic reforms designed to deprive Japan of the basis for any resurgence of militarism or authoritarian rule. Most significant among these was an agrarian land reform program, founded precisely on the "belief that the social and economic condition of the Japanese countryside was a powerful causal factor in bringing about Japan's aggressive policies in Asia."[5] While specific provisions of the reforms varied by region and locality, in general, lands owned by absentee landlords and in holdings over ten acres per household were bought by the government and resold to former tenants who could secure loans at low interest rates. As a result, by 1950, the rate of land tenancy declined from almost 50 percent to 10 percent, and rent controls alleviated the burden of high rents on agrarian households.[6]

This effort was paralleled in the industrial sphere by the dissolution of zaibatsu. In the view of SCAP authorities, the powerful financial cliques had formed the core of Japan's military-industrial structure and had inhibited the rise of a middle class that would support democratic rule in Japan. In an initial round of reforms, eighty-three zaibatsu holding companies were dissolved, "*zaibatsu* leaders including members of the founding families, were purged and were prohibited from further activity in the financial world," and antimonopoly laws were passed. A second wave of zaibatsu dissolution to affect over a thousand more companies was scheduled for February 1948. This plan was abandoned, however, when the sudden chill in U.S.-Soviet relations in 1947 sent the Occupation into "reverse course." The deepening of the cold war now dictated that Japan was no longer to be treated as a vanquished enemy to be weakened but rather as a valuable Pacific ally to be strengthened against the Soviet Union.[7]

The sudden shift in Occupation policy had an immediate negative effect on the left. In the early years of the Occupation, the left had benefited tremendously by the purge of right-wing politicians and release of political prisoners. Freedom of press and association enabled Marxists to revive their political activities and to publish again freely. In this context, the Communist Party was reborn in 1945, its objective remaining a two-stage revolution and its immediate tasks "to eliminate the emperor system, democratize Japan, and carry out land reform."[8] Likewise, late in the same year, Suzuki Mosaburō, an original member of the Rōnō-ha, took the lead in founding the Japanese Socialist Party (JSP).[9] Like the JCP, the new Socialist Party promoted the establishment of democracy and eventually socialism in Japan. Unlike the JCP, however, the Socialist Party—the left wing of which essentially coincided with the prewar Rōnō-ha—followed Yamakawa's initiative in advocating a peaceful path to socialism in Japan (*heiwa kakumei*).[10]

In the salutary conditions of the early years of the Occupation, both parties rapidly gained a following. Progressive labor legislation offered socialists a forum for popularizing their ideas. As the proportions of workers unionized soared from zero to almost 60 percent between 1945 and 1949, these workers quickly came under the influence of the JCP and the JSP. Occupation authorities were initially tolerant as the Communist Party came to dominate the All Japan Congress of Industrial Unions (Sangyōbetsu Rōdō Kumiai Kaigi, or Sanbetsu), while the Socialist Party became the major influence in the Japanese Confederation of Labor (Nihon Rōdō Sōdōmei, or Sōdōmei). Under the "reverse course," however, SCAP suppressed the general strike Sanbetsu had planned for February 1, 1947; in August 1948, SCAP issued political order No. 201, making it illegal for government employees to strike; and the following year, revisions were made in early liberal labor laws, while new legislation resembled the more restrictive Taft-Hartley model. These efforts culminated by 1950 in a "red purge," in which Communist leaders were removed from labor unions.[11]

As a result of this turn against the left, the unions found it more difficult to recruit youth to the left-wing movement. But the reversal of the Occupation's democratizing policies also had the effect of providing the left with ammunition for its critique of the Japanese state and society in the postwar era. Marxists could now call for a higher level of economic and political democracy than the United States was prepared to pursue in its desire to bolster Japan as an integral part of its security system in the Pacific. Not only was the zaibatsu-busting program aborted in midstream; but the effects of the land reform were also somewhat ambiguous. As Ronald Dore has noted, "the benefits of the reform" were not distributed very equally.[12] Similarly, while SCAP had drafted a constitution in which Article Nine embraced the goal of world peace and pledged that Japan would maintain no standing land, sea, or air forces, Marxists could argue that what Japan had in the form of the Self-Defense Forces (Jieitai) was in fact a standing army. Moreover, the terms of the 1952 Security Treaty permitted the United States to use its military bases in Japan to launch military actions in the Pacific. This provision could well have enabled Japan to be drawn into war by virtue of its alliance with the United States, even while it maintained no significant standing military forces of its own. After the collapse of the short-lived Democratic-Socialist coalition government in 1948, these issues rapidly became a focus of conflict between the conservative parties and the left.

In subsequent years, the long-term effects of the SCAP reforms could be called into greater question, when the mid-1950s saw a turn away from the early Occupation's democratizing efforts on the part of Japan's now independent government. In 1954, the law was revised to recentralize the police, and in the late 1950s the powers of the police were enhanced still further to respond to riots and internal security threats. Similarly, both education and local administration were recentralized, strengthening the power of the Ministry of Education and recalling the powers of the prewar Home Ministry. Finally, in 1956, and more recently again in the late 1970s and early 1980s, there have been efforts to revise the constitution, spearheaded by conservatives unhappy with the diminution of the status of the emperor and Japan's military dependence on the United States. In the meantime, even the minimal Self-Defense Forces have remained controversial—

the majority of law professors in Japan believe them to be unconstitutional, although the Supreme Court has been unwilling to counter government actions with such a ruling[13]—yet Japanese defense spending has risen steadily, particularly in recent years under pressure from the United States.[14] These issues remain the source of fierce controversy between the ruling Liberal Democratic Party (LDP) and those socialists and communists who suffered under the authoritarian rule of the 1930s and fear encroachments on democracy and civilian authority in postwar Japan.

As might be expected, however, there has also been much disagreement among Marxists themselves on these issues, and they were soon introduced onto the agenda of the postwar debate on Japanese capitalism. First, the nature of Japanese fascism and imperialism emerged early in the postwar period as the new focal point of the debate. Then, as they turned their attention to the character of Japanese capitalism after the war, both Rōnō-ha and Kōza-ha were compelled to ask how the changes initiated under the Occupation affected their prewar paradigms of Japanese development. To what extent had the Occupation's agrarian land reforms fundamentally altered conditions in the Japanese countryside? How had its limited attack on the zaibatsu affected Japanese "monopoly capitalism"? If the reforms were significant and effective, how were they to be integrated into the Rōnō-ha's interpretation of pre- and postwar state power, and what were their implications for the Kōza-ha's evaluation of the imperial institution as a semi-feudal absolutist regime? What was the significance of the Occupation authorities' political reforms? Did they constitute a sort of bourgeois revolution from above? And if so, how did that affect the Rōnō-ha view of the Meiji Restoration as a bourgeois revolution and the Kōza-ha/JCP view that the revolution in Japan remained a two-stage affair that had to begin with a bourgeois-democratic revolution? Both factions were compelled to introduce a powerful external factor—the American Occupation—into a theoretical paradigm of political and economic development that rested heavily on internal determinants: the forces and relations of production. Somehow the changes that occurred during the Occupation needed to be accommodated to that model and considered carefully in developing new strategies and tactics for socialist revolution in postwar Japan.

Finally, the peculiar character of the U.S.-Japan alliance presented additional problems for Marxists in postwar Japan. Was Japan in a quasi-colonial position, as the JCP claimed? Or should the alliance, as revised in the 1960 version of the Security Treaty, be appreciated for its releasing Japan from the obligation of maintaining its own effective military forces and from the alarming prospect of a militarist revival? In either case, the implications of Japan's strategic dependence on the United States had to be incorporated into an appropriate understanding of the nature of the existing Japanese state and the tasks of the coming revolution.

The consideration of complex issues such as these sharply divided the Socialist and Communist parties and introduced a plethora of new divisions within the Marxist community such as had not existed in the prewar controversy on Japanese capitalism. Beginning from the very founding of the JSP and rebirth of the JCP, factional splits proliferated and new political parties emerged. In this respect, the Kōza-ha seems to have been more vulnerable, for the Rōnō-ha's prewar emphasis on Japan's high level of economic development and its evaluation of the imperial institution as a relatively insignificant political issue prepared it well for the liberalization of the Occupation period and Japan's remarkable economic development in the 1960s.

The political fragmentation resulting from the intensity of the postwar controversy has seriously inhibited the ability of the Left as a whole to mobilize enough votes to allow any single socialist party to break the 30 percent barrier and challenge the dominance of the LDP. Nevertheless, pursued in academic as well as political circles, the postwar debate on Japanese capitalism took the prewar controversy as its point of departure and then transcended its bounds. In turn, it has become the basis for the consolidation of theoretical gains by Japan's Marxists on issues less specific to Japan. As the discussion to follow will suggest, these endeavors are of broader significance to scholars of world development, especially late development, as well as to Marxist advocates of socialism in other industrial capitalist societies.

The Controversy on the Prewar Crisis: Imperialism and Fascism

In the painful aftermath of Japan's defeat in 1945, among the first issues to stir the interest of its newly liberated Marxists were the developments that had led Japan down the path to war in the 1930s. The controversies on the origin and nature of Japanese imperialism and "fascism" allowed the Rōnō-ha and Kōza-ha to confront, in theoretical terms, the political events they had tried vainly to avert. How were they, as Marxists working now with the benefit of hindsight, to interpret the rise of Japanese militarism in the 1930s? Was this fascism? If so, how was it to be compared and contrasted with analogous phenomena in Germany and Italy, and where did it fit into the Marxist schema of the development of industrial capitalism? Similarly, to return to the question first posed by Takahashi Kamekichi two decades earlier, how was Japanese expansionism in Asia to be analyzed in Marxian terms?

These were issues that Marxists had been forbidden to pursue precisely when they became most urgent, as political crisis escalated in the 1930s; and scholars of both the major prewar Marxist factions attacked them eagerly in the late 1940s. Predictably, these issues were more provocative for Marxists of the Kōza-ha. Their view of Japan as a semi-feudal country, the economic and political development of which lagged qualitatively behind that of its counterparts in the West, made an analysis of its militaristic expansionism in Leninist terms problematic. It will be recalled that Noro Eitarō had encountered this same difficulty when he engaged Rōnō-ha advocate Inomata Tsunao in debate over Takahashi's petty imperialism thesis. Now, attacking the question of imperialism anew, Kōza-ha scholars took the prewar controversy as their point of departure. The theoretical difficulties inherent in their position that Japan was both highly developed in the industrial and semi-feudal in the agrarian and political spheres quickly came to the fore and caused a split within the Kōza-ha itself.

Imperialism and the Imperial Institution

The controversy on "militaristic feudalistic imperialism" between Shiga Yoshio and Kamiyama Shigeo, both leaders in the postwar revival of the JCP, had its roots in the Comintern's analysis of Japanese imperialism in the early 1930s. In his report to the Executive Committee of the Comintern in March 1932, O. Kuusinen had observed that Japan's bourgeois-democratic revolution had been "incomplete," and that political power in Japan was now shared by the feudalistic emperor system, landlords, and monopoly capital. Consequently, while Japan's drive for territorial expansion could be explained in part as an effort by the capitalist bourgeoisie to resolve its pressing economic difficulties, "in a certain sense one can [also] speak of a militaristic feudalistic imperialism in Japan."[15] This view was echoed in the 1932 Theses, which were preoccupied with the problem of Japanese expansionism in the wake of the Manchurian Incident. "The aggressiveness of monopoly capitalism in Japan," according to the theses, "is compounded by the militaristic adventurism of absolutist militaristic-feudalistic imperialism."[16] It was in agreement with the theses on this point that Yamada Moritarō had formulated his classic description of Japanese expansionism as a "militaristic semi-feudal imperialism."[17]

This dual definition of Japanese imperialism's reliance on both capital and a semi-feudal agrarian base had occasioned a brief controversy among Shinobu Seizaburō, Aikawa Haruki, and others, and in 1946, Shinobu revived the controversy by resuscitating the notion that Japan, along with tsarist Russia, had engaged in a "militaristic-feudalistic imperialism."[18] Shinobu was immediately criticized by Kamiyama, who used the occasion to attack Shiga, and the Shiga-Kamiyama debate erupted across a broad range of issues, including the nature of the emperor system and the question of

Japanese fascism. Citing Lenin's observations on Roman and British colonial policy, Kamiyama argued that imperialism was not peculiar or unique to capitalism, but had existed in some form in every historical epoch, each following its own particular laws; hence, there had been slavery imperialism, military-feudal imperialism in feudal society, and modern capitalistic imperialism. Thus, tsarist Russia and the Japanese "absolutist emperor system" from the late 1880s had pursued a militaristic-feudalist imperialism, reflecting the fact that they were making the transition from feudalism to capitalism. Modern capitalistic imperialism was essentially different from this kind of expansionist activity, Kamiyama asserted. Yet, Kamiyama also claimed that, reflecting its dual economic base, Japanese imperialism from the Russo-Japanese War through the 1940s had comprised both these feudalistic and capitalistic forms. To this extent, Japan's aggressive international behavior could not be understood without an analysis of the competition and cooperation between Japanese capital seeking to guarantee and to monopolize overseas markets and the emperor system, with its military element's efforts to protect its own special interests.[19]

Kamiyama's interpretation represented something of a compromise between the prewar Rōnō-ha and Kōza-ha positions. On the one hand, his notion of a "dual imperialism" (*nijū no teikoku-shugi*) implied that Japanese capitalism had in fact attained a sufficiently high level of development to generate the modern imperialism of which Lenin had written. In this sense, he made a departure from the work of prewar Kōza-ha theorists like Yamada. Nevertheless, Kamiyama remained within the orthodox Kōza-ha framework as he stressed the independence of the imperial institution and its leading role in Japanese aggression but did "not recognize the hegemony of the bourgeoisie," as Rōnō-ha Marxists did. Instead, Kamiyama adhered to the Kōza-ha characterization of the imperial regime as "absolutist" and saw the era after the Manchurian Incident as "the strengthening of the emperor system's reactionary rule," rather than as fascism.[20]

Ironically, however, Shiga's critique of Kamiyama's dual imperialism thesis made him more vulnerable to charges of approaching a Rōnō-ha perspective. Shiga argued that during the 1930s and 1940s the further development of capitalism in Japan had changed the "class character" of the emperor system. No longer was the emperor system simply absolutist. Rather, Shiga asserted somewhat cryptically, "with the development of monopoly capital after World War I, the landlord[-bourgeoisie] bloc under the hegemony of the bourgeoisie made the emperor system its class power." As a result, during the war years of 1931 to 1945, Shiga claimed, "the emperor system, as an imperialist power, was made to do fascist tasks"; in other words, Japan had experienced a "military fascism."[21] While this argument drew criticism from Kamiyama for its Rōnō-ha inclinations,[22] Shiga, like

Kamiyama, retained the Kōza-ha view of the emperor system as absolutist. Moreover, as Rōnō-ha critic Kojima Hinehisa has noted, Shiga too had developed a kind of dualistic interpretation of Japanese imperialism: he perceived the economic basis as ''modern'' and the political superstructure as ''feudalistic-militaristic,'' and he had simply grafted the imperial institution, as conceived by the Kōza-ha, onto ''fascism,'' while the two concepts were fundamentally incompatible.[23]

Kojima's rejection of the duality between economics and politics as a critical flaw in Shiga's interpretation highlights a theme that became the crux of the debate on Japanese capitalism. As Rōnō-ha and Kōza-ha Marxists endeavored to analyze Japanese imperialism from a historical perspective, the periodization of Japanese expansionism turned on the assessment of the relative significance of economic and political determinants of international behavior. This concern became pivotal as the Shiga-Kamiyama controversy on the nature of imperialism was accompanied by a conflict over how to date the origins of Japanese imperialism that involved the Rōnō-ha and yet again split the Kōza-ha. Inoue Kiyoshi launched this debate when he proposed to date the establishment of Japanese imperialism from 1900, earlier than Inomata Tsunao's citation of the Russo-Japanese War. Like Inomata, Inoue stressed external factors and internal political conditions in his analysis. Inoue pointed to Japan's entry into the international conflict surrounding the Boxer Rebellion in China, as well as a domestic alliance between the Japanese bourgeoisie and an absolutist emperor system, a link sealed by the revision of the Election Law and the birth of Itō Hirobumi's Seiyūkai party. These events marked a critical change in Japanese class relations, in Inoue's view: the Peace Police Law was passed to suppress the labor and agrarian movements, in accordance with the interests of bourgeois and landlords alike. As a result, the establishment of zaibatsu monopolies was facilitated, marking a step toward the stage of finance capitalism that Lenin had identified with modern imperialism.[24]

The international component of Inoue's analysis was echoed in Dōi Matsu'ichi's argument dating Japanese imperialism from the 1900 to 1902 period. Dōi drew on the insight of fellow Marxist Eguchi Bokurō that the ''uneven development'' of the countries of the world had made it inappropriate to use a single country's stage of capitalist development as a gauge of its propensity or capacity for imperialism. Not only was it impossible to assume that late-developing countries like Japan and Russia would follow the same course as the pioneering capitalist states of Western Europe.[25] In addition, Eguchi asserted, the international dynamics of uneven development made it likely that (semi-)feudal powers (presumably in league with an aspiring bougeoisie) in late-developing states would strengthen the military forces in order to break the *yukizumari* of capitalist development. In short,

Eguchi argued that the phenomenon of uneven development had altered the internal and external behavior patterns of leaders of countries in transition from feudalism to capitalism.[26] Accordingly, Dōi cited three factors in support of his contention that Japanese imperialism had come into being at the turn of the century: (1) the formation of monopolies shortly after the Sino-Japanese War; (2) Japan's international role as a facilitator of British imperialism, marked by its participation in the Boxer incident and its 1902 alliance with Britain; and (3) the transformation of the Meiji regime from an absolutist emperor system to a landlord-bourgeois alliance. In this interpretation, the Russo-Japanese War was an imperialist war fueled by the emperor system's hunger for territory and the imperialist bourgeoisie's search for markets.[27]

This early dating of Japanese imperialism was opposed by two groups who cited the post-Russo-Japanese War era as the proper point of demarcation. What distinguished the two groups from Inoue, Eguchi, and Dōi was their stress on internal factors; but the Kōza-ha and Rōnō-ha critics differed on the relative significance they attributed to political versus economic factors. Those loyal to the classic Kōza-ha perspective insisted that international factors should not obscure the fact that the absolutist imperial institution had remained precisely that, despite some reorganization through the Russo-Japanese War. Thus the war with Russia was not classic imperialism in the Leninist sense, but was led by the emperor system endeavoring to resolve its own "structural crisis." Rōnō-ha critics of Inoue likewise drew on their faction's prewar orthodoxy: the essence of modern imperialism lay in the formation of monopoly capital, wrote Ōuchi Tsutomu and others, and this economic basis must be emphasized in any effort to periodize the rise of Japanese imperialism. While Dōi and Inoue cited the strengthening of bank capital, the formation of cartels, and the emergence of the four largest zaibatsu, these could not constitute proof of the existence of a monopoly capitalism sufficient to promote imperialism before the Russo-Japanese War; but the Rōnō-ha had no difficulty in establishing its presence after the 1907 panic. The rise of monopoly capitalism in Japan, in this view, was easily documented to have occurred between 1905 and World War I, and the annexation of Korea and substantial exports of capital were external behaviors reflecting this trend in Japan's internal development. For Rōnō-ha critics, domestic and international political factors were an insufficient basis for the analysis of Japanese imperialism.[28]

What made the Rōnō-ha position especially cogent was that it underscored the difficulties the Kōza-ha encountered in using its view of the emperor system as "absolutist" to explain Japanese imperialism. How could one apply a Leninist conception of imperialism to a system the development of which one believed to have been constrained by powerful semi-feudal elements? Dōi had tried to circumvent this problem by describing a shift in the emperor system from "absolutism" to the product of a landlord-bourgeoisie bloc. But, given the classic Marxist treatment of absolutism,[29] the distinction between these two forms of regime was muddled at best. Moreover, if the position of the bourgeoisie had changed enough to spur imperialistic activity, then would it not be logical to assume that the changed superstructure reflected the more powerful position of capital in the base—i.e., to adopt the Rōnō-ha position?

Clearly, much of the controversy on the origins of Japanese imperialism turned on the issue of how one should interpret the nature of the imperial system from Meiji to Shōwa. In the prewar period, Rōnō-ha and Kōza-ha had already clashed on this issue, but in the postwar era, it became possible to treat the rise of militarism and authoritarianism in the late 1930s and 1940s as well.

Fascism and the Path to War

Like the controversy on imperialism, the debate on fascism was aroused both by a need to understand the past and—in the context of the cold war, the Occupation's reverse course, and hostilities in Korea—by a desire to prevent its recurrence. Once again, because of the difficulties of reconciling a view of the emperor system as absolutist with a phenomenon commonly associated with industrial capitalism—fascism, in this case—the controversy split the Kōza-ha into at least three groups, while the Rōnō-ha readily achieved a consensus.

Its consistent emphasis on signs of highly developed industrial capitalism in Japan led the Rōnō-ha to argue that Japan had in fact seen the rise of fascism. Shortly after the Manchurian Incident, Sakisaka Itsurō and other Rōnō-ha writers had warned of the impending rise of fascism in Japan.[30] After the war, Yamakawa Hitoshi initiated the effort to formulate a coherent Rōnō-ha interpretation of Japanese fascism. In his view, the bourgeoisie, seeking an escape from its economic woes, embarked on a militarist course. Gradually, "political power shifted from the grasp of the political parties, the proper representatives of bourgeois political forces, to fascist forces based on the combination of the military, bureaucracy, and zaibatsu." As the military and bureaucracy had already become "assimilated into the forces of the bourgeoisie," the rise of fascism marked the shift of the bourgeoisie to a "reactionary" role. Ōuchi Hyōe, Sakisaka, Tsuchiya Takao, and Takahashi Masao elaborated upon this argument. Fascism had "used the ideology of the middle class and then acted on behalf of finance capital" to resolve the economic crisis by linking state power to monopoly capital more closely than ever before. For the Rōnō-ha, then, fascism in general was a product of systemic crisis in the era of monopoly capitalism. Unlike its rise in Germany and Italy, however, in Japan fascism was introduced not in the guise of political party movements, but rather on the basis of the military and bureaucrats. This peculiarity was a consequence of the endemic weakness or "underdevelopment" of democratic traditions and institutions, such as was reflected in the wide authority and prerogatives attributed to the bureaucracy.[31]

The Rōnō-ha had willingly acknowledged that semi-feudal "remnants" existed in the prewar state, and their view of the rise of fascism, built on the premise of highly developed monopoly capitalism, incorporated an appreciation of those elements in a single coherent interpretation. By contrast, confrontation with the issue of fascism immediately splintered the Kōza-ha, and once again Shiga and Kamiyama were at the center of the controversy. From the perspective of his notion of Japan's dual imperialism, Kamiyama and most other Kōza-ha thinkers simply adhered to the '32 Theses and their premise that the emperor system was absolutist and "relatively autonomous." What the Rōnō-ha called fascism Kamiyama chose to term "absolutist reaction."[32] The problem with Kamiyama's view was that it was essential to recognize the role of economic crisis in provoking Japanese expansion in Asia, and for this it was necessary to recognize and analyze the economic changes that had adversely affected Japanese capitalism. It was to this omission that Shiga Yoshio directed his critique of Kamiyama:

> The development of Japanese finance capital and the intensification of its contradictions by the world economic depression caused fascism to grow dramatically between 1931 and 1945. Comrade Kamiyama has fallen into the position of explaining the essential difference between militaristic-feudalistic imperialism and fascism conceptually by means of a formula, so he cannot clarify the relationship between the emperor system and fascism. The 1931 invasion did not signify a retaliation by the emperor system in an effort to recover losses from about 1918-1919 to 1930. [Rather, this] was an imperialist war [undertaken] by a rapidly developed Japanese capitalism for the redivision of colonies.

Nevertheless, while recognizing the increasing significance of the capitalist component of Japan's dual economy, Shiga concluded that "the emperor system continued to be a state power with great independence; and from 1931 to 1945, the absolutist emperor system, as an imperialistic force, came to be made to execute fascist tasks."[33]

Shiga's critique had resolved one problem in the Kōza-ha's orthodox approach to the question of Japanese fascism; but his own analysis ultimately raised more problems than it solved. If capitalism had gained in significance in Japan in the 1920s and 1930s, sufficiently indeed to propel an "imperialist war,'' then why did Shiga continue to characterize the imperial institution as ''absolutist''? And how was it possible for the emperor system to have had ''great independence'' and still be compelled, presumably by capital, to act as a fascist power? Shiga did make something of an advance in Japanese Marxist theory when he introduced into its discourse the notion of the ''relative autonomy of the state'' in capitalist society—an idea that gained much attention among French structuralist Marxists only in the 1970s.[34] Nevertheless, Shiga failed to capitalize on the flexibility that such a notion offered to Kōza-ha orthodoxy. By maintaining the premise of imperial absolutism, Shiga implied that Japan in the 1930s was not a fully capitalistic society, and thus his notion of the relative autonomy of the state did not really serve to illuminate the growth of fascism in the 1930s. As long as Shiga clung to the Rōnō-ha's definition of fascism as a phase in the domination of monopoly capital and insisted on applying it to the war years, the logical inconsistencies noted here could not be avoided, and his stubborn adherence to the appraisal of Japanese state power as absolutist was untenable.

Apparently, Shiga was not unaware of these difficulties, for when he published his work on the theory of the state a year later, he slightly revised his interpretation of Japanese fascism. Now he argued that after the Russo-Japanese War, monopoly capital gained supremacy among the bourgeoisie, and as a result, ''while the emperor-system state had had both an absolutist origin and structure [in the Meiji period], it was transformed into an imperialist state of monopoly capital.'' In short, the emperor-system state, initially founded on petty agricultural cultivation and landlordism, remained intact, but came to operate as the agent of monopoly capital in the years after World War I. In the 1920s and 1930s, monopoly capital was increasingly fused with state power, and when the economic crisis made it impossible for the state to control class struggle with its existing resources, the emperor system turned to a ''fascist mode.'' The result was ''military fascism,'' which quickly engulfed not only the military, but the police, the judiciary, and the intelligence network.[35]

Shiga's interpretation drew supporters, but many of these primarily because of his critique of Kamiyama, rather than because of satisfaction with his analysis. Accordingly, Kōza-ha Marxists like Hattori Shisō and Moriya Fumio introduced further revisions into Shiga's treatment of fascism. Moriya was uncomfortable with Shiga's notion of the autonomy of the emperor system and the insistence that the imperial institution had taken a fascist route without having undergone any structural change in its original absolutist content. Thus, he introduced an idea of ''*tennō-sei* fascism,'' which incorporated such a structural change initiated from above by ''military fascists.''[36] Similarly, Hattori approached the Rōnō-ha view when he argued that the Japanese state had "shed its absolutist character" in the Taishō and Shōwa periods.[37]

A less satisfactory Kōza-ha response to the issue of fascism was fashioned out of a compromise between the Shiga and Kamiyama interpretations. This was a decidedly minority view, one that arose out of an effort to distinguish between structure and function in order to retain the view of the emperor system as absolutist but also to recognize fascism. In this view, it was possible to conceive that Japanese capitalism—now in the monopoly stage—embraced absolutism in structure and fascism in function. In other words, there was a time lag in which structural transformation came to accord with functional change. Thus by the 1930s, Japan's political system remained primarily absolutist in structure, as the emperor system remained intact, even while it had increasingly functioned as a fascist regime. This view, shared by historian Koyama Hirotake, Watanabe Tetsu, and others, could sustain a viable link between absolutism and fascism by means of a new definition of absolutism, one that could accommodate "the hegemony of finance capital" in the economy and the increasing political power of the bourgeoisie. Hence, they postulated a change after the Russo-Japanese War from a "classic absolutism," in which "the bourgeoisie does not yet even partially hold political power," to an absolutism consisting of a bloc of landlords and bourgeoisie sharing power.[38]

Needless to say, Rōnō-ha Marxists were as critical of this interpretation as they were of other Kōza-ha interpretations. For them, there was no need to cling to the concept of absolutism, in either its classic or its revised form; moreover, the distinction between structure and function appeared dubious, "formalistic," and "mechanistic," for in their view, the transformation to fascism had occurred in both spheres, which were in fact inseparable, in any event. Ironically, the Kōza-ha's prewar work on the state had been more compelling than that of the Rōnō-ha precisely because it seemed to point to the factors most conducive to the rise of militarism in the 1930s. Yet, whether or not one finds merit in the Kōza-ha's postwar efforts to systematize an interpretation of the rise of militarism in the 1930s, the controversies on imperialism and fascism offered a foretaste of the dilemmas that would plague JCP loyalists as they analyzed the much greater changes that occurred during the American Occupation.

The Debate on Japanese Capitalism in the Politics of Postwar Japan

In the early postwar years, then, the issues of wartime imperialism and fascism posed a challenge to Marxists of the two prewar factions, as they tried to integrate into their paradigms of Japanese development an analysis of the crisis of the 1930s and 1940s—a crisis that Takahashi Kamekichi had foreseen when he first provoked the debate on Japanese capitalism. Now, a still more difficult task remained: the interpretation of the significance of the wide-ranging and externally generated reforms of the American Occupation for a Marxist understanding of contemporary Japanese economics and politics. The updated view would in turn serve as the basis for new strategies and tactics to achieve socialist revolution in the new environment. As in the prewar era, which saw rapid economic change initiated from above, postwar Japanese development did not fit easily into the orthodox Marxian schema that rested on the spontaneous internal evolution of production forces. Once again, the Japanese case represented a peculiar situation, and, as a result, the difficulty of balancing the universal elements of the Marxist world-view with a judicious appreciation for the "specialness" of the Japanese experience became even more problematic than it had been before the war.

Not surprisingly, each faction tended to respond to this challenge by reinforcing the tendencies that had characterized its treatment of Japanese development in the prewar period. The Rōnō-ha found in the escalating economic growth following the Occupation reforms confirmation of its original thesis that Japan was an advanced capitalist country dominated by monopoly capital. Ironically, then, for Rōnō-ha Marxists, the reforms had significance but had to be downplayed in order to sustain the validity of the same assertion they had made two decades earlier. On the other hand, once again, the postwar era saw a split within the Kōza-ha, as the need to show consistency with prewar views made it difficult to agree on just how much significance should be attributed to the economic and political reforms of SCAP. Thus, particularly after the Occupation entered its reverse course, many Kōza-ha Marxists, like Moriya and Toda Shintarō, adhered to their prewar views more stubbornly than ever, without registering any change therein as a result of SCAP's agrarian, industrial, and political reform measures. In their view, landownership remained semi-feudal, supporting a political power that continued to be absolutist in the form of the emperor system. A minority of Kōza-ha Marxists rejected the constraints of the 1951 Theses, which essentially maintained the analysis and strategy of the '32 Theses, to attribute great significance to the postwar reforms. In the view of this group, the land reforms had successfully dissolved semi-feudal landownership, and as a result of this dramatic change in the economic base, the imperial institution had been transformed from an absolutist system to a bourgeois monarchy comparable to those elsewhere.

Since they proceeded so directly and predictably from positions adopted before the war, the approaches to these new issues adopted by the two original prewar factions are interesting not primarily for their role in extending the debate on Japanese capitalism into the postwar period. Indeed, the heated controversies on these narrow issues have fueled the misperception that "there is still no 'Marxism' in Japan [but only] a multitude of ideologies inspired by Marxism and Marxism-Leninism."[39] Rather, the significance of these debates lies elsewhere. First, the arguments of the two factions defined the battle lines of the day-to-day political competition between the postwar Socialist and Communist parties. Without an understanding of the evolution of the postwar debate on Japanese capitalism, it is difficult to fathom the reasons for the disagreement between the two parties on issues such as U.S.-Japan relations, the fate of the emperor system in the revolutionary process, and the nature of the process of socialist revolution itself.[40] In addition, when one is careful to note the subtleties of these controversies, it becomes clear that beneath the surface of these political arguments, Marxism has been very much alive in Japan since 1945. The postwar debate formed the context that nurtured the continuing efforts of Japanese Marxists to grasp complex issues fundamental to Marxian economics, as well as the larger issues of political and economic development that were originally posed in the prewar controversy and remain of concern for those who study late development.

The Kōza-ha, the Postwar Reforms, and the Politics of the New JCP

Early in the postwar years, it was clear that those in the mainstream of the JCP were determined to maintain the old Kōza-ha position without making any significant alterations to account for the impact of SCAP's reforms. The adoption of this approach was partly attributable to changes in SCAP policies and in the international environment, which in turn affected the party's attitude toward the United States. When the JCP was first reborn, the policies adopted at its Fifth Party Congress of February 1946 dictated that the position of the '32 Theses arguing for a two-stage revolution would remain the strategic basis for party activity, but with two changes. First, the Occupation was to be viewed as a liberating force. Thus, in the interests of the bourgeois-democratic revolution that the Occupation was in effect engineering from above, the JCP should cooperate with SCAP to achieve demilitarizing and democratizing reforms. The image of the United States portrayed in the reports of JCP leaders Tokuda Kyūichi and Nosaka Sanzō was not entirely positive. In their view, the United States did represent the strongest bastion of Western capitalism and would ultimately be the enemy of socialist revolution. Nevertheless, SCAP policy was still in its democratizing reform phase, tensions between the United States and the Soviet Union were at an ebb, and there was no reason for a communist party that had only begun to enjoy political freedom to alienate SCAP any sooner than necessary.[41]

A second departure from the '32 Theses was pioneered by Nosaka, in his promotion of "peaceful revolution." This concept represented the first in a series of efforts to "Japanize" the Marxism-Leninism of the Soviet Union in response to the new postwar conditions. While the '32 Theses had dictated a Bolshevik-style revolution in which violence would inevitably have a place, Nosaka argued that the conditions of occupied Japan were such that revolutionary violence would not necessarily play the decisive role it might have had in the repressive atmosphere of the 1930s. The conditions in which the party now operated had changed dramatically from the prewar era; and they did not resemble the Russia for which Lenin had prescribed the original vanguard party idea. Now the JCP could compete legally in parliamentary politics and could operate—again legally—to capture a mass following in organizations such as labor unions to press on toward socialist revolution. The united front from above and from below was the keynote of this tactic. As Nosaka had observed the Chinese Communists do during his wartime exile in China, the JCP would seek a broad base of class support from workers, peasants, and progressive bourgeois elements, such as intellectuals. While the JCP would be the leading force of the alliance, as the vanguard of the proletariat, it should seek alliance with other progressive political elements, specifically the Socialist party.[42] This "peaceful revolution" would help to complete the bourgeois-democratic revolution first initiated by the Meiji Restoration and pushed further by the Occupation forces. The seeds of dissatisfaction with SCAP, however, were already evident in the conviction, consistent with the '32 Theses, that its democratization effort would not be total. The JCP still called for the abolition of the emperor system, land reform, amelioration of labor conditions, and full civil rights under a new constitution, and it was yet unclear how far SCAP was genuinely prepared to go in its reform efforts.

At the outset, the sanguine view that the Occupation had taken over the tasks left undone by Japan's own bourgeoisie gained adherents among Kōza-ha Marxists participating in the postwar controversy on Japanese capitalism. As early as December 1945, Yamamoto Masami, a party member and union activist since the 1920s, had made this argument in the *Tokyo shinbun*. In his view, under the Occupation, "the military cliques were eliminated, the bureaucratic cliques were finally losing their relative independence, . . . the so-called familistic zaibatsu were also beginning to be dissolved, and even the landownership of parasitic landlords was being touched."[43] Nakanishi Kō went a step further to argue at the JCP's Sixth Party Congress of December 1947 and in a series of articles in 1947 and 1948 that it was no longer appropriate for the party to advocate the demise of an absolutist emperor system as a part of its united front strategy. As a result of its defeat in war and the Occupation reforms, Nakanishi argued, the "old system received a severe blow." The emperor system was no longer representative of a landlord-bourgeoisie bloc dominating a society in transition but rather had changed in nature. Now the reforms had removed its semi-feudal economic base, and "political power had moved fundamentally into [the hands of] monopoly capital." This view of the embourgeoisement of the emperor system led Nakanishi to advocate the transition to a socialist revolution rather than the Tokuda-Nosaka strategy of completing the transition to bourgeois democracy.[44]

Interestingly, this view drew support from Yamada Moritarō, who was continuing his scholarly investigation of the development of the Japanese economy as a professor at the University of Tokyo. In 1949, Yamada wrote that SCAP's agrarian land reforms had effectively dissolved semi-feudal landownership in Japan. Revising the position that had become the keynote of the Kōza-ha's prewar orthodoxy, Yamada argued:

> Japanese militaristic semi-feudalistic capitalism, which was constructed on the soil of a semi-feudal landownership system, semi-serf petty cultivation, which originated in the Meiji Restoration and especially in the land tax reforms of 1873, collapsed along with Japan's defeat in the war. The militaristic, semi-feudalistic Japanese capitalism, which was a threshold in Japanese history, here brought an end to its historical life extending across almost three-quarters of a century from the Meiji Restoration until the defeat in war. One stage ends, and a new, higher threshold is demarcated. The basic process of this epoch [of democratic reforms] must be a revolutionary reorganization of the basis of the old formation, [the semi-feudal landownership system and semi-serf petty cultivation]. . . . [The land reforms] form the most important task in Japan in the era of democratic revolution.[45]

In short, Yamada argued that the reforms had "opened a new path liberating Japanese agriculture" from its backward past and had established a new basis for the reconstruction of the Japanese economy as a whole. In this sense, the SCAP reform measures were more revolutionary than had been the Meiji regime's revolution from above.[46]

This view of the Occupation as a postwar bourgeois-democratic revolution from above posed theoretical problems that compensated for the new flexibility it gave to Kōza-ha Marxists. It posited the United States—an external "reactionary" and imperialistic power, in the view of most Marxists—rather than Japan's bourgeoisie as the agent of a progressive democratic revolution. Moreover, as Rōnō-ha critics were quick to point out, once the reverse course had begun, how then was one to interpret this "revolution" in Marxian terms? In the view of the Rōnō-ha, as long as the Kōza-ha persisted in its erroneous argument that prewar Japan had been dominated by "semi-feudalistic" and absolutist forces, it was necessary for them to posit a major break, in the form of a revolution from above, from prewar to postwar in order to account for the significant democratizing changes that occurred during the Occupation years.[47]

In any event, this sanguine interpretation of the Occupation reforms was firmly rejected by the mainstream of the JCP leadership and the Kōza-ha itself, particularly under the combined impact of SCAP's reverse course and the cold war. To the extent that the view of the postwar reforms as part of a bourgeois-democratic revolution was resurrected later in the decade, that interpretation was tempered by the more negative evaluation of American influence in Japan. In 1947, this tortuous process of change in party strategy and tactics began. That year, at the Sixth Party Congress, the attitude toward the United States became more ambivalent, while Nosaka defended his strategy of peaceful revolution through a united front by attacking Nishikawa and others who argued that the emperor system had undergone a fundamental change in character. Recognizing the limits of SCAP's policies, Nosaka asserted that the reforms had been inadequate and had left intact the three pillars of the prewar system: the bureaucracy, the landed elite in the countryside, and monopoly capitalism. Moreover, as Nosaka was now less optimistic about the ultimate democratizing impact of the postwar reforms, his language concerning the nature of the revolutionary process also hardened. It was now clear that the notion of peaceful revolution was only a temporary tactic, and the party could well be forced to use violence if circumstances were to change.[48]

For the Soviets, however, Nosaka was still too conciliatory toward the United States, and his peaceful revolution strategy seemed heretical; the Cominform launched a harsh attack on him in 1950. While Nosaka somehow managed to maintain his position in the party despite Cominform efforts to oust him, the Soviets gained satisfaction in the party's acceptance of the 1951 Theses. This new program condemned the United States for having brought Japan not democracy but "only chains and slavery," and it stubbornly maintained that despite the SCAP efforts, semi-feudal landownership persisted in Japan.[49] This view was echoed by Kōza-ha participants in the scholarly controversy. In 1953, when a new *Kōza* was published, it treated the reforms primarily as an effort by American imperialism to subordinate Japan and its economy to its dominance of the world economy, and, especially with the success of the Chinese revolution and the outbreak of the Korean War, to make Japan a part of its anti-Soviet alliance. The JCP had now determined that from the outset, "the foundation of American imperialism toward Japan was the abortion of democratic revolution in Japan, and that its anti-Communist attacks, a major pillar of that [policy], substantially encouraged the anti-Communist forces of right-wing social democrats [i.e., the Socialist party]."[50] Thus, it was not surprising that the new *Kōza* asserted that the SCAP reforms "had only reorganized, in a subordinating manner, a semi-feudalistic Japanese monopoly capitalism."[51]

Suddenly, then, the JCP and its Kōza-ha supporters were unwilling to credit the United States with much positive influence on Japanese development. This uncharitable view had had its advocates from the very beginning of the Occupation, in the form of Kōza-ha Marxists who brought their prewar estimation of Japan unaltered into the postwar era. Moriya Fumio and Toda Shintarō, for example, advocated this view, which received official JCP support in the '51 Theses. While some change in state power was acknowledged to have occurred after the war, the Japanese government under the American Occupation was said to be reactionary and subordinate to the United States. "The Yoshida [Shigeru] government represented the reactionary interests" of "the emperor, the old reactionary military cliques, especially privileged bureaucrats, parasitic landlords, and monopoly capitalists." The land reforms, like other Occupation reforms, in the view of this group, constituted mere window dressing; they had in fact, as the new *Kōza* also observed, preserved the "semi-feudal relations of the emperor system, landlord landownership, etc."[52]

What were the bases for this cynical Kōza-ha view of the land reforms? There were several aspects of the reforms themselves that were objectionable, according to Moriya and other *Kōza* contributors. First, the reforms did not redistribute land to the peasants gratis, but rather former tenants were required to buy it, usually by going into debt. Thus, the reforms gave nothing to the poorest farmers who had no money to buy land. Moreover, tenancy was permitted to continue within the limit of one *chōho* per landowner; the mountain, forest, and wilderness lands were virtually unaffected; rents, now paid in cash, still imposed severe exploitation on the peasants; and farmers continued to be pressed by heavy taxes and deliveries of rice at state-established prices.[53] In addition, the reforms did not fundamentally change the dynamics that had kept Japanese agriculture backward. As Kōza-ha scholar Watanabe Yōzō has noted, to the extent that the reforms placed an emphasis on landownership rights rather than on the usage of the land for cultivation, land use by the new landholders was not encouraged. Thus, land continued to be seen primarily as an investment, a factor that helps to account for the fact that only a tiny minority of those who own agrarian lands even today seek to maximize the productivity of the land as a source of livelihood, or as a source of capitalistic profit.[54] Finally, by 1956, Yamada too had changed his position on the positive impact of the land reforms. True, the land reforms had dissolved the core of landlord ownership by releasing 19.4 million *chōho* of tenant lands, and agriculture recorded some remarkable growth as a result of those reforms. Nevertheless, in the long term, the land reforms did not resolve the backwardness of Japanese agriculture. Instead, by dispersing the lands in small parcels, the reforms had stabilized the countryside with an even smaller scale agriculture than had characterized the petty cultivation of the prewar era. As a result, the contradiction between the continued dominance of large monopolies in the industrial sphere—recalling SCAP's abandonment of zaibatsu dissolution—and small-scale agricultural cultivation was worsened. "Agriculture alone" remained distinguished by the dispersed isolated plots of an earlier era, and, as a result, it could grow only to certain limits. Hence, Yamada was able to explain the "stagnation" that began to characterize agriculture in the 1955 to 1960 period.[55]

During the late 1950s, advocates of the optimistic and cynical interpretations of the American role in Japan struggled for primacy within the JCP. Gradually, a compromise position emerged, one that would recognize the salutary effects of reforms that had abolished the absolutist character of the prewar imperial regime but also permit the JCP for the first time to assume a nationalistic posture condemning American efforts to render Japan subservient and dependent. Miyamoto Kenji, the distinguished literary critic who has been the party's foremost leader since the early 1960s, made a move in this direction in his 1958 report to the Seventh Party Congress. Miyamoto recognized that politically and economically, the reforms had introduced important changes into the Japanese landscape: "Along with the loss of the emperor's absolute right [sovereignty], the structure that made the military, the Naimushō, the Privy Council, the Upper House, and the bureaucracy relatively independent political forces has been dissolved, . . . and the Diet has been accorded the position of the highest organ of national sovereignty. These [changes] have opened the way for monopoly capital to take hold of the structure of political rule more directly than before." Economically, the previous antagonism between peasants and landlords had been replaced by that between farmers and "their exploitation and usurpation by American imperialism and the [Japanese] monopoly capitalism that is subordinate to it."[56] Japan was now to be viewed as a more highly developed capitalistic country than the Kōza-ha had perceived it to be before the war. Yet, the role of domestic monopoly capital was downplayed in Miyamoto's analysis, as it was portrayed as a creature of the United States. Japanese monopoly capital was able to achieve its remarkable growth after the war, Moriya and others observed, only with the substantial aid it received from the United States.[57]

Miyamoto's ideas were not incorporated into the party's program (*tōsho*) of 1958, but they did become the basis for the 1961 program adopted at the party's Eighth Congress, and they have generally been retained by the party to the present. It is important to note that the acceptance of Miyamoto's compromise interpretation permitted the JCP to justify a continuation of the two-step revolutionary strategy of the '32 Theses. Insofar as the Occupation reforms did not result in full economic and political democratization, this had to be pursued before a socialist revolution could be undertaken. In addition, the thesis of Japan's subordination aroused substantial conflict within the JCP over just how successful the United States had been in making Japan a quasi-colony,[58] but all were agreed that the U.S. role was such as could justify a revolutionary movement of national independence in Japan—also a task of the classic bourgeois-democratic revolution. The dilemma of ascribing to the United States the leading role in the bourgeois-democratic tasks of the Occupation reforms, raised by the early interpretations of Yamada and other Kōza-ha writers, was simply avoided without resolution. One bothersome contradiction remained embedded in the new Kōza-ha perspective, however. If the United States had tried to limit the complete democratization of Japan, as the JCP now argued, then SCAP's putative bourgeois-democratic revolution did not occur, and thus the postwar reforms did not really constitute a revolution at all. If this revolution did occur despite U.S. efforts to obstruct it, this contradicted the JCP's claim that American power over Japan was sufficiently great as to impair Japan's national independence.[59]

Since the early 1960s, then, the Kōza-ha has revised its assessment of postwar Japan to account for the changes introduced by the Occupation reforms, without giving undue credit to the United States. To this extent, the Kōza-ha has demonstrated flexibility in its efforts to interpret the postwar changes within its Marxist paradigm of Japan in the prewar era. Now, the imperial system is still targetted in the JCP's two-stage revolutionary strategy, but more for its lingering "ideological legitimacy which is incompatible with democracy"—as a symbol of Japan's backwardness, in short[60]—and for the instrument that it offers to those like Prime Minister Yasuhiro Nakasone, who would exploit the public's lingering religious and sentimental attachment to the emperor to turn back the gains of democracy and help to restore "emperor-system fascism" to Japan. The emperor system is no longer viewed as "absolutist"; rather, the Kōza-ha acknowledges the tremendous postwar growth of Japanese capitalism and now, like the Rōnō-ha, sees the state as representative of the dominance of monopoly capitalism.[61]

These perspectives have not led the JCP to be especially creative in devising party strategy in response to these acknowledged changes in postwar Japan. The most daring effort at such innovation came early, in the "structural reform" theory (*kōzō kaikaku ron*), which emerged in the mid-1950s within the JCP. Influenced by Italy's Communist leader Palmiro Togliatti, Kasuga Shōjirō, a JCP activist since the 1920s, argued that the Japanese and Italian contexts were sufficiently similar to suggest that the JCP should Japanize and adopt the tactics of Togliatti's party. Kasuga and others in this group were members of the party's international faction (so called because of their close relationship with the Soviet party since the Cominform's attack on Nosaka) and denounced what they claimed was a Stalinist betrayal of Leninism. Beginning in 1955, the Kasuga group argued for inner party democracy; but they also espoused a fundamental revision of the JCP policies of the Stalin era. Repudiating the two-stage revolution formula, along with the party's call for the completion of a democratic revolution, this group recognized greater change in postwar Japan than did the mainstream of the JCP. Their alternative was to pursue socialist revolution immediately, directing their energies against the now dominant monopoly capital. Their strategy of socialist revolution would differ significantly from that envisaged by the mainstream of the JCP, however. Structural reformists argued that evolutionary changes in capitalism over the century demanded a new revolutionary strategy. For example, stock ownership of capital had spread to larger numbers of people, economic dependence on colonial exploitation had ended, and in the welfare state the lot of the worker had improved substantially.

These new circumstances made both parliamentary reforms and a direct, violent revolutionary onslaught on the state obsolete. Workers should participate in and encourage reforms within the existing capitalist structure, such as profit-sharing, worker participation in management, and welfare policies. These efforts had to be combined with a parliamentary political struggle designed to reshape national policy to serve the interests of labor rather than of monopoly capital. Incremental reforms would gradually result in a fundamental change in the power structure and facilitate the evolution of socialism in Japan. Given its resonance with Eduard Bernstein's evolutionary socialism, it is not surprising that the Kasuga group's approach was denounced by the mainstream of the JCP, and on the eve of the party's Eighth Congress, Kasuga and six other leading members of the party withdrew from the party. Thereafter, they espoused their views through the United Socialist League (Tōitsu Shakai-shugi Dōmei), while the Communist Party has pursued a course of two-stage revolution that accepts the need for parliamentary tactics.[62]

The rejection of Kasuga's structural reformism has not prevented the JCP from following a moderate course since the 1960s. While the Socialists have called for immediate socialist revolution since the 1960s, the JCP has stressed the completion of Japan's bourgeois-democratic revolution as a prerequisite for that socialist revolutionary stage. The JCP's primary strength in this strategy lies in its critical perspective vis-à-vis the domination of the Liberal Democratic Party. The Kōza-ha has jumped eagerly on current issues such as official worship by state ministers at Yasukuni shrine (where those who died for the glory of the Meiji state are entombed), the legitimacy of the Jieitai and the danger of the revival of fascism with expanded military spending under the LDP, and the tight control the LDP has maintained over school textbooks to enhance reverence for the emperor and the country's military past. The Kōza-ha has exploited these issues in their attack on the incompleteness of contemporary Japanese democracy.[63] In the meantime, the JCP's strategic creativity is limited to its pursuit of parliamentary tactics, while the Socialists, long dominated by left-wing adherents of the Rōnō-ha, have evolved their own version of Kasuga's alternative, in the doctrine of "peaceful revolution."

The Rōnō-ha, the Occupation Reforms, and the Politics of the Japanese Socialist Party

In contrast to the theoretical difficulties the Kōza-ha encountered in interpreting the postwar reforms, the Rōnō-ha readily accommodated the changes in postwar Japan to its paradigm of Japanese development. As represented in the treatment of the postwar years in its thirteen-volume series on *The Development of Capitalism in Japan*,[64] the Rōnō-ha interpretation both recognized the positive achievements of SCAP and accounted for the Occupation's reverse course, without in any way compromising the schema of Japanese development the group had articulated in the prewar period. Although the Rōnō-ha interpretation was not directly adopted as a basis for the strategy and tactics of the Japanese Socialist Party, the link between the original Rōnō-ha, led by Sakisaka Itsurō until his recent death, and the Socialist Party has been close, if somewhat problematic in recent years. More importantly, the Rōnō-ha's ability to accommodate the changing circumstances of postwar Japan has enabled its scholars to move on in new, theoretically stimulating directions.

RŌNŌ-HA SCHOLARSHIP IN THE POSTWAR ERA. Rōnō-ha scholars are still engaged in research on the impact of the Occupation reforms,[65] but to date they have argued that the Occupation reforms revived and consolidated the monopoly capitalism that had already existed in the prewar years.

> The policies of the Occupation of course were directly implemented as one part of America's global policy, and in that sense, resulted in Japan's being positioned in one corner of the American camp. What is important for us, however, is to discern the logic of state monopoly capitalism that permeates [those policies]. Needless to say, that does not mean only that the Occupation policies were state monopoly capitalistic, as viewed from the American side. Rather, what is more im-

> portant is the fact that for Japan, the Occupation policies carried out the task of reviving its capitalism under a state monopoly capitalist system. In other words, . . . [the Occupation reforms] washed away from Japanese capitalism those elements that were irrational for monopoly capital, and carried out the function of building a system of state monopoly capitalism that had greater stability.[66]

Rōnō-ha scholars have acknowledged that these intentions were not expressed explicitly by SCAP, which claimed at first to be trying to diminish Japan's industrial, and therefore military, capability. Even the agrarian land reforms could be justified in such terms: by expanding the base of the country's capacity for domestic consumption, pressure for external expansion in search of markets would be reduced, and the influence of the landed upper classes would also be diminished. Nevertheless, the "objective situation," Rōnō-ha scholars argue, indicated that the United States was not so indulgent in "allowing the establishment of a democratic and peaceful Japan." Like the Kōza-ha, Rōnō-ha scholars noted the impact of the deepening of the cold war, the CCP victory in China, and the Korean War on the American decision to make Japan a powerful American ally in the Pacific. To do that, they asserted, the United States had no choice but "to rebuild Japan as a stabilized state monopoly capitalist country," and in so doing, reversed certain measures that had begun to democratize Japan both economically and politically.[67]

It would appear, then, that while Rōnō-ha treatment of the reforms by Ōuchi Tsutomu, Ōshima Kiyoshi, and others easily explained the reverse course, to explain SCAP's early democratizing efforts was more problematic. The early years of SCAP's liberal policies, however, have found a place in the Rōnō-ha paradigm. The policies are treated as efforts to eliminate the "old historical fetters" that had prevented Japanese monopoly capitalism from reaching its fullest development in the prewar period. These "fetters" were precisely the same "semi-feudal" elements that the Kōza-ha had argued prevented Japan from fitting neatly into the category of a capitalist society. Political factors like the emperor system, the House of Peers and Privy Council, the independence of the supreme command, the familial-based zaibatsu, and the backwardness of labor organization, along with "social elements like the traditional family system and higher education system," were "unsuitable" for monopoly capitalism—all were impediments that Japanese monopoly capital had been unable to alter or abolish in the prewar years. The landlord system in the countryside also served to impede Japanese development, in this interpretation, but it too had to await the Occupation reforms of the early postwar years to be eliminated.[68]

Herein lay the key to the Rōnō-ha's interpretation of the postwar reforms.

Unlike the Kōza-ha, the Rōnō-ha did not fall into the uncomfortable position of exaggerating the significance of the postwar reforms in order to account for the sudden elimination of a dominant "feudal landownership." For the Rōnō-ha, what remained in the countryside was not a feudal land system, but only feudalis*tic* "thought, emotions, and customs." And these persisted not because of the survival of feudal landownership, but because "Japanese agriculture could not shake itself free from the premodern small farm form." Small-scale cultivation, based on a low level of technology and supporting a subsistence economy, Ōuchi Hyōe, Uno Kōzō, and others argued, "could not destroy feudalistic thought, sentiments, and habits." Thus, while the Rōnō-ha conceded that a "feudal character" remained in landlord-tenant relations, these were only in the realm of superstructure rather than base, and they were reinforced by the survival of the village community (*kyōdōtai*) form, which had previously been bound up in the structure of rural feudalism.[69]

The land reforms of SCAP, then, eliminated the landlord system and presumably eased the way to the abolition of the feudalistic characteristics that had plagued the countryside through the war. Like the Kōza-ha, the Rōnō-ha saw the reforms as radical policies of the bourgeoisie, but, since the latter did not recognize the dominance of feudalism in the countryside before the war, it was unnecessary to infuse the land reforms with bourgeois revolutionary significance. This interpretation was strengthened by the argument that, unlike many of SCAP's other reform efforts, the land reforms had originally emerged out of the initiative of the Japanese government itself, that is, they were not entirely externally initiated.[70]

As for other postwar reforms, such as the zaibatsu dissolution policy, the Rōnō-ha took note of SCAP's underlying conviction that the financial cliques were "semi-feudal." Rejecting this premise as erroneous, the Rōnō-ha saw the zaibatsu rather as a "necessary product of the development of Japanese capitalism to a certain stage"; but thereafter, the zaibatsu became fetters on its higher development to the stage of state monopoly capitalism. SCAP's attacks on the zaibatsu simply pushed forward a process that had already been generated internally and facilitated the establishment of alternative forms of industrial structure, centered on the heavy industrial and chemical sector. The zaibatsu dissolution effort, Kajinishi and others claimed, achieved success, but the coordinated effort to eliminate concentration of capital and monopolies in general faltered at the outset. This occurred, they explained, because the anti-zaibatsu effort was consonant with the internal direction of Japanese capitalism moving toward state monopoly capitalism, while the effort to eliminate concentration and monopoly was not.[71]

At first glance, this appears to be a curious argument, given the fact that the plans to dissolve the zaibatsu were never driven to completion. The argument seems to have been constructed to accord with the Rōnō-ha's previously conceived schema. Nevertheless, the manner in which this argument has been supported, indeed rather cogently, demonstrates a relatively new feature of the postwar Rōnō-ha—an ability to make room for the peculiarities of Japanese economic and political development that were neglected in the faction's prewar debate with the Kōza-ha. Moreover, this argument is based heavily on empirical work on the concentration of capital in Japan. The key to the new interpretation lies in the comparison that is drawn between Japan's zaibatsu and classic forms of monopoly capitalism identified in Western Europe at the turn of the century by Rudolf Hilferding and V. I. Lenin. The zaibatsu were a form of the concentration of capital that was unique to Japan; and the properties that made them distinctive also made them incompatible with mature monopoly capitalism. Most broadly speaking, one account argues that the organizations "had a remarkable familistic character," and "the principle of closed domination by a single family was deeply rooted and upheld."[72]

This point alone, stressed by the authors of the *Development of Capitalism in Japan* series, is inadequate, because it leaves the Rōnō-ha vulnerable to the charge that what it saw in the zaibatsu was simply the same variety of backwardness that the Kōza-ha had perceived, identified as qualitatively different from any enterprise structure in the West, and labelled as "semi-feudal." After all, the Rōnō-ha itself had also regarded the traditional family system as "feudalistic" in a superstructural sense. More supportive of the Rōnō-ha position is the following distinction offered by economist Shibagaki Kazuo:

> The first [distinctive characteristic of Japan's zaibatsu] is that they were a form of the *konzern* which was topped by a holding company and which spread its wings in diversified management through share holdings over practically the whole field of undertakings in production, commodity circulation and finance. This is . . . why the *Zaibatsu* are called "comprehensive *konzerns*." . . . The nucleus in the production sector was made of primitive industries such as mining [instead of manufacturing], while on the other hand the commodity circulation and finance sector . . . had a relatively high importance. The cartels . . . were placed in a subordinate position to the *Zaibatsu konzern* as institutions charged with . . . supplementing or complementing the control by the *konzerns*. For this reason, the *Zaibatsu* as monopolies were characterized not as simple market monopolies but as "monopolies of capital as such" which contained such simple market monopolies within themselves in subordinate positions, and further that they

> were practically devoid of the organic interconnectedness in production technology which characterizes modern monopolies in general.[73]

The Occupation's attack on the zaibatsu was successful insofar as "it initiated the transformation of zaibatsu combines into enterprise groups." These groups differed from the prewar zaibatsu in that they lacked a central holding company based on the assets of zaibatsu family members; an informal horizontal link joined independent companies, replacing the vertical or pyramidical control of the zaibatsu; and the personalized ownership of capital was eliminated, so that the "persons actually owning capital were not so readily identifiable as the zaibatsu families once were." The new groups, now free of the conservative control of older members of established zaibatsu families, were more "progressive" and "entrepreneurial" in spirit; and the autonomy of member companies often led them into situations in which members of a single group competed with one another.[74]

The U.S. Occupation as an external force, however, could only accelerate a process that had already begun to occur in the 1930s. At that time, as Japan's heavy manufacturing and chemical industries grew, corporations became more open, the zaibatsu were transformed, and certain leading zaibatsu families lost their pivotal positions. Yet this change was not sufficient to eliminate zaibatsu from their dominant economic positions at the end of the war. The Occupation reforms completely transformed this situation by fully removing the closed familistic character of the zaibatsu.[75] As economist Ōuchi Tsutomu has noted, what occurred under the Occupation in Japan had largely already been achieved in Western Europe and America in the period when state monopoly capitalism was formed in the 1930s. Japan's economic backwardness, combined with the exigencies of the wartime economy, imposed restraints that limited the extent to which such "rationalization" in the interest of higher capitalist development could occur. Such rationalization did occur under SCAP—inspired by the "image of the New Deal"—and indeed the fact that these reforms occurred so purposefully under foreign domination benefited Japan's postwar economy in the long run. It was precisely the contrast between the willy-nilly process by which this occurred in Europe and the United States, on the one hand, and the thorough deliberation with which it was pursued in Japan, on the other, Ōuchi argues, that accounts for the remarkable success of Japan's economy under state monopoly capitalism vis-à-vis the West in the years since the reforms.[76]

Crucial to this Rōnō-ha analysis is the conception of state monopoly capitalism developed by Ōuchi:

> State monopoly capitalism is a form of capitalism in which the mechanism of accumulation by finance capital has incorporated the state as

> one of its essential components whose function it is to intervene with its fiscal policy into capital-wage-labor relations in order to ensure full employment and to avoid crisis. Often called the "popular state" or the "welfare state," the state conceals class relations in various ways under the pretext of advancing the "public interest." Through its various measures ostensibly for the sake of the "public interest," the state ensures accumulation by finance capital which has lost its autonomy, and hides under a public veil the naked reality of class domination by private monopolies.

The more subtle linkages among the enterprise groups that succeeded the prereform zaibatsu fit nicely into the framework of this state monopoly capitalism. Similarly, the new prohibition on private cartels that could "invite strong antagonism from consumers and small- and medium-sized companies" proved to be beneficial to Japanese growth because such private cartels were less suitable for the more sophisticated variety of capitalism than were cartels formed—as they are in Japan now—with government approval "under the guise of protecting 'national interests.' "[77] In short, Ōuchi's conception of state monopoly capitalism and the Rōnō-ha's use of it to interpret the postwar reforms formed the bases for a systematic exposition of the Japanese economy's remarkable success in the postwar era. In this respect, the boundaries between the Rōnō-ha and the Uno school become increasingly blurred: Ōuchi has been identified with both. Nevertheless, it is useful to identify the Rōnō-ha in its "pure" form with its postwar theoretical leader, Sakisaka Itsurō, in terms of its close political linkage with the Socialist party; while the economic school of Uno Kōzō, who once asserted that true economic scholars did not try to apply their ideas to daily political practice,[78] has concentrated on the theoretical achievements that have begun to gain attention and respect in the West.

THE POSTWAR RŌNŌ-HA AND THE JSP. One indicator of this distinction between the Uno and Rōnō factions appears in the analysis of the land reforms by Sakisaka, the scholar who succeeded Kushida Tamizō as leading Rōnō-ha figure in the postwar era. Sakisaka concurred with other Rōnō-ha Marxists in repudiating the Kōza-ha's two alternative views of the agrarian land reforms and other Occupation policies. Unlike Ōuchi, however, he did not stress the analysis of Japanese monopoly capitalism with a view toward identifying its special as well as universal characteristics. Rather, Sakisaka characterized the Occupation's land policies as "a reformation of modern, private landownership introduced at the expense of large landowners in order to mitigate the serious political crisis of the capitalist class." This view coincided with the prewar Rōnō-ha interpretation of the Meiji Restoration as Japan's bourgeois-democratic revolution.[79] This interpretation, now brought forward into the postwar era (and shared by Uno Marxists as well), became the theoretical basis for the left wing of the Socialist party and its espousal of an immediate socialist revolution that would strengthen democracy in Japan.

Like the JCP and the ruling LDP, the Socialist party has been convulsed by factionalism almost from its birth, and the dissension has resulted as much from theoretical differences as from personality conflicts. Within three years after the party was founded in November 1945, such factional conflict began to cause splits in the young party's membership. Without narrating all the details of these successive ruptures,[80] it is sufficient to note that by early 1950, a left-right split had emerged at the Fifth Party Congress. Although this rupture was repaired at a Special Congress summoned in August the same year, in 1951 Yamakawa Hitoshi and Ōuchi Hyōe, leading Rōnō-ha Marxists from the prewar era, formed the Socialist Association (Shakai-shugi Kyōkai). The Kyōkai, a group of left-wing socialist intellectuals who could not accept the Kōza-ha variety of Marxism, was originally formed without organizational affiliation, but since the late 1950s, the group has been a powerful force operating within the Socialist party, infusing the party with Marxist-Leninist spirit and endeavoring to make it a "class" party in pursuit of socialist revolution in opposition to the "social-democratic" tendencies the JCP indiscriminately associates with the JSP in general.[81]

The Kyōkai, which in fact has included some Uno Marxists along with Rōnō-ha associates of Sakisaka, publishes its own organ, *Shakai-shugi* [Socialism]. Under Yamakawa, the Kyōkai's "left" position emerged early in 1951, in the left-right split in the controversy on unarmed neutrality aroused by the issue of the Security Treaty with the United States. Supporting the left wing on this issue, Yamakawa argued that Japan must repudiate pressures from the United States and the party's right wing to rearm and must maintain a neutralist international posture. From this point into the 1960s, and indeed to the present, this has remained the posture of the JSP. The left wing's dominance on this issue lay behind the Socialist party's role in the virulent public opposition to the renewal of the Security Treaty on the basis of a platform of "positive neutrality" in 1960.[82]

During the Yamakawa years, the Kyōkai distinguished itself by advocating three points. First was the notion that a socialist Japan would maintain this international position of unarmed neutrality. Second, the Kyōkai agreed with the notion of "polycentrism," a concept proposed by Yugoslavia's Tito and the object of major emphasis in Nikita Khrushchev's launching of de-Stalinization in 1956. This view repudiated Great Russian chauvinism and insisted that the Soviet experience represented but one path to socialism, of which there were many. Finally, and most importantly for the future of the Socialist party, was the notion elaborated by Sakisaka that, given Japanese conditions and especially the newly liberalized and relatively democratic postwar context, the Japanese path to socialism would be a peaceful revolution (*heiwa kakumei*).[83]

After Yamakawa's death, the leading figure in the Kyōkai became Sakisaka, who had studied Marxian economics under Uno and Tsuchiya Takao at Tokyo Imperial University and taught after the war at Kyūshū University. There, through lectures and Marxist-Leninist study groups, Sakisaka drew younger members into the Kyōkai over the years. Through the 1960s, the Kyōkai increasingly expanded its organizational activities among young activists and heightened its theoretical influence on JSP policy. This influence became particularly pronounced after the left-right conflict within the party was aggravated by the Security Treaty revision issue and finally resulted in an effort to expel the right-wing faction of Nishio Matsuhiro in 1959 and 1960. After a group of thirty-three joined Nishio in leaving the party to establish the non-Marxist Social Democratic Party (Shakai Minshutō), the influence of Sakisaka's Kyōkai reached its apex. Now, as the party began to debate its own version of "structural reform," advocated by party secretary Eda Saburō, it resolved to look more closely at the theoretical basis for its strategy and tactics.[84]

In January 1962, at its Twenty-first Party Congress, the party established a theoretical organ, the Socialist Theory Committee (Shakai-shugi Riron I'inkai) which began its work later that year under the leadership of Suzuki Mosaburō and Katsumata Sei'ichi. The result of its efforts was the *Nihon ni okeru shakai-shugi e no michi* [The path to socialism in Japan]. This document closely followed the notion of peaceful revolution of Sakisaka's Kyōkai, and it marked the closest relationship between Rōnō-ha theory and JSP practice when it was officially adopted as the party's program. Nevertheless, there were aspects of the *Michi* that departed from the perspective of the Kyōkai under Yamakawa, and it was these points that aroused considerable resistance to Sakisaka's influence within the JSP and eventually within the Kyōkai itself. Unlike Yamakawa, and indeed unlike the JCP as well, which had turned from the Soviet Union and toward China by the early 1960s, Sakisaka held a distinctly pro-Soviet orientation. Although Sakisaka argued that Japan's revolution would pursue its own peaceful course, he did not criticize the shortcomings of the Soviet experience; nor did he limit the validity of Marxism-Leninism to the Soviet Union.[85] He envisaged the JSP as a party ideologically based on Marxism-Leninism, and his vision of post-revolutionary Japan accepted the desirability of continued class struggle, a democratic dictatorship of the proletariat, as well as the need for a centralized state that would own large industry and land.[86] This document has remained the official basis of JSP policy until the present.

In recent years, this dominance of Sakisaka's Kyōkai over the Marxist left wing of the JSP and indeed over the party itself as a whole has been increasingly challenged. The Kyōkai's role in party management, its centralized and closed character, and the *Michi* itself have all aroused criticism over the years, and by 1977, this criticism had evolved into an intraparty struggle between the Kyōkai and its opponents. It is difficult to assess the effect of this split on the Socialist party as a whole partly because, as the party's right wing is quick to stress, the influence of the Kyōkai itself weakened as an older Sakisaka retired from teaching and was unable to participate as directly and easily in party affairs. In addition, in the four decades since its founding, the membership composition of the Socialist party has changed: there is a larger proportion of members drawn from the labor movement as opposed to intellectual circles.[87] Nevertheless, as the intraparty split evolved as a conflict between the Marxism-Leninism of the Kyōkai and a view more akin to Eda's espousal of "socialism through the accumulation of gradualist reforms," the party's Forty-second Party Congress of March 1978 established the Socialist Theory Center, chaired by Katsumata. The party's Central Executive Committee ordered the center to reexamine the *Michi*, giving special attention to the conception of socialism outlined in the document.[88] When this group did not accomplish these tasks promptly, another group of scholars who were critical of the *Michi*—including Ōuchi Tsutomu, Lower House Dietman Hori Masao, Tokyo University economist Baba Hiroji, and others—organized the Workers' Self-Management Research Conference (Rōdōsha Jishu Kanri Kenkyū Kaigi) in 1978 to discuss these issues. Asserting that Sakisaka's view of the transition to socialism in Japan, represented in the *Michi*, is poorly expressed and "unrealistic," the Workers' Self-Management group has undertaken its own systematic critique of the *Michi* and has endeavored to articulate an alternative Marxist vision of socialism that could provide a new basis for the revolutionary—not reformist—strategy and tactics of the Socialist party.[89]

The endeavors of this group, recorded in their quarterly publication *Studies in Workers' Self-Management*, are significant for an assessment of postwar Japanese Marxism for two reasons. First, they coincide with a split within the Kyōkai itself as well as efforts to establish a "New Socialist Party" under the new party chairman Ishibashi Masashi. In April 1984, a group of scholars and professors led by Fukuda Yutaka of Hōsei University left the Kyōkai. Many of the reasons for this group's disenchantment with Sakisaka's version of Marxism-Leninism echo the objections of the Ōuchi-Hori group. Both groups reject the pro-Soviet stand that permits not even mild criticism of Soviet intervention in Czechoslovakia, Poland, or Afghanistan; the adherence to Marx's "obsolete" thesis of the progressive and absolute impoverishment of the workers; and the retention of the Soviet model of postrevolutionary society. Finally, the Workers' Self-Management group also stresses crucial issues that confront a socialist party in any advanced capitalist society that has experienced democratization and the growth of a welfare state: How does one make socialism more popular, more appealing in such a context?[90] By raising such fundamental issues, Marxist opponents of Sakisaka's Kyōkai are engaged in a venture that has been matched in few if any other advanced capitalist societies and warrants the attention of Marxists in the West.

These theoretical efforts by descendants of the prewar *Rōnō* school are given additional significance by recent events within the Socialist party. In 1983, Ishibashi announced an effort to move the Socialist party in a more "pragmatic direction," to permit the party to exceed the 30 percent limit on the number of Diet seats it has been able to gain since 1955. This effort involves distancing the party from its Marxist roots in the belief that as long as it espouses a doctrine that is associated with an alien power (the Soviet Union) that is perceived negatively by the public, it will never gain enough popular support to unseat the LDP as the ruling political party. Part of the difficulty faced by Japan's Socialists also derives from their historical position as an opposition party. The JSP must come to be viewed as a party that can rule, will govern the country with a "responsible" domestic and foreign policy, and will not impose drastic and unsettling changes on the people. Accordingly, the amelioration of JSP relations with the United States and Ishibashi's *iken gōhō ron* (unconstitutional but legal thesis) mark steps in this direction. Ishibashi has altered the party's traditional questioning of the legitimacy of the Self-Defense Forces, arguing that while they may in fact be unconstitutional (*iken*), they were established in accordance with law. This position suggests that the JSP will no longer push the issue in Diet debates, and it makes the party appear to be content with the status quo with respect to the Jieitai.

These developments have alarmed many Rōnō-ha Marxists, and in this respect, the work of those involved in the Workers' Self-Management group represents an effort to assure that the party does not jettison Marxism itself along with Sakisaka's *Michi*, for lack of an attractive and viable alternative. To maintain the sharp edge of its attack on the Nakasone government—one area in which there is agreement between the JSP and the JCP—and assure the attainment of the final goal of socialism, this effort must succeed. A tentative step in this direction was made late in 1983, when the party's Socialist Theory Center finally produced a document entitled "Our New Conception of Socialism," which was influenced by the Workers' Self-Management group.[91] Significantly, these vigorous theoretical activities around the JSP are closely linked to the more exclusively scholarly research of Marxists who are involved with the innovative Uno school.

THEORETICAL CONTRIBUTIONS OF THE POSTWAR ERA

As this description of the postwar activities of the Rōnō-ha and Kōza-ha would indicate, the debate on Japanese capitalism has had a profound effect on the scholarship and politics of postwar Japan. Although many would stress that the debate in its original form no longer exists, it is far more important that the political concerns of these Marxists have had a long-lasting impact on the way in which Japanese political and economic history has been conceptualized in Japan to the present. Although the postwar years saw the introduction of alternative paradigms of political development, especially from the United States, the Marxist controversies, with both sides supported by impressive pioneering empirical research, have dominated the discussion of prewar Japanese development, wartime militarism and fascism, the postwar reforms, and rapid economic growth after the war, as well as the persistent shortcomings of Japanese democracy. Often despite their debts to other approaches, modernization scholars in Japan must at least respond to the arguments of Marxist scholars, and in the cases of leading scholars in politics, law, comparative history, and economics, non-Marxists often incorporate concepts borrowed from Marxism into their work.

While Kōza-ha Marxists continue to be associated with historical and comparative studies and Rōnō-ha scholars with empirical studies of contemporary capitalism, both sides have made important contributions to the theoretical debates on larger issues pursued by Marxists throughout the world. Both factions have drawn on the particular elements of the Japanese experience—its late development, revolution from above in the Meiji, military crisis, and rapid postwar development—to offer perspectives of universal significance for scholars of political development. While this discussion thus far has stressed the work of postwar Marxists on Japan in particular, both factions have achieved theoretical gains that must be noted in any final assessment of the significance of the debate on Japanese capitalism. These achievements were consolidated and pushed forward in the freer postwar academic atmosphere, but they were built atop the efforts of prewar Marxists. Therefore, they are more appropriately viewed as the culmination of the sustained scholarship that has characterized the entire debate on Japanese capitalism, prewar and postwar.

The most notable theoretical accomplishments of Rōnō-ha scholarship are represented in the theory and metatheory of Uno Kōzō (1897-1977). His work encompasses the most original results of the debate on Japanese capitalism and, as a result, has gained a wide following. According to one

Uno scholar, "there are probably around two hundred professional scholars who could be classified as Uno theorists—or about one-fifth of the total of Japanese Marxist economists," and many of these are associated with the prestigious University of Tokyo.[92] Uno is closely linked with the prewar Rōnō-ha insofar as he shared its assessment of the Meiji Restoration as a bourgeois-democratic revolution, and those in his school today support this Rōnō-ha view in opposition to the Kōza-ha. Although Uno himself was not deeply involved in the prewar debate, in the prewar years, he began to work on the ideas that would form the core of his postwar work.

In a proposition that is widely viewed as an effort to separate theory from practice, Uno asserted that pure economics and socialist political activity were two separate spheres, even if both involved the Marxian critique of capitalism and the espousal of socialism. The two activities had different purposes and should not be confused: research was dedicated to the end of discovering the laws that govern capitalist society; but these were abstract principles that should not be applied carelessly to the realm of political activism. As Uno conceived it, Marxist economic research should proceed in three stages. In the first, pure theory, the economist endeavored to discover the nature of pure capitalism. In this view, even Marx's *Capital*, which was based closely on an analysis of the British system, required a process of abstraction to reach the level of pure theory. This was the stage of research to which Uno devoted his career, and its results appeared in his *Keizai genron* (1950-1952), published in English as *Principles of Political Economy: Theory of a Purely Capitalist Society*. Pure theory has a three-part structure. The first takes the first two parts of *Capital* and analyzes the three forms of commodity, currency, and capital circulation; the second, the theory of production, based on part three of volume 1 and all of volume 2 of *Capital*, studies the production of surplus value, the accumulation of capital, forms of wages, capital circulation, and reproduction. Finally, the theory of distribution is based on volume 3's description of the process of capitalist production as a whole. Uno addressed the theory of profits, ground rent, and interest in that order (instead of Marx's original order), and this portion of the theory is most problematic, in that it ends with an analysis of classes and the commoditization of capital.[93]

The second stage or level of economic research would develop the "stages theory of world capitalist development" on the basis of the principles uncovered in stage one. Uno had already formulated this second "stage theory" in his *Theory of Economic Policy* (1935), where he argued that world capitalism had evolved through three distinct stages, in each of which a certain kind of capital was dominant. The first stage was mercantilism, in which protectionist mercantilist policies were pursued by nations in search of profits, and British merchant capital, particularly in the woolen industry, was predominant. The second stage was liberalism, in which Britain, with its cotton textile industry, achieved economic predominance on the basis of laissez-faire policies. Finally, the third stage was imperialism, in which the finance capitals that had developed with the concentration of capital in heavy industry in England, Germany, and the United States became dominant.[94] The second level of economic research would concentrate on the concrete study of the dominant forms of capital in each of these three stages of world capitalist development—British mercantile woolen, British cotton textiles in the liberal era, and British, German, and American finance capital in the imperialist stage. Each stage represented the specific modes of capital accumulation that characterized (1) the original emergence of capitalism; (2) its period of growth after the industrial revolution; and (3) its period of full maturity, respectively. The second era, in which liberalism was the economic policy pursued deliberately to promote the interests of industrial capitalism, most closely approached "pure capitalism." In this period, the 1846 abolition of grain regulation, for example, represented a suppression of the interests of British landlords demanding protectionist measures in favor of capitalists calling for free trade. In the imperialist age, the era of capitalism at its apex, German heavy industry, especially steel, was not only predominant but also became a model of finance capital. Imperialism, in Uno's view, represented the policy of finance capital and included both the use of protectionist duties and dumping and the occupation of colonies abroad through capital export.[95] Uno and his followers encountered some difficulties in analyzing the American case, for example, in terms of these stages, and these problems are reflected in the disparities among the commentaries on his work that have been written by his followers. Nevertheless, this second stage of Uno's economic research has occupied the second generation of Uno scholars; and the third stage, that most relevant to daily practice, remains on the agenda of the postwar Rōnō-ha.

The third level of economic research was "the analysis of the current situation," and this was "the ultimate objective of economic study." This work had to proceed on the basis of the achievements of the first two levels of research, and it encompassed a complex process that could not be understood on the basis of economic study alone. Uno himself participated in this stage of research only as a member of study groups at the University of Tokyo; and his followers have continued this energetically, as has Ōuchi Tsutomu, in his studies of Japanese agriculture and its relationship to Japanese capitalism as a whole. These began with Ōuchi's work on the postwar reforms and resulted in some of the leading studies on Japanese agriculture,[96] "the weak point for capitalism," according to Uno. In addition, Ōuchi developed his own variant of Uno's theory of the stages of world capitalist development, one that considered both advanced countries and later developing countries in each stage. For example, while England had the upper hand in the liberal stage of capitalist development, Germany was relatively disadvantaged; and this situation was reversed in the imperialist stage, with Germany now in the dominant position and England less advantaged. Finally, Uno's work has inspired outstanding scholarship by Tohara Shirō on German finance, by Ōshima Kiyoshi on Japanese agriculture, and by Shibagaki Kazuo on Japanese zaibatsu and postwar enterprise groups, as well as by Ōuchi on state monopoly capitalism.[97]

Uno's work has begun to gain attention in the West, as evidenced by the translation into English of his major work on the theory of pure capitalism. Moreover, the recognition by some American Marxists of the accomplishments of Japanese Marxism in treating such abstract concepts as the theory of value represents a direct reference to those of the Uno school who approached the issue by means of Uno's notion of pure capitalism.[98] In addition, Uno's conception of the stages of the development of world capitalism, as well as Ōuchi's extension thereof, calls to mind the Marxian analysis of the dynamics of the world capitalist system developed by Immanuel Wallerstein and by dependency theorists.[99] Like Kōza-ha theorists who treated the notion of fascism and invoked the notion of the potential autonomy of the state, Japanese Marxists confronting conditions of late development and its special implications—including the threat of dependency (Takahashi Kamekichi) and the potential for "revolution from above"—were driven yet again to develop paradigms that would account for those specific features decades before Western scholars attacked the same issues. Moreover, perhaps because Japan eventually overcame its so-called backwardness, the Rōnō-ha treatments tend to be less determinist than the pessimistic work of dependency theorists and may contain lessons of value for scholars of late development elsewhere.

The Rōnō-ha's prewar stress on Japan's universal characteristics as a capitalist country, then, led its descendants to focus on the dynamics of capitalist and especially mature capitalist systems. Similarly, in part because they had emphasized the peculiarities of the fusion of feudal and capitalist formations in their study of Japan, the Kōza-ha's theoretical contributions are concentrated in the analysis of the precapitalist society (as in its work on the AMP in the prewar period and Ōtsuka Hisao's work on the village community after the war) and the transition from feudalism to capitalism.

One major Kōza-ha contribution has appeared in the form of Takahashi Kōhachirō's work on the bourgeois-democratic revolution. Educated in occidental history at Tokyo Imperial University, where he taught after the war, Takahashi quickly established an international reputation for his efforts to incorporate Western work on economic history with Kōza-ha scholarship on Japan to produce new insights into the process of the transition to capitalist society. By 1950, Takahashi had already published two works that soon became classics of postwar Japanese social science. In *A Historical Treatise on the Establishment of Modern Society* (1947) and *The Structure of Bourgeois Revolutions* (1950), Takahashi argued that the collapse of feudal society and the rise of modern capitalism could be understood only in relation to the emergence and subsequent decline of an independent peasantry.[100] This thesis became a key element in the controversy between Western Marxists Maurice Dobb and Paul Sweezy, in which Takahashi became an active participant.

The Dobb-Sweezy debate revolved around the issue of whether the development of world trade was the decisive factor producing the growth of Western industrial capitalism. Takahashi was critical of points in the arguments of both Dobb and Sweezy; but he showed more agreement with Dobb when he argued that capitalism had emerged out of the growth of production forces within the feudal system itself. This growth in internal production forces in turn necessitated a bourgeois-democratic revolution. The impetus for that revolutionary change, in other words, could not come from factors external to feudalism itself. To study the modern dissolution of the strata of direct producer peasants was, Takahashi asserted, to examine the development of these internal forces. In short, the liberation of peasants from feudal bonds was the key to the bourgeois revolution and the formation of industrial capital.

In a subsequent contribution to the Dobb-Sweezy debate, Takahashi applied his knowledge of Western and Japanese development to offer some provocative conclusions. This essay, which appeared in English in an edited volume on *The Transition from Feudalism to Capitalism*, makes an exciting contribution to our understanding of the factors that determined the differences between the path from feudalism to capitalism pursued by Western Europe, on the one hand, and the path of late developers like Germany and Japan, on the other. In particular, his analysis makes it clear why in the latter cases, a bourgeois-democratic revolution from below did not occur, but rather state intervention was necessary to produce a bourgeois revolution of sorts from above. The point of departure for Takahashi's argument is the passage in chapter 20, volume 3 of Marx's *Capital* describing the "two ways" a society could make the transition from feudalism to capitalism. In the first, " 'the producer becomes a merchant and a capitalist'—'this is the really revolutionary way' "—and (2) " 'the merchant takes possession in a direct way of production,' 'preserves it [the old mode of production] and uses it as its premise,' but becomes eventually 'an obstacle to a real capitalist mode of production and declin[es] with the developing of the latter.' "[101]

In the course of his controversy with Sweezy, Dobb had asserted what in fact Kōza-ha Marxist Ōtsuka Hisao had discovered two decades earlier from his work on European history. In what must be regarded as a major theoretical contribution from the Kōza-ha, Ōtsuka had found that in the seventeenth-century English revolution, small- to middle-level yeoman farmers were the progressive force, while merchants, largely associated with the Royalist party, were "often found to be allied with feudal reaction [absolutism]."[102] This meant that the destruction of feudal absolutism "marked the first step toward the subordination of merchant capital to industrial capital."[103]

It is easy to see how the Kōza-ha's analysis of the transition to capitalism in Japan would be conducive to such an insight, for Yamada Moritarō and others had identified the close alliance between mercantile capital of zaibatsu, encouraged by the state, and the feudal forces in the countryside. The political product of this alliance they defined as absolutism, and Kōza-ha Marxists were convinced that a revolution was still required to achieve the fruits of bourgeois democracy in Japan. What Ōtsuka and Takahashi did was to use the work of Noro, Yamada, and Hirano to explain why the bourgeois-democratic revolution should have been delayed in Japan and not in England. The comparison not only with Germany, the case most like Japan, but also with Western Europe enabled Ōtsuka and Takahashi to transcend the excesses of the prewar Kōza-ha's stress on Japanese uniqueness by posing the issues in the universal terms of Marx's *Capital*.[104] In the Dobb-Sweezy debate, Takahashi argued that the crucial difference between the British experience and that of Japan and Germany was the difference between the dominance of Way I and Way II. Following Way I, the British and French revolutions occurred on the basis of "the class of free and independent peasants and the class of small- and middle-scale commodity producers." In both cases the latter group struggled against "*haute bourgeoisie* originating in the feudal land[ed] aristocracy, the merchant and financial monopolists," for example, English Independents versus Royalists and Presbyterians and French Montagnards versus Monarchiens, Feuillants, and Girondins. The victory of the middle class over the aristocracy meant the success of both revolutions.[105]

Takahashi went on to point out that the circumstances in Japan and Germany were precisely the opposite:

> The classical bourgeois revolutions of Western Europe aimed at freeing producers from the system of "constraints" (feudal land property and guild regulations) and making them free and independent commodity producers; in the economic process it was inevitable that they should be dissociated, and this differentiation (into capital and wage-labour) forms the internal market for industrial capital. It need

> hardly be said that what constituted the social background for the completion of the bourgeois revolution of this type was the structural disintegration of feudal land property peculiar to Western Europe. On the contrary, in Prussia and Japan, the erection of capitalism under the control and patronage of the feudal absolute state was in the cards from the very first.[106]

Ultimately, the manner in which feudalism was constituted played a major role in all cases in determining why this disparity between Japanese/German development and that of Western Europe should have emerged.

This insight formed the crux of Takahashi's provocative conclusions. In France and England, feudal landholding and serfdom "either disintegrated in the process of the economic development, or were wiped out structurally and categorically in the bourgeois revolution." Thus, "petty commodity producers" were released from feudal bonds in a manner that facilitated industrial capitalist production. By contrast, in Japan and Prussia, feudal land organization remained stubbornly intact despite the growth of production forces straining feudal bonds. Thus, the "bourgeois" reforms like the *Bauernbefreiung* and the Meiji land tax reforms tended to reinforce the position of semi-feudal landowners. As a result, "since capitalism had to be erected on this kind of soil, on a basis of fusion rather than conflict with absolutism, the formation of capitalism took place in the opposite way to Western Europe, predominantly as a process of transformation of putting-out merchant capital into industrial capital."[107]

In short, the closeknit integrity of Prussian and Japanese feudalism determined that these countries would follow Way II (merchant → manufacturer) rather than Way I (producer → merchant) to industrial capitalism. The consequence was that the alliance of capital with feudal interests and absolutism was inimical to the establishment of modern democracy. The "bourgeois" reforms that did occur in these settings, such as they were, were provoked by external factors—the military threat from the West in Japan's case—rather than from within, and were undertaken from above rather than from below. Finally, when democracy was achieved in both Japan and Germany, it was the accomplishment of an occupying power rather than that of the native bourgeoisie. Yet what Takahashi concluded from this historical evidence was that it was not the German and Japanese experiences that were the exception. Instead, "the fact that modern capitalism and bourgeois society may be said to have taken on their classic form in Western Europe indicates . . . an inherent fragility and instability of feudal land property there." European capitalism, then—and not the development pattern of Germany and Japan—appears to have been a historical accident.[108]

This schema did much to elucidate the reasons for the political backwardness of Japan despite its outward signs of a high level of capitalistic development in the prewar period. Democracy, the role of the state in socio-economic change, and the impediments imposed by the past on the future—these have been the themes of Kōza-ha scholarship, and they have remained its forte to the present. Taken together with Rōnō-ha studies of the economic aspects of Japanese capitalism from the 1920s on and on the schematization of the highest forms of capitalist development, the participants in the debate on Japanese capitalism offer much to our understanding of the nature of the crisis of development that Japan faced in the 1930s and an understanding of the strengths and weaknesses of its postwar achievements. Those who seek the keys to the crises of development encountered in Asia, Latin America, and Africa as well as to the continuing challenges posed to highly developed Western capitalist systems can learn a great deal from the debate on Japanese capitalism as the accomplishments of Japan's Marxist scholars are introduced into the international discourse on the origins and development of capitalism.

NOTES

PREFACE

1. Cabral suggested that the undesirable class cleavages to be remedied by socialist revolution had been introduced by Western imperialism into a society that was originally harmonious; and Nyerere injected *ujamaa*, or the "familyhood" that had characterized Tanzania's traditional agrarian community, into his socialist ideal. See Germaine A. Hoston, "Emperor, Nation, and the Transformation of Marxism to National Socialism in Prewar Japan," p. 46.

CHAPTER ONE

1. Ōishi Ka'ichirō, " 'Nihon shihon-shugi hattatsu shi kōza' kankō jijō" [The circumstances of the publication of the "Symposium on the history of the development of Japanese capitalism"], in *Nihon shihon-shugi hattatsu shi kōza* [hereafter cited as *Kōza*], Supplement, p. 10.

2. Ōuchi Tsutomu, *Fashizumu e no michi*.

3. Imai Sei'ichi, *Taishō demokurashii*, insert. Cf. John Whitney Hall, *Japan: From Prehistory to Modern Times*, Delacorte World History (New York: Dell, 1970), chap. 17. A comprehensive history of the period is offered by Shinobu Seizaburō in two monumental works: *Taishō demokurashii shi* [History of Taishō democracy], 3 vols. (Tokyo: Nihon Hyōron-sha, 1954-1959); and *Taishō seiji shi*.

4. These will be treated further below.

5. For a comparative analysis of Russian and Japanese industrialization, see Cyril E. Black et al., *The Modernization of Japan and Russia*.

6. William W. Lockwood, *The Economic Development of Japan*, p. 98.

7. Kazushi Ohkawa and Henry Rosovsky, *Japanese Economic Growth*, p. 16; cf. Ushiyama Keiji, "Nihon shihon-shugi kakuritsu-ki," p. 56.

8. Lockwood, *Economic Development of Japan*, p. 188.

9. John K. Fairbank, Edwin O. Reischauer, and Albert M. Craig, *East Asia: Tradition and Transformation* (Boston: Houghton Mifflin, 1973), p. 666.

10. Ohkawa and Rosovsky, *Japanese Economic Growth*, pp. 37-38. Also see Watanabe, Tsunehiko, "Industrialization, Technological Progess, and Dual Structure."

11. See Rudolf Hilferding, *Finance Capital* (1910), and the discussion of his work in Wolfgang J. Mommsen, *Theories of Imperialism*, pp. 36-39.

12. Economist Hayashi Yū'ichi offers the following tabulation on the growth of cartels in the 1920s:

Year	Heavy Industry	Chemicals	Textiles	Foodstuffs	Total
-1914	—	5	1	1	7
1915-1926	5	6	1	—	12
1927-1929	6	1	3	2	12

Hayashi Yū'ichi, "Dokusen shihon-shugi kakuritsu-ki," p. 118.

13. Lockwood, *Economic Development of Japan*, pp. 60, 507.

14. Ohkawa and Rosovsky, *Japanese Economic Growth*, p. 82.

15. Ibid., pp. 17-18; Lockwood, *Economic Development of Japan*, p. 25.

16. Ohkawa and Rosovsky, *Japanese Economic Growth*, pp. 27-30.

17. Lockwood, *Economic Development of Japan*, p. 203.

18. Shūichi Kato, "Taishō Democracy as the Pre-Stage for Japanese Militarism," p. 226.

19. Lockwood estimates that total population increased from about 36 million in 1880 to over 69 million by 1935. (*Economic Development of Japan*, p. 155.) Meanwhile, the area of arable land expanded from about 4,313,000 *chō* in 1878 to 6,090,000 *chō* in 1922, but recorded no further growth, remaining at 6,081,000 *chō* in 1927. Although the proportion of the population in urban centers increased during this period, the number of agrarian households remained fairly constant. Thus, between 1910 and 1925, the density of rural population actually increased slightly, from 8.87 to 9.85 persons per square *chō* (1 *chō* = 2.45 acres). Takahashi Kamekichi, *Nihon shihon-shugi hattatsu shi*, pp. 335, 399.

20. Ohkawa and Rosovsky, *Japanese Economic Growth*, p. 282, table 3.

21. Kōzō Yamamura, "Japanese Economy," p. 309.

22. Ohkawa and Rosovsky, *Japanese Economic Growth*, pp. 98, 96.

23. Yamamura, "Japanese Economy," pp. 304-305.

24. Aikawa Haruki, "Nōson keizai to nōgyō kyōkō," p. 35; cf. Hall, *Japan*, p. 312.

25. Lockwood, *Economic Development of Japan*, pp. 56-57.

26. Komine Kazuo, "Senji kokka dokusen shihon-shugi-ki," p. 191; and Hayashi, "Dokusen shihon-shugi kakuritsu-ki," p. 149. For an analysis of the tenants' movement, see Ann Waswo, "The Origins of Tenant Unrest," pp. 374-397.

27. This term was accepted in the 1920s largely on the basis of the work of the economist Takahashi Kamekichi, especially his *Nihon shihon-shugi keizai no kenkyū* and *Nihon keizai no yukizumari to musan-kaikyū no taisaku*. A detailed discussion of Takahashi's analysis of the economic crisis and its role in provoking the debate on Japanese capitalism follows in chapter 4.

28. Kato, "Taishō Democracy," p. 218.

29. Lockwood, *Economic Development of Japan*, p. 40.

30. Ohkawa and Rosovsky, *Japanese Economic Growth*, p. 33, table 2.3.

31. Ibid., p. 25, table 2.1.

32. See table 2 in Takahashi, *Nihon shihon-shugi hattatsu shi*, p. 227.

33. George Oakley Totten, III, *The Social Democratic Movement in Prewar Japan*, pp. 31-32.

34. Ibid., p. 213.

35. A discussion of the so-called *ana-boru* debate is to be found in Germaine A. Hoston, "State and Revolution in China and Japan," pp. 515-518.

36. The best example of a pessimistic account of Taishō politics is Robert A. Scalapino, *Democracy and the Party Movement in Prewar Japan*. Treated more loosely as the period from 1900 to the Pacific War, the Taishō period represents to other Western scholars an era of crisis, which eventually contributed to the rise of militarism and fascism in Japan. See, e.g., Bernard S. Silberman, "Conclusion." On the "Era of Party Rule," see Peter Duus, "The Era of Party Rule" and *Party Rivalry and Political Change in Taishō Japan*.

37. Hall, *Japan*, p. 314.

38. This cynical view of Taishō democracy was apparent early, in Marxist contributions to the debate on Japanese capitalism, particularly within the Kōza-ha. See chapter 7. To the critique of Taishō democracy that follows, it might be objected that similar criticisms of elitism in functioning Western democracies have been articulated convincingly by Joseph Schumpeter, Vilfredo Pareto, C. Wright Mills, Gastano Mosca, and others. Nevertheless, it is argued here that Taishō democracy failed not simply to fulfill an illusory notion of democracy in the West; rather, it failed in the eyes of contemporary political observers, like Yoshino Sakuzō, to fulfill its own promise of what democracy could be.

39. See Richard J. Smethurst, *A Social Basis for Prewar Japanese Militarism*. About 40 percent of first-year students in the Rikugun Shikan Gakkō (Military Academy) were of agrarian background. (Fujiwara Akira, *Gunjishi*, p. 157.)

40. According to Shinobu Seizaburō, the establishment of right-wing groups accelerated beginning in 1923:

Era:	Meiji						Taishō	
Year of Founding:	1880	1894	1897	1901	1906	1912	1914	1916
Number of Groups:	1	1	1	1	1	1	1	1

Taishō									
1917	1918	1919	1920	1921	1922	1923	1924	1925	1926
1	1	2	2	1	4	13	11	13	19

Shōwa							Total
1927	1928	1929	1930	1931	1932	1933	
19	24	17	26	65	144	131	501

Shinobu, *Taishō seiji shi*, p. 752. Baba Yoshitsugi, "Waga kuni ni okeru saikin no kokka-shugi naishi kokka-shakai-shugi undō ni tsuite" [On the recent nationalist and national socialist movement in our country], Shihō kenkyū dai jūkyū shū hōkokusho jū [Judicial studies, collection no. 19, report no. 10], quoted by Shinobu, *Taishō seiji shi*, p. 752.

41. Kato, "Taishō Democracy," p. 229.

42. See Duus, "Era of Party Rule" and *Party Rivalry and Political Change*.

43. Scalapino, *Democracy and the Party Movement*, p. 113.

44. Shinobu, *Taishō seiji shi*, p. 858.

45. Totten, *Social Democratic Movement*, p. 56. Population figures are found in Ohkawa and Rosovsky, *Japanese Economic Growth*, p. 310.

46. Totten, *Social Democratic Movement*, p. 56.

47. Scalapino, *Democracy and the Party Movement*, pp. 256-257.

48. Kato, "Taishō Democracy," p. 229.

49. That this was the popular view is suggested not only by mass participation in the democratic movement from below, but also in Scalapino's observation that there was a strong tendency for urban districts to send unaffiliated representatives to the Diet, because "many urban voters looked with disfavor on both major parties." (*Democracy and the Party Movement*, p. 256n.)

50. Party president, director, secretary, parliamentary director, and parliamentary secretary constituted party leadership positions. Between 1900 and 1920, the percentage of Seiyūkai party leaders who had been higher officials in the central government (*kōtō kanri*) increased fivefold, from 3 to 16 percent; and the proportion of those with business background or associations rose less dramatically, from 38 to 50 percent, over the same period. The proportion of leaders with prior experience as local prefectural assembly members declined from 74 to 24 percent. See Masumi Junnosuke, "Nihon seitō shi ni okeru chihō seiji no sho mondai" [Some problems of local politics in the history of Japanese political parties], *Kokka gakkai zasshi* (Tokyo), no. 76 (1963): 38. Between 1890 and 1924, the average age of Diet members rose significantly, from 42.3 to 51 years, suggesting an ossification of party power structures. In 1890, 40 percent were 31 to 39 years old (the minimum age was 31 by law); only 10 percent of Diet members were in this age group in 1924, when 56 percent (in contrast with only 17 percent in 1890) were over 49 years old. See Shimura Gi'ichi, ed., *Kokka taikan* (Tokyo: Sangyō Keizai-sha, 1954), p. 649, cited by Duus, *Party Rivalry and Political Change*, p. 15.

51. Maruyama Masao, *Thought and Behavior in Modern Japanese Politics* (London, 1963), p. 128, quoted in Bernard S. Silberman, "The Bureaucratic Role in Japan," p. 215.

52. Duus, *Party Rivalry and Political Change*, p. 4.

53. Ibid.

54. See Richard H. Mitchell, *Thought Control in Prewar Japan*, especially chap. 3.

55. Yamakawa Hitoshi, "Shōnin shinsei" and "Nihon ni okeru demokurashii no hattatsu to musan-kaikyū no seiji undō."

56. The distinction between the Rōnō-ha and Kōza-ha positions on this issue is, of course, far more complex and will be pursued in greater detail in chapter 7. Shinobu Seizaburō, a Marxist scholar with Kōza-ha leanings, for example, emphasizes the role of the emperor as capitalist alongside his role as landlord. He offers the following data on the emperor's stock holdings circa 1918:

Company	Number of Shares	Value (yen)
Nihon Ginkō [Bank of Japan]	208,000	20,800,000
Shōkin Ginkō [Specie Bank]	209,318	21,550,231

Company	Number of Shares	Value (yen)
Kōgyō Ginkō [Enterprise Bank]	45,450	1,420,312
Taiwan Ginkō [Bank of Taiwan]	30,264	1,891,000
Tōyō Takushoku Ginkō [Eastern Colonial Bank]	50,000	1,875,000
Teikoku (Mitsui) Ginkō [Imperial (Mitsui) Bank]	29,110	1,280,140
Hokkaidō Tankō [Hokkaido Coal Mine and Steamships]	153,976	6,700,200
Nihon Yūsen [Japan Mail Steamers] (also called the New York Line)	161,100	8,260,534
Ōji Seishi [Ōji Paper]	60,608	13,582,250
Kantō Haiden [Kantō Electric]	34,759	1,737,950
Minami-Manshū Tetsudō [Southern Manchurian Railway]	84,375	3,290,560
Taiwan Seitō [Taiwan Sugar Manufacture]	39,600	1,980,000

In addition to a total of ¥87,983,583 in stocks, the emperor also held ¥138,221,513 in domestic bonds; ¥26,347,217 in foreign loans; and ¥58,546,024 in corporate bonds.The total holdings of the emperor were thus ¥311,098,337. Through these holdings the emperor was linked especially closely to the Mitsui zaibatsu "and played a large role in Nihon Yūsen companies and colonial enterprises for the purpose of overseas development." (Shinobu, *Taishō seiji shi*, pp. 1343, 1342.)

57. On the basis of a government survey, Shinobu reports that the emperor's land holdings included:

Imperial estate	920 *chōho* (1 *chōho* = 2.45 acres)
Forests	1,298,781 *chōho*
Farmlands	39,835 *chōho*
Building sites	228 *chōho*
Other	12,445 *chōho*
Total	1,352,209 *chōho*

(Ibid., p. 1342.) Since Japan's total land area is about 142,811 square miles (37, 305, 730 *chōho*), the emperor's landholdings comprised a significant 3.6 percent of Japan's total land area, of which less than 20 percent is arable.

58. Kato, "Taishō Democracy," p. 225.

59. Even liberal thinker Yoshino Sakuzō affirmed Japan's special interests in China and failed to condemn the Twenty-one Demands. (Ibid., p. 224n.)

60. According to Imanaka Tsugimaro, the military was allocated the following shares of the total national budget:

1877: 19%	1907: 33%	1920: 48%	1923: 33%
1887: 28%	1913: 33%	1921: 49%	1925: 29%
1897: 49%	1919: 46%	1922: 42%	1927: 28%

(Imanaka Tsugimaro, *Nihon seiji shi shinko* [New materials on Japanese political history], Tokyo, 1948, vol. 2, p. 441, cited in Scalapino, *Democracy and the Party Movement*, p. 229n.)

61. Duus, *Party Rivalry and Political Change*, p. 196.

62. "Nihon Kyōsantō kōryō sōan," in Ishidō Kiyotomo and Yamabe Kentarō, comps., *Kominterun Nihon ni kansuru tēze shū*, p. 7.

63. Kato, "Taishō Democracy," p. 224.

64. Onabe Teruhiko, *Nijū seiki*, vol. 4, p. 464.

65. Kōtoku Shūsui, "Shakai-shugi to kokka" (1902) [Socialism and the state], in Kōtoku Shūsui, *Shakai-shugi shinzui*, pp. 61-64.

66. According to Takahashi Kamekichi, as of 1907, women and girls comprised 60 to 70 percent of Japanese workers; of these, up to 80 percent of female workers in the textile industry were under twenty years of age. (*Nihon shihon-shugi hattatsu shi*, p. 230.)

67. Gail Lee Bernstein, *Japanese Marxist*, p. 40.

68. Matsuzawa Hiroaki, *Nihon shakai-shugi no shisō*, p. 36.

69. Tanaka Masato has pointed out that this interpretation did not necessarily prescribe opposition to the traditional *kokutai*. Indeed, before the Russo-Japanese War, many Meiji socialists saw in Western captalism and its structure of economic exploitation a threat to the *kokutai*. Thus, their aim was to change economic organization, not necessarily political organization, and socialism could easily be reconciled with nationalism. See Tanaka Masato, *Takabatake Motoyuki*, p. 3.

70. Katayama Sen, *Waga shakai-shugi* (Kishimoto Eitarō, comp., Jitsugyō no Nihon-sha han), p. 257, quoted in Matsuzawa, *Nihon shakai-shugi no shisō*, p. 36, and pp. 37-40.

71. For an account of the socialist movement during this period, see Arahata Kanson, "Heimin-sha jidai."

72. Totten, *Social Democratic Movement*, pp. 25, 26.

73. Kida Jun'ichirō, *Meiji no risō*, pp. 208-209.

74. For a full discussion of Kōtoku's thought, see F. G. Notehelfer, *Kōtoku Shūsui*, chaps. 5, 6.

75. Koyama Hirotake, *Nihon Marukusu-shugi shi*, pp. 15-16; Sakai Toshihiko, *Nihon shakai-shugi undō shiwa* [Historical narrative of the Japanese socialist movement], in Sakai Toshihiko, *Sakai Toshihiko zenshū*, 6:284; Hyman Kublin, *Asian Revolutionary*, pp. 194-196; and Notehelfer, *Kōtoku Shūsui*, chap. 6 passim.

76. These arguments appeared in V. I. Lenin, *What Is To Be Done?* (1902) and *The State and Revolution* (1917), both included in *The Lenin Anthology*, ed. Robert C. Tucker (New York: W. W. Norton, 1978).

77. *Nikkan heimin shimbun*, no. 16 (February 5, 1907), p. 1, in *Meiji shakai shugi shiryō shū*, vol. 4, p. 69, quoted in Notehelfer, *Kōtoku Shūsui*, p. 142.

78. Koyama, *Nihon Marukusu-shugi shi*, p. 17; cf. Sakai, *Nihon shakai-shugi undō shiwa*, 6:285, and Arahata Kanson, *Kanson jiden*, 1:132-148.

79. Arahata Kanson, "Roshiya kakumei no koro," p. 181; Gail Lee Bernstein, "The Russian Revolution," pp. 330-331; and Arahata, *Kanson jiden*, 1:384.

80. Arahata, *Kanson jiden*, 1:384; Arahata, "Roshiya kakumei," p. 180; Inu-

maru Gi'ichi, "Nihon Marukusu-shugi no genryū," p. 8; Arahata Kanson, *Nihon shakai-shugi undō shi*, p. 113. See also Takeuchi Yoshitomo, "Nihon no Marukusu-shugi," pp. 17-18.

81. Kazama Jōkichi, *Mosukō to tsunagaru Nihon Kyōsantō no rekishi*, p. 22, quoted in Travers Edgar Durkee, "The Communist International and Japan, p. 12; and Inumaru, "Nihon Marukusu-shugi," p. 8.

82. Quoted in Kikuchi Masanori, *Roshiya kakumei to Nihonjin*, p. 269; and Kondō Kenji, *Ichi museifu-shugisha no kaisō*, p. 79.

83. Bernstein, "Russian Revolution," pp. 333-335.

84. Takabatake Motoyuki, "Kokka shakai-shugi no hitsuzen-sei," p. 175, quoted in Tanaka Masato, "Takabatake Motoyuki ron: Taishō shakai-shugi no bunka" [On Takabatake Motoyuki: the differentiation of Taishō socialism], *Shirin* 53.2 (March 1970): 46.

85. Tanaka, "Takabatake Motoyuki ron," p. 41.

86. Tanaka, *Takabatake Motoyuki*, pp. 111-113.

87. Sakai, *Nihon shakai-shugi undō shiwa*, p. 289.

88. Tanaka, "Takabatake Motoyuki ron," pp. 38-39, 44-45; and Tanaka, *Takabatake Motoyuki*, p. 120.

89. Ibid., pp. 142, 121-123.

90. Yamakawa Hitoshi, "Roshiya no shihai kaikyū," 5:249-253; Yamakawa Hitoshi, "Sobieto seiji no tokushitsu to sono hihan," 2:386, 389-390, 393-396; Koyama, *Nihon Marukusu-shugi shi*, p. 20; and Inumaru, "Nihon Marukusu-shugi," pp. 11-12.

91. Tanaka, "Takabatake Motoyuki ron," p. 46; cf. Arahata Kanson, "Yamakawa Hitoshi ron."

92. Takeuchi, "Nihon no Marukusu-shugi," p. 18; Koyama, *Nihon Marukusu-shugi shi*, p. 19; and Inumaru, "Nihon Marukusu-shugi," pp. 9-11. See, for example, Yamakawa Hitoshi, "Daisan Intanashonaru," 3:236-239.

93. Durkee, "Communist International," pp. 15-21; and Moriya Fumio (Denrō) *Nihon Marukusu-shugi riron no keisei to hatten*, p. 15.

94. Takeuchi, "Nihon no Marukusu-shugi," p. 18; Sakai, *Nihon shakai-shugi undō shiwa*, p. 288.

95. Moriya, *Nihon Marukusu-shugi*, p. 15; Durkee, "Communist International," p. 36; and Koyama, *Nihon Marukusu-shugi shi*, pp. 22-23.

96. Moriya, *Nihon Marukusu-shugi*, pp. 15-16; Inumaru, "Nihon Marukusu-shugi," p. 30; and Koyama, *Nihon Marukusu-shugi shi*, p. 23.

97. For a detailed discussion of the conception of the *kokutai* (national polity) and its implications for Japanese Marxism, see Hoston, "State and Revolution in China and Japan," 1:218-232. On the formation of Meiji official ideology, see Joseph Pittau, *Political Thought in Early Meiji Japan*; Ishida Takeshi, *Meiji seiji shisō shi kenkyū*, pt. 1; Takeda Kiyoko, "Tennō-sei shisō no keisei," pp. 270, 297-303.

98. See Harold Joseph Wray, "Changes and Continuity in Japanese Images of the *Kokutai*."

99. Takeda, "Tennō-sei shisō no keisei," p. 269.

100. On Shintō thought, see Atsuko Hirai, "Ancestor Worship in Yatsuka Hozumi's State and Constitutional Theory," in *Japan's Modern Century*, ed. Edmund Skrzypczak (Tokyo: Sophia University and Charles E. Tuttle, 1968). On Tokugawa Confucian thought on the emperor, see David Magarey Earl, *Emperor and Nation in Japan*. On the German influence, see S. An, "Meiji shoki in okeru Doitsu kokka shisō no jūyō ni kansuru ichi kōsatsu," pp. 121, 140-142.

101. See Robert Cornell Armstrong, *Light from the East*, p. 3.

102. Suzuki Yasuzō, *Kenpō seitai to Roesureru*, p. 142.

103. Takeda, "Tennō-sei shisō no keisei," p. 284; and Ienaga Saburō, "Nihon ni okeru kyōwa-shugi no dentō."

104. See Minobe Tatsukichi, "Kunshu no kokuhō-jō no chi'i"; Minobe Tatsukichi, *Kenpō satsuyō*. Cf. Miyazawa Toshiyoshi, *Tennō-kikan setsu jiken—shiryō wa kataru*; Nakase Ju'ichi, "Meiji kenpō-ka ni okeru tennō kikan setsu no keisei"; Nakase Ju'ichi, "Tennō kikan setsu kakuritsu katei ni okeru Minobe riron no tokushitsu"; Nakase Ju'ichi, "Tennō kikan setsu no genryū"; and Ukai Nobushige, "Minobe hakushi no shisō to gakusetsu." For an English-language treatment, see Frank O. Miller, *Minobe Tatsukichi*, p. 65 and passim.

105. See Uesugi Shinkichi, *Kenpō jutsugi*; Uesugi Shinkichi, *Kokutai kenpō oyobi kensei*, pt. 1; and Uesugi Shinkichi, "Kokutai ni kansuru isetsu." Cf. Kakei Katsuhiko, *Dai Nihon teikoku kenpō no konpon gi* for *tennō*-centered state theory following Hozumi and Uesugi. The latter work includes a color diagram of the Japanese polity with the *tennō* at the center.

106. Interview with Ukai Nobushige, Tokyo, July 23, 1979.

107. Interview with Fujita Shōzō, Tokyo, August 3, 1979. Cf. Fujita Shōzō, *Tennō-sei kokka no shihai genri*, pp. 5-114.

108. Wray, "Changes and Continuity in Japanese Images of the *Kokutai*," p. 64; interview with Fujita Shōzō, Tokyo, August 3, 1979.

109. See the memoir of Minobe's son, Minobe Ryōkichi, "Sore de mo tennō wa kikan de aru"; cf. Miyazawa Toshiyoshi, "Kikan setsu jiken to Minobe Tatsukichi sensei."

110. Richard Storry, *The Double Patriots: A Study of Japanese Nationalism* (Boston: Houghton Mifflin, 1957), pp. 162, 66.

111. Wray, "Changes and Continuity in Japanese Images of the *Kokutai*," p. 103; Ishida, *Meiji seiji shisō shi kenkyū*, pp. 7-8; and Ishida, "Ideolorogii to shite no tennō-sei," p. 39.

112. Political scientist Fujita Shōzō has emphasized that "Japanese political thinkers could have no notion of abstract right. One consequence of this was that during the Taishō period [Japanese leaders of the suffrage movement] understood universal suffrage as the 'demand of the age' rather than as 'right.' " When suffrage was won it accrued to the advantage of the emperor system because "our people rejoice in being treated as concrete personalities with human emotions rather than [in terms of] abstract right." (Fujita Shōzō, *Tenkō no shisō shi-teki kenkyū*, pp. 11-12.)

113. See Ishida, *Meiji seiji shisō shi kenkyū*, pp. 3-149 passim.

114. See Robert N. Bellah, *Tokugawa Religion: The Values of Pre-Industrial Japan* (Glencoe, Ill.: The Free Press, 1957; Boston: Beacon Press, 1970), pp. 13, 14.

115. George M. Wilson, *Radical Nationalist in Japan*, p. 22.

116. Japan, Department of Education, *Kokutai no Hongi*, p. 176.

117. See Germaine A. Hoston, "*Tenkō*"; and Patricia Golden Steinhoff, "*Tenkō*."

118. See Germaine A. Hoston, "Emperor, Nation, and the Transformation of Marxism to National Socialism in Prewar Japan."

119. Kobayashi Morito, *Tenkōsha no shisō to seikatsu*, pp. 7-8.

120. Bernstein, *Japanese Marxist*, p. 68.

121. Ibid., chap. 4; and Sumiya Etsuji, *Nihon keizaigaku shi*, chap. 1 passim.

122. [Kawakami Hajime], *Keizai to jinsei* [Economics and human existence] (1911), in *Kawakami Hajime chosakushū* [Collected works of Kawakami Hajime], quoted in Bernstein, *Japanese Marxist*, p. 67.

123. See Kita Ikki, *Nihon kaizō hōan taikō*, and Kita Ikki, *Kokutai ron oyobi junsei shakai-shugi* [The theory of national polity and pure socialism], in *Kita Ikki chosakushū*. Cf. the excellent studies by George Wilson, *Radical Nationalist in Japan*, especially chap. 2, and "Kita Ikki's Theory of Revolution," *Journal of Asian Studies* 26.1 (November 1966): 89-99.

124. Takabatake, "Kokka shakai-shugi no hitsuzen-sei," p. 175, quoted in Tanaka, "Takabatake Motoyuki ron," p. 43.

125. See Tanaka, "Takabatake Motoyuki ron."

126. See Akamatsu Katsumaro, "Nihon shihon-shugi hattatsu no tokushusei to musan-kaikyū seitō"; Akamatsu Katsumaro, "Kagaku-teki Nihon-shugi e" [Toward scientific Japanism], *Shinjin*, November 1924; and Moriya, *Nihon Marukusu-shugi*, p. 72.

127. See Hoston, "State and Revolution in China and Japan," 4:954-965.

Chapter Two

1. See Koyama Hirotake, *Nihon shihon-shugi ronsō shi*; Kojima Hinehisa, *Nihon shihon-shugi ronsō shi*, p. 12; Uchida Jōkichi and Nakano Jirō, *Nihon shihon-shugi ronsō*; cf. George Oakley Totten, III, *The Social Democratic Movement in Prewar Japan*, p. 192.

2. "Nihon ni kansuru ketsugi (Ni-nana nen tēze)." A translation appears in George M. Beckmann and Okubo Genji, *The Japanese Communist Party*, Appendix D. A more detailed discussion of the Comintern theses follows below.

3. A chronological listing of major contributions to the debate can be found in Uchida and Nakano, *Nihon shihon-shugi ronsō*, Appendix. Cf. Cecil H. Uyehara, *Leftwing Social Movements in Japan*, chap. 4.

4. This study will not examine the groups of academic Marxists whose work in philosophy, science, and literature was marginally, if at all, related to the debate on Japanese capitalism. Noro Eitarō's Nihon Shihon-shugi Kenkyūkai (Association for the Study of Japanese Marxism) was but one of many offshoots of the so-called

Puro-ka (Puroretaria Kagaku Kenkyūkai, the Association for Research in Proletarian Science) (1929-1934). Closely affiliated with the JCP, the association endeavored to propagate Marxist thought to the masses and to deepen research from a Marxist perspective in connection with proletarian cultural organizations. For a detailed discussion of the Puro-ka and its activities, see Koyama Hirotake, *Nihon Marukusu-shugi shi*, pp. 49-93 passim.

5. Ibid., pp. 48-49.

6. On the role of the "thought police," see Richard H. Mitchell, *Thought Control in Prewar Japan*. One source offers the following statistics on the numbers of arrestees under the Peace Preservation Law (numbers in parentheses represent those actually prosecuted):

1928 (including the 3.15 Incident)	3,426	(530)
1929 (including the 4.16 Incident)	4,942	(339)
1930	6,124	(461)
1931	10,422	(307)
1932	13,938	(646)
1933	14,624	(1,285)
1934	3,994	(469)
1935	1,772	(113)
1936	1,645	(159)
1937	1,291	(210)

Takabatake Michitoshi, "Ikkoku shakai-shugisha," 1:191. Besides smaller local trials, a large joint trial of 200 leading members of the JCP was held in Tokyo District Court from June 1931 to October 1932; 187 defendants received sentences ranging from two years to life imprisonment. See Patricia Golden Steinhoff, "*Tenkō*," pp. 3-5.

7. Published in Tokyo by Iwanami Shoten, 1932-1933. The original version of the *Kōza*, particularly the latter volumes, was heavily censored as official pressures on the left peaked in 1932 and 1933. In anticipation of this censorship, the organizers of the *Kōza* selected Iwanami Shoten, a prestigious scholarly press, hoping that the censors would be discouraged by the rigorous standards of the publisher Iwata Yoshimichi. (See Hani Gorō, "Nihon shihon-shugi hattatsu shi kōza gojū shūnen ni yosete," p. 33.) Only in June 1982, on the fiftieth anniversary of the publication of the *Kōza*, was the *Kōza* reprinted by Iwanami Shoten in its entirety, with censors' deletions restored, thus making the original complete text available to the public for the first time.

8. Koyama, *Nihon Marukusu-shugi shi*, p. 74; Sano Hiroshi, "Mosukō to Nihon Kyōsantō no kankei shi," p. 100; and Uchida and Nakano, *Nihon shihon-shugi ronsō*, p. 45.

9. The full title of Yamada's work was *Nihon shihon-shugi bunseki—Nihon shihon-shugi ni okeru saiseisan katei ha'aku* [An analysis of Japanese capitalism: A grasp of the reproduction process in Japanese capitalism]. Cf. the subtitle of Lenin's work—*The Process of the Formation of a Home Market for Large-Scale Industry*, the requisite for the domestic reproduction of capitalism in Russia. The intent of

Lenin's work, however, had been to refute the populist claim that capitalism was not developing as it had in Western Europe and therefore that a proletarian socialist revolution in the Marxian conception was not possible in Russia. Lenin demonstrated the inevitability of such a revolution given the auspicious inroads capitalism had already made in the predominantly agrarian economy. By contrast, Yamada's purpose was to emphasize the extent of Japan's backwardness, hence the impossibility of an immediate socialist revolution. What the two authors shared was their determination to show that their countries fit Marx's universal model of economic development through specific stages.

10. Koyama, *Nihon Marukusu-shugi shi*, pp. 74-75; and Shakai Keizai Rōdō Kenkyūjo, *Nihon shihon-shugi ronsō shi*, pp. 4-5.

11. On the tensions within the Rōnō-ha and their reflection in the faction's changes in membership and publications, see Hōsei Daigaku, Ōhara Shakai Mondai Kenkyūjo, comp., *Rōnō/Zen'ei: bekkan*, pp. 55-80. From 1973 to 1976 the Ōhara Institute supervised the reprinting of the Rōnō-ha organs *Rōnō* and *Zen'ei* in their entirety.

12. See this characterization of Yamakawa in Koyama Hirotake and Kishimoto Eitarō, *Nihon no hikyōsantō Marukusu-shugisha*.

13. Uchida and Nakano, *Nihon shihon-shugi ronsō*, pp. 79-81. Cf. Yamakawa Hitoshi. *Yamakawa Hitoshi jiden*, p. 429.

14. Koyama and Kishimoto, *Nihon no hikyōsantō*, p. 143.

15. Published in the May-June issue of *Marukusu-shugi*. See Uchida and Nakano, *Nihon shihon-shugi ronsō*, p. 103; Koyama, *Nihon Marukusu-shugi shi*, p. 46; and Koyama and Kishimoto, *Nihon no hikyōsantō*, p. 140.

16. Uchida and Nakano, *Nihon shihon-shugi ronsō*, p. 102.

17. See its "Theses on the Revolutionary Movements of Colonies and Semi-Colonies," which were applied directly to the Japanese case. (Koyama and Kishimoto, *Nihon no hikyōsantō*, p. 148.)

18. Ibid., pp. 148-149; interview with Takahashi Masao, Tokyo, Japan, May 5, 1984. Rōnō-ha sympathizer Tsushima Tadayuki argues that Inomata's work was not even a strictly one-stage revolutionary theory, but rather almost a "compromise between the single stage strategic doctrine and two-stage strategic theory." (*"Nihon shihon-shugi ronsō" shiron*, p. 8.)

19. Steinhoff, "*Tenkō*," pp. 249-250. Sakisaka Itsurō was arrested in the Popular Front Incident and Ōuchi Hyōe in the Professors Group Incident. Ōuchi's status in the debate is somewhat unusual. He and Tsuchiya contributed a section on financial policy to the *Kōza*, but this was less an interpretative contribution than a presentation of materials. (Hani, "Kōza gojū shūnen ni yosete," p. 29.) In his written prison statement in late 1941, Ōuchi repeatedly disavowed any association with the Rōnō-ha and its views. Indeed, he asserted that while he recognized some truths in Marxism, he was not sympathetic to it nor had he participated in any activity on the basis of such sympathies. (Ōuchi Hyōe, "Jōshinsho," pt. 1, pp. 4-6; pt. 2, pp. 4-8.) Because they had no ties to the JCP, Rōnō-ha members like Ōuchi were generally more difficult to associate with their faction than were Kōza-ha members. Indeed, the

Rōnō-ha was both organizationally and intellectually far less cohesive than the Kōza-ha. (See Shibagaki Kazuo, "Nihon keizai kenkyū ni okeru senzen to sengo," p. 17.)

20. See Arahata Kanson, *Kanson jiden*, 1:396-410; and Hoston, "State and Revolution in China and Japan," 2:505-518.

21. *Yamakawa Hitoshi jiden*, pp. 428-429.

22. Yamakawa opposed the Comintern and JCP interpretation that "ruling Japan is an absolutism in the form of the emperor system, and Japan is an absolutist state. Therefore, the aim of the proletariat's political struggle is the overthrow of the emperor system, and the strategic objective of the proletariat is the revolution of bourgeois democracy. When the bourgeois-democratic revolution has been achieved, only then will socialist revolution become the strategic aim of the proletariat. (In this respect, [the relationship between the two revolutions in the JCP view] is the same as the relationship between Russia's March and November revolutions. . . . At the time . . . this view was called the theory of two-stage revolution.)" (Ibid., p. 430.)

23. Matsuda Michio, "Yamakawa Hitoshi," in Suzuki Tadashi, ed., *Nihon no Marukusu-shugisha* [Japan's Marxists] (Nagoya: Fūbai-sha, 1969), p. 52.

24. Tsushima, *"Nihon shihon-shugi ronsō" shiron*, p. 151.

25. Noro Eitarō, "Nihon shihon-shugi hattatsu shi kōza—shu'i sho" [A symposium on the history of the development of Japanese capitalism—letter of intent], quoted in Koyama, *Nihon Marukusu-shugi shi*, p. 66.

26. Koyama, *Nihon Marukusu-shugi shi*, pp. 66-67.

27. See chapter 3 below.

28. Hani, "Kōza gojū shūnen," p. 31; interview with Ikumi Taku'ichi, Tokyo, June 17, 1982; and Kazama Yasoji, " 'Nihon shihon-shugi hattatsu shi kōza' hakkan gojū nen," pp. 196-197.

29. The prehistory of the debate is defined broadly here to embrace the Comintern theses that appeared in 1931 and 1932, since these intensified the Rōnō-ha–Kōza-ha controversy. Therefore, some Japanese scholars date the debate proper from 1932 rather than 1927 and treat the earlier period as "prehistory." The original version of Koyama Hirotake's definitive account of the debate referred to the earlier period as "the debate on democratic revolution" and the 1932 to 1945 period as "the debate on Japanese capitalism." See Koyama Hirotake, *Minshu kakumei ronsō shi*, and Shakai Keizai Rōdō Kenkyūjo, ed., *Nihon shihon-shugi ronsō shi*. Cf. Ōishi Ka'ichirō, "Nihon shihon-shugi ronsō to nōgyō-tochi mondai" [The debate on Japanese capitalism and the agrarian/land problem], in *Rekishi kagaku taikei* [Outline of historical sciences], vol. 9 (Tokyo: Rekishi Kagaku Kyōgikai, 1976), pp. 260-304.

30. The two doctrines were often linked in the works of Meiji socialists. Both Katayama Sen's *Waga shakai-shugi* [My socialism] (1903) and Kōtoku Shūsui's *Shakai-shugi shinzui* [The essence of socialism] (1903), the two most influential socialist works of their time, made this linkage explicitly. In both works, "scientific socialism [or Marxism] was grasped as evolutionary socialism, and the theory of

class struggle also was interpreted in connection with the concept of the survival of the fittest.'' Takeuchi Yoshitomo, ''Nihon no Marukusu-shugi,'' p. 12.

31. On Engels as a revisionist, see Shlomo Avineri, *The Social and Political Thought of Karl Marx*, Cambridge Studies in the History and Theory of Politics (Cambridge: Cambridge University Press, 1968), chap. 6; Donald Clark Hodges, ''Engels' Contribution to Marxism,'' *Socialist Register 1965* (London), p. 297; Leopold Labedz, ed., *Revisionism*, pp. 179-187, 344-346, and 349n; George Lichtheim, *Marxism*, pp. 58-61, 234-258; Herbert Marcuse, *Soviet Marxism: A Critical Analysis* (New York: Columbia University Press, 1958), pp. 138, 142-145; Robert Tucker, *Philosophy and Myth in Karl Marx*, p. 184; and Jean-Paul Sartre, *Critique de la raison dialectique* (Paris, 1960), pp. 121-135. A defense of Engels's contribution is presented in Leszek Kolakowski, *Main Currents of Marxism*, vol. 1, *The Founders*, pp. 399-408. Also see Rosa Luxemburg's critique of Lenin's reinterpretation of Marxism, in *The Russian Revolution: Leninism or Marxism?* (Ann Arbor: University of Michigan Press, 1961). In contrast, Hodges sees Lenin's interpretation of ''the contribution of dialectics'' not as ''the formulation of the most general interconnections in nature, society, and human thought,'' but rather in ''the use of these formulas as guides towards further specialized investigations within these areas.'' Lenin thus returns ''to the original context of Marx's thought'' (p. 308).

32. Hodges, ''Engels' Contribution to Marxism,'' pp. 297, 298, 299, 302, 304, 307.

33. Matsuzawa Hiroaki, *Nihon shakai-shugi no shisō*, p. 26; Onabe Teruhiko, *Nijū seiki*, 4:465.

34. Arahata Kanson, *Nihon shakai-shugi undō shi*, p. 20.

35. Yamakawa, *Yamakawa Hitoshi jiden*, p. 380.

36. Arahata, *Kanson jiden*, 1:99, 100; and Arahata Kanson, ''Heimin-sha jidai.''

37. *Nihon shakai undō jinmei jiten*, s.v. Kōtoku Shūsui; Arahata, *Kanson jiden*, 1:111-113, 132-135; and Arahata, *Nihon shakai-shugi undō shi*, pp. 107-108.

38. Takeuchi, ''Nihon no Marukusu-shugi,'' p. 13; and Matsuzawa, *Nihon shakai-shugi no shisō*, p. 41.

39. Matsuzawa, *Nihon shakai-shugi no shisō*, p. 40; Takeuchi, ''Nihon no Marukusu-shugi,'' p. 11. A third pioneering work, often cited along with these, was by Sakai and Morichika Unpei, *Shakai-shugi kōryō*. In all three works, the term *value* (*kachi*) was mistranslated as *kakaku*, which can be interpreted as either ''value/worth'' or ''price,'' thus obscuring the concept of surplus value in Marx's work. See Moriya Fumio, *Nihon Marukusu-shugi riron no keisei to hatten*, pp. 11n, 12.

40. Matsuzawa, *Nihon shakai-shugi no shisō*, p. 40.

41. By comparison with German leaders of the Second International, Lenin was virtually unknown in Japan until the October Revolution. In the June 1917 issue of the *Shin shakai*, for example, Sakai characterized Lenin as an anarchist. (Inumaru Gi'ichi, ''Nihon Marukusu-shugi no genryū,'' p. 8; Arahata, *Kanson jiden*, 1:384; Yamakawa, *Jiden*, p. 369; Moriya, *Nihon Marukusu-shugi*, p. 11; and Koyama, *Ni-*

hon Marukusu-shugi shi, p. 20.) Plekhanov's influence may be partly attributable to the fact that Japanese socialists had had prior contact with him (the historic handshake between Katayama and Plekhanov) at the Sixth Congress of the Second International in Amsterdam in 1904. Similarly, the dominance of Bukharin's influence as a theorist over that of Lenin may be explained by Bukharin's contact with Sakai and others in Tokyo en route to Russia in 1917. (Moriya, *Nihon Marukusu-shugi*, pp. 52, 53.)

42. During Bukharin's leadership of the Comintern, Japanese Marxists tended to defer more readily to his views, as one who understood Japan better than his colleagues. Because of his brief stop in Japan in 1917, he was regarded by the Japanese as the single Comintern leader most qualified to deal with the peculiarities of the Japanese situation. (Arahata Kanson, *Kyōsantō o meguru hitobito*, p. 31.) Moreover, Bukharin is credited with authorship of the JCP's original 1922 Draft Program and the 1927 Theses. See Kondō Eizō, *Kominterun no misshi*, p. 269; Uchida and Nakano, *Nihon shihon-shugi ronsō*, pp. 47-48; interview with Nakamura Takafusa, Tokyo, July 11, 1979 and July 17, 1979; Kazama Jōkichi, *Mosukō to tsunagaru Nihon Kyōsantō no rekishi*, 1:1-5; Tateyama Taka'aki, *Nihon Kyōsantō kenkyo hishi*, pp. 220-222; Koyama, *Nihon Marukusu-shugi shi*, pp. 47-48. Cf. Travers Edgar Durkee, "The Communist International and Japan," pp. 41-46; and Rodger Swearingen, "The Japanese Communist Party and the Comintern," pp. 50-51.

43. Moriya, *Nihon Marukusu-shugi*, p. 43; and interview with Arahata Kanson, Tokyo, August 17, 1979. Rōnō-ha academic Marxist Ōuchi Hyōe complained in 1936 that in Japan "Marxism was translated Bukharinistically" and adopted "Narodnikly," especially by the Kōza-ha. (Ōuchi, "Kaihan no tame ni.") In fact, however, Bukharin's influence became very pronounced in Rōnō-ha writings, especially in the application of his notion of state monopoly capitalism to Japan. (Interview with Nakamura Takafusa, Tokyo, July 17, 1979; interview with Taniuchi Yuzuru, Tokyo, August 3, 1979.) Other basic texts included Karl Kautsky's *Shihon-ron chūkai* [Commentary on *Capital*]; Lenin's *What Is To Be Done?*, *State and Revolution*, and *Left-Wing Communism, an Infantile Disorder*; Joseph Stalin's *Foundations of Leninism*, *History of the Communist Party of the Soviet Union*; writings by Soviet economist Yevgeny Varga; and, later, articles from the magazine *International* (1927-1933). (Matsuzawa, *Nihon shihon-shugi no shisō*, p. 195.)

44. In 1927, Hakuyō-sha published the ten-volume *Reinin chosaku shū* [Collected works of Lenin], and in 1928 *Sutārin-Buhārin chosaku shū* [Collected works of Stalin and Bukharin]. The same year Kaizō-sha published *Marukusu-Engerusu zenshū* [Complete works of Marx and Engels] (Moriya, *Nihon Marukusu-shugi*, pp. 42-43). For a more detailed account of the early importation of Marxism into Japan, see Hoston, "State and Revolution in China and Japan," 1:44-55.

45. In the early 1920s, young students who learned Marxism through English or German texts were fascinated with "the theory of dialectics . . . and with theories of overcoming and sublating Hegel via Marx." Lukács's *History and Class Consciousness* and Karl Korsch's *Marxism and Philosophy* were most influential in this respect. Yet there was far more interest in the idealism of Kant and neo-Kantian thought than in Hegel. (Moriya, *Nihon Marukusu-shugi*, pp. 127, 119.)

46. Daniel Tarschys, *Beyond the State*, p. 90 and chap. 3.

47. Moriya, *Nihon Marukusu-shugi*, p. 21; Shakai Keizai Rōdō Kenkyūjo, *Nihon shihon-shugi ronsō shi*, p. 6; and interview with Nakamura Takafusa, Tokyo, July 11, 1979.

48. Koyama and Kishimoto, *Nihon no hikyōsantō*, pp. 11, 12.

49. Matsushima Ei'ichi, "Nihon ni okeru Marukishizumu no tenkai," p. 9.

50. For an insightful discussion of these tensions, see Gail Lee Bernstein, *Japanese Marxist*.

51. Ibid., pp. 94-95; and Kushida Tamizō, "Kawakami Hajime kyōju no *Binbō monogatari* o yomu" [Reading Professor Kawakami Hajime's *Binbō monogatari*], *Kokka gakkai zasshi* (April 1917). Many, including Kawakami himself, have credited Kushida's critique of the former's moralism with Kawakami's subsequent dedication to the study of Marx's economics and even with the establishment of Marxism as academic subject matter in Japan. See Fujita Shōzō, "Aru Marukusu-shugisha," p. 84; and Kawakami Hajime, *Jijōden*, 4:123. The many points of conflict on Marxism between Kawakami and Kushida are chronicled in Kawakami Hajime, *Kawakami Hajime yori Kushida Tamizō e no tegami*, pp. 117-118.

52. See Amano Keitarō, *Kawakami Hajime bunkenshi*, pp. 193, 195, 197-198, 200-202.

53. Kawakami, *Jijōden*, 1:159-160.

54. Amano, *Kawakami Hajime bunkenshi*, pp. 70-71; and Kawakami, *Jijōden*, 1:211-212.

55. Koyama, *Minshu kakumei ronsō shi*, p. 6.

56. Uyehara, *Leftwing Social Movements in Japan*, p. 144.

57. Ibid., p. 140.

58. Koyama, *Minshu kakumei ronsō shi*, pp. 6-7. Uyehara gives the date of publication of *Nihon shakai-shi* as 1926 (Kaizō-sha) (*Leftwing Social Movements in Japan*, p. 140).

59. See especially Sano Manabu, *Minzoku to kaikyū*, and Hoston, "Emperor, Nation, and the Transformation of Marxism to National Socialism."

60. Uyehara, *Leftwing Social Movements in Japan*, p. 140.

61. Many of these articles, dated 1927 through 1930, are collected in Sano Manabu, *Seiji-ron*.

62. Takabatake maintained his claim to be a Marxist even after he formulated his *kokka shakai-shugi* (national/state socialism) doctrine. See Germaine A. Hoston, "Marxism and National Socialism in Taishō Japan"; Tanaka Masato, "Takabatake Motoyuki ron—Taishō shakai-shugi no bunka" [On Takabatake Motoyuki: The differentiation of Taishō socialism], *Shirin* 53.2 (March 1970): 33-86; and Tanaka Masato, *Takabatake Motoyuki*.

63. Inumaru Gi'ichi, "Nihon Marukusu-shugi no genryū," p. 18.

64. The 1927 Theses called for an "ideologically tempered, trained Leninist centralized mass communist party with firm/resolute faith." ("Nihon ni kansuru ketsugi," p. 45); cf. the discussion of the party's role in the '32 Theses, in "Nihon ni okeru jōsei to Nihon Kyōsantō no ninmu ni kansuru tēze," especially pp. 95-98, 101.

65. Kuno Osamu and Tsurumi Shunsuke, *Gendai Nihon no shisō*, pp. 36-37; and interview with Fukushima Shingō, Tokyo, July 31, 1979.

66. See V. I. Lenin, *What Is To Be Done?*

67. Uchida and Nakano, *Nihon shihon-shugi ronsō*, p. 33.

68. Yamakawa, *Yamakawa Hitoshi jiden*, pp. 427-428; Tsushima, *''Nihon shihon-shugi ronsō'' shiron*, p. 4; Koyama, *Nihon Marukusu-shugi shi*, p. 26. In 1907-1908 Yamakawa's Marxism was heavily influenced by the Russian anarchist Peter Kropotkin as well as by Japanese anarchist Kōtoku Shūsui. (See Thomas Duane Swift, ''Yamakawa Hitoshi and the Dawn of Japanese Socialism,'' pp. 176-177.) Generally Yamakawa's thought evolved as follows: ''theory of direct action → tendencies toward syndicalism → the 'change of direction' theory → participation in the formation of the Japanese Communist Party → dissolution of the party → Rōnō-ha Marxism.'' (Tanaka, ''Takabatake Motoyuki ron,'' p. 34.)

69. Koyama, *Nihon Marukusu-shugi shi*, pp. 45-46.

70. Yamakawa and Arahata Kanson insisted that the strategy was formulated independently of Comintern direction, but the influence of the Comintern is difficult to deny. See Beckmann and Okubo, *Japanese Communist Party*, p. 52.

71. Koyama, *Nihon Marukusu-shugi shi*, p. 27. Cf. Yamakawa, *Yamakawa Hitoshi jiden*, p. 433.

72. Koyama, *Nihon Marukusu-shugi shi*, pp. 25-28; and Koyama and Kishimoto, *Nihon no hikyōsantō*, pp. 13-14.

73. Koyama and Kishimoto, *Nihon no hikyōsantō*, p. 138.

74. See Arahata, *Kanson jiden*, vol. 2, chaps. 6, 7 passim; and Nabeyama Sadachika, *Watakushi wa kyōsantō o suteta*, p. 74.

75. Nabeyama, *Watakushi wa kyōsantō o suteta*, pp. 117-119. By contrast, Fukumoto would assert that ''Japan's bourgeoisie had still been unable to destroy the so-called absolutist-autocratic forces.'' (''Rōnō seitō to rōdō kumiai'' [The workers' and farmers' political party and labor unions], *Marukusu-shugi* [Marxism] [January 1926]: 10-13, quoted in Koyama and Kishimoto, *Nihon no hikyōsantō*, pp. 119-120.)

76. A detailed discussion of the Comintern theses follows in chapter 3.

77. See Kondō, *Kominterun no misshi*, pp. 268-271; and Inumaru, ''Nihon Marukusu-shugi no genryū,'' pp. 50-51.

78. Beckmann and Okubo, *Japanese Communist Party*, pp. 107-108; cf. Koyama, *Nihon Marukusu-shugi shi*, p. 29. In *Marukusu-shugi*, Fukumoto published under the pen name Hōjō Kazuo.

79. Kawakami Hajime, the Marxist pioneer who was criticized harshly by Fukumoto, disliked Fukumoto and his style intensely. Kawakami deplored the way Fukumoto ''mowed down people from petty officials to the world of criticism'' with what Kawakami considered bogus ''incantations'' from Leninism. Kawakami, *Jijōden*, 1:196-197, 228-229. Cf. Bernstein, *Japanese Marxism*, chap. 9 passim.

80. ''1927 Theses,'' trans. in Beckmann and Okubo, *Japanese Communist Party*, p. 305.

81. Koyama, *Nihon Marukusu-shugi shi*, pp. 29-30; and Kazama Jōkichi, *Mosukō to tsunagaru Nihon Kyōsantō no rekishi*, pp. 164-165.

82. According to one contemporary analysis, Fukumotoism was a combination of Lenin's organizational theory and George Lukács's dialectical materialism, as set forth in *History and Class Consciousness*. See Takeuchi, "Nihon no Marukusu-shugi," pp. 28-29.

83. Ibid., pp. 30-32.

84. Ibid., p. 32.

85. See Kazama, *Mosukō to tsunagaru*, pp. 164-165.

86. Ibid., p. 175.

Chapter Three

1. Lenin's interpretation of imperialism appeared in *Imperialism, the Highest Stage of Capitalism*, published in 1915. Bukharin had penned an article on the "Theory of the Imperialist State" and submitted it to Lenin for publication. Lenin criticized the essay for its "semi-anarchistic" tendencies and refused to publish it, but he clearly drew on Bukharin's ideas. In 1915 Bukharin had already completed his book, *Imperialism and World Economy*, several months before Lenin had finished his *Imperialism*, but Bukharin's book was not published until 1918. In 1915-1916, Bukharin opposed Lenin's view of the potency of nationalism in the imperialist age, but by 1923-1926, as an active Comintern leader, he had changed his views. See Stephen F. Cohen, *Bukharin and the Bolshevik Revolution*, pp. 25-43.

2. Ibid., p. 292.

3. Ibid., pp. 255, 31 (italics in original). Cf. Nikolai Bukharin, *Imperalism and World Economy*, chaps. 10, 11, and 13; and "Teorija 'organizovannoj bezkhozja-istvennosti,' " pp. 183-184.

4. On Bukharin's role in the Comintern and its policies in Asia, see Cohen, *Bukharin and the Bolshevik Revolution*, pp. 215, 292-293; and Edward Hammond, "Bukharin and the Chinese Revolution."

5. Jane Degras, "United Front Tactics in the Comintern 1921-1928," in *St. Antony's Papers*, no. 9: *International Communism*, ed. David Footman (Carbondale, Ill.: Southern Illinois University Press, 1960), pp. 11, 15. Degras interprets the theses of the Fifth Comintern Congress as a continuation of, rather than as a change in, united front tactics.

6. Others on the subcommittee included Finland's O. Kuusinen (a close associate of Bukharin), Bela Kun of Hungary, O. Piatnitsky, B. A. Vasiliov, Katayama Sen, Britain's J. T. Murphy, and Comintern representative to Japan Jacob Janson. Kazama Jōkichi, *Mosukō to tsunagaru Nihon Kyōsantō no rekishi*, pp. 176-187.

7. Degras, "United Front Tactics," pp. 15-18. Cf. Conrad Brandt, *Stalin's Failure in China, 1924-1927*, chap. 6; and Robert C. North, *Moscow and Chinese Communists*, chaps. 6 and 7.

8. Degras points out that this shift coincided with the beginning of the CPSU's domestic policy of "forced industrialization and the 'liquidation' of the kulaks as a class." ("United Front Tactics," pp. 21-22.)

9. "Nihon ni kansuru ketsugi," p. 43.

10. Ibid.

11. See Nakamura Takafusa, " 'Nihon shihon-shugi ronsō' ni tsuite."

12. See North, *Moscow and Chinese Communists*, chap. 9.

13. Interview with Nakamura Takafusa, Tokyo University, Tokyo, July 11, 1979.

14. Inomata wrote of "the fusion of finance capital with the state and state capital" in Japan but added, "We had previously called such a process of [moving] toward monopoly-state capitalism 'state capitalist trust.' However, this term must not [be used as it may] cause [us] to recall 'organized capitalism'; so we will not use it any longer." (Inomata Tsunao, *Nihon no dokusen shihon-shugi*, pp. 122, 124, 125.)

15. Uchida Jōkichi and Nakano Jirō, *Nihon shihon-shugi ronsō*, p. 47.

16. The extent to which the problem of revolutionary strategy in the East was conceived by the Soviets as the problem of revolution among oppressed, colonial, and underdeveloped nations is striking. See Stuart R. Schram and Hélène Carrère d'Encausse, *Marxism and Asia: An Introduction with Readings* (London: Allen Lane, Penguin Press, 1969), "Introduction," pt. 2.

17. There are two versions of the origins of the Draft Program. One version holds that Bukharin wrote the platform at the February 1922 Far Eastern People's Congress, whereupon Tokuda Kyūichi took it back to Japan. The first JCP meeting held at Shakujii in November 1922 discussed the Draft Program. (An alternative date given for the Shakujii meeting is March 1923, but this appears to be erroneous.) For this version, see Nabeyama Sadachika, *Watakushi wa kyōsantō o suteta*, pp. 61-62; and Travers Edgar Durkee, "The Communist International and Japan," pp. 41-42. The second account, used here because of its extensive support among primary sources, is that the platform was drafted primarily by Bukharin, as leader of the Comintern's Japan Commission at the 4th Congress. (Durkee, "Communist International," p. 42; and Kazama, *Mosukō to tsunagaru Nihon Kyōsantō no rekishi*, pp. 1-4.) The program remained a draft, because the first large-scale arrests of JCP members occurred on June 5, 1923, before the party could finish deliberating on it (Kazama, *Mosukō to tsunagaru Nihon Kyōsantō no rekishi*, pp. 86-87).

18. Durkee, "Communist International," p. 42. Contrary to the insistence of Uchida Jōkichi that the Draft Program "was not the private creature" of Bukharin but "was established by the efforts of responsible leaders of the Japanese proletarian movement [like Katayama] and Comintern leading revolutionaries" (Uchida and Nakano, *Nihon shihon-shugi ronsō*, p. 47), in fact the role of Bukharin in 1922 and thereafter in establishing JCP strategy is not to be underestimated. See Kazama, *Mosukō to tsunagaru Nihon Kyōsantō no rekishi*, p. 86; and Kondō Eizō, *Kominterun no misshi*, pp. 187, 268-269.

19. Kazama, *Mosukō to tsunagaru Nihon Kyōsantō no rekishi*, pp. 89-90.

20. Sano Hiroshi, "Mosukō to Nihon Kyōsantō no kankei shi," p. 98.

21. Kazama, *Mosukō to tsunagaru Nihon Kyōsantō no rekishi*, p. 89. Sano Hiroshi writes that in 1927, Bukharin criticized the 1922 Draft Program for having exaggerated the backwardness of Japanese society. "Mosukō to Nihon Kyōsantō no kankei shi," p. 98.

22. "Nihon Kyōsantō kōryō sōan," p. 5; cf. Uchida and Nakano, *Nihon shihon-shugi ronsō*, p. 48; and Durkee, "Communist International," pp. 42-43.

23. "Nihon Kyōsantō kōryō sōan," p. 16.

24. Inumaru Gi'ichi, "Nihon Marukusu-shugi no genryū," p. 18.

25. Whatever the merits of Bukharin's interpretation, the overall Russian predisposition to see Japan as backward even in comparison with prerevolutionary Russia may be a manifestation of "Orientalism," in which the East is treated as a great, undifferentiated, backward mass, "an element in a Romantic redemptive project." See Edward W. Said, *Orientalism*, p. 154 and chap. 1 passim. As Gail Bernstein has noted, Japanese intellectuals viewed tsarist Russia as backward in comparison to Japan. See Gail Lee Bernstein, "The Russian Revolution," p. 329.

26. G. Voichinsukii [Gregory Voitinsky], "Nihon ni okeru kaikyūsen (sankō ron)," pp. 10, 11.

27. Baruch Knei-paz, *The Social and Political Thought of Leon Trotsky*, p. 81.

28. See John W. Hall, *Japan: From Prehistory to Modern Times* (New York: Dell, 1970), p. 311.

29. Knei-paz, *Social and Political Thought of Leon Trotsky*, pp. 81-82; cf. *Itogi i Perspectivy* [Results and Prospects] (Moscow, 1919), pp. 233-236, and *1905*, 4th Russian ed. (Moscow, [1925]), pp. 46-47.

30. *Itogi i Perspectivy*, pp. 258 and 259, quoted in Knei-paz, *Social and Political Thought of Leon Trotsky*, p. 138.

31. Voichinsukii, "Nihon ni okeru kaikyūsen," p. 15.

32. Knei-paz, *Social and Political Thought of Leon Trotsky*, p. 121.

33. "Nihon Kyōsantō kōryō sōan," pp. 6-7; cf. Durkee, "Communist International," pp. 43-44. The Draft Program also made such "bourgeois-democratic" demands as freedom of press, assembly, and strikes, "abolition of the House of Peers," and the abolition of the existing military, police, and secret police organizations.

34. George M. Beckmann and Okubo Genji, *The Japanese Communist Party, 1922-1945*, pp. 66-78.

35. Yamakawa Hitoshi, "Nihon ni okeru demokurashii no hattatsu to musan-kaikyū no seiji undō," pp. 107-111.

36. Beckmann and Okubo, *Japanese Communist Party*, pp. 75-76.

37. Ichikawa Shōichi, *Nihon kyōsantō tōsō shōshi* [A brief history of the struggle of the Japanese Communist Party] (N.p., 1945), pp. 80, 83, quoted by Beckmann and Okubo, *Japanese Communist Party*, p. 76.

38. "Nihon shihon-shugi ronsō," in *Shakai kagaku dai jiten* [Encyclopedia of the social sciences] (Tokyo: Kaizō-sha, 1936), 14:305.

39. Uchida and Nakano, *Nihon shihon-shugi ronsō*, pp. 70-76.

40. Koyama Hirotake and Kishimoto Eitarō, *Nihon no hikyōsantō*, pp. 145-146.

41. The "1927 Theses," in Beckmann and Okubo, *Japanese Communist Party*, pp. 302, 300.

42. Ibid., pp. 297-298.

43. Ibid., pp. 294-295.

44. Ibid., p. 299.

45. Ibid., p. 297.

46. Ibid., p. 298.

47. Yamakawa Hitoshi, "Shōnin shinsei."

48. Durkee, "Communist International," pp. 95-96; and Koyama and Kishimoto, *Nihon no hikyōsantō*, pp. 141-142.

49. Tsushima Tadayuki, *"Nihon shihon-shugi ronsō" shiron*, pp. 29-30.

50. Koyama and Kishimoto, *Nihon no hikyōsantō*, p. 142; cf. Koyama Hirotake, *Nihon Marukusu-shugi shi*, pp. 43-44.

51. The theses were published in translation as appendices for the February issue of *Shakai shisō* [Social thought] and the March issue of *Marukusu-shugi*, which had now become the organ of orthodoxy opposed to the Rōnō-ha publication. Koyama and Kishimoto, *Nihon no hikyōsantō*, p. 141.

52. The following were designated candidate Central Committee members: Kawata Kenji, Matsuo Naoyoshi, Kasuga Shōjirō, Fujii Tetsuo, Tokuda Eiji, Takahashi Sadaki, Sōma Ichirō, Kawai Etsuzō, and Murao Satsuo. See Kazama, *Mosukō to tsunagaru*, pp. 187-188.

53. This is the emphasis in Durkee, "Communist International," p. 152; cf. Uchida and Nakano, *Nihon shihon-shugi ronsō*, p. 24n.

54. See Sano, "Mosukō to Nihon Kyōsantō no kankei shi," p. 101.

55. The 1931 Draft Political Theses opened with an analysis of the crisis engulfing world capitalism and its implications for Japanese imperialism. See "Nihon Kyōsantō seiji tēze sōan," pp. 46-49.

56. Tsushima, *"Nihon shihon-shugi ronsō" shiron*, p. 7.

57. Sano, "Mosukō to Nihon Kyōsantō no kankei shi," p. 101.

58. George M. Beckmann, "Japanese Adaptations of Marx-Leninism," p. 107.

59. Tsushima, *"Nihon shihon-shugi ronsō" shiron*, p. 128.

60. Durkee, "Communist International, p. 155.

61. Ibid., pp. 155-158, 178; and Beckmann and Okubo, *Japanese Communist Party*, pp. 196-205.

62. Durkee, "Communist International," pp. 163-164.

63. "Nihon Kyōsantō seiji tēze sōan," pp. 55-56.

64. Ibid., p. 50.

65. The 1931 Draft Political Theses, quoted in Tsushima, *"Nihon shihon-shugi ronsō" shiron*, p. 131.

66. "Nihon Kyōsantō seiji tēze sōan," p. 53.

67. Ibid., pp. 51-52.

68. Ibid., p. 54.

69. "Nihon Kyōsantō seiji tēze sōan," p. 75; cf. Durkee, "Communist International," pp. 161-162.

70. Koyama, *Nihon Marukusu-shugi shi*, p. 61.

71. The '27 Theses had been issued by the Executive Committee. See Tsushima, *"Nihon shihon-shugi ronsō" shiron*, pp. 7-8; Durkee, "Communist International," pp. 178-179; and Sano, "Mosukō to Nihon Kyōsantō no kankei shi," pp. 101-102.

72. Kuusinen had also written a report on "Japanese Imperialism and the Nature of the Japanese Revolution." See "Nihon teikoku-shugi to Nihon kakumei no sei-

shitsu,'' in *Kominterun Nihon ni kansuru tēze shū*, comp. Ishidō and Yamabe, pp. 102-119.

73. Sano, ''Mosukō to Nihon Kyōsantō no kankei shi,'' p. 102. Cf. Durkee, ''Communist International,'' pp. 181-182.

74. Okano [Nosaka], ''The General Election and the Tasks of the Communists in Japan,'' *Inprecorr*, no. 6 (February 11, 1932), p. 99, quoted in Durkee, ''Communist International,'' p. 183.

75. Koyama, *Nihon Marukusu-shugi shi*, pp. 62-63.

76. ''Shin tēze happyō ni saishi dōshi shokun ni tsugu'' [We announce to our comrades the new theses on the Japan problem], in *Kominterun Nihon ni kansuru tēze shū*, comp. Ishidō and Yamabe, pp. 120, 121, 127. Cf. Durkee, ''Communist International,'' pp. 188-189.

77. ''The Situation in Japan and the Tasks of the Japanese Communist Party,'' *Communist International*, 9.7 (April 15, 1932), pp. 221-222, quoted in Durkee, ''Communist International,'' p. 183.

78. Koyama, *Nihon Marukusu-shugi shi*, p. 57.

79. ''Nihon ni okeru jōsei to Nihon Kyōsantō no ninmu ni kansuru tēze,'' pp. 84, 83.

80. Ibid., pp. 81-82, 83.

81. Ibid., p. 85.

Chapter Four

1. Interview with Fukushima Shingō, Tokyo, July 31, 1979; and Kuno Osamu and Tsurumi Shunsuke, *Gendai Nihon no shisō*, pp. 36-37.

2. In fact, virtually all the contributions to the *Kōza* had been completed before the 1932 Theses were published, whereupon some revisions were made. (Interview with Ikumi Taku'ichi, Tokyo, June 17, 1982.) This view of the Kōza-ha, however, is especially popular among its critics associated with the Rōnō-ha, *tenkōsha* (Marxists who abandoned the JCP in support of the national war effort in the 1930s), and the so-called dissolutionist faction (Kaitō-ha), which advocated an ''Imperial Household-centered socialism'' in the late 1920s. For the Rōnō-ha view, see, for example, Tsuchiya Takao, *Nihon shihon-shugi shi ronshū*, p. 6; and Tsushima Tadayuki, *''Nihon shihon-shugi ronsō'' shiron*, p. 6. On the dissolutionist view that JCP policies, following Comintern-formulated strategy, could not handle the peculiarities of Japan's emperor system, see Sano Manabu, ''Sano Manabu jōshinsho,'' pt. 1 passim. For Sano's own views as a *tenkōsha*, see his ''Gokuchū-ki,'' pp. 94-95; cf. Kobayashi Morito, *Tenkōsha no shisō to seikatsu*, pp. 7-8.

3. The theory was first presented in Takahashi Kamekichi, ''Nihon shihon-shugi no teikoku-shugi-teki kiso'' [The imperialistic position of Japanese capitalism], *Taiyō* [The sun]. Related points in support of the ''petty imperialism'' thesis were offered in Takahashi Kamekichi, ''Makki ni okeru teikoku-shugi no henshitsu'' [The change in the quality of imperialism in the last stage], *Shakai kagaku* [Social science].

4. On the history of the Asiatic mode of production notion, see Karl A. Wittfogel,

Oriental Despotism, chap. 9 passim. An excellent analysis of the reasons for Marx's and Engels's abandonment of the notion appears in Leszek Kolakowski, *Main Currents of Marxism*, vol. 1, *The Founders*, p. 350.

5. Kojima Hinehisa, *Nihon shihon-shugi ronsō shi*, pp. 140-141; and Ōishi Ka'ichirō, "Nihon shihon-shugi ronsō to nōgyō-tochi mondai," 9:269-271.

6. Takahashi was purged during the Occupation for his part in the war effort. A long list of his associations with the government appears in Takahashi Kamekichi, *Takahashi keizai riron keisei no rokujū nen*, 2:9-12 (Appendix).

7. Ibid., 1:80-81, and preface.

8. Many scholars have cited the role of rural distress in the rise of Japanese militarism in the 1930s. At the same time that peasant associations were proliferating under left-wing tutelage, a tide of *nōhon-shugi* (agrarianism) thought swept through the country with the agricultural crisis of the 1920s. *Nōhon-shugi* became increasingly identified with the right in the 1930s. (Abe Hitoshi and Uchida Mitsuru, comps. *Gendai seiji-gaku shō jiten* [Concise dictionary of contemporary political science], [Tokyo: Yūhikaku, 1978], s.v. *nōhon-shugi*.) See Kazushi Ohkawa and Henry Rosovsky, *Japanese Economic Growth*, pp. 230-231; and the full-length studies by Richard J. Smethurst, *A Social Basis for Prewar Japanese Militarism*; and Thomas R. H. Havens, *Farm and Nation in Modern Japan*.

9. Takahashi, *Takahashi keizai riron*, pp. 57-65, 108-111.

10. Takahashi is listed as one of the founding members of this group. Also on the membership roster was Kada Tetsuji, head of the Tō-A Burokku Keizai Kenkyū I'inkai (Committee for the Study of the Economy of the East Asian Bloc). Shōwa Kenkyūkai, *Burokku keizai ni kansuru kenkyū*, p. 2. During the Sino-Japanese War, Takahashi himself published extensively in support of the government's policies at home and abroad. These works are too numerous to list them all here, but major works included *Sensō to Nihon keizairyoku* [War and Japanese economic power] (1937); *Junsenji moto no zaisei to keizai* [Finance and economy under war preparation] (Tokyo: Chikura Shobō, 1937); *Chōkisenka no zaisei keizai* [Finance and economics under protracted war] (Tokyo: Chikura Shobō, 1938); *Senji keizai tōsei no gen dankai to sono zento* [The present stage of wartime economic control and its future prospects] (1938); *Nihon senji keikaku keizai ron* [The economic theory of Japan's wartime planning] (1939); *Senji keikaku keizai no tenkai to bukka tōsei* [The development of the war-planning economy and commodity price control] (Tokyo: Chikura Shobō, 1939); *Senji keizai no gensei to infure mondai* [The present state of the wartime economy and the inflation problem] (1940); and *Senji keizai to shin keizai taisei* [The wartime economy and the new economic system] (1940). A complete list of Takahashi's works appears as an appendix to volume 2 of his *Takahashi keizai ron*.

11. His postwar three-volume study of Japanese development is still very highly regarded and heavily cited today even among Japanese socialists who dispute Takahashi's Marxist credentials. See Takahashi Kamekichi, *Taishō-Shōwa zaikai hendōshi*. (Interview with Moriya Fumio, Tokyo, June 5, 1982; and Shibagaki Kazuo, "Nihon keizai kenkyū ni okeru senzen to sengo.") Surviving Marxist contemporaries of Takahashi exhibit marked disdain for his stature as a Marxist theorist, while

acknowledging his empirical contributions to the study of Japanese economic development. (Interview with Sakisaka Itsurō, Tokyo, June 7, 1982; interview with Takahashi Masao, Tokyo, June 4, 1982.)

12. Interview with Takahashi Masao, Tokyo, June 4, 1982; and interview with Takahashi Masao, Tokyo, June 17, 1982. This was before Bukharin began to reevaluate Bolshevik views and argue that "capitalist stabilization" was occurring worldwide on the basis of a closer relationship between state and economy ("state capitalism") in Western economies. Lenin's theory of imperialism as the "highest stage of capitalism" and his view that World War I represented "imperialist war" supported the predominant Bolshevik (hopeful) view of the 1920s, that capitalism was on the verge of collapse. Bukharin's reconsideration was crushed, along with his own political power in the Soviet Union, by Stalin in 1928 and 1929. See Stephen F. Cohen, *Bukharin and the Bolshevik Revolution*, chap. 8. The *yukizumari* notion continues to appear in a variety of forms in Japanese economic scholarship. See, for example, Shibagaki Kazuo, "The Logic of Japanese Imperialism."

13. Interview with Moriya Fumio, Tokyo, June 5, 1982. This was far superior to the only other two similar efforts: Sano Manabu, *Nihon keizai-shi taikei*; and Honjō Eijirō, *Nihon shakai shi*. The *yukizumari-ron* is described below and in Moriya Fumio, *Nihon Marukusu-shugi riron no keisei to hatten*, p. 76. Cf. Shibagaki, "Nihon keizai kenkyū ni okeru senzen to sengo," p. 16n.

14. Takahashi himself brought the debate to a close with an article entitled "Gen dankai no sho meisetsu no yame o sasu" [Put an end to some fallacious theories of the present stage], *Taiyō* (December 1927). The most influential of the many critiques directed against Takahashi will be discussed below. Takahashi's intent to provoke the leadership of the left was indicated explicitly in the title of the book in which he reprinted his petty imperialism essays: *Sayoku undō no riron-teki hōkai—uyoku undō no riron-teki konkyo* [The theoretical collapse of the left-wing movement—the theoretical basis of the right-wing movement].

15. Takahashi, *Takahashi keizai riron*, p. 114.

16. The essay in *Shakai kagaku* entitled "Makki ni okeru teikoku-shugi no henshitsu" did not present the petty imperialism theory as such, but it made some important supporting points. There, Takahashi argued that the Leninist notion of the "inevitability of wars" among imperialist powers had become outdated. Having divided the world into spheres of influence, the powers were now status quo powers who had much more to lose than to gain from war. Hence their participation in the League of Nations, arms control talks, the "Open Door" in China, and other efforts to prevent war. The significance of this point was that the advanced capitalist powers had suddenly changed the "rules of the game" at precisely the time Japan needed to embark on imperialistic (but not "imperialist") ventures to sustain its own capitalistic development.

17. These works are *Nihon shihon-shugi keizai no kenkyū; Makki no Nihon shihon-shugi keizai to sono tenkan* [The last stage of Japan's capitalist economy and its conversion] (1925); *Nihon keizai no kaibō* [An analysis of Japan's economy] (1925); *Nihon keizai no yukizumari to musan-kaikyū no taisaku* [The deadlock of the Japanese economy and the countermeasures of the proletariat] (1926); and *Meiji Taishō*

nōson keizai no hensen [Changes in the Meiji and Taishō rural economy] (1926). The most coherent and refined presentation of Takahashi's analysis of Japanese development appears in *Nihon shihon-shugi hattatsu shi* (Tokyo: Nihon Hyōron-sha, 1928). Citations here are taken from the 1929 revised and expanded edition. Having wearily drawn the debate to a close at the end of 1927, Takahashi avoided using the term "petty imperialism" in this work, although all the major elements of the original thesis (with minor revisions) are there.

18. Takahashi, "Nihon shihon-shugi no teikoku-shugi-teki chi'i," pp. 39-41.

19. V. I. Lenin, *Imperialism, the Highest Stage of Capitalism*, p. 106.

20. Takahashi, "Nihon shihon-shugi no teikoku-shugi-teki chi'i," pp. 91, 44-45, 47-48, 91-92.

21. The dual or "differential" structure of the Japanese economy refers to "the presence of two sectors, one traditional and the other modern, operating with different organization, techniques, and incentives." Since World War I, the traditional sector (agrarian and small-scale industrial sector) has fallen further and further behind the "modern" urban sector in terms of changes in productivity, wage levels, and growth rates. See Ohkawa and Rosovsky, *Japanese Economic Growth*, pp. 198, 37-39; and Tsunehiko Watanabe, "Industrialization, Technological Progress, and Dual Structure," pp. 110-134.

22. Sano Manabu, "Waga haigai-shugisha no teikoku-shugi sensō ron" [The theory of imperialist war of our chauvinists], *Marukusu-shugi* [Marxism] 37 (May 1927): 24.

23. Takahashi, "Nihon shihon-shugi no teikoku-shugi-teki chi'i," pp. 84-87.

24. See Kazushi Ohkawa and Henry Rosovsky, "Economic Fluctuations in Prewar Japan"; William W. Lockwood, *The Economic Development of Japan*, pp. 55-64; and Yujiro Hayami and Saburo Yamada, "Technological Progress in Agriculture," p. 140.

25. Takahashi, *Nihon shihon-shugi hattatsu shi*, p. 332; Takahashi, *Nihon keizai no yukizumari to musan-kaikyū no taisaku* (hereafter cited as *Nihon keizai no yukizumari*), pp. 17-21.

26. Takahashi, *Nihon shihon-shugi hattatsu shi*, pp. 332-338, 358; and Takahashi, *Nihon keizai no yukizumari*, pp. 22-25, 36-37.

27. This argument closely resembled the allusion Takabatake Motoyuki made to the possibility of a "proletarian imperialism." Takabatake had argued that Lenin, too, if not consciously so, had been a nationalist, and that Japan's fear of Russian imperialism should not diminish with the birth of the Soviet Bolshevik regime. Takabatake cited Thomas Hobbes on the potential for war preceding the birth of the state and an analysis of new possibilities for postcapitalist developments unforeseen by Marx (in the manner of Nikolai Bukharin) to construct an innovative Marxist doctrine of national socialism. See Tanaka Masato, "Takabatake Motoyuki ron—Taishō shakai-shugi no bunka" [On Takabatake Motoyuki: The differentiation of Taishō socialism], *Shirin* 53.2 (March 1970): 33-86; Takeda Kiyoko, "Kakumei shisō to tennō-sei"; and Tanaka Masato, *Takabatake Motoyuki*, chap. 8.

28. Takahashi, *Nihon shihon-shugi hattatsu shi*, pp. 357-372; and Takahashi, *Nihon keizai no yukizumari*, pp. 38-39.

29. See Takahashi, "Makki ni okeru teikoku-shugi," passim; and Takahashi, *Ni-*

hon keizai no yukizumari, pp. 22-28. Cf. Takahashi Kamekichi, "Gunshuku teigi no teikoku-shugi-teki imi to Nihon no tachiba," pp. 93-104 passim.

30. Takahashi Kamekichi, *Shina keizai no hōkai to Nihon*, p. 23.

31. Takahashi, *Nihon shihon-shugi hattatsu shi*, pp. 371-373.

32. Takahashi, "Nihon shihon-shugi no teikoku-shugi-teki chi'i," pp. 61-62. Japan experienced a balance of payments surplus only during the brief wartime period 1915-1919. The temporary excess of international credits had a negative impact on the Japanese economy during the following decade. See Yasuzo Horie, "Foreign Capital and the Japanese Capitalism after World War I," pp. 39-41; and Ohkawa and Rosovsky, *Japanese Economic Growth*, pp. 298-299.

33. Takahashi, *Nihon shihon-shugi hattatsu shi*, pp. 272-275.

34. Much later, during the war, Takahashi published works on the subject, including *Kyōeiken keizai kensetsu ron* [The theory of the economic construction of the Co-Prosperity Sphere] (Tokyo: Tōshi Keizai-sha, 1942); *Dai Tō-A kyōeiken no rinen to sono kōsō* [The ideal of the Greater East Asia Co-Prosperity Sphere and its conception] (Tokyo: Tōyō Keizai Shinpō-sha, 1944); *Tō-A keizai burokku ron* [The theory of the East Asian economic bloc] (1939); *Tō-A kensetsu sen to zaisei keizai no sai-hensei* [The war for East Asian construction and the reorganization of the financial economy] (Tokyo: Chikura Shobō, 1939).

35. Takahashi, "Nihon shihon-shugi no teikoku-shugi-teki chi'i," pp. 46, 47.

36. Ibid., p. 45.

37. Takahashi, *Shina keizai no hōkai to Nihon*, pp. 23-26.

38. Ibid.

39. See Takahashi, *Nihon shihon-shugi hattatsu shi*, chap. 7 passim.

40. Takahashi felt that the outbreak of the Manchurian Incident in 1931 vindicated his petty imperialism theory. He argued that it set off "a war of territorial expansion for resolving the surplus population problem." When the war expanded to embrace the whole of the Pacific, it became "a war for the liberation of the imperialist colonies of Europe and America"; and the war, he wrote in 1977, indeed succeeded in that respect. The Pacific War was not, he asserted, "an imperialist war of the character that our left-wing camp worshipped." (Takahashi, *Takahashi keizai riron*, p. 118.)

41. George Lukács, *Lenin: A Study on the Unity of His Thought*, trans. Nicholas Jacobs (Cambridge: MIT Press, 1971), pp. 50, 59 (emphasis in the original).

42. Although the theses differed in their emphases, the JCP's Draft Program, 1927 Theses, and 1932 Theses all stressed the limitations on Japan's capitalistic development as expressed in its "semi-feudal" superstructure. All are contained in Ishidō Kiyotomo and Yamabe Kentarō, comps., *Kominterun Nihon ni kansuru tēze shū*. Translations appear in George M. Beckmann and Okubo Genji, *The Japanese Communist Party*. See the detailed discussion in chapter 3.

43. Takahashi's critics included Inomata Tsunao, Noro Eitarō, Sano Manabu, Asano Akira, Hamada Tetsuzō, Naruse Mitsuo, and others. The most influential critiques are in Inomata Tsunao, *Teikoku-shugi kenkyū*; Noro Eitarō, *Puchi-teikoku-shugi ron hihan*, also reprinted in *Noro Eitarō zenshū*, vol. 1; and Sano, "Waga hai-gai-shugisha." For a summary of these critiques, see Baba Hiroji, "Taigai kankei," pp. 96-99; and Kojima, *Nihon shihon-shugi ronsō shi*, pp. 140-146.

44. Sano's essay, "Waga haigai-shugisha," concentrated on Takahashi's interpretation of imperialism as an international phenomenon. In response to Takahashi's essay, "Makki ni okeru teikoku-shugi no henshitsu," Sano argued that the changes Takahashi described in international affairs were superficial: "imperialist peace" was really no different from "imperialist war" since both were essentially imperialistic policies. Takahashi's conclusion that the notion of the "inevitability of imperialistic wars" had become outdated was incorrect, Sano argued. Here, as elsewhere in the essay, Sano appears to have been confused about the point of Takahashi's argument. His is the least coherent critique, and the discussion that follows, therefore, will address Inomata's and Noro's views.

45. See Noro Eitarō, " 'Puchi teikoku-shugi' ron no ninshiki." Cf. Kojima, *Nihon shihon-shugi ronsō shi*, pp. 141-143.

46. See Inomata Tsunao, "Waga kuni shihon-shugi no gendankai no mondai" (August 1927), in Inomata, *Teikoku-shugi kenkyū*, p. 206.

47. Ibid., pp. 206-207, 347; and Kojima, *Nihon shihon-shugi ronsō shi*, pp. 143-144, 146n.

48. Noro Eitarō, "Puchi teikoku-shugisha no konmei," pp. 140-141.

49. Kojima, *Nihon shihon-shugi ronsō shi*, pp. 145, 146n.

50. Uno, a Marxist critic of both the Kōza-ha and the Rōnō-ha, argued that there were three historical stages in the development of world capitalism: "mercantilism," "liberalism," and "imperialism." Development would be slightly different from the model of "pure capitalism" depending on the world-historical stage in which economic development began. Uno first presented this argument in 1935, in his *Keizai seisaku ron*, vol. 1, but the theory was not refined and developed until the 1950s. (Heavy official censorship prohibited the publication of the other volume of the *Keizai seisaku ron* until after the war.) See chapter 9 below. Responding to Japan's "backwardness," both Takahashi and Uno preceded by over forty years today's world systems approach developed by Immanuel Wallerstein and dependency theorists in analyzing the impact of the world capitalist system on late-developing states. On these contemporary schools, see Albert Szymanski, *The Logic of Imperialism* (New York: Praeger, 1981), chap. 3.

51. Trotsky observed in Russia that rapid industrialization had occurred under military pressure from more advanced capitalist countries and was achieved through technological "borrowing" and massive state intervention. The result was a mixture of old indigenous and new imported forms of economic and political organization, "hybrid" forms that could not be found in Marx's original model. Trotsky realized that "backwardness" meant not merely a chronological lag in development but a qualitative difference in the pattern of development itself. See Baruch Knei-paz, *The Social and Political Thought of Leon Trotsky*, chaps. 3 and 4.

52. See Germaine A. Hoston, "*Tenkō*."

Chapter Five

1. "Theses on Japan Adopted in the Session of the Presidium of the Executive Committee of the Comintern on July 15, 1927," translated in Beckmann and Okubo, *The Japanese Communist Party*, pp. 303-306.

2. Durkee, "The Communist International," pp. 112-116.

3. These were "Wagakuni shihon-shugi no antei no kata botsuraku no kata" (July 1927) and "Wagakuni shihon-shugi no gendankai no mondai" (August 1927). See Uchida Jōkichi and Nakano Jirō, *Nihon shihon-shugi ronsō*, p. 316.

4. This essay was first published in the November 1927 issue of *Taiyō* [Sun] and was subsequently reprinted in Inomata's *Gendai Nihon kenkyū*. See Uyehara, *Left-wing Social Movements in Japan*, item IV-52.

5. It should be noted that since Yamakawa believed Japan was sufficiently developed to move directly into a proletarian socialist revolution, his use of the notion of united front differed from the narrower Comintern usage referring to an alliance between workers and peasants in less developed countries. Yamakawa's united front envisaged a coalition of diverse proletarian and peasant-based political parties engaged in a one-stage rather than two-stage revolutionary process. See the discussion of Yamakawaism in chapter 2.

6. See the essays in Inomata Tsunao, *Nihon puroretariāto no senryaku to senjutsu*. Inomata's work on the state is treated in chapter 7 below.

7. See Shakai Keizai Rōdō Kenkyūjo, ed., *Nihon shihon-shugi ronsō shi*, p. 11. The split with Yamakawa and the consequent demise of the magazine *Rōnō* were caused by a political dispute on party unity within the newly founded Nihon Taishūtō (Japan Masses Party). Even after his break with Yamakawa's faction, Inomata continued to write "on the basis of a Rōnō-ha theoretical perspective." (See "Inomata [Tsunao] shi jōshinsho," pt. 2. Cf. *Nihon shakai undō jinmei jiten*, s.v. Inomata Tsunao, Yamakawa Hitoshi.)

8. Originally published by Chūō Kōron-sha in 1937 and banned immediately, this work was reissued in 1948 by Kōdō-sha with a commentary by Rōnō-ha economist Ōuchi Hyōe. Paralleling Noro's premature departure in 1934, Inomata yielded his position as leading non-Communist Party theorist to economist Sakisaka Itsurō in the period from 1932 to 1937. Except for the book on the agrarian problem mentioned below and an essay addressed "To the Controversy on Feudal Remnants" ("Hōken isei ronsō ni yosete," *Chūō kōron* [October 1936]), Inomata did not contribute to the debate in this period. See Tsushima Tadayuki, *"Nihon shihon-shugi ronsō" shiron*, p. 11.

9. These were *Kin'yū shihon ron* [The theory of finance capital] (1925), based on Rudolf Hilferding's theory of finance capital, and *Teikoku-shugi kenkyū* [Studies on imperialism] (1928), which includes several critical essays directed against Takahashi Kamekichi.

10. Shakai Keizai Rōdō Kenkyūjo, *Nihon shihon-shugi ronsō shi*, p. 11.

11. Koyama Hirotake, *Nihon Marukusu-shugi shi*, pp. 39, 40.

12. "1927 Theses," in Beckmann and Okubo, *Japanese Communist Party*, pp. 298, 297.

13. Neither Noro nor other Kōza-ha theorists adhered to all the specific details of the Comintern view; indeed, they could not do so, since those who drafted the Comintern documents knew very little of Japanese development. For example, neither Noro nor Hirano Yoshitarō accepted the premise of large landownership in late Edo and early Meiji Japan that was implied in the '27 Theses. Notably, an essay published by Noro in *Shakai mondai kōza* in June 1927 (see note 16) preceded the ap-

pearance of the July Theses in Japan, but prefigured their argument concerning the semi-feudal characteristics of Japanese society.

14. See Yamada Moritarō, *Nihon shihon-shugi bunseki*, preface. This abstruse work by Tokyo Imperial University economist Yamada, the components of which originally appeared in the *Nihon shihon-shugi hattatsu shi kōza*, offered the most comprehensive analysis of Japanese economic development during the Meiji period and became the leading economic document of the Kōza-ha perspective. This study was not published until after the "manufacture debate."

15. See Noro Eitarō, "Nihon ni okeru tochi shoyū kankei ni tsuite—nakanzuku iwayuru 'hōken-teki zettai-shugi seiryoku no kaikyū-teki busshitsu-teki kiso' no mondai o chūshin to shite" [On landownership relations in Japan: With particular attention to the problem of the "class and material basis of the so-called feudalistic absolutist forces"], *Shisō* [Thought] 84 (May-June 1929): 47-55 (199-207). The agrarian problem is addressed in detail in chapter 8.

16. Both these studies were undertaken under the scholarly auspices of the Sangyō Rōdō Chōsajo. Hattori's work was published both in the *Marukusu-shugi kōza* [Symposium on Marxism], vols. 4-5 (February-March 1928) and as a monograph in 1929. Parts of Noro's study were published in *Shakai mondai kōza* [Symposium on social problems] (Tokyo: Shinchō-sha), vols. 11, 13 (June 1927), and *Marukusu-shugi kōza*, vols. 5, 7, 13 (March 1928, June 1928, March 1929). The thirteen-volume *Marukusu-shugi kōza*, published between November 1927 and March 1929, was a product of the Seiji Hihan-sha, and thus those who published in it were originally prominent Fukumotoists. After the '27 Theses were published in February-March 1928 and the critique of Fukumotoism was publicized, all subsequent *Marukusu-shugi kōza* articles were critical of Fukumotoism, in compliance with the new theses. See Shakai Keizai Rōdō Kenkyūjo, *Nihon shihon-shugi ronsō shi*, pp. 10-11.

17. See Maurice Dobb, *Studies in the Development of Capitalism*; and the essays collected in Rodney Hilton, ed., *The Transition from Feudalism to Capitalism.*

18. "The 1927 Theses," pp. 297-298.

19. Ibid., p. 298.

20. For a brief summary of this Rōnō-ha view, see Yamakawa Hitoshi, "Seiji-teki tōitsu sensen e!" pp. 176-179.

21. See Yasukichi Yasuba, "Anatomy of the Debate on Japanese Capitalism."

22. Hattori Shisō, *Meiji ishin shi.*

23. Hattori Shisō, "Ishin shi hōhō-jō no sho mondai," p. 93 (hereafter cited as "Hōhō-jō no sho mondai").

24. Hattori, *Meiji ishin shi*, p. 17.

25. Ibid., pp. 18-19.

26. In the Marxist sense, "absolutist monarchy" refers to a transitional form of state during the passage from the feudal to the capitalist modes of production. According to "the conclusions of . . . Soviet and English Marxist historians, . . . the absolute monarchy is a form of feudal state." In its centralization, such a state differed from the classic decentralized feudal state, but its ruling class remained feudalistic. Its historical mission was to help "prepare the conditions for the develop-

ment of capitalism''; centralization served this end by allowing the state to tax the peasantry to gain a larger surplus, to integrate the regions and localities to establish the prerequisites of a national market, and ''to control the movements of the labour force by *national* regulation, since the local organs of feudal power no longer sufficed'' as feudal society was weakened by its own internal contradictions. See Christopher Hill, ''A Comment,'' in Hilton, ed., *Transition from Feudalism to Capitalism*, pp. 120-121 (emphasis in original).

27. Hattori, *Meiji ishin shi*, pp. 110, 114, 115-116.

28. Ibid., pp. 117-118, 139, 145-146.

29. Hattori, ''Hōhō-jō no sho mondai,'' pp. 96-97. Hattori also makes this point repeatedly in his memoir of the controversy. What he appears to have been referring to as ''Bukharinist'' are, first, the mechanistic ''equilibrium'' approach that dominated Nikolai Bukharin's *Historical Materialism* and, second, the emphasis on the international context and the role of the powers in disturbing the forces existing within Japan before the opening of the ports. See Hattori Shisō, ''Ma'nyufakuchua ronsō ni tsuite no shokan,'' passim; and Shakai Keizai Rōdō Kenkyūjo, *Nihon shihon-shugi ronsō shi*, p. 46.

30. Hattori, ''Hōhō-jō no sho mondai,'' pp. 98-103; Shakai Keizai Rōdō Kenkyūjo, *Nihon shihon-shugi ronsō shi*, pp. 46-47; cf. Kojima Hinehisa, *Nihon shihon-shugi ronsō shi*, p. 97.

31. Tsuchiya Takao, ''Bakumatsu dōran-ki no keizai-teki bunseki,'' *Chūō kōron* (October 1932), p. 76, quoted in Hattori, ''Hōhō-jō no sho mondai,'' pp. 102-103.

32. See Ishihama Tomoyuki, ''Nihon ni okeru shihon-shugi no seiritsu''; and Hani Gorō, ''Tōyō shihon-shugi-teki hassei'' [The capitalistic birth of the East], originally published in *Shigaku zasshi* [Historiography], vol. 43 (February-May 1932), reissued as ''Tōyō ni okeru shihon-shugi no keisei'' [The formation of capitalism in the East], in Hani Gorō, *Meiji ishin shi kenkyū*.

33. Manufacture in this sense was characteristic of the early stages of capitalistic production. See Karl Marx, *Capital*, vol. 1: *A Critical Analysis of Capitalistic Production*, chap. 14.

34. Hattori, ''Hōhō-jō no sho mondai,'' pp. 102-106.

35. Similar points were made in Ogawa Shin'ichi, ''Meiji ishin ni kansuru oboegaki'' [A note on the Meiji Restoration], *Puroretaria kagaku* [Proletarian science] (March 1930); Nomura Kōsaku, ''Nihon ni okeru jinushi-teki tochi shoyū no kiki'' [The crisis of landlord landownership in Japan], *Puroretaria kagaku* (November 1930); and Takahashi Sadaki, ''Meiji ishin shi sono ta'' [The history of the Meiji Restoration and other matters], *Puroretaria kagaku* (January 1931).

36. ''Meiji ishin no kakumei oyobi hankakumei'' (February 1933) (hereafter cited as ''Kakumei oyobi hankakumei'').

37. Hattori, ''Kakumei oyobi hankakumei,'' pp. 3-5. On the last point, Hattori also cites Hani Gorō, ''Bakumatsu ni okeru shakai keizai jōtai kaikyū kankei oyobi kaikyū tōsō'' [The social and economic situation, class relations, and class struggles in the late Tokugawa era], in *Kōza*, p. 3:60.

38. Hattori, ''Kakumei oyobi hankakumei,'' pp. 5-8.

39. Marx, *Capital*, 1:367.

40. Ibid., 1:336. Hattori Shisō, " 'Gen mani' jidai no rekishi-teki jōken," originally published in *Rekishi kagaku* (March-April 1934), included under the title "Ma'nyufakuchua jidai no rekishi-teki jōken" in *Hattori Shisō chosaku shū*, 1:223-268 (hereafter cited as "Rekishi-teki jōken").

41. Hattori Shisō, "Hōhō oyobi sairyō no mondai," originally published in *Rekishi kagaku* (August 1933), in *Hattori Shisō chosaku shū*, 1:197-222. Hattori collected the *Rekishi kagaku* essays on manufacture in *Ishin shi no hōhōron*; beginning with the fourth edition, this book was titled *Meiji ishin shi kenkyū*.

42. See Hattori, "Mani ronsō no shokan," pp. 274-276. The results of some of his later work were presented in "Bakumatsu Akida han no momen shijō oyobi momen kigyō"; "Nihon ma'nyufakuchua shiron" [Historical treatise on Japanese manufacture] (May 1935); "Meiji zen-hanki no ma'nyufakuchua" [Manufacture in the first half of the Meiji period], included in *Keizai kagaku* [Econometrics] (January 1936); and "Meiji senshoku keizai shi" [History of the Meiji dyeing and weaving economy] (May 1937).

43. V. I. Lenin, *The Development of Capitalism in Russia*, pp. 546-547.

44. Ibid., p. 547.

45. According to Maurice Dobb, in the putting-out system, "production was subordinated to 'merchant manufacture.' " This was common in "the early period of capitalism." In this system, the merchant capitalist purchased raw materials and supplied them to individual craftsmen, who processed the materials on the basis of handicrafts work methods, in exchange for compensation (wages). The merchant then took the finished products and sold them on the market. See Dobb, *Studies in the Development of Capitalism*, pp. 17, 17n. In this putting-out system, the merchants' "buying-up capital appeared as intermediary between the producers and the market, gradually dominated [the producers], and finally made them *de facto* wage laborers to the extent of paying processing wages." (Ara Kenjirō et al., comps., *Keizai jiten*, s.v. *toiya-sei kanai kōgyō*.) The presence of *toiya-sei* industry and its form of capitalist domestic labor are significant for seeking in manufacture the origins of capitalist production. As Dobb notes, "the only difference between manufactory and domestic production was that in the former a number of looms were set up side by side in the same building, instead of being scattered in the workers' homes," because the technical basis of production was handicrafts and "the work was highly industrialized." Dobb identified this as more common than "examples of factories owned by capitalists who employed workers directly on a wage-basis" in sixteenth-century England during the manufacture period proper. (Dobb, *Studies in the Development of Capitalism*, p. 138.)

46. Hani, "Bakumatsu ni okeru shakai keizai jōtai" (pt. 1), p. 63.

47. Hattori, *Meiji ishin shi*, quoted in Hattori, "Hōhō-jō no sho mondai," p. 112.

48. Marx, *Capital*, 1:367-368.

49. Hattori, "Hōhō-jō no sho mondai," pp. 117-120.

50. Hattori, "Mani ronsō no shokan," p. 335.

51. Shakai Keizai Rōdō Kenkyūjo, *Nihon shihon-shugi ronsō shi*, p. 48.

52. Hattori, "Mani ronsō no shokan," p. 335.

53. Dobb, *Studies in the Development of Capitalism*, p. 18.

54. Lenin, *Development of Capitalism in Russia*, p. 446n, under the subheading "Capitalist Domestic Industry as an Appendage of Manufacture."

55. See Hattori, "Hōhō oyobi sairyō no mondai," pp. 201ff.

56. Hattori, "Hōhō-jō no sho mondai," p. 114.

57. "Since the production and the circulation of commodities are the general prerequisites of the capitalist mode of production, division of labour in manufacture demands, that division of labour in society at large should previously have attained a certain degree of development." (Marx, *Capital*, 1:353.)

58. Hattori, "Hōhō-jō no sho mondai," p. 123.

59. Ibid., pp. 123-124.

60. Ibid., pp. 125-130.

61. Hattori, "Kakumei oyobi hankakumei," pp. 8-9.

62. Hattori, "Hōhō-jō no sho mondai," pp. 120-121; and Hattori, "Hōhō to sairyō no mondai," p. 207.

63. Shakai Keizai Rōdō Kenkyūjo, *Nihon shihon-shugi ronsō shi*, pp. 57-59. Hattori, "Rekishi-teki jōken," pp. 226, 227, 244-249, 259n, 260n, 261n. It should also be noted that in the course of the manufacture debate, the subjects of agrarian rents and the Asiatic mode of production were also pursued. These are discussed in chapters 6 and 8.

64. Hattori, "Hōhō oyobi sairyō no mondai," p. 205.

65. Marx, *Capital*, 1:353-354.

66. Hattori, "Rekishi-teki jōken," pp. 237-242; Hattori, "Hōhō-jō no sho mondai," pp. 121-123.

67. Hattori, "Hōhō oyobi sairyō no mondai," p. 205.

68. Ibid., p. 198; Hattori, "Hōhō-jō no sho mondai," pp. 129-130.

69. In the parallel controversy between Tsuchiya and Hattori on *bakumatsu* agriculture, the two men's positions were precisely the opposite. Tsuchiya argued that "sprouts of modernity" existed in "new landlords" and wage labor, while Hattori maintained the Kōza-ha position of the essential continuity of feudal characteristics in the village. Thus, while Tsuchiya pointed to modern capitalist characteristics in both industry and agriculture, the Kōza-ha's position stressed the incongruence, or uneven development, of feudalistic elements in agriculture alongside modern capitalistic industry. (Kojima, *Nihon shihon-shugi ronsō shi*, pp. 100n-101n.)

70. Tsuchiya Takao, "Tokugawa jidai no ma'nyufakuchua," originally published in *Kaizō* [Reconstruction] (September 1933) (hereafter cited as "Tokugawa jidai no mani").

71. Kojima, *Nihon shihon-shugi ronsō shi*, p. 100n.

72. Tsuchiya, "Tokugawa jidai no mani," pp. 138-139.

73. Ibid., pp. 140-142.

74. Ibid., pp. 142-147.

75. Ibid., pp. 148-153.

76. Ibid., pp. 153-156.

77. Ibid., pp. 156-161.

78. Cf. Dobb, *Studies in the Development of Capitalism*, pp. 20-21, on the persistence of the "feudal tegument."

79. Hattori, "Hōhō oyobi sairyō," pp. 198-220.

80. These were "Edo jidai no keizai," in *Iwanami kōza: Nihon rekishi* [Iwanami symposium: Japanese history] (October 1933); and "Edo jidai ni okeru kanai kōnai kōgyō," *Rekishi chiri* [History and geography] (October 1933). See Shakai Keizai Rōdō Kenkyūjo, *Nihon shihon-shugi ronsō shi*, p. 55.

81. This counterattack was published in two essays: "Ishin shi kenkyū no chūshin ronten," originally published in *Kaizō* (January 1934); and "Nihon ma'nyufakuchua zusetsu," originally published in *Rekishi-gaku kenkyū* [Historical studies] (February 1934).

82. Marx, *Capital*, 1:368. The misunderstanding here seemed to be on Tsuchiya's part, since the following passage in *Capital* suggested that mechanization was one of the elements to which Marx was referring.

83. Tsuchiya, "Ishin shi no chūshin ronten," passim; and Shakai Keizai Rōdō Kenkyūjo, *Nihon shihon-shugi ronsō shi*, pp. 55-56.

84. Tsuchiya, "Nihon ma'nyufakuchua zusetsu," pp. 180-188.

85. Ibid., pp. 189, 188. Subsequent efforts by Tsuchiya to match Hattori's foray into primary historical materials on the Tokugawa economy continued to lead Tsuchiya to conclusions opposite those of Hattori. In a study of the textile industry, for example, he once again found that while there was some development of manufacture, on the whole, "domestic industry under the putting-out system was the main form." (Tsuchiya Takao, "Tokugawa jidai no orimonogyō ni okeru toiya-sei kanai kōgyō," originally published in *Keizai* [Economics] [July-August 1934], in Tsuchiya, *Nihon shihon-shugi shi ronshū*, pp. 243-244.)

86. Hattori himself saw this diversity as the "strength" of the Kōza-ha. See Hattori, "Hōhō-jō no sho mondai," p. 95.

87. The '31 Theses were in effect as the *Kōza* was being prepared. Hattori later recalled that the '32 Theses were drafted on March 20, 1932 by the Far Eastern Bureau of the Comintern. Since the first volume of the *Kōza* was published in May, and therefore was in press by April, the Kōza-ha did not even know of the new theses when volume one was prepared. Kawakami Hajime translated the theses when they were finally relayed to Japan via the German edition of *Communist International*, and the Japanese version was published in a special July 2 issue of *Akahata* [Red flag]. By this time volume two of the *Kōza* had already been published. Needless to say, Noro and other Kōza-ha members did not agree with the '31 Theses even when they were official policy. Moreover, according to Hattori, until the *Kōza* was completed, none of its contributors, except Noro, Ikumi Taku'ichi, Hirado Ryōei, Kazahaya Yasoji, Henmi Shigeo, and Akisasa Masanosuke, belonged to the Japanese Communist Party. (Hattori, "Mani ronsō no shokan," pp. 291-293, 310.)

88. Marx, *Capital*, 1:358; Karl Marx, "The British Rule in India," pp. 653-658. For a full analysis of Hani's and Hirano's view of Japan's Asiatic characteristics, see chapter 6.

89. See Hirano Yoshitarō, "Jiyū minken," p. 11.

90. Yamada, *Nihon shihon-shugi bunseki*, passim.

91. Hattori, "Mani ronsō no shokan," pp. 300-302. Hattori was forced to aban-

don his plans to work exclusively in the Yuiken as he was drawn into extended controversy over his manufacture thesis.

92. Kobayashi Ryōsei, "Bakumatsu girudo no tokushitsu ni kansuru ichi kōsatsu" [A look at the special character of late Tokugawa guilds], *Kaizō* [Reconstruction] (October 1933), p. 26, cited by Shakai Keizai Rōdō Kenkyūjo, *Nihon shihon-shugi ronsō shi*, p. 52.

93. Shakai Keizai Rōdō Kenkyūjo, *Nihon shihon-shugi ronsō shi*, p. 57, citing the following essays: Aikawa Haruki, "Tokugawa hōken-sei no hōkai katei" [The process of the collapse of Tokugawa feudalism], *Rekishi kagaku* (February 1934); and Kobayashi Ryōsei, "Ishin shi waikyoku no ichi ruikei" [One pattern of distortion in Restoration history], *Rekishi kagaku* (February 1934).

94. Yamada Shōjirō, "Nōgyō ni okeru shihon-shugi no hattatsu," *Kōza*, 7:12, cited by Shakai Keizai Rōdō Kenkyūjo, *Nihon shihon-shugi ronsō shi*, p. 49.

95. Hirano, "Jiyū minken," p. 12n.

96. Hattori, "Mani jidai no rekishi-teki jōken," pp. 258n-259n, 256-257.

97. Tsuchiya, "Bakumatsu mani no sho ronten," pp. 171-172.

98. Hirano, "Jiyū minken," p. 13n.

99. Ibid.

100. Shakai Keizai Rōdō Kenkyūjo, *Nihon shihon-shugi ronsō shi*, p. 54.

101. Ibid., p. 53.

102. Ibid., p. 54.

103. Tsuchiya, "Bakumatsu mani no sho ronten," p. 167.

104. Hattori, "Mani ronsō in tsuite no shokan," p. 306.

105. During the war, the controversy was revived in the form of the debate on "dispersed manufacture" (*bunsan mani*). The theory of dispersed manufacture was advocated by Horie Hideichi, Toyoda Shirō, and Shinobu Seizaburō. The theory was based on the methodology of the historical school of Ōtsuka Hisao, a Tokyo Imperial University professor of economics who was of Kōza-ha lineage and stressed Japan's peculiarities in comparative historical perspective. The notion of dispersed manufacture arose out of a discussion of whether the classic form of manufacture described by Marx in *Capital* (vol. 1, chap. 26) was concentrated—*manufactures réunies*, in which workers worked within the same workshop—or dispersed—manufacture in which independent handicraftsmen worked separately under the domination of a single capitalist (as in the putting-out system). While advocates of the *bunsan mani* thesis were critical of Hattori's original schema of the manufacture period, in fact they carried the theory forward in another form. By emphasizing the peculiarities of Japan's development in comparison with that of England, these theorists saw Japan's manufacture as more dispersed in character than that of England. Horie argued, for example, that Japan's modern silk goods industry should be called dispersed manufacture, since it had developed more into *toiya-sei* domestic industry rather than manufacture in the form of manufactories. This dispersed manufacture had a different class basis since it did not gather free wage laborers in a single workshop, but made workers only de facto wage laborers, allowing craftsmen to work in their own shops and cutting them off from the markets for both raw materials and finished products. Moreover, although both kinds of manu-

facture relied on cooperation and a division of labor, factory manufacture relied on industrial capital, while *toiya-sei* capital was essentially identified with the development of domestic industry under the putting-out system. (See Horie's essays in *Keizai ronshū* [August, September, and October 1942], now collected in Horie Hide'ichi, *Kindai sangyō shi kankyū*.) Toyoda, in advocating the notion of dispersed manufacture, argued that *toiya-sei* domestic industry alone did not comprise a special stage in the development of industrial capitalism, but rather was "a form of the domination of production by commercial capital which takes its socio-economic content only when joined with the production forms of the small enterprise, manufacture, and large industrial stages of development." Capitalist domestic labor was most broadly used in the manufacture stage. Thus, domestic industry under the putting-out system in the manufacture period was a variation of classical manufacture called *bunsan mani*. (See Toyoda Shirō, "Kindai sangyō shi kenkyū no seika ni tsuite" [On the results of research on the history of modern industry], *Mita gakkai zasshi* [Journal of the Mita Learned Society], October 1942, also included in Toyoda Shirō, *Shakai keizaishigaku no konpon mondai*, especially pp. 178-179.) Shinobu Seizaburō, once a student of Hattori, also adopted this notion. (See his *Kindai Nihon sangyō shi josetsu* and "Saihensei o habamu nōka keizai" [The farm economy hindering reorganization], *Teikoku Daigaku shinbun* [Imperial University news] [September 7, 1942].) After the war, critiques of the *bunsan mani* notion emerged. See the discussions in Kojima, *Nihon shihon-shugi ronsō shi*, pp. 98n-99n, 124-135, 127n, 128n; Hattori, "Mani ronsō ni tsuite no shokan," pp. 280-281.

106. Takahashi Kōhachirō, "Contribution to the Discussion," in Hilton, ed., *The Transition from Feudalism to Capitalism*, pp. 94-96.

Chapter Six

1. Said asserts that "Orientalism," "a style of thought based on an ontological and epistemological distinction made between 'the Orient' and (most of the time) 'the Occident,' " is "a Western style for dominating, restructuring, and having authority over the Orient" "by making statements about it, authorizing views of it, describing it, teaching it, settling it, ruling over it" (pp. 2-3). While Said's discussion focuses primarily on the Western European literary tradition of Orientalism with respect to the Middle East, he also correctly identifies Orientalism in Marx's treatment of the East as a stagnant, passive, undifferentiated mass. See Edward W. Said, *Orientalism*, especially pp. 153-156.

2. Franco Venturi, "Oriental Despotism," pp. 133, 134-135.

3. Karl Marx, "The British Rule in India," pp. 657-658 (emphasis in the original).

4. "Marx on the History of His Opinions," in *The Marx-Engels Reader*, ed. Robert C. Tucker, p. 5.

5. Anne M. Bailey and Josep R. Llobera, eds., *The Asiatic Mode of Production: Science and Politics*, p. 1.

6. Jean Chesneaux, "Le mode de production asiatique," p. 2. Also see Jean Chesneaux, "Où en est la discussion sur le 'mode de production asiatique'?" [parts

1, 2, and 3]. For another account of the controversy, see the work that became its focal point after the birth of the People's Republic of China: Karl A. Wittfogel, *Oriental Despotism*, chap. 9.

7. See Maurice Godelier, "The Concept of the 'Asiatic Mode of Production' and Marxist Models of Social Evolution."

8. E. J. Hobsbawm, "Karl Marx's Contribution to History," in *Ideology in Social Science: Readings in Critical Social Theory*, ed. Robin Blackburn (New York: Random House, Vintage Books, 1973), p. 273.

9. T. Shanin, "The Third Stage," p. 301. See the notes appended to Perry Anderson, *Lineages of the Absolutist State*. Similarly, Hindess and Hirst have concluded that "Wittfogel's conception of Oriental despotism is a continuation of the Western misconception of the Orient (a conception in which the West flattered itself . . .) and a projection into the pre-capitalist era of the modern concept of 'totalitarianism' (the modern variant of the concept in which the West recognises its own virtues in the absolute evil of another)." (Barry Hindess and Paul Q. Hirst, *Pre-Capitalist Modes of Production*, pp. 213-214.)

10. See Germaine A. Hoston, "Marxism and National Socialism in Taishō Japan"; Tanaka Masato, *Takabatake Motoyuki*; and Tanaka Masato, "Takabatake Motoyuki ron—Taishō shakai-shugi no bunka" [On Takabatake Motoyuki: The differentiation of Taishō socialism], *Shirin* 53.2 (March 1970): 33-86.

11. See chapter 4. For a fuller explication of the implications of Takahashi's theory in terms of the integrity of Marxist theory, see Germaine A. Hoston, "Marxism and Japanese Expansionism."

12. Others, including Wittfogel, have attributed the demise of the concept to its potential applicability to the Soviet regime. See Wittfogel, *Oriental Despotism*, pp. 395ff; cf. George Lichtheim, *Marxism*, pp. 147, 147n; and Konstantin F. Shtepa, *Russian Historians and the Soviet State* (New Brunswick: Rutgers University Press, 1962), pp. 47-48.

13. Leszek Kolakowski, *Main Currents of Marxism*, vol. 1: *The Founders*, p. 350.

14. See V. I. Lenin, *The Development of Capitalism in Russia*, 1st ed., pp. 195-197; and the discussion in Samuel H. Baron, "The Transition from Feudalism to Capitalism in Russia."

15. "Japan, with its purely feudal organisation of landed property and its developed *petite culture*, gives a much truer picture of the European middle ages than all our history books." Karl Marx, *Capital*, vol. 1: *A Critical Analysis of Capitalist Production*, p. 718n. The exhaustive analysis of the issue of the Asiatic mode of production during the debate on Japanese capitalism demonstrates that this identification of Japan as feudalistic did not resolve the matter of oriental society in the minds of Japanese Marxists. Continued interest in the subject is indicated by the recent publication of such works as Takimura Ryūichi, *Ajia-teki kokka to kakumei*; Moriya Fumio, *Nihon shihon-shugi shōshi*, esp. vol. 1, chap. 1; and Tanaka Sōgorō, *Tennō no kenkyū*, esp. chap. 1, sec. 4.

16. Of the Rōnō-ha Marxists, only Inomata Tsunao explored the "Asiatic" characteristics of Japanese society in any depth, and he did so in writings on the agrarian

problem only after breaking his ties to the Rōnō-ha circa 1930. Like the Kōza-ha, Inomata found certain elements of the Asiatic mode of production concept useful in explaining the continued backwardness of Japan's agrarian sector. See Inomata Tsunao, *Nōson mondai nyūmon* and the discussion below.

17. Rōnō-ha scholars avoided the oriental society issue in part because they begged the question of the nature of Japan's emperor system (see chapter 7). While they conceded that the emperor system was a remnant of the past with "feudalistic" hues, Rōnō-ha Marxists believed that it would eventually disappear ("wither away"?) spontaneously as the revolution culminated in socialism. (Interview with Arahata Kanson, Takahashi Masao, and Watanabe Fumitarō, Tokyo, August 17, 1979.)

18. For an example of this application of the oriental society conception, see Hirano Yoshitarō, *Dai Ajia-shugi no rekishi-teki kiso*. After the war, Hirano established his own institute, the Chūgoku Kenkyū-jo, to conduct scholarly research on China untarnished by any motivation to support imperialist designs. I am indebted to Ishida Takeshi for this observation on the pattern of Hirano's work on China. One good example of Hirano's postwar endeavors on China is his article, "Chūgoku to Nihon no kindaika no hikaku." Both before and after his *tenkō*, however, Hirano was consistent in using the Asiatic mode of production conception and in emphasizing the negative impact of Japan's "Asiatic" characteristics on its capitalistic development. (Interview with Hirano Yoshitarō, Tokyo, July 27, 1979.)

19. Karl Wittfogel has identified at least two separate descriptions, coinciding with the popular distinction between the young and the old Marx. He argued that in the early version Marx emphasized the political role of the despot resting on isolated agrarian villages, while in the later version he stressed "the technical side of large-scale water works." (See *Oriental Despotism*, pp. 369-386.) Maurice Godelier rejects this view and sees a coherent model of the Asiatic mode of production in Marx's work. It should be noted, however, that in resurrecting the concept, he has disposed of the "dead elements" in earlier formulations, including (1) the notion of "despotism" employed in an ideological sense, and (2) the "image" of a stagnating Asia. (Godelier, "Concept of the 'Asiatic Mode of Production,' " pp. 214-215.)

20. Donald M. Lowe, *The Function of "China" in Marx, Lenin, and Mao*, pp. 11-14. In Engels's *Origin of the Family, Private Property and the State* (1884), the conception was completely omitted.

21. All these elements were present in the 1853 correspondence and the *Grundrisse der Kritik der Politischen Ökonomie*, the manuscript of notes toward *Capital* which was completed in 1855-1859 but was unpublished until 1939. See also George Lichtheim, "Oriental Despotism," in George Lichtheim, *The Concept of Ideology and Other Essays* (New York: Random House, 1967), p. 67.

22. Engels to Marx, June 6, 1853, in Marx and Engels, *Selected Correspondence*, p. 66.

23. Frederick Engels, *Herr Eugen Dühring's Revolution in Science (Anti-Dühring)*, pp. 198, 200, 165. Cf. Marx, *Capital*, vol. 1, chap. 16, par. 12 (p. 514) on the impact of natural conditions on historical development and the need for irrigation in the East.

24. Maurice Godelier, "The Concept of the Asian Mode of Production and the Marxist Model of Social Development," p. 39.

25. Marx, *Capital*, vol. 3: *The Process of Capitalist Production as a Whole*, chap. 37, par. 39 (p. 634); cf. *Capital*, vol. 1, chap. 14, par. 9 (p. 357); and Engels, *Anti-Dühring*, p. 195.

26. Marx to Engels, June 2, 1853, in Marx and Engels, *Selected Correspondence*, p. 65 (italics in the original).

27. Marx, *Capital*, vol. 3, chap. 20, par. 25 (p. 331); vol. 1, chap. 14, par. 9 (p. 357); vol. 3, chap. 47, sec. 3 (p. 796); and vol. 1, chap. 13, par. 22 (p. 333).

28. Ibid., vol. 3, chap. 47, sec. 2, par. 1 (p. 791).

29. Ibid., sec. 3 (p. 796).

30. Lichtheim, *Marxism*, p. 158.

31. Bryan S. Turner, *Marx and the End of Orientalism*, pp. 6-7; cf. Ernest Mandel, *The Formation of the Economic Thought of Karl Marx* (London and New York: n.p., 1971), pp. 127, 128, 124.

32. Compare the recent arguments of Bryan S. Turner and Louis Althusser and Etienne Balibar (*Reading Capital*). Turner agrees that "there is an epistemological break in Marx's work and that Marx's journalism does not provide the basis for a scientific analysis of Asian social formations." The argument made here does not rest on such a formalistic and ultimately untenable distinction between the young and old Marx. More to the point, given Marx's ignorance about the Far East, citing Hindess and Hirst, Turner asserts that "it is possible to question the theoretical coherence of the construction of the AMP [Asiatic mode of production] by showing that the AMP represents an arbitrary combination of relations and forces of production." (Turner, *Marx and the End of Orientalism*, p. 82.)

33. Marx, *Capital*, vol. 3, chap. 36, par. 13 (p. 597).

34. Karl Marx and Frederick Engels, "Manifesto of the Communist Party," in *Marx-Engels Reader*, pp. 476-477.

35. Marx, *Capital*, vol. 3, chap. 20, par. 28 (pp. 333-334).

36. Lichtheim, *Marxism*, p. 152. Cf. Eric J. Hobsbawm's argument that Marx's statement "does not . . . imply any simple unilinear view of history, not a simple view that all history is progress. It merely states that each of these systems is in crucial respects further removed from the primitive state of man." (Introduction to Karl Marx, *Pre-Capitalist Economic Formations*, p. 38.)

37. Marx, *Pre-Capitalist Economic Formations*, p. 97; cf. Lichtheim, *Marxism*, pp. 148-152; and John M. Maguire, *Marx's Theory of Politics*, pp. 214-216.

38. Maguire, *Marx's Theory of Politics*, p. 213.

39. Ibid., pp. 217-218.

40. Marx and Engels, Preface to the second Russian edition (1882), "The Communist Manifesto," p. 334.

41. Samuel H. Baron, "Plekhanov's Russia," pp. 390, 392, 393. On Plekhanov's populist thought, see S. H. Baron, "Plekhanov, Trotsky, and the Development of Soviet Historiography," p. 382; and Samuel H. Baron, *Plekhanov: The Father of Russian Marxism* (Stanford: Stanford University Press, 1966), chap. 4.

42. George Plekhanov, *Sochineniya* [Collected Works], 10:154 and 20:12, quoted by Baron, "Development of Soviet Historiography," pp. 383, 384.

43. Baron, "Plekhanov's Russia," pp. 400, 396, 398, 399.

44. The notion of old Russia as an independently developed Asiatic society permeated his major work, *The History of Russian Social Thought*, begun in 1909 and published in 1914-1917. See Baron, "Development of Soviet Historiography," pp. 382-384.

45. Ibid., p. 385; and Baron, "Plekhanov's Russia," p. 401.

46. Along with the role of superstructure acting on the economic base and the notions of uneven and combined development, these elements of the Asiatic mode of production theory came to be attributed officially to Lenin after Plekhanov was denounced by M. N. Pokrovsky in the 1920s. (See Baron, "Development of Soviet Historiography," pp. 393, 388.) *Fundamental Problems of Marxism* was among the first works of Russian Marxism to be introduced into Japan, and it was widely read by 1925. There is no evidence to indicate that Plekhanov's influence in Japan suffered under the impact of Pokrovsky's denunciation of him again with Stalin's support in 1929. (See Shtepa, *Russian Historians and the Soviet State*, chap. 4 passim.)

47. Marx, *Capital*, vol. 3, chap. 51, par. 3 (p. 877); and Marx, *Pre-Capitalist Economic Formations*, pp. 70, 88. Cf. Maurice Meisner, "The Despotism of Concepts," pp. 103-104. Maurice Godelier argues that Marx underestimated the "geographical scope" of the concept, which in fact refers "to certain stages in the transition to class society" and could be found in "the empires of pre-Columbia America, the African kingdoms, the Mycenaean empires." ("Concept of the Asiatic Mode of Production," p. 39.)

48. George V. Plekhanov, *Fundamental Problems of Marxism* (New York: International Publishers, 1969), pp. 49-55.

49. Plekhanov, *Fundamental Problems*, pp. 64, 57 (italics in original).

50. Lenin, *Development of Capitalism in Russia*, pp. 176-177.

51. Samuel H. Baron, "The Transition from Feudalism to Capitalism in Russia," p. 721.

52. Ibid.

53. Lenin, *Development of Capitalism in Russia*, pp. 195-197 (italics in original).

54. Aikawa Haruki, " 'Ajia-teki seisan yōshiki' to Nihon hōken-sei ni kansuru ronsō," p. 58.

55. The contributions of Yevgeny S. Iolk and M. Godes to the Leningrad Conference are mentioned repeatedly throughout the writings examined here. The proceedings of the conference were translated by Kōza-ha scholar Hayakawa Jirō and published in Japanese in 1933. See Sovēto Marukusu-shugi Tōyō Gakusha Kyōkai, comp., *Ajia-teki seisan yōshiki ni tsuite*.

56. His essays included "Ekonomicheskie problemy revolutsij v Kitae" [Economic problems of the revolution in China], *Planovoe khozjajstvo* [Planned economy], no. 12 (1925); "Osnovnye problemy Kitajskoj revolutsij" [Fundamental problems of the Chinese revolution], *Bol'shevik*, no. 8 (1928); and "Novaja nauchnaja literatura o Kitae" [The new scientific literature on China], *Pravda* [Truth], January 6, 1929, and "Perspektivy kitajskoj revolutsij: Zakluchitelnij vazdel" [Per-

spectives of the Chinese revolution: the final chapter), in L. Mad'iar, *Ocherki po ekonomike Kitaia* (Moscow, 1930). For a comprehensive bibliography of Soviet scholarship on China during this period, see V. N. Nikiforov, *Sovetskie istoriki o problemax Kitaja*, pp. 368-397. Both Varga (1879-1964) and Mad'iar (1891-1940) seem to have been associated fairly closely with Comintern leader Nikolai Bukharin at this time. It is noteworthy that the rejection of the Asiatic mode of production theory espoused by N. S. Riazanov, Varga, and Mad'iar occurred at the same time as Bukharin's permanent fall from power in the Soviet Union in 1929. See Stephen F. Cohen, *Bukharin and the Bolshevik Revolution*, chap. 9.

57. Riazanov (1870-1938), who compiled the first edition of the twenty-seven-volume *Complete Works of Marx and Engels*, was another victim of Joseph Stalin's purges. Accused of counter-revolutionary crimes in 1931, he was purged, and died (executed?) in 1938.

58. Wittfogel, *Oriental Despotism*, p. 401.

59. Mad'iar's most important work in identifying the Asiatic mode of production in China was *Ekonomika sel'skovo khoziajstva v Kitae* (1928). Other major early writings included *Ocherki po ekonomike Kitaja* (1930); *Sovremennoe sosto'janie kitajskoj revolutsii* (1929); and "Dve agrarnye programmy v kitajskoj revolutsii" [Two agrarian programs in the Chinese revolution], *Problemy Kitaja* [Problems of China], no. 4-5 (1930).

60. See L. I. Mad'iar, "The Legitimacy of the AMP [Asiatic Mode of Production]," in *The Asiatic Mode of Production*, ed. Bailey and Llobera, pp. 76-94.

61. The only work listed by Godes in the Nikiforov bibliography is *Shto takoe kemalistiskii put' i bozmozhen li on v Kitae?* [What is the Kemalist road (Kemal Ataturk) and is it possible in China?] (Leningrad, 1928). Iolk's writings did not appear until 1930: "K voprosy ob osnovakh obshchestvennovo stroja drevnova Kitaja"; "O zadachakh Marksistsko-Leninskovo izuchenija kolonial'nikh i polukolonial'nikh stran"; Review of M. Kokin and G. Papajan, *"Tszintjan": Agrarnij stroj drevnevo Kitaja* ["Jingtian": The agrarian system of ancient China] and "K voprosy ob 'Aziatskom' sposobe proizvodstva" [On the problem of the 'Asiatic' mode of production].

62. Wittfogel, *Oriental Despotism*, p. 402.

63. E. S. Iolk, "The AMP and the Class Struggle," in *Asiatic Mode of Production*, ed. Bailey and Llobera, p. 97.

64. See Benjamin I. Schwartz, *Chinese Communism and the Rise of Mao*, pp. 122-123. Cf. Wittfogel, *Oriental Despotism*, pp. 405, 405n.

65. Mad'iar, "Legitimacy of the AMP," pp. 93-94.

66. M. Godes, "The Reaffirmation of Unilinealism," in *Asiatic Mode of Production*, ed. Bailey and Llobera, pp. 102, 104; Iolk, "AMP and Class Struggle," p. 98.

67. Godes, "Reaffirmation of Unilinealism," pp. 103-104.

68. Aikawa Haruki, "Ajia-teki seisan yōshiki no riron no handō-sei." Although this essay established the terms of the Japanese controversy on the Asiatic mode of production, Aikawa was by no means the first to discuss the concept. This role fell to the scholar Fukuda Tokuzō, who discussed the Asiatic mode of production in his 1927 work, "Yuibutsu shikan keizai shi no shuttatsuten no saiginmi" [A reconsid-

eration of the historical materialist point of departure for economic history]. Subsequently, in 1929 and 1930, both Noro Eitarō and Hattori Shisō discussed the concept in their writings, and Terajima Kazuo penned a critique of Mad'iar. Finally, in July 1932, Hani Gorō's essay, "Tōyō ni okeru shihon-shugi no keisei" [The formation of capitalism in the Orient], was published in *Shigaku zasshi* [Journal of historiography] and was followed by Moritani Katsumi's essay, "Tōyō shakai ni okeru Heigeru to Marukusu" [Hegel and Marx in oriental society], published in January 1933. Aikawa Haruki, " 'Ajia-teki seisan yōshiki' ni kansuru danshō," p. 246. (Originally published in *Hōsei Daigaku shinbun* [Hōsei University news], no. 43-44 [May 23, 1934-June 15, 1934].)

69. Aikawa, " 'Ajia-teki seisan yōshiki' ni kansuru ronsō," pt. 1, p. 57.

70. Mad'iar, "Legitimacy of the AMP," pp. 93, 94.

71. Aikawa Haruki, "Hanchū to shite no 'Ajia-teki seisan yōshiki' "; and Aikawa, " 'Ajia-teki seisan yōshiki' ni kansuru dansho (A)," pp. 242-243.

72. Aikawa, " 'Ajia-teki seisan yōshiki' ni kansuru dansho (A)," p. 246.

73. Here Aikawa agreed with the views expressed by Hirano Yoshitarō in his epilogue to the Japanese edition of Wittfogel's *Economy and Society of China*, published in January 1934.

74. Aikawa, " 'Ajia-teki seisan yōshiki' ni kansuru danshō (A)," pp. 246-252.

75. Moritani Katsumi, "Iwayuru 'Ajia-teki seisan yōshiki' sairon," pp. 41-52.

76. Ibid., pp. 52-54, 56-57.

77. Ibid., pp. 56, 57, 60-62.

78. Ibid., pp. 62-65. The details of Aikawa's interpretation were presented in his periodization of Japanese history. This is more fully explored below.

79. Ibid., pp. 66-75.

80. See Hani Gorō, "Tōyō shihon-shugi-teki hassei" [The capitalistic birth of the East], *Shigaku zasshi* [Journal of historiography] 43 (February-May 1932). This essay was subsequently revised and published under the title "Tōyō ni okeru shihon-shugi no keisei" [The formation of capitalism in the East] in Hani Gorō, *Meiji ishin shi kenkyū*. Citations here are taken from the latter.

81. Hani Gorō, "Ajia-teki seisan yōshiki," p. 186.

82. Ibid.

83. Akizawa Shūji, "Dorei shoyūsha-teki shakai keizai kōsei no igi," p. 14 (emphasis in original).

84. Hayakawa Jirō, " 'Ōchō jidai' no 'kokka-teki tochi shoyū' ni tsuite," pp. 81, 82.

85. Akizawa, "Dorei shoyūsha-teki shakai," pp. 21-23.

86. Hattori Shisō, "Ishin shi hōhō-jō no sho mondai," pp. 138-139.

87. Quote by Marx from *Capital*, vol. 1, p. 459 in the Shinho-sha edition, cited by Hayakawa and translated by the author. Hayakawa, " 'Ōchō jidai,' " pp. 82-83, 82n-83n.

88. An earlier article by Hayakawa Jirō, published in *Rekishi kagaku* [Historical science], March 1933, quoted in ibid., p. 82n.

89. Hayakawa Jirō, "Tōyō kodaishi ni okeru seisan yōshiki no mondai," pp. 277-280.

90. On the controversy on Chinese social history, see Benjamin Schwartz, "A Marxist Controversy on China"; Benjamin Schwartz, "Some Stereotypes in the Periodization of Chinese History"; He Ganzhi, *Zhongguo shehui shi wenti lunzhan*; Arif Dirlik, *Revolution and History*; and Germaine A. Hoston, "State and Revolution in China and Japan," chap. 5.

91. Hayakawa, "Tōyō kodaishi mondai," pp. 283-284, 290 (Marx's words translated from Japanese by the author).

92. Ibid., pp. 291-292.

93. Ibid., pp. 284-285.

94. Hayakawa Jirō, "Iwayuru tōyō shi ni okeru 'dorei shoyūsha-teki kōsei no ketsujo' o ika ni setsumei subeki ka," p. 294 (hereafter cited as "Iwayuru 'dorei shoyūsha-teki kōsei no ketsujo' "). See Hayakawa Jirō, "Sano Manabu cho 'Nihon rekishi' sono ta ni okeru gobyū."

95. Hayakawa Jirō, "Dorei shoyūsha-teki kōsei no tōyō-teki keitai no mondai," pp. 322-323.

96. Hayakawa, "Iwayuru 'dorei shoyūsha-teki kōsei no ketsujo,' " pp. 295-296.

97. Ibid., pp. 295-297.

98. Hayakawa, "Dorei shoyūsha-teki kōsei," pp. 325-327.

99. Ibid., pp. 323-325.

100. Here was a point of agreement with Akizawa, Hayakawa's critic, although Hayakawa himself acknowledged the veracity of Marx's observation that commerce alone could not cause the emergence of a new mode of production (*Capital*, vol. 3). See Hayakawa, "Iwayuru dorei shoyūsha-teki kōsei no ketsujo," pp. 303-307. Hirano also shared Hayakawa's views on the differences between Asian and classical slavery and the role of commerce in the underdevelopment of the East. In "Asiatic" or total slavery, in which slaves were owned along with the land by the despotic monarch, slaves were not used to promote commodity circulation, but for state projects, he argued. By contrast, in classic Greek and Roman slavery, slaves were owned by private families and were used to produce commodities for exchange or sale. Where the Greek or Roman state acted to expand commercial activity, the Asian despotic state acted to repress it, or itself acted as a merchant in trade relations with other countries, usurping this function from a private sector that did not exist. (Interview with Hirano Yoshitarō, Tokyo, July 27, 1979.)

101. Hayakawa, "Iwayuru 'dorei shoyūsha-teki kōsei no ketsujo,' " pp. 303-307.

102. Ibid., pp. 307-308.

103. Ibid., p. 300.

104. Hayakawa, "Dorei shoyūsha-teki kōsei," pp. 313-314, 316, 320-321.

105. Hayakawa, "Iwayuru 'dorei shoyūsha-teki kōsei no ketsujo,' " pp. 299-302; Hayakawa, "Dorei shoyūsha-teki kōsei," pp. 317-318.

106. Hayakawa Jirō, "Jōdai ni okeru 'be,' " pp. 164-165.

107. Ibid., pp. 160-164.

108. Hayakawa, "Dorei shoyūsha-teki kōsei," pp. 164-166, 172-174.

109. Ibid., pp. 175-176; Hayakawa, " 'Ōchō jidai' no 'kokka-teki tochi shoyū' ni tsuite," pt. 1, pp. 86, 89.

110. Tsuchiya Takao, *Nihon keizai shi gaiyō* (Tokyo: Iwanami Shoten, 1934), p. 35, quoted in Aikawa Haruki, "Nihon dorei-sei ni kansuru kiso ronten," p. 330.

111. Hori Toshio, *Nihon kodaishi zenshin no tame ni* [For the progress of ancient Japanese history] (November/December 1932), cited by Aikawa, "Nihon dorei-sei ni kansuru kiso ronten," pp. 331-332.

112. Aikawa Haruki, "Ajia-teki seisan yōshiki no Nihon rekishi e no 'tekiyō' ron ni kanren shite," pp. 41-44; Aikawa, " 'Ajia-teki seisan yōshiki' ni kansuru ronsō," pt. 1, pp. 57-64.

113. Aikawa, "Ajia-teki seisan yōshiki ni kanren shite," pp. 44-48.

114. Aikawa, "Nihon dorei-sei ni kansuru kiso ronten," pp. 336-338.

115. Ibid., pp. 344-346, 348.

116. This was disputed by Miura Tsuneo, since the Japanese state had been born, presumably of class divisions, long before the Taika reforms. Yet Miura's critique did not generate a cogent alternative to the views of Hayakawa and Aikawa, which were the most fully elaborated among the periodizations of Japanese history that emerged in the 1930s. See Miura Tsuneo, "Nihon no dorei-sei ni kansuru saikin no tairon."

117. Akizawa, "Dorei shoyūsha-teki shakai," pt. 1, p. 12.

118. Ibid., pp. 3-7.

119. Ibid., pp. 24-25.

120. Ibid., p. 26.

121. Akizawa Shūji, "Nihon ni okeru kokka-teki tochi shoyū no mondai."

122. Akizawa, "Dorei shoyūsha-teki shakai," pt. 2, pp. 75-76.

123. Ibid., pp. 77-80 (italics in original).

124. Ibid., pp. 80-81.

125. Ibid., pp. 81-87.

126. Ibid., pp. 92-95.

127. Ibid., pp. 95-97.

128. Ibid., pp. 98-101.

129. Ibid., pp. 101-102.

130. "Theses on the Situation in Japan and the Tasks of the Communist Party" (May 1932), in Beckmann and Okubo, *The Japanese Communist Party, 1922-1945*, p. 337.

131. This distinction was drawn in Aikawa Haruki, "Dorei-sei narabi ni hōken-sei no 'Ajia-teki' keitai," pp. 281-282.

132. Hayakawa, " 'Ōchō jidai' no 'kokka-teki tochi shoyū' ni tsuite," pt. 1, pp. 83-84.

133. Ibid., p. 85.

134. Ibid., pp. 87-88.

135. Ibid., pp. 89-90.

136. Ibid., pp. 90-91.

137. Hirano did not devise a formal periodization of Japanese history, nor does his general interpretation of the Asiatic mode of production described here appear in his writings. The primary source here is the author's interview with Hirano, Tokyo, July 27, 1979. Other of Hirano's *Kōza* contributions discussed the Asiatic features

of Japanese development from Tokugawa to Meiji. See *Nihon shihon-shugi hattatsu shi kōza*. Hirano's essays have been collected and published also as *Nihon shihon-shugi shakai no kikō*.

138. See Hirano Yoshitarō, "Jiyū minken."

139. Interview with Hirano Yoshitarō, Tokyo, July 27, 1979.

140. Hattori Shisō, "Ishin shi hōhō-jō no sho mondai," pp. 141-145, originally published in *Rekishi kagaku* (April-June 1933).

141. Hirano, *Nihon shihon-shugi shakai no kikō*, pp. 227-228, 228n.

142. Ibid., pp. 228-230, 230n.

143. Ibid., p. 230n-231n; and Hirano Yoshitarō, *Burujoa minshu-shugi kakumei*, pp. 85-88.

144. Hirano, *Nihon shihon-shugi shakai no kikō*, pp. 233-234.

145. Ibid., p. 231; Hirano, *Burujoa minshu-shugi kakumei*, p. 84; and Hirano, "Jiyū minken," pp. 14-16.

146. Hirano, *Nihon shihon-shugi shakai no kikō*, p. 257n. The issue of the survival of feudal relations in the countryside is explored more fully in chapter 8.

147. Aikawa, "Hanchū to shite no 'Ajia-teki seisan yōshiki,' " pp. 263-264; Aikawa, "Dorei-sei no 'Ajia-teki' keitai," pp. 283-284.

148. Aikawa Haruki, "Nihon hōken-sei no 'tenkei'-teki kōzō: iwayuru 'Ajia-teki hōken-sei' kitei no yōki" [The "typical" structure of Japanese feudalism: The sublation of the definition of so-called "Asiatic feudalism"], in Aikawa, *Rekishi kagaku no hōhōron*, pp. 294-299.

149. Ibid., pp. 299-317.

150. Godes, "Reaffirmation of Unilinealism," pp. 103-104.

151. E. Iolk, " 'Ajia-teki' seisan yōshiki no mondai ni yosete," Russian ed., in *Marukusu-shugi no hata no moto ni*, Japanese ed., p. 80, quoted in Hani, "Tōyō ni okeru shihon-shugi no keisei," pp. 60-61, 55.

152. Hani, "Tōyō ni okeru shihon-shugi no keisei," pp. 64-65.

153. Ibid., pp. 96-114 passim.

154. Ibid., pp. 118-150 passim.

155. Ibid., p. 21.

156. Shiga Yoshio, *Kokka ron*, p. 110.

Chapter Seven

1. John W. Dower, "Introduction: E. H. Norman, Japan, and the Uses of History," in *Origins of the Modern Japanese State*, ed. John W. Dower, pp. 17-19, 114.

2. Dower, ed., *Origins of the Modern Japanese State*, p. 315.

3. Marx, *Capital*, 3:791.

4. Marx, "The Civil War in France (1871)," p. 629. Cf. Louis Althusser, "Ideology and Ideological State Apparatuses," in Louis Althusser, *Lenin and Philosophy and Other Essays*, trans. Ben Brewster (New York: Monthly Review Press, 1971), pp. 142-143.

5. See especially the writings of Nicos Poulantzas: *Political Power and Social*

Classes (London: New Left Books and Sheed and Ward, 1973, 1975); "The Problem of the Capitalist State"; and *State, Power, Socialism* (London: N.p., 1978). These writings, however, refer primarily to the capitalist state rather than to the state in general.

6. Theda Skocpol, *States and Social Revolutions*, p. 29.

7. Trimberger argues that "the propropriation [sic] of surplus in Tokugawa Japan fits . . . [the] definition [by Samir Amin] of a tributary mode of production as distinct from feudalism." (Ellen Kay Trimberger, "State Power and Modes of Production," pp. 85-88, 92-93; cf. Ellen Kay Trimberger, *Revolution from Above: Military Bureaucrats and Development in Japan, Turkey, Egypt, and Peru* [New Brunswick, N.J.: Transaction Books, 1978].)

8. "Dependency" and "world systems" analyses of this process may be criticized for ascribing excessive significance to external factors while neglecting indigenous sources of economic and political change. Nevertheless, the world systems approach has produced the most systematic analysis of the dynamics of the historical development of the world capitalist economy. See Immanuel Wallerstein, *The Modern World-System*, 2 vols. (New York: Academic Press, 1974, 1975); and Immanuel Wallerstein, "A World-System Perspective on the Social Sciences," pp. 350-351.

9. See Joji Watanuki, "State Formation and Nation-Building in East Asia"; Ishida Takeshi, *Meiji seiji shisō shi kenkyū*, pt.1; Mary Clabaugh Wright, *The Last Stand of Chinese Conservatism: The T'ung-chih Restoration, 1862-1874* (Stanford: Stanford University Press, 1957), chap. 12; Benjamin Schwartz, *In Search of Wealth and Power: Yen Fu and the West* (Cambridge: Harvard University Press, Belknap Press, 1964), pp. 42-67, chap. 7; Philip C. Huang, *Liang Ch'i-ch'ao and Modern Chinese Liberalism*, Publications on Asia of the Institute for Comparative and Foreign Area Studies, no. 22 (Seattle: University of Washington, 1972), chap. 4; Joseph R. Levenson, *Confucian China and Its Modern Fate*, vol. 1, *The Problem of Intellectual Continuity*, chap. 7.

10. Interview with Hayashi Takehisa, Tokyo, Japan, June 23, 1982; interview with Shibagaki Kazuo, Tokyo, Japan, June 23, 1982; Shibagaki Kazuo, "The Early History of the Zaibatsu," p. 549; Shibagaki Kazuo, "The Logic of Japanese Imperialism," pp. 74-77. Uno's interpretation of Japanese development in light of the international context predated Wallerstein's world systems analysis by four decades. See Uno Kōzō, *Keizai seisaku ron*, and chap. 9 below.

11. Reinhard Bendix, "Tradition and Modernity Reconsidered," pp. 334-335. On the role of the state in the capitalist development of Western Europe, see Otto Hintze, "Economics and Politics in the Age of Modern Capitalism," p. 427; and Charles Tilly, "Reflections on the History of European State-Making," in *The Formation of National States in Western Europe*, ed. Charles Tilly, Studies in Political Development, no. 8 (Princeton: Princeton University Press, 1975).

12. Bendix, "Tradition and Modernity Reconsidered," p. 335. See the discussion of the "tensions" in this process in Edward A. Shils, "Political Development in the New States," p. 281; cf. Hedley Bull, "The State's Positive Role in World Affairs," p. 121.

13. Kazushi Ohkawa and Henry Rosovsky, "A Century of Japanese Economic

Growth," in *The State and Economic Enterprise in Japan: Essays in the Political Economy of Growth*, ed. William W. Lockwood, Studies in the Modernization of Japan (Princeton: Princeton University Press, 1965), pp. 51-52, 52n. Cf. Alexander Gerschenkron, "The Approach to European Industrialization: A Postscript," in Gerschenkron, *Economic Backwardness in Historical Perspective*; and Reinhard Bendix, "Preconditions of Development," pp. 312-329.

14. See Kazushi Ohkawa and Henry Rosovsky, *Japanese Economic Growth*, pp. 198, 37-39; and Tsunehiko Watanabe, "Industrialization, Technological Progress, and Dual Structure."

15. Marx, *Capital*, 3:791-792. This and other ambiguities in Marx's work on the state have engendered at least two competing perspectives on the state among contemporary Marxists. The first, the "critical perspective," drawn primarily from Marx's early writings, stresses the relationship between the state and society as a whole. This Hegelian view sees the state as a realm of alienation. Although it is created by civil society, the state is always potentially autonomous because it gradually arrogates to itself powers above and against society itself. This view is congenial both to the discussion of the potential autonomy of the state and to the analysis of a situation, as in prewar Japan, in which the characteristics of base and superstructure appear to be in conflict. A second, "scientific," perspective treats primarily the relationship between the state and the social classes that are components of society. Adopted by Lenin and other post-Marx Marxists who lacked access to or chose to deemphasize Marx's early writings, this perspective identifies the state not only as the product of class society, but also as the instrument or agent of the ruling socio-economic class. Generally, Japanese Marxist studies of the state until about 1930 (including those of Yamakawa Hitoshi and Inomata Tsunao) adopted the "scientific perspective" on the state that had been imported into Japan as part of historical materialism. However, subsequent analyses, particularly the *Kōza* writings of Hirano Yoshitarō, Hani Gorō, and Hattori Shisō, also drew on such early works as Marx's *Critique of Hegel's "Philosophy of Right"* and *The German Ideology*. This variety of sources offered participants in the debate on Japanese capitalism considerable latitude in their treatment of the Japanese state from Meiji to Shōwa. For a detailed discussion of the dual conception of the state in Marx, see Germaine A. Hoston, "State and Revolution in China and Japan," 1:105-137; and Alan Wolfe, "New Directions in the Marxist Theory of Politics," p. 133.

16. The term *tennō-sei* remains especially popular among Kōza-ha Marxists and in certain academic circles. Its use by the Kōza-ha signified the importance of the operation of the imperial institution as a system with deep socio-economic roots. The Rōnō-ha never treated the institution as a system, tending to prefer the term *tennō*, and seemed to regard it as a meaningless appendage of an essentially bourgeois-democratic state. (Interview with Maruyama Masao, Tokyo, June 17, 1982.)

17. Interview with Arahata Kanson, Takahashi Masao, and Watanabe Fumitarō, Tokyo, August 17, 1979; cf. Uchida Jōkichi and Nakano Jirō, *Nihon shihon-shugi ronsō*, p. 33.

18. Given the difference between the Rōnō-ha's and the Kōza-ha's approaches to the emperor system in the debate on Japanese capitalism, one might ask if there was

any correlation between the propensity to *tenkō* and factional affiliation (*Rōnō* versus *Kōza*). This discussion would suggest that *Rōnō* Marxists would have *tenkō*ed more readily than *Kōza* Marxists. In addition to their neglect of the emperor system, leaders of the Rōnō-ha, like Arahata Kanson and, to a lesser extent, Yamakawa Hitoshi, were deeply involved in the early anarchist movement and continued to exhibit anarchist proclivities throughout their careers. A comparison of *tenkō* among Marxists of the two factions would be very difficult, however. Kōza-ha Marxists with strong JCP ties were imprisoned first, while the Rōnō-ha's abstention from illegal activity protected them until the mid-1930s. In addition, reliable and unbiased data for statistical study are not readily available. Factional affiliations of the large numbers of *tenkōsha* would be especially hard to identify, since one was not officially a "member" of one faction or the other.

19. See Patricia Golden Steinhoff, "*Tenkō*," p. 159 and chap. 5 passim.

20. See Harold Joseph Wray, "Changes and Continuity in Japanese Images of the *Kokutai*."

21. This thesis is discussed in more detail in Germaine A. Hoston, "*Tenkō*."

22. On the family conception of the state (*kazoku kokka*), see Ishida, *Meiji seiji shisō shi kenkyū*, pt. 1, especially chap. 1, sec. 2.

23. Takeda Kiyoko, "Tennō-sei shisō no keisei," p. 269.

24. Joseph Pittau, *Political Thought in Early Meiji Japan*, pp. 132, 145; Takeda, "Tennō-sei shisō no keisei," pp. 273-275; cf. Ishida Takeshi, "Ideorogii to shite no tennō-sei," p. 39. On the mythology concerning the emperor, see Robert Cornell Armstrong, *Light from the East*, p. 3.

25. Interview with Ukai Nobushige, Tokyo, July 23, 1979; interview with Maruyama Masao, Tokyo, June 17, 1982.

26. Interview with Ishida Takeshi, Tokyo, August 11, 1979; interview with Ukai Nobushige, Tokyo, July 23, 1979; interview with Fujita Shōzō, Tokyo, August 3, 1979. Cf. Fujita Shōzō, *Tennō-sei kokka no shihai genri*, pp. 5-114.

27. See Hori Makoto, "Meiji shoki no kokka ron." Hozumi studied in Germany from 1884 to 1888 and studied German public law at Heidelberg, Berlin, and Strausburg universities. British constitutional theory is more often identified with the progressive constitutional monarchic movement and the party movement. Hozumi's course as an orthodox scholar of the Meiji Constitution was heavily influenced by his work in Germany, but his notion of the emperor-centered Japanese state was firmly vested in the late Tokugawa *kokutai* idea. See Nakase Ju'ichi, "Meiji kenpōka ni okeru tennō-kikan setsu no keisei," pp. 62, 66; Ishida Takeshi, *Nihon kindai shisō shi ni okeru hō to seiji*, p. 166; and Suzuki Yasuzō, *Nihon kenpō-gaku shi kenkyū*, part 1.

28. Kawakami Hajime noted that although university professors were often regarded as advocates of dangerous ideas in the 1920s and the sale of their work was often banned, censorship was desultory, and university professors enjoyed a broad range of freedom in their writing. This circumstance reflected "the authority and prestige Japanese professors enjoyed in society despite the rule of a militaristic police-type imperial regime." See Kawakami's *Omoide*, pp. 213-214.

29. See Joseph O'Malley, "Editor's Introduction," in Marx, *Critique of Hegel's*

"*Philosophy of Right*," pp. xiii-xiv; Robert C. Tucker, "The Political Theory of Classical Marxism," in Robert C. Tucker, *The Marxian Revolutionary Idea* (New York: W. W. Norton, 1969), p. 80; and Wolfe, "New Directions in the Marxist Theory of Politics," p. 131.

30. Uchida and Nakano, *Nihon shihon-shugi ronsō*, p. 33.

31. Claus Offe, "Structural Problems of the Capitalist State," pp. 31-32. The instrumentalist is one of the two major contemporary Marxist approaches to the state. The other, the structuralist approach, will be discussed below.

32. David A. Gold, Clarence Y. H. Lo, and Erik Olin Wright, "Recent Developments in Marxist Theories of the Capitalist State (I)," pp. 32-33. Ralph Miliband's work best typifies this school. See his *The State in Capitalist Society* (New York: Basic Books, 1969); "The Capitalist State"; and "Poulantzas and the Capitalist State." Other examples include: G. William Domhoff, *Who Rules America?* (Englewood Cliffs, N.J.: Prentice-Hall, 1967); Gabriel Kolko, *The Triumph of Conservatism* (Chicago: Quadrangle, 1967); Joyce Kolko and Gabriel Kolko, *The Limits of Power* (New York: Harper & Row, 1972); S. Menshikov, *Millionaires and Managers* (Moscow: Progress Publishers, 1969); and James Weinstein, *The Corporate Ideal in the Liberal State* (Boston: Beacon Press, 1968).

33. Yamakawa Hitoshi, *Yamakawa Hitoshi jiden*, pp. 428-429.

34. Karl Marx and Frederick Engels, "Manifesto of the Communist Party," in Tucker, ed., *Marx-Engels Reader*, p. 337.

35. Significantly, this alternative strategy was presented more effectively in two of Inomata's essays: "Hiyorimi-shugi-teki senryaku to 'senryaku-teki' hiyorimi-shugi" [Opportunistic strategy and "strategic" opportunism], *Rōnō* (February-March 1928); and "Puroretaria kakumei ni okeru burujoa minshu-shugi tōsō no yakuwari" [The tasks of the bourgeois-democratic struggle in the proletarian revolution], *Rōnō* (September and December 1928). See Koyama Hirotake and Kishimoto Eitarō, *Nihon no hikyōsantō Marukusu-shugisha*, pp. 143-144.

36. *Hanbatsu*, or clique of feudal clans, referred to the dominance of the new Meiji regime by the Chōshū, Satsuma, and Tosa clans, which had led the rebellion against the Tokugawa shogunate.

37. Yamakawa objected specifically to the interpretation of Japanese politics offered by Y. Varga, in "Nihon shihon-shugi no busshitsu to sono seisaku" [The substance of Japanese capitalism and its policies], *International* (November 1927). See Yamakawa Hitoshi, "Seiji-teki tōitsu sensen e!" pp. 174-183.

38. Ibid., pp. 183-201.

39. At this point, the Comintern had been forced to face the demise of the Communist Party it had created just two years before, but Yamakawa neglected this context.

40. Ibid., pp. 215n, 216n, 217-218.

41. Tsushima Tadayuki, "*Nihon shihon-shugi ronsō*" *shiron*, pp. 13-14. Cf. Uchida and Nakano, *Nihon shihon-shugi ronsō*, p. 45.

42. Ibid., p. 19; Inomata Tsunao, *Gendai Nihon kenkyū*, pp. 113-114.

43. Inomata's 1932 work on monopoly capitalism in Japan contained a chapter entitled "*Kokka shihon-shugi*" [State capitalism]. Its six subsections indicate the

influence of Bukharin's theoretical work on Inomata: *Dokusen shihon-shugi to kokka* [Monopoly capitalism and the state]; *Dokusen-teki kokka shihon* [Monopolistic state capital]; *Kokka oyobi kokka-shihon no kin'yū shihon e no setsugō jūzoku* [The union and subordination of the state and state capital to finance capital]; *Tsugi no ippo—fukamaru gōsei e* [The next step: Toward deepening synthesis]; *Kokka ni yoru keizai tōsei* [Economic control by the state]; and *Futa-tsu no kokka shihon-shugi* [Two (kinds of) state capitalism(s)]. (Inomata Tsunao, *Nihon no dokusen shihon-shugi*, chap. 7, pp. 107-135.)

44. See Okada Sōji, "Nihon shihon-shugi no kiso mondai" [Basic problems of Japanese capitalism], *Kaizō* (August 1934): 21, cited by Uchida and Nakano, *Nihon shihon-shugi ronsō*, pp. 244-245.

45. Ibid., pp. 113-114 (emphasis in original); Uchida and Nakano, *Nihon shihon-shugi ronsō*, pp. 19-20.

46. Niijima Issaku (pseud. of Inomata Tsunao), "Nihon musan-kaikyū undō ni kansuru tēze. (1) Nihon shihon-shugi no gensei," pp. 12-14.

47. Ibid.

48. Inomata, *Gendai Nihon kenkyū*, p. 157.

49. [Inomata], "Tēze. (1) Nihon shihon-shugi no gensei," p. 13; Inomata, *Gendai Nihon kenkyū*, p. 158.

50. [Inomata], "Tēze. (1) Nihon shihon-shugi no gensei," pp. 13-14; and Inomata, *Gendai Nihon kenkyū*, pp. 146-148.

51. Ibid., pp. 148-149, 158-159, 153-154, 152; and Niijima Issaku [Inomata Tsunao], "Nihon musan-kaikyū undō ni kansuru tēze. (2) Seiji jōsei," pp. 13-14.

52. Inomata, *Gendai Nihon kenkyū*, p. 161.

53. Ibid., pp. 146-148, 162-166; [Inomata], "Tēze. (2) Seiji jōsei," p. 24.

54. [Inomata], "Tēze. (1) Nihon shihon-shugi no gensei," pp. 14-15; Inomata, *Gendai Nihon kenkyū*, pp. 167-168; and [Inomata], "Tēze. (2) Seiji jōsei," p. 25.

55. Inomata, *Gendai Nihon kenkyū*, pp. 114-115, 135-136, 141 (emphasis in original). Here Inomata opposed Takahashi Kamekichi's view that the petty bourgeoisie was more numerous and therefore that "the real power of industrial rule still remains with the petty bourgeois stratum." Such an argument was as ludicrous, Inomata argued, as the notion that "because poor peasants were the vast majority in prewar Russia, they exercised the real power over Russian production." (Ibid., p. 135.)

56. Ibid., p. 145.

57. [Inomata], "Tēze. (2) Seiji jōsei," pp. 25-27; and Inomata, *Gendai Nihon kenkyū*, p. 144.

58. Ibid., pp. 109-114, 171; Tsushima, *"Nihon shihon-shugi ronsō" shiron*, pp. 56-57; and [Inomata], "Tēze. (2) Seiji jōsei," pp. 25-26.

59. Inomata, *Gendai Nihon kenkyū*, pp. 115-117, 25-27, 44-50; and [Inomata], "Tēze. (2) Seiji jōsei," p. 27.

60. See Nikolai Bukharin, "K teorii imperialisticheskogo gosudarstva" [Toward a theory of the imperialist state], *Revoljutsiia pravda: Sbornik pervyi* (M. 1925): 5-32; quotations here as translated in Stephen Cohen, "Bukharin, Lenin and the Theoretical Foundations of Bolshevism," pp. 438, 439, 441; and Sidney Heitman,

"Between Lenin and Stalin: Nikolai Bukharin," in *Revisionism*, ed. Leopold Labedz, pp. 81-82.

61. Heitman, "Between Lenin and Stalin," p. 82; and Bukharin, "K teorii imperialisticheskogo gosudarstva," pp. 15-18, 21-22, 25, 27, and 18, 28, 30, quoted in Cohen, "Bukharin, Lenin," pp. 441-443.

62. Nikolai Bukharin, "Imperialism and World Economy," in *Essential Works of Socialism*, ed. Irving Howe (New Haven: Yale University Press, 1976), pp. 387-388. Rōnō-ha Marxists report that the influence of Bukharin's work on the capitalist state was widespread in 1927-1929 and remained high through the 1930s. (Interview with Ōuchi Tsutomu, Tokyo, June 11, 1982; interview with the Honorable Minobe Ryōkichi, Tokyo, June 8, 1982; interview with Hayashi Takehisa, June 23, 1982.)

63. Inomata cites a piece by Bukharin entitled "Shihon-shugi no antei to musan-kaikyū no kakumei" [The stability of capitalism and the proletarian revolution]. This is probably the pamphlet mentioned above. See Inomata, *Gendai Nihon kenkyū*, pp. 18-23; and [Inomata], "Tēze. (1) Nihon shihon-shugi no gensei," pp. 11-12.

64. The "scissors price gap" refers to a structural crisis in which either agricultural prices are so high that industrial workers cannot buy food or, as Inomata stresses, the agricultural sector suffers disproportionately because low agricultural prices paired with high industrial prices prevent agricultural workers from buying industrial goods because of loss of income.

65. Inomata Tsunao, *Kyokutō ni okeru teikoku-shugi*; and [Inomata], "Tēze. (1) Nihon shihon-shugi no gensei," p. 12.

66. [Inomata], "Tēze. (1) Nihon shihon-shugi no gensei," pp. 12-21.

67. Inomata, *Gendai Nihon kenkyū*, pp. 25-27, 44-50.

68. [Inomata], "Tēze. (1) Nihon shihon-shugi no gensei," pp. 17-18; and Inomata, *Gendai Nihon kenkyū*, pp. 119-120.

69. Inomata, *Nihon no dokusen shihon-shugi*, p. 110; Inomata, *Gendai Nihon kenkyū*, pp. 117-118; and Inomata, *Kyokutō ni okeru teikoku-shugi*, p. 374.

70. Inomata, *Kyokutō ni okeru teikoku-shugi*, pp. 374-376; and Inomata, *Nihon no dokusen shihon-shugi*, pp. 110-111, 113.

71. Inomata, *Kyokutō ni okeru teikoku-shugi*, pp. 376-379; and Inomata, *Nihon no dokusen shihon-shugi*, pp. 113-117, 122-125.

72. Inomata, *Nihon no dokusen shihon-shugi*, p. 112.

73. Ibid., pp. 119-121; Inomata, *Kyokutō ni okeru teikoku-shugi*, pp. 381-382; and Inomata, *Gendai Nihon kenkyū*, pp. 125-128. Compare Takahashi Kamekichi's analysis of the same phenomenon in chapter 4.

74. Inomata, *Nihon no dokusen shihon-shugi*, pp. 125-131; and Inomata, *Kyokutō ni okeru teikoku-shugi*, pp. 377-384, 388-389.

75. Inomata, *Nihon no dokusen shihon-shugi*, pp. 111-112; cf. Inomata, *Kyokutō ni okeru teikoku-shugi*, pp. 374-375. Shidehara Kijurō was foreign minister in the Hamaguchi Cabinet; Sengoku Mitsugu, railroad minister in the first and second Katō Cabinets and a founder of the Minseitō; Sakurauchi Mitsugu, an industrialist and politician; Yamamoto Teijirō and Yamamoto Jōtarō were both industrialists and politicians; Kuhara Fusanosuke was an industrialist and politician who served in Tanaka

Gi'ichi's Seiyūkai Cabinet; Mutō Sanji was an industrialist and politician; and Takahashi Korekiyo was the zaibatsu member and politician who played a leading role in the Tanaka Cabinet's handling of the 1927 panic.

76. Inomata, *Kyokutō ni okeru teikoku-shugi*, p. 395.

77. In opposition to Takahashi's theory of petty imperialism, Inomata attacked the view that the state's predominance in the capitalist economy revealed its adoption of socialist principles. Inomata heatedly repudiated Takahashi's muddling of socialism and capitalism:

> We must clearly distinguish [between] two state capitalisms. The state capitalism we have described is the state capitalism of the bourgeois state. This, *in its essence*, has no point in common with the state capitalism of the proletarian state.
>
> The state capitalism of the proletarian state forms a transitional form toward perfect socialism appearing within the framework of socialism, and as a rule, the major industries are held by the state for the sake of workers and poor peasants; and thus, while intervening in private enterprise for the sake of workers and peasants, [the state] leads it to destruction.
>
> The "control" of monopoly capitalism, whether that is made by capitalists or created by the state, is essentially different from the control of socialism. The subject of control—the class—is different. Consequently, the aim is different [and] the result is different. . . . The control of monopoly-state capitalism is penetrated from A to Z with *capitalist principles*.

Inomata, *Nihon no dokusen shihon-shugi*, pp. 132-133; Inomata, *Kyokutō ni okeru teikoku-shugi*, pp. 389-391, emphasis in the original.

78. Inomata Tsunao, *Teikoku-shugi kenkyū*, pp. 111-112, quoted by Moriya Fumio, *Nihon Marukusu-shugi riron no keisei to hatten*, pp. 57-58.

79. See Inomata Tsunao, *Botsuraku shihon-shugi no daisan ki*, especially pp. 6, 16. Cf. Moriya, *Nihon Marukusu-shugi*, pp. 53-59; and Inomata Tsunao, "Puroretaria senryaku ni okeru burujoa minshu-shugi tōsō no yakuwari (2)," p. 111.

80. [Inomata], "Tēze. (1) Nihon shihon-shugi no gensei," p. 21.

81. Inomata Tsunao, "Shihon-shugi Nihon no teikoku-shugi," p. 149.

82. Ibid., pp. 123-124, 146-147.

83. Inomata Tsunao, "Doronuma ni kanbotsu shita 'puchi teikoku-shugisha' (zokkō)," pp. 307-308; and Inomata Tsunao, "Nihon teikoku-shugi no shin dankai no mondai," pp. 198, 206.

84. Inomata, "Doronuma ni kanbotsu shita," pp. 311-314; and Inomata, "Shihon-shugi Nihon," p. 147.

85. Inomata, "Nihon shihon-shugi no gensei," pp. 21-23.

86. Inomata, *Gendai Nihon kenkyū*, pp. 94-97.

87. Ibid., pp. 97-98, 102.

88. Ibid., pp. 102-105.

89. Inomata Tsunao, "Waga senryaku ni okeru burujoa minshu-shugi-teki tōsō no yakuwari (1)," pp. 100-103; Inomata, *Gendai Nihon kenkyū*, pp. 133-134.

90. See Inomata Tsunao, "Nihon musan-kaikyū no ippan senryaku," p. 5; and Inomata, "Puroretaria senryaku," p. 114

91. Tsushima, *"Nihon shihon-shugi ronsō" shiron*, pp. 106, 111, 114-127. Mid-

dle peasants would be temporary allies in the initial, bourgeois-democratic, phase of the revolution, and as the revolution was radicalized, poor peasants would share in the dictatorship of the proletariat. See Inomata, *Gendai Nihon kenkyū*, p. 134; Inomata, "Waga senryaku," pp. 98-100; and Inomata, "Nihon musan-kaikyū no ippan senryaku," pp. 4-5.

92. Inomata, "Tēze. (2) Seiji jōsei," p. 25.

93. Karl Marx and Frederick Engels, "The German Ideology," in Tucker, ed., *Marx-Engels Reader*, pp. 112-139.

94. Offe, "Structural Problems of the Capitalist State," p. 34.

95. Gold, Lo, and Wright, "Recent Developments," p. 36.

96. Ibid. See also Amy Beth Bridges, "Nicos Poulantzas and the Marxist Theory of the State," pp. 163-164.

97. This structuralist thrust of Kōza-ha writings is particularly evident in Hirano Yoshitarō's work on the state. See his *Nihon shihon-shugi shakai no kikō*; *Nihon shihon-shugi shakai no mujun*; *Kokka kenryoku no kōzō*; and *Kokka—sono genjitsu to henkaku*.

98. Koyama Hirotake, *Nihon Marukusu-shugi shi*, pp. 34-35; cf. Shakai Keizai Rōdō Kenkyūjo, *Nihon shihon-shugi ronsō shi*.

99. Shiga Yoshio, quoted in Uchida and Nakano, *Nihon shihon-shugi ronsō*, pp. 69-70 (emphasis is Uchida and Nakano's).

100. See Hattori Shisō, "Zettai-shugi ron," originally published in *Marukusu-shugi kōza* [Symposium on Marxism], vol. 9 (1928); and Hattori Shisō, "Zettai-shugi no shakai-teki kiso."

101. Hattori, "Zettai-shugi ron," pp. 384, 389.

102. Koyama, *Nihon Marukusu-shugi shi*, pp. 63-64.

103. "Nihon ni okeru jōsei to Nihon Kyōsantō no ninmu ni kansuru tēze," p. 83 and Kūshinen [Kuusinen], "Nihon teikoku-shugi to Nihon kakumei no seishitsu," pp. 114-115.

104. Moriya Fumio, *Tennō-sei kenkyū*, p. 137.

105. Hirano, *Burujoa minshu-shugi kakumei*, pp. 58-59.

106. Moriya, "Tennō-sei no busshitsu-teki kiso," p. 26.

107. See Tsuchiya Takao and Okazaki Saburō, *Nihon shihon-shugi hattatsu shi gaisetsu*, pp. 1, 65-80.

108. See Yamakawa, "Seiji-teki tōitsu sensen e!" pp. 176-183; cf. "Nihon ni kansuru ketsugi (Ni-nana nen tēze)," especially pp. 30-35.

109. Moriya, "Tennō-sei no busshitsu-teki kiso," p. 27; cf. Kūshinen, "Nihon teikoku-shugi to Nihon kakumei no seishitsu," pp. 104-105; and the critique in Tsushima, *"Nihon shihon-shugi ronsō" shiron*, pp. 151-152.

110. Hirano, *Nihon shihon-shugi shakai no kikō*, p. 273.

111. Noro Eitarō, *Nihon shihon-shugi hattatsu shi*, p. 162; cf. Noro Eitarō, "Nihon ni okeru tochi shoyū kankei ni tsuite—nakanzuku iwayuru 'hōken-teki zettai-shugi seiryoku no kaikyū-teki busshitsu-teki kiso' no mondai o chūshin to shite" [On landownership relations in Japan: With particular attention to the problem of the "class and material basis of the so-called feudal absolutist forces"], *Shisō* [Thought] 84 (May-June 1929): 47-55 (199-207) passim. Compare Hirano's observations discussed below.

112. Noro, *Nihon shihon-shugi hattatsu shi*, especially pp. 121-136 and 271-280; and Noro, "Nihon ni okeru tochi shoyū kankei," p. 201. Cf. Uchida and Nakano, *Nihon shihon-shugi ronsō*, pp. 23-25; and Koyama, *Nihon Marukusu-shugi shi*, pp. 69-70.

113. The Kōza-ha has found itself in a similar position in criticizing the emperor system in the postwar period as well. It may be correct that democracy in Japan continues to be hindered by the existence of the emperor system, but the Kōza-ha's need to anchor that claim by finding semi-feudal production relations in the countryside years after the American Occupation's sweeping land reforms has placed it in a position that is difficult to sustain. See Moriya, "Tennō-sei no busshitsu-teki kiso," p. 33 and the extended discussion in chapter 9 below.

114. Noro, "Nihon ni okeru tochi shoyū kankei," p. 205.

115. Ibid., p. 203 (emphasis in original); cf. Hirano Yoshitarō, "Meiji ishin ni okeru seiji-teki shihai keitai" (hereafter cited as "Ishin seiji"), pp. 23-24.

116. Noro, "Nihon ni okeru tochi shoyū kankei," pp. 205-207.

117. Hirano, "Ishin seiji," pp. 4-5; Hirano, *Nihon shihon-shugi shakai no kikō*, p. 266.

118. Hirano, "Ishin seiji," pp. 6n, 11-12n.

119. Ibid., pp. 6n, 7-11; cf. Uchida and Nakano, *Nihon shihon-shugi ronsō*, p. 188.

120. Cf. W. A. Beasley, *The Meiji Restoration* (Stanford: Stanford University Press, 1972), pp. 337ff., 382-383.

121. Hirano, "Ishin seiji," pp. 5-6, 13-16. Cf. Hani Gorō, "Bakumatsu ni okeru seiji-teki shihai keitai," pp. 38-39, 45-46; cf. Yamada Moritarō, *Nihon shihon-shugi bunseki*, p. 216.

122. Hirano, "Ishin seiji," pp. 9-10. See also Hirano, *Nihon shakai no kikō*, pp. 2-4.

123. Hirano, "Ishin seiji," pp. 10, 16-19, 56n; and Hirano, *Nihon shakai no kikō*, pp. 263-267.

124. Hirano, "Ishin seiji," p. 57; cf. Uchida and Nakano, *Nihon shihon-shugi ronsō*, pp. 188-189.

125. Uchida and Nakano, *Nihon shihon-shugi ronsō*, pp. 200-201, 217-221, 243-244; Yamada, *Bunseki*, pp. 205, 74-75.

126. Hirano, "Ishin seiji," pp. 58-59n.

127. Hirano Yoshitarō, "Burujoa minshu-shugi undō shi" [History of the bourgeois-democratic movement], in *Kōza*, 3:5-7, 18-20.

128. Yamada, *Bunseki*, p. 173.

129. See Hattori, "Zettai-shugi ron," passim.

130. See Shinobu Seizaburō, *Nihon no dokusen shihon-shugi*.

131. Cf. Barrington Moore, *Social Origins of Dictatorship and Democracy*.

Chapter Eight

1. See Kazushi Ohkawa, *The Growth of the Japanese Economy since 1878*, table 2, p. 246.

2. William W. Lockwood, *The Economic Development of Japan*, p. 451; cf. figures for primary industry in Ohkawa, *Growth Rate of the Japanese Economy*, p. 17, table 1; p. 26, table 8.

3. Uchida Jōkichi and Nakano Jirō, *Nihon shihon-shugi ronsō*, p. 25.

4. Kojima Hinehisa, *Nihon shihon-shugi ronsō shi*, p. 282n. For the long-range impact of this controversy on ground rent, see Makoto Itoh, *Value and Crisis*, pp. 17-22.

5. Nakamura Takafusa, " 'Nihon shihon-shugi ronsō' ni tsuite," p. 186n.

6. This is true of Inomata's work during his association with the Rōnō-ha. After breaking with Yamakawa and his faction around 1930, Inomata published a major work on the agrarian problem. This was *Nōson mondai nyūmon* [Introduction to the agrarian problem]. Significantly, in this volume Inomata placed far greater stress on the problem of "feudal remnants" in the countryside; and he also relied heavily on an interpretation of the long-range effects of the Asiatic mode of production on Japanese development. In both these respects, this latter work more closely resembled that of the Kōza-ha. Accordingly, this Inomata work, including its treatment of the Asiatic mode of production concept, is discussed in this chapter along with Kōza-ha writings.

7. As Lockwood notes, "This price decline . . . was an initial stage in the whole series of events which accelerated Japan's transition to industrialism in the next decade. In prewar Japan agriculture was never to recoup its former position." (*Economic Development of Japan*, p. 451.) It is significant that the controversy on agriculture intensified at precisely this critical time.

8. "Nihon Kyōsantō kōryō sōan," p. 5.

9. See chapter 3; and "Nihon ni kansuru ketsugi," p. 33. The Comintern's stress on the increasing concentration of capital, particularly in finance, has been supported by more recent scholarship. See, for example, Kōzō Yamamura, "The Japanese Economy," especially pp. 310-324.

10. "Nihon mondai ni kansuru ketsugi," p. 33.

11. "Nihon Kyōsantō seiji tēze sōan," p. 51.

12. "Nihon ni okeru jōsei to Nihon Kyōsantō no ninmu ni kansuru tēze," pp. 81-85.

13. Tsushima Tadayuki, *"Nihon shihon-shugi ronsō" shiron*, pp. 14-15.

14. Nakamura, " 'Nihon shihon-shugi ronsō' ni tsuite," p. 195.

15. Nishiyama Take'ichi, "Nōgyō mondai no kihon-teki ichi kōsatsu," *Shakai kagaku* [Social Science] (August 1927): 369-372, quoted by Moriya Fumio, *Nihon Marukusu-shugi riron no keisei to hatten*, p. 106.

16. See Yamamura, "Concentration, Conflicts, Crises," pp. 304-305.

17. Ann Waswo, "The Origins of Tenant Unrest."

18. See the discussion in Yasukichi Yasuba, "Anatomy of the Debate on Japanese Capitalism."

19. Shibagaki Kazuo, "Nihon keizai kenkyū ni okeru senzen to sengo," pp. 19-20.

20. Waswo, "Origins of Tenant Unrest," pp. 386-389.

21. Yamakawa Hitoshi, "Seiji-teki tōitsu sensen e!" pp. 180-183.

22. See Yamada Moritarō, *Nihon shihon-shugi bunseki*, especially pp. 161-216. The Kōza-ha interpretation is discussed in more detail below.

23. In addition to the works cited here, see the following for the Rōnō-ha argument: Tsuchiya Takao, *Nihon shihon-shugi shi ronshū*; and Tsuchiya Takao and Okazaki Saburō, *Nihon shihon-shugi hattatsu shi gaisetsu*.

24. Sakisaka Itsurō, " 'Nihon shihon-shugi bunseki' ni okeru hōhōron," pp. 5, 19-23, originally published in *Kaizō* [Reconstruction] (October 1935); and Sakisaka Itsurō, "Shihon-shugi ni okeru kōzō-teki henka no mondai" [The problem of structural change in capitalism], *Chūō Kōron* [Central review] (December 1935), p. 40, cited in Uchida and Nakano, *Nihon shihon-shugi ronsō*, p. 252.

25. Inomata Tsunao, "Puroretaria senryaku ni okeru burujoa minshu-shugi tōsō no yakuwari (2)," pp. 108-109. Cf. Inomata, "Gendai Nihon burujoajii no seiji-teki chi'i."

26. Originally entitled "Nōmin undō no konpon mondai to tōmen no mondai" [Fundamental questions and immediate problems of the peasant movement], this essay was also published as chapter 10, "Nōmin undō no senryaku-teki igi" [The strategic significance of the peasant movement], in Inomata's *Gendai Nihon kenkyū*.

27. Inomata, *Gendai Nihon kenkyū*, pp. 355-356, quoted in Ōshima Kiyoshi, "Inomata Tsunao no nōgyō ron/senryaku ron," part 1, p. 30.

28. Inomata, *Gendai Nihon kenkyū*, p. 360, cited in Ōshima, "Inomata Tsunao no nōgyō ron/senryaku ron."

29. Inomata Tsunao, *Nihon musan kaikyū undō no hihan*, p. 8.

30. Ōshima, "Inomata Tsunao no nōgyō-ron," pt. 1, p. 30.

31. Inomata, *Gendai Nihon kenkyū*, p. 150.

32. Ibid., pp. 362, 363; and Ōshima, "Inomata Tsunao no nōgyō-ron," pt. 2, pp. 78-79.

33. Ōshima, "Inomata Tsunao no nogyō-ron," pt. 2, p. 79; and Uchida and Nakano, *Nihon shihon-shugi ronsō*, p. 156.

34. Uchida and Nakano, *Nihon shihon-shugi ronsō*, p. 145; and Shibagaki, "Nihon keizai kenkyū," p. 20.

35. Marx, *Capital*, 3:618.

36. Inomata Tsunao, "Tochi mondai to hōken isei," pp. 144-147, originally published in *Kaizō* (January 1930); and Ōshima, "Inomata Tsunao no nōgyō-ron," pt. 2, pp. 78-81.

37. Inomata, "Tochi mondai to hōken isei," p. 156.

38. Ōshima, "Inomata Tsunao nōgyō-ron," pt. 2, p. 81.

39. See Marx, *Capital*, vol. 3, part 6, especially chaps. 37 and 38.

40. Kushida Tamizō, "Burujoa minshu-shugi kakumei no ichi zuhyō to shite no 'sagaku jidai-hyō' " ["The diagram of differential ground rent" as a schematization of the bourgeois-democratic revolution], *Hihan* [Critique], September 1931; [*Kushida Tamizō*] *zenshū* [Complete writings of Kushida Tamizō], 3:156, quoted in Moriya, *Nihon Marukusu-shugi riron*, p. 134. Cf. Kojima, *Nihon shihon-shugi ronsō shi*, p. 278.

41. Hijikata Seibi, "Jidai-ron yori mitaru Marukusu kachi-ron no hōkai," *Keizaigaku ronshū* [Collected essays in economics], 6.4, cited by Kojima, *Nihon shi-*

hon-shugi ronsō shi, p. 278; and Y. Takada, "The Value of Marx's Value Theory," *Keizai ronsō* (Kyoto) 30.1 (1930), cited by Itoh, *Value and Crisis*, p. 20.

42. Kojima, *Nihon shihon-shugi ronsō shi*, p. 279.

43. Marx, *Capital*, 3:646.

44. Kojima, *Nihon shihon-shugi ronsō shi*, pp. 279-280; Itoh, *Value and Crisis*, pp. 20-21; and Ara Kenjirō et al., comps., *Keizai jiten*, s.v. *sagaku jidai*.

45. Marx, *Capital*, 3:620.

46. Kojima, *Nihon shihon-shugi ronsō shi*, p. 280.

47. Sakisaka Itsurō, *Jidai-ron kenkyū*, p. 29, quoted in Moriya, *Nihon Marukusu-shugi riron*, p. 136; and Itoh, *Value and Crisis*, pp. 21-22. Cf. Marx, *Capital*, 3:639.

48. Moriya, *Nihon Marukusu-shugi riron*, pp. 136-138.

49. Kushida Tamizō, "Waga kuni kosakuryō no tokushitsu ni tsuite" [On the special characteristics of our country's rents], *Ōhara shakai mondai kenkyūjo zasshi* 8.1 (June 1931), quoted by Yasuba, "Debate on Japanese Capitalism," p. 68.

50. Inomata, "Tochi mondai to hōken isei," quoted in Ōshima, "Inomata Tsunao nōgyō-ron," pt. 2, p. 87.

51. Inomata, *Nihon musan kaikyū undō no hihan*, p. 10; and Inomata Tsunao, "Hiyorimi-shugi-teki senryaku ka 'senryaku-teki' hiyorimi-shugi ka" [Opportunistic strategy or "strategic" opportunism?] (March 1928), pt. 2, in Inomata, *Nihon puroretariāto no senryaku to senjutsu*, pp. 65-66.

52. Inomata, *Gendai Nihon kenkyū*, pp. 130, 357-359; Inomata, *Nihon musan kaikyū undō no hihan*, p. 21; and Inomata Tsunao, "Waga senryaku ni okeru burujoa minshu-shugi-teki tōsō no yakuwari," pp. 92-94.

53. Inomata, "Puroretaria senryaku ni okeru burujoa minshu-shugi tōsō," p. 114.

54. Ibid.; and Inomata Tsunao, "Nihon musan-kaikyū no ippan senryaku," pp. 9-10.

55. Inomata, *Gendai Nihon kenkyū*, pp. 185-186.

56. Inomata Tsunao, "Hiyorimi-shugi senryaku," p. 66 (originally published in *Rōnō*, March 1928); cf. Inomata, "Waga senryaku ni okeru burujoa minshu-shugi-teki tōsō," p. 106.

57. Niijima Issaku [Inomata Tsunao], "Nihon musan kaikyū undō ni kansuru tēze. (I) Nihon shihon-shugi no gensei," p. 16; and Inomata, "Nihon musan-kaikyū no ippan senryaku," p. 3.

58. Inomata, *Gendai Nihon kenkyū*, p. 134; Inomata, "Waga senryaku ni okeru burujoa minshu-shugi-teki tōsō," pp. 98-100; and Inomata, "Nihon musan-kaikyū no ippan senryaku," pp. 4-5.

59. Inomata, "Tochi mondai to hōken isei," pp. 144-147.

60. Kushida Tamizō, *Nōgyō mondai*, *Kushida Tamizō zenshū*, 3:340, 341, quoted in Yasuba, "Debate on Japanese Capitalism," pp. 69-70.

61. See "Nihon ni kansuru ketsugi," p. 32; and "Nihon ni okeru jōsei to Nihon Kyōsantō no ninmu," p. 76.

62. See especially Hirano Yoshitarō, "Meiji ishin ni okeru seiji-teki shihai kei-

tai,'' especially p. 27; and Aikawa Haruki, ''Nōson keizai to nōgyō kyōkō,'' especially pp. 5-9.

63. Noro Eitarō, *Nihon shihon-shugi hattatsu shi*, cited in Moriya, *Nihon Marukusu-shugi riron*, pp. 106-107.

64. Watanabe Masanosuke, ''Hōkoku no yōten'' [Essential points of the report], in *Gendai shi shiryō* [Materials on current history], 14:27, quoted by Moriya, *Nihon Marukusu-shugi riron*, p. 107.

65. Noro, *Noro Eitarō zenshū*, 1:243, quoted by Moriya, *Nihon Marukusu-shugi riron*, p. 109.

66. Noro Eitarō, ''Nihon ni okeru tochi shoyū kankei ni tsuite: nakanzuku iwayuru 'hōken-teki zettai-shugi seiryoku no kaikyū-teki busshitsu-teki kiso' no mondai o chūshin to shite'' [On landownership relations in Japan: With particular attention to the problem of ''the class and material basis of so-called feudal absolutist forces''], *Shisō* [Thought] 84 (May-June 1929): 51.

67. Moriya, *Nihon Marukusu-shugi riron*, pp. 109-110.

68. Ibid., p. 54.

69. Yamada, *Bunseki*, p. 4.

70. See Karl Marx, ''The Eighteenth Brumaire of Louis Bonaparte,'' in *The Marx-Engels Reader*, ed. Tucker, especially pp. 606-607; and the discussion in chapter 7 supra.

71. Uchida and Nakano, *Nihon shihon-shugi ronsō*, pp. 198-199; Yamada, *Bunseki*, pp. 196-200; and Aikawa, ''Nōson keizai to nōgyō kyōkō,'' pp. 5-7.

72. Noro, ''Nihon ni okeru tochi shoyū kankei ni tsuite,'' p. 52.

73. Noro Eitarō, ''Inomata Tsunao shi cho 'Gendai Nihon burujoajii no seiji-teki chi'i' o hyōsu,'' in *Noro Eitarō zenshū*, 1:294, quoted in Ōshima, ''Inomata Tsunao no nōgyō-ron,'' pt. 1, p. 20.

74. See Yamada Moritarō, ''Meiji ishin nōgyō henkaku,'' pp. 22-27; Aikawa, ''Nōson keizai to nōgyō kyōkō,'' p. 38; cf. Hirano Yoshitarō, ''Kashō nōmin ni yoru jidai,'' p. 14.

75. See Yasuba, ''Debate on Japanese Capitalism,'' p. 69. Cf. the analysis by Sekiya Tomesaku summarized in Moriya, *Nihon Marukusu-shugi riron*, pp. 125-126.

76. Hirano, ''Kashō nōmin ni yoru jidai,'' p. 3.

77. Hirano, *Nihon shihon-shugi shakai no kikō*, pp. 257n-259n.

78. Yamada, *Bunseki*, p. 5.

79. Hirano, ''Kashō nōmin ni yoru jidai,'' pp. 3-4, 27-32.

80. Ibid., pp. 32, 33.

81. See, for example, Hirano's discussion of ''stagnancy in ground rents in kind of an Asiatic feudal character,'' in ibid., pp. 37-39; and Aikawa, ''Nōson keizai to nōgyō kyōkō,'' pp. 5-11.

82. This was ''Kyūbō no nōson,'' published in *Kaizō* (n.d.). See Ōshima, ''Inomata Tsunao no nōgyō-ron,'' pt. 1, p. 26.

83. Inomata, *Nōson mondai nyūmon*, pp. 4-5, 29-64 passim.

84. Ibid., pp. 105-130.

85. Ibid., p. 4.

86. See Karl Marx, "Contribution to the Critique of Hegel's Philosophy of Right: Introduction," in *Marx-Engels Reader*, ed. Tucker, p. 59 (emphasis in original); and the complete text in Karl Marx, *Critique of Hegel's "Philosophy of Right."*

87. See Moore, *Social Origins of Dictatorship and Democracy*.

88. See Noro's preface to the *Kōza* for this statement of purpose.

89. See Thomas R. H. Havens, *Farm and Nation in Modern Japan*, chaps. 12, 13 passim; Richard J. Smethurst, *A Social Basis for Prewar Japanese Militarism*; and Waswo, "Origins of Tenant Unrest," p. 379.

90. Waswo, "Origins of Tenant Unrest," pp. 389-394.

91. Havens, *Farm and Nation in Modern Japan*, p. 310.

92. See R. P. Dore, *Land Reform in Japan* (London: Oxford University Press, 1959), p. 393; and Smethurst, *Social Basis for Prewar Japanese Militarism*, p. 179.

93. Havens, *Farm and Nation in Modern Japan*, p. 319.

Chapter Nine

1. For an analysis of *tenkō* in terms of Japanese development and the national question in Marxism, see Germaine A. Hoston, "*Tenkō*."

2. Patricia Golden Steinhoff, "*Tenkō*," pp. 6, 10n; cf. Kuno Osamu and Tsurumi Shunsuke, *Gendai Nihon no shisō*, pp. 53-54. Not all those who *tenkō*ed jettisoned Marxism along with their Communist affiliations. Many, like Sano Manabu and the so-called Kaitō-ha (a group of imprisoned Marxists led by Mizuno Shigeo, who preceded Sano in *tenkō* in 1930), elected to adapt Marxism to the Japanese cultural context by reinterpreting it as a form of national or state socialism. See Germaine A. Hoston, "Emperor, Nation, and the Transformation of Marxism"; and Takabatake Michitoshi, "Ikkoku shakai-shugisha."

3. Some who had participated in the debate on Japanese capitalism began to write in support of Japanese expansion in Asia, reflecting their *tenkō* in new writings. An example of this is Hirano Yoshitarō's work on the Pacific war as a struggle for "the liberation of Greater Asia by Asians for Asians" from British and American imperialism. See Hirano Yoshitarō, *Dai Ajia-shugi no rekishi-teki kiso*. After the war, Hirano atoned for this by establishing his own Institute for China Studies (Chūgoku Kenkyūjo) to conduct serious scholarly research on China from a Marxist point of view.

4. As early as 1952, public opinion surveys taken by *Yomiuri shinbun* revealed that the Japanese people held more of an emotional attachment to the emperor rather than a belief that the power of the emperor should be increased. (See Takeshi Ishida, "Popular Attitudes toward the Japanese Emperor"; cf. Ishida Takeshi, "Ideorogii to shite no tennō-sei"; and Ishida Takeshi, *Kindai Nihon seiji kōzō no kenkyū*, p. 308, table.) More recent surveys taken by *Asahi shinbun* reveal that even this sentimental attachment has declined significantly since the 1950s: only an average of 21.8 percent report such an attachment. (Usui Toshio, " 'Fūka' no uchigawa ni tadayou yawarakai 'shiji,' " p. 8.)

5. See R. P. Dore, *Land Reform in Japan* (London: Oxford University Press, 1959), p. 115.

6. Ibid., chaps. 6-8, especially p. 175, table 8.

7. Takafusa Nakamura, *The Postwar Japanese Economy*, pp. 23-25.

8. Beckmann and Okubo, *The Japanese Communist Party*, p. 275.

9. *Nihon shakai undō jinmei jiten*, s.v. Suzuki Mosaburō; and *Shakai-shugi Kyōkai tēze*, p. 9.

10. Yamakawa claimed support for his vision of "peaceful revolution" from Marx's view that there was no single model of socialism, and from the belief that "Marx, Engels, and Lenin had said that 'one can attain socialism by a peaceful process.' " *Shakai-shugi Kyōkai tēze*, p. 9. Cf. "Nihon Shakaitō kōryō (kettō-ji)," p. 21. A more detailed discussion on the JSP and JCP will follow below.

11. Nakamura, *Postwar Japanese Economy*, pp. 28-29; and Robert A. Scalapino, *The Japanese Communist Movement, 1920-1966* (Berkeley: University of California Press, 1967), p. 68. Subsequently, labor union workers were also blamed for the death of the president of Japan National Railroads and were indicted for two separate train accidents. Since the mid-1960s, it has been speculated that the government took advantage of the incidents to suppress the unions.

12. Dore, *Land Reform in Japan*, p. 175.

13. I am indebted to Ukai Nobushige for these insights into the constitutional problems posed by the Jieitai. See also the brief reference to these issues in Ukai Nobushige, *Kenpō* [The constitution] (Tokyo: Iwanami Shoten, Iwanami Shinsho, 1956, 1981), pp. 69n-70n and the lengthy discussion in Fukushima Shingo, *Nihon no "bōei" seisaku* [Japan's defense policy] (Tokyo: Tōkyō Daigaku Shuppan-kai, 1978), especially chap. 9 and appendix.

14. See Ishida, "Popular Attitudes toward the Emperor," p. 32. For figures on defense spending since 1958, see *Zen'ei* [Vanguard] 479, Special Expanded Issue (May 1982): *Seiji Keizai Sōran (1982)* [Compendium of Politics and Economics] (Tokyo), p. 127, table I-2.5.

15. Kūshinen, "Nihon teikoku-shugi to Nihon kakumei no seishitsu," pp. 104, 114, 106-107.

16. "Nihon ni okeru jōsei to Nihon Kyōsantō no ninmu ni kansuru tēze," p. 79.

17. This thesis was based on Yamada's *Kōza* analysis of Japanese capitalism. See Yamada, *Nihon shihon-shugi bunseki*.

18. See Shinobu Seizaburō, "Nihon teikoku-shugi no shūen" [The demise of Japanese imperialism], *Keizai hyōron* (April 1946), cited by Kojima Hinehisa, *Nihon shihon-shugi ronsō shi*, p. 148.

19. See Kamiyama Shigeo, "Nihon teikoku-shugi no seikaku no mondai ni yosete," pp. 200-215.

20. Kojima, *Nihon shihon-shugi ronsō shi*, pp. 148-153. Cf. Moriya Fumio, *Tennō-sei kenkyū*, p. 175n.

21. Shiga Yoshio, "Gunji-teki hōken-teki 'teikoku-shugi' ni tsuite."

22. See Kamiyama Shigeo, *Kokka riron*, p. 84.

23. Kojima, *Nihon shihon-shugi ronsō shi*, pp. 153-154.

24. Inoue Kiyoshi, "Nihon teikoku-shugi no keisei" [The formation of Japanese imperialism], in *Kindai Nihon no keisei* [The formation of modern Japan], comp. Rekishigaku Kenkyūkai (June 1953), cited by ibid., pp. 155-156.

25. Cf. the ideas of Takahashi Kamekichi, in Germaine A. Hoston, "Marxism and Japanese Expansionism," pp. 16-20.

26. Eguchi Bokurō, *Teikoku-shugi to minzoku*, pp. 71-73.

27. Dōi Matsu'ichi, "Teikoku-shugi no seiritsu to Nichi-Ro sensō," in *Jidai kubun-jō no riron-teki sho mondai* [Theoretical problems of periodization], comp. Rekishigaku Kenkyūkai, cited by Kojima, *Nihon shihon-shugi ronsō shi*, pp. 156-158.

28. Kojima, *Nihon shihon-shugi ronsō shi*, pp. 158-162.

29. In Marx and Engels, absolutism seemed to refer to a period of transition, especially from feudal to capitalist society, in which class conflict yields not a dominant class but a balance among classes, as between the nobility and the bourgeoisie in the absolute monarchies of the eleventh through eighteenth centuries or proletariat versus bourgeoisie under Bonapartism. See Frederick Engels, *Origin of the Family*, p. 231; Frederick Engels, "Hungary and Panslavism" (1849), in *The Russian Menace to Europe*, by Karl Marx and Frederick Engels, ed. Paul W. Blackstone and Bert F. Hoselitz (Glencoe, Ill.: Free Press, 1952), pp. 58-59; and Karl Marx, "The Eighteenth Brumaire of Louis Bonaparte," in *The Marx-Engels Reader*, ed. Tucker, p. 515.

30. See Sakisaka Itsurō, "Fasshizumu no shakai-teki kiso" [The social basis of fascism], *Zenshin* [Advance] (succeeded *Rōnō* in July 1932) 1.2 (August 1932); Takahashi Masao, "Fasshizumu seiritsu no shi-teki kōsatsu" [A historical examination of the establishment of fascism] (2 parts), *Zenshin* 1.1 (July 1932): 47-59 and 1.4 (October 1932): 268-285; and Takahashi Masao [Nakajima Kiyoshi], "Fashizumu kenkyū" [A study of fascism], *Rōnō* 6.3 (March 1932): 240-244.

31. See Okazaki Saburō, "Fashizumu"; Ōuchi Hyōe, Sakisaka Itsurō, Tsuchiya Takao, and Takahashi Masao, *Nihon shihon-shugi no kenkyū*; and Kojima, *Nihon shihon-shugi ronsō shi*, pp. 179-181.

32. Kamiyama Shigeo, *Tennō-sei ni kansuru riron-teki sho mondai*, pp. 121-122.

33. Shiga Yoshio, *Sekai to Nihon*, pp. 47-48, cited by Kojima, *Nihon shihon-shugi ronsō shi*, p. 176.

34. Kamiyama too, of course, had referred to the "relative autonomy"' of the emperor system. (See *Tennō-sei ni kansuru riron-teki sho mondai*.) Nevertheless, this notion had a more central position in Shiga's analysis. See Moriya, *Tennō-sei kenkyū*, p. 175n. It is significant that the notion of the potential or relative autonomy of the state has received so much attention among structuralists. This stress seems to have arisen out of dissatisfaction with the assumption of "capitalist rationality" that appears to be inherent in the instrumentalist approach of Marxists like Ralph Miliband. See Fred Block, "The Ruling Class Does Not Rule," p. 8; Raymond Williams, "Base and Superstructure in Marxist Cultural Theory," *New Left Review* 82 (1973); and Nicos Poulantzas, "The Problem of the Capitalist State," pp. 238-253.

35. Shiga Yoshio, *Kokka-ron*, pp. 149-150, 157-159.

36. See Moriya, *Tennō-sei kenkyū*, pp. 175n-176n; and Moriya Fumio, "Nihon

teikoku-shugi no shi-teki bunseki,'' *Chōryū* (August 1948), cited by Kojima, *Nihon shihon-shugi ronsō shi*, p. 182n; cf. Hirano Yoshitarō, *Nihon shihon-shugi shakai no mujun*, pt. 4.

37. Hattori Shisō, ''Dai Nihon teikoku-shugi,'' in *Hattori Shisō chosaku-shū*, p. 239, cited by Kojima, *Nihon shihon-shugi ronsō shi*, p. 178.

38. Kojima, *Nihon shihon-shugi ronsō shi*, pp. 174-176, 181n; Moriya, *Tennō-sei kenkyū*, p. 179; and the discussion in Koyama Hirotake, *Nihon shihon-shugi ronsō no shin dankai*, chap. 5.

39. Alan Rix, ''Marxism in Japan: Theory versus Tradition,'' in *Marxism in Asia*, ed. Colin Mackerras and Nick Knight (London: Croom Helm and St. Martin's Press, 1985).

40. Cf. Takauchi Shun'ichi, *Gendai Nihon shihon-shugi ronsō*, pp. 16-18.

41. The definitive discussion of these changes in JCP policy is to be found in Scalapino, *Japanese Communist Movement*, pp. 54-56.

42. See Nihon Kyōsantō, *Nihon Kyōsantō no rokujū nen*, 1:154-171, and Scalapino, *Japanese Communist Movement*, pp. 56-57.

43. Yamamoto Masami [Yumoto Masao], ''Gendankai to rōdōsha kaikyū'' [The current stage and the working class], *Tōkyō shinbun* [Tokyo News], December 2, 5, 1945, cited by Kojima, *Nihon shihon-shugi ronsō shi*, pp. 212-213.

44. Nakanishi Kō, ''Ikensho'' [Letter of my views], cited by Andō Jinbee, ''Sengo shakai-shugi kakumei-ron no senku,'' and *Nihon shakai undō jinmei jiten*, s.v. Nakanishi Kō.

45. Yamada Moritarō, ''Nōchi kaikaku no rekishi-teki igi'' [The historical significance of the land reforms], in *Tōkyō Daigaku keizaigaku-bu shōritsu sanjū shūnen kinen ronbun shū* [Collected essays commemorating the thirtieth anniversary of the establishment of the Economics Department of the University of Tokyo], vol. 2: *Sengo Nihon keizai no sho mondai* [Problems of the postwar Japanese economy] (Tokyo: Yūhikaku, 1949), p. 139.

46. Yamada, ''Nōchi kaikaku no rekishi-teki igi,'' cited by Shibagaki Kazuo and Saeki Naomi, ''Sengo Nihon keizai no kihon mondai'' [Basic problems of the postwar Japanese economy], in *Nihon keizai kenkyū nyūmon* [Introduction to Japanese economic studies], ed. Saeki Naomi and Shibagaki Kazuo (Tokyo: Tōkyō Daigaku Shuppan-kai, 1972), pp. 50-51.

47. Kojima, *Nihon shihon-shugi ronsō shi*, p. 213; and Shibagaki and Saeki, ''Sengo Nihon keizai no kihon mondai,'' pp. 51-52.

48. Scalapino, *Japanese Communist Movement*, pp. 59-60.

49. Ibid., pp. 60-63, 80-81; Kojima, *Nihon shihon-shugi ronsō shi*, p. 214.

50. Nihon Kyōsantō, *Nihon Kyōsantō no rokujū nen*, 1:176 (insertions by the author).

51. *Nihon shihon-shugi kōza* [Symposium on Japanese capitalism], 1:338, cited by Shibagaki and Saeki, ''Sengo Nihon keizai no kihon mondai,'' p. 50.

52. '' 'Nihon shihon-shugi kōza' no shuppatsu no tame ni'' [For the beginning of the *Symposium on Japanese capitalism*], in *Nihon shihon-shugi kōza*, vol. 1, cited by Kojima, *Nihon shihon-shugi ronsō shi*, pp. 208-209.

53. See Inoue Kiyoshi and Kondō Yasuo et al., ''Nōchi kaikaku to han-hōken sei,'' in *Nihon shihon-shugi kōza*, vol. 5; and Yamada Shōjirō et al., ''Nōmin shū-

datsu to nōgyō kiki [The exploitation of peasants and agricultural crisis], in *Nihon shihon-shugi kōza*, vol. 6, both cited by Kojima, *Nihon shihon-shugi ronsō shi*, p. 212n.

54. Watanabe Yōzō, "Gendai minshu-shugi hōgaku to 'Nihon shihon-shugi hattatsu shi kōza,' " pp. 118-119; and interview with Watanabe Yōzō, Tokyo, Japan, April 14, 1984.

55. See Yamada Moritarō, comp., *Kenkaku-ki no jidai hanchū* [The category of ground rent in the reform era] (Tokyo: Iwanami Shoten, 1956), cited in Shibagaki and Saeki, "Sengo Nihon keizai no kihon mondai," p. 51n.; Yamada Moritarō, "Nihon nōgyō saiseisan kōzō no kiso-teki bunseki" [A basic analysis of the structure of reproduction of Japanese agriculture], Senshū Daigaku Tochi Seido Shiryō Hoson-kai, 1962, p. 10, cited by Moriya Fumio, "Gendai Nihon no seiji kikō" [The political structure of contemporary Japan], in *Kōza Gendai Nihon to Marukusu-shugi*, 1:137-138. See the statistics on proportions of full- and part-time farm households and the net decline in the population employed in agriculture from 1955 on, in Nakamura, *Postwar Japanese Economy*, p. 194, table 5.19. Also, compare with Yamada's view Nakamura's observations concerning the land reform: "Aimed at preventing the revival of a landlord system like that of the prewar era, the Agricultural Land Act was passed in 1952, imposing severe restrictions on land transfers, tenure, tenant rents, etc. However, this law also had the undeniable effect of preserving without modification the much more dispersed, minutely fragmented pattern of landownership" (p. 195).

56. Miyamoto Kenji, Report on the Party Program to the Seventh Party Congress, quoted in Kojima, *Nihon shihon-shugi ronsō shi*, pp. 215-216.

57. Moriya, "Gendai Nihon no seiji kikō," p. 129.

58. Space does not permit a detailed discussion of the intra-JCP controversies on the revival of Japanese imperialism and the subordination of Japan to the United States. It may be noted briefly, however, that those who saw Japan as largely independent of the United States, like Uchida Jōkichi and Satō Noboru, tended to be linked with the "structural reform" faction (see below) and believed that Japanese imperialism was reviving, and that therefore Japanese monopoly capitalism was the main enemy of socialist revolution in Japan. Those, like Toyota Shirō and Moriya Fumio, who saw Japan as very much subordinate to the United States argued that the revival of Japanese imperialism was incomplete, and thus made a stronger case for a two-stage revolution. See Kojima, *Nihon shihon-shugi ronsō shi*, pp. 251-265; and Takauchi, *Gendai Nihon shihon-shugi ronsō*, chaps. 2-5.

59. Cf. Kojima, *Nihon shihon-shugi ronsō shi*, p. 217.

60. Watanabe, "Gendai minshu-shugi hōgaku," pp. 116, 109.

61. Ibid., p. 116; Moriya, *Tennō-sei kenkyū*, pp. 252-253; and Watanabe Yōzō, *Gendai Nihon shakai to minshu-shugi*.

62. Scalapino, *Japanese Communist Movement*, pp. 102-113; *Gendai jinbutsu jiten* (Tokyo: Asahi Shinbun-sha, 1977), s.v. Kasuga Shōjirō; and interview with Ikumi Taku'ichi, Tokyo, Japan, June 17, 1982.

63. See, for example, the discussion of the impending "crisis of democracy" in Japan in Watanabe, "Gendai minshu-shugi hōgaku" passim; interview with Okudaira Yasuhiro, Tokyo, Japan, April 2, 1984; Okudaira Yasuhiro, *Hyōgen no jiyū*,

vol. 1: *Riron to rekishi* (Tokyo: Yūhikaku, 1983), pp. 336-347; and Saitō Yasuo, "Seikyō bunri no gensoku to Yasukuni jinja hōan."

64. Kajinishi Mitsuhaya, Ōshima Kiyoshi, Katō Toshihiko, and Ōuchi Tsutomu, *Nihon ni okeru shihon-shugi no hattatsu*, 13 vols., *Nihon shihon-shugi no botsuraku* [The fall of Japanese capitalism], 8 vols., vol. 5: *Dokusen shihon no fukkatsu (1945-1950): Iwayuru keizai no minshuka* [The revival of monopoly capital (1945-1950): The so-called democratization of the economy], 2d ed. (Tokyo: Tōkyō Daigaku Shuppan-kai, 1977). This was essentially the Rōnō-ha's response to the postwar *Kōza*.

65. This group, approaching the Occupation reforms from the perspective of the theory of state monopoly capitalism, is working in the form of a special committee organized at the Institute of Social Science at the University of Tokyo. Working since 1970, the committee publishes its own periodic research bulletin. (Shibagaki and Saeki, "Sengo Nihon keizai no kihon mondai," p. 53n.) This group includes those who prefer to identify themselves as members of the Uno school, formed on the basis of the work of Uno Kōzō, who belonged to neither faction in the prewar era but was closer to the Rōnō-ha and may be viewed as a descendant therefrom. There is substantial overlap between the Rōnō-ha and the Uno school. (The Uno school is discussed in more detail below.) Ōuchi Tsutomu is credited with the most systematic exposition of the theory of state monopoly capitalism. See Baba Hiroji, *Gendai shihon-shugi no tōshi*; and Baba Hiroji, "Kokka dokusen shihon-shugi ron o megutte."

66. Kajinishi et al., *Nihon shihon-shugi no botsuraku*, 5:1470-1471.

67. Ibid., pp. 1471-1472.

68. Ibid., pp. 1472-1473.

69. Ibid., pp. 1449-1450, 1451n; Uno Kōzō, "Waga nōson no hōken-sei"; and Ōuchi Hyōe, "Nōson minshuka no michi chikakarazu."

70. Kajinishi et al., *Nihon shihon-shugi no botsuraku*, 5:1451.

71. Ibid., pp. 1220-1223; and Shibagaki Kazuo, "Dissolution of Zaibatsu and Deconcentration of Economic Power," p. 52.

72. Kajinishi et al., *Nihon shihon-shugi no botsuraku*, 5:1218.

73. Shibagaki Kazuo, "The Early History of the Zaibatsu," p. 535.

74. Shibagaki, "Dissolution of Zaibatsu," pp. 50-53.

75. Kajinishi et al., *Nihon shihon-shugi no botsuraku*, 5:1218-1220.

76. See Ōuchi Tsutomu, "Sengo kaikaku e no futatsu no apurōchi," p. 180; and Shibagaki and Saeki, "Sengo Nihon keizai no kihon mondai," pp. 54-56.

77. Shibagaki, "Dissolution of Zaibatsu," p. 54.

78. Interview with Baba Hiroji, Institute of Social Science, University of Tokyo, May 1, 1984; and interview with Ukai Nobushige, Tokyo, Japan, April 27, 1984. Although in the prewar era Uno believed, along with most Marxists, that theory and practice could not be separated, in accordance with his stage theory of the development of Marxist scholarship (see below), in the postwar years he became fearful of the abuse of pure theory by political activists and disdainful of practical politicians who fancied themselves theorists. For a defense of this controversial view, see also Uno Kōzō, "Riron to jissen."

79. Makoto Itoh, *Value and Crisis*, p. 36.

80. For a brief summary of these splits in the Socialist party, see Hori Masao, "Shakai-shugi seitō to shite no sokunin," p. 4.

81. Hayano Tōru and Inaka Yoshiaki, "Sayoku riron, kenji ka tenkan ka"; and *Gendai jinbutsu jiten*, s.v. Yamakawa Hitoshi; cf. the account of Takahashi Masao, according to which the Kyōkai, under Yamakawa and Ōuchi, was originally dedicated to "social democracy" and became attached to Marxism-Leninism only after Yamakawa's death (1958), when Sakisaka succeeded to Yamakawa's leading position. Early in the 1950s, Takahashi split with Sakisaka over the latter's attachment to Marxism-Leninism and "uncritical view" of the Soviet Union. Interview with Takahashi Masao, Tokyo, Japan, May 5, 1984; and Takahashi Masao, *Happō yabure*, pp. 250-251.

82. *Nihon shakai undō jinmei jiten*, s.v. Yamakawa Hitoshi; *Gendai jinbutsu jiten*, s.v. Yamakawa Hitoshi; and J.A.A. Stockwin, " 'Positive Neutrality'—the Foreign Policy of the Japanese Socialist Party," *Asian Survey* 2.9:36-38.

83. *Gendai jinbutsu jiten*, s.v. Yamakawa Hitoshi. This concept might be compared with the views of the "structural reformists" of the JCP. However, it should be noted that the JSP's own notion of "structural reformism," articulated by Eda Saburō, was rejected. See n. 84.

84. Eda argued in favor of a gradual transformation to socialism through incremental reforms and opposed Sakisaka's peaceful revolution, which allowed the need to use police power to repress reactionary opposition after the revolution in order to hasten the transformation to complete socialism. (Interview with Ōuchi Tsutomu, Tokyo, Japan, April 27, 1984.) This view gained adherents within the party, but under pressure from the Kyōkai it was finally decisively defeated within the party by the mid-1960s. Eda finally left the party in March 1977 and formed his own Socialist Citizens' Alliance (Shakai Shimin Rengō) (*Gendai jinbutsu jiten*, s.v. Eda Saburō; Hori, "Shakai-shugi seitō," p. 6). For Sakisaka's critique of structural reformism, see the essays collected in Sakisaka Itsurō, *Nihon kakumei to Shakaitō*, chap. 4.

85. According to Takahashi, Yamakawa and Sakisaka disagreed on the universal validity of the Leninist version of Marxism (Yamakawa saw Leninism as valid only for Russia) and the assessment of the Soviet Union as a socialist society (Yamakawa argued that the October Revolution had so distorted the original Marxist perspective of history that the result was not socialism). See Takahashi Masao, *Shakaitō no himitsu*, pp. 188-189; and interview with Takahashi Masao, Tokyo, Japan, May 5, 1984.

86. See "Nihon ni okeru shakai-shugi e no michi," especially pt. 2, chaps. 1, 2; and interview with Ōuchi Tsutomu, Tokyo, Japan, April 27, 1984. For an explanation of Sakisaka's differences with the Communist Party and the Rōnō-ha roots of Kyōkai thought, see the essays collected in Sakisaka Itsurō, *Nihon Kyōsantō ron*; Sakisaka Itsurō, *Zoku Nihon Kyōsantō ron*; and interview with Sakisaka Itsurō, Tokyo, Japan, June 7, 1982; June 14, 1982.

87. Only about 2 or 3 of the Socialist Party's 156 Diet representatives belong to the Kyōkai, although many more of those now in office were once associated with it. Hayano and Inaka, "Sayoku riron"; interview with Ōuchi Tsutomu, April 27, 1984; and interview with Hori Masao, Tokyo, Japan, May 4, 1984.

88. Hayano and Inaka, "Sayoku riron"; and Hori, "Shakai-shugi seitō," pp. 6-7.

89. Interview with Ōuchi Hyōe, April 27, 1984. For a sustained critique of the *Michi* undertaken within the Workers' Self-Management Research Conference, see Baba Hiroji, " 'Nihon ni okeru shakai-shugi e no michi' hihan."

90. Others who left the Kyōkai with Fukuda include Kamakura Takai (Saitama University), Misono Hitoshi (Tokyo Keizai Daigaku), Nagasaka Satoshi (Ōita Daigakuin, Kyūshū), Isayama Tadashi (Niigata University), and Yoshida Shintarō (Tōhoku University). (Interview with Ōuchi Tsutomu, Tokyo, Japan, April 27, 1984; and Hayano and Inaka, "Sayoku riron.") At the same time, Takahashi Masao, long a critic of Sakisaka, is also engaged in a similar enterprise, along with another group of scholars. (Interview with Takahashi Masao, Tokyo, Japan, May 5, 1984.)

91. Interview with Ōuchi Tsutomu, April 27, 1984; interview with Hori Masao, May 4, 1984; and interview with Minobe Ryōkichi, May 7, 1984.

92. Itōh, *Value and Crisis*, p. 38.

93. Baba Hiroji, "Uno riron to gendai shihon-shugi ron," pp. 172-173. See Uno Kōzō, *Keizai genron*; Uno Kōzō, *Kachi-ron*; Uno Kōzō, *Kyōkō-ron*; and Uno Kōzō, *Shihon-ron no keizaigaku*.

94. Uno Kōzō, *Keizai seisaku ron*; Ōuchi Shūmei, Kamakura Takao, Hayashi Takehisa, and Saeki Naomi, *Uno Kōzō*, chap. 2; and interview with Hayashi Takehisa, Tokyo, Japan, June 16, 1982.

95. Baba, "Uno riron," pp. 175-179.

96. Ibid., pp. 180-181. See, for example, Ōuchi's *Nihon shihon-shugi no nōgyō mondai*, the recipient of a publication award from Mainichi Press; Ōuchi Tsutomu, *Nihon nōgyō no zaisei-gaku*; and Ōuchi Tsutomu, *Nōgyō kyōkō ron*.

97. Baba, "Uno riron," pp. 186-190.

98. See the discussion of the work of the Uno school on this concept in Itoh, *Value and Crisis*, chap. 2.

99. See the introduction to Immanuel Wallerstein, *The Modern World-System: Capitalist Agriculture and the Origins of the European World-Economy in the Sixteenth Century* (New York: Academic Press, 1974); and Samir Amin, *Unequal Development: An Essay on the Social Formations of Peripheral Capitalism*, trans. Brian Pearce (New York: Monthly Review Press, 1976), chap. 4.

100. See Takahashi Kōhachirō, *Kindai shakai seiritsu shi ron*; and Takahashi Kōhachirō, *Shimin shakai no kōzō*.

101. Takahashi Kōhachirō, "A Contribution to the Discussion," in *The Transition from Feudalism to Capitalism*, ed. Rodney Hilton, pp. 88-89.

102. Maurice Dobb, "A Reply," in *Transition from Feudalism to Capitalism*, ed. Hilton, p. 64.

103. Takahashi, "Contribution to the Discussion," p. 88.

104. See Ōtsuka Hisao, *Kindai Ōshū keizai shi josetsu*; and Ōtsuka Hisao, "Nōson no orimoto to tōshi no orimoto."

105. Takahashi, "Contribution to the Discussion," p. 95.

106. Ibid., pp. 95-96.

107. Ibid., p. 96.

108. Ibid., pp. 96 and 74.

SELECT BIBLIOGRAPHY

Foreign Language Sources

BOOKS

Aikawa Haruki. *Rekishi kagaku no hōhōron* [The methodology of historical science]. Tokyo: Hakuyō-sha, 1935.

Amano Keitarō. *Kawakami Hajime bunkenshi* [A bibliography of the writings of Dr. Hajime Kawakami]. Tokyo: Nihon Hyōron Shinsha, 1956.

Ara Kenjirō, Uchida Tadao, and Fukuoka Masao, comps. *Keizai jiten* [Dictionary of economics]. Tokyo: Kōdan-sha Gakujutsu Bunko, 1980.

Arahata Kanson. *Hidari no menmen—Jinbutsu ron* [Men of the left]. Tokyo: Hayakawa Shobō, 1951.

———. *Kanson jiden* [Autobiography of (Arahata) Kanson]. 2 vols. Tokyo: Iwanami Shoten, Iwanami Bunko, 1975.

———. *Kyōsantō o meguru hitobito* [Men around the Communist Party]. [Tokyo]: Kōbundō, 1950.

———. *Nihon shakai-shugi undō shi* [History of the Japanese socialist movement]. Tokyo: Mainichi Shinbun-sha, 1948.

———. *Roshia ni hairu* [Going to Russia]. Tokyo: Kibōkaku, 1924.

Baba Hiroji. *Gendai shihon-shugi no tōshi* [An examination of contemporary capitalism]. Tokyo: Tōkyō Daigaku Shuppan-kai, 1981.

Eguchi Bokurō. *Teikoku-shugi to minzoku* [Imperialism and nations]. Tokyo: Tōkyō Daigaku Shuppan-kai, 1954.

Fujita Shōzō. *Tenkō no shisō shi-teki kenkyū—Sono ichi sokumen* [The intellectual historical study of *tenkō*: One aspect]. Tokyo: Iwanami Shoten, 1975.

———. *Tennō-sei kokka no shihai genri* [The ruling principles of the emperor-system state]. 2d ed. Tokyo: Mirai-sha, 1978.

Fujiwara Akira. *Gunjishi: Nihon gendai shi taikei* [Military history: Outline of Japan's contemporary history]. Tokyo: N.p., 1961.

Hani Gorō. *Hani Gorō rekishi ron chosaku shū* [Collected historical writings of Hani Gorō]. 4 vols. Tokyo: Aoki Shoten, 1967.

———. *Hani Gorō senshū* [Selected writings of Hani Gorō]. 2 vols. Tokyo: Iwasaki Shoten, 1950.

———. *Meiji ishin shi kenkyū* [Studies on the history of the Meiji Restoration]. Tokyo: Iwanami Shoten, Iwanami Bunko, 1978.

Hattori Shisō. *Hattori Shisō chosaku shū* [Collected works of Hattori Shisō]. 7 vols. Tokyo: Riron-sha, 1955, 1960.

———. *Ishin shi no hōhōron* [Methodology of the history of the Restoration]. Tokyo: Hakuyō-sha, 1933.

———. *Meiji ishin shi* [History of the Meiji Restoration]. Tokyo: Sanryū Shobō, 1948.

Hattori Shisō. *Meiji ishin shi kenkyū* [Studies on the history of the Meiji Restoration]. N.p.: Sanwa Shoten, 1947; Kureha Shoten, 1948.

Hayakawa Jirō. *Hayakawa Jirō chosaku shū* [Collected writings of Hayakawa Jirō]. 4 vols. Tokyo: Mirai-sha, 1977.

Hayashi Shigeru and Nishida Taketoshi, comps. *Heimin shinbun ronsetsu shū* [Collected articles of the *Heimin shinbun*]. Tokyo: Iwanami Shoten, Iwanami Bunko, 1961.

He Ganzhi. *Zhongguo shehui shi wenti lunzhan* [The controversy on problems in Chinese social history]. Qingnian zixue congshu, no. 3. Shanghai: Shenghuo Shudian, 1937.

Hirano Yoshitarō. *Burujoa minshu-shugi kakumei: Sono shi-teki hatten* [The bourgeois-democratic revolution: Its historical development]. Hirano Yoshitarō ronbun shū [Collected works of Hirano Yoshitarō]. Tokyo: Nihon Hyōron-sha, 1948.

———. *Dai Ajia-shugi no rekishi-teki kiso* [The historical basis of Pan-Asianism]. Tokyo: Kawade Shobō, 1945.

———. *Kokka kenryoku no kōzō* [The structure of state power]. Hirano Yoshitarō shin chosaku shū—Minzoku kaihō no riron-teki sho mondai [New collected works of Hirano Yoshitaro: Theoretical problems of national liberation], no. 2. [Tokyo]: Riron-sha, 1954.

———. *Kokka—Sono genjitsu to henkaku* [The state: Its reality and revolution]. Tokyo: Hōritsu Bunka-sha, 1973.

———. *Nihon shihon-shugi shakai no kikō—Shi-teki katei yori no kyūmei* [The structure of Japanese capitalist society: An inquiry from the (perspective of the) historical process]. Tokyo: Iwanami Shoten, 1934, 1949, 1959.

———. *Nihon shihon-shugi shakai no mujun* [Contradictions in Japanese capitalist society]. Hirano Yoshitarō shin chosaku shū—Minzoku kaihō no riron-teki mondai [New collected works of Hirano Yoshitarō: Theoretical problems of national liberation], no. 1. [Tokyo]: Riron-sha, 1954.

Honjō Eijirō. *Nihon shakai shi* [History of Japanese society]. N.p., 1924.

Horie Hide'ichi. *Kindai sangyō shi kenkyū* [Studies in the history of modern industry]. Tokyo: Nihon Hyōron-sha, 1948.

Hōsei Daigaku. Ōhara Shakai Mondai Kenkyūjo [Ōhara Institute for the Study of Social Problems], comp. *Rōnō/Zen'ei: bekkan* [*Rōnō* and *Zen'ei*: Supplement]. Nihon shakai undō shiryō [Historical materials on Japan's social movement]. Tokyo: Hōsei Daigaku Shuppan-kyoku, 1982.

Ichikawa Shōichi. *Nihon Kyōsantō tōsō shōshi* [A brief history of the struggle of the Japanese Communist Party]. N.p., 1945.

Imai Sei'ichi. *Taishō demokurashii* [Taishō democracy]. Vol. 23 of *Nihon no rekishi* [A history of Japan]. Tokyo: Chūō Kōron-sha, Chūkō Bunko ed., 1974.

Inomata Tsunao. *Botsuraku shihon-shugi no daisan ki—Nihon shihon-shugi wa botsuraku shinai ka* [The third stage of declining capitalism: Will Japanese capitalism collapse?]. N.p.: Taishū Kōron-sha, 1930.

———. *Gendai Nihon kenkyū—Marukishizumu no tachiba yori* [Studies on contemporary Japan: From a Marxist perspective]. Tokyo: Kaizō-sha, 1929, 1934.

———. *Kin'yū shihon ron (1925)* [The theory of finance capital]. Tokyo: Shōkō Shoin, 1948.

———. *Kyokutō ni okeru teikoku-shugi* [Imperialism in the Far East]. Keizai-gaku zenshū [Complete economic writings], no. 24. Tokyo: Kaizō-sha, 1932.

———. *Nihon musan kaikyū no senryaku* [The strategy of the Japanese proletariat]. N.p.: Bungei Sensen Shuppan-bu, n.d.

———. *Nihon musan kaikyū undō no hihan: Kominterun no hihan o yomite* [A critique of the Japanese proletarian movement: Reading the Comintern's criticism]. Musan-sha panfuretto [Musan-sha pamphlet], no. 16. N.p.: Musan-sha, 1928.

———. *Nihon no dokusen shihon-shugi: Kin'yū shihon no kyōkō taisaku* [Japanese monopoly capitalism: Finance capital's policy toward the panic]. Tokyo: Nanboku Shoin, 1932.

———. *Nihon puroretariāto no senryaku to senjutsu: Zasshi ''Rōnō'' keisei ronbun shū* [The strategy and tactics of the Japanese proletariat: Collected essays published in the magazine *Rōnō*]. Tokyo: Tosho Shinbun-sha, 1973.

———. *Nōson mondai nyūmon* [Introduction to the agrarian problem]. Tokyo: Chūō Kōron-sha, 1937; Kōdo-sha, 1948.

———. *Teikoku-shugi kenkyū* [Studies on imperialism]. Tokyo: Kaizō-sha, 1928.

Ishida Takeshi. *Kindai Nihon seiji kōzō no kenkyū* [Studies on the structure of contemporary Japanese politics]. Tokyo: Mirai-sha, 1956.

———. *Meiji seiji shisō shi kenkyū* [Studies in the history of Meiji political thought]. Tokyo: Mirai-sha, 1954.

———. *Nihon kindai shisō shi ni okeru hō to seiji* [Law and politics in the history of modern Japanese thought]. Tokyo: Iwanami Shoten, 1976.

Ishidō Kiyotomo and Yamabe Kentarō, comps. *Kominterun Nihon ni kansuru tēze shū* [Collected Comintern theses on Japan]. Tokyo: Aoki Shoten, Aoki Bunko, 1961.

Iwanami kōza: Nihon rekishi [Iwanami symposium: Japanese history]. Vol. 16: *Kindai* [The modern age]. Tokyo: Iwanami Shoten, 1962.

Kajinishi Mitsuhaya, Ōshima Kiyoshi, Katō Toshihiko, and Ōuchi Tsutomu. *Nihon ni okeru shihon-shugi no hattatsu* [The development of capitalism in Japan]. 13 vols. Tokyo: Tōkyō Daigaku Shuppan-kai, 1977.

Kakei Katsuhiko. *Dai Nihon teikoku kenpō no konpon gi* [The basic meaning of the constitution of the Greater Japanese Empire]. N.p., N.d.

Kamiyama Shigeo. *Kokka riron* [The theory of the state]. Tokyo: Iwasaki Shoten, 1950.

———. *Tennō-sei ni kansuru riron-teki sho mondai* [Theoretical problems concerning the emperor system]. Rev. and enlgd. ed. Tokyo: Minshu Hyōron-sha, 1956.

Katayama Sen. *Waga shakai-shugi* [My socialism]. N.p., 1903.

Katsumata Sei'ichi and Kitayama Airō, comps. *Nihon Shakaitō kōryō bunken shū* [Collected documents of the Japanese Socialist Party]. Tokyo: Nihon Shakaitō Chūō Honbu Kikanshi-kyoku, 1978.

Kawakami Hajime. *Jijōden* [Autobiography]. 5 vols. Tokyo: Iwanami Shoten, 1952.

———. *Kawakami Hajime yori Kushida Tamizō e no tegami* [Letters from Kawakami Hajime to Kushida Tamizō]. Edited by Ōuchi Hyōe and Ōshima Kiyoshi. Tokyo: Hōsei Daigaku Shuppan-kyoku, 1974.

———. *Omoide* [Memoirs]. N.p.: Nihon Minshu-shugi Bunka Renmei, 1946.

Kawakami Hajime and Ōyama Ikuo, comps. *Marukusu-shugi kōza* [Symposium on Marxism]. 13 vols. N.p.: Seiji Hihan-sha, 1927-1929.

Kazama Jōkichi. *Mosukō to tsunagaru Nihon Kyōsantō no rekishi* [History of the Japanese Communist Party in relationship to Moscow]. Edited by Sano Manabu and Nabeyama Sadachika. Tokyo: Fuman-sha, 1951.

Kida Jun'ichirō. *Meiji no risō* [Ideals of the Meiji period]. Tokyo: San'ichi Shobō, 1965.

Kikuchi Masanori. *Roshia kakumei to Nihonjin* [The Russian Revolution and the Japanese]. Tokyo: Chikuma Shobō, 1973.

Kita Ikki. *Kita Ikki chosaku shū* [Collected works of Kita Ikki]. 3 vols. Tokyo: Misuzu Shobō, 1959, 1972.

Kobayashi Morito. *Tenkōsha no shisō to seikatsu* [The thought and lives of *tenkōsha*]. Tokyo: Daidō-sha, 1935.

Kojima Hinehisa. *Nihon shihon-shugi ronsō shi* [History of the debate on Japanese capitalism]. Tokyo: Arisue, 1976.

Kondō Eizō. *Kominterun no misshi: Nihon Kyōsantō sosei hiwa* [Secret agent of the Comintern: The secret history of the creation of the Japanese Communist Party]. Tokyo: Bunka Hyōron-sha, 1949.

———. *Kondō Eizō jiden* [Autobiography of Kondō Eizō]. Kyoto: Hiei Shobō, 1970.

Kondō Kenji. *Ichi museifu-shugisha no kaisō* [Memoirs of an anarchist]. Tokyo: Heibon-sha, 1965.

Kōtoku Shūsui. *Shakai-shugi shinzui* [The essence of socialism]. 1903. Reprint, Tokyo: Iwanami Shoten, Iwanami Bunko, 1953.

Kovalev, S. I. et al. *Istorija drevnevo mira* [History of the ancient world]. Part 1, *Drevnij Vostok i Gretsija* [The ancient East and Greece]. Moscow: N.p., 1935.

Koyama Hirotake. *Minshu kakumei ronsō shi* [History of the debate on the democratic revolution]. Tokyo: Itō Shoten, 1947.

———. *Nihon Marukusu-shugi shi* [History of Japanese Marxism]. Tokyo: Aoki Shoten, 1956.

———. *Nihon shihon-shugi ronsō no shin dankai* [The current stage in the debate on Japanese capitalism]. Tokyo: Aoki Shoten, 1956.

———. *Nihon shihon-shugi ronsō shi* [History of the debate on Japanese capitalism]. 2 vols. Tokyo: Aoki Shoten, 1953.

Koyama Hirotake and Kishimoto Eitarō. *Nihon no hikyōsantō Marukusu-shugisha: Yamakawa Hitoshi no shōgai to shisō* [Japanese non-Communist party Marxist: The life and thought of Yamakawa Hitoshi]. Tokyo: San'ichi Shobō, 1962.

Kōza Gendai Nihon to Marukusu-shugi [Symposium: Contemporary Japan and Marxism]. 4 vols. Tokyo: Aoki Shoten, 1966.

Kuno Osamu and Tsurumi Shunsuke. *Gendai Nihon no shisō: Sono itsutsu no uzu* [Contemporary Japanese thought: Five whirlpools]. Tokyo: Iwanami Shoten, 1956; Iwanami Shinsho, 1978.

Kushida Tamizō. *Kushida Tamizō zenshū* [Complete writings of Kushida Tamizō]. 5 vols. N.p., 1935.

Mad'iar, L. *Ekonomika sel'skovo khoziajstva v Kitae* [The economy of agriculture in China]. Moscow and Leningrad: N.p., 1928.

———. *Ocherki po ekonomike Kitaja* [Studies on the economy of China]. N.p., 1930.

———. *Sovremennoe sosto'janie kitajskoj revoljutsii: Discussija v Kommunisticheskoj Akademii* [The present status of the Chinese revolution: Discussion at the Communist Academy]. Moscow: N.p., 1929.

Matsuzawa Hiroaki. *Nihon shakai-shugi no shisō* [Japanese socialist thought]. Tokyo: Chikuma Shobō, 1973.

Minobe Tatsukichi. *Kenpō satsuyō* [Outline of the constitution]. Tokyo: Yūhikaku, 1924.

Miyazawa Toshiyoshi. *Tennō-kikan setsu jiken—shiryō wa kataru* [The emperor-organ theory incident: The historical record speaks]. 2 vols. Tokyo: Yūhikaku, 1970.

Moritani Katsumi. *Ajia-teki seisan-yōshiki ron* [On the Asiatic mode of production]. Tokyo: Ikusei-sha, 1937.

Moriya Fumio. *Nanajū nendai igo no Nihon shihon-shugi* [Japanese capitalism since the 1970s]. Nagoya: Shinshū Shirakaba, 1984.

———. *Nihon Marukusu-shugi no rekishi to hansei* [The history of and reflections on Japanese Marxism]. Tokyo: Gōdō Shuppan, 1980.

———. *Nihon Marukusu-shugi riron no keisei to hatten* [The formation and development of Japanese Marxist theory]. Tokyo: Aoki Shoten, 1967.

———. *Nihon shihon-shugi hattatsu shi* [The history of the development of Japanese capitalism]. Tokyo: Aoki Shoten, 1969.

———. *Nihon shihon-shugi shōshi* [A brief history of Japanese capitalism]. 2 vols. Tokyo: Shin Nihon Shuppan-sha, 1974.

———. *Sengo Nihon shihon-shugi—Sono bunseki to hihan* [Postwar Japanese capitalism—An analysis and a critique]. Tokyo: Aoki Shoten, 1971.

———. *Tennō-sei kenkyū* [Studies on the emperor system]. Tokyo: Aoki Shoten, 1979.

Nabeyama Sadachika. *Watakushi wa Kyōsantō o suteta—Jiyū to sokoku o motomete* [I abandoned the Communist Party: Seeking freedom and the fatherland]. Tokyo: Daitō Shuppan-sha, 1949.

Nihon Kyōsantō. *Nihon Kyōsantō no rokujū nen* [Sixty years of the Japanese Communist Party]. 2 vols. and supplemental chronology. Tokyo: Shin Nihon Bunko, 1983.

Nihon no rekishi [A history of Japan]. 26 vols. Tokyo: Chūō Kōron-sha, Chūkō Bunko, 1974.

Nihon shakai undō jinmei jiten [Biographical dictionary of Japan's social movement]. Tokyo: Aoki Shoten, 1979.

Nihon shihon-shugi hattatsu shi kōza [Symposium on the history of the development of Japanese capitalism]. 7 vols. and supplement. Tokyo: Iwanami Shoten, 1932-1933, reissued, 1982.

Nihon shihon-shugi kōza [Symposium on Japanese capitalism]. Tokyo: Iwanami Shoten, 1953-1955.

Nikiforov, V. N. *Sovetskie istoriki o problemax Kitaja* [Soviet historians on problems of China]. Moscow: N.p., N.d.

Noro Eitarō. *Nihon shihon-shugi hattatsu shi* [History of the development of Japanese capitalism]. Tokyo: Tettō Shoin, 1930; Iwanami Shoten, Iwanami Bunko, 1954.

———. *Noro Eitarō zenshū* [Complete writings of Noro Eitarō]. 2 vols. Tokyo: Shin Nihon Shuppan-kai, 1965.

———. *Puchi teikoku-shugi ron hihan* [Critique of the theory of petty imperialism]. Tokyo: San'ichi Shobō, 1949.

Onabe Teruhiko. *Nijū seiki* [''The Twentieth Century'']. Vol. 4: *Meiji no hikari to kage* [Light and shadows of the Meiji period]. Tokyo: Chūō Kōron-sha, 1978.

Ōtsuka Hisao. *Kindai Ōshū keizai shi josetsu* [Introduction to the economic history of modern Europe]. N.p., 1944.

Ōuchi Hyōe, Sakisaka Itsurō, Tsuchiya Takao, and Takahashi Masao. *Nihon shihon-shugi no kenkyū* [Studies on Japanese capitalism]. 2 vols. Tokyo: Kōdo-sha, 1948.

Ōuchi Shūmei, Kamakura Takao, Hayashi Takehisa, and Saeki Naomi. *Uno Kōzō: Chosaku to shisō* [Uno Kōzō: His works and thought]. Tokyo: Yūhikaku Shinsho, 1979.

Ōuchi Tsutomu. *Fashizumu e no michi*. Vol. 24 of *Nihon no rekıshi* [A history of Japan]. Tokyo: Chūō Kōron-sha, Chūkō Bunko, 1974.

———. *Nihon shihon-shugi no nōgyō mondai* [The agrarian problem of Japanese capitalism]. Tokyo: Nihon Hyōron-sha, 1949.

———. *Nihon nōgyō no zaisei-gaku* [The study of the finance of Japanese agriculture]. N.p., 1950.

———. *Nōgyō kyōkō ron* [Theory of agricultural crisis]. N.p., 1954.

Rekishi Kyōiku Kenkyūjo, comp. *Nihon shi jiten* [Encyclopedia of Japanese history]. Tokyo: Ōbun-sha, 1978.

Sakai Toshihiko. *Sakai Toshihiko zenshū* [Complete works of Sakai Toshihiko]. 6 vols. Tokyo: Chūō Kōron-sha, 1933.

Sakai Toshihiko and Morichika Unpei. *Shakai-shugi kōryō* [The socialist program]. N.p., 1907.

Sakisaka Itsurō. *Jidai-ron kenkyū* [Studies on the theory of ground rent]. Tokyo: Kaizō-sha, 1948.

———. *Nihon kakumei to Shakaitō* [The Japanese revolution and the Socialist Party]. Tokyo: Nihon Shakai-shugi Kyōkai, 1972.

———. *Nihon Kyōsantō ron* [On the Japanese Communist Party]. Tokyo: Shakai-shugi Kyōkai, 1973.

———. *Nihon shihon-shugi no sho mondai* [Problems of Japanese capitalism]. [Tokyo]: Kōdo-sha, 1948; Shakai-shugi Kyōkai Shuppan-kyoku, 1976.

———. *Zoku Nihon Kyōsantō ron* [More on the Japanese Communist Party]. Tokyo: Shakai-shugi Kyōkai, 1974.

Sano Manabu. *Minzoku to kaikyū* [Nation/race and class]. Minshu shiriizu [Democracy series], no. 3. Tokyo: Kinrō Jihōsha, 1949.

———. *Nihon keizai-shi gairon* [Outline of Japanese economic history]. [Waseda Taibun-sha], 1923.

———. *Seiji-ron* [Political essays]. Sano Manabu gakushū [Collected studies of Sano Manabu], no. 4. [Tokyo]: Kibōkaku, 1930.

Shakai-kagaku jiten [Dictionary of social science]. Tokyo: Shin Nihon Shuppan-sha, 1978.

Shakai Keizai Rōdō Kenkyūjo, ed. *Nihon shihon-shugi ronsō shi* [History of the debate on Japanese capitalism]. Tokyo: Itō Shoten, 1947.

Shakai-shugi Kyōkai tēze [Theses of the Socialist Association]. Tokyo: Shakai-shugi Kyōkai, 1971.

Shiga Yoshio. *Kokka ron* [The theory of the state]. Nauka bunko [Nauka library], no. 10. Tokyo: Nauka-sha, 1949.

———. *Sekai to Nihon* [The world and Japan]. N.p.: Gyōmyō-sha, 1948.

Shinobu Seizaburō. *Kindai Nihon sangyō shi josetsu* [Preface to the history of modern Japanese industry]. Tokyo: Nihon Hyōron-sha, 1942.

———. *Nihon no dokusen shihon-shugi* [Japan's monopoly capitalism]. Tokyo: Aoki Shoten, 1948.

———. *Taishō demokurashii shi* [History of Taishō democracy]. Tokyo: Keisō shobō, 1968.

———. *Taishō seiji shi* [History of Taishō politics]. Tokyo: Keisō Shobō, 1968.

Shōwa Kenkyūkai. *Burokku keizai ni kansuru kenkyū* [Studies on the bloc economy]. Tokyo: Seikatsu-sha, 1939.

Sovēto Marukusu-shugi Tōyō Gakusha Kyōkai [Association of Soviet Marxist Scholars of the Orient], comp. *Ajia-teki seisan yōshiki ni tsuite* [On the Asiatic mode of production]. Translated by Hayakawa Jirō. Tokyo: Hakuyō-sha, 1933, 1948.

Sumiya Etsuji. *Nihon keizaigaku shi* [History of Japanese economics]. Kyoto: N.p., 1958.

Suzuki Yasuzō. *Kenpō seitai to Roesureru* [Roesler and the framing of the constitution]. Tokyo: Tōyō Keizai Shinpō-sha, 1942.

———. *Nihon kenpō-gaku shi kenkyū* [Studies in the history of Japanese constitutional law]. Tokyo: Keisō Shobō, 1975.

Takahashi Kamekichi. *Gendai Nihon keizai no kenkyū* [Studies on the contemporary Japanese economy]. Tokyo: Kaizō-sha, 1927.

———. *Kyōeiken keizai kensetsu ron* [The theory of the economic construction of the Co-Prosperity Sphere]. Tokyo: Tōshi-keizai-sha, 1942.

———. *Makki no Nihon shihon-shugi keizai to sono tenkan* [The last stage of Japan's capitalist economy and its conversion]. Tokyo: Hakuyō-sha, 1925.

———. *Meiji Taishō nōson keizai no hensen* [Changes in the Meiji and Taishō rural economy]. Tokyo: Tōyō Keizai Shinpō-sha, 1926.

———. *Nihon keizai no kaibō* [An analysis of Japan's economy]. Tokyo: Tōyō Keizai Shinpō-sha, 1925.

———. *Nihon keizai no yukizumari to musan-kaikyū no taisaku* [The deadlock of the Japanese economy and the countermeasures of the proletariat]. Tokyo: Hakuyō-sha, 1926.

———. *Nihon senji keikaku keizai ron* [The economic theory of Japan's wartime planning]. Tokyo: Chikura Shobō, 1939.

———. *Nihon shihon-shugi hattatsu shi* [History of the development of Japanese capitalism]. Rev. and enlgd. ed. Tokyo: Nihon Hyōron-sha, 1929.

———. *Nihon shihon-shugi keizai no kenkyū* [Studies on the Japanese capitalist economy]. Tokyo: Hakuyō-sha, 1924.

———. *Nihon zaibatsu no kaibō* [An analysis of Japanese zaibatsu]. Tokyo: Chūō Kōron-sha, 1930.

———. *Sayoku undō no riron-teki hōkai—Uyoku undō no riron-teki konkyo* [The theoretical collapse of the left-wing movement—The theoretical basis of the right-wing movement]. Tokyo: Hakuyō-sha, 1927.

———. *Senji keikaku keizai no tenkai to bukka tōsei* [The development of the war-planning economy and commodity price control]. Tokyo: Chikura Shobō, 1939.

———. *Senji keizai no gensei to infure mondai* [The present state of the wartime economy and the inflation problem]. Tokyo: Chikura Shobō, 1940.

———. *Senji keizai tōsei no gendankai to sono zento* [The present stage of wartime economic control and its future prospects]. Tokyo: Chikura Shobō, 1938.

———. *Senji keizai to shin keizai taisei* [The wartime economy and the new economic system]. Tokyo: Kōdan-sha, 1940.

———. *Sensō to Nihon keizairyoku* [War and Japanese economic power]. Tokyo: Chikura Shobō, 1937.

———. *Shihon-shugi makki no kenkyū* [Studies on the late stage of capitalism]. Tokyo: Kaizō-sha, 1927.

———. *Shina keizai no hōkai to Nihon* [The collapse of the Chinese economy and Japan]. Tokyo: Chikura Shobō, 1936.

———. *Shin dankai no Nihon keizai seisaku* [Japan's economic policy in the new period]. Tokyo: Chikura Shobō, 1935.

———. *Taishō-Shōwa zaikai hendōshi* [History of economic fluctuations in the Taishō and Shōwa periods]. Tokyo: Tōyō Keizai Shinpō-sha, 1954-1955.

———. *Takahashi keizai riron keisei no rokujū nen* [Sixty years in the formation of Takahashi (Kamekichi's) economic theory]. 2 vols. Tokyo: Tōshi Keizai-sha, 1976.

———. *Tō-A keizai burokku ron* [The theory of the East Asian economic bloc]. Tokyo: Chikura Shobō, 1939.

Takahashi Kōhachirō. *Kindai shakai seiritsu shiron* [A historical treatise on the establishment of modern society]. Tokyo: Ochanomizu Shobō, 1947, 1953.

———. *Shimin shakai no kōzō* [The structure of bourgeois society]. Rev. and enlgd. ed. Tokyo: Ochanomizu Shobō, 1980.

Takahashi Masao. *Happō yabure: Watakushi no shakai-shugi* [Breakdown on all sides: My socialism]. Tokyo: TBS Buritanika (Britannica), 1980.

———. *Shakaitō no himitsu* [Secrets of the Socialist Party]. Tokyo: Chōbun-sha, 1981.

Takauchi Shun'ichi. *Gendai Nihon shihon-shugi ronsō* [The contemporary debate on Japanese capitalism]. Tokyo: San'ichi Shobō, 1973.

Takeuchi Yoshitomo, ed. *Marukishizumu* [Marxism]. Gendai Nihon shisō taikei [Outline of contemporary Japanese thought], no. 21. Tokyo: Chikuma Shobō, 1965.

Takimura Ryūichi. *Ajia-teki kokka to kakumei* [The Asiatic state and revolution]. Tokyo: San'ichi Shobō, 1978.

Tanaka Masato. *Takabatake Motoyuki: Nihon no kokka shakai-shugi* [Takabatake Motoyuki: Japanese national socialism]. Tokyo: Gendai Hyōron-sha, 1978.

Tanaka Sōgorō. *Tennō no kenkyū* [Studies on the emperor]. Tokyo: San'ichi Shobō, 1974.

Tateyama Taka'aki. *Nihon Kyōsantō kenkyo hishi* [Secret history of the arrests of the Japanese Communist Party]. Tokyo: Bukyō-sha, 1929.

Toyoda Shirō. *Shakai keizaishigaku no konpon mondai* [Fundamental problems in the study of social and economic history]. Tokyo: Kenshin-sha, 1949.

Tsuchiya Takao. *Nihon shihon-shugi shi ronshū* [Collected essays on the history of Japanese capitalism]. Tokyo: Ikusei-sha, 1937.

Tsuchiya Takao and Okazaki Saburō. *Nihon shihon-shugi hattatsu shi gaisetsu* [Outline of the history of the development of Japanese capitalism]. Tokyo: Yūhikaku, 1937, 1948.

Tsushima Tadayuki. *"Nihon shihon-shugi ronsō" shiron* [Treatise on the "debate on Japanese capitalism"]. Tokyo: Kōdo-sha, 1947.

Uchida Jōkichi and Nakano Jirō. *Nihon shihon-shugi ronsō: Rekishi hen* [The debate on Japanese capitalism: A historical volume]. Rev. and enlgd. ed. Tokyo: Shinkō Shuppan-sha, 1952.

Uesugi Shinkichi. *Kenpō jutsugi* [Explication of the constitution]. Tokyo: Yūhikaku, 1913.

———. *Kokutai kenpō oyobi kensei* [The *kokutai* constitution and constitutional government]. Tokyo: Yūhikaku, 1916.

Uno Kōzō. *Kachi-ron* [The theory of value]. Tokyo: Kawade Shobō, 1947.

———. *Keizai genron* [Principles of political economy]. 2 vols. Tokyo: Iwanami Shoten, 1950-1952.

———. *Keizai seisaku ron* [Theory of economic policy]. Tokyo: Kōbundō Shobō, 1935.

———. *Kyōkō-ron* [The theory of crisis]. Tokyo: Iwanami Shoten, 1953.

———. *Nōgyō mondai joron* [Preface to the agrarian problem]. Tokyo: Kaizō-sha, 1947.

———. *Shihon-ron no keizaigaku* [The economics of *Capital*]. Tokyo: Iwanami Shoten, Iwanami Shinsho, 1969.

Watanabe Yōzō. *Gendai Nihon shakai to minshu-shugi* [Contemporary Japanese society and democracy]. Tokyo: Iwanami Shinsho, 1982.

Yamada Moritarō. *Nihon shihon-shugi bunseki: Nihon shihon-shugi ni okeru saiseisan katei ha'aku* [An analysis of Japanese capitalism: A grasp of the reproductive process in Japanese capitalism]. Tokyo: Iwanami Shoten, 1934, 1949.

Yamakawa Hitoshi. *Yamakawa Hitoshi jiden* [Autobiography of Yamakawa Hitoshi]. Edited by Yamakawa Kikue and Sakisaka Itsurō. Tokyo: Iwanami Shoten, 1961.

———. *Yamakawa Hitoshi shū* [Collected works of Yamakawa Hitoshi]. Edited by Takabatake Michitoshi. Kindai Nihon shisō taikei [Outline of modern Japanese thought], no. 19. Tokyo: Chikuma Shobō, 1976.

———. *Yamakawa Hitoshi zenshū* [Complete works of Yamakawa Hitoshi]. Tokyo: Keisō Shobō, 1966.

ARTICLES

Aikawa Haruki. " 'Ajia-teki seisan yōshiki' ni kansuru dansho (A)" [Fragment on the "Asiatic mode of production" (A)] (May/June 1934). In *Rekishi kagaku no hōhōron* [The methodology of historical science], pp. 240-279. Tokyo: Hakuyō-sha, 1935.

———. "Ajia-teki seisan yōshiki no Nihon rekishi e no 'tekiyō' ron ni kanren shite: Hayakawa-shi shoron no hōhōron-teki na ginmi" [On the theory of the "application" of the Asiatic mode of production to Japanese history: A methodological look at Hayakawa's argument]. *Rekishi kagaku* [Historical science] 2 (May 1933): 40-48.

———. " 'Ajia-teki seisan yōshiki' no riron no handō-sei" [The reactionary nature of the theory of the "Asiatic mode of production"]. *Shakai* [Society] (April 1933).

———. " 'Ajia-teki seisan yōshiki' to Nihon hōken-sei ni kansuru ronsō" (1) ["The Asiatic mode of production" and the debate on Japanese feudalism]. *Rekishi kagaku* [Historical science] 2.8 (October 1933).

———. "Dorei-sei narabi ni hōken-sei no 'Ajia-teki' keitai" [The slave system and the "Asiatic" form of feudalism]. In *Rekishi kagaku no hōhōron* [The methodology of historical science], pp. 281-290. Tokyo: Hakuyō-sha, 1935.

———. "Hanchū to shite no 'Ajia-teki seisan yōshiki' " [The "Asiatic mode of production" as a category]. In *Rekishi kagaku no hōhōron* [The methodology of historical science], pp. 263-279. Tokyo: Hakuyō-sha, 1935.

———. "Nihon dorei-sei ni kansuru kiso ronten—Awasete dorei-sei no 'tōyō-teki keitai' hihan" [Basic points at issue concerning Japanese slavery: With a critique of the "oriental form" of slavery]. In *Rekishi kagaku no hōhōron* [The methodology of historical science], pp. 329-352. Tokyo: Hakuyō-sha, 1935.

———. "Nōson keizai to nōgyō kyōkō" [The agrarian economy and the agricultural recession]. In *Nihon shihon-shugi hattatsu shi kōza* [Symposium on the history of the development of Japanese capitalism], vol. 7. Tokyo: Iwanami Shoten, 1932-1933; reprint ed., 1982.

———. "Tokugawa hōken-sei no hōkai katei" [The process of the collapse of Tokugawa feudalism]. *Rekishi kagaku* [Historical science] (February 1934).

Akamatsu Katsumaro. "Nihon shihon-shugi hattatsu no tokushusei to musan-kaikyū seitō" [The peculiarities of Japanese capitalist development and the proletarian political party]. *Shinjin* [New man] (September 1924).

Akizawa Shūji. "Dorei shoyūsha-teki shakai keizai kōsei no igi: Dorei-sei no Nihon-teki keitai" [The significance of the slaveowner socio-economic formation:

The Japanese form of slavery], pt. 1. *Keizai hyōron* [Economic review] 2.16 (December 1935): 2-26.

———. "Dorei shoyūsha-teki shakai keizai kōsei no igi: Dorei-sei no Nihon-teki keitai" [The significance of the slaveowner socio-economic formation: The Japanese form of slavery], pt. 2. *Keizai hyōron* [Economic review] 3.17 (January 1936): 75-103.

———. "Nihon ni okeru kokka-teki tochi shoyū no mondai" [The problem of state landownership in Japan]. *Keizai hyōron* [Economic review] 2.16 (December 1935): 64-81.

An, S. "Meiji shoki ni okeru Doitsu kokka shisō no juyō ni kansuru ichi kōsatsu: Burunchuri to Katō Hiroyuki o chūshin to shite" [The reception of J. C. Bluntschli's theory of the state by Hiroyuki Katō in early Meiji Japan]. in *Nihon seiji gakkai nenpō, 1975: Nihon ni okeru Sei-Ou seiji shisō* [Annual bulletin of the Japanese Political Science Association, 1975: "Western Political Thoughts in Japan"], pp. 113-156. Tokyo: Iwanami Shoten, 1976.

Andō Jinbee. "Sengo shakai-shugi kakumei-ron no senku—'Nakanishi riron' " [Pioneer in the postwar theory of socialist revolution—"Nakanishi theory"]. *Gendai no riron.* [Contemporary theory] 104 (September 1972): 5-12.

Arahata Kanson. "Heimin-sha jidai" [The era of the Heimin-sha]. *Chūō kōron* [Central review] 1097-1107 (August 1978-July 1979).

———. "Roshiya kakumei no koro" [At the time of the Russian Revolution]. *Sekai* [World] 265 (December 1967): 177-182.

———. "Yamakawa Hitoshi ron" [On Yamakawa Hitoshi]. *Kaizō* [Reconstruction] (January 1931).

Baba Hiroji. "Gendai shihon-shugi no tōshi: Shihon-shugi no hōkai katei ni okeru shakai henkaku no hōkō" [The analysis of contemporary capitalism: The direction of social change in the process of the collapse of capitalism]. *Rōdōsha jishu kanri kenkyū* [Studies in workers' self-management] 12 (November 1982): 10-24.

———. "Kokka dokusen shihon-shugi ron o megutte" [On the theory of state monopoly capitalism]. *Shakai kagaku kenkyū* [Studies in social science] 27.2 (1975).

———. " 'Nihon ni okeru shakai-shugi e no michi' hihan" [A critique of "The path to socialism in Japan"]. *Rōdōsha jishu kanri kenkyū* [Studies in workers' self-management] 5 (August 1979): 8-107.

———. "Taigai kankei" [Foreign relations]. In *Nihon keizai kenkyū nyūmon* [Introduction to Japanese economic studies]. Edited by Saeki Naomi and Shibagaki Kazuo. Tokyo: Tokyo Daigaku Shuppan-kai, 1972.

———. "Uno riron to gendai shihon-shugi ron" [Uno theory and the theory of contemporary capitalism]. *Shakai kagaku kenkyū* [Studies in social science] 34.1 (July 1982): 171-197.

Bukharin, Nikolai. "Teorija 'organizovannoj bezkhozjaistvennosti' " [The theory of "organized mismanagement"]. In *"Organnizovannyi kapitalizm": Diskussija v Komakademii* ["Organized capitalism": A discussion at the Communist Academy]. 2d ed. Moscow, 1930.

Chesneaux, Jean. "Le mode de production asiatique: Quelques perspectives de recherche'' [The Asiatic mode of production: Some research perspectives]. *La Pensée* [Thought] 114 (April 1964).

———. ''Où en est la discussion sur le 'mode de production asiatique'?'' [Wherefore the discussion on the ''Asiatic mode of production''?], pts. 1 and 2. *La Pensée* [Thought] 122 (July-August 1965).

———. ''Où en est la discussion sur le 'mode de production asiatique'?'' [Wherefore the discussion on the ''Asiatic mode of production''?], pt. 3. *La Pensée* [Thought] 129 (October 1966).

Fujita Shōzō. ''Aru Marukusu-shugisha: Kawakami Hajime'' [A Marxist: Kawakami Hajime]. In *Tenkō no shisō shi-teki kenkyū: Sono ichi sokumen* [The intellectual historical study of *tenkō*: One aspect], pp. 64-87. Tokyo: Iwanami Shoten, 1975.

Hani Gorō. ''Ajia-teki seisan yōshiki'' (1940) [The Asiatic mode of production]. In *Hani Gorō rekishi ron chosaku shū* [Collected historical essays of Hani Gorō], 4:185-187. Tokyo: Aoki Shoten, 1967.

———. ''Bakumatsu ni okeru seiji-teki shihai keitai'' [The form of political domination in the late Tokugawa period]. In *Nihon shihon-shugi hattatsu shi kōza* [Symposium on the history of the development of Japanese capitalism], vol. 1. Tokyo: Iwanami Shoten, 1932-1933, reprint ed., 1982.

———. ''Bakumatsu ni okeru shakai keizai jōtai kaikyu kankei oyobi kaikyū tōsō'' [The socio-economic situation, class relations, and class struggles in the late Tokugawa era]. In *Nihon shihon-shugi hattatsu shi kōza* [Symposium on the history of the development of Japanese capitalism], vols. 3 and 4. Tokyo: Iwanami Shoten, 1932-1933, reprint ed., 1982.

———. ''Nihon shihon-shugi hattatsu shi kōza gojū shūnen ni yosete'' [On the fiftieth anniversary of the Symposium on the history of the development of Japanese capitalism]. *Tosho* [Books] no. 394 (June 1982).

———. ''Tōyō ni okeru shihon-shugi no keisei'' [The formation of capitalism in the East] (February-May 1932). In *Meiji ishin shi kenkyū* [Studies on the history of the Meiji Restoration], pp. 13-150. Tokyo: Iwanami Shoten, Iwanami Bunko, 1978.

Hattori Fumio. ''Nihon shihon-shugi kenkyū no dōko to kadai'' [Trends and themes in the study of Japanese capitalism]. *Keizai hyōron* [Economic review] 5.4 (April 1956): 85-91.

Hattori Shisō. ''Bakumatsu Akida han no momen shijō oyobi momen kigyō'' [The cotton cloth market and cotton cloth weaving industry in the late Tokugawa Akida *han*]. *Rekishi kagaku* [Historical science] (March, May, July 1935).

———. '' 'Gen mani' jidai no rekishi-teki jōken'' [Historical conditions of the ''manufacture'' period proper]. *Rekishi kagaku* [Historical science] (March-April 1934).

———. ''Hōhō oyobi sairyō no mondai'' [Problems of method and materials]. In *Hattori Shisō chosaku shū* [Collected works of Hattori Shisō], 1:197-222. Tokyo: Riron-sha, 1955, 1960.

———. ''Ishin shi hōhō-jō no sho mondai'' [Methodological problems in the history of the Restoration] (April-June 1933). In *Hattori Shisō chosaku shū* [Collected works of Hattori Shisō], 1:91-194. Tokyo: Riron-sha, 1955, 1960.

———. "Ma'nyufakuchua jidai no rekishi-teki jōken" [Historical conditions of the manufacture period]. In *Hattori Shisō chosaku shū* [Collected works of Hattori Shisō], 1:223-268. Tokyo: Riron-sha, 1955, 1960.

———. "Ma'nyufakuchua jidai sairon" [More on the manufacture era]. In *Hattori Shisō chosaku shū* [Collected works of Hattori Shisō], 1:195-268. Tokyo: Riron-sha, 1955, 1960.

———. "Ma'nyufakuchua ronsō ni tsuite no shokan" [Thoughts on the manufacture debate] (July 1952). In *Hattori Shisō chosaku shū* [Collected works of Hattori Shisō], 1:269-336. Tokyo: Riron-sha, 1955, 1960.

———. "Meiji ishin no kakumei oyobi hankakumei" [Revolution and counter-revolution in the Meiji Restoration] (February 1933). In *Nihon shihon-shugi hattatsu shi kōza* [Symposium on the history of the development of Japanese capitalism], vol. 1. Tokyo: Iwanami Shoten, 1932-1933, reprint ed., 1982.

———. "Zettai-shugi no shakai-teki kiso" [The social basis of absolutism]. In *Tennō-sei ni kansuru sho mondai* [Problems concerning the emperor system]. Edited by Nihon Kindai Shi Kenkyūkai. Tokyo: Kawade Shobō, 1954.

———. "Zettai-shugi ron: Marukishizumu ni okeru zettai-shugi no gainen" [On absolutism: The concept of absolutism in Marxism]. In *Marukishizumu* (1) [Marxism], pp. 381-410. Compiled by Uchida Yoshihiko, Ōtsuka Hisao, and Matsushima Ei'ichi. Gendai Nihon shisō taikei [Outline of modern Japanese thought], no. 20. Tokyo: Chikuma Shobō, 1966.

Hayakawa Jirō. "Dorei shoyūsha-teki kōsei no tōyō-teki keitai no mondai" [The question of the oriental form of the slaveowner formation] (July 1935). in *Hayakawa Jirō chosaku shū, II: Nihon kodaishi kenkyū to jidai kubun ron* [Collected writings of Hayakawa Jirō, vol. 2: Studies in the history of ancient Japan and theories of periodization], pp. 309-327. Tokyo: Mirai-sha, 1977.

———. "Iwayuru tōyō shi ni okeru 'dorei shoyūsha-teki kōsei no ketsujo' o ika ni setsumei subeki ka?" [How should one explain the so-called "lack of a slaveowner formation" in Eastern history?] (April 1935). In *Hayakawa Jirō chosaku shū, II: Nihon kodaishi kenkyū to jidai kubun ron* [Collected writings of Hayakawa Jirō, vol. 2: Studies in the history of ancient Japan and theories of periodization], pp. 294-308. Tokyo: Mirai-sha, 1977.

———. "Jōdai ni okeru 'be'—Sono naiyō, igi oyobi rekishi" [The *'be'* in antiquity—Its content, significance, and history]. In *Hayakawa Jirō chosaku shū, II: Nihon kodai shi kenkyū to jidai kubun ron* [Collected writings of Hayakawa Jirō, vol. 2: Studies in the history of ancient Japan and theories of periodization], pp. 30-178. Tokyo: Mirai-sha, 1977.

———. " 'Ōchō jidai' no 'kokka-teki tochi shoyū' ni tsuite" [On "state landownership" in the "dynastic period"], pt. 1. *Rekishi kagaku* [Historical science] 2.6 (August 1933): 81-91.

———. "Sano Manabu cho 'Nihon rekishi' sono ta ni okeru gobyū: Nihon ni okeru dorei shoyūsha-teki shakai keizai-teki kōsei no sonpi ni kansuru ronsō no gakusetsu shi no ichibu to shite" [Errors in Sano Manabu's *Nihon rekishi* and other works: One part of the academic history of the debate of the existence of the slave-owner socio-economic formation in Japan]. *Rekishi kagaku* [Historical science] (September 1933): 48-58.

———. "Tōyō kodaishi ni okeru seisan yōshiki no mondai" [The problem of modes of production in ancient Eastern history]. In *Hayakawa Jirō chosaku shū, II: Nihon kodaishi kenkyū to jidai kubun ron* [Collected writings of Hayakawa Jirō, vol. 2: Studies in the history of ancient Japan and theories of periodization], pp. 275-293. Tokyo: Mirai-sha, 1977.

Hayano Tōru and Inaka Yoshiaki. "Sayoku riron, kenji ka tenkan ka: Nyū-shakaitō ni hamon" [Left-wing theory, stick to it, or change it? Ripples within the New Socialist Party]. *Asahi shinbun* [Asahi news], May 15, 1984.

Hayashi Yu'ichi. "Dokusen shihon-shugi kakuritsu-ki: Dai-ichiji taisen kara Shōwa kyōkō made" [The period of the establishment of monopoly capitalism: From World War I to the Shōwa crisis]. In *Nihon nōgyō shi: Shihon-shugi no tenkai to nōgyō mondai* [History of Japanese agriculture: The development of capitalism and the agrarian problem], pp. 113-162. Edited by Teruoka Shūzō. Tokyo: Yūhikaku, Yūhikaku Sensho, 1981.

Hirano Yoshitarō. "Chūgoku to Nihon no kindaika no hikaku—Sono kiten to shite no Taihei Tenkoku to Meiji Ishin" [A comparison of the modernization of China and Japan: The Taiping Heavenly Kingdom and the Meiji Restoration as their starting points]. *Chūgoku kenkyūjo kiyō: Chūgoku kindaika to Nihon* [Bulletin of the China Institute: China's modernization and Japan] 2 (October 1963): 1-75.

———. "Jiyū minken: Sono seishitsu, undō no gendo, naibu-teki kihon tairitsu no kiso kōsatsu" [Civil rights: An examination of their character, the limits of the movement, and the basis of its fundamental internal contradictions]. *Kaizō* [Reconstruction] (December 1933): 2-22.

———. "Kashō nōmin ni yoru jidai: Kiga-teki seikatsu no tame no ryōsai kosaku oyobi jidai no seishitsu/keitai" [Ground rents (paid) by excessively small-scale peasants: The character and form of petty rents and ground rents for a life of starvation]. *Keizai hyōron* [Economic review] 3.21 (May 1936): 2-41.

———. "Meiji ishin ni okeru seiji-teki shihai keitai" [The form of political rule in the Meiji Restoration]. In *Nihon shihon-shugi hatttatsu shi kōza* [Symposium on the history of the development of Japanese capitalism], vol. 5. Tokyo: Iwanami Shoten, 1932-1933, reprint ed., 1982.

Hori Makoto. "Meiji shoki no kokka ron" [The theory of the state in the early Meiji period]. In *Kokka gakkai gojū shūnen kinen—Kokkagaku ronshū* [Commemoration of the fiftieth anniversary of the Kokka Gakkai: A collection of essays on state theory], pp. 711-744. Tokyo: Yūhikaku, 1937.

Hori Masao. "Shakai-shugi seitō to shite no sokunin" [(Our) responsibility as a socialist political party]. *Rōdōsha jishu kanri kenkyū* [Studies on workers' self-management] 5 (August 1979): 4-7.

Ienaga Saburō. "Nihon ni okeru kyōwa-shugi no dentō" [The tradition of republicanism in Japan]. *Shisō* [Thought] (August 1958).

Inomata Tsunao. "Buhārin" [Bukharin]. *Kaizō* [Reconstruction]. (February 1929): 48-58.

———. "Doronuma ni kanbotsu shita 'puchi teikoku-shugisha' (zokkō)" [The "petty imperialists" who have sunk into the quagmire (sequel)]. In *Teikoku-shugi kenkyū* [Studies on imperialism], pp. 247-402. Tokyo: Kaizō-sha, 1928.

———. "Gendai Nihon burujoajii no seiji-teki chi'i" [The political position of the contemporary Japanese bourgeoisie] (September 7, 1927). In *Gendai Nihon kenkyū: Marukishizumu no tachiba yori* [Studies on contemporary Japan: From a Marxist perspective], pp. 135-192. Tokyo: Kaizō-sha, 1929, 1934.

———. "Hiyorimi-shugi-teki senryaku ka 'senryaku-teki' hiyorimi-shugi ka (2)" [An opportunistic strategy or "strategic" opportunism (2)] (March 1928). In *Nihon puroretariāto no senryaku to senjutsu—Zasshi "Rōnō" keisei ronbun shū* [The strategy and tactics of the Japanese proletariat: Collected essays published in the magazine *Rōnō*], pp. 47-84. Tokyo: Tosho Shinbun-sha, 1973.

———. "Nihon musan-kaikyū no ippan senryaku" [The general strategy of the Japanese proletariat] (November 10, 1927). In *Nihon puroretariāto no senryaku to senjutsu—Zasshi "Rōnō" keisai ronbun shū* [The strategy and tactics of the Japanese proletariat: Collected essays published in the magazine *Rōnō*], pp. 3-10. Tokyo: Tosho Shinbun-sha, 1973.

———. "Nihon musan-kaikyū undō ni kansuru tēze. (1) Nihon shihon-shugi no gensei" [Theses on the Japanese proletarian movement. 1: The present state of Japanese capitalism]. In *Nihon puroretariāto no senryaku to senjutsu——Zasshi "Rōnō" keisei ronbun shū* [The strategy and tactics of the Japanese proletariat: Collected essays published in the magazine *Rōnō*], pp. 11-23. Tokyo: Tosho Shinbun-sha, 1973.

———. "Nihon musan-kaikyū undō ni kansuru tēze. (2) Seiji jōsei" [Theses on the Japanese proletarian movement. 2: The political situation]. In *Nihon puroretariāto no senryaku to senjutsu——Zasshi "Rōnō" keisei ronbun shū* [The strategy and tactics of the Japanese proletariat: Collected essays published in the magazine *Rōnō*], pp. 24-27. Tokyo: Tosho shinbun-sha, 1973.

———. "Nihon teikoku-shugi no shin dankai no mondai" [The question of the new stage of Japanese imperialism] (August 1927). In *Teikoku-shugi kenkyū* [Studies on imperialism], pp. 165-211. Tokyo: Kaizō-sha, 1928.

———. "Puroretaria senryaku ni okeru burujoa minshu-shugi tōsō no yakuwari (2)" [The role of bourgeois-democratic struggle in the strategy of the proletariat (2)] (December 1928). In *Nihon puroretariāto no senryaku to senjutsu—Zasshi "Rōnō" keisai ronbun shū* [The strategy and tactics of the Japanese proletariat: Collected essays published in the magazine *Rōnō*], pp. 108-114. Tokyo: Tosho Shinbun-sha, 1973.

———. "Shihon-shugi Nihon no teikoku-shugi" [The imperialism of capitalist Japan] (June 1927). In *Teikoku-shugi kenkyū* [Studies on imperialism], pp. 113-163. Tokyo: Kaizō-sha, 1928.

———. "Tochi mondai to hōken isei" [The land problem and feudal remnants] (December 7, 1929). In *Nihon musan kaikyū no senryaku* [The strategy of the Japanese proletariat], pp. 137-162. N.p.: Bungei Sensen Shuppan-bu, 1930.

———. "Waga senryaku ni okeru burujoa minshu-shugi-teki tōsō no yakuwari (1)" [The role of bourgeois-democratic struggle in our strategy] (September

1928). In *Nihon puroretariāto no senryaku to senjutsu—Zasshi ''Rōnō'' keisai ronbun shū* [The strategy and tactics of the Japanese proletariat: Collected essays published in the magazine *Rōnō*], pp. 85-107. Tokyo: Tosho Shinbun-sha, 1973.

———. ''Wagakuni shihon-shugi no antei no kata botsuraku no kata'' [The pattern of stability and the pattern of decline of Japanese capitalism]. *Chūō kōron* [Central review] (July 1927).

———. ''Wagakuni shihon-shugi no gendankai no mondai'' [Problems in the present stage of our country's capitalism]. *Shakai kagaku* [Social science] (August 1927).

Inumaru Gi'ichi. ''Nihon Marukusu-shugi no genryū'' [The origins of Japanese Marxism]. In *Gendai no ideorogii* [Contemporary ideology], vol. 2, *Nihon no Marukusu-shugi* [Japanese Marxism]. Edited by Ikumi Takuichi. Tokyo: San'ichi Shobō, 1961.

Iolk, Y. S. '' 'Ajia-teki' seisan yōshiki no mondai ni yosete'' [On the question of the ''Asiatic'' mode of production]. *Marukusu-shugi no hata no moto ni* [Under the banner of Marxism] 3 (October/December 1931).

———. ''K voprosy ob osnovakh obshchestvennovo stroja drevnevo Kitaja'' [On the problem of the major social systems of ancient China]. *Problemy Kitaja* [Problems of China] 2 (1930).

———. ''O zadachakh Marksistsko-Leninskovo izuchenija kolonial'nikh i polukolonial'nikh stran'' [On problems of the Marxist-Leninist study of colonial and semi-colonial countries]. *Problemy Kitaja* [Problems of China] 2 (1930).

———. Review of M. Kokin and G. Papajan, *''Tszintjan'': Agrarnij stroj drevnevo Kitaja* [''Jingtian'': The agrarian system of ancient China]. *Problemy Kitaja* [Problems of China] 4-5 (1930).

Ishida Takeshi. ''Ideorogii to shite no tennō-sei'' [The emperor system as ideology]. *Shisō* [Thought] 336 (June 1952): 32-43.

Ishihama Tomoyuki. ''Nihon ni okeru shihon-shugi no seiritsu'' [The establishment of capitalism in Japan]. *Kaizō* [Reconstruction] (October 1932).

Kamiyama Shigeo. ''Nihon teikoku-shugi no seikaku no mondai ni yosete: 'Gunji-teki teikoku-shugi' no gainen ni tsuite'' [On the problem of the nature of Japanese imperialism: On the concept of ''militaristic imperialism'']. In *Tennō-sei ni kansuru riron-teki sho mondai* [Theoretical problems concerning the emperor system]. Rev. and enlgd. ed. Tokyo: Minshu Hyōron-sha, 1956.

Kawamura Zenjirō. ''Kaisetsu'' [Commentary]. In *Hattori Shisō chosaku shū* [Collected works of Hattori Shisō], 1:337-342. Tokyo: Riron-sha, 1955, 1960.

Kazama Yasoji. '' 'Nihon shihon-shugi hattatsu shi koza' hakkan gojū nen—Sono rekishi-teki igi to konnichi-teki igi'' [Fifty years since the publication of the ''Symposium on the history of the development of Japanese capitalism'': Its historical significance and its present significance]. *Keizai* [Economics] (June 1982).

Komine Kazuo. ''Senji kokka dokusen shihon-shugi-ki: Shōwa kyōkō kara haisen made'' [The period of wartime state monopoly capitalism: From the Showa panic to the defeat in the war]. In *Nihon nōgyō shi: Shihon-shugi no tenkai to nōgyō mondai* [History of Japanese agriculture: The development of capitalism and the agrarian problem], pp. 163-226. Edited by Teruoka Shūzō. Tokyo: Yūhikaku, Yūhikaku Sensho, 1981.

Kūshinen [Kuusinen, O.]. ''Nihon teikoku-shugi to Nihon kakumei no seishitsu'' [Japanese imperialism and the nature of the Japanese revolution] (1932). In *Kominterun Nihon ni kansuru tēze shū* [Collected Comintern theses on Japan], pp. 102-128. Compiled by Ishidō Kiyotomo and Yamabe Kentarō. Tokyo: Aoki Shoten, Aoki Bunko, 1961.

Mad'iar, L. ''Osnovnye problemy Kitajskoj revolutsij'' [Fundamental problems of the Chinese revolution]. *Bol'shevik* [Bolshevik] 8 (1928).

Matsuda Michio. ''Yamakawa Hitoshi'' [Yamakawa Hitoshi]. In *Nihon no Marukusu-shugisha* [Japan's Marxists]. Edited by Suzuki Tadashi. Nagoya: Fubai-sha, 1969.

Matsushima Ei'ichi. ''Nihon ni okeru Marukishizumu no tenkai'' [The development of Marxism in Japan]. In *Marukishizumu* (I) [Marxism], pp. 7-72. Compiled by Uchida Yoshihiko, Ōtsuka Hisao and Matsushima Ei'ichi. Gendai Nihon shisō taikei [Outline of modern Japanese thought], no. 20. Tokyo: Chikuma Shobō, 1966.

Minobe Ryōkichi. ''Sore de mo tennō wa kikan de aru: Aru kenpō gakusha no shōgai'' [Even so, the emperor is an organ: The life of a certain constitutional scholar]. In *Kumon suru demokurashii* [Democracy in anguish], pp. 61-96. Tokyo: Bungei Shunjū Shinsha, 1959.

Minobe Tatsukichi. ''Kunshu no kokuhō-jō no chi'i'' [The position of the monarch in state law]. *Hōgaku shirin* 50 (November 15, 1903): 1-6.

Miura Tsuneo. ''Nihon no dorei-sei ni kansuru saikin no tairon'' [The recent controversy on Japanese slavery]. *Yuibutsu kenkyū* [Studies on materialism] 8 (1933): 164-173.

Miyazawa Toshiyoshi. ''Kikan setsu jiken to Minobe Tatsukichi sensei'' [Professor Minobe Tatsukichi and the organ theory affair]. *Hōritsu jihō* [Legal times] 20 (August 1948): 42-44.

Moritani Katsumi. ''Iwayuru 'Ajia-teki seisan yōshiki' sairon'' [More on the so-called ''Asiatic mode of production'']. *Rekishi kagaku* [Historical science] (September 1935): 41-75.

Nakamura Takafusa. '' 'Nihon shihon-shugi ronsō' ni tsuite'' [On ''the debate on Japanese capitalism'']. *Shisō* [Thought] 624 (June 1976): 185-197.

Nakase Ju'ichi. ''Meiji kenpōka ni okeru tennō-kikan setsu no keisei'' [The formation of the emperor-organ theory under the Meiji constitution]. *Hōritsu jihō* [Legal times] 34.4 (April 1962): 59-71.

———. ''Tennō-kikan setsu kakuritsu katei ni okeru Minobe riron no tokushitsu'' [The special character of Minobe's theory in the process of the establishment of the emperor-organ theory]. *Dōshisha hōgaku* [Dōshisha law review] 72 (June 1962): 155-195.

———. ''Tennō-kikan setsu no genryū'' [Origins of the emperor-organ theory]. *Rekishi hyōron* [Historical review] (February-August 1962).

''Nihon Kyōsantō kōryō sōan'' [Draft program of the Japanese Communist Party] (1922). In *Kominterun Nihon ni kansuru tēze shū* [Collected Comintern theses on

Japan], pp. 5-9. Compiled by Ishidō Kiyotomo and Yamabe Kentarō. Tokyo: Aoki Shoten, Aoki Bunko, 1961.

"Nihon Kyōsantō seiji teze sōan (1931)" [1931 Draft Political Theses]. In *Kominterun Nihon ni kansuru tēze shū* [Collected Comintern theses on Japan], pp. 46-75. Compiled by Ishidō Kiyotomo and Yamabe Kentarō. Tokyo: Aoki Shoten, Aoki Bunko, 1961.

"Nihon mondai ni kansuru shin tēze happyō ni saishi dōshi shokun ni tsugu" [To all comrades on the occasion of the proclamation of the new theses on the Japan problem]. In *Kominterun Nihon ni kansuru tēze shū* [Collected Comintern theses on Japan], pp. 120-128. Compiled by Ishidō Kiyotomo and Yamabe Kentarō. Tokyo: Aoki Shoten, Aoki Bunko, 1961.

"Nihon ni kansuru ketsugi (Ni-nana nen tēze)" [Resolution on Japan (The '27 Theses)]. In *Kominterun Nihon ni kansuru tēze shū* [Collected Comintern theses on Japan], pp. 28-45. Compiled by Ishidō Kiyotomo and Yamabe Kentarō. Tokyo: Aoki Shoten, Aoki Bunko, 1961.

"Nihon ni okeru jōsei to Nihon Kyōsantō no ninmu ni kansuru tēze (san-ni tēze)" [Theses on the situation in Japan and the responsibilities of the Japanese Communist Party ('32 Theses)]. In *Kominterun Nihon ni kansuru tēze shū* [Collected Comintern theses on Japan], pp. 76-101. Compiled by Ishidō Kiyotomo and Yamabe Kentarō. Tokyo: Aoki Shoten, Aoki Bunko, 1961.

"Nihon ni okeru shakai-shugi e no michi" [The path to socialism in Japan]. In *Nihon Shakaitō kōryō bunken shū* [Collected documents of the Japanese Socialist Party]. Compiled by Katsumata Sei'ichi and Kitayama Airō. Tokyo: Nihon Shakaitō Chūō Honbu Kikanshi-kyoku, 1978.

"Nihon Shakaitō kōryō (kettō-ji)" [Program of the Japanese Socialist Party (at the time of its founding)]. In *Nihon Shakaitō kōryō bunken shū* [Collected documents on the program of the Japanese Socialist Party]. Compiled by Katsumata Sei'ichi and Kitayama Yoshio. Tokyo: Nihon Shakaitō Kikanshi-kyoku, 1978.

Niijima Issaku [Inomata Tsunao]. "Nihon musan kaikyū undō ni kansuru tēze. (1) Nihon shihon-shugi no gensei" [Theses on the Japanese proletarian movement. (1) The current state of Japanese capitalism]. (December 1927-January 1928). In *Nihon puroretariāto no senryaku to senjutsu—Zasshi "Rōnō" keisai ronbun shū* [The strategy and tactics of the Japanese proletariat: Collected essays published in the magazine *Rōnō*], pp. 11-23. By Inomata Tsunao. Tokyo: Tosho Shinbunsha, 1973.

Noro Eitarō. " 'Puchi teikoku-shugi' ron no ninshiki" [An understanding of the theory of "petty imperialism"] (September 1927). In *Noro Eitarō zenshū* [Complete writings of Noro Eitarō], 1:113-157. Tokyo: Shin Nihon Shuppan-sha, 1965.

———. "Puchi teikoku-shugisha no konmei" [The confusion of the petty imperialists]. In *Noro Eitarō zenshū* [Complete writings of Noro Eitarō], 1:133-157. Tokyo: Shin Nihon Shuppan-sha, 1965.

Ōishi Ka'ichirō. "Nihon shihon-shugi ronsō to nōgyō-tochi mondai" [The debate on Japanese capitalism and the agrarian/land problem]. In *Rekishi kagaku taikei*

[Outline of historical sciences], 9:260-304. Tokyo: Rekishi Kagaku Kyōgikai, 1976.

Okazaki Saburō. "Fashizumu" [Fascism]. In *Gendai Nihon shihon-shugi taikei* [Outline of contemporary Japanese capitalism], 7 vols. Compiled by Ōuchi Hyōe, Arisawa Hiromi, Uno Kōzō, and Sakisaka Itsurō. Tokyo: Kōbundō, 1957-1958.

Ōshima Kiyoshi. "Inomata Tsunao no nōgyō ron/senryaku ron" (1) [The agricultural and strategic theory of Inomata Tsunao]. *Shisō* [Thought] 595 (January 1974): 18-33.

———. "Inomata Tsunao no nōgyō ron/senryaku ron" (2) [The agricultural and strategic theory of Inomata Tsunao]. *Shisō* [Thought] 596 (February 1974): 78-102.

Ōtsuka Hisao. "Nōson no orimoto to tōshi no orimoto" [Country clothiers and town clothiers]. *Shakai keizai shigaku* [Social and economic history] 8.3/4 (1938).

Ōuchi Hyōe. "Kaihan no tame ni" [Introduction to the revised edition]. In *Nōson mondai nyūmon* [Introduction to the agrarian problem]. Tokyo: Kōdo-sha, 1937.

———. "Nōson minshuka no michi chikakarazu" [The path of democratization of the agricultural village is not at hand]. *Sekai* [The world] (August 1946).

Ōuchi Tsutomu. "Gendai shihon-shugi no kiki to wa nani ka? Rōdōryoku no hōsetsu no rekishi-teki tenbō" [What is the "crisis of contemporary capitalism"? A historical view of the subsumption of labor power]. *Rōdōsha jishu kanri kenkyū* [Studies in workers' self-management]. 12 (November 1982): 34-50.

———. "Michi no kihon-teki rinen" [The fundamental ideas of the "Michi"]. *Rōdōsha jishu kanri kenkyū* [Studies in workers' self-management] 5 (August 10, 1979): 108-133.

———. "Nihon shihon-shugi ron no kenkyū ni tsuite" [On the study of the theory of Japanese capitalism]. *Keizai hyōron* [Economic review] 5.4 (April 1956): 76-84.

———. "Sengo kaikaku e no futatsu no apurōchi" [Two approaches to the postwar reforms]. *Shakai kagaku kenkyū* [Studies in social science] 21.5/6 (1970).

———. "Shakai-shugi no kōsō" [The conception of socialism]. *Rōdōsha jishu kanri kenkyū* [Studies in workers' self-management] 3 (February 1979).

———. "Shihon-shugi to shakai-shugi" [Capitalism and socialism]. *Rōdōsha jishu kanri kenkyū* [Studies in workers' self-management] 12 (November 1982): 4-9.

Saitō Yasuo. "Seikyō bunri no gensoku to Yasukuni jinja hōan" [The principle of the separation of state and religion and the Yasukuni shrine case]. *Jurisuto* [Jurist] 748 (September 1, 1981): 28-35.

Sakisaka Itsurō. " 'Nihon shihon-shugi bunseki' ni okeru hōhōron" [The methodology in (Yamada's) "Analysis of Japanese Capitalism"] (October 1935). In *Nihon shihon-shugi no sho mondai* [Problems of Japanese capitalism], pp. 3-33. N.p.: Kōdo-sha, 1947; Tokyo: Shakai-shugi Kyōkai Shuppan-kyoku, 1976.

Sano Hiroshi. "Mosukō to Nihon Kyōsantō no kankei shi" [A history of relations between Moscow and the Japanese Communist Party]. *Chūō kōron* [Central review] 65.3 (March 1950): 96-103.

Sano Manabu. "Gokuchū-ki" [Prison diary]. In *Tenkō jūgo-nen* [Fifteen years since *tenkō*], pp. 81-153. By Nabeyama Sadachika and Sano Manabu. Rōdō minshu shiriizu [Labor democracy series], no. 7. Tokyo: Rōdō Shuppan-bu, 1949.

Shibagaki Kazuo. "Nihon keizai kenkyū ni okeru senzen to sengo" [Prewar and postwar in Japanese economic research]. In *Nihon keizai kenkyū nyūmon* [Introduction to Japanese economic studies], pp. 15-35. Edited by Saeki Naomi and Shibagaki Kazuo. Tokyo: Tōkyō Daigaku Shuppan-kai, 1972.

Shiga Yoshio. "Gunji-teki hōken-teki 'teikoku-shugi' ni tsuite" [On militaristic feudalistic "imperialism"]. In *Sekai to Nihon* [The world and Japan]. N.p.: Gyōmyō-sha, 1948.

Shioda Shobee. "Nihon Shakaitō no rekishi-teki seikaku" [The historical character of the Japanese Socialist Party]. *Keizai hyōron* [Economic review] (June 1953): 2-10.

Takabatake Michitoshi. "Ikkoku shakai-shugisha—Sano Manabu/Nabeyama Sadachika" [One-country socialists: Sano Manabu and Nabeyama Sadachika]. In *Tenkō* [*Tenkō*] 1:164-200. Edited by Shisō no Kagaku Kenkyūkai. Tokyo: Heibon-sha, 1959, 1965.

Takabatake Motoyuki. "Kokka shakai-shugi no hitsuzen-sei" [The inevitability of state socialism]. In *Hihan Marukusu-shugi* [Criticizing Marxism]. Tokyo: Nihon Hyōron-sha, 1934.

Takahashi Kamekichi. "Gunshuku teigi no teikoku-shugi-teki imi to Nihon no tachiba" [The imperialistic implications of disarmament proposals and Japan's position]. In *Sayoku undō no riron-teki hōkai—Uyoku undō no riron-teki konkyo* [The theoretical collapse of the left-wing movement—The theoretical basis of the right-wing movement], pp. 93-104. Tokyo: Hakuyō-sha, 1927.

———. "Makki ni okeru teikoku-shugi no henshitsu" [The change in the quality of imperialism in the last stage]. In *Sayoku undō no riron-teki hōkai: Uyoku undō no riron-teki konkyo* [The theoretical collapse of the left-wing movement: The theoretical basis of the right-wing movement], pp. 1-38. Tokyo: Hakuyō-sha, 1927.

Takeda Kiyoko. "Kakumei shisō to tennō-sei—Takabatake Motoyuki no kokka shakai-shugi o chūshin ni" [Revolutionary thought and the emperor system: The state/national socialism of Takabatake Motoyuki]. In *Kindai Nihon seiji shisō shi* [History of modern Japanese political thought], 2:252-300. Compiled by Hashikawa Bunzō and Matsumoto Sannosuke. Kindai Nihon shisō shi taikei [Outline of the history of modern Japanese thought], no. 4. Tokyo: Yūhikaku, 1970.

———. "Tennō-sei shisō no keisei" [The formation of the emperor system ideology]. In *Iwanami Kōza: Nihon rekishi* [Iwanami symposium: Japanese history], vol. 16: *Kindai* [The modern age], pp. 267-311. Tokyo: Iwanami Shoten, 1962.

Takeuchi Yoshitomo. "Nihon no Marukusu-shugi" [Japanese Marxism]. In *Marukishizumu* (II) [Marxism], pp. 7-58. Edited by Takeuchi Yoshitomo. Gendai Nihon shisō taikei [Outline of contemporary Japanese thought], no. 21. Tokyo: Chikuma Shobō, 1965.

"Tokushū: Shakai minshu-shugi no kenkyū" [Special issue: Studies on social democracy]. *Keizai hyōron* [Economic review] (June 1953): 1-90.

Tsuchiya Takao. "Ishin shi kenkyū no chūshin ronten: Bakumatsu ma'nyufakuchua no sho mondai" [Central points at issue in the study of Restoration history: Some problems of late-Tokugawa manufacture] (January 1934). In *Nihon shihon-shugi shi ronshū* [Collected essays on the history of Japanese capitalism], pp. 162-178. Tokyo: Ikusei-sha, 1937.

———. "Nihon ma'nyufakuchua zusetsu" [Explanatory diagram of Japanese manufacture] (February 1934). In *Nihon shihon-shugi shi ronshū* [Collected essays on the history of Japanese capitalism], pp. 179-190. Tokyo: Ikusei-sha, 1937.

———. " 'Shin jinushi ron' no saikentō" [A re-examination of the theory of new landlords]. In *Nihon shihon-shugi shi ronshū* [Collected essays on the history of Japanese capitalism], pp. 3-26. Tokyo: Ikusei-sha, 1937.

———. "Tokugawa jidai no ma'nyufakuchua" [Manufacture in the Tokugawa era] (September 1933). In *Nihon shihon-shugi shi ronshū* [Collected essays on the history of Japanese capitalism], pp. 137-161. Tokyo: Ikusei-sha, 1937.

———. "Tokugawa jidai no orimonogyō ni okeru toiya-sei kanai kōgyō" [*Toiya-sei* domestic industry in the textile industry in the Tokugawa period] (July-August 1934). In *Nihon shihon-shugi shi ronshū* [Collected essays on the history of Japanese capitalism], pp. 191-244. Tokyo: Ikusei-sha, 1937.

———. "Yamada shi 'bunseki' ni okeru yōeki rōdō ron hihan" [A critique of the theory of slave labor in Yamada's "Analysis"]. In *Nihon shihon-shugi shi ronshū* [Collected essays on the history of Japanese capitalism], pp. 77-102. Tokyo: Ikusei-sha, 1937.

Uesugi Shinkichi. "Kokutai ni kansuru isetsu" [Different opinions concerning the *kokutai*]. In *Taishō shisō shū* [Collection of Taishō thought], 1:3-13. Compiled by Imai Sei'ichi. Kindai Nihon shisō taikei [Outline of Modern Japanese thought], no. 33. Tokyo: Chikuma Shobō, 1978.

Ukai Nobushige. "Minobe hakushi no shisō to gakusetsu—Sono rekishi no igi" [The thought and theory of Dr. Minobe: Its historical significance]. *Hōritsu jihō* [Legal times] 20 (August 1948): 45-49.

Uno Kōzō. "Riron to jissen: keizaigaku to shakai-shugi" [Theory and practice: Economics and socialism]. In *Shihonron no keizaigaku* [The economics of *Capital*], pp. 141-192. Tokyo: Iwanami Shoten, Iwanami Shinsho, 1969.

———. "Waga nōson no hōken-sei" [The feudal nature of our agricultural villages]. In *Nōgyō mondai joron* [Preface to the agrarian problem]. Tokyo: Kaizō-sha, 1947.

Ushiyama Keiji. "Nihon shihon-shugi kakuritsu-ki: 1880 nendai-matsu kara daiichiji taisen made" [The period of the establishment of Japanese capitalism: From the late 1880s to World War I]. In *Nihon nōgyō shi: Shihon-shugi no tenkai to nōgyō mondai* [History of Japanese agriculture: The development of capitalism and the agrarian problem], pp. 49-112. Edited by Teruoka Shūzō. Tokyo: Yūhikaku, Yūhikaku Sensho, 1981.

Usui Toshio. " 'Fūka' no uchigawa ni tadayou yawaraki 'shiji' " [Soft "support" floating within "the influence of the ruler"]. *Asahi Journal* 26.19 (May 4, 1984).

Voichinsukii, G. [Gregory Voitinsky]. "Nihon ni okeru kaikyūsen (sankō ron)" [Class struggle in Japan (reference paper)] (1922). In *Kominterun Nihon ni kansuru tēze shū* [Collected Comintern theses on Japan], pp. 10-27. Compiled by Ishidō Kiyotomo and Yamabe Kentarō. Tokyo: Aoki Shoten, Aoki Bunko, 1961.

Watanabe Yōzō. "Gendai minshu-shugi hōgaku to 'Nihon shihon-shugi hattatsu shi kōza' " [Contemporary democratic law and the *Symposium on the history of the development of Japanese capitalism*]. *Bunka hyōron* [Cultural criticism] 264 (March 1983).

Yamabe Kentarō. "Kōryō mondai no rekishi" (I) [History of the issues of the program]. *Zen'ei* [Vanguard] (September-December 1957): 109-128.

Yamada Moritarō. "Meiji ishin ni okeru nōgyō-jō no sho henkaku" [Changes in agriculture during the Meiji Restoration]. In *Nihon shihon-shugi hattatsu shi kōza* [Symposium on the history of the development of Japanese capitalism], vol. 7. Tokyo: Iwanami Shoten, 1932-1933, reprint ed., 1982.

Yamakawa Hitoshi. "Daisan Intanashonaru" [The Third International] (April 1921). In *Yamakawa Hitoshi zenshū* [Complete writings of Yamakawa Hitoshi], 3:236-239. Tokyo: Keisō Shobō, 1966.

———. "Nihon ni okeru demokurashii no hattatsu to musan-kaikyū no seiji undō" [The development of democracy in Japan and the political movement of the proletariat] (November 1923-April 1924). In *Yamakawa Hitoshi shū* [Collected writings of Yamakawa Hitoshi], pp. 105-135. Edited by Takabatake Michitoshi. Tokyo: Chikuma Shobō, 1976.

———. "Roshiya no shihai kaikyū" [Russia's ruling class] (July 1923). In *Yamakawa Hitoshi zenshū* [Complete writings of Yamakawa Hitoshi], vol. 5. Tokyo: Keisō Shobō, 1966.

———. "Seiji-teki tōitsu sensen e! Musan seitō gōdō-ron no konkyo" [Toward a political united front! The basis of the argument for the merger of proletarian political parties] (November 10, 1927). In *Yamakawa Hitoshi shū* [Collected writings of Yamakawa Hitoshi], pp. 174-218. Edited by Takabatake Michitoshi. Kindai Nihon shisō taikei [Outline of modern Japanese thought], no. 19. Tokyo: Chikuma Shobō, 1976.

———. "Sobieto seiji no tokushitsu to sono hihan: Puroretarian dikuteitōshippu to demokurashii" [The characteristics of the Soviet government and the critique of it: Proletarian dictatorship and democracy] (1919). In *Yamakawa Hitoshi zenshū* [Complete writings of Yamakawa Hitoshi], vol. 2. Tokyo: Keisō Shobō, 1966.

Unpublished Sources

Arahata Kanson, interview, Tokyo, Japan, August 17, 1979.

Arahata Kanson, Takahashi Masao, and Watanabe Fumitarō, interview, Tokyo, Japan, August 17, 1979.

Doi Takako, interview, Tokyo, Japan, June 25, 1982.

Durkee, Travers Edgar. "The Communist International and Japan, 1919-1932." Ph.D. dissertation, Stanford University, 1953.

Fujita Shōzō, interview, Tokyo, Japan, August 3, 1979.

Fukushima Shingō, interview, Tokyo, Japan, July 31, 1979.

Hayashi Takehisa, interview, Tokyo, Japan, June 16, 1982.

Hirano Yoshitarō, interview, Tokyo, Japan, July 27, 1979.

Hori Masao, interview, Tokyo, Japan, May 4, 1984.

Hoston, Germaine A. "State and Revolution in China and Japan: Marxist Perspectives on the Nation-State and Social Revolution in Asia." 4 vols. Ph.D. dissertation, Harvard University, 1981.

Ikumi Taku'ichi, interview, Tokyo, Japan, June 17, 1982.

"Inomata [Tsunao] shi jōshinsho" [Inomata (Tsunao)'s written statement]. Tokyo District Court, Hōritsu jimusho. Part 2. March 15, 1941 (Handwritten manuscript). Ōhara Shakai Mondai Kenkyūjo [Ōhara Institute for the Study of Social Problems], Hōsei University, Tokyo, Japan.

Itō Makoto, interview, Tokyo, Japan, June 11, 1982.

Kuwabara Takeo, interview, Kyoto, Japan, April 19, 1984.

Maruyama Masao, interview, Tokyo, Japan, June 17, 1982; May 8, 1984.

Minobe Ryōkichi, interview, Tokyo, Japan, July 30, 1979; May 7, 1984.

Moriya Fumio, interview, Tokyo, Japan, August 6, 1979; June 5, 1982.

Nakamura Takafusa, interview, Tokyo, Japan, July 11, 1979; July 17, 1979.

Okudaira Yasuhiro, interview, Tokyo, Japan, April 2, 1984.

Ōuchi Hyōe. Jōshinsho [Written statement]. Tokyo Criminal Court, no. 2. (Handwritten manuscript). September 1941.

Ōuchi Tsutomu, interview, Tokyo, Japan, June 11, 1982; April 27, 1984.

Sakisaka Itsurō, interview, Tokyo, Japan, June 7, 1982; June 14, 1982.

Sano Manabu. "Sano Manabu jōshinsho—Kaito-ha ni tsuite" [Sano Manabu's written statement: On the dissolutionist faction]. Handwritten. February 1931.

Shibagaki Kazuo, interview, Tokyo, Japan, June 23, 1982.

Steinhoff, Patricia Golden. "*Tenkō*: Ideology and Societal Integration in Prewar Japan." Ph.D. dissertation, Harvard University, 1969.

Swearingen, Rodger. "The Japanese Communist Party and the Comintern, 1919-1943: A Study of the Relationship Between the Japanese Party and Moscow and the Success of the Japanese Special Higher Police (Thought Police) in Combating Communism in Japan." Ph.D. dissertation, Harvard University, 1953.

Swift, Thomas Duane. "Yamakawa Hitoshi and the Dawn of Japanese Socialism." Ph.D. dissertation, University of California at Berkeley, 1970.

Takahashi Masao, interview, Tokyo, Japan, August 17, 1979; June 4, 1982; May 5, 1984.

Taniuchi Yuzuru, interview, Tokyo, Japan, August 3, 1979.

Ukai Nobushige, interview, Tokyo, Japan, July 23, 1979.

Watanabe Yōzō, interview, Tokyo, Japan, April 3, 1984; April 14, 1984.

Wray, Harold Joseph. "Changes and Continuity in Japanese Images of the *Kokutai* and Attitudes and Roles Toward the Outside World: A Content Analysis of Japanese Textbooks, 1903-1945." Ph.D. dissertation, University of Hawaii, 1971.

Yamakawa Hitoshi. "Shōnin shinsei" [Witness's summons]. May 30, 1944. Handwritten manuscript. Ōhara Institute for the Study of Social Problems, Hōsei University, Tokyo, Japan.

English Language Sources

BOOKS

Althusser, Louis and Balibar, Etienne. *Reading Capital*. London: New Left Books, 1970.

BIBLIOGRAPHY

Anderson, Perry. *Lineages of the Absolutist State*. London: New Left Books, 1974.

Armstrong, Robert Cornell. *Light from the East: Studies in Japanese Confucianism*. Toronto: University of Toronto, 1914.

Bailey, Anne M. and Llobera, Josep R., eds. *The Asiatic Mode of Production: Science and Politics*. London: Routledge and Kegan Paul, 1981.

Beckmann, George M. and Okubo Genji. *The Japanese Communist Party, 1922-1945*. Stanford: Stanford University Press, 1969.

Bernstein, Gail Lee. *Japanese Marxist: A Portrait of Kawakami Hajime, 1879-1946*. Harvard East Asian series, no. 86. Cambridge: Harvard University Press, 1976.

Black, Cyril E. et al. *The Modernization of Japan and Russia*. New York: Free Press, 1975.

Brandt, Conrad. *Stalin's Failure in China 1924-1927*. Cambridge: Harvard University Press, 1958; New York: W. W. Norton, Norton Library, 1966.

Bukharin, Nikolai. *Imperialism and World Economy*. New York: International Publishers, 1929; New York and London: Monthly Review Press, 1973.

Cohen, Stephen F. *Bukharin and the Bolshevik Revolution: A Political Biography, 1888-1938*. New York: Random House, 1971; Vintage Books, 1975.

Deutscher, Isaac. *The Prophet Armed: Trotsky, 1879-1921*. New York: N.p., 1954.

Dirlik, Arif. *Revolution and History: Origins of Marxist Historiography in China, 1919-1937*. Berkeley and Los Angeles: University of California Press, 1978.

Dobb, Maurice. *Studies in the Development of Capitalism*. New York: International Publishers Co., 1947; rev. ed., 1963.

Dower, John W., ed. *Origins of the Modern Japanese State: Selected Writings of E. H. Norman*. New York: Random House, Pantheon Books, 1975.

Duus, Peter. *Party Rivalry and Political Change in Taishō Japan*. Cambridge: Harvard University Press, 1968.

Earl, David Magarey. *Emperor and Nation in Japan: Political Thinkers of the Tokugawa Period*. Seattle: University of Washington Press, 1964.

Engels, Frederick. *Herr Eugen Dühring's Revolution in Science (Anti-Dühring)*. Translated by Emile Burns. Edited by C. P. Dutt. New York: International Publishers Co., New World Paperbacks, 1935.

———. *Origin of the Family, Private Property and the State: In Light of the Researches of Lewis H. Morgan*. Edited by Eleanor Burke Leacock. New York: International Publishers Co., New World Paperbacks, 1972.

Gerschenkron, Alexander. *Economic Backwardness in Historical Perspective*. Cambridge: Harvard University Press, 1962.

Havens, Thomas R. H. *Farm and Nation in Modern Japan: Agrarian Nationalism, 1870-1940*. Princeton: Princeton University Press, 1974.

Hilton, Rodney, ed. *The Transition from Feudalism to Capitalism*. London: New Left Books and Atlantic Highlands, N.J.: Humanities Press, 1976.

Hindess, Barry and Hirst, Paul Q. *Pre-Capitalist Modes of Production*. London and Boston: Routledge and Kegan Paul, 1975.

Itoh, Makoto. *Value and Crisis: Essays on Marxian Economics in Japan*. New York: Monthly Review Press, 1980.

Japan, Department of Education. *Kokutai no Hongi: Cardinal Principles of the National Entity of Japan*. Translated by John Owen Gauntlett. Edited by Robert King Hall. Cambridge: Harvard University Press, 1949.

Knei-paz, Baruch. *The Social and Political Thought of Leon Trotsky*. Oxford: Oxford University Press, Clarendon Press, 1978.

Kolakowski, Leszek. *Main Currents of Marxism: Its Origins, Growth, and Dissolution*. Translated by P. S. Falla. 3 vols. Oxford: Oxford University Press, Clarendon Press, 1978.

Kublin, Hyman. *Asian Revolutionary: The Life of Sen Katayama*. Princeton: Princeton University Press, 1964.

Labedz, Leopold, ed. *Revisionism: Essays on the History of Marxist Ideas*. New York: Frederick A. Praeger, 1962.

Lenin, V. I. *The Development of Capitalism in Russia: The Process of the Formation of a Home Market for Large-Scale Industry*. Moscow: Progress Publishers, 1964.

———. *Imperialism, the Highest Stage of Capitalism*. Peking: Foreign Languages Press, 1973.

———. *What Is To Be Done? Burning Questions of Our Movement*. New York: International Publishers Co., New World Books, 1969.

Levenson, Joseph R., *Confucian China and Its Modern Fate: A Trilogy*. Berkeley and Los Angeles: University of California Press, 1958, 1964, 1965.

Lichtheim, George. *Marxism: An Historical and Critical Study*. New York: Frederick A. Praeger, 1961.

Lockwood, William W. *The Economic Development of Japan: Growth and Structural Change, 1868-1938*. Princeton: Princeton University Press, 1954.

Lowe, Donald M. *The Function of "China" in Marx, Lenin, and Mao*. Berkeley and Los Angeles: University of California Press, 1966.

Maguire, John M. *Marx's Theory of Politics*. Cambridge: Cambridge University Press, 1979.

Marx, Karl. *Capital*. 3 vols. Edited by Frederick Engels. New York: International Publishers Co., New World Paperbacks, 1967.

———. *Critique of Hegel's "Philosophy of Right."* Edited with an Introduction by Joseph O'Malley. Translated by Annette Jolin and Joseph O'Malley. Cambridge Studies in the History and Theory of Politics. Cambridge: Cambridge University Press, 1970, paperback ed., 1977.

———. *Pre-Capitalist Economic Formations*. Translated by Jack Cohen. Edited by Eric J. Hobsbawm. New York: International Publishers Co., New World Paperbacks, 1965.

Marx, Karl and Engels, Frederick. *Selected Correspondence*. Translated by Dona Torr. Marxist Library. New York: International Publishers Co., 1942; reprint ed., Westport, Conn.: Greenwood Press, 1975.

Miller, Frank O. *Minobe Tatsukichi: Interpreter of Constitutionalism in Japan*. Berkeley and Los Angeles: University of California Press, 1965.

Mitchell, Richard H. *Thought Control in Prewar Japan*. Ithaca and London: Cornell University Press, 1976.

Mommsen, Wolfgang J. *Theories of Imperialism*. Translated by P. S. Falla. New York: Random House, 1980.

Moore, Barrington. *Social Origins of Dictatorship and Democracy: Lord and Peasant in the Making of the Modern World*. Boston: Beacon Press, 1966.

Nakamura, Takafusa. *The Postwar Japanese Economy: Its Development and Structure*. Translated by Jacqueline Kaminski. Tokyo: University of Tokyo Press, 1981.

North, Robert C. *Moscow and Chinese Communists*. 2d ed. Stanford: Stanford University Press, 1963.

Notehelfer, F. G. *Kōtoku Shūsui: Portrait of a Japanese Radical*. Cambridge: Cambridge University Press, 1971.

Ohkawa, Kazushi. *The Growth Rate of the Japanese Economy since 1878*. Tokyo: Kinokuniya Bookstore Co., 1957.

Ohkawa, Kazushi and Rosovsky, Henry. *Japanese Economic Growth: Trend Acceleration in the Twentieth Century*. Studies on Economic Growth in Industrialized Countries. Stanford: Stanford University Press and London: Oxford University Press, 1973.

Pittau, Joseph. *Political Thought in Early Meiji Japan, 1868-1889*. Harvard East Asian Series, no. 24. Cambridge: Harvard University Press, 1967.

Said, Edward W. *Orientalism*. New York: Pantheon, 1978; Random House, Vintage Books, 1979.

Scalapino, Robert A. *Democracy and the Party Movement in Prewar Japan*. Berkeley and Los Angeles: University of California Press, 1962.

Schwartz, Benjamin I. *Chinese Communism and the Rise of Mao*. Cambridge: Harvard University Press, 1951.

Skocpol, Theda. *States and Social Revolutions: A Comparative Analysis of France, Russia, and China*. Cambridge: Cambridge University Press, 1979.

Smethurst, Richard J. *A Social Basis for Prewar Japanese Militarism: The Army and the Rural Community*. Berkeley and Los Angeles: University of California Press, 1974.

Tarschys, Daniel. *Beyond the State: The Future Polity in Classical and Soviet Marxism*. Swedish Studies in International Relations, no. 3. Stockholm: Läromedelsförlagen, Scandinavian University Books, 1972.

Titus, David Anson. *Palace and Politics in Prewar Japan*. New York: Columbia University Press, 1974.

Totten, George Oakley, III. *The Social Democratic Movement in Prewar Japan*. Studies on Japan's Social Democratic Parties, vol. 1. New Haven: Yale University Press, 1966.

Tucker, Robert C. *Philosophy and Myth in Karl Marx*. 2d ed. Cambridge: Cambridge University Press, 1972.

———, ed. *The Marx-Engels Reader*. Rev. ed. New York: W. W. Norton, 1978.

Turner, Bryan S. *Marx and the End of Orientalism*. Controversies in Sociology, no. 7. Edited by T. B. Bottomore and M. J. Mulkay. London: George Allen and Unwin, 1978.

Uyehara, Cecil H. *Leftwing Social Movements in Japan: An Annotated Bibliog-*

raphy. Studies on Japan's Social Democratic Parties. Tokyo and Rutland, Vt.: Charles E. Tuttle Co., for Fletcher School of Law and Diplomacy, Tufts University, 1959.

Wilson, George M. *Radical Nationalist in Japan: Kita Ikki, 1883-1937*. Cambridge: Harvard University Press, 1969.

Wittfogel, Karl A. *Oriental Despotism: A Comparative Study of Total Power*. New Haven: Yale University Press, 1957; New York: Random House, Vintage Books, 1981.

ARTICLES

Baron, S. H. "Plekhanov, Trotsky, and the Development of Soviet Historiography." *Soviet Studies* 26.3 (July 1974): 380-395.

———. "Plekhanov's Russia: The Impact of the West upon an 'Oriental' Society." *Journal of the History of Ideas* 19.3 (June 1958): 388-404.

———. "The Transition from Feudalism to Capitalism in Russia: A Major Soviet Historical Controversy." *American Historical Review* 77.3 (June 1972): 715-729.

Beckmann, George M. "Japanese Adaptations of Marx-Leninism: Modernization and History." *Asian Cultural Studies* 3, Studies on the Modernization of Japan (October 1962).

Bendix, Reinhard. "Preconditions of Development: A Comparison of Japan and Germany." In *Comparative Perspectives: Theories and Methods*, pp. 312-329. Edited by Amitai Etzioni and Fredric L. Dubow. Boston: Little, Brown, 1970.

———. "Tradition and Modernity Reconsidered." *Comparative Studies in Society and History* 9.3 (April 1967): 292-346.

Bernstein, Gail Lee. "The Russian Revolution, the Early Japanese Socialists, and the Problem of Dogmatism." *Studies in Comparative Communism* 9.4 (Winter 1976): 327-348.

Block, Fred. "The Ruling Class Does Not Rule: Notes on the Marxist Theory of the State." *Socialist Revolution* 33 (May-June 1977): 6-28.

Bridges, Amy Beth. "Nicos Poulantzas and the Marxist Theory of the State." *Politics and Society* 4.2 (Winter 1974): 161-190.

Bull, Hedley. "The State's Positive Role in World Affairs." *Daedalus* 108.4 (Fall 1979): 111-124.

Cohen, Stephen. "Bukharin, Lenin and the Theoretical Foundations of Bolshevism." *Soviet Studies* 21.4 (April 1970): 436-457.

Duus, Peter. "The Era of Party Rule: 1905-1932." In *Modern East Asia: Essays in Interpretation*. Edited by James B. Crowley. New York: Harcourt, Brace & World, 1970.

Godelier, Maurice. "The Concept of the Asian Mode of Production and the Marxist Model of Social Development." *Soviet Anthropology and Archeology* 4.2 (1965).

———. "The Concept of the 'Asiatic Mode of Production' and Marxist Models of Social Evolution." In *Relations of Production: Marxist Approaches to Economic Anthropology*. Edited by David Seddon. Translated by Helen Lackner. London: Frank Cass & Co., 1978.

Gold, David A., Lo, Clarence Y. H., and Wright, Erik Olin. "Recent Developments in Marxist Theories of the Capitalist State (1)." *Monthly Review* 27.5 (October 1975): 29-43.

Hammond, Edward. "Bukharin and the Chinese Revolution." *Modern China* 1.4 (October 1975): 463-472.

Hayami, Yujiro and Yamada, Saburo. "Technological Progress in Agriculture." In *Economic Growth: The Japanese Experience since the Meiji Era*. Edited by L. Klein and K. Ohkawa. Homewood, Ill.: Richard D. Irwin, Inc. and Nobleton, Ontario: Irwin-Dorsey Limited, 1968.

Hintze, Otto. "Economics and Politics in the Age of Modern Capitalism." In *The Historical Essays of Otto Hintze*, pp. 422-452. Edited by Felix Gilbert. New York: Oxford University Press, 1975.

Hodges, Donald Clark. "Engels' Contribution to Marxism." *Socialist Register* (London) (1965): 297-310.

Horie, Yasuzo. "Foreign Capital and the Japanese Capitalism after World War I." *Kyoto University Economic Review* 20.1 (April 1950): 38-59.

Hoston, Germaine A. "Emperor, Nation, and the Transformation of Marxism to National Socialism in Prewar Japan: The Case of Sano Manabu." *Studies in Comparative Communism* 18.1 (Spring 1985): 25-47.

———. "Marxism and Japanese Expansionism: Takahashi Kamekichi and the Theory of 'Petty Imperialism.' " *Journal of Japanese Studies* 10.1 (January 1984): 1-30.

———. "Marxism and National Socialism in Taishō Japan: The Thought of Takabatake Motoyuki." *Journal of Asian Studies* 44.1 (November 1984): 43-64.

———. "*Tenkō*: Marxism and the National Question in Prewar Japan." *Polity* 16.1 (Fall 1983): 96-118.

Ishida, Takeshi. "Popular Attitudes toward the Japanese Emperor." *Asian Survey* 2.2 (April 1962): 29-39.

Kato, Shūichi. "Taishō Democracy as the Pre-Stage for Japanese Militarism." In *Japan in Crisis: Essays on Taishō Democracy*. Edited by Bernard S. Silberman and H. D. Harootunian. Princeton: Princeton University Press, 1974.

Marx, Karl. "The British Rule in India." In *The Marx-Engels Reader*. Edited by Robert C. Tucker. Rev. and enlgd. ed. New York: W. W. Norton, 1978.

———. "The Civil War in France (1871)." In *The Marx-Engels Reader*. Edited by Robert C. Tucker. Rev. and enlgd. ed. New York: W. W. Norton, 1978.

Meisner, Maurice. "The Despotism of Concepts: Wittfogel and Marx on China." *China Quarterly* 16 (October-December 1963): 99-111.

Miliband, Ralph. "The Capitalist State: Reply to Nicos Poulantzas." *New Left Review* 59 (January 1970): 53-60.

———. "Poulantzas and the Capitalist State." *New Left Review* 82 (November-December 1973): 83-92.

Offe, Claus. "Structural Problems of the Capitalist State." *German Political Studies* 1 (1974): 31-56.

Offe, Claus and Ronge, Volker. "Theses on the Theory of the State." *New German Critique* 6 (Fall 1975): 137-147.

Ohkawa, Kazushi and Rosovsky, Henry. "Economic Fluctuations in Prewar Japan: A Preliminary Analysis of Cycles and Long Swings." *Hitotsubashi Journal of Economics* 3.1 (October 1962): 10-33.

Poulantzas, Nicos. "The Problem of the Capitalist State." In *Ideology in Social Science: Readings in Critical Social Theory*. Edited by Robin Blackburn. New York: Random House, Vintage Books, 1973.

Schwartz, Benjamin. "A Marxist Controversy on China." *Far Eastern Quarterly* 13.2 (February 1954): 143-153.

———. "Some Stereotypes in the Periodization of Chinese History." *The Philosophical Forum* 1.2 (New series) (Winter 1968): 219-230.

Shanin, T. "The Third Stage: Marxist Social Theory and the Origins of Our Time." *Journal of Contemporary Asia* 6.3 (1976): 289-308.

Shibagaki, Kazuo. "Dissolution of Zaibatsu and Deconcentration of Economic Power." *Annals of the Institute of Social Science* (Tokyo) 20 (1979).

———. "The Early History of the Zaibatsu." *The Developing Economies* (Tokyo) 4.4 (December 1966): 535-566.

———. "The Logic of Japanese Imperialism." *Annals of the Institute of Social Science* (Tokyo) 14 (1973): 70-87.

Shils, Edward A. "Political Development in the New States." *Comparative Studies in Society and History* 2 (April 1960): 265-292.

Silberman, Bernard S. "The Bureaucratic Role in Japan, 1900-1945: The Bureaucrat as Politician." In *Japan in Crisis: Essays on Taishō Democracy*. Edited by Bernard S. Silberman and H. D. Harootunian. Princeton: Princeton University Press, 1974.

———. "Conclusion: Taishō Japan and the Crisis of Secularism." In *Japan in Crisis: Essays on Taishō Democracy*. Edited by Bernard S. Silberman and H. D. Harootunian. Princeton: Princeton University Press, 1974.

Trimberger, Ellen Kay. "State Power and Modes of Production: Implications of the Japanese Transition to Capitalism." *The Insurgent Sociologist* 7.2 (Spring 1977): 85-98.

Venturi, Franco. "Oriental Despotism." *Journal of the History of Ideas* 24.1 (January-March 1963).

Wallerstein, Immanuel. "A World-System Perspective on the Social Sciences." *British Journal of Sociology* 27.3 (September 1976).

Waswo, Ann. "The Origins of Tenant Unrest." In *Japan in Crisis: Essays on Taishō Democracy*. Edited by Bernard S. Silberman and H. D. Harootunian. Princeton: Princeton University Press, 1974.

Watanabe, Tsunehiko. "Industrialization, Technological Progress, and Dual Structure." In *Economic Growth, the Japanese Experience since the Meiji Era*, pp. 110-134. Edited by L. Klein and K. Ohkawa. Homewood, Ill.: Richard D. Irwin, Inc. and Nobleton, Ontario: Irwin-Dorsey Limited, 1968.

Watanuki, Joji. "State Formation and Nation-Building in East Asia." *International Social Science Journal* 23.3 (1971): 421-434.

Wolfe, Alan. "New Directions in the Marxist Theory of Politics." *Politics and Society* 4.2 (Winter 1974): 131-159.

Yamamura, Kōzō. "The Japanese Economy, 1911-1930: Concentration, Conflicts, and Crises." In *Japan in Crisis: Essays on Taishō Democracy*. Edited by Bernard S. Silberman and H. D. Harootunian. Princeton: Princeton University Press, 1974.

Yasuba, Yasukichi. "Anatomy of the Debate on Japanese Capitalism." *Journal of Japanese Studies* 2.1 (Autumn 1973): 63-82.

INDEX

LIBRARY OF CONGRESS CATALOGING-IN-PUBLICATION DATA

Hoston, Germaine A., 1954-
Marxism and the crisis of development in prewar Japan.

Bibliography: p.
Includes index.
1. Communism—Japan—History—20th century.
2. Japan—Economic conditions—1918-1945.
3. Japan—Politics and government—1926-1945. I. Title.
HX413.H67 1986 335.43'0952 86-42846
ISBN 0-691-07722-3 (alk. paper) ISBN 0-691-10206-6 (pbk.)

GPSR Authorized Representative: Easy Access System Europe - Mustamäe tee 50, 10621 Tallinn, Estonia, gpsr.requests@easproject.com

www.ingramcontent.com/pod-product-compliance
Lightning Source LLC
LaVergne TN
LVHW011107300926
849160LV00008B/295
9780691610139